Reading and Writing in the Academic Community

Why Do You Need This New Edition?

If you're wondering why you should buy this new edition of *Reading and Writing in the Academic Community,* here are seven great reasons!

1 The book has been expanded from four parts to five. New in this edition is Part I, "The Composing Process," orienting students to writing as process, an approach that is emphasized throughout the rest of the book.

2 In Part II, "Reading Sources and Incorporating Them into Your Writing," a new chapter is devoted to summarizing, and expanded treatment of the summary essay is included.

3 Part III, "Responding to, Analyzing, and Evaluating Sources," focuses on essays that examine single sources.

4 Part IV, "Synthesizing Sources," covers essays that draw on multiple sources, including summary of multiple sources, an objective synthesis, an essay written in response to multiple sources, an argument essay, and a research paper.

5 Additional sample student essays have been added to Parts II, III, and IV.

6 New chapter themes in Part V, "Reading Selections," include "Cyberhood," "Adolescent Pregnancy," and "Creativity and Ownership."

7 The Appendix on MLA and APA documentation reflects the latest versions of these two styles.

Reading and Writing in the Academic Community

Fourth Edition

MARY LYNCH KENNEDY
State University of New York at Cortland

HADLEY M. SMITH
Ithaca College

Prentice Hall

Upper Saddle River   London   Singapore
Toronto   Tokyo   Sydney   Hong Kong   Mexico City

Editorial Director: Joe Opiela
Senior Acquisitions Editor: Brad Potthoff
Project Manager, Editorial: Jessica A. Kupetz
Editorial Assistant: Nancy C. Lee
Director of Marketing: Tim Stookesberry
Executive Marketing Manager: Megan Galvin-Fak
Marketing Manager: Sandra McGuire
Marketing Assistant: Jean-Pierre Dufresne
Senior Operations Specialist: Sherry Lewis
Cover Art Director: Jayne Conte
Cover Design: Bruce Kenselaar

Manager, Rights and Permissions: Zina Arabia
Manager, Research Development: Elaine Soares
Manager, Cover Visual Research & Permissions:
  Karen Sanatar
Image Permission Coordinator: Annette Linder
Composition/Full-Service Project Management:
  Karen Berry/Laserwords Maine
Copyeditor: Natalia F. Morgan
Printer/Binder: R. R. Donnelley & Sons
Text Font: 10/12 Minion

Credits and acknowledgments borrowed from other sources and reproduced, with permission, in this textbook appear on appropriate page within text or on pages 517–520.

Library of Congress Cataloging-in-Publication Data

Kennedy, Mary Lynch
   Reading and writing in the academic community / Mary Lynch Kennedy, Hadley M. Smith.—4th ed.
      p. cm.
   Includes index.
   ISBN 0-205-68946-9
  1. English language—Rhetoric—Problems, exercises, etc.   2. Research—Methodology—Problems, exercises, etc.   3. Academic writing—Problems, exercises, etc.   4. College readers.   I. Smith, Hadley M.   II. Title.
   PE1478.K395 2009
   808'.0427—dc22

                                                                    2009016865

10 9 8 7 6

Prentice Hall
is an imprint of

www.pearsonhighered.com

Student
ISBN-10:   0-205-68946-9
ISBN-13: 978-0-205-68946-0

Exam
ISBN-10:   0-205-68947-7
ISBN-13: 978-0-205-68947-7

Brief Contents

Contents

PART II Reading Sources and Incorporating Them into Your Writing   49

CHAPTER 2 Reading Sources   50

CHAPTER 3 Paraphasing, Quoting, and Acknowledging Sources   79

CHAPTER 4 Summarizing Sources   111

PART V Reading Selections   377

Preface

TO THE STUDENT

WRITING IN THE ACADEMIC COMMUNITY

When you come to college, you join a new community. It consists of a group of people who share knowledge, beliefs, and values and operate according to a set of agreed-upon norms. The type of writing done in this community is well established, and it follows certain expectations and conventions. In some ways, it is like high-school writing. You will find yourself writing for similar purposes—to respond, compare and contrast, argue, and analyze. But in other ways, college writing is different.

The purpose of *Reading and Writing in the Academic Community* is to help you learn how to communicate successfully with the members of the "academic community," a group that includes teachers, scholars, and artists as well as you and your fellow students. Individuals in the academic community hold widely diverse opinions, but they all share a special interest in language and interact regularly by writing and by reading one another's work. Written communication is not identical in all fields of study, but members of the academic community share certain standards and conventions for written expression. When students write for academic audiences, sometimes they become confused and frustrated. But once they learn the language conventions that govern the academic community, they see that this new way of reading, writing, and thinking is not so difficult to accomplish.

The best way to learn the language conventions of the academic community is to master a variety of strategies for reading and writing. Most important is learning how to comprehend assigned reading and use it in your own compositions. Assume that you are taking a Western civilization course and you have received the following essay assignment:

Draw on your textbook and related reading to explain why existentialism, Marxism, and Christianity were considered major intellectual trends of the twentieth century.

The assignment requires you to perform three tasks: (1) read complex texts; (2) summarize, paraphrase, and quote various authors; and (3) weave textual material into your essay. But do you think your professor will be satisfied if all your essay does is summarize relevant passages from the textbook and other reading you have done? Probably not. College professors expect more than report writing. They want students to move beyond simply restating the information in reading sources to transforming that information to support their thesis statements or points of view. A student who is transforming knowledge rather than retelling it will write the history essay to convince her audience that Marxism had a greater impact on the twentieth century than existentialism or Christianity. She will do more than report on existentialism, Marxism, and Christianity as major intellectual trends. Her goal will be more complex. She will analyze and synthesize the readings for a specific rhetorical purpose: to persuade her readers that one trend had a greater effect on the twentieth century than did the others. Expert academic writers make statements that go beyond those in the original texts, and in so doing they transform the sources rather than simply translate them.

A major convention of academic writing is the citing of evidence from print sources. Think of how you might draw upon reading sources to write about television in a course on child development. You could use ideas from assigned readings to convince your audience that television advertising targeted at children should be banned. In a sociology class, you could summarize articles in order to compare and contrast the level of violence in Japanese and American television programs. In an engineering course, you could draw on reading sources to explain the design and delivery of interactive television systems and as a political science student, you could summarize research to illustrate how televised debates have affected American presidential elections. In each situation, you would write with a different purpose and audience in mind.

College writing assignments often have a greater degree of specificity than high-school assignments. Another important difference is that they require you to engage other writers' texts. When you use textual sources, you are expected to do more than simply report to your audience the set of facts or body of material that you have read. You are expected to alter the reading material so that it fits your own writing purpose. For example, a high-school writing assignment might ask you to write an essay on the causes of the growth of poverty in the United States, whereas a comparable college assignment might ask you to evaluate the views of Lester C. Thurow and Barbara Ehrenreich on the feminization of poverty. The college assignment focuses on a particular feature of poverty and requires you to read, analyze, and perhaps compare the texts of two authors and evaluate their positions. You will have to summarize, paraphrase, and quote the reading materials in your essay, and you will also have to keep in mind that your professor is more interested in your appraisal of Thurow's and Ehrenreich's views than in your explanation of them.

The academic community shares certain expectations for the way writers use language and develop ideas. Unless you follow these conventions, readers will not take your writing seriously. To a large extent, your success in college depends on your ability to learn the language that the academic community writes and speaks.

GOALS OF THIS TEXTBOOK

Unfortunately, some students never internalize the conventions of academic writing. They puzzle over "what the teacher wants" and have difficulty adjusting to the demands of different professors. But all professors are part of the academic community, so their fundamental expectations are similar. Once you master the genres and conventions of academic writing, you should never have to relearn them. What is the best way to do this? The trick is to "overlearn" the strategies for effective reading and writing to the point where they become automatic. Once you have a ready command of these strategies and they have become habits of mind, you will not have to give them a second thought. You will be free to focus on being imaginative and finely crafting your prose. You will be able to accomplish your goals as an academic writer most effectively when you can execute certain processes without effort.

This book has three objectives:

1. To help you attain the habits of mind needed for the process of academic reading and writing
2. To give you a ready command of the genres, stylistic features, and conventions of academic writing
3. To show you that once you have practiced and internalized these genres and conventions, you can use them to communicate your ideas about any topic

Throughout *Reading and Writing in the Academic Community,* our foremost consideration is your purpose for writing academic essays. The book is divided into five parts. Part I, "The Composing Process," encourages you to become a process-oriented writer who engages fully in prewriting, drafting, revising, and editing. Part II, "Reading Sources and Incorporating Them into Your Writing," describes how to read thoughtfully and extract facts and concepts from the academic texts that will serve as sources for your essays. Part III, "Responding to, Analyzing, and Evaluating Sources," explains how to draw on your prior knowledge and use your thinking abilities as you compose source-based essays. Part IV, "Synthesizing Sources," provides instruction on combining material from various sources as you write essays that serve a variety of purposes.

Parts III and IV are both driven by a central question: What do you want to get across to readers in your academic community? At the heart of each essay you write is the particular purpose you want to accomplish. On one occasion, you may decide that the best way to get your readers to understand a difficult issue is to compare and contrast two authors' views. Another time, your aim is to persuade your readers of your viewpoint. In another paper, you may want to analyze and evaluate other writers' views.

Whatever your purpose for writing, you can fulfill it more easily if you know how to organize your essay using patterns that reflect your thinking. In each chapter in Parts I, II, III, and IV, we show you how student writers typically arrange texts for various purposes, and we guide you through the process of composing essays of your own.

We begin Part I with a description of the process that leads to successful writing. In Chapter 1, we take you through the steps in writing an academic essay. In this chapter, you will find pointers for creating titles and openers; developing a thesis; and crafting paragraphs, including introductions and conclusions. You will also learn a number of useful strategies for revising preliminary drafts of your essays

Since so much of your college writing requires you to draw on sources, a key ability is critical reading. That is why Part II focuses on the reading process. Chapter 2 offers you a set of powerful strategies for assertive reading and shows you how to apply them to your assignments. Chapter 3 and 4 introduce you to three basic conventions of academic writing—paraphrasing, quoting, and summarizing—and provide you with extensive practice using these techniques. Parts III and IV cover the forms of writing that are most commonly assigned in college courses. Chapter 5 explains how to write essays in which you draw on your prior experience and knowledge to respond personally to sources. In Chapter 6, we take up analysis and evaluation. We first show you how to write a systematic rhetorical analysis of a reading source.

Then we explain how to compose an essay in which you evaluate the strengths and weaknesses of a source according to a set of established criteria. Finally, we take you through the process of writing an essay in which you analyze an issue objectively, "unpacking" it so that your reader can understand its complexities. In Chapter 7, we cover synthesis essays that involve combining ideas from several different sources. We discuss assignments that ask you to compare and contrast the views of two or more writers on the same topic. We also show how to write four other types of papers that draw on multiple sources and, in some cases, your own knowledge and experience: a summary of multiple sources, an objective synthesis, an essay written in response to multiple sources, and a synthesis essay written for a specific purpose.

The focus of Chapter 8 is developing strong arguments supported by reliable reading sources. We take you through the process of clarifying and refining issues, probing both sides of controversies, composing an arguable thesis, and marshaling a body of solid evidence to make a strong case. Chapter 9 sets forth a process for conducting independent library research: posing questions and setting research goals, searching for information in print and electronic sources, and composing a research paper. In this chapter, we make a special effort to explain the use of computerized catalogs and indexes and the Internet so that you will feel confident using these powerful tools to obtain information for your research papers.

Throughout Parts I, II, III, and IV, we make extensive use of sample student essays. As we analyze these models, we guide you through the process of composing similar essays of your own.

Part V of the book is an anthology of compelling, high-interest reading selections. Chapters 10 to 14 focus on provocative, timely topics: grades in higher education, human identity and community in cyberspace, adolescent pregnancy, creativity and the ownership of intellectual property, and the role of race in American society. Following Part V are three appendices that serve as useful reference guides for writers. Appendix A includes updated information on MLA and APA documentation styles. Appendix B serves as a mini handbook on sentence grammar, usage, and mechanics. Appendix C provides advice for improving sentence clarity and style.

As you analyze the reading sources and write essays for the assignments in this book, you will master the basic conventions of academic writing. Eventually, the conventions and processes described in this book will become second nature, and you will be able to execute the processes with very little effort.

TO THE INSTRUCTOR: HIGHLIGHTS OF THE FOURTH EDITION

The fourth edition of *Reading and Writing in the Academic Community* continues to present a comprehensive rhetoric covering assertive, critical reading and the major types of academic writing students encounter as undergraduates and an anthology of timely, high-interest readings. A distinct strength of the book is that it makes few assumptions about students' prior experience in the academy and provides explicit, step-by-step instruction in active reading strategies, paraphrasing, quoting, summarizing, writing essays in response to readings, writing essays that analyze and evaluate sources, synthesizing sources to write essays for a variety of purposes, developing arguments, and conducting research.

The book has been expanded from four parts to five. New in this edition is Part I, "The Composing Process," which orients students to writing as process, an approach that is emphasized throughout the rest of the book. In Part II, "Reading Sources and Incorporating Them into Your Writing," we have devoted a new chapter to summarizing and expanded our treatment of the summary essay. Part III, "Responding to, Analyzing, and Evaluating Sources," focuses on essays that examine single sources while Part IV, "Synthesizing Sources," covers essays that draw on multiple sources including summary of multiple sources, an objective synthesis, an essay written in response to multiple sources, an argument essay, and a research paper. Additional sample student essays have been added to Parts II, III, and IV.

In Part V, "Reading Selections," we continue to focus on timely, provocative topics. New chapter themes include "Cyberhood," "Adolescent Pregnancy," and "Creativity and Ownership." We continue to accompany each reading selection with a prereading activity and reading comprehension questions that encourage students to (1) grasp the informational content, (2) decide what genre, organizational plan, and stylistic features the author uses, and (3) analyze rhetorical context, such as the context of the piece and the author's purpose with regard to his or her audience. As in earlier editions, several writing assignments accompany each reading, and a further selection of writing assignments is presented at the end of each topically related chapter of readings. Finally, the Appendix on MLA and APA documentation styles has been brought up to date.

ACKNOWLEDGMENTS

We owe special thanks to the students at Cornell University, Ithaca College, and the State University of New York at Cortland who contributed essays to this book. We are greatly indebted to Christina Haas and Linda Flower for the concept of "rhetorical reading," to Marlene Scardamalia and Carl Bereiter for "knowledge telling" and "knowledge transforming," to Victoria Stein for "elaboration," and to Linda Flower for "writer-based and reader-based prose." We have also drawn on the work of other researchers and writers, including Edward Corbett, Peter Elbow, Donald Murray, and Mina Shaughnessy.

At Prentice Hall, we have had the privilege of working with an outstanding team: Leah Jewell, Brad Pottoff, Jessica Kupetz, Jennifer Conklin, Gina Aloe, Nancy Lee, and Sandra McGuire. We are indebted to Karen Berry at Laserwords Maine for her excellent production work on our fourth edition.

We are also grateful to our reviewers for their helpful suggestions and insightful analysis: Lindsay Lewan, Arapahoe Community College; Jim McKeown, McLennan Community College; Kate Lavia, North Carolina State University; Joseph McCarren, Slippery Rock University; Alexandria Casey, Graceland University; Wanda Lloyd, North Carolina State University; and William Smith, Weatherford College.

Finally, we want to thank Nancy Siegele, Timm Smith, and Bill Kennedy for their help, humor, and support in getting us through yet another revision of the textbook.

Mary Lynch Kennedy
Hadley M. Smith

PART I

The Composing Process

CHAPTER 1

Writing as Process

Which scenario best describes your past experiences with writing?

A. You receive a writing assignment that is due in two weeks. Not long before the essay is due (sometimes the night before), you read the assigned material, take a few notes, and sit down at the computer to pound out a finished product. If you have time, you read over the essay for typos before handing it in. A week later, maybe longer, the teacher returns your paper. You check out the grade, glance at the teacher's comments, and stash the essay in your notebook.

B. You receive an assignment that directs you to write an essay in stages. The first draft is due in one week, a second draft a week later, and perhaps a final draft a week after that. Before you compose the preliminary draft, you do some prewriting activities, reading the assigned material and responding to it in your course journal. You use these prewriting notes to write your essay. When you bring your essay to class, you give it to a group of peers or to the teacher. These reviewers make suggestions for revision. You rethink the paper, make revisions, and resubmit it. The teacher returns the paper with comments and a grade. You check out the grade; read over the comments, especially those referring to the improvements you made; and store the essay in your notebook.

These scenarios represent two different approaches to writing. Scenario A focuses on the finished product, whereas scenario B values the *process* as much as the product. The product-oriented writer tries to create a perfect, polished essay in one try. The process-oriented writer works at assignments in phases: *prewriting, drafting, revising,* and *editing.* The product-oriented writer considers composing a solitary activity. The process-oriented writer engages in collaborative activities, sometimes in prewriting discussions and often in peer review groups.

In this book, we take a process approach to reading and writing. Whenever you generate ideas, read texts, and organize your materials for writing, you engage in prewriting. When you begin to compose the paper, you enter the *drafting* phase. After you complete a draft and receive some feedback from your teacher or peers, you rework your paper in the *revising* phase. You expand on important points, delete irrelevant material, and clarify anything that confused your readers. Finally, you move to *editing*. At this phase, you focus on the surface features of your writing, checking for problems with usage, spelling, punctuation, and mechanics.

We want to emphasize that although we refer to reading, prewriting, drafting, revising, and editing as phases, writers do not necessarily proceed from one stage to the next in a systematic fashion. The process is recursive. The various activities can occur at any point in the process. Revising can take place while you are drafting your essay or after you have completed a full-blown draft. As we wrote this textbook, we revised some of it at the drafting stage, most of it at the revision stage as we completed each chapter, and a few parts at a later date after we had completed the entire manuscript.

You need not work through the reading and writing process in lockstep fashion, marching methodically from one stage to the next. But you should be aware that some types of pacing are more productive than others. When you are drafting your essay, if you stop every few minutes to fret about spelling, punctuation, or correct usage, you may end up with disjointed, disconnected prose. The beauty of the process approach to writing is it allows you to concentrate on generating ideas while you are drafting. Editing comes later.

You should also be aware that writers may use different composing styles, depending on their purposes. A writer completing a complex history assignment may spend much more time on prewriting activities—reading, underlining and annotating the materials, and taking notes—than would a writer who is composing an essay drawing on prior knowledge or personal experience.

RESISTANCE TO PROCESS WRITING

The following excerpt comes from an e-mail one of us received from a student the morning an essay was due:

> ...It's [name deleted] from your academic writing course. I had grand ambitions tonight of pulling the classic college-esque 'all-nighter' to finish a biology project, chemistry lab report, and your writing paper. Unfortunately, things aren't going as smoothly as I planned—it's 5 AM and the chem report is almost done, while the bio project and paper are as blank as I'd imagine your facial expression will be when reading this. With class in 4 hours and 15 minutes (its actually 5:09 right now according to my computer clock), I am doubting how much I will get done on your assignment. I have 387 words, but it's mostly fragmented paragraphs with incomplete ideas. If i manage to crawl into your class this morning the shell of a shell of the man i usually am (that's not a typo, but you may have to read it a few times to understand it. Actually, I really have no idea how much of my language in this makes sense at all. The amount of caffeine that i've consumed is enough to kill a small horse, and my eyes are having trouble focusing), I will most likely have a shitty essay at best, with some pretty cool ideas that never get expanded upon. My essay is about the relationship and integration of television and the internet, and I'm having a lot of trouble finding articles to support my claim. I've used ProQuest,

> Lexis-Nexis, EbscoHost, and Google. I've never used databases before, and I'm having a lot of trouble finding review articles on the relation between the internet and society, tv and society, and just statistics about either (i.e., how many people own/watch tv, the amount of time the average user spends on the internet, etc.). I know how terrible it is that I'm sending this so late in the game. I hate to put professors in positions like this. The only time I can meet this week is on Friday after 11 AM.
>
> The worst part about this is the entire e-mail is 533 words, which is longer than my essay.

Many of our students believe that they write best "under pressure." Some intentionally begin work on essays the night before a due date because they think that approach works well for them. Even those who admit that they are not able to write well under pressure often believe that they might develop that ability with practice. Virtually all our students claim to know someone who is able to start working on an essay the night before it is due and by morning produce A-quality work.

While students may want to believe that last minute drafting is effective, the evidence indicates that successful writers rely on a process that involves multiple drafts and extends over time. Virtually all teachers of writing are committed to the process approach because the research in our discipline demonstrates the importance of process. The following excerpt, taken from a recent research study, indicates the consensus of those who study writing:

> Writing in marathon sessions is a kind of blocked practice that students and perhaps even some of their professors use to meet deadlines. Such writing binges can cause anxiety, exhaustion, and writer's block (Boice, 1985, 1997). Professional writers typically compose on a consistent schedule of a few hours per day at most (Kellogg, 2006). (Kellogg and Raulerson)

In addition to the conclusions of scholarly inquiry into writing, anecdotal evidence from hundreds of famous writers indicates that even the most proficient wordsmiths, those with years of successful publishing experience, must go through a process of drafting and revision that cannot be compressed into a short time frame. For example, consider Joyce Carol Oates, known for her excellence as a writer of novels, short stories, poems, essays, and reviews. Since Oates is one of the most prolific writers of our times, we might assume that she has mastered the art of writing under pressure. However, at a reading she gave in 2003 at Ithaca College, Oates explained that she depends upon a writing process that extends over time. She compared writing a first draft to pushing a peanut over a filthy floor using only her nose. Only after she crosses the floor can she get up, see where she has been to get "the big picture," and then begin revising. Oates also stated that a writer can only write a good first sentence after he or she has written the last sentence; in other words, revision produces good sentences. She described her process for writing a novel as writing the first half and then rewriting that half while simultaneously writing the second half. She also reported that the short story she read to us earlier in the evening had been written and published years before, but she still made revisions for the reading up until twenty minutes before she took the stage. Other accomplished writers' descriptions of the writing process echo that of Oates. Writing takes time. Good writing results from getting down a draft and then returning to it repeatedly and tinkering with it until it works. There are no shortcuts.

As Anne Lamott points out in her best selling book *Bird by Bird*, developing writers should take heart in the fact that first drafts are always rough:

> Almost all good writing begins with terrible first efforts. You need to start some-where. Start by getting something—anything—down on paper. A friend of mine says that the first draft is the down draft—you just get it down. The second draft is the up draft—you fix it up. You try to say what you have to say more accurately. And the third draft is the dental draft, where you check every tooth, to see if it's loose or cramped or decayed, or even, God help us, healthy. (25–26)

We are encouraged by Oates' and Lamott's testimonies as they indicate to us that everyone, even the best writers, struggle with first drafts but that anyone who commits to the writing process will improve. Don't expect too much from your first drafts, but, on the other hand, don't be discouraged by them.

Exercise 1.1

Write a one-paragraph description of how you wrote essays in high school. Consider the following questions: How did you come up with ideas for your writing? What organizational plans did you use? Did you create outlines? Did you write first drafts without notes? Did you ask friends, family members, or teachers to read your rough drafts? If so, what types of feedback did you receive, and how did you respond? When you proofread, what specific issues of usage, spelling, punctuation, and mechanics did you focus on?

Now consider the overall writing process you have used. Over how many days did the process extend? What were the strengths of your approach to writing assignments? What were the weaknesses? Which parts of the process were the easiest for you, and which parts were the hardest? Write another paragraph in response to these questions.

In class, compile a joint list of students' strengths and weaknesses. Discuss why students' responses vary.

PREWRITING

Prewriting is also called *invention.* A root of *invention* is the Latin word *invenire,* meaning to discover or find. It is the period in which writers discover what they want to say. They explore what they already know about a topic, searching for ideas, using problem-solving methods, making connections, and conducting inquiries. In Chapter 2, we discuss strate-gies for tapping prior knowledge and experiences: freewriting, brainstorming, and journal writing (see pages 53–58).

As a college writer, you will spend a substantial amount of time prewriting: analyzing your assignments, specifying your purposes for writing, establishing your audience, and reading your sources. As you read each source, decide what you want to obtain from it. Remember to look beyond content. Also consider form, organization, stylistic features, and rhetorical context. As you underline, annotate, and take notes, plan how you will use the reading source in your essay. Then reread part or all of the text, reread your notes, record additional notes, and do more planning. When you have done all this rereading, noting, and planning, you are ready to write your first draft.

For assignments that require you to use reading sources in your writing, the key to success lies at the prewriting stage. This is the period just before you sit down at the computer to type out a complete draft of your paper. It is the time for reading and rereading the text, annotating, taking notes, and planning your essay. You will find that it is far more efficient to select relevant parts of the reading source, bring your prior topic knowledge into play, and organize your ideas at this stage than to rack your brain and refer continually to the reading source *while* you are drafting your essay.

ANALYZE THE ASSIGNMENT

When you receive your assignment, put on your rhetorical glasses and think about audience and purpose. Work within the context of the rhetorical situation: just as the author of the source you are about to read has written to his or her readers for a reason, you are writing your essay for a reason. You are trying to affect or influence your readers in a certain way.

Consider student Nora Gold, who received the following assignment in her first-year writing course:

> How should our society balance the rights and responsibilities of developing teens? Write a 1000-word essay in which you take a position on an issue concerning the legal rights of minors in American society. You might consider the laws and governmental policies specific to minors that pertain to one of the following issues: alcohol use, abortion, consent to sexual activity, voting, municipal curfews, or sentencing youthful offenders. Conduct research on your topic and use at least three sources in your essay. Write for an general audience unfamiliar with the sources you cite.

This assignment asks the writer to take a position and write an argument essay, a type of essay we discuss in depth in Chapter 8. Whenever you analyze an assignment, determine the essay type or "genre" that is called for. Other genres that we cover in this textbook include summary essays (Chapter 4), response essays (Chapter 5), essays of analysis and evaluation (Chapter 6), synthesis essays (Chapter 7), and research papers (Chapter 9).

You may need to ask your instructor for more detail about aspects of the assignment. For instance, we have noticed that our colleagues in various disciplines use the term "critique" in distinct ways: some assume that a critique includes both a summary of a source as well as a response to it, while others think that a critique should include only analysis of the source and no summary. Some instructors believe that papers should be written for a general readership while others want papers directed to those knowledgeable about the field. You need to pose questions about the assignment up front rather than wait until the essay is well under way, as some students are inclined to do.

Some genres are particular to academic disciplines. For example, in the world of business, cost–benefits analysis is a common form for written expression. Proposed corporate ventures are often presented in this balance sheet approach, where potential gains are weighed against risks and potential losses. All academic disciplines are characterized by certain thinking strategies or methodologies. An important part of learning to write in a particular discipline is identifying and becoming skilled at using the methods of analysis specific to that the field of study.

Another way to better understand writing assignments is to think about how the instructor expects you to use the course content in your writing. Bloom's Taxonomy of Educational Objectives provides a means of achieving this understanding. Educational psychologist Benjamin Bloom analyzed the intellectual demands of academic tasks and came up with the following classifications: knowledge, comprehension, application, analysis, synthesis, judgment. In the following list, we use Bloom's scheme as the basis for questions you might ask about the goals of your writing assignments:

Analyzing writing assignments using Bloom's Taxonomy

To what extent is the goal of the assignment to show

- knowledge: I am aware of the information presented in the course?
- comprehension: I understand fully the information presented in the course?
- application: I can apply the information presented in the course outside the context in which I learned it?
- analysis: I can break down concepts taught in the course into their components and understand the relationships among those components?
- synthesis: I can make connections among various parts of the course content to arrive at a conclusion of my own?
- judgment: I can arrive at and defend my own viewpoints about the course content?

Keep in mind that any given assignment may touch on more than one of the categories in Bloom's Taxonomy. For example, a judgment might be supported by analysis and synthesis of course content elements.

Don't hesitate to ask for explanations of your assignments, but make sure your questions have meaningful content. Avoid the "Just tell me what you want" demand. Try asking your instructor the following questions:

**QUESTIONS TO ASK INSTRUCTORS
ABOUT WRITING ASSIGNMENTS**

- For whom am I writing? The professor? My classmates? Someone else?
- Do you have a sample of a strong student essay that you can show me?
- Which documentation style shall I use?
- Which organizational plans will work best for this assignment?
- What percentage of the essay should be taken from sources and what percentage should be my own ideas?

Exercise 1.2

Describe a particular situation in which you did not understand what a professor wanted in a writing assignment (don't use our class) and as a result produced a paper that was off target. What was the nature of your confusion? To what extent was the confusion your fault and to what extent did the professor make unwarranted assumptions about what would be obvious to students?

Establish a Focus

From among the options mentioned in the assignment on page 6, Nora is drawn to the topic of youth curfews, since she grew up in a community that enforces a midnight curfew on teens under seventeen years of age, and she has been involved in many discussions of that law, particularly with her parents.

As do most teens in her community, Nora opposes the curfew law. Several of her friends were caught violating the curfew on weekends and were detained at the police station until their parents picked them, an experience that the teens felt was embarrassing and unfair. On the other hand, Nora knows the curfew was instituted following a series of late night accidents which claimed teens' lives. The parents of one of those who died mounted the campaign for the curfew. As Nora thinks about the goal of her essay, she realizes it will not be enough to merely reiterate her opinion and relate the experiences of her friends. In order to appeal to a broad audience, one that includes both young and older readers, she will need to do more than explain her own viewpoint; she will need to draw on outside sources that will substantiate her point of view.

In this particular example, the student starts out the writing process with an opinion she has developed in the past and identifies an audience that is not inclined to agree with her and needs to be convinced. We should note, however, that many times students begin the writing process with an assigned topic about which they have no opinion. In those cases, opinions emerge through reading and responding to sources, processes that we describe in Chapter 2 (52–58) and Chapter 5 (146–150). Even in cases where writers begin with a viewpoint they want to defend, it is advantageous to consider a range of opinions at the prewriting stage. As we explain in Chapter 8, strong arguments are grounded in a clear understanding of and response to viewpoints contrary to the writer's.

Two weeks before her essay is due, Nora begins to collect information on her topic. She reasons that her topic will be covered in newspaper and magazine articles since it is an issue of public concern; consequently, she decides to check databases at her college library that cover periodicals written for a broad readership. She travels on the Internet to the Web site of her college library and accesses Proquest Research Library, a database that she has used in the past to access journal and magazine articles. She tries "Curfews" as a subject search term, and Proquest responds with a list of related subject headings including "Curfews and teens." She selects "Curfews and teens," and Proquest provides a long list of related articles, starting with the most recently published. Nora reads through the titles of the articles that were published over the last ten years and selects those that seem most relevant to her topic. She then conducts similar searches on General OneFile, another general purpose database and LexisNexus, a database that emphasizes legal content. On all three databases, Nora locates numerous articles related to her topic.

While youth curfews is relatively easy to research, other topics may require a more sophisticated approach. In Chapter 9 (pages 331–344), we explain in detail how to use online databases to tackle challenging research tasks. In this case, Nora is able to locate material easily; her work is to sift through the sources and select those that best serve her purposes as a writer. She narrows down the list of articles to those that seem most promising and then prints them out.

READ AND RESPOND TO SOURCES

In Chapter 2, we stress the importance of active reading, a process in which you interact with and respond to the text as you read. As Nora reads the articles she has printed out, she writes marginal comments that record her responses to the text. Here is an excerpt of her response to the article "Nunez and Beyond: An Examination of Nunez v. City of San Diego and the Future of Nocturnal Juvenile Curfew Ordinances" by Jeff Beaumont:

Juvenile curfews implicate serious constitutional issues involving minors' and parents' fundamental rights. They infringe on minors' First Amendment freedoms of speech and association, as well as the fundamental right of free movement. Minors—like adults—possess these fundamental rights, and any infringement therein requires strict scrutiny.

This is exactly what I want to prove.

However, because the United States Supreme Court has not yet ruled on the constitutionality of nocturnal juvenile curfews, lower federal courts addressing these fundamental rights issues have been unable to meet a consensus. Federal courts' inconsistent and divergent treatment of minors' rights in relation to those of adults is a result [*122] of the erroneous application of Bellotti v. Baird [n280] in the context of juvenile curfews. Federal courts, such as the Ninth Circuit, continue to apply Bellotti despite the absence of the Supreme Court's willingness to extend Bellotti beyond the context of abortions. Even

The Supreme Court needs to take leadership on this issue. But then, the current Court is conservative and might not place as much value on youth rights as I do.

assuming that the Supreme Court would extend Bellotti, juvenile curfews do not implicate "the peculiar vulnerability of children; their inability to make critical decisions in an informed, mature manner; and the importance of the parental role in childrearing." [n281] Moreover, the imposition of juvenile curfews

Apparently, Bellotti v. Baird has to do with abortions. How does this case relate to curfews?

on minors burdens—not strengthens—parents' fundamental right to rear their children.
Thus, as one court stated, juvenile curfews are
like "a bull in a china shop of constitutional   *I could use this quotation!*
values." [n282]

When she is finished reading Beaumont's article, Nora jots down her thoughts on
how she might use the material in her essay. Here is an excerpt from Nora's journal:

> Beaumont supports the idea that curfews violate the constitutional rights of young
> people. One point he raises that I hadn't read elsewhere is that curfews interfere
> with minors' First Amendment rights. He says that curfews "significantly restrict
> minors' access to public forums, thereby preventing minors from exercising their
> First Amendment freedoms." This makes sense. If you can't go out in public, then
> it limits your ability to express yourself or get information from others.
>
> Beaumont and other writers on this topic refer to the Bellotti v. Baird case.
> According to Beaumont, the case involved a Massachusetts law that required minors
> to obtain their parents' consent before they could have abortions. I understand that
> the abortion and curfew issues both involve the constitutional rights of minors and
> thus might have some common ground, but I don't think it will help my argument to
> bring up the abortion issue. People react so strongly to the debate over abortion
> rights that it might be a distraction from what I want to say about curfews.

Nora's marginal notes and journal entries are examples of the active reading strategies that we discuss in Chapters 2 and 5. Her goal at this stage is to record her thoughts
about the readings, material that she will be able to draw on as she begins her preliminary
writing.

DRAFTING

From what we just described, you can see that throughout the prewriting phase, you continually shift back and forth between your role as reader and your role as writer. As you begin
drafting, the writer role takes on more importance, but you don't give up the reader role.
Throughout the drafting stage, you may find it necessary to refer to the reading sources to
retrieve a quotation, verify a piece of information, or flesh out a note.

Before you begin to write a first draft, reflect on the prior knowledge you have already
brought into play. You have tapped your prior knowledge of the topic to produce a pool of
responses to the reading source, and you have invoked your prior knowledge of organization
and structure to discover an organizational plan. At this point, you will summon up two other
types of prior knowledge: (1) knowledge of the basic features of writing—elements like titles,
introductions, sentences, paragraphs, transitions and connecting ideas, and conclusions—and
(2) knowledge of strategies for summarizing, paraphrasing, and quoting sources.

DEVELOP A THESIS

The preliminary or *working thesis* is the central idea that you intend to develop in your
paper. You might think of it as a capsule summary of your entire essay. It reflects your

rhetorical purpose and the effect you want to have on the audience. It may also indicate your organizational plan. In an argument essay, it may express your level of agreement (or disagreement) with the source or indicate ways you will extend or build on the source. We call the thesis *preliminary* at the prewriting stage because writers often revise their thesis statements later in the writing process.

One of the principal characteristics of the academic essay is that it is *thesis-driven*. This means that the thesis is revealed early in the essay and everything that follows serves to support it. You may find this convention unappealing because it forces you to reveal the end before you have told the story and thus may sound like a formula for boredom. All the same, the convention of beginning with a thesis statement is strong in the academic tradition, and your readers will expect you to observe this practice. The thesis for an academic essay should accomplish the following goals.

GOALS OF A THESIS STATEMENT

- Provide a comprehensive statement of the writer's intentions and the central idea
- Indicate the complexity of the writer's thinking
- Suggest how the essay will be organized
- Be consistent with the discussion in the body of the essay and with the conclusion

You may be asking, "How can I come up with a thesis statement at the outset of the drafting process if I'm not yet sure about the point I wish to make in my essay?" If this is the case, review marginal notes and journal entries as follows.

- **See if one type of response predominates.**
- **See if a good number of responses were triggered by a particular source idea.**
- **Classify your responses.** Select workable categories and discard the rest. You might highlight the responses in which you agree or disagree with the author of the source and then work only with these as you draft your essay.

Another way to work toward a thesis statement is by *freewriting*, which involves writing nonstop for ten minutes or more without worrying about spelling, grammar, or punctuation. The goal is to force yourself to get words down and thus get past the psychological barrier of the blank page or screen. Allow ideas to flow freely and follow your stream of consciousness. For this technique to work, you have to keep writing without a pause for at least ten minutes. Once you have completed your ten-minute writing blitz, you read through what you have written searching for main ideas that might form part of your thesis statement.

In his book *Writing With Power*, Peter Elbow, a renowned expert on writing instruction, describes the value of freewriting: "Freewriting makes writing easier by helping you with the root psychological or existential difficulty in writing: finding words in your head and putting them down on a blank sheet of paper. So much writing time and energy is spent *not* writing: wondering, worrying, crossing out, having second, third, and fourth thoughts" (14).

Nora decides to use freewriting as she works on her thesis statement. She first reviews her assignment and looks through her written responses to the articles she read. Then she puts her readings and notes aside and writes nonstop for ten minutes, attempting to capture the main idea that she wants to develop in her essay. Later, she looks through her freewriting and notices that the following excerpt seems to capture what she wants to say in her essay:

> I didn't find a single source that included any information that really proves that teen curfews help reduce crime or make young people any safer. What good are they? Why have them at all? Politicians, of course, love curfews. If they pass curfews, they seem like they are tough on crime, which gets them votes. So it seems they are willing to stomp on the civil liberties of teenagers just for a few votes! This is totally unfair!

Using this freewriting excerpt as a starting point, Nora develops the following preliminary thesis statement:

> Even though curfews are supposed to reduce youth crime, there is no real evidence that they work. What is clear is that curfews infringe on the civil liberties of young people. Apparently, politicians are willing to sacrifice those civil liberties in order to appear tough on crime.

This preliminary thesis statement serves as a starting point for Nora as she writes the first draft of her essay. Subsequent revisions result in the thesis statement as it appears in her final draft:

> Teen curfew laws, such as the one enforced in San Diego, are being established in cities across the United States for the alleged purpose of reducing youth crime. These laws will do little to deter those teens who are criminally inclined and are unfair to the millions of young people who have done nothing to deserve being held under house arrest. Enforcing teen curfews amounts to penalizing young people so that adults can enjoy a false sense of security and politicians can give the impression that they are tough on crime.

You may be surprised that this preliminary thesis statement is three sentences long since you may have been told that a thesis statement should be a single sentence. The length and the complexity of a thesis statement depend on the writer's rhetorical purpose. Thesis statements in academic essays are often two, three, or more sentences. If you have a complex reaction to the topic, the thesis of your essay may be lengthy. Consider a thesis statement that took up the entire second paragraph of our student Steven Siegele's essay:

> The courts have ruled that people under the age of eighteen have constitutional rights that may be affected by curfew laws. Curfews potentially impinge on First Amendment rights to freedom of expression and assembly, the Fourth Amendment principle of probable cause, and the Fourteenth Amendment right to equal protect under the law. In addition, it has been argued that curfews violate parents' right to determine what is best for their children, a right which, according to the Supreme Court, is protected by the Constitution. On the other hand, the Supreme Court has ruled in many cases that individual rights must sometimes take a back seat to what is good for society in general. As was once stated by the Court, freedom of speech does

not give one the right to yell "Fire" in a crowded theater. Curfews are justified only when the authorities can demonstrate clearly that they do more good than harm.

As his thesis indicates, Steven wants his audience to understand how the courts need to balance individual rights with the greater good of society. His point is to urge caution in establishing that balance. He has a complicated objective, and it takes an entire paragraph to express it. Some thesis statements are much more compact, like the one written by student Colin Smith:

> I oppose curfews because they single out people for harassment based on their age alone. We should be judged by our actions, not by the number of years we've lived.

Lisa Rodriguez's thesis is longer than Colin's but shorter than Steven's paragraph:

> As long as the rate of crime in our society remains unacceptably high, we must continue to provide the police with the means to maintain law and order. Curfews are one of the tools that the police need to control urban crime. I do feel, however, that the penalties for curfew violation should be relatively mild. Curfews should serve primarily as a justification for police to stop and check up on teens who are out on the streets.

As our examples indicate, the length and the complexity of a thesis statement depend on the writer's rhetorical purpose.

You may be surprised that several of these thesis statements contain the first-person pronouns—*our, we, I*. Personal pronouns are appropriate in certain types of academic writing, particularly in response essays. It is difficult to write from personal experience without using *we, I, my,* or *me.* These pronouns also help writers label their own views so that they are not confused with those of the source authors. Personal pronouns appear in respected professional journals, but they are discouraged in some academic writing contexts. In the sciences, lab reports are generally written to sound objective and impersonal ("The sample was analyzed for trace elements" rather than "I analyzed the sample for trace elements"). Ask your professor if you are unsure about using personal pronouns in your assignment.

We should stress that your preliminary thesis statement is subject to change throughout the writing process. Too often students think that they have to make sense of the topic and come up with a full-blown thesis before they begin to write the essay. Writing is a creative process that advances your thinking. Often your ideas about a topic will develop as you draft the essay. If you hold tenaciously to your initial thesis, you won't be able to take advantage of the new thinking that the writing process inspires.

We discuss revising entire essay drafts later in the chapter, but we briefly touch on thesis revision here because writers typically revisit their thesis statements repeatedly as they work on their initial drafts. One result of in-process revisions is to enrich the thesis and make it more comprehensive. In the following example, notice how the successive revisions of a preliminary thesis statement reflect increasing complexity of thought. The thesis is written in response to Jerry Farber's essay "A Young Person's Guide to the Grading System," which appears on pages 385–388.

Preliminary Thesis	I am against the grading system.
First Revision	I believe the grading system runs counter to the goals of education.
Second Revision	I believe grades are counterproductive because they focus students' attention on scores rather than knowledge.
Third Revision	Even though many students believe that they need grades for motivation, grades are counterproductive because they distract students from the most important goal of education: gaining knowledge.

In the third revision, the writer takes a stand, "grades are counterproductive . . . ." She also acknowledges an opposing position, "many students . . . ." This thesis indicates the writer's path of development. She will support her own position against grades, but she will also respond to students who favor grades. The wording of the thesis tells readers that they can expect the writer to organize the essay as an argument. In general, you will help readers if you can write a thesis that indicates your organizational plan.

The following table lists the most common organizational plans. Notice how the intended organizational plan for the essay is signaled in each of the following thesis statements. The topic for this example is affirmative action in college admissions. Notice also that the thesis statements do not express the writers' viewpoints on affirmative action. Although the term *thesis* is often used to refer to an argumentative position, it has a much broader meaning in the academic community. The thesis statement specifies your *intention* in writing—what you hope to accomplish but not always your opinion. In many cases, your intention in writing will not be to win an argument but rather to present an issue objectively for the benefit of your readers, and that intention would still be labeled your thesis statement. For a discussion of thesis statements that express argumentative positions, see pages 291–294 in Chapter 8.

ORGANIZATIONAL PLAN	THESIS STATEMENT
Time order	During the 1960s and early 1970s, it was widely accepted that affirmative action policies were beneficial, particularly in the college admission process. After the *Baake* decision in 1978, however, arguments against affirmative action grew louder and reached a crescendo in the 1990s.
Comparison and contrast	The supporters and critics of using affirmative action in college admission decisions disagree on a range of social issues. Among them are what constitutes merit, how America should address class-based education deprivation, and which rights are protected by the Fourteenth Amendment.
Case in point	Opponents of affirmative action would argue that my adopted brother from Guatemala and I should receive the same treatment in the college admission process. On the other hand, proponents of affirmative action would maintain that my brother should be given special advantages.

Each of these thesis statements provides the reader with a roadmap for how the essay will proceed and will help the reader follow the writer's train of thought as the essay develops. A strong thesis statement establishes the basis for a unified and coherent essay.

As you approach the end of the revision process, make sure that your thesis is consistent and comprehensive. It must be consistent with the discussion in the body of your essay and with the perspective that comes through in your conclusion. If the drafting process has altered your perspective on the issue, modify the thesis so that it is consistent with this shift. Read the introduction and then immediately read the conclusion to check for consistency. The thesis should be comprehensive enough to capture the major viewpoints the essay presents.

A final piece of advice is to avoid a banal thesis statement that includes an opinion but makes only a superficial attempt to come to grips with the topic. Imagine that you are writing an essay in response to an article that defends human cloning. After reading the article, you decide you are opposed to human cloning and write the following thesis statement:

> I am opposed to human cloning because it involves asexual reproduction of a human being.

This statement indicates opposition to human cloning and then provides a brief definition of cloning as if it were a reason to reject the technology. It leaves readers with a question: Why does the writer find "asexual reproduction" troubling? Since there are a number of possible answers to this question, readers can only guess how the writer would answer it.

The next sample thesis includes a reason for the writer's belief but still does not indicate that the writer weighed the evidence or thought about the issue in any depth.

> I oppose human cloning because it is an unnatural process that no normal person would be willing to undergo.

The offhand dismissal of proponents of cloning makes the writer seem immature. You risk losing the respect of your reader at the outset if your thesis indicates a superficial approach to the topic. Take advantage of the thesis statement to indicate the full complexity of your viewpoint, as in the following example:

> I oppose human cloning for the same reason that I oppose selective breeding and other eugenic technologies: because it is based on the assumption that some individuals' genes are better than those of others. If this assumption becomes widely accepted, it will jeopardize the basic human rights of those who are judged genetically inferior.

SELECT AN ORGANIZATIONAL PLAN

After you come up with a preliminary thesis, your next step is to decide which organizational format to use. Table 1-1 identifies the most common patterns and gives a brief description of the purpose of each.

TABLE 1-1   Patterns for Developing and Organizing Ideas

Pattern	Writer's Purpose
Time order, narration, process	To present ideas or events in a chronological sequence; to tell what happened (narration) or to describe a sequence of actions (process)
Antecedent and consequence, cause and effect	To present causes (antecedents) or examine effects or outcomes (consequences); to reveal the causes of a particular outcome or phenomenon or to explain its consequences, usually by explaining the relationship between the causes and the effects
Description	To present the physical attributes, parts, or setting of the topic, often out of a desire to give a personal impression of the person, place, or thing being described
Statement and response	To present a statement and give a reaction, often in a question-and-answer, problem-and-solution, or remark-and-reply format
Comparison and contrast	To present the similarities or differences between objects, approaches, or viewpoints
Example	To present illustrations or instances that support an idea
Analysis or classification	To divide the topic into parts (analyze) or to group parts or facets of the topic according to some principle or characteristic (classify)
Definition	To explain a word, concept, or principle
Analogy	To show the similarity between things that otherwise bear little or no resemblance; to explain something by comparing it point by point with something similar

An organizational plan you may have learned in middle school or high school is the five-paragraph theme.

Introduction	Introduce your topic. At the end of the paragraph, state your thesis.
Three body paragraphs	In each paragraph, present a reason why you hold your position.
Conclusion	Sum up your main points, speculate about the implications of what you have just said, or call your readers to action.

The five-paragraph format is appropriate in some cases, but don't rely on it in college-level papers. One of the principal reasons this format is taught so widely is that it provides a general-purpose organizational plan students can rely on when writing under time pressure, especially during standardized tests, when they do not have the leisure to think carefully about the organizational structure that best fits the situation. The five-paragraph plan may serve as a security blanket when you are under pressure to produce a coherent essay in a very limited time, but it also shackles your writing. Your ideas about the topic should determine how you organize your essay, but your ideas will be distorted if you force them into an inappropriate pattern. Our recommendation is that you approach exams with a handful of writing plans in mind rather than a single all-purpose format.

As Nora considers how she will develop her thesis, she realizes that there are four principal assertions she intends to defend:

1. Curfews don't actually reduce youth crime.
2. After-school programs can help reduce youth crime.
3. Politicians propose curfews to give the appearance of being tough on crime.
4. Curfews lead to reductions in the civil liberties of young people.

As she thinks about these four assertions, she realizes that they all involve cause-and-effect relationships. For each of the four, she will have to demonstrate a causal relationship between two factors. She also considers how the four assertions connect together and reorders them as follows:

1. Curfews lead to reductions in the civil liberties of young people.

   Nora reasons that her entire argument rests on this point: if adults do not perceive that curfews have serious negative consequences, then they would be inclined to give them a try.

2. Curfews don't actually reduce youth crime.

   Once she has demonstrated the negative consequences of curfews, then Nora reasons she can weigh those consequences against the dubious claims that curfews reduce crime.

3. Politicians propose curfews to give the appearance of being tough on crime.

   Nora figures that some readers may question her point 2, since they assume that curfews would not be established if they weren't effective. Her point 3 responds to that concern by identifying the political motives behind curfews.

4. After-school programs can help reduce youth crime.

   Nora thinks that presenting an alternative method of reducing youth crime and demonstrating that it works is a logical way to end her discussion. She reasons that in response to points 1 to 3, some skeptical readers might say to themselves, "But we can't just do nothing at all about youth crime." Point 4 provides a possible solution that might be applied in the future.

Nora now has a rough plan for how she will organize the first draft of her essay. Of course, she may modify this initial plan as the essay develops. As she writes her first draft, she may discover new ways of connecting ideas that did not occur to her before she began to write.

WRITE A FIRST DRAFT

Next, we will describe drafting an essay sequentially, starting with the title and ending with the conclusion. We do not mean to suggest that you will follow this order. The title may be a later addition to the essay. You may find it easier to write the introduction after you compose the body. Whatever you do, don't stare at the blank page waiting for the title or first sentence to come to you. Start wherever you feel ready to write, and return later to the parts that caused initial hesitation. As she begins to draft her essay, Nora decides to begin with point 2 from her organizational plan: demonstrating that curfews do not reduce crime. She begins with point 2 because she is confident that she has collected enough information to prove this point and has a good notion of what she wants to say in this section of her essay. She starts with the section of the essay that she feels she is best prepared to write.

Title Your Essay

Wait to title your essay until after you have revised your first draft. That way, if you've changed direction, you will not have to retitle it. Your title should express the position you take in the essay or relate to your thesis in some other way. Create titles that indicate your perspective and, if possible, capture the essence of the issue you are addressing. For example, assume that you are writing an essay in response to "Time to Do Everything But Think," an article written by *New York Times* columnist David Brooks on the topic of technology. A straightforward title like "A Response to David Brooks's 'Time to Do Everything But Think'" fails to indicate that the topic under discussion is the social impact of wireless communication. Compare this matter-of-fact title to the examples in the box below.

TITLING YOUR ESSAY

- Let the title reflect your organizational plan. An essay that develops according to the comparison-and-contrast pattern might be titled "The Wireless Human: Master or Slave?"
- Borrow an apt phrase from the reading source or from your essay. In paragraph 5 of his article, Brooks states, "He's a speed freak, an info junkie." An essay written in response to Brooks might be titled "Info Junkies."
- State the general topic and then, after a colon, your perspective or stance—for example, "Wireless Communication: A New Technology That Is Dominating Our Lives."
- Phrase the title as a question—for example, "Will Wireless Technology Change Society?"
- Use another well-known quotation or saying, such as "Faster Than a Speeding Bullet: The Wireless Culture."

Nora uses the third of these options and titles her essay "Curfew Laws: Demonizing Teens." She wants her title to announce the topic and to suggest her perspective on the issue. She also hopes the provocative phrase "Demonizing Teens" will capture her audience's attention.

Establish a Style

Before you write your first draft, you should make a conscious decision about the writing style that will be appropriate for your assignment and audience. Academic writing always involves making decisions about style based on content and audience. At this early stage of the writing process, you will set general stylistic goals. Don't get bogged down in wording, turns of phrase, and sentence structure. When you are revising and editing your essay, you will revisit the issue of style and use specific strategies for improving the style of your paper. In Appendix C, we offer specific strategies for improving style.

To illustrate how writers tailor style to content, we'd like you to read excerpts from two articles in the same issue of *College English,* a journal written for English professors. Each of the writers, Eleanor Berry and Lee Ann Carroll, addresses the same group of readers, but because of the nature of her subject matter, she conceives of her audience in a distinct way.

> While the method of grammetrical analysis and the notion of counterpoint as constituting a prosody, as developed and deployed by Wesling and Hartman, serve to illuminate ways that poets eschewing meter can induce an experience of rhythm and affect readers' attention and construction of meaning, they do not fully address the need for a means of classifying the many modes of versification encompassed by the term "free verse." (Berry)

> It is not that students know too few stories, but that they know too many. Students experience every day how the lines between genres are blurred—in news presented as entertainment, docu-dramas, shock-jockey talk shows as the most public forums for political debate. Contrasting different forms over the course of a semester makes clearer how conventions both permit and constrain us to speak in different ways. (Carroll)

Professor Berry discusses poetic forms, a discipline that has a history and a related vocabulary. She sees her audience as scholars with knowledge of poetic forms and the field's specialized vocabulary. Professor Carroll writes about a broader topic, the teaching of first-year composition. She views her readers as classroom teachers, and she uses everyday language and an informal voice to speak to them. Both examples fit underneath a broad umbrella of academic writing styles that range from conversational to highly formal, from terse to expansive. Some students view the academic writing style as a starchy, uncomfortable uniform that they must don to write course papers. It should be seen as a vast wardrobe that allows the writer to make choices about content and audience.

As the examples from *College English* show, academic writers may employ different styles for readers of the same publication. But the readership has to be comfortable with diversification. Some readerships are not, and the journals that appeal to them expect uniformity in writing style and even give prospective authors style sheets that they must follow. Just as scholars have to adjust their writing style to the publication, students have to tailor their style to particular assignments. Prior to writing her essay, Nora Gold revisits her assignment:

> How should our society balance the rights and responsibilities of developing teens? Write a 1000-word essay in which you take a position on an issue concerning the legal rights of minors in American society. You might consider the laws and governmental policies specific to minors that pertain to one of the following issues: alcohol use, abortion, consent to sexual activity, voting, municipal curfews, or sentencing youthful offenders. Conduct research on your topic and use at least three sources in your essay. Write for a general audience unfamiliar with the sources you cite.

Nora notes that the last sentence of the assignment specifies "a general audience," so she knows she is not writing exclusively for the professor, for other students in her writing or sociology classes, or for other members of the college community. She figures that she should use words that will be accessible to a relatively wide range of readers and should avoid academic jargon that might put off nonacademics. She looks through the sources she intends to draw on and decides to model her style on articles from *The Economist* and *National Catholic Reporter*, respected publications intended for wide readerships. She notes that some of her source articles are taken from academic publications, *New York University Law Review* and *Harvard Law Review*, and she concludes that she should present ideas from those sources in language that will make them accessible to a broader audience.

Some people speak of a writer's style as his or her trademark. They talk about Hemingway's clipped sentences and repeated adjectives and Faulkner's long, convoluted sentences. The truth is that writers make stylistic choices based on the publication and audience. Asked to write for *People* magazine, Eleanor Berry would not adopt the scholarly style she uses for her article in *College English.*

To show you how an academic writer alters her style to accommodate the publication and its intended audience, we reprinted the opening paragraphs from articles written by Sherry Turkle, a professor of sociology at M.I.T. and an expert on machine–human interaction. The first article appeared *UNESCO Courier,* a publication meant for a general adult readership. The second article was published in *Social Research,* a venue for academic research studies in the social sciences. The readers of this journal are college professors and social scientists. Note the differences in Turkle's writing styles.

From *UNESCO Courier*

Children have always used their toys and playthings to create models for understanding their world. Fifty years ago, the genius of Swiss psychologist Jean Piaget showed it is the business of childhood to take objects and use how they "work" to construct theories of space, time, number, causality, life and mind. At that time, a child's world was full of things that could be understood in simple, mechanical ways. A bicycle could be understood in terms of its pedals and gears, a windup car in terms of its clockwork springs. Children were able to take electronic devices such as basic radios and (with some difficulty) bring them into this "mechanical" system of understanding.

From *Social Research*

Computers offer themselves as models of mind and as "objects to think with" for thinking about the self. They do this in several ways. There is, first of all, the world of artificial intelligence research—Marvin Minsky once called it the enterprise of "trying to get computers to do things that would be considered intelligent if done by people." In the course of this effort, some artificial intelligence researchers explicitly endeavor to build machines that model the human mind. Second, there is the world of computational objects in the culture—the toys, the games, the simulation packages, the computational environments accessed through Internet connections. These objects are evocative; interacting with them provokes reflection on the nature of the self.

For many decades computers had a clear cultural identity as linear, logical, mechanistic machines. Here I tell a story of a change in the cultural identity of the computer and consequently in the kind of mirror that computers offer for thinking about the self. Computational theories of intelligence now support decentered and emergent views of mind; experience with today's computational objects encourages rethinking identity in terms of multiplicity and flexibility.

These two passages are not dramatically different, but the stylistic distinctions make sense given each publication's audience. In the first excerpt, Turkle uses straightforward language and provides examples—a bicycle, a windup car, a radio—that will appeal to a broad readership. She makes a point of identifying Jean Piaget for a population who may be unfamiliar with this developmental psychologist. In the passage from *Social Research,* Turkle quotes a fellow scholar, uses enumeration, and adopts a serious tone. Reread the closing sentence of the passage from *Social Research:* "Computational theories of intelligence now support decentered and emergent views of mind; experience with today's computational objects encourages rethinking identity in terms of multiplicity and flexibility." Language of this complexity does not appear anywhere in the *UNESCO Courier* excerpt. Readers unfamiliar with the field of artificial intelligence will not understand "decentered and emergent views of the mind." But the passage from *Social Research* remains an example of good academic writing. Those who read in the field of artificial intelligence will recognize its efficient use of language and the validity of Turkle's stylistic choices.

Appendix C (pages 505–515) includes some specific strategies for improving style that can be applied as you draft or revise your essay.

STRATEGIES FOR IMPROVING STYLE COVERED IN APPENDIX C

- Avoid inflated language.
- Vary the structure and length of your sentences.
- Strengthen your verbs.
- Make your writing concise by cutting ineffective words and expressions and eliminating needless repetition.
- Liven up your writing with detail.
- Avoid sexist language.

Play it safe and discuss issues of style with your professors before you write your papers. Many professors assign only one or two papers per course, so you don't have the luxury of writing the first paper without assistance just to see how the instructor will respond, a strategy that many students use in high school. When you receive your first writing assignment, ask the professor to describe his or her expectations for style. Ask about the level of formality the professor expects, and find out about any special stylistic requirements, such as use of discipline-specific vocabulary or avoidance of passive voice. See if your professor can give you examples of successful student papers from past semesters. These models will tell you a lot about stylistic expectations.

While you should write in a style that meets the demands of particular courses, don't lose sight of your personal development as a stylist. See yourself as expanding your stylistic options rather than just complying with a temporary set of style guidelines that you will abandon at the semester's end. When adjusting to a professor's stylistic preferences, you are still growing as a writer and learning approaches that will prove useful down the road.

Exercise 1.3

Search through the readings assigned in your current courses and locate three paragraphs that are written in distinctly different styles. Look for good-sized paragraphs like the ones we supplied by Turkle. Photocopy each paragraph. For each excerpt, write a description of the author's writing style and an explanation of why that style is (or is not) appropriate for the publication and its intended audience.

Exercise 1.4

Describe a particular situation in which you did not understand the style of writing a professor or high-school teacher wanted in a writing assignment (don't use our class) and as a result produced a paper that was off target. What was the nature of your confusion? To what extent was the confusion your fault, and to what extent did the professor make unwarranted assumptions about what would be obvious to students?

Write an Introduction

Introductions prepare readers for what comes next. In your introduction, you will accomplish several objectives. We have listed them in the box below.

HOW TO WRITE EFFECTIVE INTRODUCTIONS

- Use an opener that will interest the reader.
- Announce the topic.
- Disclose a thesis or attitude toward the topic.
- Establish your style and voice.

Let's see how Nora Gold develops the introduction to her essay on page 43.

Notice how Nora leads the reader smoothly and logically from one idea to the next. She begins by engaging the reader with an example that illustrates dramatically how curfews are unreasonable and unfair. The opening example also introduces the topic of her essay and suggests her viewpoint. Then she mentions that curfews are established to reduce youth crime, a goal that clearly was not served in her opening example; thus, she has begun to contrast her position with those of her opponents. She next begins to develop her thesis, stating that curfews do not deter criminals; they punish those who mean no harm. Finally, she suggests why ineffective and unfair curfews are established: they give the appearance of addressing a politically sensitive issue. Nora's writing style is consistent throughout the paragraph: she establishes a serious tone that seems appropriate for an issue of social concern. Her style is certainly appropriate for an academic essay, yet she avoids sounding stilted.

The opening sentences of an essay should engage the readers and encourage them to read on. The opening also establishes the writer's voice as formal or informal, academic, or conversational. Some forms of academic writing require you to open your paper in a designated way and write in a very professional voice. Formal research studies often open with a one-paragraph abstract that summarizes the study's principal findings in straightforward, objective language. Response essays allow for much more freedom, for example, an informal opening that speaks directly to the reader. If you have difficulty deciding how to begin, use one of the techniques listed below. The examples of essay openers were written in response to an assignment on the topic of cloning human beings.

ESSAY OPENERS

Technique	*Example*
Quotation (from the reading source or elsewhere)	"Human embryos are life-forms, and there is nothing to stop anyone from marketing them now, on the same shelves with Cabbage Patch dolls" (Ehrenreich 86). Perhaps we are headed to a future where, as Ehrenreich suggests in her article "The Economics of Cloning," we will purchase rather than bear our children.
Question	Many parents want their children to have certain family characteristics—their grandfather's hair, their aunt's height, their father's eyes—but would you want a child who was an exact replica, a clone, of you or your spouse?
Anecdote, brief story, or scenario	Imagine you were born a clone, an exact copy of your mother or father, rather than a combination of genetic material from them both.
Fact or statistic	When human embryos were first cloned, President Clinton issued an executive order banning any further human cloning in government-sponsored research.
Generalization	Despite our fascination with genetic technologies, many of us recoil from the idea of cloning human beings.
Contradiction	Although cloning may multiply the odds that infertile couples will conceive, it may also multiply the chances of a genetic disaster.
Thesis statement	Cloning human beings threatens our very future as a species.
Background	Cloning, a biological process that makes it possible to produce an exact replica of a living organism, has been applied to simple life forms for years. Now it is possible to clone complex animals, even humans.

Avoid using paper openers that will bore or turn off your readers. If your opening sentences alienate readers, it is difficult to win them back in the paragraphs that follow. The following paper openers are used too often and sound trite.

OVERUSED OPENINGS YOU SHOULD AVOID

Opening	*Example*
Clichés or platitudes	As we consider the rapid growth of wireless communication, we should keep in mind that fools rush in where angels fear to tread.
Dictionary definitions of well-known words	According to *Webster's International Dictionary, thinking* means....
Restatement of the assignment	In "Time to Do Everything But Think," David Brooks attempts to demonstrate that wireless....
An obvious statement of your purpose	In this essay, I give my reactions to David Brooks's article "Time to Do Everything But Think."

Reread the preliminary thesis you wrote at the prewriting stage (page 10) and decide if you want to revise it before incorporating it into your introduction. Make sure that it still captures the principal perspective that you want to develop. The thesis statement is often located at the end of the introduction—after the opening, explanation of the general topic, and identification of the source—but it can occur anywhere within the introduction, even in the very first line. Wherever you place it, be sure to provide your reader with enough context to understand it fully. As we explained, a thesis statement may be several sentences long.

The introduction can include more than one paragraph. Long academic essays often have an introduction that contains many paragraphs. Shorter essays can also have multiparagraph introductions. For lengthy, complex thesis statements, a two-paragraph introduction may work best. Another consideration is to use a dramatized scenario or vignette to open a paper that runs to several paragraphs. Follow the opening paragraphs with a paragraph that zeroes in on the topic and presents the thesis.

Write the Body of the Essay

The essay you compose at this stage should be a preliminary draft, not a polished, final copy. Think of this first draft as a discovery draft, an opportunity to find out more about what you want to say.

As you draft the body, follow the organizational plan you chose at the prewriting stage—time order, statement and response, point-by-point, or another pattern. Develop sections and paragraphs that fit into your plan. If your prewriting plan proves unworkable or you discover a new direction for the paper, rethink your organizational strategy.

Recall that before she began to draft her essay, Nora determined that she would develop four central points in the following order:

1. Curfews lead to reductions in the civil liberties of young people.
2. Curfews don't actually reduce youth crime.
3. Politicians propose curfews to give the appearance of being tough on crime.
4. After-school programs can help reduce youth crime.

On page 17, we explain Nora's rationale for this particular sequence. Also recall that Nora concluded that each of these four points involved establishing cause-and-effect relationships. Nora's approach is to work on these points separately and then, when all four are completed, write the transitions that connect them.

Paragraphs. Develop paragraphs that are unified and coherent. Make sure that each paragraph develops a central idea and that all the sentences contribute to this idea in some way. As you read the following paragraph, notice how each sentence develops the point that curfew laws violate teens' constitutional rights.

> From several different perspectives, youth curfews represent an attack on Americans' civil liberties. The Supreme Court has ruled that "neither the Fourteenth Amendment nor the Bill of Rights is for adults alone" (qtd. in Herman). The most obvious constitutional problem is that curfews grant police the power to detain citizens for nothing more than appearing young (Budd 23). This blatant age discrimination is arguably a violation of the constitutional principle of equal protection under the law, a Fourteenth Amendment right (Diviaio). Some curfew laws include provisions that fly in the face of Fourth Amendment protections against unreasonable search and seizure. For instance, a law passed in Cicero, Illinois, gives police the right to seize the vehicles of teenagers who violate the local curfew ("Lights Out"). Court challenges to curfew laws have defended teens' "fundamental right to free movement" (Herman) as well as their rights to travel to and from evening jobs and even to stand or sit on their own sidewalks ("Juvenile Curfews"). Finally, some curfew laws may violate teens' First Amendment rights if they restrict opportunities for young people to attend religious services or school meetings held in the evening ("Juvenile Curfews").

At the outset of the paragraph, Nora asserts that curfew laws curtail civil liberties, and subsequent sentences identify the specific rights (Fourteenth, Fourth, and First Amendment rights) that are affected. The overall structure of the paragraph is a claim backed up by several supporting examples. That structure stands out for the reader and results in a paragraph that is unified.

Also strive to make your paragraphs coherent. In a coherent paragraph, repeated words and ideas, rewording of ideas, and transitional expressions (*also, for example, thus, similarly, consequently,* and so on) show the reader the logical links among the sentences. We give you additional pointers on coherence later in this chapter.

Integrate Source Material

As you draft the body of your essay, include relevant material from sources in the form of summaries, paraphrases, and quotations. Later in this book, we discuss in detail how to summarize sources (Chapter 4) and how to paraphrase and quote from sources (Chapter 3). We also discuss how to document summaries, paraphrases, and quotations so that your audience will be able to identify the sources from which they are taken. At this point, we will merely list several principles of using sources that are crucial at the drafting stage:

USING SOURCES AS YOU DRAFT YOUR ESSAY

- Each quotation must be enclosed within quotation marks. Do not alter the wording of the quotation except when you interpolate or cut material, adding ellipses (see pages 100–101).

- Every summary and paraphrase must be converted from the language of the original into your own words. Change both vocabulary and sentence structure.

- Every summary, paraphrase, and quotation must be cited to the source from which it was derived. The citation must appear within the text of the essay and must indicate precisely the extent of the material taken from the source. Typically, an in-text citation gives the source author's last name or, for a source without an identified author, the source title. A full bibliographic reference to the source must appear in the Works Cited list at the end of the essay.

Note in the following paragraph how Nora Gold integrates documentation into her paragraph:

> More and more frequently, American communities are relying on curfews in their efforts to battle youth- and gang-related crime. Over seventy percent of the largest two hundred cities in the United States had youth curfews by the late 1990s (Diviaio). Typical curfew hours are 11:00 p.m. on weeknights and 12:00 p.m. on Fridays and Saturdays, and these restrictions usually apply to individuals under eighteen ("Juvenile Curfews"). In addition to curfews passed by city and town governments, certain privately owned shopping malls have established teen curfews. According to the International Council of Shopping Centers, shopping malls in no fewer than ten states have established youth curfews ("Mall Madness"). In many cases, mall curfews deny entry on Friday and Saturday after 6:00 p.m. to anyone under eighteen unless they are under the supervision of someone over twenty-one ("Mall Madness"). The combination of strict public and private sector curfews could essentially confine teens to home and school unless they are accompanied by an adult.

Paraphrase from Diviaio

Paraphrase from the article "Juvenile Curfews"

Paraphrase from the article "Mall Madness"

Paraphrase from the article "Mall Madness"

Make sure that as you draft, you put summaries and paraphrases into your own language and that you document all material that comes from sources. If you partially reword source material as you draft, assuming that you will change the wording more when you revise, you run the risk of forgetting which sections need further work. Similarly, if you leave out documentation as you draft, you may, at the revising stage, find it hard to determine what material came from which source. These oversights can lead to charges of plagiarism (see pages 89–90), a serious academic offense that can lead to expulsion.

Notice that Nora identifies her sources in *parenthetical citations*. Immediately after she draws on information from a source, Nora inserts within parentheses either the author's name or, in the case of articles published anonymously, an abbreviated version of the article's title. She constructs her citations according to the Modern Language Association (MLA) documentation style. We will provide much more information about MLA documentation style in Chapters 2 and 9 and in Appendix A.

Write the Conclusion

Human beings seem hard-wired to want beginnings and endings. Just as readers need an introduction to orient them to your essay, they need an ending that leaves them with a sense of closure. Your closing paragraph should do more than summarize your argument or restate your thesis. Use one of the following techniques.

TECHNIQUES FOR WRITING CONCLUDING PARAGRAPHS

- Stress the significance of your thesis rather than simply repeating it. Encourage your readers to look beyond the thesis to an important future goal.
- Predict consequences.
- Call your readers to action.
- Come full circle to an idea mentioned in the introduction
- Use any of the devices for paper openers (see pages 23–24).

Read Nora Gold's closing paragraph on page 47. Notice how she uses three distinct techniques to achieve closure: (1) stressing the significance of her essay topic, (2) predicting consequences, and (3) coming full circle back to her opening example. Writers often construct conclusions using more than one closing technique.

Construct a List of Sources

As you complete your initial draft, make sure you construct a list of the sources that you referred to in your essay. Nora's list of sources appears on pages 47–48. Nora is using MLA documentation style, so she constructs a Works Cited list according to the guidelines published in the *MLA Manual and Guide to Scholarly Publishing*, 3rd edition. We provide an abbreviated version of those guidelines in Appendix A. Don't leave the Works Cited list for the night before the essay is due, as you may not have enough time to locate lost citations or to check style manuals for complex citation formats.

REVISING

The essence of editing is easy come easy go. Unless you really say to yourself, "What the hell. There's plenty more where that came from, let's throw it away," you can't really edit. You have to be a big spender. Not tightass. (39)

Every word omitted keeps another reader with you. Every word retained saps strength from the others. Think of throwing away not as negative—not as crumpling up sheets of paper in helplessness and rage—but as a positive, creative, generative act. Learn to play the role of the sculptor pulling off layers of stone with his chisel to reveal a figure beneath. Leaving things out makes the backbone or structure show better. (41)

In the preceding passages taken from the book *Writing Without Teachers*, Peter Elbow describes the essence of revision: you must be willing to let go of much or even all of what appears in your first draft. It is, of course, hard work to hammer out a draft, and it is difficult to part with the words that you struggled to produce. All the same, you need to approach revision with the idea that everything is subject to change or even deletion.

After you have composed a draft of your essay, set it aside and come back to it in a day or two. You will acquire fresh insights in the interim. It is also beneficial to have someone else read your draft and give you feedback. Your teacher may arrange to have peer review groups in class. If not, if it is all right with your instructor, ask your roommate, a family member, or a friend to review your draft.

The reviewer of your essay will find the following questions helpful. The same questions can guide your own rereading of your draft.

✓ *Checklist for Revising a First Draft*

_____   1. Does the essay have an appropriate title?

 2. As you consider style and voice,

_____   do you hear the writer's voice throughout the entire essay? (Can you describe it?)

_____   is the style of the essay appropriate for its content and audience?

 3. Does the introduction accomplish the following:

_____   use an opener that will interest the reader?

_____   announce the topic?

_____   disclose a thesis or attitude toward the topic?

_____   establish a style and voice?

 4. As you consider the overall organization of the essay,

_____   is the writer's rhetorical purpose clear? (How does the writer attempt to influence or affect readers?)

_____   does everything in the draft lead to or follow from one central thesis? (If not, which ideas appear to be out of place?)

_____   is the organizational plan or form appropriate for this kind of paper? (If not, can you suggest another format?)

_____   does the writer provide transitions or connecting ideas? (If not, where are they needed?)

 5. As you consider the writer's use of sources,

_____   throughout the essay, when referring to the source, does the writer supply necessary documentation?

_____ are there clear transitions or connectives that differentiate the writer's own ideas from those of the source author?

_____ does the paper end with a list of sources used?

_____   6. Does the conclusion do more than simply restate the main idea? Does it leave the reader with a sense of closure?

The process of getting advice on your writing may be difficult both for you and for your reviewer. Many of us tighten up in response to criticism; some even feel compelled to defend themselves. Reviewers are typically aware that their comments may not be well received and thus may hesitate to point out difficulties in drafts. We recommend that you ask for an honest response to your writing, listen carefully to the feedback you get, take notes, and then return to those notes in a day or two. At that point, you will be in a position to benefit from the feedback you received without feeling too defensive.

Once you have feedback from one or more readers and have reread the draft yourself, devise a revision plan and begin a second draft of your essay. You may want to start with the introduction and work through sequentially to the conclusion, or you may decide to start with the sections of the essay that, based on the feedback you received and your own rereading of draft, seem to need the most work.

There is no generic formula for revision, since each initial draft has its unique strengths and weaknesses. We can, however, provide a case in point and describe the revision process of student Jane Wolf. We will show the first draft and revision of Jane's essay and then discuss the changes that she made. Jane wrote this essay for her introductory computer science course. The assignment was to read a book on the social consequences of computers and then submit a short essay of response to the book. Jane selected _The Intimate Machine,_ in which Neil Frude argues that humans may one day have fulfilling emotional relationships with intelligent machines.

First Draft

Wolf 1

Jane Wolf

Professor Kennedy

English 131

15 July 2008

Intimate Machine Paper: First Draft

A book titled _The Intimate Machine_ describes a machine that could be programmed to act like a friend. The machine would "be programmed to behave in a congenial manner" and "to be charming, stimulating, and easygoing," to "sometimes take the initiative," and "to have a personality of its own" (Frude 169). The machine would provide people with many of the benefits of friendship. It would carry on a conversation and take an active interest in humans. It could even become intimate with them. Such an idea is not so far-fetched. People already use machines for therapeutic purposes, and they play chess with computers. People may be shocked by the idea of having a machine as a friend, but they should not condemn something that could benefit so many lonely people (157-87). I disagree with Frude, and I worry that machines have already replaced too many people today. I think it is far better for people to befriend people than to become intimate with machines.

Machines already function as therapists and teammates. They also teach classes. When my economics professor cannot make the class, he sends us a video lecture to watch in his place. Machines have also replaced bank tellers, telephone operators, and checkout cashiers. If this trend continues, we will soon have robot waiters, nurses, and mechanics, and, finally, machine friends. We will have less and less human contact in our daily lives.

I would argue that it is important to bring more and more people together than to separate them by introducing machines as friends. A lonely person may get some enjoyment from conversing with a "charming, stimulating, and easygoing" machine, but the satisfaction would be much greater if the person had genuine human contact. It is true that the machine would always be available, but the person would know that it had not come of its own free will.

    Some people will find the prospect of having a friendly, intimate machine tempting. But I would urge them to reconsider their position. Instead of putting so much research time and money into developing friendly machines, why not study ways to bring people together and enhance human relations? People need spontaneous, human love, not a programmed simulation.

4

REVISED DRAFT

Jane Wolf

Professor Kennedy

English 131

15 July 2008

How do you regard your personal computer, as a "tool," a "colleague" or a "friend"? You might be surprised that anyone would consider a machine a friend, but in

Do We Want Programmed Friends?

~~Intimate Machine Paper: First Draft~~

Neil Frude explains that

~~A book entitled~~ *The Intimate Machine* ~~describes a~~ machine s

~~that~~ could be programmed to act like ~~a~~ friend. The machine would "~~be programmed to~~ behave in a congenial manner" and "~~to~~ be charming, stimulating, and easygoing," *It would* ~~to~~ "sometimes take the initiative," and "~~to~~ *it would* have a personality of its own"

Frude claims that

(Freud 169). ~~The~~ machine would provide ~~people~~ *us* with many of the *with us* benefits of friendship. It would carry on a conversation and *our affairs. We* take an active interest in ~~humans. It~~ could even become *says Frude.* intimate ~~with them~~. Such an idea is not so far-fetched. People already use machines for therapeutic purposes, and they play *Frude points out that we* chess with computers. ~~People~~ may be shocked by the idea of *we* having a machine as a friend, but ~~they~~ should not condemn

1

Wolf 2

something that could benefit so many lonely people (157-87). I disagree with Frude ~~and~~ I worry that machines have already replaced too many people ~~today~~. ~~I think~~ It is far better for people to befriend people than to become intimate with machines.

[2] As Frude points out ^Machines already function as therapists and ~~teammates~~ partners for games. They also teach classes. When my economics professor ~~cannot make the~~ is unable to attend class, he sends ~~us~~ a video lecture to watch in his place. Machines have also replaced bank tellers, telephone operators, and checkout cashiers. If this trend continues, we will soon have robot waiters, nurses, and mechanics, and, finally, machine friends. We will have less and less human contact in our daily lives and less understanding of each other's wants and needs.

[3] ~~I would argue that~~ It is important to bring ~~more and more~~ people together rather ~~than~~ ~~to~~ separate them by introducing machines as friends talking to a machine. A lonely person may get some enjoyment ~~from~~ about politics or sharing a secret or juicy piece of gossip ~~conversing with a "charming, stimulating, and easygoing" machine~~, but the satisfaction would be much greater if ~~the person had~~ there were genuine human contact. It is true that ~~the machine would always be available~~ A human friend would respond less predictably and would probably have more authentic stories to tell, but the person would know that it had not come on its own free will. Nor would it be able to turn itself on. It would be totally dependent on the human user.

[4] Some people will find the prospect of having a friendly, intimate machine tempting. But I would urge them to reconsider their position. Instead of putting so much research time and money into developing friendly machines, why not study ways to bring people together and enhance human relations? People need spontaneous, human love, not a programmed simulation.

```
                                                            Wolf 3

                              Work Cited

Frude, Neil. The Intimate Machine. New York: New American
        Library, 1983. Print.
```

REVISE THE TITLE AND OPENING

Starting with the title, let us discuss some of the additions, deletions, and other changes Jane made. As we mentioned earlier, you will probably title your essay after you have revised your preliminary draft. Jane decided to phrase her title as a question: "Do We Want Programmed Friends?" Notice that she did not underline or italicize the essay title or place it in quotation marks.

Next, compare the opening sentences of the two drafts.

First Draft

```
A book titled The Intimate Machine describes a machine that could
be programmed to act like a friend.
```

Revised Draft

```
How do you regard your personal computer--as a "tool," a "colleague,"
or a "friend"?
```

The first draft begins with a statement of fact. Although this is an acceptable way to open an essay, Jane thought it was too formal, so she decided to address the reader with a question instead. Notice that the new opening also does a better job of establishing the writer's voice.

REVISE THE BODY PARAGRAPHS

If you refer to Jane's preliminary draft, you will see that the main way she altered the body paragraphs was by adding details. Paragraph 2 was already adequately developed with examples, but Jane needed to add details in order to flesh out paragraph 3. Both of these body paragraphs follow directly from the introduction. In paragraph 2, Jane develops the statement, "I worry that machines have already replaced too many people," and in paragraph 3, she explains why it is "better for people to befriend people than to become intimate with machines."

In this response essay, Jane could have developed the body paragraphs by quoting, paraphrasing, or summarizing pertinent ideas from the source and forging a connection between those ideas and her own thoughts. Also, she could have used any of the patterns of development (cause and effect, comparison and contrast, example, and so forth; see Table 1-1) to develop her body paragraphs. We describe the process of writing a response essay in Chapter 5.

REVISE THE CONCLUSION

Jane left her closing paragraph untouched because she was satisfied with its form and content. She brings her essay to a close by acknowledging that some people may not share her view and calling on her readers to change their outlook and set new priorities for the future.

ADD ATTRIBUTION

Comparing Jane's two drafts, you can see that in the revised version, she signals her reader each time she presents one of Frude's points. In the first draft, the reader is not always sure where Frude's ideas end and Jane's begin. The addition of attribution— "Frude claims that...," "...says Frude," "Frude points out..."—helps the reader make this differentiation.

IMPROVE FOCUS AND DEVELOPMENT

Well-written papers have a clear, sharply defined focus. When you reread your first draft, check to see if you present a consistent perspective throughout the entire piece. Make sure that you have not started off with a thesis that expresses your intention but then drifted away from it in the subsequent paragraphs. Also make sure that you have not started off with one intention as expressed in your thesis but ended up with another position.

If you drifted away from your original goal, examine each sentence to determine how the shift took place. You may need to eliminate whole chunks of irrelevant material, add more content, or rearrange some of the parts. If this is the case, ask yourself these questions:

- What should I add so that my audience can follow my train of thought more easily?
- What should I eliminate that does not contribute to my central focus?
- What should I move that is out of place or needs to be grouped with material elsewhere in the paper?

After you make these changes, read over your work to make sure that the new version makes sense, conforms to your organizational plan, and shows improvement.

IMPROVE COHESION

When you are satisfied with your focus and development, check that the ideas in the essay connect with each other. Your readers should be able to follow your train of thought by referring to preceding sentences, looking ahead to subsequent sentences, and being mindful of transitions and other connective devices. The following are some common connective devices.

- Repeating words or parts of words
- Substituting synonyms or related words
- Using personal pronouns and demonstrative pronouns (*this, that*) with easily recognizable referents

- Using explicit or implied transitions that signal relationships such as addition, exemplification, opposition, similarity, cause, effect, or time order
- Substituting a general term for a more specific term or terms

To illustrate, here is a paragraph from an essay student Maura Kennedy wrote in response to John Knowles's novel *A Separate Peace*. We have highlighted and labeled some of the connective devices. See if you can find others.

A Separate Peace shows that sarcasm helps us to escape from stating the truth straightforwardly. Gene, the [Repeats word] weaker character, uses sarcasm to express disapproval, [Synonym] whereas [Transition: contrast] Finny, the symbol of strength, blatantly states his [Repeats word] disapproval. Gene uses sarcasm because [Transition: cause] he feels resentment toward Finny. His [Pronoun] indignation [Synonym] stems from jealousy. This [Demonstrative pronoun] becomes evident after Finny charms his way out of trouble for wearing the Devon tie as a belt. Gene explains, "He had gotten away with everything. I felt a sudden stab of disappointment." Later, [Transition: Time] he [Pronoun] adds, "That was because [Transition: contrast] I just wanted to see some more excitement; that [Repeats word] must have been it" (Knowles 21). Although Gene's jealousy almost causes him to dislike Finny, he cannot admit this painful fact, [General term] and he [Pronoun] covers it up.

Exercise 1.5

Identify the connective devices in the following paragraphs from Maura Kennedy's essay written in response to John Knowles's novel *A Separate Peace*.

I have often tried to cover up the truth as well. I once had a very close friend, "Sally," whom I gradually came to despise. I kept telling myself that Sally was conceited and cared about no one but herself. I later realized that I, being shy, was jealous of her outgoing personality and her ability to make people like her. Just as Gene realizes that he and Finny aren't "competitors," that Finny has always thought of him as his best friend and would never do anything to hurt him, I realized the same about my friend. Then I became even more annoyed, because even though I was rude to Sally, she still thought of me as her best friend. My annoyance caused a resentment that eventually ended our friendship. By the time I realized this, we were both better friends with other people. Gene also realizes too late that his competition with Finny "was so ludicrous [he] wanted to cry" (Knowles 58). I too found this out after Sally and I had stopped being best friends. And like Gene, I still think about it today, three years later.

Gene, meanwhile, fools himself by making up stories. So does Finny. When Gene gets Leper's telegram, he immediately imagines Leper escaping from spies. He lets himself believe this because deep down he knows that whatever has happened to Leper probably isn't as exciting as his imaginative prediction. When Leper's real reason for "escaping" shatters his hopes, Gene must deal with the unpleasant truth that he had been avoiding. Although Finny's character is in many ways stronger than Gene's, Finny also makes up his own stories about the war in order to escape from reality. Finny doesn't want to accept the fact that he won't be fighting in the war. Because he doesn't like this idea, he tries to convince himself and others that there is really no war at all. To him, "the fat old men" in the government have made up the war (Knowles 107). He finally faces the truth about the war when he sees Leper. Knowles shows that even strong people like Finny delude themselves rather than recognize an unpleasant truth.

MOVE FROM WRITER-BASED TO READER-BASED PROSE

We have stressed the importance of considering your audience as you make stylistic decisions. One way to do this, as composition theorist Linda Flower points out, is to learn to distinguish between writer-based prose and reader-based prose. When you are getting your ideas down on paper, you put words down in the order in which they come to you. You record what makes sense to you, but you exert minimal effort to communicate these ideas to someone else. This type of egocentric writing is called *writer-based prose*. It is meaningful personally, but it may not make sense to a larger audience. In contrast, *reader-based prose* clearly conveys the writer's ideas to other people. The writer does not assume that the reader will understand automatically, so she provides information that will facilitate the reader's comprehension. It is easy to forget about audience amid all the complications of producing the first draft of an academic essay. That's why first drafts are quite often writer-based. An important function of revising is to convert this writer-based prose to something the reader can readily understand.

For an illustration of writer-based prose, read the following excerpt from a student's early draft. The topic is technological advancements, and Emily is responding to an article written by Bill Joy, cofounder and chief scientist of Sun Microsystems. The assignment asked students to select an article from their anthology and write a response that would appeal to their classmates. As you read, make note of features that are writer-based.

```
                                                          Korf 1

     Emily Korf

     Professor Smith

     Academic Writing I

     17 April 2008

                       Humans  and  Technology

          The article deals with the author's ideas about the interaction

     between humans and technology in the next century. Joy backs up his

     views with numerous examples and with references to conversations

     he has had with experts in the field. After reading his article,

     I feel that I agree with many of the points Joy raises.
```

From the outset, the student assumes the audience is familiar with both the assignment and the article on which it is based. The introduction begins, "The article deals with . . ." as if the reader knows in advance the article that will be discussed. The first sentence indicates that "the author" has "ideas" about "the interaction between humans and technology," but the student doesn't tell us about the nature of those ideas. What is Bill Joy's position? Does he fear or embrace technology? The introduction doesn't answer these questions. The student is writing for someone who already knows the author's viewpoint, not for classmates who may not have read the article. Similar failures to consider the audience occur throughout the paragraph.

Note how Emily transforms her introductory paragraph from writer-based prose to reader-based prose.

```
                                                          Korf 1

     Emily Korf

     Professor Smith

     Academic Writing I

     17 April 2008

                       Human  Obsolescence

          In "Why the Future Doesn't Need Us," Bill Joy, the cofounder

     and chief scientist of Sun Microsystems, expresses his fear that

     twentieth-century technology might exterminate the human species.
```

> His particular concern is that the world might be overrun by
> genetically engineered life forms capable of reproduction or
> self-replicating computerized robots. Joy backs up his views with
> strong evidence by providing numerous examples and references to
> respected scientists and computer experts, such as Ray Kurzweil
> and Hans Moravec. I agree with Joy that researchers must
> consider carefully how the technologies they produce will
> affect the larger society.

What does the revision tell you that the first draft does not? You learn the title of the article, the author's name and affiliation, Joy's position on technology, and Emily's reaction to that position. If you lay the two drafts side by side, you will see that Emily has cracked open the vague words in the first version. "Article" has been expanded to "Why the Future Doesn't Need Us"; "author" has become "Bill Joy, cofounder and Chief Scientist of Sun Microsystems"; "ideas" has become "his fear that twentieth-century technology might exterminate the human species" and "that the world might be overrun by genetically engineered life forms capable of reproduction or self-replicating computerized robots"; "experts" has become "Ray Kurzweil and Hans Moravec"; and "points" has become "researchers must consider carefully how the technologies they produce will affect the larger society." Emily has learned to write with detail.

As you revise your first drafts, make sure you have provided your readers with context or background for the material you have taken from sources. Add lots of detail and specific information. Unless the assignment indicates that the audience has read the sources, do not assume that your readers share your prior knowledge and experience.

REVISE SENTENCES FOR CLARITY AND STYLE

Earlier in this chapter in our discussion of stylistic choices, we stressed the importance of clear expression. Revise any sentences in your draft that might not communicate your ideas clearly to a reader. A classmate or friend can help you locate the sentences that need work by reading through your draft and putting a checkmark in the margin next to each sentence that seems unclear. Some of the sentences your reader checks may sound fine to you since you know your intended meaning, but you need to rework those sentences all the same. When someone can't follow a sentence you have written, the problem is with the sentence, not the reader.

As you revise for clarity and style, consult Appendix C: Revising for Style, where we provide strategies for making improvements in the following areas:

STRATEGIES FOR IMPROVING STYLE COVERED IN APPENDIX C

- Avoid inflated language.
- Vary the structure and length of your sentences.

- Strengthen your verbs.
- Make your writing concise by cutting ineffective words and expressions and eliminating needless repetition.
- Liven up your writing with detail.
- Avoid sexist language.

As you revise sentences, it will help to keep in mind the following advice that Joseph Williams provides in his book *Style: Lessons in Clarity and Grace,* ninth edition:

> Express actions [in sentences] in verbs.... Make the subjects of those verbs the characters associated with those actions. (51)

This basic principle of revision will help you restructure confusing sentences so that the central meaning stands out for your reader.

PROOFREADING

We use the term "proofreading" to refer to the process of checking for details: spelling, punctuation, word usage, and grammar. Of course, you often catch your own mistakes as you write and revise, so proofreading typically begins early in the writing process, as soon as you begin to get words on the page. That said, focusing too intently on proofreading in early drafts may interrupt your train of thought and sap your creativity. Much of the published advice on writing recommends getting your thoughts down, expanding on them fully, and organizing them coherently before you worry about matters of correctness. Even for those who prefer to edit as they write, it is important to proofread carefully as the final step in the writing process.

All students have the experience of handing in papers they have proofread carefully, only to receive them back with instructors' comments pointing out errors that seem obvious to the students in retrospect. Professors miss errors in their own writing. As we worked on this fourth edition of our textbook, we detected several errors that had been repeated in our three previous editions, errors that we and our editors did not see while proofreading the manuscripts and page proofs of the earlier editions.

Why do we overlook, at least on occasion, obvious errors in our written work? Part of the answer, undoubtedly, has to do with the way our brains process information when we read. We think of our eyes as smoothly scanning the printed page, but our eyes actually move across the page in small jumps, called saccades. We take in information from the page only when the eye is still, not when it is making a jump. When the eye takes in information from the page, the brain processes the meaning and structure of the text and makes predictions on what will come next. Based on these predictions, the brain instructs the eye to make successive saccades across the page, pulling in new information from the page and filling in any gaps to make meaning. This process of filling in the gaps makes it possible for us to read quickly rather than having to stop to perceive each word and figure out how it fits into the context of the surrounding text. But another result is that we sometimes make unconscious predictions about what will come up next in the text that are off the mark. These faulty predictions may make us stumble over words when we are reading out loud. Once we catch the problem, we backtrack to get the right words. If, however, the inaccurate prediction fits into the structure and meaning of the rest of the sentence, we may never notice that the word or phrase that the brain expected was different from what appeared on the page. The brain's efforts to fill the gaps as we read accounts for our unconscious ability to mentally "correct" errors as we proofread but still fail to correct the written text. In other words, we read what we meant, not what we actually wrote.

So how do we proofread if our brains work against us by hiding our own errors? The key to accurate proofreading is to establish a list of the errors you typically make and then develop a method for locating each of those errors in your drafts. For many common errors, the "Find" or "Search" functions on word processing programs can help you locate and correct problems. For example, if you tend to confuse "there" and "their," use the Find function to locate each occurrence of those words in your draft and check to make sure you use the correct spelling in each instance. This method counteracts your natural tendency to mentally "correct" errors since you are not processing the sentences in a meaningful sequence but rather just focusing on sentence parts.

Keep a list of your own problem areas. The night before you submit an essay, proofread it by using the Find function to locate each of these potential problem areas in your draft.

Another way to circumvent your brain's auto correction mechanism is to proofread your sentences in reverse order, beginning with the last sentence in the essay and working backward to the first. This technique breaks up the logical sequence of your sentences, which reduces the likelihood that your brain will attempt to make those subconscious predictions of what is coming next; consequently, it is easier to notice errors.

Appendix B: Editing for Correctness contains explanations of the following common proofreading concerns:

Sentence Structure
>   Clauses and Sentences (485–488)
>   Sentence Fragments (488–489)
>   Run-On Sentences and Comma Splices (489–491)
>   Elliptical Constructions (491)
>   Dangling Constructions (492)
>   Parallel Structure (492–493)

Verbs
>   Subject-Verb Agreement (493–494)
>   Tense Switching (494–495)

Pronouns
>   Clear Antecedents (495–496)
>   Other Mismatches between Pronouns and Their Antecedents (496)
>   Pronoun Consistency (496–497)

Misused Words (497–499)

Punctuation
>   Commas (499–501)
>   Apostrophes (501–503)
>   Semicolons and Colons (503–504)

SPELLING

Use the spelling checker, but be aware that it will not detect all errors. For example, consider the following sentence:

> The orchestra preformed works by Bach and Hayden.

The third word in the sentence should be "performed" rather than "preformed." "Preformed" is actually a word which refers to something that is formed in advance of use, so the spelling checker will not mark it as an error. For the most part, spelling software is not sophisticated enough to analyze the context of words.

A WORD ABOUT AUTO CORRECT

If you use the "Auto correct" function of your spelling checker, the software will change spellings automatically as you type. While this feature helps you get ideas down without having to interrupt your flow of thought to look up spellings, it may introduce errors by guessing incorrectly. A comparative study of error patterns in first-year college writing found that "wrong word" errors have increased dramatically over the last two decades, and the study authors suggest that spelling checkers may be responsible (Lunsford and Lunsford). For example, if you are working rapidly and mistakenly type "defintly" rather than "definitely," the spelling checker may insert the correction as "defiantly." A common problem with the Auto correct function is that the spelling checker will interpret a person's name as a misspelling and then attempt to correct it, for example, changing the last name "Littel" to "Little." As we have stressed earlier, it is important in academic writing to cite the source of borrowed ideas or language. Be careful that the authors' names you cite are spelled correctly.

As with other proofreading concerns, you can reduce your spelling errors by keeping a list of frequent misspellings and then searching for those misspelling using the Find function of your word processor.

Good editing skills depend on your knowledge of sentence structure, punctuation, usage, and spelling, but even more important is your commitment to getting it right and your willingness to invest time attending to detail. As we explained earlier, even if you know grammatical conventions thoroughly, you'll make mistakes in initial drafts because your primary focus is on getting thoughts down on paper, not on comma placement and spelling. As you edit your papers, you have to train your eyes and brain to detect commonplace errors. Otherwise, you will be using your time inefficiently.

SUBMITTING THE FINAL DRAFT

When you have finished proofreading your paper, print out your final draft on the best quality printer you have access to. Use black ink only. If you are relying on your own printer, don't wait until the night before the essay is due to make sure you have black ink in your printer cartridge. Check each page for ink smears, paper tears, and other printing errors. Make sure that each page is there, including the Works Cited list.

The advice in the preceding paragraph may seem self-evident, but students who have worked hard on essays sometimes undermine their efforts by failing to check the final draft for obvious problems. If you submit an essay that is missing pages, you may lose credit since, from the instructor's perspective, the essay is not finished until it can be evaluated.

A SUMMARY OF THE WRITING PROCESS

Prewriting
- Analyze the assignment
- Establish a focus
- Read and respond to sources

Drafting
- Develop a thesis
- Select an organizational plan
- Write a first draft
  - Title your essay
  - Establish a style
  - Write an introduction
  - Write the body of the essay
  - Integrate source material
  - Write the conclusion
  - Construct a list of sources

Revising
- Revise the title and opening
- Revise the body paragraphs
- Revise the conclusion
- Add attribution
- Improve focus and development
- Improve cohesion
- Move from writer-based to reader-based prose
- Revise sentences for clarity and style

Proofreading

Submitting the final draft

Here is a copy of Nora Gold's final draft. As you read through it, notice how she combines material from a number of reading sources in order to make a statement about teen curfews.

Gold 1

Nora Gold

Professor Smith

Academic Writing I

30 March 2008

Curfew Laws: Demonizing Teens

In the summer of 1996, sixteen-year-old Asha Sidhu was
arrested by the San Diego police, taken to the station,
interrogated by officers, accused of various offenses, and held
for hours, all without her parents' being informed (Allen 4).
What crime did she commit? She was out after the 10:00 p.m.
curfew. Even though she was only two blocks from her home and
was out with her parents' permission, the San Diego curfew law
gave the police the right to treat this honor student as if she
were a common criminal (4). Teen curfew laws, such as the one
enforced in San Diego, are being established in cities across
the United States for the alleged purpose of reducing youth
crime. These laws will do little to deter those teens who are
criminally inclined and are unfair to the millions of young
people who have done nothing to deserve being held under house
arrest. Enforcing teen curfews amounts to penalizing young
people so that adults can enjoy a false sense of security and
politicians can give the impression that they are tough on crime.

More and more frequently, American communities are relying
on curfews in their efforts to battle youth- and gang-related
crime. Over seventy percent of the largest two hundred cities in
the United States had youth curfews by the late 1990s (Diviaio).
Typical curfew hours are 11:00 p.m. on weeknights and 12:00 p.m.
on Fridays and Saturdays, and these restrictions usually apply
to individuals under eighteen ("Juvenile Curfews"). In addition

to curfews passed by city and town governments, certain privately owned shopping malls have established teen curfews. According to the International Council of Shopping Centers, shopping malls in no fewer than ten states have established youth curfews ("Mall Madness"). In many cases, mall curfews deny entry on Friday and Saturday after 6:00 p.m. to anyone under eighteen unless they are under the supervision of someone over twenty-one ("Mall Madness"). The combination of strict public and private sector curfews could essentially confine teens to home and school unless they are accompanied by an adult.

From several different perspectives, youth curfews represent an attack on Americans' civil liberties. The Supreme Court has ruled that "neither the Fourteenth Amendment nor the Bill of Rights is for adults alone" (qtd. in Herman). The most obvious constitutional problem is that curfews grant police the power to detain citizens for nothing more than appearing young (Budd 23). This blatant age discrimination is arguably a violation of the constitutional principle of equal protection under the law, a Fourteenth Amendment right (Diviaio). Some curfew laws include provisions that fly in the face of Fourth Amendment protections against unreasonable search and seizure. For instance, a law passed in Cicero, Illinois, gives police the right to seize the vehicles of teenagers who violate the local curfew ("Lights Out"). Court challenges to curfew laws have defended teens' "fundamental right to free movement" (Herman) as well as their rights to travel to and from evening jobs and even to stand or sit on their own sidewalks ("Juvenile Curfews"). Finally, some curfew laws may violate teens' First Amendment rights if they restrict

Gold 3

opportunities for young people to attend religious services or

school meetings held in the evening ("Juvenile Curfews").

 Some people might argue that it is worth sacrificing the

4

constitutional rights of teenagers in order to protect all

Americans, young and old, from crime. There is, however, little

evidence that curfews make our country any safer. On the

surface, it seems unlikely that curfews would deter anyone with

serious criminal intentions. Budd points out that teens who are

willing to risk spending years in jail for committing serious

crimes, such as burglary or assault, are unlikely to fear the

relatively minor penalties for violating curfew laws (22). Crime

statistics support this notion. According to Budd, no studies

have provided empirical evidence that curfews actually work

(22). For example, San Diego officials claim their curfew law

helped reduce juvenile crime; Budd points out, however, that the

crime rate decline occurred only during hours of the day not

covered by the curfew (22-23). According to legal scholar

Danielle Diviaio, research studies indicate that curfews are not

a significant factor in deterring crime. These studies show,

among other things, that "curfews do not work because (1) most

crime happens during non-curfew hours, (2) juveniles who do not

fear getting caught for a crime will not fear violating juvenile

curfew laws" (Diviaio). In the case of Ramos v. Town of Vernon,

the court ruled that the government could not prove that the

curfew law under consideration had any impact on gang activity

or youth safety (Divialo).

 If curfews appear to violate teens' rights and do not even

5

accomplish their intended purpose of reducing crime, why are

more and more cities establishing curfews? One reason that
curfews appeal to politicians and adult citizens is that they
give the appearance of attacking crime without asking the
taxpayers to provide much additional funding. According to Rice
University sociologist Steven Kleinberg, "People feel insecure
economically, and so there's resistance to dealing with
delinquency through measures that require an investment.... In
this climate of thought, it's a helpful belief to say, 'It's
their [teens'] fault'" (Allen 5). Curfews remain in place
because Americans under age eighteen cannot vote and thus lack
the political power to resist unfair laws. As Budd points out,
"Such a blunt and overreaching crime-fighting technique would
clearly be unenforceable against adults." Legal scholar David
Herman points out that children cannot make effective use of the
democratic process to overturn laws that were passed for
political motives:

> Even if it turns out that a curfew does nothing to prevent
> juvenile crime and victimization, children are unlikely
> to be able to bring about the repeal of the ineffective
> ordinance. The law will remain in place, therefore,
> although it imposes great restrictions on children's
> freedom with little appreciable benefit.... There is a
> danger ... that the curfews are actually enacted to benefit
> adults' interest in aesthetics, peace and quiet, or even
> their distaste for the lifestyles of certain young
> people.... While reducing juvenile crime and victimization
> may be compelling interests, removing unpleasant-looking
> youths from the nighttime streets is not.

Gold 5

Sociologists have argued that youth crime can be addressed effectively only through programs that help teens develop into productive adults, such as after-school tutoring and sports, rather than laws that attempt to keep them off the streets (Allen 4-5). Rather than addressing social problems that affect teens, the focus of curfew laws is seemingly "to make adults feel better" ("Lights Out"). Surely, our efforts and money should go into programs for troubled youth that appear to work rather than senseless curfew enforcement, which, although inexpensive, does nothing.

"The image of dissolute youth roaming the streets in search of victims is now a fixture of our political rhetoric, and curfews offer a satisfying and uncomplicated solution" (Budd 23). A curfew is a simplistic and ineffective response to teen crime. Until we develop and support effective programs to address poverty, domestic violence, drug abuse, and a host of other social problems, teen crime will continue. Harassing thousands of innocent teenagers, such as Asha Sidhu, will do nothing to make our streets safer.

Gold 6

Works Cited

Allen, John. "U.S. Teens Face Rash of Get-Tough Actions As
     Nation's Fear Grows." *National Catholic Reporter* 10 Jan.
     1997: 4-5. *General OneFile.* Web. 16 March 2008.
Budd, Jordan C. "Juvenile Curfews: The Rights of Minors vs. the
     Rhetoric of Public Safety." *Human Rights* Fall 1999.
     American Bar Association. Web. 16 March 2008.

Diviaio, Danielle. "The Government Is Establishing Your Child's
        Curfew." *St. John's Journal of Legal Commentary* 21.3 (Spring-
        Summer 2007): 797-835. *LexisNexis Academic.* Web. 16 Mar. 2008.

Herman, David A. "Juvenile Curfews and the Breakdown of the
        Tiered Approach to Equal Protection." *New York University
        Law Review* 82 (Dec. 2007): 1857-93. *LexisNexis Academic.*
        Web. 16 Mar. 2008.

"Juvenile Curfews and the Major Confusion Over Minor Rights."
        Harvard Law Review 118 (May, 2005): 2400-21. *LexisNexis
        Academic.* Web. 16 Mar. 2008.

"Lights Out." *The Economist* 18 Sept. 1999: 30. Print.

"Mall Madness." *Know Your World Extra* 11 Jan. 2008: 8-9.
        Proquest Research Library. Web. 16 March 2008.

Exercise 1.6

Study Nora's essay, and then answer the following questions.

1. What is Nora's overall purpose? What point is she making? How does she get that message across to her readers?
2. What aspects of the essay remind you of things you have been taught in the past about writing?
3. What aspects of the essay are at odds with what you have been told about writing? Can you account for any discrepancy?
4. How does Nora's essay differ from essays you have written in high school?
5. What is the relationship between Nora's ideas and those of the authors of the sources she cites?
6. Which approach is Nora using: simply telling her readers the contents of the reading sources, giving her readers a new understanding of information in the reading sources, or using that information as support for her own thesis or point of view?

PART II

Reading Sources and Incorporating Them into Your Writing

CHAPTER 2

Reading Sources

READING ACADEMIC TEXTS

College students sometimes have difficulty comprehending assigned reading. Even when they understand the text, they find it hard to communicate that understanding in writing. Why do students who were accomplished readers in high school experience problems with reading comprehension? In this chapter, we give you some insight into this phenomenon. Read each of the following passages and then summarize the main ideas.

Passage 1

Man is spirit. But what is spirit? Spirit is the self. But what is the self? The self is a relation which relates itself to its own self, or it is that in the relation [which accounts for it] that the relation relates itself to its own self; the self is not the relation but [consists in the fact] that the relation relates itself to its own self. Man is a synthesis of the infinite and the finite, of the temporal and the eternal, of freedom and necessity, in short it is a synthesis. A synthesis is a relation between two factors. So regarded, man is not yet a self. (Kierkegaard 146)

Passage 2

One of childhood's saddest figures is the one who hangs around the fringes of every group, walks home alone after school, and sobs in despair, "Nobody wants to play with me." Children can be unpopular for many reasons, sometimes because they are withdrawn or rebellious. They may walk around with a "chip on the shoulder," showing unprovoked aggression and hostility. Or they may act silly and babyish, showing off in immature ways. Or they may be anxious and uncertain, exuding such a pathetic lack of confidence that they repel other children, who don't find them fun to be with. (Papalia and Olds 233)

Most students have difficulty with the passage by the Danish philosopher Kierkegaard but no problem with the passage by Papalia and Olds. Kierkegaard's vocabulary is no more complex than that of Papalia and Olds, so what accounts for the disparity in comprehensibility? A fundamental difference between the two passages is that Kierkegaard's definition of "self" is theoretical and abstract, whereas Papalia and Olds's description of unpopular children is grounded in everyday experience. Readers comprehend not just by recognizing vocabulary but also by relating the content to prior knowledge and experience. As you read Passage 2, you may picture an unpopular child whom you know. Because you already have the background knowledge to make this image concrete, the text is easy to understand. As you read Passage 1, you are stumped. Since you haven't thought much about the philosophical definition of self, the text is enigmatic.

Another factor that contributes to comprehension is text organization. The Papalia and Olds passage is easy to understand because it follows a logical, conventional pattern. It starts with the effect of unpopularity—the lonely child—and goes on to list the causes of the problem. The Kierkegaard passage is difficult to grasp because it doesn't follow a familiar pattern.

You can make sense of the child passage because you have a working knowledge of the concept of *unpopularity* and the organizational pattern of cause and effect. Your stored mental images of these phenomena are called *schemata*. You have schemata for any number of things, for example, how a college course is conducted. When you entered the classroom on the first day of your writing course, you probably took a seat, faced the front of the room, and waited for your professor to begin since you have experienced that routine innumerable times in your career as a student. If your professor had not come to the front of the room but rather had taken a seat in the back, opened his book, and began reading quietly, you would undoubtedly have felt confused, because the circumstances would not fit with your mental schema for how a class functions. We acquire schemata from our experiences in the world and we rely on our schemata to make sense of new situations we encounter. If new circumstances are at odds with our existing schemata, we try as best we can to make tentative links to what we already know.

Strategies designed to improve reading comprehension typically begin with activities that involve surveying the reading source to get an idea of its content and generating preliminary links between that content and the reader's prior knowledge. These prereading activities activate the reader's preexisting schemata for the source topic and thus prepare the ground for understanding the text. In the past, you have probably learned one or more prereading strategies. When you have difficulty understanding a text, it is because you lack the appropriate background and cannot make connections between its content and your mental schemata.

Exercise 2.1

Read "Race, Higher Education, and American Society" by Yolanda T. Moses on pages 458–469. As you read, write "yes" in the margin next to passages that match up with your prior knowledge and "no" next to passages that are unrelated to your experience. Are the passages marked "yes" easier to understand than those marked "no"? Estimate the percentage of the selection that is recognizable and the percentage that is unfamiliar.

Next, read Jerry Farber's essay "A Young Person's Guide to the Grading System" on pages 385–388 and annotate the margin as you did for the Moses reading. Again, estimate the percentage of the selection that is recognizable and the percentage that is unfamiliar. Based on the percentages for Farber and Moses, which selection should be easier to understand? Which do you think you actually did understand better?

A COMPREHENSIVE STRATEGY FOR THE READING PROCESS

Despite the gaps that exist between texts and prior knowledge, it is possible to improve your reading comprehension. The key is to approach texts from several perspectives. In this chapter, we describe a powerful reading strategy that will enable you to do so.

COMPREHENSIVE READING STRATEGY

- Grasp the *content,* the main idea, and details.
- Determine how the text functions: its *genre, organization,* and *stylistic features.*
- Identify the *rhetorical context:* the context in which the author is writing and the effect he or she means to achieve.

As you use each strategy, ask yourself the following questions.

STRATEGY	QUESTIONS
Reading for content	What is the main idea?
	How is the main idea supported and developed?
	What other content is important?
Reading for genre, organization, and stylistic features	Is the text in an identifiable genre?
	How do the different parts function?
	How is the text organized?
	What are the text's distinctive stylistic features?
Reading for rhetorical context	What is the author's purpose?
	How is the author trying to affect the audience?
	What are the circumstances surrounding the production of the text?

When you use these strategies, you read in three different but not necessarily separate ways. All three approaches can be used simultaneously and harmoniously. For the purposes of this discussion, however, we present the strategies one by one.

READING FOR CONTENT

When we read for content, we read for concepts, main ideas, and supporting information. This reading requires versatility and various degrees of exertion. We scan the front page of the newspaper to find out the latest developments in a current political crisis; we thumb through *Consumer Reports* to locate facts on a car we're interested in buying; we study a textbook to learn details about an important historical event; and we debate with the premise of a journal article we wish to incorporate in our own writing.

When you read for content, you must be *active*. This means reading with a purpose instead of passively processing print. An example of active reading is reading a scholarly article to discern the author's position on a topic you are researching for a term paper. Your purpose is clear: to find expert opinions you can quote in support of your argument. The following strategies will help you to be an active reader.

STRATEGIES THAT PROMOTE ACTIVE READING

- Call up your prior knowledge, experience, and feelings about the topic.
- Preview the text and derive questions that will guide your reading.
- Annotate the text and take notes.

Calling Up Prior Knowledge, Experience, and Feelings

Prior knowledge and experience enable you to construct meaning for new information. You will comprehend difficult texts with ease if you can relate them to existing conceptual frameworks. This is why people who have read extensively in a subject find it easy to understand complex texts written in that area. Prior knowledge prepares them to receive new information. Prior experience may bias you in certain ways, but it makes comprehension possible. As a process-oriented reader, you will benefit from your prior knowledge and experience *before* you read, *while* you are reading, and *after* you have completed the text.

USING PRIOR KNOWLEDGE IN THE READING PROCESS

- Tap your prior knowledge *before* you read.
- Probe for links between the content and your prior knowledge *while* you are reading.
- Look for additional links *after* you have read through the text.

These strategies enable you to take full advantage of what you already know as you unpack the meaning of the text. At the same time, they make you aware of how prior knowledge and experience influence your reading. Two ways to tap prior knowledge and experience are **freewriting** and **brainstorming.**

As we explained in Chapter 1 (pages 11–12), freewriting involves writing anything that comes to mind about a topic. Write nonstop for ten minutes and don't worry about usage, spelling, or mechanics. Jot down whatever is in your head. Here is an excerpt from the freewriting a student completed prior to reading Moses's "Race, Higher Education, and American Society" in Chapter 14 of this book. She is writing in response to the title of the Moses article.

> When I was looking at colleges, all the material we received from their admissions offices stressed diversity. All the brochures showed students of various races and ethnic backgrounds, which appealed to me. One of the main reasons I wanted to attend college away from home was to meet people who are not just the same as those I grew up with. It's not that I was tired of my friends from back home, but I felt that I needed to move out of my comfort

zone and give myself room for personal growth. My parents also wanted me to attend a college with a diverse student body. They thought the experience would prepare me better for the American workforce of the future that will be increasingly diverse. That's why they had me study Spanish in high school rather than French as they did. When I actually visited campuses, I found that they were actually less diverse than my high school, which came as a big surprise. It seems that the colleges I was considering wanted diversity but that it was still a goal that they were working toward. Perhaps the article by Moses will explain why campuses are still less diverse than American society as a whole.

Brainstorming uses a process of free association. To begin the process, skim the text for key words or phrases that are pivotal to the assignment. Then list the associations that come to mind when you think about these target concepts. Don't bother to write complete sentences; just list words and phrases. Give your imagination free rein. Here's a short list of words and phrases a student generated after skimming Moses's article:

What I learned in the past about the role of race in American education

- Brown v. Topeka Board of Education Supreme Court decision
- separate but equal
- affirmative action
- reverse discrimination
- test scores and college admissions
- recruiting for diversity: fair to everyone?
- school desegregation: Little Rock, South Boston
- the documentary film Eyes on the Prize shown on PBS
- comparison of urban and suburban high schools
- busing
- athletic recruitment and race
- elimination of affirmative action in California and Texas
- student organizations based on race and ethnic background: racist?
- campus housing units that are based on race and ethic background: racist?
- ethnic studies majors and minors at colleges
- diversity awareness programs in the dorms
- college speakers that focus on issues of diversity

Freewriting and brainstorming help you to access prior knowledge of key concepts and make fuller sense of your background. These procedures also make you more conscious of your opinions and biases so you won't inadvertently confuse your views with those of the author. All the same, because you comprehend texts by relating known concepts to new ideas, you can never be completely objective. Your understanding is always a function of what you already know.

Previewing and Deriving Questions

After you have tapped your prior knowledge, set some goals for what you expect to get from the text. Then preview the text by reading the introduction, headings, and any print in special type. If you are reading a textbook, use the reader aids that accompany each chapter: preview outlines, introductory and concluding sections, and review questions. Then generate questions about the content. For example, what do you expect to find out? What more do you want to know about the topic? Answer these questions as you read. This tactic works best if you write out the questions beforehand and record the answers as you come to them. If you enter the questions and answers in a reading journal or log, you can reread them at a later date. Too often, students spend hours reading information-rich texts only to find several days later that they remember nothing and must reread the material. The extra time it takes to preview a text and formulate reading questions represents a real savings compared to the extra time needed for rereading the text.

Annotating the Text and Taking Notes

Another strategy that promotes active reading is to enter into a dialogue with the author by *annotating* the text as you read. *Annotating* means making marginal notes, underlining or highlighting important concepts, and recording brief responses to what the author says. The following example shows a student's annotations of paragraph 6 from Yolanda Moses's article. The student uses the right margin to highlight important concepts and record personal reactions.

> Modern anthropology's roots lie in nineteenth-century European natural history traditions, with their focus on the classification and comparison of human populations and their search for indicators of "mental capacity." Cultural anthropologists such as L.H. Morgan and E.B. Tylor worked with physical anthropologists of the time to "scientifically" reconstruct human prehistory and to rank human groups along a unilinear evolutionary path from "savagery" to "civilization." Morgan considered mental development crucial to a group's evolutionary progress. Physical indicators of evolutionary rank were developed, including such attributes as the degree of facial projection and the position of the foramen magnum. Measurements of cranial dimensions and proportions ("the cephalic index") were initially proposed as indicators of advancement. Cranial size and the weight and morphological complexity of the brain were other measures used to infer the "mental capacity" of

Margin annotations:

View of 19th century anthropologists on race.

Morgan and Tylor

Does this imply that we are still evolving? That we are smarter, in general, than ancient Egyptians and ancient Greeks?

Is this called phrenology?

various groups (e.g., "races," sexes, immigrant groups) according to their "natural" "intellectual endowments," which presumably identified their overall evolutionary rank (Mukhopadhyay and Moses 1997:518).

Totally unfair!!!

An effective annotation technique is to use prior knowledge to *elaborate* the text. *Elaborations* are associations, extensions, illustrations, or evaluations. Elaborate by suggesting situations the author has not envisioned and by providing analogies, examples, or counterexamples. Here is how a student elaborates on ideas in paragraph 27 of Moses's article.

As I stated earlier, in this section I am going to discuss how salient words such as "merit" and "quality" are used in the admissions process and how a single standardized test such as the SAT figures more prominently, not less, in the arguments used by conservatives to describe why minorities are not qualified (read "worthy") to attend elite institutions. The SAT exam and the vocabulary of "worthiness" that tends to be used in connection with it create an artificial environment that reinforces the myth that individual merit and intelligence can only be measured by scores on such tests. The fact that minorities and women consistently do worse on these tests is assumed to mean that there must be some underlying immutable, natural reason for this.

Why use SAT scores at all for college admissions? Why not rely primarily on high school grades? Don't the grades, accumulated over many years of education, say more about how a person will perform in college than a single test taken on one particular day? Some people just don't test well when under time pressure. The two people from my high school class who got the highest scores on the SAT are really not the classmates I would feel confident going to in the future as my doctor or lawyer. Test taking skill is only a small part of what makes someone a good student who will go on to be a competent professional.

As you annotate, don't overuse highlighting markers. When you read through a text the first time, you may have difficulty deciding what's important. Every concept seems worthy of special attention. But if you highlight a large percentage of the text, you'll have a lot to reread when you study for an exam or search for ideas for papers. Another problem is that highlighting is a passive, mechanical activity. It only gives the illusion that you are engaged with the text. Instead of highlighting, write out summary statements and reactions. Writing forces you to process information, restate it in your own words, and react to it. The ultimate goals of annotating are to involve you intellectually with the text and give you access to it without rereading. Writing marginal notes is the best way to accomplish this.

The most successful strategy for reading difficult texts is to use the preview-and-question method or some other type of note-taking method along with marginal annotations. Keep in mind, however, that sometimes one system is more practical than the other. Since you can't annotate library materials, you have to take separate notes.

If texts are easy to read and have straightforward content, you can streamline note-taking and annotating procedures to capture only the most basic ideas. But remember that it's natural to forget much of what you've read; even relatively simple ideas slip from memory unless you write them down.

Whether you take separate notes or annotate, it's helpful to write out your reactions to the text. Designate a notebook as your reading journal or log. Reactions can include agreements and disagreements, questions for the author, and judgments on the text's relevance or acceptability. The written responses are another way of relating your prior knowledge to the author's ideas. Reacting as you read is especially important if you intend to write a paper that gives your views on the text. To get the juices flowing, ask the following questions.

QUESTIONS FOR REACTION

- What do you already know about this topic from books, magazines, television, school or college courses, personal experience, or conversation?
- What is the relationship between your prior knowledge and the content being presented in the text?
- Do you have personal opinions or biases on this topic? With what parts of the author's discussion do you agree or disagree?

Answering these questions will help you link content to relevant information that you already know.

Notice how the goals of summarizing and reacting are represented both in marginal notes and in a journal entry for paragraph 12 of Moses's article:

Over the past five to seven years, practitioners have been revisiting and reexamining the nature of race in both biological and cultural anthropology (e.g., Harrison 1995; Goodman 1996; Lieberman and Jackson 1995; Blakey 1987; Marks 1995; Sacks 1994; Shanklin 1994). The conclusion of most of us is that "race" does not exist as a biological phenomenon, but rather that it is socially and culturally constructed. Having said that, we also have said how important it is to understand that this statement does not explain why people *look* different. Most lay

Current views on basis of race: cultural or biological?

Current anthropologist: race is culturally constructed.

people, and some cultural anthropologists, do not know how to explain human variability in ways that are easily understood. So, in the absence of reasonable anthropological explanation, many people tend to fall back on what they know, or what they think they know. The media and peers tend to reinforce uninformed stereotypes, and eventually these stereotypes become belief. For example, why were the sociobiological themes of Shockley's and Jensen's writings so popular with conservatives in the 1970s, and why was *The Bell Curve* such a best-seller only recently? Just a few years ago I proposed that it was because both books reinforce easy stereotypes that have long been held in this society, namely, that people of color and women are inferior to White males, and that our cultural institutions subliminally reinforce these notions in many ways, from advertising to loan policies, to work laws, to wages.

Hard to explain human variability.

Racial stereotypes are definitely reinforced in the media. Music videos (including, ironically, those on BET) often reinforce the stereotype of the Black male as a "gangsta." Black woman are often presented as sexual objects in these videos. "Uninformed stereotypes" to be sure!

I've never heard of The Bell Curve. I'll Google it.

Journal Notes

Modern anthropologists agree that the concept of race is created by our culture, not our biological makeup. This reminds me of the movie Black and White, which focused on a group of affluent White teenagers who were making a conscious decision to become "Black," by adopting speech patterns and stereotypical behavior associated with African Americans. The film portrayed the teens as more or less "posers" with a shallow understanding of Black culture. One of the points the film seems to make is that you can't just choose to be Black, that racial identity is formed by how society treats you as you grow up, which is based, in part, on your skin color.

Also useful is a *double-entry journal.* For this type of journal, you create two columns. In the left-hand column, you copy key passages from the text. In the right-hand column, you write your reactions, questions, interpretation, or evaluation.

Reading actively by taking notes, annotating, and reacting is important when your ultimate goal is to write about the text. Notes and annotations are the raw material for summaries and paraphrases, two forms of writing we discuss in Chapter 3. Responses recorded in marginal notes and freewriting are the basis for response essays. In Chapters 5 and 6, we discuss how you can move from these initial responses to essays of personal reaction and analysis. Active reading not only helps you understand the ideas in reading sources, it sets you well on the way to writing source-based essays.

Exercise 2.2

Read Kay Hymowitz's article, "Gloucester Girls Gone Wild" on pages 417–419. Use the active reading techniques described so far, and practice the process approach to reading. First, preview the text and use freewriting to activate your prior knowledge of the topic. Next, read the article and use the preview-and-question technique to take separate notes. Annotate the text as well. After you have finished reading, write your overall reactions to Hymowitz's argument.

READING FOR GENRE, ORGANIZATION, AND STYLISTIC FEATURES

To become a proficient college reader and writer, you have to pay attention to what authors are *doing* as well as saying. In addition to reading for content, you need to consider the genre, the organizational pattern, and the stylistic features of the text.

Just as you have prior knowledge related to content, you have expectations about the ways authors set up their texts. Since you've had at least twelve years of reading practice by the time you enter college, you know a great deal about genres, structures, and features of texts. You already know that stories have elements like setting, plot, and theme; business letters contain an inside address and salutation; poems sometimes rhyme and have uneven lines; and newspaper articles are constructed with the most important facts in the first paragraph and the less essential information later in the piece. In other words, you have developed conceptual frameworks for each genre. This type of knowledge is crucial to reading comprehension.

Genre

Your knowledge of the word *genre* may be restricted to your English teachers' discussions of textual forms: the genre of the novel, the short story, or the poem. Today, genre is understood as a broader concept. It refers to a wide range of standardized activities. In the classroom setting, you could speak of pedagogical genres—for example, the genre of show-and-tell in primary school and the genre of the in-place final examination in the university. Each of these activities has recognizable features and conventions. Each is a regularized or structured response to a recurring event. Everything we write can be described in terms of genre. These written genres are the focus of our discussion.

Most likely, you have no difficulty recognizing the literary genres we mentioned above or nonliterary genres like the news article, editorial, or biography. As you become more familiar with academic writing, you will be able to identify specialized genres like the psychological research article, the scientific lab report, and the philosophical essay of reflection. In this book, we concentrate on classroom genres which play a major role in college composition courses: the response essay, the comparison-and-contrast essay, the synthesis essay, the argument essay, the rhetorical analysis essay, the evaluation essay, and the research paper (See Table 2-1).

TABLE 2-1   Classroom Genres in Academic Writing

Essay Type	Characteristics
Summary Essay	Includes title, author, thesis, and key elements of the text. The essay reflects the organizational pattern of the source and closes by placing the source in a larger context.
Response Essay	Includes identification of the text to which the writer is responding, indication of the focus of the essay, commentary, and reactions.
Comparison-and-Contrast Essay	Presents a thesis based on the elements being compared or contrasted. The essay usually follows one of two patterns of organization. In the *point-by-point* pattern, the writer shifts back and forth between the elements being compared; in the *block* pattern, the writer explains one item completely before turning to the other.
Synthesis Essay	Includes a thesis or unifying theme around which the writer organizes material selected from two or more texts. The writer sets the context for the reader by giving appropriate background information on the reading sources. Clear connectives differentiate the writer's ideas from those of the authors of the other texts.
Argument Essay	Includes an argumentative thesis, background information on the issue, support for the position being argued, mention of positions in opposition to the writer's, and response to opposition.
Analysis Essay	Includes identification of the text being analyzed, background information, statement of the writer's purpose for writing, summary of main points of the source, and examination of the author's presentation. Shows how the author's technique and various parts of the text contribute to the theme and the author's purpose.
Evaluation Essay	Includes identification of the text being evaluated, background information, statement of the writer's purpose for writing, summary of the main points of the source, and consideration of the author's presentation. The essay includes comments on the author's success in achieving his or her purpose, usually by reviewing stylistic features and techniques. Discusses overall strengths and weaknesses.
Research Paper	Starts with a question or problem that requires collecting facts, opinions, and perspectives from books, magazines, newspapers, or other sources. The author makes sense of information derived from a variety of sources. May include literature review, analysis, or evaluation.

Readers familiar with the genres of academic writing have expectations about organization, textual features, and authors' intentions. When reading an argument essay, they assume the writer will lay out both sides of the controversial issue, make concessions to people holding opposing views and refute their claims, and marshal convincing evidence to support the thesis. Knowledge of genre is indispensable if you want to read with full comprehension. Make a conscious effort to learn new genres whenever possible. The reading selections in Part V of this book will give you a good start.

Exercise 2.3

Select one of the readings in Part V of this book. Identify the genre and list the characteristics on which you based your decision.

Patterns of Organization and Development

Just as you come to college already knowing something about genre, you also bring knowledge of the basic organization of texts. You can identify introductions, conclusions, theses or main idea statements, and topic sentences of paragraphs. In your own essays, you've used organizational plans, such as cause and effect or comparison and contrast. Writers use a variety of these patterns, depending on their purpose for writing. Review the organizational plans for academic writing that we presented in Table 1-1 (page 16).

Occasionally, writers tell their readers how they are going to organize material. In the introductory paragraph of her article, Moses informs us that she will explore three premises.

"Race, higher education, and American society" are three topics that I care deeply about and have written and talked about separately on many other occasions. In this article I want to bring them together in a way that helps me to lay out three major observations that I have been thinking about as I go about my work as an anthropologist, as a spokesperson for higher education—especially public education—and as someone who still believes in the potential of American society to deliver its promise of an equitable, culturally pluralistic society. (459)

When writers explain what they are doing or direct you to read in a certain way, you know what to expect. When they don't supply this information, you have to determine the pattern of development yourself.

A key to unlocking the meaning of a text is to identify the pattern of organization. A writer may use a single organizational pattern, but more likely he or she will use overlapping patterns. An initial, quick reading often gives you a sense of the text's overall organizational pattern. Keep this pattern in mind, and then, when you do a close reading, annotate the places where the author has used other patterns of development. Consider how one of our students annotated a paragraph from an article by musicologist Michael J. Budds:

Time order — In retrospect, it seems possible to identify a number of factors that help explain this radical change in musical taste. First of all, the popular song tradition of Tin Pan Alley, which had been centered in New York City and had flourished for more than three generations, began to show signs of wear. The search for fresh and compelling expression within the rather well-defined style became increasingly difficult. The traumatic events of World War II, moreover, made the sanitized worldview delivered in the *— Cause and effect* snappy dance songs and dreamy love ballads

Example —

that were hallmarks of the genre seem inappropriate or irrelevant to the new generation of youngsters. At the same time that Tin Pan Alley was reaching its peak in the songs of Gershwin, Kern, Rodgers, and Porter, two minority song traditions that had evolved from longstanding folk practice—the urban blues of black America and the country and western songs of rural white Southerners—entered the popular arena and reached a larger audience thanks to a process of commercialization that included recordings, radio stations, and more venues for live performance. The inexpensive portable transistor radio, a by-product of wartime technology, enabled young people to acquaint themselves with rhythm and blues as well as country and western music without parental knowledge or supervision.

The general plan for the paragraph is cause and effect; Budds identifies the various causes of a "radical change in musical taste." But within this overall pattern, Budds describes a time-ordered sequence of events and gives examples.

Exercise 2.4

Identify the patterns of development that the authors use in the following passages. Choose from the nine patterns presented in Table 1-1 (page 16). Remember that in some instances, patterns of development may overlap.

1. Page 394, paragraph 2, Stephen Ray Flora and Stacy Suzanne Poponak, "Childhood Pay for Grades Is Related to College Grade Point Averages"
2. Page 403, paragraphs 12 and 13, Sherry Turkle, "Cyberspace and Identity"

Stylistic Features

In addition to identifying the genre and organizational pattern of texts, proficient readers pay attention to stylistic features. They look at the writer's sentences and word choice, tone, and reliance on other textual sources. For a clearer understanding of stylistic features, first read the following passages and then read our comparison of Moses's and Farber's styles of writing.

Moses (paragraph 7)

Efforts to refine devices for measuring linked physical and mental traits existed well into the twentieth century. Such endeavors stimulated the development of psychometrics and the intelligence tests first used in World War I on nearly two million American military recruits. Consistent with Euro-American racial ideology, these tests were eventually put to civilian use. Psychologists interpreted results of these tests as indicators of heredity-based, innate intelligence and compared group scores to support ideologies of natural racial superiority and inferiority (Mukhopadhyay and Moses 1997:518). Anthropology helped establish an elaborate set of ideological principles, based on racial and biological determinism, which to this day deeply influence how the world understands human variation and its relations to human behavior. This racial worldview has provided a rationale for slavery, colonial and neocolonial domination, racial segregation, and discrimination and miscegenation laws, and it has fueled the eugenics and anti-immigration movements in the United States.

Farber (paragraph 4)

Learning happens when you *want* to know. Ask yourself: did you need grades to learn how to drive? To learn how to talk? To learn how to play chess—or play the guitar—or dance—or find your way around a new city? Yet these are things we do very well—much better than we handle that French or Spanish that we were graded on for years in high school. Some of us, though, are certain that, while we might learn to drive or play chess without grades, we still need them to force us to learn the things we don't really want to learn—math, for instance. But is that really true? If for any reason you really want or need some math—say, algebra—you can learn it without being graded. And if you don't want it and don't need it, you'll probably never get it straight, grades or not. Just because you pass a subject doesn't mean you've learned it. How much time did you spend on algebra and geometry in high school? Two years? How much do you remember? Or what about grammar? How much did all those years of force-fed grammar do for you? You learn to talk (without being graded) from the people around you, not from gerunds and modifiers. And as for writing—if you ever do learn to write well, you can bet your sweet ass it won't be predicate nominatives that teach you. Perhaps those subjects that we would never study without being graded are the very subjects that we lose hold of as soon as the last test is over.

COMPARISON OF THE STYLISTIC FEATURES OF THE TEXTS

Moses	*Farber*
All relatively long sentences. Sentences contain lengthy phrases or clauses.	Varied sentence length. Sentences are medium length or short, some only two to four words. He uses intentional fragments.
Some words, such as "psychometrics," are challenging. Language is formal.	Accessible, everyday words. Language is very informal.
Formal tone.	Informal tone.
Third-person point of view.	Second-person point of view, addressing the reader directly with the pronoun *you*.
Cites other sources and relies on readers' knowledge of history and scholarly concepts such as "neocolonialism."	Includes no references to outside sources. Makes a number of appeals to the reader's experience

Our analysis is based on five features of the text: *choice of sentences, words, tone, point of view,* and *reliance on other textual sources.* We looked first at sentence type, length, and complexity. All of Moses's sentences are straightforward statements, whereas almost half of Farber's sentences are questions addressed to the reader. Moses's sentences are relatively long, and some contain lengthy phrases: "Consistent with Euro-American racial ideology." Farber varies the length of his sentences between medium-sized and very short sentences. Some of Farber's sentences contain dependent clauses, but these longer sentences are balanced by intentional sentence fragments like "Or what about grammar?" that add to the informal tone.

Our next consideration was the authors' word choice. Moses uses words such as *miscegenation* and *eugenics.* Farber uses common, everyday language and an informal vocabulary bordering on vulgarity in *you can bet your sweet ass.* In general, Farber's language is down to earth while Moses includes words that are not commonly used outside the academic community.

The above features—sentence type, length, and complexity as well as word choice—contribute to the author's voice and tone. Moses's tone is formal and scholarly; Farber's is informal and chatty. Another feature contributing to tone is point of view. Moses writes in the third person; Farber addresses the reader in the second person, *you.*

The last stylistic feature we examined is called *intertextuality.* Intertextuality is the relationship between texts. It refers to the way writers relate other texts to their own text, often by incorporating the other texts in the form of direct quotations, paraphrases, summaries, or other types of references. Moses bolsters her position by referring to a previous publication. She also relies on the readers' knowledge of academic concepts, such as *biological determinism.* Farber doesn't refer to prior publications or academic concepts. Instead, he asks questions that evoke his readers' personal experiences.

Our textual analysis leads us to conclude that Moses writes in a formal style characteristic of many genres of academic writing. She uses long sentences, sophisticated language, a scholarly tone, and references to prior publications. In contrast, Farber has a relaxed, conversational style that we associate with informal writing. For a more detailed explanation of stylistic choices in academic writing, see pages 18–21.

We have provided a detailed analysis of the Moses and Farber passages in order to show you the roles stylistic features play in writing. We don't expect you to perform an exhaustive textual analysis each time you read a text. However, knowledge of the five stylistic features we have discussed—sentence type, length, and complexity; word choice; tone; point of view; and intertextuality—will better enable you to read critically and appreciate how the writer's style contributes to the text. On the occasions when you wish to delve deeper, ask yourself the following questions.

QUESTIONS FOR ANALYZING THE STYLISIC FEATURES OF TEXTS

- Does the writer vary the type of sentences? Do all the sentences function as statements, or do some ask questions, give commands, or express exclamations?
- What does the length of the sentences convey?
- What can you say about sentence complexity? Are the sentences simple and unpretentious or complex, remote, and scholarly?
- Does the writer put verbs into active or passive voice?
- Does the writer use difficult or specialized words?

> - How would you describe the point of view, voice, and tone? Does the writer use the first person (I, we), the second person (you), or the third person (he, she, it, they)?
> - How often does the writer draw on other sources? How do the references to other texts further the writer's agenda?
> - What do your answers to the preceding questions indicate about the author's writing style? Write a paragraph summarizing the style.

Your professors will undoubtedly assign texts that are more like Moses's than Farber's. As Moses does, scholarly writers frequently draw on evidence from prior publications or original research, taking care to cite and document their sources. They adopt formal tones and use lengthy, rather complex sentences. They often use specialized vocabulary or technical terms as well. But you will also be assigned texts by academic writers who use conversational, less formal writing styles like Farber's. One style is not necessarily more appropriate than the other.

It is difficult to make generalizations about academic writing style or describe it as a distinct entity. In academia, there are many different writing styles ranging from the prescribed style of the scientific research article in an upper level chemistry course to the relaxed style of free verse in an introduction to creative writing. Disciplines such as economics, finance, and accounting require textual features like headings and subheadings, enumeration, and figures and charts. Other disciplines, like engineering, stress the importance of visual and numeral texts.

In your own work, you will learn to write in styles that are appropriate to the rhetorical situation. The lab reports you write in biology will be formal, with concise sentences describing procedural matters. The personal essays you compose in English will be less formal with free-flowing sentences rich in descriptive detail. In later chapters, we include examples of professional and student writing that illustrate a range of styles and techniques.

Intertextuality

Of all the stylistic features we have discussed, the one that best characterizes academic discourse is the practice of drawing on other texts. Academic texts depend on other texts for their meaning. Sometimes writers simply refer to other sources, but more often they paraphrase, quote, or summarize them, always citing the author and providing bibliographic information for their readers. Let us illustrate with another example from Moses's article:

> Greater access to higher education for minorities has translated into better performance on standard school tests for their children. Grissmer, Kirby, Berends, and Williamson (1994) showed tremendous increases in the verbal and math proficiency scores of Black thirteen-to-seventeen-year-olds between 1970 and 1990 as measured by the National Assessment of Educational Progress (NAEP) Test. (463)

Moses refers to ideas in Grissmer, Kirby, Berends, and Williamson's book, *Student Achievement and the Changing Family,* published in 1994. She names the scholars and puts in parentheses the date of the publication. If readers want to know the book's title or if they wish to learn more about the research, they can consult the alphabetical list of references on the last pages of the Moses selection (see pages 468–469) and then locate the book in the library.

Another distinctive feature of academic writing is content endnotes or footnotes. When writers want to give their readers additional information but don't want to interrupt the flow of the text, they provide a reference numeral in the text and include the extra information in a footnote or in a list titled "Notes" at the end of the selection. Here is an example from Michael J. Budds's scholarly article on popular music.

> Song texts of mainstream America had long been influenced by the high culture of Europe, however watered down for middle-class consumption. Romantic love, the subject of the vast majority of all songs, was treated in a highly idealistic, typically sentimental manner. Although rarely profound, the language tended toward the poetic, preferring a high-priced vocabulary filled with euphemism and fully respectful of an unwritten, but widely sanctioned code of public propriety. Songs with texts overstepping this sensibility were banned by radio stations or deleted from the musical scores of Broadway and Hollywood.[7] Early in the nineteenth century, for example, Stephen Foster's Jeanie was "borne like a vapor on the summer air."
>
> 7. The grand exception appears to be songwriter/composer Cole Porter (1891–1964), whose witty but suggestive lyrics earned for him the nickname "the genteel pornographer" from Cecil Smith in *Musical Comedy in America* (New York: Theatre Arts Books, 1950).

The convention of drawing on other texts is not confined to academic writing. Writers whose work originally appeared in newspapers or popular magazines tend to cite, paraphrase, quote, and summarize sources without supplying bibliographic information for the reader. The convention of meticulously citing sources is not always observed outside the academic community. Sometimes magazine writers even cite facts without explaining where they came from, and depending on their editorial policies, some newspapers publish stories based on the statements of unnamed sources. In Chapter 3, we explain in detail how you, as an academic writer, should follow conventions for citing sources.

Exercise 2.5

For this exercise, analyze the stylistic features of passages from three reading selections:

> Stephen Ray Flora and Stacy Suzanne Poponak, "Childhood Pay for Grades Is Related to College Grade Point Averages," paragraph 1, page 394.
> Liz Mandrell, "Zen and the Art of Grade Motivation," paragraph 13, page 380.
> Kay Hymowitz, "Gloucester Girls Gone Wild," paragraph 4, page 418.

As you read each article, record answers to the questions for analyzing the stylistic features of texts on pages 64–65.

READING FOR RHETORICAL CONTEXT

For proficient readers, the rhetorical context of a text is as important as its content and stylistic features. The word *rhetorical* relates to *rhetoric*. Many people who hear the word *rhetoric* think of pretentious language. "Politicians' speeches are all rhetoric" means that politicians use empty or inflated language. Either they do not say very much or they divert attention from where it should be. When we speak of rhetoric in this book, we do not mean pompous language. We mean *an author's attempt to use language to achieve an intended effect on an audience.* An important word here is *intended.* Both writing and reading are intentional. They are deliberate actions, guided by a purpose or goal.

We wrote this textbook with a clear purpose: to show you how to become competent readers and writers in the academic community. As you read this book, you should have a clear purpose: to learn how to write for your college courses. Without purpose, the acts of reading and writing are meaningless.

When you are reading for content, genre, organization, and stylistic features, you are focusing on the text itself. This type of analysis is called *textual analysis.* But another type of analysis is also important: *contextual analysis.* Contextual analysis examines *the author's purpose and motivation for writing the text, the intended audience, the circumstances surrounding the text's production, the author's position toward other writers and other texts, and the larger conversation of which the text is part.* As rhetoric scholar Jack Selzer argues,

> Textual analysis, strictly speaking, need not attend to such matters; it can proceed as if the item under consideration "speaks for all time" somehow, as if it is a sort of museum piece unaffected by time and space just as surely as, say, an ancient altarpiece once housed in a church might be placed on a pedestal in a museum. Museums have their functions, and they certainly permit people to observe and appreciate objects in an important way. But just as certainly as museums often fail to retain a vital sense of an art work's original context and cultural meaning; in that sense museums can diminish understanding as much as they contribute to it. Contextual rhetorical analysis, however, as an attempt to understand communications through the lens of their environments, does attend to the setting or scene out of which any communication emerges. It does strive to understand an object of analysis as an integral part of culture. (292)

Equally as important as the environment in which the text was written is the environment in which the text is read. You also need to consider the rhetorical context of the **act of reading**— the reader's purpose and the circumstances surrounding the reading. In this section, we present sets of questions for analyzing both contexts as a means of improving comprehension. You can answer some of these questions by drawing inferences from the text itself. Other questions require you to undertake research. We first discuss the context of the text itself and then move on to the context of your own act of reading.

Context of the Text

To illustrate the process of analyzing the rhetorical context of a text, we walk you through an analysis of Jerry Farber's "A Young Person's Guide to the Grading System" on pages 385–388. Take time to read the essay carefully before you continue.

> ### QUESTIONS FOR ANALYZING THE RHETORICAL CONTEXT OF A TEXT
>
> - For whom is the author writing, and what do you perceive as the effect the author intends to have on this audience?
> - What do you know about the author's background and credibility?
> - What prompted the author to write the text? Can you identify a circumstance, event, or social practice?
> - How is the author drawing on other writers and other texts? How does he or she view what others have said about the topic?

To answer these questions, you have to take two courses of action. You have to step inside the author's head to discover his or her intentions, and you have to conduct research into the circumstances surrounding the text's production. In some cases, the writer's motives are obvious. When you receive an advertisement in the mail, you know that the ad writers want to convince you to buy something. They are also attempting to please their employers and earn a paycheck. True, they may have other motives that you can't discern—for instance, striving to win a promotion or an advertising industry award—but their primary goals are clear. The goals of academic writers are not as obvious as those of advertisers. The text itself gives you insights into the imperative—the feeling, view, incident, or phenomenon—that inspired the author to write, but you also need to do some research.

For whom is the author writing, and what do you perceive as the effect the author intends to have on this audience? This is a crucial question for determining the rhetorical context. A proficient writer tailors the text to the needs of a particular group of readers. If you can identify the audience, you're well on your way to determining what the author is trying to accomplish. An important factor is where the text was published. Was it published in book form or as an article in an academic journal or a popular magazine? Academic writers write for the university community, whereas staff writers for news magazines like *Newsweek* or *Time* direct their articles to a general audience. Certain writers address readers of a particular political persuasion. Writers for *The National Review* anticipate a readership that is conservative, whereas writers for *The Nation* expect their readers to be liberal.

Farber's essay originally appeared in book form as part of a collection of essays he published in 1970. In the essay, he mentions educational reform at all levels, but most of his comments relate to the undergraduate college. He speaks directly to students, referring to their experiences with the grading system, but he also addresses an audience other than students. In his last paragraph, he asks, "But what about the students themselves? Can they live without grades? Can they learn without them?" Here he addresses an audience concerned about students—perhaps professors, college administrators, or parents.

Next, we ask about Farber's impact on these two audiences. What does he expect them to do or think after reading the essay? This question gets to the heart of writers' goals. Some writers want to prompt overt changes in the behavior of readers. For example, the writer of an article on ozone depletion warns readers to reduce their use of air conditioners and aerosol cans. Other authors intend to change opinions. The author of a biography of Mozart encourages readers to accept a new interpretation of the composer's significance. Many writers work to make more subtle changes in readers' perspectives. A journalist provides conflicting information on a Supreme Court decision. She does not want her readers to favor or oppose the court decision. In the tradition of news reporting, she wants to provide them with accurate and detailed information that will help them arrive at sound decisions of their own. The writer's intended impact is to prompt independent and informed thought in the reader.

Farber's intentions are clear. He wants to persuade his readers to adopt his position on grades and his broader plan for an educational system that depends less on what he terms "Mickey-Mouse requirements." In contrast, Moses's essay is not overtly argumentative in tone. Yet Moses intends to influence her audience. Presumably, she wants her readers to derive from her article a new way of understanding certain aspects of American culture. Specifically, she wants to provide her readers with a theoretical framework for understanding the role race plays in American higher education.

What do you know about the author's background and credibility? The introductory material preceding the Farber selection gives a brief biographical sketch.

> Jerry Farber, a civil rights activist and professor of English and comparative literature at San Diego State University, is author of many books and articles of social and literary criticism. His work had an impact on the student movement of the late 1960s and early 1970s. The following essay was published in 1970 in a collection of essays and stories entitled *The Student as Nigger.* Farber is using the analogy in the title to describe students as slaves of teachers and administrators.

Further research tells us that Farber (born 1935) wrote for the *Los Angeles Free Press* from 1965 to 1968 and taught at California State University at Los Angeles from 1962 to 1968 and later at the University of Paris. He is the author of two other books, *The University of Tomorrowland* (1972) and *A Field Guide to the Aesthetic Experience* (1982). This information makes clear that Farber is a credible author and scholar. We found this biographical material by going to www.google.com and searching for *Jerry Farber* and *The Student as Nigger,* the author's name and the title of the book in which the essay was published.

What prompted the author to write the text? Can you identify a circumstance, event, or social practice? As was the case for question 1, we can answer this question in part by analyzing the text itself, but we also have to do some research. Farber focuses the essay on a common educational practice: grading. He argues passionately that he is vehemently opposed to the A through F grading system. We can infer that he wrote the essay to express his outrage, to convince his readers that grades hinder learning, and to provoke them to support educational reform. Farber wrote the essay over forty years ago. To discover more about the circumstances, events, and social practices of the time, we set out to do some research.

We found that the Lone Star College Kingwood Library maintains a comprehensive Web site devoted to American cultural history in the nineteenth and twentieth centuries, including a series of Web guides for each decade. A visit to *http://lonestar.edu/decades.html* and a click on *1960–1969* tells us that college campuses were highly volatile centers of debate in the 1960s. It was a time of social unrest: civil rights demonstrations, antiwar rallies, and unprecedented student protest directed toward many facets of American society, including education. Knowing the historical period when Farber wrote enables us to put his essay in a rich, multilayered context. Even though the essay still has relevance today, it is part of a larger cultural conversation that took place five decades ago. Another useful Web site for historical research is Best of History Web Sites: *http://www.besthistorysites.netl.*

How is the author drawing on other writers and other texts? How does he or she view what others have said about the topic? Many academic texts are multivocal because they represent the voices of many different writers. As we noted earlier, academic writers often draw on the words and utterances of other writers. Sometimes the author simply mentions another writer or text. Other times the text is quoted, paraphrased, or summarized. Writers draw on other texts to acknowledge what other individuals have written about the topic, to provide the reader with background, to support their position, and to develop their argument.

We can categorize the ways authors use sources to build arguments according to the following scheme. A writer constructs a *one-dimensional argument* by presenting a thesis and supporting it with texts that argue a similar viewpoint. A writer creates a *two-dimensional argument* by drawing on sources for direct support and also for counterarguments. A two-dimensional argument anticipates and deals with views that are contrary to those of the writer. Farber makes a two-dimensional argument: he anticipates what supporters of grades might say about his proposal to eliminate grades and responds to their concerns. Farber does not refer to other writers or make explicit use of other texts. As we explained earlier, we cannot make generalizations about academic writing.

Exercise 2.6

Break into groups of four. Each group selects one of the readings from Part V of this book or another selection of the group's choice and carefully reads the text. Each member of the group is responsible for preparing a response to one of the four questions for analyzing the rhetorical context of a text on page 68. After each member contributes his or her response, the group leader synthesizes the four responses and reports to the class.

Rhetorical Context of Your Reading

As a critical reader, you should be just as aware of the circumstances surrounding the process of your own reading as you are of the circumstances surrounding the production of the assigned text. Keep in mind that there are degrees of separation between you and the author. Take the book you are reading right now as an example. We wrote Parts I, II, III, and IV with you in mind. We address the text directly to students, and we envision these students as members of a college writing class. The reading selections in Part V of this book were originally published elsewhere. They were written for other audiences in response to other rhetorical situations. Liz Mandrell addresses English teachers in "Zen and the Art of Grade Motivation," an article originally published in *English Journal*. It is important to acknowledge that the audience the writer had in mind is not the only audience that ends up reading the text.

When you read a text, either one that is assigned or one chosen independently, be sure to enunciate clear-cut goals. For novels and popular magazines, your goal is pure enjoyment. For academic texts, your goal is more functional. In college writing courses, you will be asked to read sources and then write about them. If your assignment is to summarize the source, you will read with the goal of extracting and rewording the author's main ideas. If your assignment is to respond to the text, you will read for the purpose of generating reactions to the author's argument. Effective readers tailor their reading goals and strategies to the task at hand.

Reading to write, reading a text in preparation for a writing assignment, also requires a clear rhetorical purpose. This purpose should guide your reading as well as your writing. It should speak to the two roles you are assuming: reader and writer.

The first step in reading to write is making sure that you fully understand the writing assignment. Examine the assignment carefully. Underline key words that are crucial to your aim and purpose in writing. Ask yourself the following questions.

QUESTIONS TO ASK ABOUT ASSIGNMENTS

- What is the topic or issue you will be writing about?
- As you read, can you find key words or phrases that signal material that is relevant to your topic?
- Who is the audience for your paper, and what are this audience's needs?
- Does the assignment require you to adopt a particular perspective on the issue, a recognizable genre, or a particular plan of development?
- Do you already hold a position on the issue that you intend to develop or defend?

Answering these questions helps you develop a mind-set for the assignment. Then you can fit relevant parts of the text into this mental image as you read.

For example, assume that you are asked to write an essay in which you summarize and respond to Moses's article on race and higher education. In this case, you will read with two distinct purposes: to identify Moses's main points and to relate your own opinion and knowledge about race and education to Moses's discussion. Your notes and annotations will reflect these two reading goals. However, if your assignment is to write an essay explaining the evolution of affirmative action in higher education, your reading will focus on turning points in the history of that issue. Your reading goals will also change depending on whether your essay is intended for an audience of professors or an audience of students.

When you receive a writing assignment, articulate a rhetorical purpose that will drive your reading of the text. The purpose will suggest a method of structuring the textual information. Consider the following rhetorical purposes and the corresponding plans for organizing the material in Moses's article.

PURPOSE	PLAN
Explain anthropologists' assertion that race is culturally rather than biologically determined	Group by the arguments for and against both biological and cultural determinism
Argue for or against affirmative action	Group by reasons affirmative action is either helpful or harmful to society
Explain the history of the anthropological scholarship on race	Group anthropological concepts in time order
Describe the impact that the concept of biological determinism has had on American society	Group by various aspects of American culture that have been influenced by the concept of biological determinism

When you read with the goal of fitting the source information into a specific rhetorical plan, you read more efficiently and you're better able to extract relevant ideas from complex texts. A major advantage of rhetorical reading is that it is active and goal-driven. If you read just to get through the required number of pages, you will recall little, especially if the text is challenging. Rhetorical reading is purposeful reading. It increases the likelihood that you will comprehend the material, and it lays the groundwork for writing.

READING AND INTERPRETATION

In this chapter, we recommended a variety of reading strategies. As we mentioned earlier, there is more than one way to understand a text. Scholars argue long and hard about the meaning of a single passage in a text important to their discipline. Or they discover a new interpretation of a text that was long assumed to be adequately understood. It should come as no surprise that when students with varying degrees of prior knowledge read the same text, they may interpret it differently. Similarly, students who read for a particular purpose interpret a text differently from readers with other goals. A text may have several interpretations, some of which conflict. Often class discussions center on comparing and contrasting various interpretations of texts.

Sometimes our students argue that the author's intended meaning is sacrosanct and more important than the reader's interpretation. Even if this were true, we can't be sure that we have arrived at the definitive interpretation of the text. We cannot contact an author each time we are in doubt about what his or her text means. Viewing the author as the ultimate judge of debates about meaning does not help us solve the everyday problems of interpretation. Once ideas appear in print, readers have to interpret them as best they can.

Are we implying that you are a prisoner of your prior knowledge and experience, doomed to a subjective interpretation of every text you read? Not necessarily. Many texts have unambiguous meanings upon which most readers agree. In this chapter, our objective is to make you aware of the factors that influence your interpretation of texts so that you can see beyond the bounds of your own experiences. Once you recognize you are reading Farber's article from the perspective of a student in the twenty-first century, you are free to speculate about how students in the 1960s and 1970s reacted to the essay. As you become more aware of how the rhetorical situation affects your understanding, you become a better reader.

Exercise 2.7

The purpose of this exercise is to give you practice using the three reading strategies we presented in this chapter: (1) reading for content; (2) reading for genre, organization, and stylistic features; and (3) reading for rhetorical context. Read one of the selections in Part V of this book or a selection assigned by your professor. Approach the reading by following the process described in Table 2-2 (see p. 73). Record answers *before* you read, *as* you read, and *after* you have read the article.

TABLE 2-2   Summary of the Guidelines for the Reading Process

Before You Read

1. Call up your prior knowledge and feelings about the topic (see pages 53–54).
2. Preview the text and derive questions that will guide your close reading (see page 55).

As You Read

1. Annotate the text and take notes (see pages 55–58).
2. Identify the genre. Given the genre, what expectations do you have about the way the article will be organized?
3. Identify how the author has organized his or her ideas. What is the principal pattern of development? Does it overlap with other patterns? (see pages 61–62)
4. Identify the stylistic features of the text by answering the following questions:
   - Does the writer vary the type of sentences? Do all the sentences function as statements, or do some ask questions, give commands, or express exclamations?
   - What does the length of the sentences convey?
   - What can you say about sentence complexity? Are the sentences simple and unpretentious or complex, remote, and scholarly?
   - Does the writer put verbs in active or passive voice?
   - Does the writer use difficult or specialized words?
   - How would you describe the point of view, voice, and tone? Does the writer use the first person (I, we), the second person (you), or the third person (he, she, it, they)?
   - How often does the writer draw on other sources? How do the references to other texts further the writer's agenda?

After You Read

Identify the rhetorical context of the text by answering following questions:

- For whom is the author writing, and what do you perceive as the effect the author intends to have on this audience?
- What do you know about the author's background and credibility?
- What prompted the author to write the text? Can you identify a circumstance, event, or social practice?
- How is the author drawing on other writers and other texts? How does he or she view what others have said about the topic?

Identify the rhetorical context of your own reading by answering the following questions:

- What is the topic or issue you will be writing about?
- As you read, can you find key words or phrases that signal material that is relevant to your topic?
- Who is the audience for your paper, and what are this audience's needs?
- Does the assignment require you to adopt a particular perspective on the issue, a recognizable genre, or a particular plan of development?
- Do you already hold a position on the issue that you intend to develop or defend?

Exercise 2.8

The purpose of this exercise is to give you practice using the text you selected for the previous exercise to write an essay for a specified rhetorical purpose. Select one of the following purposes, or formulate a rhetorical goal of your own.

1. Agree or disagree with the author's thesis, viewpoint, or central assertion.
2. Explain the author's perspective for an audience of high-school students.
3. Compare and contrast the reading selection to another text you have read.

When you have written a preliminary draft of your essay, exchange papers with a classmate. Use the following questions to direct your reading of your peer's draft. Give complete answers so that the writer can use your comments to revise the paper.

QUESTIONS FOR PEER REVIEWERS

- Is the writer's rhetorical purpose clear? What point does the writer make, and how does he or she affect or influence the reader?
- What audience does the writer have in mind?
- Is the essay well organized? What pattern of development is used?
- Does the essay hold your attention? Which parts are most interesting to you?
- What do you like best about the essay?

When you get your paper back from your classmate, use the comments to revise your essay.

TACKLING DIFFICULT COURSE READINGS

The Yolanda Moses article that we analyzed in this chapter is a first-rate example of academic writing: Moses writes for an educated audience interested in the role of race in American higher education. She maintains a scholarly tone, and she includes numerous references to publications in the field. Even though the article is scholarly, it is readable because the subject matter is familiar and the language is accessible. But not all the reading you are assigned in college courses will be as easy to understand. Consider the opening paragraph of Paulo Freire's *The Pedagogy of the Oppressed,* a classic academic text frequently assigned in education courses:

> While the problem of humanization has always, from an axiological point of view, been man's central problem, it now takes on the character of an inescapable concern. Concern for humanization leads at once to the recognition of dehumanization, not only as an ontological possibility but as a historical reality. And as man perceives the extent of dehumanization, he asks himself if humanization is a viable possibility. Within history, in concrete, objective

contexts, both humanization and dehumanization are possibilities for man as an uncompleted being conscious of his incompletion.

This passage poses comprehension problems comparable to the ones we confronted when we read the Kierkegaard passage on page 50. Kierkegaard assumes his readers are already familiar with ongoing academic discussions of the definition of self. Freire assumes his readers are familiar with "the problem of humanization." The Freire passage presents the additional challenge of difficult vocabulary, with words like *axiological* and *ontological.* In fairness to Freire, we should mention that his book is translated into English from his native language of Portuguese. We don't know if the text is more readable in the original, but we do know that the English translation is difficult reading for students in our teacher education programs.

The strategies we covered earlier in the chapter will help you unpack the meaning of demanding academic texts, but you need additional techniques as well.

STRATEGIES FOR COMPREHENDING COMPLEX TEXTS

1. Allow adequate time to read.
2. Work with classmates.
3. Use a dictionary.
4. Read sentence by sentence.
5. Ask questions in class.

1. Allow adequate time to read. A significant barrier to understanding complex texts is attempting to complete the reading the night before it is due. If you open your books only when tests are looming and you don't make academic reading part of your daily schedule, you will find yourself skimming complex readings with minimal comprehension.

Complex academic texts take longer to read than magazine articles, newspapers, or novels. Paulo Freire's short book, *The Pedagogy of the Oppressed,* would take a period of days, possibly weeks, to comprehend, whereas a thriller novel of the same length could be read in a single sitting.

No shortcut will significantly reduce reading time for complex texts. Study-skill strategies like skimming and reading headings and subheadings do not work well for dense academic prose. Academic readings vary in difficulty, so preview your reading assignments well in advance of the deadlines. That way you can gauge how much time you will need to complete them. As a rule of thumb, start difficult readings several days before they are due.

2. Work with classmates. Gather several classmates together for study sessions devoted to the collaborative reading of complex texts. Your professors may encourage or even require you to participate in collaborative learning groups that meet outside of regular class hours. If not, go ahead and form groups of your own. Group members pool their intellectual resources to unlock the meaning of difficult texts, and they encourage and motivate each other to succeed. Reading complex texts is hard work; it helps to share the load.

The group activity can be as simple as taking turns reading aloud, stopping at points where anyone loses the train of thought. Or group members could read silently, stopping periodically, perhaps at the end of a page, to discuss the content. If you wish to structure the activity, you could engage in an exercise called **reciprocal reading** with a group of three. Group members read the text independently, marking the spots where comprehension breakdown occurs. When the group convenes, the members take turns reading the designated passages aloud. After reading a passage, the student does what we call a **think aloud.** She rereads the passage out loud, sentence by sentence, and tells the others the thoughts that are going through her head. In other words, she makes audible to her listeners the mental process she engages in while reading. In so doing, she demonstrates where and how her comprehension broke down. Then the other two members of the group take turns assuming the role of reader, reading the passage and then thinking aloud. After all three think alouds, the group members reach a consensus on their comprehension and interpretation of the difficult text. If questions and doubts persist, they consult with the professor.

Although collaborative reading is a slow process, it is more efficient than working alone. Within a group, you are less likely to become frustrated and lay the complex text aside. The encouragement and fellowship of the group keeps you on task. In our culture, we view reading as a solitary activity that is best done in complete silence. It doesn't have to be that way. In the Middle Ages, literate Europeans read aloud, even when no one else was around. Hearing the words provides another avenue for understanding the content.

3. Use a dictionary. Since spell checkers are widely available, many students think they don't need a dictionary. But a college-level dictionary is invaluable, especially for looking up the definitions of complex words like *humanization, axiological,* and *ontological,* from the Freire passage we examined earlier. Using *Webster's New World Dictionary of the American Language,* third college edition, we obtained the following definitions for Freire's terms:

> humanize: to make humane; make kind, merciful, considerate, etc.; civilize; refine

> axiology: the branch of philosophy dealing with the nature of values and the types of value, as in morals, aesthetics, religion, and metaphysics

> ontology: the branch of metaphysics dealing with the nature of being, reality or ultimate substance

The definition of *ontology* includes the word *metaphysics,* defined as "the branch of philosophy that deals with first principles and seeks to explain the nature of being or reality." Dictionary definitions take us a long way toward understanding Freire's paragraph. We conclude that it means

> The problem of getting people to treat each other humanely has always been philosophers' most important concern, but now it has become a central problem for everyone.

4. Read sentence by sentence. You may need to tackle dense texts sentence by sentence in order to avoid becoming overwhelmed by the language. Part of the difficulty in reading the Freire paragraph is that one difficult sentence follows another. Because of this cascade effect, readers become increasingly confused as they proceed through the paragraph. Try to unpack each sentence rather than read a paragraph or more and then pause to consider what was said. Armed with our dictionary definitions, we were able to decipher Freire's passage one sentence at a time. Try to figure out each sentence by yourself before reading our paraphrases. Freire's text is followed by the paraphrase.

While the problem of humanization has always, from an axiological point of view, been man's central problem, it now takes on the character of an inescapable concern.

> The problem of getting people to treat each other humanely has always been philosophers' most important concern, but now it has become a central problem for everyone.

Concern for humanization leads at once to the recognition of dehumanization, not only as an ontological possibility but as a historical reality.

> Once we begin to focus on getting people to treat others humanely, we become more aware of inhuman behavior, both as a theoretical possibility and as an occurrence in everyday life.

And as man perceives the extent of dehumanization, he asks himself if humanization is a viable possibility.

> There is so much inhumane behavior in the world that one begins to wonder if it is possible to get people to treat each other humanely.

Within history, in concrete, objective contexts, both humanization and dehumanization are possibilities for man as an uncompleted being conscious of his incompletion.

> In actuality, people are capable of behaving both humanely and inhumanely, but we realize that we have the potential to develop further.

When the language is simplified, Freire's assertions are not so daunting. By looking up a few key terms and zeroing in on the text sentence by sentence, we get to the core of Freire's ideas.

5. Ask questions in class. Students who have difficulty understanding assigned readings lay low in class discussions because they want to avoid embarrassment. To succeed in college, you need to become an active learner who admits to having problems with comprehension. On the days you are confused about the reading assignment, you should be active in class. Here are questions to ask your professor.

1. How was the author educated?
2. What is his or her principal field?
3. Who is the intended audience? For whom did the author write the text?
4. What basic background knowledge do we need to understand the text?
5. How is the author using... (insert a word)?
6. In this sentence, does the author mean (give your paraphrase of the text)?

These questions show the professor that you are making an effort to understand the reading. Avoid questions that pass responsibility off to the professor, such as "Freire's too hard to read. What is his point?" Make sure you actually do the reading instead of relying on your professor to explain the concepts contained in the texts. Some students can do well in high-school courses without reading their textbooks, since all the content is covered in class. College professors may not go over reading assignments that they expect students to have already read and fully understood. Instead, they supplement the reading with additional material and offer commentary. The responsibility for keeping up with and comprehending course readings is on your shoulders, not your professor's.

Exercise 2.9

Working with four or five other students, use the Strategies for Comprehending Complex Texts on page 75 to write a summary of the following passage from Walter J. Ong's classic work *The Presence of the Word: Some Prolegomena for Cultural and Religious History:*

> The alphabet, useful and indispensable as it has certainly proved to be, itself entails to some extent delusional systematization if not necessarily schizophrenia properly so called. The alphabet, after all, is a careful pretense. Letters are simply not sounds, do not have the properties of sounds. As we have seen, their whole existence and economy of operation is in a temporally neuter space rather than within the living stream of time. With alphabetic writing, a kind of pretense, a remoteness from actuality, becomes institutionalized.

CHAPTER 3

Paraphrasing, Quoting, and Acknowledging Sources

SUMMARIZING, PARAPHRASING, AND QUOTING

Since many writing assignments require you to draw on books, articles, lecture notes, and other written texts, it's important to learn how to use reading sources to their best advantage. The ability to take information from reading sources and use it in a piece of writing addressed to one's own audience is useful not only in academic writing, but in business and professional settings. When writers prepare annual reports for stockholders in large corporations, they summarize hundreds of individual reports, studies, and analyses. They repackage information that was originally produced for accountants, managers, engineers, and other professionals so that the general public can easily understand it. For in-house business documents, writers often take information that was originally intended for one audience, for instance, technical experts, and make it intelligible for another audience, say, the sales staff. Much of the writing that goes on in business, government, and other professions involves reducing, processing, and translating information for a designated audience or purpose.

Writers use three basic techniques to represent information they acquire from sources. First, they *summarize* the information by focusing on key elements and compacting or omitting details. Whether summaries are brief or comprehensive, they are attempts to capture the overall message. Second, they *paraphrase* selected parts of sources by translating the text into their own words. Finally, they *quote* directly from original sources. In this chapter, we focus on paraphrasing and quoting. In Chapter 4, we will cover summarizing.

SETTING RHETORICAL GOALS

When you summarize, paraphrase, and quote, even though you are working with another person's ideas, you are still guided by your own *rhetorical purpose*. Recall from Chapter 1 that *your rhetorical purpose is your reason for writing and the desired effect that you hope to have on your audience.* When you incorporate sources into your writing, you do not passively transfer them from one document to another. You make many decisions about how to tailor them to your own purpose.

Your rhetorical purpose dictates the amount of source material to include in your paper and the form the material will take. Your purpose provides you with answers to a number of questions:

- Will you summarize the author's thesis and entire supporting argument or simply summarize the main points?
- Will you paraphrase the author's thesis or other important points?
- Will you quote selectively from the text you are borrowing?

Students sometimes think that when they summarize, paraphrase, and quote a text, they must convey it exactly as it is written. Accuracy is important whenever you draw on a source. You cannot distort the message to make it appear that the text states something its author did not intend. But the way you use the source depends on your own intentions. Two writers can draw on the same text in very different ways.

Consider two assignments. For the first assignment, your psychology professor asks you to write a three-page paper summarizing major theories for the causes of schizophrenia. You scan relevant sections of your assigned readings and class notes and write brief summaries of each theory. Given the page requirement, you make each summary concise, providing only enough information for the reader to understand the broad outlines of the theory. For the second assignment, your professor asks you to write a four-page argument defending what you believe is the most plausible explanation for schizophrenia. For this assignment, you summarize the passages describing the theory you favor and paraphrase and quote evidence that supports the theory. You also consider evidence that argues against competing theories. Your essay will contain details that you do not include in the paper that summarizes the principal theories. To illustrate, we use excerpts from student papers written in response to these two assignments. Student A summarizes a passage from R. D. Laing's book *The Politics of Experience* as part of her three-page summary of chief theories for the causes of schizophrenia. Student B writes a four-page defense of Laing's theory.

Student A

R. D. Laing maintains that schizophrenia is not a disease but rather a means to escape or even resolve an impossible situation. According to this view, people become schizophrenic when they are caught in a double bind, usually in a family setting, so that any course of action (or inaction) they take leads to psychic stress. They extract themselves from these unlivable situations by "going crazy." Laing supports his theory by analyzing the families of schizophrenics and attempting to identify the double binds that he believes produced the patients' conditions (100-30).

Student B

In the 1960s, R. D. Laing began to question the traditional assumption that schizophrenia is a physiological illness. Traditional psychiatric practices relied heavily on using drugs that reduce schizophrenic symptoms while largely ignoring the underlying

causes. Laing, however, identified the actual root of the problem:
the family. By analyzing the dynamics of schizophrenics' families,
he demonstrated that schizophrenia results when a family creates
an environment that places one family member in a double bind. In
this untenable situation, all of the unfortunate victim's options
for acting or thinking lead to emotionally unacceptable consequences, and schizophrenia becomes a refuge from an impossible
life. Laing's theory goes to the heart of the schizophrenic's
problem and thus suggests to the therapist a course of action,
whereas treating the symptoms of schizophrenia with drugs leaves
the basic cause intact (100-30).

Both students provide essentially the same information about Laing's theory. But Student A writes an objective summary while Student B reveals that he advocates Laing's views and rejects the medical model for schizophrenia. As this example demonstrates, the task at hand and the writer's rhetorical purpose determine how the source material is used.

You may have noticed that each summary ends with numbers enclosed within parentheses. These are the page numbers of the material in Laing's book that students are summarizing. The title of the book, its publisher, and the date of publication are listed at the end of the essay. The student provides the page numbers in the body of the paper itself so that the reader knows that the ideas presented in the paper appear on pages 100 to 130 in the original text. When you cite short, single-page print sources or electronic sources that are not broken up into individual pages, you do not need to include page numbers in the body of your paper.

Even though we urge you to let your rhetorical purpose determine how you use sources in your writing, we caution you not to distort sources deliberately. As an academic writer, you have the right to defend your opinion, but you should never use sources in a way that changes or hides their intended meaning. This is sometimes done in advertising. Ad writers twist the meaning of a source to suit their rhetorical purpose of convincing readers to purchase a product. When they cite experiments that demonstrate a product's usefulness or superiority, sometimes they refer only to the parts of the studies that portray the product in the most favorable light. Staff writers for *Consumer Reports,* a magazine published by a nonprofit organization, might summarize the same studies in their entirety and thereby reveal the limitations of the product. Or they might compare the studies with other experiments that prove that other products work as well or better. Academic writers are expected to conform to a standard of objectivity that is more like the one for *Consumer Reports* than the one for advertising. Certainly, scholars often write about controversial matters and present source material in ways that best support their personal views, but they are always expected to represent the source material accurately. Make sure that you do not twist the words of authors you use as sources or put your own words into their mouths.

Exercise 3.1

Before class, turn to pages 379–383 and read "Zen and the Art of Grade Motivation" by Liz Mandrell. Write out answers to the accompanying questions.

During class, break up into groups of three or four students. Each group will be assigned one of the following rhetorical purposes.

1. Write an essay for teachers suggesting ways they can resist the pressure to inflate grades.
2. Argue that grades should be eliminated in higher education.
3. Explain why grades have risen in recent years on campuses across the nation.
4. Argue that academic standards should be raised on your campus.

    Discuss with your group how you would use Mandrell's article to write an essay for your assigned rhetorical purpose. Appoint a spokesperson to report your group's consensus to the class.

CONSIDERING YOUR AUDIENCE

When you summarize, paraphrase, and quote portions of reading sources, you tailor the material for your own audience. Your readers may have needs that differ from the needs of the readers of the original text. It is important to envision your own audience as you work with the sources.

    Before you incorporate sources into your writing, ask the following questions.

QUESTIONS ABOUT AUDIENCE

- Are you writing for your professor or for a broader audience?
- Is your audience in the academic community?
- Are you writing for a general audience or for specialists?
- What will your audience already know about the topic?
- Will you need to explain basic concepts or provide background for the source material to make sense?
- Will your audience be biased either for or against what the source says?
- Can you predict how your audience will react to the source?
- What is the overall impact that you want to have on your audience?
- How will your writing inform, influence, or change your audience?

Answers to these questions help you clarify your readers' needs so that you can present the source information in ways they can comprehend.

    To see how considerations of audience affect summary writing, read two passages excerpted from summaries of Stephen Goode and Timothy W. Maier's article "Inflating the Grades." In the margin of your book, speculate on the audience for whom each passage is intended.

Passage 1

According to Goode and Maier, the use of student evaluations as a measure of teaching success may provide a motive for grade inflation. Students often give good teaching evaluations to teachers who give them good grades on their work. The pressure to inflate grades is particularly strong, Goode and Maier point out, on part-time faculty members, who typically have short-term contracts and no job security. If their student evaluations are not strong, these part-timers may very well lose their jobs, so they may be reluctant to risk the anger of students who are displeased with their grades. Full-time faculty members in permanent, tenure-track positions may, from their position of greater security, resist the pressure for higher grades. They are more willing to take the stance of Professor Mark Edmundson of the University of Virginia: "I do feel a certain amount of pressure. Fending it off is part of the job" (qtd. in Goode and Maier 10).

Passage 2

On the surface, grade inflation might seem like a benefit to students who will get a higher GPA for less effort. But Goode and Maier point out that grade inflation may actually diminish the value of college students' academic achievements. According to Kiki Petrosino, a student at the University of Virginia, "I've got the good grades. But part of me would like so much to have my A stand out. I wish my A would mean more" (qtd. in Goode and Maier 11). Goode and Maier list a number of campuses where the percentage of A's and B's is very high, in some cases over 80%. Under these circumstances, good grades cease to mean very much. But it will be difficult to revive the value of the A unless students are "willing to accept the possibility of a C grade" (Goode and Maier 11).

The first passage is excerpted from a report to college presidents on the causes of grade inflation. The second comes from an article in a campus newspaper on the consequences of grade inflation for students. You may have noticed that even though both passages summarize the same text, their emphasis, tone, form, and content are tailored for the designated audiences.

Notice that in both passages, "qtd. in," the abbreviation for "quoted in," appears within parentheses. This phrase indicates that the Goode and Maier text contains quotations that are used in the summary passages. For example, the second passage quotes Kiki Petrosino, a University of Virginia student whom Goode and Maier apparently interviewed and quoted in their article. The student who wrote Passage 2 must make sure her readers know that the Petrosino quotation appears in Goode and Maier's text. It is not a quotation the writer came up with on her own. She informs her readers of the origin of the quotation by putting "qtd. in Goode and Maier" and the page number in parentheses.

Sometimes readers have difficulty understanding ideas attributed to sources. If you anticipate this happening, use additional texts or your own knowledge to provide background, definitions, or context that will help your readers understand what the source is saying. For example, assume that you are writing a paper on racial profiling, the police practice of targeting nonwhites as potential criminals, which has been the subject of recent public discussion. Your primary source is a lengthy article on racial profiling. A section of the article compares racial profiling perpetrated by police officers to the actions of Bernhard Goetz, New York City's notorious "subway vigilante," but the article does not explain the Goetz incident. If you don't know the details of the Goetz incident yourself, you have to look for another source that provides this background information. Then you must explain to your readers that Goetz was a white civilian who in 1984 shot four African American teenagers who he thought intended to mug him in a New York City subway car.

If you're sure that your readers will not need background information, you can reduce summarizing or paraphrasing to the simple process of transforming material meant for one audience to material comprehensible to other readers. Later in this chapter, we describe this process in more detail. The important thing to remember is to identify the specified audience whenever you receive a writing assignment. If the audience is not stipulated, ask the professor for guidance or define an appropriate audience on your own. Avoid writing only to yourself. Egocentric writing does not communicate effectively to anyone else. Egocentric summary writing can serve as a prompt to help you recall the source, but it is of little help to someone who has not read the original text. When you draw on textual sources, always have your audience clearly in mind.

Exercise 3.2

Read John Perry Barlow's "Cyberhood vs. Neighborhood" on pages 408–413. As you read, look for indications of the audience Barlow has in mind. Is he writing for a college-educated audience? For computer addicts? For everyday Americans? For technophobes? Write a paragraph that describes Barlow's intended audience. Be sure to defend your answer with references to Barlow's text.

IDENTIFYING YOUR SOURCES

As we mentioned in the opening paragraph of this chapter, all types of writers draw from sources when they compose texts. The difference between academic writers, news writers, and writers for popular magazines is that academic writers *always* attribute the source material to its author and provide their readers with information about the original publication. Writers for newspapers, magazines, and other popular materials rarely use footnotes, parenthetical citations, or reference lists. No matter what type of source academic writers use—newspaper, popular magazine, scholarly journal, book, reference material, sound recording, image, interview, Web site, blog, e-mail, or other online material—their standard operating procedure is to identify each piece of information that is borrowed from sources. You should strictly observe the convention of citing and documenting sources in all your college courses. Failure to adhere to it, even in short pieces of writing, is unacceptable and considered to be plagiarism.

Often students have trouble adjusting to the academic convention of acknowledging sources because they are accustomed to nonprint media and popular forms of writing in which sources are not cited and documented. Television ads claim, "Tests show that …" without specifying where and by whom these tests were conducted. Newspapers quote sources without revealing their identity. *Time* and *Newsweek* often quote authorities without citing pages and providing documentation. The general public overlooks the importance of identifying sources, but academic readers are demanding. They want to know which ideas are original, which ideas are from elsewhere, and where each borrowed idea originated.

To illustrate how academic writing differs from popular writing in its handling of sources, we excerpted two passages, one from Michael Budds's "From Fine Romance to Good Rockin'—and Beyond: Look What They've Done to My Song," a chapter from a scholarly book, and the other from Philip O'Donnell's "Ours and Theirs: Redefining Japanese Pop Music," an article from *World and I,* a popular magazine.

Budds

Serious loss of income and loss of control forced industry executives to adopt a defensive posture. Leaders of the recording industry went so far as to condemn the music of their competitors as socially irresponsible and morally corrupting. The editors of *Billboard* and *Variety,* trade magazines of the profession, called for self-policing and raised the specter of government censorship as the ultimate solution to the dilemma.[6]

[6]See the editorials "Control the Dim-Wits," *Billboard* LXVI (25 Sept. 1954); and Abel [Green], "A Warning to the Music Business," *Variety* CXCVII:12 (23 Feb. 1955), 2.

O'Donnell

According to the Recording Industry Association of Japan (RIAJ), foreign artists in 1992 had a market share of less than 24 percent. That figure has remained relatively constant for over a decade, and domestic music has been consistently outselling imports for thirty years.

Budds acknowledges his sources, "the editors of *Billboard* and *Variety.*" The [6] at the end of Budds's final sentence is called a superscript. It refers the reader to endnote 6, where Budds cites the specific sources, editorials from *Billboard* and *Variety.* If readers wish, they can locate and consult the two sources. O'Donnell offers statistics from the Recording Industry Association of Japan, but he does not provide complete bibliographic information for this source. We are not criticizing O'Donnell or the magazine that printed his article. We're simply pointing out that standards for identifying, citing, and documenting sources are less strict in the popular press than in academic publications. As a student writer, you must adhere to academic standards for citing sources, not to the less rigorous standards in the magazines and newspapers that you read regularly.

The precise way in which source material is cited varies depending on the academic discipline, but there are general guidelines that cover most subject areas.

CONVENTIONS FOR CITING SOURCES IN ACADEMIC WRITING

- Cite each source you use and each piece or block of information you draw from the source.
- Identify where each fact or idea came from.
- Make documentation clear enough that readers can differentiate your ideas or assertions from those you have borrowed from the sources.
- Provide complete citations to sources either in footnotes or endnotes or in a list of works cited at the end of the piece.

These citations enable readers to locate the exact page on which the borrowed fact or idea appears in the original document. The citation should be thorough enough that readers can locate the original source in the library or online. Compare two students' summaries of David Rothenberg's "Learning in Finland: No Grades, No Criticism," an article from the *Chronicle of Higher Education.* In the first, the writer fails to attribute the source material to Rothenberg. In the second, the writer refers to Rothenberg by name and includes a page reference in parentheses.

Matt's Summary

In Finland, it is difficult to get admitted to the most prestigious universities, but once students are in, the competition stops. College students' work is never graded, and students can't fail a course, even if they do not submit the "required" work. When students submit work that falls short of expectations, they are rarely criticized or asked to revise. Finnish professors discourage competition among students, and critique is just not part of the Finnish educational culture. Students ultimately graduate by completing a final exam or project and may take as many years as they like to reach this goal.

Rob's Summary

According to David Rothenberg, who spent a semester as a visiting professor in Finland, it is difficult to get admitted to the most prestigious Finnish universities, but once students are in, the competition stops. College students' work is never graded, and students can't fail a course, even if they do not submit the "required" work. Rothenberg notes that when students submit work that falls short of expectations, they are typically not criticized or asked to revise. Finnish professors discourage competition among students, and "critique is just not part of the Finnish educational culture" (B9). Students ultimately graduate by completing a final exam or project, and Rothenberg explains that they may take as many years as they like to reach this goal.

Matt gives us no indication of the source of the ideas. Because Matt is appropriating Rothenberg's ideas and words as his own, he is guilty of plagiarism even if he lists Rothenberg's article on his works cited or reference page at the end of his essay. Rob does a good job of crediting his source. He begins by citing Rothenberg, and he cites him throughout the summary. Once the author's name, quotation marks, and the page number are added, we know immediately that Rob is summarizing and quoting from Rothenberg. Notice also how Rob attributes the material to Rothenberg, using tag words like "According to David Rothenberg," "Rothenberg notes," and "Rothenberg explains." In academic essays, citations may become quite numerous. If a writer alternates, sentence by sentence, among various sources, every sentence may need a reference. Consider the following excerpt from Josh White's essay on gun control and the Second Amendment. Josh draws on four sources.

As Doherty points out, a key issue in the debate over the constitutional right to bear arms is whether the Second Amendment protects
an individual right to self-protection or rather establishes only a
collective right to maintain state militias. A 2008 Harris poll
indicated that two of every three American adults believe that under
the Constitution, gun ownership is an individual right ("Does the
Second Amendment"). Opponents of gun control, notably the National
Rifle Association, point out the other nine amendments in the Bill
of Rights are clearly interpreted as protecting individual rather
than collective rights, so the Second Amendment should be interpreted in the same way (Greenhouse). The justification for gun ownership is often self defense. One gay rights group has asserted in a
brief to the U.S. Supreme Court that for gay Americans who are subject to bias-related attacks, "recognition of an individual right to
keep and bear arms is literally a matter of life or death" (qtd. in
Rauch). In general, the logic for seeing the Second Amendment as an
individual right is its connection to the concept of self defense.

In three consecutive sentences, Josh paraphrases Doherty, summarizes an article identified by its title, and paraphrases Greenhouse. Later in the paragraph, Josh excerpts a quotation
from an article by Rauch. Authors' and articles' names by themselves do not give readers all the
information they need to locate and consult sources. At the end of the paper, a works cited list,
organized alphabetically by authors' last names, provides the complete identification.

White 6

Works Cited

"Does the Second Amendment Provide the Right to Bear Arms? U.S.

Adults Think So." *Business Wire*. 3 Jun 2008. *LexisNexis*

Academic. Web. 23 June 2008.

Doherty, Brian. "Guns for D.C.?" *Reason*. Mar 2008: 8. *Proquest*

Research Library. Web. 23 June 2008.

Greenhouse, Linda. "Do You Have a Right to 'Bear Arms'?" *New*

York Times Upfront. 14 Jan. 2008: 14+. *Proquest Research*

Library. Web. 23 June 2008.

Rauch, Jonathan. "The Right Kind of Gun Right." *National Journal*

15 Mar. 2008: 15-16. *Proquest Research Library*. Web. 23

June 2008.

Josh uses the Modern Language Association (MLA) documentation style. This is the most commonly used style in the humanities. Other student work in this book also uses MLA style. We discuss this style in more detail later in this chapter and give you a guide to MLA documentation in Appendix A. We will also cover the style of the American Psychological Association (APA), a style popular with social scientists and educators. If you are writing for an audience in a specialized area, you may need to use its documentation style. Consult a style manual appropriate for that discipline.

Several characteristics of MLA documentation style are evident in the excerpt from Josh's paper. In MLA style, sources are generally identified in the body of the paper by author's name. The name can be included in the sentence—for example, "As Doherty points out,"—or within parentheses at the end of the sentence—for example, "(Greenhouse)." If the original version of a source does not specify an author, then the source is referred to in the body of the essay by title. If the title is included as part of the sentence, the full title must be used, but if the title is provided within parentheses at the end of the sentence, it can be abbreviated to the first few words in the title—for example, "Does the Second Amendment."

If you use more than one article by the same author, you distinguish among them by citing both the author's name and abbreviated titles of the publications within the body of your paper:

Excerpt from Body of Student Paper

```
Turkle has studied the nature of the relationships between humans
and robots ("Cuddling Up"; "Love By Any") and the effects of
online culture on personal identity ("Looking Toward Cyberspace";
Life on the Screen).
```

On your works cited page, list the publications alphabetically.

Works Cited

```
Turkle, Sherry. "Cuddling Up to Cyborg Babies." UNESCO Courier
     Sept. 2000: 43. Print.
---. Life on the Screen: Identity in the Age of the Internet. New
     York: Simon, 1995. Print.
---. "Looking Toward Cyberspace: Beyond Grounded Sociology."
     Contemporary Sociology 28.6 (1999): 643-48. Print.
---. "Love By Any Other Name." Technos 10.3 (2001): 4-8. Print.
```

The titles that are in quotation marks are articles. The italicized titles are the names of journals (*UNESCO Courier* and *Contemporary Sociology*) and a book (*Life on the Screen: Identity in the Age of the Internet*). In the Works Cited list, "---." indicates that the author is the same one who appears in the previous entry.

In addition to providing the author's name or source's title, you must give page numbers for information taken from print sources. If you include the author's name in a sentence in your paper, put the page number, all by itself (omit "page" or "p."), in parentheses.

```
As Dyson points out, for inner-city residents, rap serves as "a
form of cultural resistance" (7) and expresses the problems their
communities face.
```

If you place both the author's name and the page number in parentheses, put the page number after the author's name. Do not use any intervening punctuation:

```
Rappers often urge young people to "get down with the program" and
reject drugs, crime, and racism (Gates 61).
```

Look back at the works cited page accompanying Josh White's essay. The "White 6" in the upper right corner of the works cited page provides the last name of the writer and the page number of the essay.

Notice that Moses's article in Chapter 14 and some other scholarly works included in this textbook do not use the MLA documentation style. Some scholarly journals use their own documentation style, and others use the standard style for their discipline.

AVOIDING PLAGIARISM

Failure to identify the source is a form of *plagiarism*. Over the past decade, accusations of plagiarism for not citing sources damaged the careers of several prominent scholars and politicians. One of the most publicized cases was that of the Pulitzer Prize–winning Harvard historian Doris Kearns Goodwin. In 1987, Goodwin published a 900-page biography, *The Fitzgeralds and the Kennedys*. Although Goodwin included 3,500 footnotes in the book, she admitted that she failed to acknowledge a number of passages that she took from sources. Because of this oversight, Goodwin's reputation suffered. Students who plagiarize are assigned penalties ranging from a reduced grade for the assignment to automatic suspension or expulsion. Be sure to consult your writing instructor, college writing center, student handbook, or college catalog for details about how plagiarism cases are handled on your campus.

To avoid plagiarism, you must do more than cite and document your sources. You must set off direct quotations with quotation marks and entirely reword and document material you paraphrase or summarize. Be sure the vocabulary and the sentence structure are significantly different from the original. It is not enough to change the words but keep the same sentence structure and order of ideas. The following examples show adequate and inadequate paraphrases.

Original

The current constitutional debate over heavy metal rock and gangsta rap music is not just about the explicit language but also advocacy, an act of incitement to violence.

Inadequate Paraphrase

```
Today's constitutional debate about gangsta rap and heavy metal
rock is not just about obscene language but also advocacy and
incitement of acts of violence.
```

Adequate Paraphrase

```
Rap and heavy metal lyrics that contain obscenities and appear
to promote violence have generated a constitutional debate over
popular music.
```

The inadequate paraphrase reshuffles the words from the original but retains the vocabulary, sentence structure, and order of ideas. There is no acceptable middle ground between an adequate paraphrase and a direct quotation. You must either reword or quote word for word. An inadequate paraphrase is considered a form of plagiarism, since it is interpreted as an attempt to pass off another writer's sentence structure and word choice as your own.

While it is hard to define precisely how much rewording is necessary to avoid plagiarism, the following guidelines can help.

GUIDELINES FOR REWORDING SOURCE MATERIAL

- As a rule of thumb, do not repeat more than three consecutive words from the original without putting them in quotation marks. You may occasionally need to repeat a three-word phrase, but whenever possible, substitute synonyms for the original words.
- Change, as best you can, the original order in which concepts are presented. For example, if the author you are paraphrasing presents a generalization and then backs it up with an example, try using the example as a lead-in to the generalization. For a sentence, relocate a phrase from the beginning of the sentence to a position near the end, or vice versa.

In our discussion of paraphrasing later in this chapter, we provide more specific techniques for rewording source material.

Remember that entirely rewording the material you obtain from a source does not make it yours. You must still cite the source so that the reader knows exactly where the information came from. Failing to document a paraphrase or summary is considered plagiarism.

Exercise 3.3

Read Cathy Gulli's article "Suddenly Teen Pregnancy Is Cool" on pages 420–426. As you read, pause at each place where Gulli uses a fact or idea that you believe comes from another source. Each time you pause, write "yes" in the margin if you think Gulli provides enough information for you to locate the original source and "no" if she does not. Can you make any generalizations about when Gulli chooses to identify sources as opposed to when she does not cite a source? If you were to convert Gulli's popular magazine article into an academic paper, how many sources would appear in the list of works cited?

THE PARAPHRASING PROCESS

Paraphrasing is a powerful operation for academic writing, but students do not use it enough. Too often, beginning academic writers rely on direct quoting when they use reading sources. Quotations are necessary only when you have a clear reason for including the precise wording of the original. We discuss some of the reasons for quoting in the next section of this chapter. A drawback of quoting is that it is a passive process of mechanically copying portions of the text. Paraphrasing is an active process that forces you to grapple with the author's ideas. In this way, paraphrasing promotes comprehension. It is no wonder that many professors ask students to paraphrase rather than quote textual sources. They know that students who can paraphrase ideas are students who understand ideas.

Whereas a summary contains only the *most important* information from the source, a paraphrase includes *all* the information. Writers paraphrase to record the total meaning of a passage. Notice the difference between the paraphrase and the summary in the following example, which draws on a sentence from Steven Vogel's "Grades and Money" (page 391).

Vogel's Sentence

Students expect that their grade will indicate the amount of time they have put into the course, as if they were hourly workers, and many faculty agree that it's important to consider "effort" when they "award" grades.

Paraphrase

```
Professors often reward students' efforts with higher grades, and
indeed, most students assume that they should receive grades that
reflect how much time they invest in schoolwork, just as if they
were being paid by the hour (Vogel 391).
```

Summary

```
Students and many professors think grades should reflect effort to
some degree (Vogel 391).
```

If you want to include only the gist or main idea of a reading source, summarize it. If you want to capture the meaning of the text in its entirety, paraphrase it. In general, writers paraphrase relatively small sections of text, often a sentence or two. When dealing with larger chunks of information, they summarize.

Begin the paraphrasing process by articulating your rhetorical purpose and defining your audience, as when summarizing. The act of clarifying how you intend to use the paraphrase and the effect you hope it will have on your audience will prepare you to paraphrase effectively.

Earlier in this chapter, we discussed how extensively you must alter the wording of the original when you paraphrase. Change both vocabulary and sentence structure, and don't repeat more than three consecutive words from the original.

STRATEGIES FOR PARAPHRASING

As with summarizing, you can sometimes paraphrase simply by rewriting the original passage for a new audience. Envision your readers and then change the original text to make it more suitable for them. Suppose that your objective is to paraphrase for an audience of middle-school students the following sentence from an article by visual anthropologist Joanna Cohan Scherer.

> Neither the photograph itself as an artifact, nor the viewer's interpretations of the subject of the photograph, nor an understanding of the photographer's intention alone can give holistic meaning to images.

Because you do not want to talk over the students' heads, you put the sentence into simpler language.

> As Scherer points out, if we want to fully understand the meaning of
> a photograph, we need to consider what actually appears in the image,
> but we must also take into account the photographer's goal and the
> various interpretations that viewers might give to the photograph.

You could simply rewrite the original, as here, keeping in mind that the audience might not understand terms like *artifact*. As the example demonstrates, paraphrasing often requires you to express abstract ideas in a more concrete form. But for many assignments, you need a more systematic approach to paraphrasing. When a passage includes difficult concepts or complex language, it may be hard to reword it and still preserve the original meaning. In these cases, try the following paraphrasing procedures.

IMPORTANT PARAPHRASING STRATEGIES

- Locate the individual statements or major idea units in the original.
- Change the order of major ideas, maintaining the logical connections among them.
- Substitute synonyms for words in the original, making sure the language in your paraphrase is appropriate for your audience.
- Combine or divide sentences as necessary.
- Compare the paraphrase to the original to ensure that the rewording is sufficient and the meaning has been preserved.
- Weave the paraphrase into your essay in accordance with your rhetorical purpose.
- Document the paraphrase.

Sometimes you may use only some of these seven strategies, and you may apply them in any order. For illustrative purposes, we paraphrase a sentence from John Leo's article, "When Life Imitates Video," using all the strategies in the order listed. Let's assume that we are writing for an audience of first-year college students. The excerpt refers to the possible role that violent video games played in motivating the Columbine High School massacre in Littleton, Colorado.

> If we want to avoid more Littleton-style massacres, we will begin taking the
> social effects of the killing games more seriously.

Locate Individual Statements or Major Idea Units

First, we determine how many major ideas are presented in the passage. We find two central units of information: (1) avoiding more school massacres and (2) taking seriously the impact of violent video games.

1. If we want to avoid more Littleton-style massacres,...
2. we will begin taking the social effects of the killing games more seriously.

Change the Order of Major Ideas, Maintaining the Logical Connections Among Them

Now we change the order of the two units of information, placing the second before the first. To accommodate this switch, we substitute "If we begin" for "we will" and "we may" for "If we want to" so that the recommendation to take seriously the social impact of killing games fits at the beginning of the sentence.

1. If we begin taking the social effects of the killing games more seriously,...
2. we may avoid more Littleton-style massacres.

Exercise 3.4

Change the order of the ideas in each of the following sentences. An example is shown.

> When Boris Pasternak was awarded the Nobel Prize for his novel *Doctor Zhivago,* Soviet authorities pressured him to reject the prize.
>
> Soviet authorities pressured Boris Pasternak to reject the Nobel Prize when he was awarded it for his novel *Doctor Zhivago.*

1. As the Industrial Revolution progressed, exploitation of child labor became a serious social problem.
2. Although there are currently several theories concerning the origin of the universe, the Big Bang theory is the one most widely held.
3. Despite the common belief that the brush is the primary tool of the painter, many well-known paintings were created entirely with pallet knives.
4. Even though the secretary of defense disagreed sharply with the president's foreign policy, she did not resign from office.

Substitute Synonyms for Words in the Original

At this stage, it is important to think about audience. Leo's original language is relatively easy to understand. If the language of the original source is too formal or sophisticated, you may want to make it more accessible to your readers. In addition, you may need to provide a context for certain types of material that you excerpt from reading sources.

Whenever you replace original text with synonyms, try to come up with synonyms without consulting a dictionary or thesaurus. Many students who have trouble substituting words rush to reference books and copy synonyms without considering how they fit into the general sense of the sentence. This is a mistake. Paraphrases filled with synonyms taken indiscriminately from a dictionary or thesaurus are awkward and confusing. Here is a procedure for finding synonyms on your own.

COMING UP WITH YOUR OWN SYNONYMS

1. Think of a word or phrase in your vocabulary that comes as close as possible to the meaning of the original word.
2. Read the original sentence, substituting your synonym for the original word. Reread the sentence to see if it makes sense. If the new word changes the meaning, come up with another synonym and try the substitution again.
3. Compare the dictionary definitions of the original word and your synonym. If the definitions do not correspond, come up with another synonym and try the substitution again.

When you are paraphrasing a passage that contains a word you don't understand, you have to supplement these strategies. Before you consult a dictionary or thesaurus, try to figure out the approximate meaning of the unfamiliar word based on its relationship to the other words in the sentence. We call this procedure using *contextual clues* to discover meaning. Use contextual clues to figure out a synonym for the italicized word in the following sentence.

> After meeting someone for the first time, we often retain a *gestalt* of what the person is like but cannot remember specific details such as eye color.

From the sentence, you learn that a *gestalt* is something other than a memory of specific details, so you can infer that it means an overall impression. Check a dictionary to see if the definition we derived from context is appropriate.

Contextual clues will not give you a complete definition of an unknown word, but they will help you unlock enough of the meaning to know what synonym to substitute for it. Always test a synonym that you figure out from contextual clues by substituting it for the word it replaces in the original sentence. If you are not sure the synonym fits, consult a dictionary to check your understanding of the original word. Also, check your synonym against the synonyms listed in the dictionary or thesaurus.

As we mentioned, if you copy a synonym without examining its fit in the original sentence, your paraphrase may not sound right, and it may distort the meaning of the original. As a last resort, consult the dictionary, using the following procedure.

LOCATING SYNONYMS IN A DICTIONARY

1. Read *all* the definitions for the word. (Do not read the synonyms.)
2. When the dictionary lists more than one definition, reread the original sentence to see which definition works best in the context.
3. Try to come up with your own synonym based on the definition.
4. Replace the original word with your synonym. Does the sentence still have its original meaning?
5. If the dictionary gives synonyms for the original word, compare them to your synonym. Do they mean the same thing?

If you use a thesaurus, make sure that you follow steps 4 and 5 so that you do not pick inappropriate synonyms. Remember that no two words mean exactly the same thing, and a synonym listed in a thesaurus is not necessarily an appropriate substitute for the original word in all contexts. Returning to our example, by substituting synonyms, doing a little more rearranging, and providing context where necessary, we arrive at the following paraphrase:

```
If we consider seriously how violent video games affect society, we
may be able to prevent future Littleton-style tragedies (Leo 14).
```

You do not have to find a substitute for every word in the sentence you are paraphrasing. You can repeat words that are essential to the meaning or have no appropriate synonyms, such as the term *Littleton-style* in our example.

Exercise 3.5

Rewrite the following paragraph from James Monaco's book *How to Read a Film* by substituting synonyms for the underlined words and phrases. Come up with your own synonyms for familiar words. If contextual clues do not unlock the meaning of unfamiliar words, use the procedure for finding synonyms in a dictionary or thesaurus.

> The theoretical <u>interrelationship</u> between painting and film <u>continues to this day.</u> The Italian Futurist movement produced obvious parodies of the motion picture; <u>contemporary</u> photographic hyperrealism continues to comment on the <u>ramifications</u> of the camera esthetic. But the connection between the two arts has never been as <u>sharp</u> and <u>clear</u> as it was during the Cubist Period. The primary <u>response</u> of painting to the <u>challenge</u> of film has been the <u>conceptualism</u> that Cubism first <u>liberated</u> and that is not <u>common</u> to all the arts. The work of <u>mimesis</u> has been left, in the main, to the recording arts. The arts of representation and <u>artifact</u> have moved on to a new, more abstract <u>sphere.</u> The <u>strong challenge</u> film presented to the pictorial arts was certainly a function of its <u>mimetic capabilities,</u> but it was <u>also due to</u> the one factor that made film <u>radically different</u> from painting: film moved. (Monaco 25)

Combine or Divide Sentences as Necessary

Since our paraphrase is well-coordinated, there is no pressing need to divide it. But for illustration, we split it into two smaller units.

```
We should consider seriously how violent video games affect
society. Then we may be able to prevent future Littleton-style
tragedies (Leo 14).
```

Compare the Paraphrase to the Original

At this juncture, before we incorporate the paraphrase into our essay, we compare it to Leo's original sentence and make any necessary revisions.

Original

If we want to avoid more Littleton-style massacres, we will begin taking the social effects of the killing games more seriously.

Paraphrase

```
If we consider seriously how violent video games affect society, we
may be able to prevent future Littleton-style tragedies (Leo 14).
```

As you compare your paraphrase to the original, ask yourself the following questions.

QUESTIONS FOR REVISING PARAPHRASES

- Did you leave out important ideas in the original source?
- Did you change the meaning of the original text by adding your own interpretation or superfluous ideas?
- Did you follow the original text too closely by neglecting to rearrange main idea units?
- Did you include too many words from the original text or repeat more than three words in a row?
- Did you substitute inappropriate synonyms that change the original meaning of the text?
- Did you choose words that are inappropriate for your audience?

Exercise 3.6

Here we present a sentence from a textbook and sample student paraphrases. Compare each paraphrase to the original to see if the writer needs to make revisions. Ask yourself the questions for revising paraphrases.

> Somatic cells, while tiny compact worlds within themselves, nevertheless do not exist in isolation; instead, cells bond together, according to their special function, and thereby form definite units or structures called tissues. (Luckman and Sorensen 138)

PARAPHRASES

1. A tissue is formed by the bonding of different somatic cells according to their common functions (Luckman and Sorensen 138).

2. Tissues that are definite units or structures are formed by cells that bond together. They bond according to the special functions they have. Somatic cells are an example of small cells that bond together to form a tissue instead of remaining separate (Luckman and Sorensen 138).

3. Somatic cells, like any other cells, do not live alone. They join together with other cells depending on their specific functions and form a substance called tissue (Luckman and Sorensen 138).

4. Tissues are formed when somatic cells collide outside their small worlds. In order for these cells to be bonded, they must match in a certain way (Luckman and Sorensen 138).

5. Tissues are formed by the bonding together of somatic cells according to their special functions (Luckman and Sorensen 138).

Weave the Paraphrase into Your Essay

We are now ready to weave the paraphrase into our essay in a way that helps further our rhetorical purpose. Consider the following example.

Essay Excerpt

> So what is causing the current outburst of deadly violence in American public schools? One explanation is that the current school-age generation has been entranced by violent entertainment, including television, films, and video games. In the wake of the massacre at Columbine High School in Littleton, Colorado, John Leo wrote that if we considered seriously how violent video games affect society, we might be able to prevent future Littleton-style tragedies (14). It is hard to imagine that children who spend hours each day "killing" in cyberspace will not be affected by the experience.

We cannot be sure that a paraphrase is successful without seeing it in context. The paraphrase must accurately reword the author's message and also fit smoothly in the passage of the essay for which it was intended. To achieve this fit in our example, we had to identify the overall subject of Leo's piece. We did this by adding "In the wake of the massacre at Columbine High School in Littleton, Colorado, John Leo wrote that...." This phrase also attributes the material to Leo.

Document the Paraphrase

Remember that failing to document a paraphrase is considered plagiarism. Always indicate the author of the source, the page numbers of the information you paraphrased, and a complete entry on the works cited page.

In addition to the seven paraphrasing strategies we have discussed, you can use graphic overviews as paraphrasing tools. If you are paraphrasing complex sentences or groups of sentences, construct a graphic overview of the text and then derive your paraphrase from the overview. For more information on constructing graphic overviews, see pages 112–115, but keep in mind that a paraphrase includes all the points from the original rather than just the key ideas.

Exercise 3.7

For this exercise, we reproduced two excerpts from student essays that draw on Steven Vogel's "Grades and Money." For each excerpt, convert the quotation to a paraphrase by using the strategies described in the text. Remember that in addition to accurately rewording the author's ideas, you have to make sure the paraphrase fits smoothly into the existing paragraph. If you have not read Vogel's article, it will help to know that Vogel is a college professor of philosophy who claims that students have come to see grades as "money," the currency of higher education. According to Vogel, professors "pay" students for their academic work with grades, and thus grades are valued more than learning.

1. The tragic aspect of the A-F grading system is that it devalues education. Under this system, students attend college not to learn but rather to accumulate an impressive portfolio of grades. Students see grades, not knowledge, as the payoff for hard academic work. "If grades are money, then learning is a cost—a painful effort one undergoes only for the reward it produces" (Vogel 391). Thus it is not that students need grades to motivate them to learn but rather that achieving the grades has itself become the ultimate goal of higher education.

2. Most students expect relatively high grades in courses where they work hard. Perhaps the exception is mathematics, where some students readily admit a lack of aptitude, but even students who recognize that they are struggling in a particular subject expect decent grades if they are trying. At the same time, students who are doing well in a subject are often not content with any grades below an A. "These honor students are in some ways the worst in terms of their fixation on grades and their constant and creative search to find ways to manipulate the system: their skill at doing so, after all, has gotten them where they are today" (Vogel 392). Since virtually all students, from the academically talented to the academically challenged, think they deserve higher grades, professors are under constant pressure to compromise their standards.

DIRECT QUOTING

When you draw on sources, make an effort to summarize or paraphrase rather than quote directly. As a general rule, repeat sources word for word only when there is an obvious rhetorical advantage to quoting, for example, when rewording the original will weaken your argument or prevent you from including particularly elegant language.

Sometimes students quote for convenience because they think it's too much trouble to paraphrase the source. But it is to your advantage to negotiate a difficult text and render its meaning in your own words. When you quote excessively, you relinquish rhetorical control and give it to the source author. You can also end up with a series of strung-together quotations in an essay that seems purposeless and disjointed.

REASONS FOR DIRECT QUOTING

Given these admonitions, when is it advisable to quote? We discuss five common purposes for quoting and give an example of each.

WHEN TO USE DIRECT QUOTATIONS

- To retain the meaning and authenticity of the original source
- To lend support to an analysis or evaluation
- To capture exactly language that supports your point

- To employ a stylistic device
- To capture language that is unusual, well crafted, striking, or memorable

A typical reason for quoting is to retain the meaning or authenticity of the original source. Assume that you are writing about whether youth curfews violate teens' constitutional rights. In your essay, you decide to quote directly from relevant parts of the United States Constitution. In this case, it would not be effective to paraphrase the Constitution, since the exact wording is crucial to its interpretation. When precise wording affects your argument, you may need to quote.

Another purpose for quoting involves analysis and evaluation. When you analyze and evaluate texts, you need to identify specific passages that support your position. We discuss analysis and evaluation essays in Chapter 6. For now, we illustrate with an excerpt from an essay in which Helen Chang analyzes journalist Linda Grant's book, *Sexing the Millennium: Women and the Sexual Revolution.*

> Although Grant makes some good points about the significance of the sexual revolution for many women's lives, one flaw in her argument lies in her overly general and sweeping definition of "women." The women Grant refers to are for the most part white and middle-class. A case in point is her statement that prior to the 1960s, women who had jobs were "sexless, repressed—spinsters whom, by implication, no man wanted or loved" (2). Perhaps this was true for the privileged classes, but many poor women did work and also had children and husbands who valued them.

If Helen had paraphrased Grant's words instead of quoting them directly, Grant's description would have lost its punch and Helen would have weakened her argument.

A third purpose for quoting is to capture exactly language that supports your point. In his essay "From Fine Romance to Good Rockin'—and Beyond: Look What They've Done to My Song," musicologist Michael Budds explains that with the advent of rock and roll, popular music lyrics became more sexually explicit. He illustrates this shift by quoting directly from a Tin Pan Alley song and then contrasting the song with early rock-and-roll lyrics. Excerpts from the lyrics Budds quotes make his point quite vividly.

Tin Pan Alley (from "All the Things You Are," lyrics by Jerome Kern)

Some day my happy arms will hold you,
And some day I'll know that moment divine
When all the things you are, are mine.

Rock and Roll (from "Sixty-Minute Man," lyrics by William Ward and Rose Marks)

If your man ain't treatin' you right, come up here and see old Dan.
I rock 'em, roll 'em all night long: I'm a sixty-minute man.

By quoting directly from the lyrics, Budds lends a sense of reality to his discussion. The exact language of the lyrics tells the reader much more about the treatment of sexuality in each song than paraphrased language would reveal.

Another reason to use a direct quotation is as a stylistic device. A common technique for opening or closing a paper is to supply a direct quotation. Consider how Charles Krauthammer, a staff writer for *Time* magazine, ends his article, "First and Last, Do No Harm," with a quotation from the Hippocratic Oath that for centuries has been the pledge doctors take when they enter the medical profession:

"I will give no deadly medicine to anyone if asked."

—The Hippocratic Oath

A final reason for quoting is to capture language that you find especially effective or memorable. Notice how our student Karla Allen employs Charles Dickens's memorable lines.

> In Charles Dickens's words, "It was the best of times, it was the worst of times" (3). While big corporations were reaping larger profits than ever before, many smaller companies and individuals found themselves out of work.

Exercise 3.8

Explain why students used direct quotations in each of the following examples.

1. Computer expert Alan Kay once stated that "although the personal computer can be guided in any direction we choose, the real sin would be to make it act like a machine" (Frude 24). As Kay indicates, we should take advantage of recent advances in artificial intelligence to produce a computer that simulates human thinking.

2. The Supreme Court's recent decisions on search warrants seem to support the logic that "if you have nothing to hide, you have nothing to fear" (Stephens 22).

3. "I'm going [to the party] because I've been invited....And I've been invited because Luciana is my friend. So there." [Her mother replied], "That one's not your friend. You know what you are to them? The maid's daughter, that's what!" (432). This brief yet dramatic confrontation draws the reader immediately into the theme of Liliana Heker's story, "The Stolen Party."

4. One of the physician's most fundamental rights is the right to choose patients. In Section VI of the Code of Ethics, the American Medical Association guarantees that "a physician is free, except in emergencies, to choose whom to serve" (Zuger and Miles 1926).

ALTERING QUOTATIONS

There will be times when you wish to alter a direct quotation by omitting or inserting words. These changes are permissible as long as you follow conventions that alert your audience to what you are doing. In the following example, we give a sentence from Michael Moffatt's "College Life: Undergraduate Culture and Higher Education," an article published in the *Journal of Higher Education,* and an excerpt from a student paper that quotes part of the sentence. The student uses *points of ellipsis,* a set of three spaced periods, to show where words have been omitted.

Original

As it is elsewhere in American middle-class culture, friendliness is the central code of etiquette in student culture, the expected code of conduct in student collectivities such as dorm-floor groups and fraternities, the one taken-for-granted politesse whose systematic breach almost always generates anger and even outrage in students. (Moffatt 52–53)

Student Essay

```
While students may tolerate outrageous and idiosyncratic behavior
in the residence halls, they will not put up with unfriendliness.
According to Moffatt, "As it is elsewhere in American middle-class
culture, friendliness is the central code of etiquette in student
culture...whose systematic breach almost always generates anger
and even outrage in students" (52-53).
```

In cases where you need to show omission at the end of quoted material, use a period followed by the three spaced points of ellipsis.

Sometimes, you will find it necessary to insert your own words into a quotation. When you *interpolate* in this way, signal this to your audience by placing your words between brackets. Notice how our student Spencer Levy uses this convention when he quotes the final sentence from Toni Cade Bambara's short story, "The Lesson."

Original

But ain't nobody gonna beat me at nuthin.

Student Essay

```
At the end of the story, when we hear Sylvia boasting that "nobody
[is] gonna beat me at nuthin," we know that she does not need our
sympathy; she simply deserves our praise.
```

By inserting the verb *is,* Spencer works the quotation into the structure of his sentence. Brackets also enable you to explain or identify quoted material. In the following example, a student uses brackets to provide context for a quotation from Jerry Farber's essay "A Young Person's Guide to the Grading System."

```
Farber points out that "many of us understand all this [that
grades are just a game we play to please teachers] and yet remain
convinced that we need to be graded in order to learn" (385).
```

The student inserts "that grades are just a game we play to please teachers" in order to explain "all this." Remember that the only time it is permissible to change a quotation or interject your own words is when you use ellipsis points or brackets.

DOCUMENTING QUOTATIONS

Enclose short quotations (up to four typed lines) in double quotation marks. Set longer quotations apart from your text by indenting them one inch, as has been done for the following quotation from Rand Cooper's article "The Dignity of Helplessness: What Sort of Society Would Euthanasia Create?," which appeared in *Commonweal* magazine.

Jones 4

At the end of his article, Cooper reminds us that physician-assisted suicide may affect not only the individuals who choose this option but the rest of society as well:

> A sense of this deep privacy drives the right-to-die movement in America today. And yet to step outside the rights framework is to ask how institutionalizing assisted suicide will affect not only those who die, but those who live on; not only individuals, but society. The fact is, our deaths are both solo journeys toward an ultimate mystery and strands in the tapestries of each other's lives. Which side of this reality will we emphasize? Whose death is it, anyway? The debate about assisted suicide should begin at the place where that question ceases to be a rhetorical one. (14)

Cooper is right that most deaths have a strong impact on those who are left behind. In this sense, we have a responsibility to consider others when we make choices about our own deaths. While we tend to think of death as a private matter, it most certainly does have a public dimension.

Notice that for a long quotation, the parenthetical citation goes outside the final punctuation. For short quotations, place the parenthetical citation between the final quotation marks and the closing punctuation:

Farber points out that "many of us understand all this [that grades are just a game we play to please teachers] and yet remain convinced that we need to be graded in order to learn" (385).

In the MLA documentation style, the parenthetical citation is an absolute requirement for quotations in academic prose. You must acknowledge the author and provide the page number of the quotation in the original text.

In our example, the phrase "Farber points out" leads in to the quotation and acknowledges the author. Many other verbs can be used to introduce quotations:

acknowledges	describes	proposes
addresses	determines	proves
adds	discovers	questions
admits	emphasizes	rationalizes
agrees (disagrees)	envisions	refers to
analyzes	evaluates	remarks
answers	examines	replies
argues	explores	reports
ascertains	expounds on	reviews
asks	finds	says
assesses	furnishes	shows
believes	identifies	states
categorizes	inquires	stipulates
cites	investigates	stresses
compares (contrasts)	lists	suggests
concludes	makes the case	summarizes
concurs	measures	surveys
considers	notes	synthesizes
critiques	observes	traces
defines	points out	views
delineates	postulates	warns
demonstrates	presents	writes

These verbs can be used as lead-ins to summaries and paraphrases as well as quotations.

As we mentioned on page 83, when you use a direct quotation that appears in a reading source, you must acknowledge both the person who originally said or wrote the words and the author of the source in which you found the quotation. For example, assume that you want to use a quotation that appears in John Leo's *U.S. News & World Report* article, "When Life Imitates Video." Leo quotes David Grossman, a retired army officer and psychologist, who claims that violent video games increase incidents of violence:

Sentence from Leo's Article

"We have to start worrying about what we are putting into the minds of our young," says Grossman.

Documentation in Student Essay

```
According to David Grossman, a retired army officer and psycholo-
gist, "We have to start worrying about what we are putting into
the minds of our young" (qtd. in Leo 14).
```

As we explained on page 83, "qtd. in" is the standard MLA abbreviation for "quoted in." The student must link both Grossman's and Leo's names to the quotation in order for the documentation to be complete.

If the sentence contains quotation marks, substitute single quotation marks for the double quotation marks that appear in the original. Then enclose the entire block you are quoting within double quotation marks, as show below:

Sentence from Leo's Article

One ad for a Sony game says: "Get in touch with your gun-toting, testosterone-pumping, cold-blooded murdering side."

Documentation in Student Essay

```
According to Leo, "One ad for a Sony game says: 'Get in touch with
your  gun-toting,  testosterone-pumping,  cold-blooded  murdering
side'" (14).
```

If you paraphrase the speaker tag and quote only the embedded quotation, all you need is the set of double quotation marks:

Documentation in Student Essay

```
According to Leo, a Sony computer game advertisement urges kids to
"get in touch with your gun-toting, testosterone-pumping, cold-blooded
murdering side" (14).
```

WEAVING QUOTATIONS INTO YOUR ESSAY

There are a number of ways to weave a quotation into your writing. You can acknowledge the author right in your text, or you can place the name in parentheses. When you acknowledge the author in the text, you can cite the name before the quotation, within the quotation, or after it. For example, let's say you are quoting the following sentence from Vogel's article:

We let grades count as money—we let education count as money—because money, nowadays, is the only value we know.

Here are five options for incorporating quotations into your essay. Option A allows you to insert the quotation without acknowledging the author in the body of the text. Instead, you place the name in parentheses.

A. "We let grades count as money—we let education count as money—because
    money, nowadays, is the only value we know" (Vogel 392).

When you use option A, remember to connect your own ideas to the quotation. Don't just plop the quotation into your essay. Lead in to it by providing transitions or connecting ideas. Inexperienced writers sprinkle their papers with direct quotations that appear to have little connection with the rest of the text. If you have difficulty coming up with connecting ideas, use option B, C, D, or E. In these options, you acknowledge the author within the text.

B. Vogel argues, "We let grades count as money—we let education count as money—because money, nowadays, is the only value we know" (392).

C. "We let grades count as money—we let education count as money—because," Vogel argues, "money, nowadays, is the only value we know" (392).

D. "We let grades count as money—we let education count as money—because money, nowadays, is the only value we know," Vogel claims (392).

A final option is to introduce a quotation with a complete sentence followed by a colon.

E. Vogel reminds us that the problem with grades in higher education reflects the values of the larger society: "We let grades count as money—we let education count as money—because money, nowadays, is the only value we know" (392).

You will find the following rules about capitalization and punctuation useful when you quote.

CAPITALIZATION

1. If the quotation is a complete sentence, begin it with a capital letter.

   According to Leo, "Video games are much more powerful versions of the military's primitive discovery about overcoming the reluctance to shoot" (14).

2. If the quotation is not a complete sentence, begin it with a lowercase letter.

   Video games that include cops as targets are, according to Leo, "exploiting resentments toward law enforcement and making real-life shooting of cops more likely" (14).

3. If the quotation is preceded by the word *that* and the quoted words become part of the structure of your own sentence, omit the comma and begin the quotation with a lowercase letter.

   Leo points out that "adolescent feelings of resentment, powerlessness, and revenge pour into the killing games" (14).

4. If you break up a quotation and insert a speaker tag, do not capitalize the opening word of the latter part of the quotation unless it begins a complete sentence or is a proper noun.

   "Did the sensibilities created by the modern video kill games," asks Leo, "play a role in the Littleton massacre?" (14).

PUNCTUATION

1. Set off the quoted material with double quotation marks: "…"
2. Set off quoted material within a quotation with single quotation marks.

   Leo notes that "psychologist David Grossman of Arkansas State University, a retired Army officer, thinks 'point and shoot' video games have the same effect as military strategies used to break down a soldier's aversion to killing" (14).

3. Separate the verb of acknowledgment from a short quotation with a comma and from a long quotation with a colon.

> Leo asks, "Can it be that all this constant training in make-believe killing has no social effects?" (14).

> Many parents assert that their children are aware of the differ-ence between video games and real life; however, these games may have more impact on children's values than most parents realize. Leo points out:
>> We are now a society in which the chief form of play for mil-lions of youngsters is making large numbers of people die. Hurting and maiming others is the central fun activity in video games played so addictively by the young. A widely cited survey of 900 fourth-through-eighth-grade students found that almost half of the children said their favorite electronic games involve violence. Can it be that all this constant training in make-believe killing has no social effects? (14)

4. Close a quotation by placing the period or comma after the parenthetical documentation of the page number.

> According to Leo, many Americans believe that video games are just a "harmless activity among children who know the difference between fantasy and reality" (14).

5. When you acknowledge a source, set off the title with italics or quotation marks. Italics tells your audience that you are quoting from a long source: a book, full-length play, journal, magazine, or long poem. Quotation marks signal a shorter work: a chapter or section in a book, an article in a journal or magazine, a poem, or a short story.

> In his novel, *The Stranger*, Albert Camus describes....

> James Joyce's short story, "The Dead," concerns....

> In Chapter 2, "Reading Sources," Kennedy and Smith discuss....

> *Romeo and Juliet*, a play by Shakespeare turned into a film by Zeffirelli, shows how....

Exercise 3.9

Scan Liz Mandrell's "Zen and the Art of Grade Motivation" (pages 379–383) and Mark Helprin's "A Great Idea Lives Forever. Shouldn't Its Copyright?" (pages 448–450) for places where the authors have quoted directly from other sources. Can you make any generalizations about how these authors use direct quotations to build their arguments? Do the authors differ in the way they use quotations?

INCORPORATING QUOTATIONS AND PARAPHRASES INTO ESSAYS

Usually, when you quote or paraphrase, your rhetorical purpose is to do much more than reproduce the content of a text. Most likely, you intend to incorporate the material in your essay. For example, you might include paraphrase or quotations from Vogel's "Grades and Money" in an essay in which you react to, analyze, or evaluate Vogel's article. For the reaction essay, you might take the stance of a college student, professor, or administrator. The source material has to fit your point of view and purpose.

Integrating quotations and paraphrases into your essay becomes more complex when you use more than one source. When you draw from a variety of sources that address the same topic, it is challenging to keep the information from each source distinct when you incorporate it in your paper. The bedrock principle of documentation is to make sure your reader is able to identify the source of every piece of information that you include in your paper. Students sometimes attempt to avoid confusion in documentation by presenting sources one at a time, each in its own paragraph. While this approach helps to avoid ambiguity, it works against synthesis, the practice of combining various ideas to derive a fresh viewpoint. As we explain in our discussion of synthesis in Chapter 7, this practice is valued highly in academia because it is an important component in independent and creative thinking. By isolating each source in its own paragraph, you make synthesis awkward at best. It is essential to develop the skill to work with several sources simultaneously while still providing accurate documentation for all the borrowed ideas.

In order to synthesize source material within a single paragraph while still documenting responsibly, it may help to think of the paragraph as a quilt in which information and ideas from various sources are combined into an interesting pattern. While you are concerned with the overall design, you still want the individual pieces to stand out. Read the following excerpt from an essay on random drug testing in public schools to see how our student, Kate Kobre, combines various sources but still highlights the boundaries between them.

Summary of two sources —

Juvenile courts were first established in America in the late nineteenth century based on the beliefs that children were less responsible than adults for their actions and were more open to rehabilitation (Drizin 4; Talbot 44). In recent years, however, these beliefs have been called into question. Over the past decade, thousands of American teenagers have been tried and sentenced as adults, including sentences of death and life in prison without parole, for crimes they committed before they turned eighteen. Across the nation, examples abound of youngsters being tried as adults. In Michigan, a fourteen-year-old boy who was

Kate's generalization

Documentation marks
source boundaries

Beginning of
information from
Talbot

References to a
person featured in
Talbot's article

End of information
from Talbot

Kate's opinion

mentally retarded was charged for hitting another youth and stealing two dollars from him
(Young 19). In Kentucky, a fourteen-year-old
involved in a robbery received a ten-year
prison sentence that he may have to serve in
adult prison (Stansky 61). In Arizona, a fourteen-year-old boy who used an unloaded
antique shotgun to scare off his property three
boys who had come to beat him up was placed
in an adult prison, where he may stay for as
long as thirty years (Talbot 42). The number of
cases where children are sentenced as adults
will most likely grow as more states pass and
enforce laws designed to get tough on young
criminals. Three states allow prosecutors to
request that children ten or older be tried as
adults and ten states have no lower age limits
at all ("Should Children").

Sentencing children to adult prisons is
a misguided practice because it keeps them
from receiving the opportunities for rehabilitation that juvenile detention centers typically
provide. Talbot reports on a case in Florida
where a thirteen-year-old girl named Jessica
was involved in a robbery and then sentenced
to an adult prison where she will remain until
she is at least twenty-two. In the adult facility,
Jessica will have no opportunity to receive
therapy and is not required to continue her
schooling. Her guidance comes primarily from
her surrogate prison mother, a twenty-nine-
year-old who is serving a life sentence for cutting the throats of two elderly people during
a robbery. Her prison meals lack the dietary elements, such as milk, that are essential for a
teenager's development (46–47). Jessica's case
illustrates that our society has become increasingly willing to write off young criminals
rather than trying to improve their lives. I
share the belief of Janet Reno, former United
States Attorney General, that "we can save each
child if we only put enough effort into it,
enough know-how, enough continuity in the
child's life" (207). Our focus should be on
providing more effective rehabilitation rather
than maximizing the level of punishment.

Evidence from
sources to support
Kate's generalization

Kate's opinion

Example that
supports Kate's
opinion

Kate's opinion

Quotation that
supports Kate's
opinion

In the first paragraph, Kate links sources in a relatively straightforward manner. The first sentence contains background information on the development of juvenile courts. The parenthetical citation at the end of the sentence contains two sources separated by a semi-colon. This indicates that the background information Kate is summarizing is contained in both of the sources. In the second sentence, Kate generalizes about trends in youth sentencing. In subsequent sentences, she provides evidence that supports this generalization. She follows each piece of evidence with parenthetical documentation, including the author's name or an abbreviated article title, which indicates the source of the evidence. These parenthetical citations serve as boundaries that show clearly what information came from which source.

The second paragraph begins with a sentence containing Kate's opinion about youth sentencing. In the next four sentences, she describes a supporting example that is taken from an article written by Talbot. It is not necessary to include documentation within every sentence that pertains to the example. The phrase "Talbot reports" signals the beginning of the material taken from Talbot, and the sentence goes on to identify "Jessica," the young woman who, Talbot explains, was sentenced to adult prison. The next sentence, which combines information from various sentences in Talbot's article, is not cited to a source, but the sentence's content, particularly the name "Jessica," links it quite obviously to Talbot. The word "Her" that begins the next two sentences refers to Jessica, and the subject matter of both sentences clearly comes from Talbot's article. The writer ends the second of these sentences with "(46–47)." The parenthetical documentation provides page references for the Talbot article, and it also establishes a boundary between the sentences describing Jessica and the next sentence in which Kate states her opinion.

We noted that in the second paragraph, Kate cites Talbot at the beginning of the block of information she takes from Talbot's article. Cite the source as soon as you begin to draw on it. A common mistake that students make is paraphrasing or summarizing a source over several sentences and failing to cite it until the end of the last sentence. This is what the student does in the following paragraph.

> As states toughen punishments for juvenile offenders, an increasing number of children end up in prisons designed for adults. These children in the general prison population are targets for physical and sexual abuse and, as a result, are more likely to commit suicide than adult prisoners. Children receive fewer educational opportunities in adult prisons than they do in juvenile facilities and have less access to counseling and rehabilitation programs. Their role models are the adult prisoners. A case in point is Jessica, who committed a robbery at thirteen for which she will remain in adult prison until she is twenty-two. Jessica receives no schooling and has been "adopted" by a twenty-nine-year-old woman who committed multiple murders (Talbot 46).

The documentation at the end of the paragraph links the case in point to Talbot's article, but the reader has no way of knowing whether or not Talbot is the source for the rest of the information in the paragraph. The paragraph refers to specific facts, such as the incidence of suicides in prison, that the writer must have derived from a source. But the reader doesn't know whether the source is Talbot or some other author the student fails to document. Make sure that all documentation is unambiguous.

Exercise 3.10

Turn to Yolanda T. Moses's article, "Race, Higher Education, and American Society" (pages 458–469), and locate the subheading "Race: Is It Biological or Cultural?" on page 460, which begins a ten-paragraph section of the article. Annotate the ten paragraphs in that section to indicate the boundaries between Moses's ideas and those taken from sources as well as the boundaries between various sources. For a model, review our annotations of the paragraphs from a student essay on page 108.

CHAPTER 4

Summarizing Sources

THE SUMMARIZING PROCESS

The term *summary* covers a wide range of activities. When students answer essay exam questions, they compress material that extends over many pages of their textbooks. When they write short papers reviewing the main ideas in journal articles, they summarize. When they write research papers, they summarize ideas from several sources in order to develop a particular perspective on an issue. They also summarize when they take notes on the main points of a class lecture.

Based on years of research, psychologist Ann Brown concluded that the ability to summarize develops in the following sequence:

1. **Knowledge-telling**—When children are first learning to summarize, they report everything they know about a topic and may fail to distinguish between what they have read about the topic and their prior knowledge of the topic.

2. **Copy-delete**—A rudimentary summarizing strategy is to move through the source sentence by sentence (or paragraph by paragraph, for longer sources) and either transcribe the content of the sentence into the summary or skip it and move on to the next sentence. Young children will often copy sentences verbatim, while more sophisticated summarizers will paraphrase the sentences. When college students encounter difficult texts, they sometimes revert to the copy-delete strategy.

3. **Deletion rules**—As they gain experience with summarizing, students learn to minimize redundancy and leave out unimportant material. Deletion rules depend upon the ability to distinguish the text's central message from less important details and elaborations.

4. **Superordinate rules**—Expert summarizers are able to reduce the length of the original by using language efficiently. For example, they may provide a generalized term or action to cover several terms or actions from the original.

5. **Awareness of prose structure**—Expert summarizers are sensitive to the prose structure of the original and can mirror that structure in their summaries.

6. **Metacognitive awareness**—Expert summarizers are aware of the various components of their summarizing abilities and can draw on strategies as appropriate to approach a wide variety of summarizing tasks.

Brown's work indicates that summarizing is not a simple, one-dimensional operation. It is a complex, challenging task that requires a full range of academic reading and writing abilities.

As we indicated in Chapter 3, your rhetorical purpose has a direct impact on the way you draw on sources in your writing. The first step in any summarizing process is to clarify this rhetorical purpose to make sure you know why you are drawing on the source. To do this, ask yourself how the reading material supports your overall thesis and how it will be received by your audience.

After you have articulated your rhetorical purpose and defined your audience, you can use any one of the following three strategies to create a summary.

APPROACHES TO SUMMARIZING

- Create a graphic overview that you can convert into a summary.
- Focus on main ideas, patterns, and rhetorical situations, and compress information to create a summary.
- Create a sentence outline that you can convert into a summary.

CREATING A GRAPHIC OVERVIEW

A graphic overview is a diagram that represents the central ideas in the original source, shows how they are related, and indicates the author's overall purpose. It reflects the three textual elements we discussed in Chapter 1: content; genre, organization, and features; and rhetorical context. Think of the overview as a framework for the text's main ideas, similar to the frameworks we discussed on pages 15–17. To construct a graphic overview, write down key words and concepts, and depict the relationships among them by drawing circles and boxes connected by lines and arrows. Use labels to show how the basic ideas are interrelated. When you summarize complex sources, it is especially helpful to create a graphic overview and use it as the outline for the summary.

Here is an excerpt from an essay by Carl Sagan called "In Defense of Robots." A graphic overview of the passage is presented in Figure 4-1.

Excerpt from "In Defense of Robots"

We appear to be on the verge of developing a wide variety of intelligent machines capable of performing tasks too dangerous, too expensive, too onerous or too boring for human beings. The development of such machines is, in my mind, one of the few legitimate "spin-offs" of the space program. The efficient exploitation of energy in agriculture—upon which our survival as a species depends—may even be contingent on the development of such machines. The main obstacle seems to be a very human problem, the quiet feeling that comes stealthily and unbidden, and argues that there is something threatening or "inhuman" about machines performing certain tasks as well as

FIGURE 4-1   Graphic Overview of the Excerpt from "In Defense of Robots"

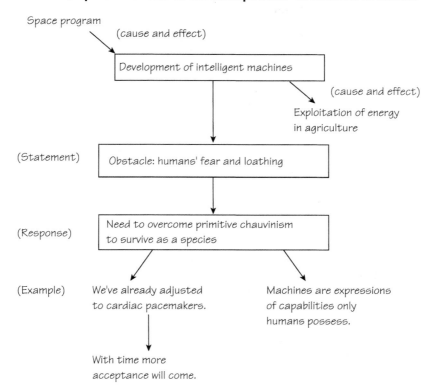

or better than human beings; or a sense of loathing for creatures made of silicon and germanium rather than proteins and nucleic acids. But in many respects our survival as a species depends on our transcending such primitive chauvinisms. In part, our adjustment to intelligent machines is a matter of acclimatization. There are already cardiac pacemakers that can sense the beat of the human heart; only when there is the slightest hint of fibrillation does the pacemaker stimulate the heart. This is a mild but very useful sort of machine intelligence. I cannot imagine the wearer of this device resenting its intelligence. I think in a relatively short period of time there will be a very similar sort of acceptance for much more intelligent and sophisticated machines. There is nothing inhuman about an intelligent machine; it is indeed an expression of those superb intellectual capabilities that only human beings, of all the creatures on our planet, now possess. (Sagan 292)

The advantage of the graphic overview is that it forces you to think about the big picture. You can manipulate chunks of information like pieces in a puzzle and determine how they best fit together. Notice that the graphic overview of Sagan's article makes clear that Sagan has three main assertions that are logically connected. It would be easy to summarize this source now that you see all the main ideas diagrammed on a single page.

FIGURE 4-2   Alternative Graphic Overview of the Excerpt from "In Defense of Robots"

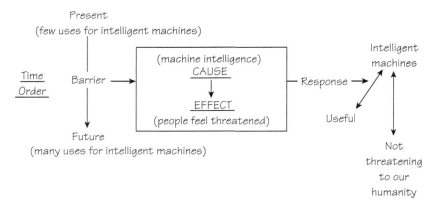

Of course, creating a graphic overview is a highly individual process. A single, definitive graphic overview does not exist for each text. Variations are possible. Consider the alternative representation of the Sagan text in Figure 4-2.

You can make a graphic overview for a source of any length—a single paragraph, a sequence of paragraphs, or a complete article—but the strategy works best if you fit the diagram on a single page so that you can see it all at once. This limits the amount of detail in the graphic overview, but if you try to cram in lots of details, you will soon lose sight of the big picture. The graphic overview works best for recording the general outlines of an author's argument. When you are working with lengthy texts and want more than a broad outline, you may find the one-page format too restrictive.

You may wish to work with computer-generated graphic overviews. We provide directions for creating a simple graphic overview with Microsoft Word. If you are working with other word processing software, consult the Help directory and search for "diagrams."

DIRECTIONS FOR CREATING A GRAPHIC OVERVIEW WITH MICROSOFT WORD

1. Open a blank Word document.
2. Go up to the main menu bar and click **Insert.**
3. Select **Text Box** from the Insert menu. When you click on your document, a box will be displayed.
4. Click on the corner of the box and drag your mouse to make the box the size you want it. Then click outside the box to deselect it.
5. Click inside the box and type in words and sentences.
6. Create additional boxes by repeating steps 3, 4, and 5.
7. Move boxes around by selecting them (click on an edge). With your cursor on the edge, drag the box around the page.

8. Connect the boxes with the following procedure:
   - Go up to the Main menu and click on **View.** Scroll down to **Toolbars.**
   - From the Toolbar menu, select **Drawing.** The drawing toolbar contains a button with a line on it. Click on this button to highlight it.
   - Bring your cursor to the edge of one box and drag it to the edge of a second box. A line will appear. Each time you wish to draw a line, go back to the line button and highlight it.
9. To delete boxes and lines, click on the edge of the box or the line in order to highlight it. Then press delete.

You can move directly from a graphic overview to a written summary by following these steps.

CONVERTING A GRAPHIC OVERVIEW TO A WRITTEN SUMMARY

1. Study each main idea in the graphic overview, and in your own words, write it out in one or more sentences.
2. Use labeled lines and arrows to show the logical connections among the main ideas, just as you did in the graphic overview.
3. Write transitional expressions that mean the same as the logical connections.
4. Combine all the sentences into a single summary using transitional expressions and making any necessary adjustments so that the sentences fit together.

In Figure 4-3, we use these steps to create a summary from the graphic overview of the Sagan passage.

Depending on the assignment, your summaries will vary in length and complexity. For long, detailed summaries, you may need to consult the original source for additional information, expand the main ideas in the graphic overview into entire paragraphs, and make the transitions more elaborate. Even though the graphic overview does not provide all the raw material for a lengthy summary, at the very least it suggests its overall structure.

The beauty of the graphic overview is that it removes you from the author's exact words and thus helps you avoid plagiarizing. Because the graphic overview allows you to visualize relationships among main ideas in a form other than sentences and paragraphs, once you understand the web of meaning, you can express it in your own words. You don't fall back on the author's language as you write your summary.

Exercise 4.1

Read "Grades and Money" by Steven Vogel on pages 389–392 and construct a graphic overview. Keep in mind the three textual elements: content; genre, organization, and features; and rhetorical context. Working from this overview, write a summary of about 200 words that captures Vogel's main ideas. Bring both the graphic overview and the summary to class. Working in groups of three or four, compare your overviews and summaries. To what extent do your graphic overviews differ? How do your summaries differ? Do the graphic overviews differ more than the summaries? If so, can you explain why?

FIGURE 4-3   Creating a Summary from a Graphic Overview

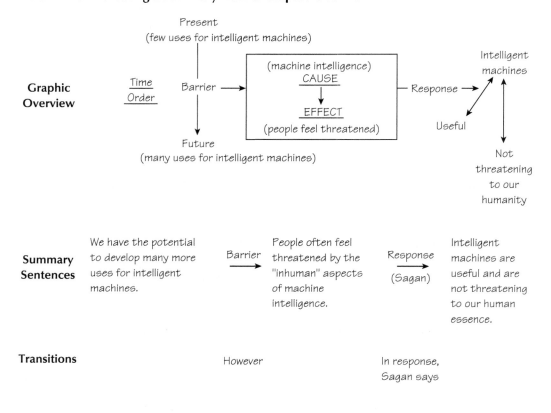

In his essay "In Defense of Robots," Carl Sagan argues that humans must overcome their prejudices against intelligent machines. He explains that we have the potential to develop many more uses for intelligent machines; however, people often feel threatened by the "inhuman" aspects of machine intelligence. In response, Sagan argues that intelligent machines are useful and are not threatening to our human essence.

COMPRESSING INFORMATION

Another powerful approach to summarizing is to analyze and manipulate the source until you have reduced it to its essentials. This process draws on a variety of summarizing strategies.

SUMMARIZING STRATEGIES

1. Annotate, label, or underline important material.
2. Delete unimportant detail, examples, and redundancy.
3. Combine ideas in sentences and paragraphs.
4. Compress words in the original text into fewer words, and provide general terms to cover several specific items.

5. Locate and emphasize the thesis and topic sentences. Invent thesis and topic sentences if none are found.
6. Identify and imitate the organizational pattern of the source.
7. Identify and incorporate the author's rhetorical purpose and the rhetorical context.

These strategies need not be applied in any particular order, and you don't have to use all seven of them for each summary you write. Simply choose the strategies that are appropriate for the source you are working with. In some cases, all you need to do to generate a short summary is explain the context and indicate the author's rhetorical purpose. In other cases, you may have to use the full range of strategies.

1. *Annotate, label, or underline important material.* As we explained in Chapter 1, annotations provide a record of your initial understanding of the text. This record is extremely useful when it comes time to write a summary. Marginal labels, underlining, and other notations also alert you to ideas that should appear in your work. By paraphrasing those ideas, you are well on the way to producing a summary.

The next three strategies often work together. We describe each of them and then show you how they work.

2. *Delete unimportant detail, examples, and redundancy.* Cross out or label as nonessential any material that you think is unimportant for your summary. Also take out information that merely repeats what was said previously. Academic sources are often highly redundant because authors repeat or illustrate complex concepts in order to give the reader more than one chance to understand them.

3. *Compress words in the original text into fewer words, and provide general terms to cover several specific items.* Compress several words or phrases into fewer words, and reduce items in the same class to a single category.

4. *Combine ideas in sentences and paragraphs.* After you delete nonessential material and categorize bits of information, you are often left with disjointed pieces of text. If you want your summary to flow smoothly, you have to rearrange key ideas, make elements parallel, or add logical connectors.

Look at how we performed the operations for strategies 2, 3, and 4 in Figure 4-4. Notice how we deleted the nonessential examples of the three cities; compressed text by substituting "urban" for the phrase "in large cities"; and combined this reconfigured material into a concise summary.

5. *Locate and emphasize the thesis and topic sentence.* As we explained in Chapter 1, the **thesis** is the focal point of a piece: the main point or the claim the author demonstrates or proves. **Topic sentences** contain the main ideas of paragraphs or other subdivisions of a text. In practice, a thesis or a paragraph's main idea may be expressed in more than one sentence, so do not assume that you should always search for a single sentence. Since thesis statements and topic sentences often include the author's most important ideas, you can build a summary by paraphrasing them and then weaving the paraphrases together into a coherent whole.

The thesis statement is typically in the first paragraph or another introductory paragraph, but it can also appear at the end of the piece. Topic sentences often come at the beginning of paragraphs, but they may appear in the middle or at the end of paragraphs as

FIGURE 4-4 Using Summarizing Strategies to Compress Information

Original Sentence from Source

Schools in large cities, such as New York, Boston, and Philadelphia, have been criticized for passing students from grade to grade for demonstrated effort, regular attendance, and good citizenship rather than for adequate academic performance.

Edited Sentence

Urban
~~S~~chools (in large cities,) ~~such as New York, Boston, and Philadelphia,~~ have been criticized for
    promoting students
(passing students from grade to grade) for (demonstrated effort, regular attendance, and good
        unjustified reasons
citizenship rather than for adequate academic performance.)

Resulting Summary Sentence

Urban schools have been criticized for promoting students for unjustified reasons (Janik 43).

well. Notice that in Sagan's paragraph (pages 112–113), the topic sentence occurs at the very end. You will find that in some paragraphs, there is no explicit topic sentence; the main idea is implied through an accumulation of details, facts, or examples. When you are summarizing such a paragraph, create a topic sentence of your own by combining ideas that will make a unified statement. Here is an example of a paragraph that does not have a distinct topic sentence.

> Buddha is said to have achieved spiritual enlightenment through meditation and fasting. Similar procedures, however, are used to prepare for divine inspiration in religions the world over. This fact has implications for how one might view the development of religion in various cultures. Indeed, this aspect of the religious experience may be a direct response to human physiological characteristics. People the world over share common experiences as a consequence of being members of the same species. It seems reasonable that they might interpret these experiences the same way.

The first sentence tells how Buddha acquired spiritual enlightenment. Buddha is used merely as an example, however, because the remaining sentences discuss a larger population—religious people throughout the world. The final sentence is a partial statement of the main idea: people everywhere have the same interpretation of certain experiences. We combine these ideas to arrive at a topic sentence:

> Human beings everywhere share certain experiences that they interpret as having religious significance.

6. *Identify and imitate the organizational pattern of the source.* The author's organizational plan will also help you summarize. A good summary reflects the structural pattern of the original text. You may recall that we advised you to change the order of texts when you paraphrase them. Summarizing follows a different procedure. Once you identify how the author has arranged the piece, you can use this pattern as the skeleton for your summary. Because organization conveys meaning, your reader should be able to follow the train of thought quite easily.

In Table 1-1 (page 16), we described nine organizational plans for academic writing: time order, narration, process; antecedent and consequence or cause and effect; description; response; comparison and contrast; example; analysis or classification; definition; and analogy. Authors may use a single plan to organize an entire piece of writing, or they may use several patterns simultaneously. As you read the source, make a marginal note about its organizational plan.

To illustrate how to base a summary on the author's organizational plan, reconsider the excerpt from Sagan's "In Defense of Robots" on pages 112–113. Which of the nine plans best describes the way this passage is organized? A strong candidate is the response plan, since Sagan is responding to the critics of machine intelligence. You could construct your summary by first explaining the perspective Sagan is reacting to (the human bias against machines) and then describing Sagan's response. The organizational plan can thus provide the backbone for your summary.

7. *Identify and incorporate the author's rhetorical purpose and the rhetorical context.* In some cases, you will include in your summary the author's rhetorical purpose and the rhetorical context of the text, particularly if you are writing a summary that will stand alone rather than one that will become a part of a longer essay. To determine the rhetorical purpose and context, ask yourself seven questions. In your summary, you may respond to some, but not necessarily all, of them.

QUESTIONS FOR DETERMINING RHETORICAL PURPOSE AND CONTEXT

- For whom is the author writing, and what role does the author assume in relation to the audience?
- In what type of publication does the text appear? If the publication is a journal, magazine, or newspaper, who are its typical readers?
- What is the author's background? Is he or she an acceptable, credible authority?
- What effect does the author intend to have on this audience?
- What feeling, view, incident, or social practice brought about the need or motivated the author to write the text?
- When was the piece published? Is it current or out of date?
- Does the author draw on other texts? If so, how does he or she view what the other writers have said about the topic?

Purpose is determined by how the author tries to affect or influence the audience. Sometimes the purpose is easily identified because it is a controlling feature of the piece, as is the case in an argumentative text or a highly opinionated editorial. Other times the author's purpose may not be self-evident. (To review the concept of rhetorical purpose, reread pages 67–72.)

The following summary of Vogel's "Grades and Money" (see pages 389–392) illustrates that once you have identified the rhetorical context and determined the author's purpose, you have created a concise, informative summary.

Summary of Vogel's "Grades and Money"

```
Steven Vogel, a philosophy professor at Denison University, notes
that his students are much more concerned about grades than he and
his peers were as undergraduates in the early 1970s. Vogel's pur-
pose in writing is to explain why the current generation of stu-
dents is so obsessed with grades. He asserts that his students
view grades as "money" received in exchange for the "work" of
learning. They have adopted this viewpoint because "money, now-
adays, is the only value we know" (392). Vogel addresses his article
to readers in his own generation, particularly academics, who might
not understand the motives of today's college students.
```

As with the graphic overview technique, the seven strategies for summary writing can be used to produce detailed or brief summaries of short and long sources. When you have written a draft of your summary, check to see that you have changed the author's wording, or else you run the risk of plagiarizing the source. Also remember to document your summary by providing your readers with information about the author, title, place and date of publication, and pages. (For a more detailed explanation of documentation, see pages 84–89.)

Exercise 4.2

Use at least two of the seven summary strategies to construct a 200-word summary of an article of your choice, either from this book or another reading source. Write for an audience of first-year college students who have not read the article.

CREATING A SENTENCE OUTLINE

A sentence outline is especially useful for creating a summary that follows the organizational format and order of the original text. If your source contains an introductory paragraph, five body paragraphs, and a conclusion, your sentence outline should reflect this organizational distribution. Write a sentence summary of each paragraph and then combine the sentences to form a coherent passage. The resulting summary is a miniature version of the original. The sentence summary technique is well suited for long textual sources that have subdivisions or follow clear-cut organizational plans.

To illustrate the process, turn to Sherry Turkle's essay, "Cyberspace and Indentity" (pages 400–407). Turkle divides her article into five sections. Your first step is to create a sentence outline by writing a sentence summary for each section. The second step is to merge these sentence summaries into a coherent paragraph.

Sentence Outline of Sherry Turkle's "Cyberspace and Identity"

Introduction (unlabeled, precedes the first subheading)

As people spend more of their time online, they will begin to see themselves as having several distinct personal identities that they can move among at will.

Virtual Personae

On any interactive Web site, a user can specify a personality, and even a physical appearance, and use it to interact with others in that particular virtual world, and at any moment the user can assume several of these identities simultaneously by cycling through two or more computer windows.

Identity, Moratoria, and Play

Cyberspace provides an environment for people to experiment with various identities without risking real-world consequences.

Expanding One's Range in the Real

Experimenting with cyberspace identities may help one develop a greater range of responses to situations that come up in the real world.

An Object to Think with for Thinking About Identity

The fact that Internet life allows an individual multiple identities raises a basic philosophical question: Does a normal, nonpsychotic human being have a core self, or is he or she composed of multiple selfs that function together?

From a Psychoanalytic to a Computer Culture?

Despite the apparent contradiction between thinking of ourselves as having multiple identities and believing that we have core personalities, both of these perspectives can work together to give us a clearer picture of who we really are.

Summary Created from the Sentence Outline

In "Cyberspace and Identity," Sherry Turkle maintains that as people spend more of their time online, they will begin to see themselves as having several distinct personal identities that they can move among at will. According to Turkle, on any interactive Web site, a user can specify a personality, and even a physical appearance, and use it to interact with others within that particular virtual world, and at any moment, the user can assume several of these identities simultaneously by cycling through two or more computer windows. Turkle notes that cyberspace provides an environment

```
for people to experiment with various identities without risking
real-world consequences, and this experimentation may help them to
develop a greater range of responses to situations that come up in
the real world. In view of the fact that Internet life allows an
individual to assume multiple identities, Turkle raises a basic
philosophical question: Does a normal, nonpsychotic human being have a
core self, or is he or she composed of multiple selves that function
together? Turkle argues that despite the apparent contradiction
between thinking of ourselves as having multiple identities and
believing that we have core personalities, both of these perspectives
can work together to give us a clearer picture of who we really are.
```

When you convert a sentence outline to paragraph form, consider making the following additions.

ADDITIONS TO THE SENTENCE SUMMARY OUTLINE

- Identify the author and the title of the reading source.
- Add appropriate transitional words and expressions.
- Supply documentation.
- Add rhetorical context when necessary.

In the summary of Turkle's article, we highlighted instances of attribution. This is where we added connectives like "according to Turkle" and "Turkle notes." For summary writing, attribution is an especially effective transitional device. For your summary to make sense, you may also need to add an introductory sentence or two to identify the rhetorical context of the original source. Since you don't want your summary to sound like a set of disconnected ideas, you should double-check that you have added enough context and transitions.

DOCUMENTING SUMMARIES

Remember that you must document all information you obtain from sources. Even if you have summarized the text in your own words, you must make its origin clear to your readers. The sample summaries in this chapter clearly indicate that the writers are borrowing information from sources.

Summarizing a source without proper documentation is considered plagiarism. Always cite the source at the point where you use it in your writing. Also include it in the works cited list at the end of your paper. (We explain how to set up a works cited list on pages 87–88.)

Exercise 4.3

Make a 250-word sentence summary outline of John Perry Barlow's article "Is There a There in Cyberspace?" (pages 408–413), and then convert the outline into a summary. Make sure that the organization of your summary reflects the plan of Barlow's article.

INCORPORATING SUMMARIES INTO YOUR ESSAYS

When you incorporate a summary in an essay that has its own purpose, you have to adapt and transform it so that it is compatible with the rest of the paper. Consider how a summary of "It's Over, Debbie," an anonymous article from the *Journal of the American Medical Association,* functions in an essay written for a specific purpose. It will help to know that the article is a first-person narrative in which a physician in training describes administering a lethal dose of morphine to a dying patient who is suffering terribly. The summary could be written from the perspective of the physician, as in the original text, in order to focus on the medical ethics of the situation. The writer could also shift the perspective of the summary to the patient and focus on an individual's right to decide when it is time to die. Look at how the summary functions in an essay written by our student, Elizabeth Goldman. Elizabeth begins with a short summary of "It's Over, Debbie." We have reproduced Elizabeth's introductory summary, the first sentence or two from each of her body paragraphs, and her conclusion. Notice how her opening summary highlights each of the three perspectives that she develops in her paper.

Goldman 1

Elizabeth Goldman

Professor Smith

Academic Writing I

22 October 2007

When the Time Comes

"Let's get this over with" were the only words spoken

by Debbie, a twenty-year-old terminal cancer patient, to the

physician on call at the hospital. Minutes later, the doctor

gave Debbie a fatal dose of morphine to end her suffering.

"It's Over, Debbie," a narrative of this event, was published

anonymously by the doctor who administered the morphine. The

details are sparse: the physician was awakened at night and told

that a cancer patient was "having difficulty getting rest." The

doctor proceeded to the cancer ward and found a young woman who

was breathing heavily and was vomiting repeatedly as a result of

her medication. An IV and nasal oxygen were helping to keep her

80-lb. body alive, but over the past two days, she hadn't eaten

1

any food. The doctor made a decision on the spot to honor the
dying woman's request for death. An older woman, very likely the
patient's mother, was also in the room and seemed "relieved" once
the morphine made Debbie relax and then die. Imagine yourself in
the role of Debbie, her mother, or the doctor. What would you do?
When I place myself in any of those roles, I come to the same
conclusion: there comes a time when it is appropriate to end a
painful and hopeless struggle to remain alive, a principle our
society and legal system needs to support.

If I become a doctor, I hope that all the technical medical   2
training on how to sustain life will not overcome my common
sense and basic compassion for others. It is true that the IV,
nasal oxygen, and other forms of treatment were keeping Debbie
alive, but what is the value to Debbie of a life that offers
nothing but suffering?

•   •   •

If I, rather than Debbie, were lying in the hospital bed,   3
suffering, I have no question that I would want to die, for my
own sake and for the peace of mind of those I love.

•   •   •

The mother's perspective is perhaps the most difficult to   4
imagine. I have read that according to therapists, the most
devastating trauma of all is being predeceased by a child. But
if my child were suffering, I hope I would be able to place her
needs ahead of my own.

•   •   •

Our society still maintains laws against committing or   5
assisting in suicide, and we have locked away Dr. Jack Kevorkian for

---

Goldman 3

his courageous defense of the right to die. We need to acknowledge

that our laws against suicide coupled with our advanced medical

technology can cruelly condemn the dying to spend their final days

in agony. Our society needs to accept, as Debbie, her mother, and

her physician did, that death is sometimes the only humane option.

Goldman 4

Work Cited

"It's Over, Debbie." *Journal of the American Medical Association*

259.2 (1998): 272. Print.

Elizabeth's essay summarizes and responds to "It's Over, Debbie." Response essays, which we will discuss in detail in Chapter 5, often include summaries of the sources that students are responding to. When you write in response to a single source, you may, as Elizabeth does, begin with a full summary of the source, followed by your response, or you may summarize and respond sequentially to individual points raised in the source.

In Chapters 7, 8, and 9, you will study how to write synthesis essays, which may include summaries of more than one source. In those chapters, we will discuss in detail how to interweave multiple summaries with your own ideas and will provide sample essays in which students summarize more than one source. One point that we will emphasize is making connections among the various sources you summarize. Make sure your essay doesn't become just a collection of free-standing summaries. You should use summaries as components that help advance your overall goal rather than as separate items that you merely list.

THE SUMMARY ESSAY

Sometimes professors ask students to write a summary for its own sake rather than incorporate it into a longer piece of writing. They may even assign a freestanding paraphrase. Your philosophy professor could ask you to write a paraphrase of an especially demanding passage of text, or your English teacher could tell you to put a poem into your own words. Professors who assign course journals or reading logs may ask you to enter paraphrases of selected passages of text.

A more common assignment than a freestanding paraphrase is a freestanding summary. A freestanding summary may be written in essay format. Typically, it includes the following elements.

ELEMENTS IN A FREESTANDING SUMMARY ESSAY

Introduction	• Engages the reader with an interesting opening
	• Identifies the source (author, title)
	• Explains the topic of the source
	• Conveys the main perspective or thesis of the source
Body	• Discusses a key element of the source in each of the body paragraphs
	• Links material together according to a clear plan, usually reflecting the organizational pattern of the source
Conclusion	• Closes the essay by broadening the focus and placing the source in a larger context

If you wish, draw on your knowledge and experience as you compose the freestanding summary. If you are well versed in the subject matter and feel comfortable and confident working with the source, let your voice surface in the summary itself. Your summary will sound less like a straightforward transfer of information and more like a personal, inventive rendition of the source material. Your audience will hear your voice at least as loudly as they hear the information you are summarizing. When you draw on your knowledge and experience while summarizing, make sure you do not put words in the author's mouth. Remember that one of the basic rules for summarizing is that you remain faithful to the original source. When you draft the summary essay, there are two conventions you should keep in mind. First, give authors' full names the first time you mention them. Thereafter, refer to them by last name only. Second, write the essay in present tense. In the following essay, our student James Henderson summarizes "Jennifer and Rachel," written by Lee Silver, a professor at Princeton University. Notice how James adheres to the conventions of summary writing and integrates the source material with his own knowledge.

Henderson 1

James Henderson

Professor Smith

Academic Writing I

28 Sept. 2006

Summary of "Jennifer and Rachel" by Lee M. Silver

How might our society change if individuals began to clone themselves to produce children rather than conceive through sexual relations? This question conjures up images of Aldous Huxley's *Brave New World*, where hordes of identical children

1

---

were "hatched" and raised in uniform batches to fulfill specific social needs. According to Lee M. Silver, author of "Jennifer and Rachel," human cloning will happen, but it will not pose the danger to our humanity or our social structure that Huxley predicted. Silver presents his own fictional account of cloning, but in his tale, a single woman named Jennifer clones herself to create a child that is entirely her own. He tells Jennifer's story to illustrate why someone might choose to be cloned, and then, through commentary on the scenario, he explains why we should not fear these products of our own brave new world.

Silver's scenario is set in the year 2049, when human cloning is technically possible but illegal in the United States. Jennifer, a financially secure woman, decides that she wants to give birth to a child and raise it alone. Several options for becoming pregnant are possible for Jennifer, but she chooses cloning because no one else's genetic material will be involved. This technology enables Jennifer to know automatically what her child's traits will be, an idea that appeals to her. After she makes her decision, she travels to the Cayman Islands, where the procedure takes place. Nine months later, Jennifer gives birth to her daughter. Rachel grows up very much like other children. Jennifer intends to tell Rachel the full story of her creation and birth as soon as she is old enough to understand the concept. Silver's scenario is certainly plausible; my cousin Louise, a single woman in her thirties, just adopted a child from Honduras, and no one questioned her desire to be a single parent. If cloning were available now, Louise might have used it.

After Silver presents the Jennifer and Rachel scenario, he anticipates and responds to the objections that some people might

Henderson 3

have to Jennifer's choice to clone herself. One objection is that as a clone of her mother, Rachel is denied the right to grow up and develop her own identity. Since Jennifer and Rachel have the same genes, will Rachel grow up to be just like her mother? Will she have the freedom to develop a personality of her own? According to Silver, the fact that Rachel and Jennifer have the same genetic makeup doesn't mean that their lives will be the same. Rachel's childhood is bound to differ from that of her mother because the environmental influences will not be the same. Mother and daughter will be members of distinct generations and grow up under different social circumstances, as is the case with other children and their parents. And after all, what teenage girl tries to grow up to be just like her mom? While most parents have certain expectations for their children, Silver sees no reason that Jennifer will burden her clone daughter with unreasonable goals. Silver is probably thinking of the many parents like my own who have their children's lives all plotted out for them. And I'm most certainly not a clone!

Silver also notes that cloning may be perceived as a violation of religious doctrines, and I know that the Vatican has, in fact, condemned human cloning. In response to this objection, Silver points out that cloning does not involve tampering with embryos, as abortion does, but rather involves only unfertilized eggs and regular body cells that, without the cloning process, would never develop into embryos. Though some people feel that the scientists who clone humans are "playing God," Silver points out that this claim applies equally to all reproductive technologies, not just to cloning.

But the critics of cloning are not finished by any means; they next point out that cloning has the potential to interfere

4

5

with evolution and thus affect the future progress of our
species. In response, Silver argues that relatively few people
will find cloning attractive and hence that such a limited use
of the technology is unlikely to affect human evolution. As for
the critics' claim that evolution must be allowed to take its
course, Silver maintains that "unfettered evolution" won't
necessarily guarantee improvement for the species.

The last objection to cloning that Silver addresses is that it **6**
might create an underground market in designer clones. The genetic
material of famous and talented individuals might be stolen and
cloned, and the resulting embryos could then be sold to parents who
want a child with outstanding characteristics. Silver agrees that
this practice is possible but maintains that it would most likely be
prohibited by law. He also questions whether many parents would want
to raise other people's clones rather than their own biological
children. I imagine that it would be very difficult to raise a child
whose talents and skills far surpassed my own. Say my son was
Michael Jordan's clone. As a nine-year-old, what would little Mike
think of my lead feet and pitiful jump shot? In any case, Silver
states that those parents who do purchase designer clones may be
disappointed since environmental influences will ensure that the
clones are significantly different from their biological parents.

Silver envisions a future where cloning will be one of the **7**
available reproductive choices, and he suggests that some of us
may have good reason to give birth to a cloned child. Though many
fear the idea of human cloning, Silver believes that this process
poses no significant risks to the clone children or to our society
at large. By the time I am ready to have a family, the Jennifer

Henderson 5

and Rachel scenario may be more than just fiction, and the debate

Silver outlines will be more than a hypothetical exercise.

Henderson 6

Work Cited

Silver, Lee. "Jennifer and Rachel." *Remaking Eden: Cloning and*

Beyond in a Brave New World. New York: Avon, 1997. Print.

We suggest that you use matter-of-fact titles for freestanding summaries. James Henderson's title, "Summary of 'Jennifer and Rachel' by Lee M. Silver," indicates the straightforward goal of his essay. Clever or elaborate titles are inappropriate for summary essays.

The following essay by Clara Eisinger comes from a legal studies class where students were given the following assignment:

> In Chapter 10 of our textbook, you read about issues related to the legal status of minors. Pick one of those issues and then locate a related Supreme Court decision. In 500 words, summarize the decision, highlighting the constitutional principles at stake involving the rights of minors.

Eisinger 1

Clara Eisinger

Legal Studies I

Professor Swensen

14 Feb. 2008

Minors and Direct Access to the Court in Belotti v. Baird

In the movie *Juno*, the sixteen-year-old protagonist makes a

string of decisions no teenager should ever make on her own. Although

her future looks promising by the time the movie reaches its ending

song, just because her string of choices worked out for her does not

mean teen pregnancy resolves itself so cleanly for other teenagers.

In fact, it does not. Often, teens and their parents have different

views about abortion. In these circumstances, does the pregnant
teen's right to control her own destiny outweigh the parents' right
to participate in important decisions affecting their child? In
Bellotti v. Baird, a court case that involved just such a
controversy, the Supreme Court ruled that if girls could prove they
are responsible, then they should have the option of obtaining an
abortion directly from a court without parental consent.

In Bellotti vs. Baird, the Court identified three ways in
which minors differ from adults. It said children are vulnerable,
are less able than adults to make important decisions for
themselves, and are subject to the authority of their parents.
According to the Court, parents play a large role in shaping
children to become responsible citizens, and so when children make
mistakes, their parents should justifiably be the first to know
and the first to guide their offspring in the right direction.
Parents are intermediaries between minors and the state.

But in Bellotti v. Baird, the Court felt that parents' and
children's rights may stand at odds. For example, a pregnant girl's
parents may want her to keep the baby against her will. Though adults
are usually allowed to limit minors' freedoms because they are
immature, in Bellotti vs. Baird, the justices believed both a girl and
her parents should be allowed to argue their particular sides of the
issue. If the girl can prove she is a mature, responsible adult and
the abortion is in her best interest, the Court thought she should
be allowed to obtain it in spite of parental objections. But if she
cannot prove her maturity, she must at least prove the abortion is
in her best interest. If she cannot prove either point, and if her
parents' arguments are stronger than hers, then she will not be
permitted to go through with the abortion. The Court did not want to

Eisinger 3

automatically grant the rights of adulthood to pregnant minors only because they face an adult problem; the justices felt that, like adults, minors still must prove they know what they want and why.

The Court in Bellotti v. Baird preferred to let families decide what to do when a girl becomes pregnant, and they preferred not to overrule parents unless absolutely necessary. They also wanted girls to consult with their parents before seeking an abortion. But when girls feel uncomfortable discussing the issue with their families, or when they risk abuse in telling their parents, justices felt states should allow direct access to the court. Therefore, they ruled the Massachusetts statute not guaranteeing direct access to court unconstitutional.

Telling parents about a pregnancy may be the hardest discussion a girl will ever have, but it is a discussion worth having. Unlike girls in movies such as *Juno*, real girls do not always make the decisions best for them, and so they need parents to decide for them, or at least help them decide.

4

5

Eisinger 4

Works Cited

Bellotti v. Baird. No. 78-329. Supreme Ct. of the US. 2 June
    1979. *Justia U.S. Supreme Court Center.* OYEZ U.S. Supreme
    Court Media. n.d. Web. 3 Feb. 2008.
Juno. Dir. Jason Reitman. Fox Searchlight, 2007. Film.

Clara organizes her essay so that the constitutional issues are prominent, particularly the conflict between the rights of teens and their parents. Rather than summarizing the Supreme Court decision section by section, Clara reorganizes the material to highlight how the rights of teens clash with those of their parents, because she believes that this conflict is the key constitutional issue at stake in the case.

Notice that Clara uses the film *Juno* to introduce her topic to her readers. A summary essay can draw on sources aside from the particular one that is being summarized. Bringing in other sources may help identity or illuminate the issues that are contained within the source that is the focus of the summary. Just make sure that those additional sources do not detract from your goal of summarizing the source specified in the assignment.

One of Clara's classmates, Alejandro Chavarria, takes a somewhat different approach to the assignment. While Clara concentrated on conflict between the rights of parents and those of their children, Alejandro focuses more on the extent to which minors are entitled to have access to the courts to plead their cases.

Chavarria 1

Alejandro Chavarria

Legal Studies I

Professor Swensen

14 February 2008

Bellotti v. Baird

In Bellotti v. Baird, the U.S. Supreme Court was asked to
look at a Massachusetts statute concerning minors and abortion.
The statute specifically forbade any minor from getting an
abortion without the consent of both living parents or a judge,
providing the parents had been notified. The Court ultimately
struck down the statute as unconstitutional because of two
problems the Court identified: 1) since the parents of the minor
had to be notified before a judge could hear the case, it unduly
burdened the minor's access to the courts, and 2) even if the
minor was found to be mature enough to handle the decision on her
own, the abortion could still be denied. In reviewing the Court's
decision, I tend to agree with most of the Court's reasoning.
Parental involvement in such an important decision as abortion
is paramount and should be highly encouraged. However, should a
minor be able to prove herself mature and responsible enough to
make the decision on her own or prove that the abortion would be
in her best interests, the operation should not be denied her.

1

Chavarria 2

In making its decision, the Court first had to make some
determinations about the legal status of minors under the
Constitution (Bellotti v. Baird). The Court determined that
minors are expected to be treated differently in the legal
system and do not enjoy all of the constitutional rights of
adults. As justification for this conclusion, the Court pointed
out the vulnerability of children, the fact that their
immaturity generally makes them incapable of making important
decisions, and the importance of parental authority in the
upbringing of children (Bellotti v. Baird).

The Court indicated in its decision that it would prefer
if such matters concerning abortion were decided outside of
the courtroom within a family (Bellotti v. Baird). But it also
acknowledged that some families are less than ideal and that a
parent's influence over his or her child may not always be in
the child's best interests. For this reason, the Court felt that
minors need direct access to the courts and that the provisions in
the Massachusetts statute requiring parental involvement in the
minor's court proceedings would interfere with that access. They
felt that this amounted to giving the parents the ultimate veto in
the matter since the parents who knew about the proceeding could
keep their children from going to the court (Bellotti v. Baird).

The Court also felt that a minor should not be denied an
abortion if she or a knowledgeable representative could prove that
she was mature enough or that it was in her best interests to have
the abortion (Bellotti v. Baird). This right was not protected in
the Massachusetts statute because of the parental notification
requirement as well as the fact that the judge could still deny
the operation even if the minor was proven to be mature enough to

Chavarria 3

make that decision on her own. This is objectionable for two very simple reasons: 1) parental involvement in court proceedings such as these may lead to granting the parents an ultimate veto in the decision and 2) allowing a judge to deny an abortion to an individual who is proven mature results in granting the judge an ultimate veto in the decision as well (Bellotti v. Baird). At some point, the decision needs to be given to the person actually dealing with this situation: the potential mother.

Chavarria 4

Work Cited

Bellotti v. Baird. No. 78-329. Supreme Ct. of the US. 2 June 1979. *Justia U.S. Supreme Court Center*. OYEZ U.S. Supreme Court Media. n.d. Web. 3 Feb. 2008.

Both Clara and Alejandro provide adequate summaries of Bellotti v. Baird. But even though the two summaries are consistent in terms of the basic facts of the case, they do differ in the aspects of Bellotti v. Baird that are emphasized: Clara highlights balance between families and courts in making decisions about abortion, while Alejandro focuses on the constitutional rights of minors with regard to abortion. If we examined the notes, annotations, and elaborations that Clara and Alejandro accumulated as they read Bellotti v. Baird, we would undoubtedly see distinctions in the ways they read the text. Any complex text leads to various reading and thus distinct summaries. We do not mean to say that all readings of a text are equally valid, and certainly there must be concrete evidence in the text to justify a particular summary of it. That said, for any complex text, there is a range of plausible readings that would lead to summaries that differ in emphasis. Clara and Alejandro's summaries, while they obviously differ, are both grounded in careful readings of Bellotti v. Baird.

Just as Clara and Alejandro's summaries reflect their own readings of the text, summaries you write will indicate the interplay between your mind and the sources you are working with. In this sense, summarizing is a creative and dynamic process, one that draws fully on your thinking abilities.

Drawing on the strategies presented in this chapter, we outline the process of summary writing in Table 4-1.

TABLE 4-1   The Process of Summary Essay Writing

Prewriting: Planning and Preparatory Activities

1. Read the assignment, and formulate your rhetorical goals.
   - Why are you writing the summary, and what desired effect do you hope to have on your audience?
   - How much of the source material should you include in the summary, and what form should this material take?
   - Will your summary be a comprehensive account of the author's thesis and argument, or will it emphasize only the author's central points?
2. Consider your audience.
   - Are you writing for your professor or for a broader audience?
   - Is your audience in the academic community?
   - Are you writing for a general audience or for specialists?
   - What will your audience already know about the topic?
   - Will you need to explain basic concepts or provide background for the source material to make sense?
   - Will your audience be biased either for or against what the source says?
   - Can you predict how your audience will react to the source?
   - What is the overall impact that you want to have on your audience?
   - How will your writing inform, influence, or change your audience?
3. Read the source for content; genre, organization, and features; and rhetorical concerns.
   - Reading for content: What is the author's thesis or main point? What are other important points?
   - Reading for genre, organization, and features: How does the author get his or her points across? What is the method of presentation? What is the pattern of organization?
   - Reading for rhetorical concerns: What is the author's purpose? How does the author intend to influence the audience? Who is this author and what is his or her background? To whom is the piece addressed? In what type of publication is it published? What is the author's relationship to the audience?

Drafting

1. Arrange summarized material in paragraphs.
2. Identify the source by title and author.
3. Insert transitions and logical connectors.
4. Supply parenthetical documentation.
5. Title your summary.
6. Create a works cited page.

Revising

If possible, have a classmate or friend read your summary and answer the questions on the following checklist. If no one is available, answer the questions yourself.

✓ *Checklist for Revising a Summary Essay*

_____   1. Have you identified the author and title of the source?

_____   2. Have you indicated the author's purpose and the point he or she is trying to make (thesis)?

_____   3. Have you referred to the rhetorical context (audience and place of publication) if it is discernible?

_____   4. Are there clear transitions and logical connectors between paragraphs?

_____   5. Are there clear transitions within paragraphs?

_____   6. Have you paraphrased instead of following the original word for word?

_____   7. Have you included too many quotations?

_____   8. Does the summary include too much detail or redundancy or too many examples?

_____   9. Have you adapted the summary to your audience's needs?

_____   10. Have you provided parenthetical documentation?

_____   11. Have you included a works cited page?

_____   12. Have you corrected sentences that sound stilted or awkward?

_____   13. Have you corrected errors in usage, punctuation, or mechanics?

_____   14. Have you corrected typographical errors or misspellings?

PART III

Responding to, Analyzing, and Evaluating Sources

CHAPTER 5

Responding to Sources

RESPONSE ESSAYS: AN INTRODUCTION

When you were young, you undoubtedly wrote personal essays drawing on life experiences. You may have written on assigned topics such as "an influential person in my life" or "an important lesson I learned." Or you might have responded to open-ended assignments that allowed you to write about relevant personal experiences; for example, "Compare your experiences to the those of the main character in the novel." In order to compose these personal essays, you had to search your memory to recall previous experiences and knowledge of the topic.

The writing assignments you receive in college will seldom ask you to write exclusively about memories and personal experiences. As we explain in Chapters 1 and 2, college professors expect students to write papers that draw on authoritative sources such as books and journal articles. That is not to say academic writers never make references to personal experiences. Occasionally, you will be asked to give personal reactions to readings. Such assignments will extend your understanding of the readings by allowing you to demonstrate the texts' relevance to your life. Consider the following assignment from a psychology class:

> As we have read in our textbook, research suggests that firstborn children experience greater anxiety throughout their lives than later-born children do. In a two-page essay, describe these research findings and test them against your own experience as a member and observer of families.

This assignment requires students to summarize material from the textbook and link it to their lives. Essays that cling to the textbook and make minimal use of personal experience will not work here; nor will essays that focus entirely on experiences. The assignment asks students to draw on two sources: the text and their own lived experience.

The writing tasks that we focus on in this chapter call for a balance between textual content and the writer's own expression. You are not being asked to offer opinions substantiated only by your own knowledge and experience. Your professors expect you to give an *informed*

140

outlook. They want to hear your point of view about a text. You could approach these assignments in an elementary fashion by summarizing the text and tagging on a few sentences of commentary or reaction. But there are much more interesting ways to go about it.

To illustrate, let us look at a student essay. Diane Abramowitz was a student in a composition class that was studying the effect that technology has on our privacy. One of the sources she was required to read was "Invasion of Privacy," a *Time Magazine* article written by Joshua Quittner in 1997. Diane received the following assignment:

> In "Invasion of Privacy," Joshua Quittner explains that he is willing to risk his personal privacy in order to take advantage of technology. Use your experiences with technology to write an essay in response to the article.

The student paper reprinted here demonstrates how personal response to a source can form the basis for an essay. Notice that Diane Abramowitz does more than simply summarize the source and add personal reaction. As you read the essay, see if you can identify Diane's purpose.

Abramowitz 1

Diane Abramowitz

Academic Writing I

Professor Smith

27 September 2007

Hackers

Opens with a scenario followed by a question

You turn on your computer and open your email expecting to read a few messages from your family and friends. Instead you find that your inbox is overflowing. It contains hundreds of messages. Some of them are returned messages with notifications about failure of delivery. Others are complaints accusing you of spamming. Does this scenario sound implausible? It's not. Until recently I was naïve enough to think that my email account was secure because I've never shared my password with anyone. Now I know that keeping my account password confidential is no guarantee that I will be exempt from email identity theft.

Three months ago someone stole my email address and sent a message to everyone in my address book. The message was

1

2

Describes personal experience

advertising a company that sells discounted electronic products. When I contacted my email provider, I was told to change my password immediately. I was also told that I should select a new password that is difficult to decipher, for example, one that combines letters, numbers, and symbols, because email thieves use programs that can easily figure out many people's passwords. I was also told never to use my email password on a website that requires a password, and I was advised to get a firewall to protect my computer.

Introduces Quittner's article

Joshua Quittner went through an experience similar to mine, but instead of his e-mail it was his phone that was attacked. He recalls this event in "Invasion of Privacy," an article published in *Time Magazine* in 1997. Quitter explains that soon after he and his wife published a book on computer hackers, someone redirected his incoming phone calls to an answering machine containing an insulting message. The phone company was able to restore the phone service initially, but the hacker struck again. Over the next six months, the hacker interfered with Quittner's phone repeatedly, despite the best efforts of the phone company. Even though Quittner found this incident

Quittner's main idea

annoying, he concludes in his article that the usefulness of electronic technologies meant more to him than the privacy he lost by using them. While I agree with Quittner that technology

Writer's thesis

improves our everyday lives significantly, I am not resigned to giving up my privacy in order to enjoy those advantages.

Quittner describes a wide range of technologies that have the potential to compromise our privacy. He explains that we leave an electronic record of our whereabouts and activities as we use ATM machines, E-Z Pass lanes, and Internet shopping sites

3

4

Abramowitz 3

Summary of Quittner's article

and even as we walk down the street past a store that uses video surveillance. Our interests, preferences, and purchasing habits are recorded as we browse the Web or make credit card purchases. A skilled Internet researcher can, starting with only a name and address, uncover much of the personal information that has been stored online. Quittner points out that we can protect ourselves, to some extent, against invasions of privacy by being more careful about the personal information we divulge and the technologies we use. He also suggests that the online business community or the government do more to protect individual privacy in cyberspace. In the final analysis, however, Quittner concludes that he is willing to risk losing some of his privacy in order to benefit from the power and convenience of technology. He has "nothing to hide" and just wants some control over who has access to his personal information.

In the years since Quittner wrote "Invasion of Privacy," the use of technology has increased at an astounding rate. He saw this coming when he wrote, "If things seem crazy now, think how much crazier they will be when everybody is wired as I am" (30). Today everyone is wired. I grew up online, and every day I use a range of technologies that Quittner does not even mention in his article. I frequently use my cell phone to text message my friends. I send email messages on my cell as well as on my computer. I download music from iTunes onto my iPod. I share a good deal of personal information on Facebook and MySpace, and in one of my classes, I was required to record my reactions to the course readings on a blog. Without a doubt, technology has made communicating more convenient and, overall, it has improved my life.

Draws on personal experience to illustrate one of Quittner's points

5

Abramowitz 4

Increased convenience has led to less personal privacy. 6
While Quittner seems resigned to giving up some of his privacy,
I don't think I should have to surrender my privacy when I go
online. Despite the fact that I have a description of myself,
photos, video clips, and lists of dozens of friends on Facebook,
I value my privacy. I restrict my profiles to friends and
family. Some of my friends do not even know that they have the
option to edit their privacy settings and set limits on the
amount of information they divulge to people. This option is
very important to me. You can't be an individual without having
secrets that you share only with those you trust. When someone
trespasses into my online time, I feel that my rights have been
violated. I don't want strangers to know what I am writing to my
friends or relatives, and I don't want anyone looking over my
shoulder while I'm surfing the Internet. Even though I am just
browsing a Web page, I don't want to be followed around wherever
I go to chat or browse. In legal terms, following people around
is known as stalking. But what can the authorities do? At this
point in time, there is legislation that protects children's
privacy on the Internet, but none that protects adults'. Certainly,
local, state, and federal authorities must take immediate steps
to ensure that our right to privacy is protected. We don't have
to accept, as Quittner does, that our privacy rights and modern
technology are simply incompatible.

Last year I rented a film called *The Net 2.0*, a thriller 7
about a computer systems analyst whose identity is stolen. Her
credit cards are inoperable and all the money in her bank
account disappears. The plot is about how she struggles to

Challenges one of Quittner's claims and gives reasons for disagreeing

Reference to a film plot that illustrates a problem associated with Quittner's point of view

reclaim her identity after she is accused of crimes she did not commit. The movie is a sequel to *The Net*, an earlier movie about identity theft and hacking. These films are not science fiction. Online identity theft is widespread and it occurs every day, but we are not powerless against it. We all need to take precautions against it such as never divulging our passwords, using passwords that are difficult to decipher, being careful when we shop on sites like EBay, and never giving our personal information to people we don't know.

"The only guys who insist on perfect privacy are hermits like the Unabomber. I don't want to be cut off from the world. I have nothing to hide. I just want some measure of control over what people know about me" (35). Although there is no such thing as perfect privacy, that doesn't mean that we don't need and deserve as much privacy as possible. The government and citizens themselves must take a much more active role in ensuring that hackers do not threaten either our national or our personal security. In the future, our individual freedom may depend as much on access to cyberspace as it now does on access to the ballot box and the podium.

Speculates about the future

8

Works Cited

The Net. Dir. Irwin Winkler. Columbia, 1995. Film.

The Net 2.0. Dir. Charles Winkler. Columbia, 2006. Film.

Quittner, Joshua. "Invasion of Privacy." *Time* 25 Aug. 1997:
    28-35. Print.

Diane has a more complex goal than merely summarizing the source and giving a brief personal reaction. Let's zero in on her rhetorical purpose. From her comments, we know that she spends a great deal of time online, and she agrees with Joshua Quittner that this technology improves one's quality of life. But Diane takes issue with Quittner's willingness to surrender a degree of personal privacy in return for the advantages that technology has to offer. Her goal as a writer is to assert that one should be able to benefit from technology without giving up privacy rights. Notice that Diane supports her position by bringing her own knowledge into play. In the first paragraph, she describes how someone used her e-mail account to send out bogus messages to hundreds of e-mail addresses. Diane uses this personal experience to introduce Quittner's article, which begins with a description of his own experience with a malicious phone hacker. In the fourth paragraph, Diane explains that she has grown up online and she gives examples to show how much she relies on the Internet for day-to-day communication. Paragraph 5 includes Diane's personal feeling about having someone read her e-mail or monitor her Web-browsing habits. Her goal is to convey the sense of violation one experiences when victimized by electronic eavesdropping.

In the first, fourth, and fifth paragraphs, Diane describes experiences from her own life and her feelings about those experiences to demonstrate that online privacy violations should be taken seriously. In the sixth paragraph, she uses the film *The Net 2.0* as an example of how our lives can be affected if we fail to institute electronic privacy safeguards. As Diane's essay shows, personal knowledge includes not only direct experiences but also second-hand experiences and knowledge gleaned from books, magazines, film, television, radio, and audio recording. You may draw on a full range of personal knowledge when you write response essays.

Exercise 5.1

Reread Diane Abramowitz's essay, listing any changes you think she might make in content, genre, organization, or stylistic features in order to achieve her rhetorical purpose more successfully. In class, compare your list to those of your classmates. Discuss any differences in perception.

WRITING RESPONSE ESSAYS

PREWRITING

Prewriting is the period when writers discover what they want to say. It includes everything you do before sitting down to pound out a first draft of your paper. When you are assigned a Response Essay, you will devote most of this time to reading the text and carefully considering your reactions to it. You will also organize these reactions, devise a preliminary thesis, and contemplate how you will support it. And you will select an organizational plan for your essay.

Do a First Reading to Get a General Impression of the Source

After you have analyzed the assignment and determined that you are being asked to write an essay in response to a reading source, turn your attention to your purpose for reading. You will read the text for the purpose of generating reactions to the author's ideas. Review the prereading and close reading strategies we discussed in Chapter 2 (pages 52–72). Your first reading may elicit little more than a general, impressionistic reaction. In the case of Joshua Quittner's article "Invasion of Privacy," our students' initial reactions ranged from "I care about my privacy and I don't want it to be invaded" to "Why worry about technology that makes our lives more convenient and safer?" After this initial reading, freewrite your reactions. Write nonstop for ten minutes or so, jotting down whatever comes to mind about the topic.

Reread and Elaborate

The second reading allows you to probe your memory and make associations between prior knowledge and experience and the propositions in the text. As we explained in Chapter 2 (pages 56–58), this strategy is called *elaboration*. To elaborate, annotate in the margins of the text or take separate notes. Here a reader elaborates on two passages from Quittner's "Invasion of Privacy."

Quittner Text	Elaboration Notes
Losing control of your telephone, of course, is the least of it. After all, most of us voluntarily give out our phone number and address when we allow ourselves to be listed in the White Pages. Most of us go a lot further than that. We register our whereabouts whenever we put a bank card in an ATM machine or drive through an E-Z Pass lane on the highway. We submit to being photographed every day—20 times a day on average if you live or work in New York City—by surveillance cameras. We make public our interests and our purchasing habits every time we shop by mail order or visit a commercial Website.	Since 9/11, the government has been accused of spying on U.S. citizens. I don't know if that's true or not, but surveillance cameras and closed circuit tvs are everywhere, even in schools.
I don't know about you, but I do all this willingly because I appreciate what I get in return: the security of a safe parking lot, the convenience of cash when I need it, the improved service of mail-order houses that know me well enough to send me catalogs of stuff that interests me. And while I know we're supposed to feel just awful about giving up our vaunted privacy, I suspect (based on what the pollsters say) that you're as ambivalent about it as I am.	We could have an unlisted phone number, but we don't have a choice about how information collected by an ATM, E-Z Pass, or surveillance camera is used. We should have the same choice of being unlisted with those services as we do with phones. At home we get dozens of catalogs we don't want at all. I read that one catalog order can generate over 100 solicitations from other companies.

Margin annotations:

I don't do it willingly! I have no choice!

I think most students value their privacy. One of the most controversial issues on campus is that the college has the authority to enter at will any of our private dorm rooms.

As you reread the source, elaborate as fully as you can. Even if some of these elaborations don't prove valuable to you, it is easier to write when you can select work from a rich pool of resources from which you can easily make selections. Review the examples of elaborating and annotating that appear in Chapter 2 (pages 55–56).

You may be asking, "How can I forge connections between information in my memory and information in the reading source when I am dealing with a topic that is new to me?" When you don't have a pool of topic-related prior knowledge that you can draw forth readily, it helps to focus on your purpose for elaborating. Remind yourself of all the different forms your elaborations can take.

Establish Purposes and Forms of Elaborations

Researchers who study composition have found that elaborations serve three purposes (Stein 148):

- To produce new ideas
- To develop critical viewpoints
- To develop ideas already stated by the author

Let us illustrate these three functions with another passage from Quittner's article. Here Quittner discusses the views of Sherry Turkle.

Text	Elaboration	Function
"It's a very schizophrenic time," says Sherry Turkle, professor of sociology at the Massachusetts Institute of Technology, who writes books about how computers and online communication are transforming society. She believes our culture is undergoing a kind of mass identity crisis, trying to hang on to a sense of privacy and intimacy in a global village of tens of millions. "We have very unstable notions about the boundaries of the individual," she says.	I see the "mass identity crisis" in youth fashion advertising. We're encouraged to develop a particular "look" that the fashion industry wants to sell. Part of the sales pitch is that this standardized "look" which will be worn by thousands of others is supposed to highlight the purchaser's individuality. Is it technology or is it our market economy that has created our society's identity crisis? My guess is that marketplace forces are at the root of the problem but that technology makes these forces even more powerful. "Be all that you can be."	Develops an idea already stated by the author

Develops a critical view

Produces a new idea |

Notice the functions the elaboration serves. It extends Turkle's point about the impact of technology by linking it to the market economy; it poses a critical question about Turkle's conclusion; and it develops a new idea using Turkle's idea as a springboard. There are countless ways you can bring your own ideas to bear on the reading source. Some of them are as follows.

STRATEGIES FOR ELABORATING ON READING SOURCES

- Agree or disagree with a statement in the text and give reasons for your agreement or disagreement.
- Compare or contrast your reactions to the topic (for example, "At first I thought…, but now I think…").
- Extend one of the author's points.
- Draw attention to what the author has neglected to say about the topic.
- Discover an idea implied by the text but not stated by the author.
- Provide additional details by fleshing out a point made by the author.
- Illustrate the text with an example, incident, scenario, or anecdote.
- Embellish the author's point with a vivid image, metaphor, or example.
- Test one of the author's claims.
- Compare one of the author's points with your own prior knowledge of the topic or with your own or others' experiences.
- Interpret the text in the light of your prior knowledge or applicable experiences.
- Personalize one of the author's statements.
- Question one of the author's points.
- Speculate about one of the author's points by
  Asking questions about the direct consequences of an idea
  Predicting consequences
  Drawing implications from an idea
  Applying the idea to a hypothetical situation
  Giving a concrete instance of a point made in the text
- Draw comparisons between the text and applicable books, articles, films, or other media.
- Classify items in the text under a superordinate category.
- Discover relationships between ideas in the text that are unstated by the author.
- Validate one of the author's points with an example or prior knowledge.
- Criticize a point in the text.
- Create hierarchies of importance among ideas in the text.
- Make a judgment about the relevance of a statement that the author has made.
- Impose a condition on a statement in the text (for example, "If…, then…").
- Qualify an idea in the text.
- Extend an idea with a personal recollection or reflection.
- Assess the usefulness and applicability of an idea.

Responding Independently and Responding with Others

During and after your reading, write brief marginal comments in the margins of the text and record longer reactions in your journal. In Chapter 2 we suggest that you use a double-entry journal in which you copy key passages from the text in the left-hand column and write your thoughts and opinions in the right-hand column. You may prefer a full-page format in which you write out your responses without copying down the text. If you use this format, be sure to make a note of the passages and pages to which you are responding. A useful prewriting activity is to share your responses with a partner or a small group. Exchange your journal with a classmate and comment on his or her reactions to the text. In the small group setting, ask each member of the group to select a sample of marginal annotations and journal entries and read them aloud. Group members will discuss responses that are similar in nature, and then they will come to consensus on a group response. You may choose to record your elaborations and extended journal entries in electronic form rather than pen and paper. You can share them with your classmates via email. Or your professor may ask you to post your comments on an electronic discussion board or class blog.

Exercise 5.2

This exercise gives you practice using different forms of elaboration. Read and reread each of the following passages, elaborate, and record your elaboration notes in a notebook or journal.

1. "Modern Romance" by Celeste Biever, page 398, paragraph 9. Elaborate on Biever's passage in the following ways:
   a. Agree or disagree with a statement in the text and give reasons for your agreement or disagreement.
   b. Extend one of the author's points.
   c. Illustrate a statement with an example, incident, scenario, or anecdote.
   d. Compare one of the author's points with prior knowledge or your own or others' experiences.

2. "Give the Girls a Break" by Nancy Gibbs, pages 427–429, entire article. Elaborate on Gibbs's article in the following ways:
   a. Discover an idea implied by the text but not stated by the author.
   b. Draw attention to what the author has neglected to say about the topic.
   c. Validate one of the author's points with an example or prior knowledge or experience.

3. "Control of Creativity? Fashion's Secret " by David Bollier and Laurie Racine, pages 444–447, paragraphs 1–4. Elaborate on the passages in the following ways:
   a. Discover an idea implied by the text but not stated by the author.
   b. Discover relationships between ideas in the text that are unstated by the author.
   c. Speculate about one of the author's points by asking questions about the direct consequences of an idea, predicting consequences, drawing implications from an idea, or applying the idea to a hypothetical situation.

Exercise 5.3

Assume that you are working on the following essay assignment.

> In "Suddenly Teen Pregnancy Is Cool?," Cathy Gulli gives her interpretation of why teenage girls in the United States willingly choose to become pregnant. In a three-page essay, summarize and respond to Gulli's views.

Turn to "Suddenly Teen Pregnancy Is Cool?" (pages 420–426) or another selection of your choice. As you read, elaborate in some of the ways we described on page 149. Jot down your elaborations in a notebook or journal.

Develop a Thesis

Even more important than generating your own ideas is deciding how to use them in your essay. If you already know the point you want to make, your rhetorical purpose will allow you to derive a *preliminary thesis* from your elaborations. Taking the Quittner assignment as an example, if you decide to argue that technological advances that make life more convenient should not come at the expense of individual privacy, you can prove your point by selecting elaborations that disagree with Quittner, draw attention to important factors he leaves out, challenge and question his ideas, make relevance judgments, or qualify his ideas and assess their applicability.

If you are not sure of the point you wish to make in your essay, review your elaborations as follows:

1. **See if one type of elaboration predominates.** Again, using the Quittner article as an example, let's assume that a good portion of your elaborations were drawn from your personal experiences. You could plan an essay in which you show how your experiences either validate or contradict Quittner's claims.

2. **See if a good number of elaborations were triggered by a particular source idea.** Let's say you elaborated at length on one of Quittner's assertions: "Popular culture shines its klieg light on the most intimate corners of our lives, and most of us play right along. If all we really wanted was to be left alone, explain the lasting popularity of Oprah and Sally and Ricki tell-all TV." If you wish, you may focus your paper on this single aspect of the topic.

3. **Classify your elaborations.** Select workable categories and discard the rest. You might highlight the elaborations in which you agree or disagree with the author of the source and then work only with these as you draft your essay.

To illustrate these procedures, we examine our student Kayla Robinson's elaborations on a set of paragraphs from Quittner's "Invasion of Privacy." As you study these elaborations, decide if one type of elaboration predominates. Are a number of elaborations triggered by a certain idea in the reading source? Do the elaborations fit into a classification scheme?

Text	**Elaborations**

Paragraph 4

I should also point out that as news director for Pathfinder, Time Inc.'s mega info mall, and a guy who makes his living on the Web, I know better than most people that we're hurtling toward an even more intrusive world. We're all being watched by computers whenever we visit Websites; by the mere act of "browsing" (it sounds so passive!) we're going public in a way that was unimaginable a decade ago. I know this because I'm a watcher too. When people come to my Website, without ever knowing their names, I can peer over their shoulders, recording what they look at, timing how long they stay on a particular page, following them around Pathfinder's sprawling offerings.

When I first read this paragraph, I didn't like the idea that someone is looking over my shoulder as I browse through Web sites. Since I'm alone when I browse, it feels like it should be private. But when I think about it, Web browsing is one of the least private activities because I am linked up to a network of literally millions of people and organizations. I know that commercial Web providers keep track of the people visiting their sites and they use small files called "cookies" to store information about my interests. That's why ads for sports products often pop up on my screen.

Paragraph 10

I don't know about you, but I do all this willingly because I appreciate what I get in return: the security of a safe parking lot, the convenience of cash when I need it, the improved service of mail-order houses that know me well enough to send me catalogs of stuff that interests me. And while I know we're supposed to feel just awful about giving up our vaunted privacy, I suspect (based on what the pollsters say) that you're as ambivalent about it as I am.

These conveniences appeal to me as well. I'd miss my ATM card and my e-mail more than the privacy I lose by using these technologies.

Paragraph 11

Popular culture shines its klieg lights on the most intimate corners of our lives, and most of us play right along. If all we really wanted was to be left alone, explain the lasting popularity of Oprah and Sally and Ricki tell-all TV.

What's a kleig light? I think it's sad that our society doesn't value privacy. TV reality shows have become popular,

Memoirs top the best-seller lists, with books about incest and insanity and illness leading the way. Perfect strangers at cocktail parties tell me the most disturbing details of their abusive upbringings. Why?

and there is a channel where you can watch live video of every moment of people's lives 24/7.

Paragraph 17

It all started in the 1950s, when, in order to administer Social Security funds, the U.S. government began entering records on big mainframe computers, using nine-digit identification numbers as data points. Then, even more than today, the citizenry instinctively loathed the computer and its injunctions against folding, spindling and mutilating. We were not numbers! We were human beings! These fears came to a head in the late 1960s, recalls Alan Westin, a retired Columbia University professor who publishes a quarterly report *Privacy and American Business*. "The techniques of intrusion and data surveillance had overcome the weak law and social mores that we had built up in the pre–World War II era," says Westin.

I didn't know this. How did they keep track of people before that? I heard that soon we'll be required to have national ID cards. What if this database of personal information is hacked?

Paragraph 23

"Most people would be astounded to know what's out there," says Carole Lane, author of *Naked in Cyberspace: How to Find Personal Information Online*. "In a few hours, sitting at my computer, beginning with no more than your name and address, I can find out what you do for a living, the names and ages of your spouse and children, what kind of car you drive, the value of your house and how much taxes you pay on it."

I don't like the idea that people can find out so much about me. Now all you have to do is google someone and you can find tons of information.

Paragraph 28

The real problem, says Kevin Kelly, executive editor of *Wired* magazine, is that although we say we value our privacy, what we really want is something very different: "We think that privacy is about information, but it's not—it's about relationships." The way Kelly sees it, there was no privacy in the traditional village or small town; everyone knew everyone else's secrets. And that was comfortable. I knew about you,

I'm creeped out about this. Companies collect information about our shopping habits. Once it's on the Internet, personal information becomes the property of strangers.

and you knew about me. "There was a symmetry to the knowledge," he says. "What's gone out of whack is we don't know who knows about us anymore. Privacy has become asymmetrical."

Paragraph 35

"Technology has outpaced law," says Marc Rotenberg, director of the Washington-based Electronic Privacy Information Center. Rotenberg advocates protecting the privacy of E-mail by encrypting it with secret codes so powerful that even the National Security Agency's supercomputers would have a hard time cracking it. Such codes are legal within the U.S. but cannot be used abroad—where terrorists might use them to protect their secrets—without violating U.S. export laws. The battle between the Clinton Administration and the computer industry over encryption export policy has been raging for six years without resolution, a situation that is making it hard to do business on the Net and is clearly starting to fray some nerves. "The future is in electronic commerce," says Ira Magaziner, Clinton's point man on Net issues. All that's holding it up is "this privacy thing."

I'm afraid that the law will never catch up with the technology. Laws change so slowly and technology advances so rapidly. New methods of electronic snooping are invented every day. As soon as a law is created to control one method, two more will be invented.

Paragraph 38

I'm with Kelly. The only guys who insist on perfect privacy are hermits like the Unabomber. I don't want to be cut off from the world. I have nothing to hide. I just want some measure of control over what people know about me. I want to have my magic cookie and eat it too.

I had to look up Unabomber. The Unabomber was a guy named Ted Kaczynski who had once been a math professor. From late 1970 to the mid 1990s he mailed bombs to people working at universities and airports (that's why he's called "Unabomber") and subsequently killed three of the recipients. He wrote a manifesto about how technology was curtailing freedom. It was published in the New York Times.

Notice that the elaborations on these paragraphs express Kayla's reluctant acceptance of Quittner's ideas. A viewpoint emerges: although any loss of personal privacy is regrettable, the advantages of the new technology make it worth sacrificing a degree of privacy. Kayla also indicates that technology advances with such speed that it will leave in its wake any efforts to protect privacy. From these elaborations she derives the following preliminary thesis:

> Quittner's claim that technological advances are having a negative impact on personal privacy is, unfortunately, true. He is also correct that the benefits of the technology are worth the loss of privacy. Even if we wanted to stop the loss of privacy, it would not be possible, given the rapid progress of technology.

Exercise 5.4

For the exercise on page 151, you jotted down elaborations in response to "Suddenly Teen Pregnancy Is Cool?" or another article of your choice. Using these elaborations, derive a preliminary thesis for a response essay. Recall the assignment:

> In "Suddenly Teen Pregnancy Is Cool?," Cathy Gulli gives her interpretation of why teenage girls in the United States willingly choose to become pregnant. In a three-page essay, summarize and respond to Gulli's views.

> As you examine your elaborations, see (1) if any one type of elaboration predominates, (2) if a good number of elaborations were triggered by a particular source idea, or (3) if you can classify the elaborations.

Select an Organizational Plan

After you come up with a preliminary thesis, your next step is to decide which organizational plan to use. First, review the organizational plans that we presented in Table 1-1 (page 16). A number of these plans are appropriate for response essays, depending on the sources and your rhetorical purpose. Two additional patterns that are commonly used for response essays are summary and response and point-by-point response. Diane Abramowitz (pages 141–145) uses the summary and response pattern:

Paragraphs 2–3	Summary of Quittner's points
Paragraphs 4–6	Diane's commentary and reaction

Diane could have used the point-by-point response pattern by taking up each of Quittner's main points and responding to them one by one. To do this, Diane would alternate between her own ideas and those expressed by Quittner, perhaps in the following manner:

Paragraph 2	Brief summary and commentary
Paragraphs 3–6	In each paragraph, summary of one of Quittner's points and response to it

Note how we use the summary and response and point-by-point alternating patterns to organize the elaborations we presented on pages 152–154.

PART OF ESSAY	SUMMARY AND RESPONSE PATTERN	POINT-BY-POINT PATTERN
Introductory paragraphs	Summarize Quittner's claim that we are sacrificing personal privacy in our pursuit of new technologies that make our lives more convenient and his belief that this trade-off is worthwhile. Explain your reluctant acceptance of Quittner's position.	Briefly summarize Quittner's claim that we are sacrificing personal privacy in our pursuit of new technologies that make our lives more convenient and his belief that this trade-off is worthwhile. Present your thesis.
Body paragraphs	Give reasons why the technological advances are worthwhile and why the losses in personal privacy are not that significant.	Alternate between Quittner's statements and your reactions. For example, first summarize the points Quittner makes in paragraphs 10 and 11 and give your reactions; then summarize the points Quittner makes in paragraph 17 and give your reactions; and so on.
Concluding paragraph	See the techniques on page 27.	See the techniques on page 27.

The summary and response and point-by-point patterns are not the only ways to organize response essays. As we mentioned earlier, your rhetorical purpose may provide the blueprint for your essay. Suppose that you disagree with Quittner's willingness to trade personal privacy for high-tech conveniences. You might develop your essay in a comparison-and-contrast format if you know of cases of devastating privacy violations that can be contrasted with the milder examples in Quittner's article. Or you might show the negative consequences of allowing convenience to take precedence over personal rights and thereby follow one of standard format for a cause-and-effect essay.

Exercise 5.5

Turn to the elaboration notes you took on "Suddenly Teen Pregnancy Is Cool?" or on another article of your choice, for the exercise on page 151. Review the notes. Then classify your elaborations and study them to discern patterns for developing and organizing your essay. Next, outline your essay according to the summary and response pattern, the point-by-point pattern, or some other plan. Recall the assignment:

In "Suddenly Teen Pregnancy Is Cool?," Cathy Gulli gives her interpretation of why teenage girls in the United States willingly choose to become
pregnant. In a three-page essay, summarize and respond to Gulli's views.

DRAFTING

To understand drafting better, reflect on the prior knowledge you have already brought into
play. You have tapped your prior knowledge of the topic to produce a pool of elaborations
on the reading source, and you have invoked your prior knowledge of organization and
structure to discover an organizational plan. At this point, you will summon up two other
types of prior knowledge: (1) knowledge of the basic features of writing—elements like
titles, introductions, sentences, paragraphs, transitions and connecting ideas, and conclusions—and (2) knowledge of strategies for summarizing, paraphrasing, and quoting
sources. To review these elements and strategies, reread the first four chapters of this book.

Exercise 5.6

Return to the elaboration notes, preliminary thesis, and organizational plan you have
developed in response to "Suddenly Teen Pregnancy Is Cool?," Cathy Gulli's interpretation of why teenage girls in the United States willingly choose to become pregnant,
or another topic of your choice. Use the guidelines we have provided in Chapter 1
to come up with a preliminary title for the essay. You may want to revise this title
after you have completed the first draft. Then write an introductory paragraph for
the essay, making sure that you (1) use a paper opener that will interest the reader,
(2) announce the topic, (3) disclose a thesis or attitude toward the topic, (4) establish
your voice as a writer, and (5) include the title, author, author's affiliation, and some
summary information about the reading source.

Write the Body of the Response Essay

The essay you compose at this stage should be a preliminary draft, not a polished, final
copy. Think of this first draft as a discovery draft, an opportunity to find out more about
what you want to say.

As you draft the body, follow the organizational plan you chose at the prewriting
stage—summary and response, point-by-point, or another pattern. Develop sections and
paragraphs that fit into your plan. If your prewriting plan proves unworkable or you discover a new direction for the paper, rethink your organizational strategy.

Summary.   The summary is an integral part of the response essay. Keep in mind that the
type of summary you write depends on your rhetorical purpose. Ask yourself if your purpose is to provide your readers with a comprehensive summary that covers all the major
aspects of the reading source. Or do you want simply to reduce the reading source to a
series of gists?

Remember that your objective is to tailor the summary to the reaction. After you organize and classify your ideas and establish your direction, adapt the summary to your purpose. You need not summarize the entire article, only the sections that relate to your purpose. The summary should highlight the passages that prompted your reaction and refer only incidentally to other portions of the text.

Paragraphs.   Develop paragraphs that are unified and coherent. Make sure that each paragraph develops a central idea and that all the sentences contribute to this idea in some way. As you read the following paragraph, notice how each sentence develops the point that our everyday activities are becoming a matter of public record.

```
As Quittner points out, we leave electronic trails behind us as we
move through our everyday lives. When my computer alarm wakes me up
at the preprogrammed time, I register my presence in cyberspace by
logging on to my e-mail account to check for any messages and then
moving on to a local weather Web site to help me decide what to wear.
I'm still barely awake when the cashier swipes my ID at the campus
coffee shop. On my way across campus, I stop by an ATM in the student
center and get cash to repay a friend from whom I borrowed over the
weekend. My first-period course meets in a networked classroom, and
the professor asks us to log on to the course Web page to download
the next assignment. It's only 9:00 a.m., and I've already created a
trail, dropping electronic breadcrumbs at four different locations.
```

Also strive to make your paragraphs coherent. In a coherent paragraph, repeated words and ideas, rewording of ideas, and transitional expressions (*also, for example, thus, similarly, consequently,* and so on) show the reader the logical links among the sentences.

Exercise 5.7

Return to the draft you are composing on "Suddenly Teen Pregnancy Is Cool?" or another topic of your choice, and work on the summary, body paragraphs, and conclusion. Make an effort to (1) adapt the summary to your rhetorical purposes, (2) develop unified and coherent paragraphs, and (3) write a conclusion that does more than simply restate the thesis.

REVISING

Working on your own or with a peer reviewer, use the following checklist to plan the revision of your response essay:

✓ *Checklist for Revising the First Draft of a Response Essay*

_____   1. Is the writer's rhetorical purpose clear? (How does the writer attempt to influence or affect readers?)

_____   2. Does everything in the draft lead to or follow from one central thesis? (If not, which ideas appear to be out of place?)

_____ 3. Will the reader understand the essay, and is the writer sensitive to the reader's concerns?

    _____ a. Does the writer provide necessary background information about the source, including title, author, and author's affiliation?

    _____ b. Is the summary of the relevant portions of the source complete, or does the writer need to add more material?

    _____ c. Throughout the essay, when referring to the source, does the writer supply necessary documentation?

    _____ d. Are there clear transitions or connectives that differentiate the writer's own ideas from those of the source author?

_____ 4. Is the organizational plan or form appropriate for this kind of paper? (If not, can you suggest another format?)

_____ 5. Is the writer's response varied, adequate, and appropriate for this kind of paper? (If not, can you explain why?)

_____ 6. Does the writer provide transitions or connecting ideas between the summary and reaction sections? (If not, where are they needed?)

_____ 7. Do you hear the writer's voice throughout the entire essay? (Can you describe it?)

_____ 8. Does the writer open the paper in a way that catches the reader's attention?

_____ 9. Does the conclusion simply restate the main idea, or does it offer new insights?

_____ 10 Does the essay have an appropriate title?

Exercise 5.8

Return to the draft of the response essay you are revising. (1) Reread the essay to see if you present a consistent perspective. (2) Examine the draft to see if you have used enough transitional expressions and connecting ideas.

EXPANDING YOUR RHETORICAL GOAL

When you write the type of response essay discussed in this chapter, you are meeting the author of the reading source halfway. You are bringing your prior knowledge and experiences to bear on the ideas you read, and then as you compose the essay, you are forging connections between your own ideas and those of the author. The reader of your essay is well aware that the reading source has triggered your particular response.

If you have a good deal of knowledge about the topic or have generated a rich pool of elaborations, you may be able to compose a different type of response essay. The reading source will still trigger your reaction, but it will serve as a springboard or taking-off point rather than a mine from which you have unearthed a good portion of your material. In other words, the essay will be driven primarily by your own ideas and conception of the topic, and you will take your own angle or approach. Your readers will still be aware that the reading source has provided you with ideas, evidence, or support for your thesis, but they will see that you have taken the initiative and are not simply reacting to another person's ideas. Rather than summarizing and responding to a text (knowledge telling), you are transforming it for your own design and purpose (knowledge transforming). The following chart contrasts response essays of both types.

TOPIC: PRIVACY AND THE INTERNET

Stock Summary and Response Essay	*Response Essay with a Self-Directed Purpose*
Source author's conception of the topic is the driving force behind the writer's essay.	The writer's conception of the topic drives the essay.
Writer's points are prompted by or derived from passages in the reading source.	The writer uses some of the source author's ideas, but the emphasis is on developing the writer's own points.
The writer is engaged in knowledge-telling, referring to passages in the text and reacting to them.	The writer is engaged in knowledge-transforming, using the text as a spring-board for his or her take on the topic.

Now let us look at a response essay that is written with a self-directed rhetorical purpose and then discuss its characteristics. Our student, Lili Wong, received the following assignment:

> Write a thoughtful essay in response to "When Poop Goes Primetime," the first chapter of Daniel J. Solove's *The Future of Reputation: Gossip, Rumor, and Privacy on the Internet*. Address your essay to classmates who have also done the reading. Solove's book is available online. You can download a PDF of Chapter 1 at http://docs.law.gwu.edu/facweb/dsolove/Future-of-Reputation/text.htm.

Solove's book examines the tension between free speech and individual rights. We are free to disclose personal information online and free to post information about other people, but this freedom has a profound impact on privacy. Solove opens *The Future of Reputation: Gossip, Rumor, and Privacy on the Internet* with a description of an incident that occurred on a subway train in South Korea. A young woman's dog pooped in the subway car, and despite complaints from the other passengers she refused to clean up the dog's mess. Someone on the train photographed the incident and posted the photos on a blog where many readers made accusatory and sometimes scathing comments. The story spread from the Korean blog to blogs in the United States and other countries, and as Solove remarks, soon everyone on the planet was reading about "the dog poop girl." Eventually the young woman's identity became known and she and her family were harassed. Distraught and shamed, she dropped out of the university she was attending. The remainder of Solove's chapter discusses how online freedom of expression is curtailing our privacy and in some cases having destructive effects on our lives. You might want to go to the Web site and read Chapter 1 of Solove's book before you examine Lili's response essay.

Lili Wong

Professor Kennedy

English 131

24 June 2008

Facing the Inevitable Truth

The Internet profoundly intrudes upon your privacy, and
there is very little you can do about it. Even if it were
possible to survive without a computer, to never surf the Net,
never write an email message, and never place an order online,
you would still have an online presence. I could easily use free
search tools to locate a great deal of personal information
about you. Public records have been computerized, and well over
a billion of them are available at Government Registry Online
Records Retrieval (http://www.governmentregistry.org). Using
this site, I can find birth and marriage certificates, property
records, court records, arrest records, military status, as well
as tons of other information about people. Your phone number and
address are easily located online, and Google Maps will even
provide me with a photo of your apartment building. In return,
you can obtain a detailed profile of me, and since I have grown
up online as you have, when you google Lili Wong, you will have
access to an amazing amount of my personal information.

Every time you boot up your computer and open your browser,
you sacrifice your privacy and even risk the possibility of
endangering your reputation. If you are like me, you do not have
the technological know-how to safeguard your privacy. But even
if you did, you still could not prevent people from posting
information about you. The truth is that you have little control

over the Internet. Daniel J. Solove, an associate professor of law at George Washington University Law School, explains that the Internet is a fairly recent phenomenon. Solove compares it to an adolescent who is young, wild, and ungovernable. In *The Future of Reputation, Gossip, Rumor, and Privacy on the Internet*, he writes

> The future of the Internet involves not only the clash between freedom and control but also a struggle within the heart of freedom itself. The more freedom people have to spread information online, the more likely that people's private secrets will be revealed in ways that can hinder their opportunities in the future. In many respects, the teenage Internet is taking on all the qualities of an adolescent—brash, uninhibited, unruly, fearless, experimental, and often not mindful of the consequences of its behavior. And as with a teenager, the Net's greater freedom can be both a blessing and a curse. (5–6)

I have friends who act like teenagers when they're on the "teenage Internet." They will do anything to get attention. They do not think about personal risk when they have online interactions with strangers, and they have no regard for anonymity when they post intimate secrets on blogs and social networking sites.

In some instances, you are guilty for voluntarily giving up your privacy. Phone conversations used to be private. If you wished to make a phone call in a public place, you entered a phone booth and closed the door behind you before you dialed the number. Years ago people wouldn't think of talking on the phone in front of strangers. Now you can easily eavesdrop on countless cell phone conversations every day. Growing up I kept a diary under lock and key, and I complained loudly the day my younger brother broke into it and read my cherished entries. Today I read blogs where people post risque photos and divulge shocking details about their private lives. They have no secrets. Until I got to college, the only people I knew intimately were my close circle of friends. I remember my middle school distributed a paper facebook to help us get to know each other, but all it contained was a headshot and short paragraph on each student. Today when I sign onto Facebook, I can access the personal profiles, blogs, photos, and videos of mere acquaintances. All of this openness comes at a price. I know that when I willingly divulge personal information on public blogs and social networking sites, I have to accept the consequences. I have heard that recruiters and employers check these sites and also do Google searches on prospective employees. A friend of mine was denied a job because of Facebook photos showing his alcohol and drug use. In cyberspace, privacy is an unreasonable expectation.

In other instances, you do not voluntarily give up your privacy. It is stolen from you. Solove gives an example of this with the story of the "dog poop girl." The girl was traveling on the subway with her dog. The dog pooped on the floor, and she refused to clean up after it. A passenger on the train photographed the incident and posted the pictures on the Internet. Someone found out the girl's identity. Bloggers criticized and ridiculed her and eventually severely damaged her reputation.

What is interesting about this case is that it could not have happened without technology. Personal data, even photos, are no longer private. As Solove explains:

> Many of us today—especially children and teenagers—are spending more of our lives on the Internet. And the more we're online, the more likely details about our lives will slip out into cyberspace. This risk is increased because it is not just we ourselves who might leak information—data about us can be revealed by our friends or enemies, spouses or lovers, employers or employees, teachers or students ... and even by strangers on the subway. We live in an age when many fragments of information about our lives are being gathered by new technologies, horded by companies in databases, and scattered across the Internet. Even people who have never gone online are likely to have some personal information on the Internet. (9–10)

It is next to impossible to privatize your name to prevent it from popping up on search engines. You can take precautions to limit access to your profiles on Facebook and MySpace, but there is not much you can do to prevent other people from posting photos or information about you without your consent. It is foolish to have expectations of privacy.

The bottom line is that there is no semblance of privacy on the Internet. When you send email, use search engines, and shop online, you no longer own your personal information. Disregard for privacy on the part of web-based corporations is rampant. They cavalierly collect information about your web

5

browsing and online shopping habits and use it for online
profiling. The Internet has been called transparent, but this
is not an accurate description because you don't know who is
collecting information about you or what they are doing with
it. Unfortunately, you cannot reclaim your privacy. The
information that has been gathered about you is forever
archived.

Perhaps trustworthy privacy protections will appear in the
future, but at this point in time they don't exist. Solove is
optimistic because he believes that the law has the potential
to stop people from posting personal information without
obtaining the person's consent. However, the law will not
prevent you and me from divulging personal information ourselves.
Solove admits that "any solution will be far from perfect, as
we are dealing with a social tapestry of immense complexity,
and the questions of how to modulate reputation, gossip, shame,
privacy, norms, and free speech have confounded us for centuries"
(13). Privacy in cyberspace is an illusion. Accept this as the
inevitable truth.

6

Work Cited

Solove, Daniel J. *The Future of Reputation: Gossip, Rumor, and*
    Privacy on the Internet. New Haven: Yale UP, 2007. Web.
    18 June 2008. <http://docs.law.gwu.edu/facweb/dsolove/
    Future-of-Reputation/text.htm>.

In this essay, Lili moves beyond a simple response to the reading source. One of Solove's claims—that the lack of privacy on the Internet has profound consequences for us—triggers her essay. But in developing the essay, Lili uses more of her own knowledge and experiences than information from the reading source. Her purpose is to add to what the author has said about the topic. She includes three quotations from the text but uses them to develop her own points. She does not limit her response to the ideas that already appear in the chapter.

To develop an essay of this type, you can follow the same preparatory procedures as for a stock summary and response essay. The difference lies in the way you use your elaborations. As we saw earlier, elaborations can become the blueprint for the standard response essay. You can often find an essay lurking in your notes. When this does not occur, either of two straightforward patterns (summary and response or point by point; see page 156) can serve as a prefabricated plan for the essay. If you have a more personal rhetorical purpose, however, try either of these two approaches:

- Pull back from your elaborations and try to reconceptualize or transform them.

- Write a preliminary draft that takes you in a new direction and triggers new ideas.

Either procedure involves a substantial amount of ruminating, reflecting on the material you have already developed, and deciding how to use and expand it in a more interesting way. The following questions will prove helpful.

QUESTIONS FOR DEVELOPING A RESPONSE ESSAY WITH A SELF-DIRECTED PURPOSE

- How can you make this material more interesting, relevant, eventful, or meaningful?
- What new angle or point of view can you take with regard to this material?
- Can you create a rhetorical situation in which you are writing to move or influence a certain group of readers for a specific reason?
- Can you address a more definite audience?
- How can you better engage the reader?
- Can you fashion a richer rhetorical situation?

After you have come up with a thesis and a fresh approach, be sure to review the source to determine how it will figure in your essay. You won't be able to proceed as you would for a stock summary and response essay because you won't be following a prefabricated plan. You will use your elaboration notes, the source, and perhaps a preliminary draft as the raw materials for your essay.

TABLE 5-1   Summary of the Guidelines for Responding to Sources

Prewriting: Planning and Preparatory Activities

1. Read the assignment, and formulate your rhetorical purpose.
    * Why are you writing the response essay, and what desired effect do you hope to have on your audience?
    * How much of the source should you summarize, and what form will the summary take?
2. Consider your audience.
    * Are you writing for your professor or for a broader audience?
    * Is your audience in the academic community?
    * Are you writing for a general audience or for specialists?
    * What will your audience already know about the topic?
    * Will you need to explain basic concepts or provide background for the source material to make sense?
    * Will your audience be biased either for or against what the source says?
    * Can you predict how your audience will react to the source?
    * What is the overall impact that you want to have on your audience?
    * How will your writing inform, influence, or change your audience?
3. Read the source to get a general impression of the content; genre, organization, features; and rhetorical concerns.
    * Reading for information: What is the author's thesis or main point? What are other important points?
    * Reading for genre, organization, and stylistic features: How does the author get his or her points across? What is the method of presentation? What is the pattern of organization?
    * Reading for rhetorical concerns: What is the author's purpose? How does the author intend to influence the audience? Who is the author, and what is his or her background? What is the rhetorical context? To whom is the piece addressed? In what type of publication is it published? What is the author's relationship to the audience?
4. Reread and elaborate.
    * Tap your memory, and make associations between your prior knowledge and the ideas in the reading source (see the strategies for elaboration of reading sources on pages 56–58).
    * Review your elaborations, and develop your thesis.
        See if one type of elaboration predominates.
        See if a number of elaborations were triggered by a particular idea in the reading source.
        Classify them.
    * Decide on a suitable organizational format.
        Summarize the relevant parts of the source, and state your position.
        Develop your commentary, or briefly summarize the source and give your view.
        As you develop your position, alternate between the ideas in the reading source and your response, or use an organizational pattern (see page 16) that is appropriate for your rhetorical purpose.

<u>**Drafting**</u>

1. Write an opening paragraph in which you accomplish the following goals:
   - Use an opening that will interest the reader.
   - Announce the topic and disclose a thesis or attitude toward it (the thesis may come later).
   - Indicate the source title, author, and author's credentials and provide some summary information about the source.
   - Establish your own voice.
2. Arrange your elaboration notes in paragraphs, and develop each paragraph to its fullest.
3. Compose a concluding paragraph in which you use one of the following techniques:
   - Stress the significance of your thesis rather than simply repeating it. Encourage your readers to look beyond the thesis to an important future goal.
   - Predict consequences.
   - Call your readers to action.
   - Use any of the devices for paper openers (see pages 23–24).

<u>**Revising**</u>

1. If possible, have a classmate or friend read over your first draft and answer the questions on pages 158–159.
2. If no one is available, leave your work for a day or two and then answer the questions yourself.

<u>**Editing**</u>

1. When you are satisfied with your revision, read your paper aloud. Then reread it line by line and sentence by sentence. Check for correct usage, punctuation, spelling, mechanics, manuscript form, and typos.
2. Run the spell checker. Then print out the paper and review the spelling yourself. Even the best spell checkers will not catch every error.
3. If your editing skills are not strong, have a friend read over your work.

CHAPTER 6

Analyzing and Evaluating Sources

The reason we analyze things is to help us understand them better. Let's say you're working hard at a part-time job, but you don't seem to be saving much money. You investigate the causes of your problem by itemizing your weekly purchases. This systematic analysis of your spending habits reveals that a surprising portion of your paycheck is being spent on the take-out dinners you buy every night on your way home from work. Analysis serves many purposes. It enables you to identify and solve problems, examine how things work, and inquire into the complexities of various phenomena.

In college, you will be asked to write analyses of issues and texts. The procedure is the same. You break the subject up into elements, facets, or parts. For this process, you use the critical thinking and reading strategies presented throughout this book: examination of content; genre, organization, features; and rhetorical situation. In this chapter we explain how to analyze a text rhetorically, how to evaluate texts and images, and how to write an in-depth analysis and evaluation.

The focus of this chapter is:

- Rhetorical analysis
- Evaluation of written texts
- Analysis and evaluation of images
- In-depth analysis and evaluation

ANALYSIS AND EVALUATION AS OPPOSED TO RESPONSE

Professors ask students to write analysis essays because they want to hear students' *own* interpretations of what they read. That's why it's important to come to your own conclusions rather than parrot the interpretations you hear in class lectures and discussions. Keep in mind that your professors expect you to base your interpretation on a systematic examination of the material, not on personal opinions or reactions. A reaction or response essay

169

is different from an analysis essay. As you saw in Chapter 5, the response essay is based on your previous knowledge of and experiences with the topic. *Response essays focus on your reaction to content, whereas analysis essays focus on your estimation of how that content is conveyed.*

The *evaluation essay,* also called a *critique, critical essay,* or *review,* is similar to an analysis in that it requires you to do a systematic examination of the reading source. The primary difference is that the evaluation essay judges the strengths and weaknesses of the source according to established criteria. The analysis essay offers an interpretation; it does not assess the source's quality or worth. For example, if you were to *analyze* Yolanda Moses's article "Race, Higher Education, and American Society" (pages 458–469), your goal would be to interpret the article by showing how the various rhetorical techniques that Moses uses contribute to her thesis. If you were to *evaluate* "Race, Higher Education, and American Society," your goal would be to measure *how well* Moses conveys her thesis. You would base this judgment on a set of clear-cut criteria.

Another difference between the two types of essays is that the evaluation essay has more of a persuasive edge than the analysis essay. For the evaluation, your aim is to get your reader to agree with you and in some cases, for instance, when you write a book review, to influence your reader to actually read the book.

The distinctions among essays of response, analysis, and evaluation are extremely important. Unless your assignment specifically calls for it, personal reaction is inappropriate in analyses and reviews.

ESSAY TYPE	STRATEGY	GOAL
Response essay (subjective)	Obtain ideas from your personal knowledge and experience and apply them to the reading material.	Express informed opinions about the subject matter.
Analysis essay (objective)	Obtain ideas from your examination of the various elements of the reading source.	Interpret how the writer's techniques convey meaning.
Evaluation essay (objective)	Obtain ideas from your examination of the various elements of the reading source and judge them according to a set of established criteria.	Show the relative strengths and weaknesses of the work.

As illustrated, response essays are *subjective,* and essays of analysis and evaluation are *objective.* When you analyze and evaluate, you do not rely on personal reactions. You base your conclusions on a reasoned examination of standards that are acceptable to your readers. You already know many of these standards—you have been using them throughout this book. In this chapter, we discuss additional criteria that are commonly used in English and composition courses. You should keep in mind, however, that various academic fields have their own standards for analyzing and evaluating written work. When you take courses in the social sciences, you will see that the criteria in those fields differ somewhat from the criteria used in the humanities. Make a point to learn the criteria for quality writing in the various academic fields, and refer to them when you read and write in each area.

RHETORICAL ANALYSIS

Before we describe the process for composing a rhetorical analysis, we want you to take a look at an essay of this type. The essay was written in response to the following assignment:

> Write a systematic analysis of a reading selection of your choice. As you interpret the text, comment on the author's rhetorical strategies.

Steve Stout wrote his essay on "Skills and Pills," written by physician Kate Scannell when she was clinical director of AIDS services at a county hospital in San Francisco. Scannell explains that when she started working at the hospital, she treated her terminally ill patients the only way she knew how, with impersonal, aggressive medical service. She relates in detail her efforts to help Raphael, a young man who was near death. Each time Raphael asked Scannell for help, she responded with her "skills and pills." She was unaware that Raphael was not asking her to treat his disease but to put him out of his suffering. One night when Scannell was off duty, another physician granted Raphael his wish. After Raphael's death, Scannell was better able to communicate with her patients. She learned to practice medicine more compassionately, with her heart as well as her skills and pills.

Stout 1

Steve Stout

Professor Kennedy

English 223

6 November 2006

The Role of Imagery in "Skills and Pills"

In her article "Skills and Pills," Kate Scannell describes the process she went through as a physician learning how to administer effectively to AIDS patients. Throughout the article, she uses a series of images that serve to emphasize and illuminate the transformation she experienced, from a devotee of medical technology to a compassionate caregiver who is aware of the limitations of medical science.

Title (focus of essay)

Paper opener giving author, title, and topic

Initial identification of author by full name

Thesis

172   Chapter 6   Analyzing and Evaluating Sources

Stout 2

Later
identification
of author by
last name
only

Summary

Textual
evidence
supporting
thesis

Use of
present
tense to
explain how
writer uses
techniques

Summary
paragraph

Summary
paragraph

Scannell, who was clinical director of services for AIDS patients at a county hospital in San Francisco, began working in the AIDS ward right after medical school. Her initial response to AIDS was to give each patient full, aggressive treatment. Describing herself as an "ever-ready gunfighter," she says, "I stalked the hallways ready for surprise developments and acute medical problems to present themselves. [When they did,] I would shoot them down with my skills and pills" (102). Scannell explains that she was listening to the voices of her old teachers in medical school, who had told her to use every intervention possible to keep her patients alive.

For months Scannell persisted in offering her brand of intensive, exhaustive medical service. Then one day she encountered Raphael. Raphael was a twenty-two-year-old AIDS patient, "a large, bloated, purple, knobby mass with eyes so swollen shut that he could not see" (103). When Raphael asked Scannell to help him, she put her "diagnostic sharpshooting abilities" to work. Each time Raphael asked for more help, Scannell responded with more medical procedures. She said that when she left the hospital that evening, she knew that she had done everything conceivable to help her patient.

That night Raphael again asked for help. The attending physician responded very differently from Scannell, however. Instead of giving Raphael skills and pills, he disconnected Raphael's intravenous and blood transfusions and gave him some morphine. "Raphael smiled and thanked the doctor for helping him, and then expired later that evening" (104).

Raphael's death changed the way Scannell practiced medicine. She describes her transformation in terms of a clothing image:

2

3

4

5

Stout 3

Block
format for
long
quotation

> Like the vision of Raphael's spirit rising free from his
> disease-racked corpse in death, the clothing fashioned for
> me by years of traditional Western medical training fell
> off me like tattered rags. I began to hear my own voices
> and compassionate sensibilities once again, louder and
> clearer than the chorus of voices of my old mentors. (104)

Scannell compares her self-discovery to an archaeological

expedition. She says, "I got crushed under mounds of rubble that

Paragraph
with textual
evidence
supporting
thesis

collected over the years of my intense and all-consuming medical

training" (104). She describes this rubble as consisting of

increased medical technology, the dictum that physicians must

save lives at all costs, and the taboos against doctors using

intuition or compassion (104).

Transformed, Dr. Scannell no longer listened to the voices   6

Conclusion

of her old teachers, and she was no longer a sharpshooter. She

listened instead to the people behind the disease. She no longer

offered these patients skills and pills; instead, she gave them

conversation and compassion.

Stout 4

Work Cited

Scannell, Kate. "Skills and Pills." *AIDS: The Women*. Ed. Ines

Rieder and Patricia Ruppett. San Francisco: Cleis, 1988.

103-05. Print.

In this essay, Steve's aim is to show his readers how one of Scannell's rhetorical strategies, her use of imagery, operates in the article. His title indicates that he will focus on "the role of imagery," and his thesis reveals that he will explain how the imagery functions. The introductory paragraph reveals that he will show how Scannell's images serve to emphasize and illuminate the transformation she experienced. In paragraphs 2, 4, and 5, he describes how Scannell uses particular images, backing up his points with quotations from the article. The main purpose of paragraph 3 is to summarize relevant parts of the article. Note that Steve does not summarize the entire article. He gives only the background information readers need to comprehend the analysis.

WRITING A RHETORICAL ANALYSIS ESSAY

Now that you have read a model analysis essay, you can practice writing one of your own. In the next section, we take you through the process Steve experienced as he wrote his analysis. The process we describe is applicable to any assignment that requires you to write a rhetorical analysis of nonfiction.

PREWRITING

Successful analysis requires careful planning. Assignments that direct you to analyze or evaluate a text are typically harder than assignments that ask you to react, compare and contrast, or argue because they require a more detailed examination of the reading source and a deeper knowledge of the author's writing techniques. Without sufficient planning, you may become lost or turn out an extended summary or reaction instead of an analysis. Without extensive preparation, it is almost impossible to write a satisfactory analytical piece.

Clarify the Assignment, Set Your Rhetorical Goal, and Consider Your Audience

When you receive your assignment, pay attention to what it asks you to do. Some assignments, like the one our student Steve received, are open-ended and allow the writer to determine the aspects of the reading source that will be examined. Other assignments may stipulate the parts of the text on which you should focus. For example, a professor might ask you to discuss the role of language in a particular piece or to comment on the structure of a work and explain why it is organized as it is. If you have questions about the type of analysis the assignment calls for, be sure to ask your professor before you proceed.

After you have clarified the assignment, decide on your rhetorical purpose by asking yourself, Why am I writing this analysis essay? What desired effect do I hope to have on my audience? Your fundamental purpose is to give your readers your interpretation of the reading source and in so doing explain how one or more characteristics of the text contribute to its meaning. Looking back at Steve's essay, you can see that his objective is to demonstrate how various images in Scannell's "Skills and Pills" help the author convey that she has experienced a dramatic transformation.

The next decisions concern your audience. Ask yourself these questions:

- What will your readers already know about the source?
- How much of the source should you summarize, and what form will the summary take?
- Will you need to explain basic concepts and provide background for the material to make sense?
- What overall impact do you hope to have on your readers?

If your audience is familiar with the piece you are analyzing, supply only a minimal amount of background information. If your audience has not read the piece, as was the case with Steve, give some general background and summarize the parts of the source that are crucial to your analysis. It isn't necessary to summarize the entire text, only enough to persuade your readers that you have a valid, reasonable interpretation.

Do a First Reading to Get a General Impression of the Source

Your first reading may leave you with little more than a general impression of the reading source. You will get an overall sense of the subject, the author's approach, and the central point, but you probably won't pay much attention to other characteristics of the text unless they are very conspicuous. At this stage, you may want to freewrite your reactions, especially if the text evokes a strong response. A reader's first reaction to Scannell's "Skills and Pills" might have been, "Wow, that doctor certainly did an about-face!" The reader might also have been unsettled by Scannell's graphic description of Raphael's ravaged body.

Reread and Ask Analysis Questions

Analyzing a reading source is largely a matter of asking the right questions about it. The second reading allows you to ask questions, annotate the text, and take analysis notes. Essentially, you will work with the same questions concerning content; genre, organization, and features; and rhetorical concerns that you have been using throughout this book. But you will add to them and make them more probing and more detailed. Your objective is to delve deeper into the material. Don't trust your memory. Write the answers to the analysis questions in your journal or notebook. The answers to these questions will serve as the basis for your analysis essay.

Examine Content

Start by examining the content. Locate the thesis or central point the author is making about the topic and identify other important points. Ask yourself which aspects of the topic are emphasized and which are downplayed or ignored. Next, examine the types of evidence the author uses, estimate whether they are sufficient, and determine whether they lead logically to the conclusions. (For a review of various types of evidence, see pages 295–303.) Finally, ask whether the author acknowledges and refutes the views of individuals who might oppose his or her argument.

Determine Genre, Organization, and Features

Identify the genre of the text. In this book, you have already examined response essays. In Chapters 7, 8, and 9, you will study synthesis essays, argument essays, and research essays. In your everyday reading, you encounter other recognizable genres such as editorials, news stories, feature articles, biographies, memoirs, autobiographies, and letters to the editor. Ask yourself how the form contributes to the meaning of the text.

Then determine the organizational pattern. Is it chronological order or narrative; cause and effect; comparison and contrast, either point-by-point or block; argument, including position, reasons, opposition, and refutation; problem and solution; statement and response; question and answer; or classification? How does the organizational pattern contribute to the meaning of the piece? Would the meaning change if the parts were arranged differently, for example, if the narrative progressed from past to present instead of present to past; if the consequences were explained before the causes; or if reasons were ordered from least important to most important instead of vice versa?

Finally, zero in on the features of the text, asking yourself how they help convey the author's points. Search for memorable or significant devices that enable you to see the subject in a new perspective, and look closely at features like language, sentence elements, images and scenes, and references and allusions.

Determine whether the language serves to heighten and illuminate the topic. Does the author use precise wording, vivid details, words that appeal to the senses, and words with emotional intensity? Is figurative language (similes and metaphors) used? A *simile* occurs when the writer draws a comparison, using *like* or *as* to show the two elements that are being compared. Kate Scannell uses simile when she writes

> Like a very weary but ever-ready gunfighter, I stalked the hallways ready for surprise developments and acute medical problems to present themselves. (102)

A *metaphor* is an implicit comparison because the *like* or *as* is not mentioned. Scannell uses metaphor when she writes

> The clothing fashioned for me by years of traditional Western medical training fell off me. (104)

Here she likens the treatments, cures, and procedures that she learned in medical school to clothing. For another example, read Professor Steven Vogel's article, "Grades and Money," on pages 389–392. Throughout the article, Vogel uses the metaphor of money.

> In my college, like most others, grades *are* money. They're the currency around which everything revolves. (390)

Next, examine sentence elements. Are you struck by rhythmic, balanced, symmetrical, and graceful sentences? Look for these characteristics in the following excerpt from an essay written by Gore Vidal about the "inventors" of the Constitution:

> But the Inventors were practical men and the federal constitution that they assembled in 1787 was an exquisite machine that, with a repair here and a twist there, has gone on protecting the property of the worthy for two hundred years while protecting in the Bill of Rights (that sublime afterthought) certain freedoms of speech and assembly which are still unknown even now to that irritable fount of America's political and actual being, old Europe. (Vidal 153)

How does this sentence help to convey the meaning of the text?

Also examine the author's use of images and scenes. *Images* are mental pictures. Recall the images Steve Stout examines in "Skills and Pills":

> Like the vision of Raphael's spirit rising free from his disease-racked corpse in death, the clothing fashioned for me by years of traditional Western medical training fell off me like tattered rags. I began to hear my own voices and compassionate sensibilities once again, louder and clearer than the chorus of voices of my old mentors. (104)

I got crushed under mounds of rubble that collected over the years of my intense and all-consuming medical training. (104)

Scenes are also mental pictures, but they have enough detail in them that they could be acted out. As illustration, we'd like you to read three scenes from an essay written by Erica Mazor, one of our students. The focus of Erica's essay is the care of people who are mentally ill. To illustrate her point that physically ill individuals will be escorted to hospitals involuntarily whereas mentally ill people will not, Erica depicts three scenes:

- An elderly man rushes across the avenue and is hit by a bus and seriously injured. He pleads with the police to take him home instead of to the hospital. The police call an ambulance, and the man is quickly transported to a nearby emergency room.
- A young woman with chronic asthma has an attack on a crowded city street. A passerby offers to assist, but she refuses his help. Worried that she is seriously ill, the man hails a cab and escorts the woman to the nearest hospital.
- A middle-aged woman, ravaged by paranoid schizophrenia, lies in the fetal position on a blanket on a subway platform. Commuters walk past her day after day. Finally, some people speak to her and offer to call the police. The woman yells at them to leave her alone. They walk away.

Each vignette enables the reader to visualize the characters and action, and in so doing, it drives home Erica's point. As you examine the text, ask yourself, Does the writer create memorable images and scenes that contribute to the meaning?

Finally, examine the author's references and allusions to determine if they illuminate or add significantly to the subject matter. Take account of the writer's formal references to other written sources as well as other types of references and allusions. An *allusion* is a reference to some other parallel concept. Describing the patients on her AIDS ward, Scannell writes:

Some patients were so emaciated by profound wasting that I could not shake disquieting memories of photographs I had seen as a little girl which depicted Auschwitz and Buchenwald prisoners. (103)

Scannell's reference to prisoners of concentration camps intensifies her description of the patients' sad state. Notice Liz Mandrell's allusion in the following description:

Robin is a young Katie Couric, all smiles and perky nose, but racked with journalistic ambition and biting cynicism. (390)

Define Rhetorical Concerns

As we explained in Chapter 2, skilled writers consciously adopt an attitude or rhetorical posture that is appropriate to their audience and subject. As you read the text, consider the writer's persona or stance and how it contributes to his or her point. In "Grades and Learning," Chapter 10 of this book, two authors write from the point of view of educators. Liz Mandrell is writing from the standpoint of a high school teacher and Steven Vogel from the standpoint of a college professor. As you read Mandrell's "Zen and the Art of Grade Motivation," pages 379–383, and Vogel's "Grades and Money," ask yourself how each writer's stance contributes to the text. How would the texts change if they had been written from the perspective of Mandrell's and Vogel's students? Also consider how the writer's voice contributes to the piece. Jerry Farber (pages 385–388) adopts a personal voice on the topic of the relationship between grades and learning, while Stephen Ray Flora and Stacy Suzanne Poponak (pages 393–394) keep themselves at a distance as they explain the effect of rewarding children for high grades.

For a summary of the analysis questions, see Questions for Analysis and Evaluation on pages 192–194.

Exercise 6.1

Apply the analysis questions to Lawrence Lessig's "Why Crush Them" on pages 442–443. Write a one-page explanation of how the analysis process affected your understanding of the reading selection.

Review Your Answers to the Analysis Questions

Soon after you finish rereading and responding to the analysis questions, pause to organize your thoughts. It is best to do this while the answers are still fresh in your mind. Planning at this stage saves time because you won't have to do extensive rereading of the source later while you are drafting. First, reexamine your rhetorical purpose. Keep in mind that your objective is to show your readers how the author of the source used specific rhetorical techniques to get his or her points across. Review your notes on the analysis questions as follows.

Look to see if a particular question produced a lengthy, substantive response.   If this is the case, go for depth rather than breadth, and focus your analysis on a single, prominent feature. For example, reading "Why Crush Them," you may have been so struck by Lawrence Lessig's tone that you wrote extensive notes in response to questions about rhetorical concerns, especially those with reference to the author's stance and voice. These notes may supply you with enough material for your analysis.

See if you can group answers that pertain to similar categories.   This is the approach our student Steve used in his essay on pages 171–173. When Steve reviewed his analysis notes, he discovered that his most promising insights were about Kate Scannell's descriptive and figurative language, particularly her imagery. Since all of the images he was considering were evoked by figurative language, he decided to subsume language under the category of imagery. As you may recall, Steve does not refer specifically to metaphors and similes; instead, he describes the images that these devices call up.

Steve also took copious notes on Scannell's moving descriptions of the AIDS patients, but he decided against including them in his essay. As you review your analysis notes, you will find that you have collected much more information than you can possibly include in your paper.

Select two or more elements for your focus.   Instead of zeroing in on a single, substantive response or categorizing related responses, focus on two or more areas. If Steve had decided to fashion his essay in this way, he might have selected four characteristics of Scannell's article: descriptive language, figurative language, images, and scenes.

Return to the relevant parts of the text to check for supporting material.   In your essay, each time you make a point about the textual features you are analyzing, you will provide textual evidence in the form of a quotation, paraphrase, or summary. At this juncture, go back to the reading source and mark all the passages that you might use to support your points. If you cannot find enough textual evidence, think about changing your focus. Decide on an organizational plan.

You can organize your analysis essay in any number of ways. The important thing is your rhetorical purpose. Your goal is to reveal to your readers how certain characteristics of the reading source contribute to its meaning. In this section, we present three typical patterns of organization and skeletal outlines of each.

Show cause and effect.   In a cause-and-effect rhetorical analysis, you show the effects of the writer's techniques (causes).

Thesis

In "Skills and Pills," the imagery and descriptive language reinforce Scannell's depiction of her transformation from an impersonal physician to a compassionate companion to her patients.

ESSAY STRUCTURE

- Introductory paragraph(s)
- One to two paragraphs explaining how imagery reinforces the transformation
- One to two paragraphs explaining how figurative language reinforces the transformation
- Concluding paragraph

Present your argument.   Another possibility is to structure your analysis along the lines of the broad argument discussed on page 176. Your goal is to persuade your readers that your interpretation is valid. State your position, and then give three or four reasons for your stand.

Thesis

Scannell's description and figurative language contribute significantly to her text.

ESSAY STRUCTURE

- Introductory paragraph(s)
- One to two paragraphs giving reasons the description is significant
- One to two paragraphs giving reasons the figurative language is significant
- Concluding paragraph

Use the structure of the reading source.   A third possibility is to follow the order of the reading source. Take up each feature in the order in which it is presented in the text. Our student Steve operated in this way. Guided by the chronological order of "Skills and Pills," he discussed the imagery at the beginning, middle, and end of the piece.

Thesis

Throughout "Skills and Pills," Kate Scannell uses a series of images that serve to emphasize and illuminate the transformation she experienced.

ESSAY STRUCTURE

- Introductory paragraph(s)
- Paragraph developing imagery at the beginning of the piece
- Paragraph developing imagery in the middle of the piece
- Paragraph developing imagery at the end of the piece

DRAFTING

Now you are ready to compose a preliminary draft of your analysis essay. Remember that this is not a final, polished draft. You will have an opportunity to revise it at a later date. Before you begin writing, decide how you want to come across to your readers. Will you offer a personal interpretation, using first-person pronouns, or write in a more formal tone? The degree of formality may be dictated by the assignment. If you are unsure about taking a particular stance, ask your professor for advice.

As you draft your essay, you may want to consult the sections on paper openers, introductions, and conclusions in Chapter 1, pages 22–27.

After you arrange the notes that you took on the analysis questions, convert them into body paragraphs in accordance with your organizational plan. As you develop each paragraph, support your points with evidence (quotations, paraphrases, or summaries) from the reading source.

A further consideration is to adhere to the special conventions that academic writers follow when composing analysis essays.

SPECIAL CONVENTIONS FOR ANALYSIS ESSAYS

- Use the present tense when explaining how the author uses particular procedures and writing techniques.

```
Raphael's death changed the way Scannell practiced medicine. She
describes her transformation in terms of a clothing image....Scannell
compares her self-discovery to an archaeological expedition.
```

Notice that Steve writes in the past tense when he is explaining what happened to Scannell, the narrator ("Raphael's death *changed* the way Scannell *practiced* medicine"), but he switches to the present tense when he explains how Scannell, the writer, uses certain techniques ("She *describes*," "Scannell *compares*").

- Identify the author of the source by first and last name initially and thereafter only by last name.
- Indent long quotations (four or more lines) in block format.

REVISING

If your instructor agrees, arrange for a classmate or friend to review your preliminary draft and give you feedback. If this is not possible, set the paper aside for a few days and then review it yourself. Respond to the following questions.

✓ *Checklist for Revising a Rhetorical Analysis Essay*

_____   1. Can you identify the writer's rhetorical purpose? Is the writer giving you an interpretation of the source and in so doing explaining how certain characteristics contribute to its meaning?

_____   2. Does everything in the draft lead to or follow from one central meaning? If not, which ideas seem to be out of place?

_____   3. Do you understand the analysis, and is the writer sensitive to your concerns?

_____   4. Does the writer provide necessary background information about the subject and enough summary of the source as well as its title and author? If not, what is missing?

_____   5. When referring to the source, does the writer supply the necessary documentation?

_____   6. Does the writer provide clear transitions and connecting ideas that differentiate his or her own ideas from those of the author?

_____   7. Does the writer refer to the author by name?

_____   8. Which organizational format does the writer use: cause and effect, argument, or order of the source? If another pattern is used, is it appropriate for an analysis essay?

_____   9. Has the writer made you aware of the bases for the analysis? Which characteristics of the source provide focus? If the bases for the analysis are unclear, explain your confusion.

_____ 10. Does the writer support each point with direct evidence (quotations, paraphrases, summaries) from the source? If not, where is evidence needed?

_____ 11. Does the writer provide smooth transitions and connecting ideas as he or she moves from one point of analysis to another? If not, where are they needed?

_____ 12. Do you hear the writer's voice throughout the essay? Describe it.

_____ 13. What type of lead does the writer use to open the paper? Is it effective? If not, why not?

_____ 14. Does the paper have an appropriate conclusion? Can you suggest an alternative way to end the essay?

_____ 15. Is the title suitable for the piece? Can you suggest an alternative?

_____ 16. Has the writer followed academic writing conventions, such as writing in the present tense when explaining how the author uses particular procedures and techniques, identifying the author initially by first name and last name and thereafter only by last name, and indenting long quotations in block format?

EDITING

When you are satisfied with your revision, read your paper aloud. Then reread it line by line and sentence by sentence. Check for correct usage, punctuation, spelling, mechanics, manuscript form, and typographical errors. If your editing skills are not strong, get a friend to read over your work.

EVALUATION

When you evaluate a reading source, you move beyond interpretation into the realm of judgment. Your purpose is to give your readers your estimation of the quality or worth of the piece. Always base your judgment on accepted criteria. Instead of explaining that a writer's evidence supports his or her argument, tell your readers *how well* the evidence serves the writer's purpose. Rather than simply explaining how descriptive language contributes to a theme, appraise the language. In addition to describing the text's strong qualities, you can point out its weaknesses.

You can't make a valid value judgment about a reading source unless you comprehend it thoroughly. For that reason, you have to analyze the text before you evaluate it. The analysis also enables you to demonstrate that you are knowledgeable about the topic. Your readers will take your evaluation seriously only if you have established this credibility.

To acquaint you with the characteristics of evaluation essays, let's look at a sample essay. Students in Professor Smith's class were asked to evaluate a text of their own choice from a list of recommended reading selections. The evaluation was to be addressed to their classmates. Jordan Conway selected "Global Warming Is Not a Threat But the Environmentalist Response Is" written by economics professor George Reisman. As the title indicates, Reisman is skeptical about global warming. He is more fearful of environmentalists' response to it than the climate change itself. Reisman's article is available online at http://www.lewrockwell.com/reisman/reisman34.html. It would be useful to read it before you study the student's evaluation essay.

Exercise 6.2

Read Jordan Conway's essay to yourself. Then break the class into three groups. Assign each group a paragraph from Jordan's essay, beginning with paragraph 3 and ending with paragraph 5. For each paragraph, assess the quality of Jordan's evaluation. Reconvene the entire class. The recorder for each group should report the group's findings.

Conway 1

Jordan Conway

Professor Smith

Academic Writing II

26 April 2008

A Questionable Argument

In 2007 the United Nations issued a report that stated that the reality of global warming is "unequivocal." Writing in response to this report, economist George Reisman disputes the fact that climate change is as serious a problem as the UN

reports. In "Global Warming Is Not a Threat But the
Environmentalist Response Is," he argues that if global warming
really is occurring, we should fear environmentalists'
response to it more than we should fear the warming itself.
Environmentalists insist that we must reduce our carbon footprint
and regulate the production and use of fossil fuels. Reisman
contends that such actions will impede economic progress, prevent
technological advances, and lead to the ruin of industrial
civilization as we know it. He says Americans should never sign
any international treaty that limits their consumption of energy.

    Reisman's argument rests on the importance of fossil fuels. He   2
says that modern civilization was built on the use of oil, coal, and
natural gas. If we limit our use of these fuels, we will incur great
losses that will result in a lower standard of living. Reisman
insists that "global warming should simply be accepted as a
byproduct of economic progress and that life should go on as normal
in the face of it" (1). He also claims that global warming will have
benefits that environmentalists fail to mention. For example, when
the climates of Canada, Siberia, and Greenland grow warmer, plants
will thrive and when ice melts in the Arctic, shipping routes will
be shortened. In the latter third of the article under a subheading
entitled "Emissions Caps Mean Impoverishment," Reisman declares,
"The environmental movement does not value industrial civilization.
It fears and hates it" (2). He closes the article by asking people
in the U.S. and the world to "turn their backs on environmentalism"
(3). Reisman misrepresents environmentalists and presents an
argument that is seriously flawed.

    A serious shortcoming is the disparaging, abrasive tone   3
Reisman uses when referring to environmentalists. He accuses

them of having a "profoundly destructive, misanthropic philosophy" (3). He says for environmentalists, human life is "of no greater value than other life forms, such as spotted owls or snail darters," and "the loss of industrial civilization is of no great consequence. It is a boon" (2). Such language is excessive and unreasonable. Reisman makes it sound as if all people who are concerned about the environment are radical, whacky tree-huggers. On the contrary, everyone who recycles trash, refrains from littering, and cleans up after his dog is an environmentalist. The overwhelming majority of environmentalists do not fit Reisman's exaggerated description.

In addition to the fact that Reisman does not give an honest view of environmentalists, he uses no references or research to back up his questionable claim that global warming "will bring major benefits to much of the world" (2). He sees the disappearance of Arctic ice as a benefit for trade routes, but he fails to mention how it will affect large numbers of species on the planet and the earth's ecology in general. Reisman admits that coastal flooding will destroy many people's homes, and he recommends that the UN work out a plan whereby "the portion of the world not threatened with rising sea levels would accept the people who are so threatened" (2). He does not explain how the UN will motivate the unthreatened people to "accept" the millions of people whose homes will be destroyed by water. Reisman goes on to say that the United States could prompt people to relocate before the flooding occurs by "making all areas determined to be likely victims of coastal flooding in the years ahead ineligible for any form of governmental aid, insurance, or disaster relief that is not already in force" (2). Again, he does not explain how this could possibly happen. As was seen at the time of Katrina, the government did not act fast enough to "prompt" people to relocate, and this was after the levee failures and flooding, not before the hurricane. Reisman accuses environmentalists of making far-fetched predictions. His own ideas are more impractical and unrealistic than theirs.

Although Reisman's argument is flawed, a positive feature   5
of the article is that it is well-suited for his audience. Resiman is Professor Emeritus of Economics at Pepperdine University and author of *Capitalism: A Treatise on Economics.* The article was published on the conservative libertarian political weblog, LewRockwell.com. He tailors his argument to readers who share his values about the importance of economic progress and increased material well being. He probably thinks he does not have to give a balanced picture of environmentalists nor present the views of those who would oppose his position because many readers of the blog feel the same way about the topic as he does.

Climate change is a real, indisputable problem. As Al   6
Gore's film, *An Inconvenient Truth*, so convincingly argues, everyone has to be part of the solution. If some of us make provisions to protect the environment and others continue to pollute it, we will cancel each other out. The U.S. has the technical know-how to take the lead in safeguarding the planet against global climate destruction. If Americans believe the bogus argument presented in "Global Warming Is Not a Threat But the Environmentalist Response Is" and they "turn their backs on environmentalism" as Reisman suggests, we will all regret it.

Conway 5

Works Cited

An Inconvenient Truth. Dir. Davis Guggenheim. Lawrence Bender,

2006. Film.

Reisman, George. *Capitalism: A Treatise on Economics.* Ottawa,

IL: Jameson, 1998. Print.

---. "Global Warming Is Not a Threat But the Environmentalist

Response Is." LewRockwell.com. 14 March 2007. Web. 4 April

2008.

Jordan begins his essay with two paragraphs summarizing Reisman's article for his classmates. At the end of paragraph 2, he states his thesis: "Reisman misrepresents environmentalists and presents an argument that is seriously flawed." Jordan devotes paragraph 3 to the first of these weaknesses, Reisman's biased, sweeping view of environmentalists. In paragraph 4 he covers the second shortcoming of the article, Reisman's lack of substantiation for his claims. In paragraph 5, he praises Reisman for tailoring his argument to his target audience. Finally, Jordan concludes by urging his readers to disregard the questionable argument presented in Reisman's article.

Even though Jordan's overall evaluation of George Reisman's argument is negative, he does mention a positive feature of Reisman's piece. Notice Jordan's language:

STRENGTH

Although Reisman's argument is flawed, a positive feature of the article is

WEAKNESSES

A serious shortcoming is the . . .
In addition to the fact that Reisman does not give an honest view of environmentalists . . .

When you write a negative review of a text, try to be fair to the author. Do your best to mention a positive quality. Before we outline the process for writing an evaluation essay, let's examine an essay that judges the effectiveness of two reading sources. In this evaluation essay, Erika Perrotte evaluates two memoirs, "Seven Years Ago I Raped a Woman" by Jack M. and "Notes from a Fragmented Daughter" by Elena Tajima.

Erika Perrotte

Professor Kennedy

Composition 101-301

27 March 2003

Finding Meaning in Memoir

Both "Seven Years Ago I Raped a Woman" by Jack M. and "Notes from a Fragmented Daughter" by Elena Tajima are effective memoirs, but for different reasons. Each possesses its own particular strengths. Jack M.'s memoir is strong because the author is excruciatingly honest and open to the reader about rape and his feelings about it, while Tajima's piece offers bold descriptions as its greatest strengths.

Jack M. does not hold back and is very straightforward with his audience. His honesty starts right in the title of his memoir, where he admits, "I raped a woman." He is not proud of what he has done and makes no excuses for himself. In this memoir, Jack does not try to rationalize his behavior or make himself look innocent. Looking back on his life "seven years ago," he admits his guilt not only for the rape incident but also for the way he treated *all* the women with whom he had sexual relations in his period of heavy drinking and "slutting" (111). He candidly states, "I was often cruel to these women" (111). Furthermore, Jack bears out his poor treatment of women when he explains that he acted only in ways that would help him ultimately achieve sexual favors. He tells us how he manipulated one of his many pick-ups: "I would do everything I could to make her go to bed with me" (111). Jack admits his shameful behavior, saying, "I would use empathy, understanding, humor, even my deepest secrets to get them on my side" (114). He continues to show his honesty by including statements such as "If the sex was good, I might see them again, but I would quickly get bored...and I would abruptly blow them off" (111). Jack is honest at all costs, and his absolute truthfulness serves as the cornerstone of his memories. He gains his readers' trust by sharing his private memories. Jack is willing to sacrifice his image as a "good guy" as he writes his memoir, thereby creating a very strong and engaging impression as a storyteller.

Jack M.'s honesty with himself and his audience creates an especially interesting element of positive personal development. The author shows how his growth as a man has made him realize the harm and pain he inflicted on his victims. And as a result of this realization, Jack also emphasizes his feelings of remorse. He is deeply ashamed of what he did, and he is taking responsibility for his actions. This former rapist convinces his readers that he has truly changed for the better: he regrets his past actions and hopes that his story will instruct others not to take his path.

3

While Jack M. centers his memoir on one specific event in his life, Elena Tajima writes about a number of incidents. Nonetheless, all of the memories that Tajima shares deal with one aspect of her life, her heritage. In "Notes from a Fragmented Daughter," she tells of her experience growing up with a mixed American and Japanese heritage. She adds positive energy to her memoir by using bold descriptions when discussing the situations that she has encountered. Tajima is descriptive throughout the memoir, painting vivid pictures of every situation. She adds details about hairstyles, car models, brand names, skin tones, and movie titles. Instead of saying a car, she says "a Volkswagen"; instead of a camera, "a Kodak Instamatic" (82). At first, the specific examples may seem like only a small part of Tajima's memoir, but I believe they are what make it so effective.

4

Tajima, like Jack M., does not hold back. She gets right to
the point and cites various events as support. She also uses many
examples to serve as justification for her feelings. For instance,
she tells of the time she visited an Asian American exhibit
featuring Oriental food. She was asked if she had cooked any of the
dishes, simply because she "looked kinda Asian" (82). She goes on
to point out that as Americans, we live "in a culture that can't
tell Chinese apart from Japanese" (82). Tajima's details and
descriptions effectively allow her readers to see what she has
dealt with due to her Asian ethnicity, and as a result the audience
tends to empathize powerfully with her. "Notes from a Fragmented
Daughter" contains bold descriptions of racist stereotypes,
including terms such as "flat-faced Chinaman" and "slant-eyed
face," descriptions used by others to describe Tajima, not to
mention people the author refers to as "idiot," "hillbilly," and
"bub," and the sexist attitude she describes as "touch-me-feel-you"
(82). Tajima's word choice includes these and a number of other
controversial terms. They are not infamously known "bad words," but
they are shocking and daring enough to catch our attention. These
words are meant to make the reader stop and think twice about how
they are being used. Without her word choice, Tajima's memoir would
lose a substantial amount of power and feeling.

The most powerful point of Tajima's memoir comes at the end
when she gives a lengthy, bold, detailed description of herself:

> A half-Japanese postmodernist Gemini feminist, existentialist
> would-be writer of bad one-act comedy revues, avid cat
> trainer, and closet reader of *mademoiselle, cosmo, signs,*
> *diacritics, elle, tv guides, architectural digest, country*
> *living, cat fancy, bird talk, mother jones, covert action,*

vogue, glamour, the new yorker, l.a. times, l.a. weekly, and

sometimes *penthouse forum.* (83)

This quotation is not only proof of the author's bold   7

descriptions but also evidence of the transition that takes

place. Tajima breaks rules. Notice that she does not capitalize

the titles of the publications she reads. No longer is she

sitting back and listening to what others have to say; she is

now silencing the oppressive white culture with her newfound

spirit. Not only is she speaking up, but she is also talking

back to everyone who has hurt her throughout her life. Tajima's

memoir begins with her being ashamed of her true identity and

ends with her bursting out with an extremely detailed and

powerful description of exactly who she is. Readers have to

admire her strength of character.

Both "Seven Years Ago I Raped a Woman" and "Notes from a   8

Fragmented Daughter" satisfy my requirements for an effective

memoir in that they are honest, descriptive, interesting, and

filled with feeling. The authors open themselves up to their

readers and use distinctive techniques for getting their points

across in bold and powerful ways.

Works Cited

M., Jack. "Seven Years Ago I Raped a Woman." *Glamour* Jan. 1992:

111-15. Print.

Tajima, Elena. "Notes from a Fragmented Daughter." *Making Face, Making

Soul: Creative and Critical Perspectives by Women of Color.* Ed.

Gloria Anzaldua. San Francisco: Aunt Lute, 1990. 82-83. Print.

In the opening paragraph, Erika introduces the two reading selections and states her thesis. In her judgment, both selections are effective memoirs because of particular strengths: the honesty and openness of Jack M.'s memoir and the bold descriptions of Tajima's. In paragraphs 2 and 3, Erika discusses the straightforward, honest nature of Jack M.'s piece, backing up each of her points with details and quotations from the text. Paragraphs 4, 5, and 6 focus on "Notes from a Fragmented Daughter." In each paragraph, Erika shows how a certain writing technique contributes to the memoir's effectiveness: in paragraph 4, Tajima's use of details; in paragraph 5, her use of examples and her word choice; and in paragraph 6, her detailed, powerful description. Paragraph 7 concludes the essay.

Both Jordan and Erika communicate clearly that they are doing more than simply interpreting the reading sources. They are using established criteria to evaluate the texts. Jordan evaluates both the strengths and weaknesses of George Reisman's argument, and his essay is much more pointed and pronounced than Erika's. Jordan exposes one flaw after another and takes Reisman to task on a number of points. Erika's entire review is complimentary.

Exercise 6.3

Reread the essays by Jordan Conway and Erika Perrotte. Which do you find more convincing? What accounts for its relative effectiveness? What are the shortcomings of the essay that you do not find as effective?

WRITING AN EVALUATION ESSAY

Now that you have studied two evaluation essays, you can practice writing one of your own. Begin the process with prewriting, and then draft, revise, and edit.

PREWRITING

As always, your first act is to set your rhetorical goal. Do this by asking yourself, Why am I writing this evaluation? and What desired effect do I hope to have on my audience? Your central goal is to use carefully selected criteria to persuade your readers of the reading source's quality, importance, or worth. Looking back at the student essays, you can see that Jordan's goal is to persuade readers that Reisman has fashioned a rather weak argument, whereas Erika's objective is to convince her audience that Jack M. and Elena Tajima have created interesting, well-crafted memoirs.

Your next decision concerns your audience:

- Are your readers already familiar with the reading source?
- How much of the source should you summarize? What form should the summary take?
- Do you need to explain basic concepts and provide background for the material to make sense?

As we mentioned earlier, the assignment will signal how much summarizing you must do. If you are evaluating a reading selection of your own choice or a text that has not been covered in class, give your readers general background information and summarize the parts of the source that they need to understand in order to profit from your evaluation.

Exercise 6.4

Take a few minutes to compare Jordan's and Erika's summaries of the reading sources. You probably haven't read all of these texts, but do you think these student writers do an adequate job? Do their evaluations leave you with unanswered questions? What additional background information about the sources do you need to know?

Read, Reread, and Analyze the Reading Source

Do a first reading to get an overall sense of the text, and then freewrite your general impressions. The purpose of the second reading is to ask a series of analysis and evaluation questions. These questions serve two functions. They help you break down the text into its major components, and they eventually become the basis for your paper. With a few additions, the questions are the same as the ones for examining a source for an analysis essay. The major difference is that some of the questions are phrased in a way that encourages evaluation as well as interpretation. Record your answers to these questions in your journal or notebook.

QUESTIONS FOR ANALYSIS AND EVALUATION

Questions about Content

- Is the author's thesis realistic?
- Do the other important points follow logically from the thesis?
- Is the author emphasizing appropriate aspects of the topic? Does the author disregard important aspects or put too much emphasis on certain points?
- Does the author acknowledge and refute the views of individuals who might oppose his or her argument?
- Does the author use a sufficient amount of evidence to support his or her points? Which points need more support or explanation? (For a review of the various types of evidence, see pages 295–303.)
- Do the author's conclusions follow logically from the evidence, or are there places where the reader has difficulty seeing the connection?
- Are the conclusions accurate? Do they have direct implications for readers, or do they have limited applicability and usefulness?

Questions about Genre, Organization, and Features

GENRE

- Is the genre appropriate for the content? Would the author have been better able to convey his or her message in another genre?

ORGANIZATION

- Is the organizational pattern clear and well conceived?
- Would the meaning be better represented if the parts were arranged differently—for example, if the thesis were disclosed in the introduction instead of the conclusion; if the narrative progressed from past to present instead of present to past; if reasons were ordered from most important to least important instead of vice versa?

FEATURES

Language

- Does the author's language serve to heighten and illuminate the topic, or is it merely adequate?
- Does the author use precise wording, vivid details, words that appeal to the senses, and words with emotional intensity?
- If the author uses figurative language, are the similes and metaphors appropriate, or are they confusing, inexact, or misleading?
- Is the author's vocabulary unnecessarily formal or pompous? Does the author use big words where common ones would do?

Sentence Elements

- Are the sentences balanced and symmetrical or disorganized and awkward?
- Is the author concise, or does he or she try to pack too many ideas into long, sprawling sentences?

Images and Scenes

- If the author creates images and describes scenes, do they vivify the text, or are they superfluous?
- What would be gained if the author included more images?
- What would be lost if images were left out?

References and Allusions

- Do the author's allusions illuminate or add significantly to the subject matter?
- What would be lost if they were left out?
- Are the references to other written sources welcome additions to the text, or do they seem superfluous?
- Are the other sources timely, or does the author rely on outdated information?

Questions about Rhetorical Concerns

- Has the author fashioned the piece for the target audience?
- Is the author's persona or stance suitable, or does it detract from the piece?
- Are the voice and tone appropriate or unnecessarily pompous or formal?
- Does the author come across as authoritative, creditable, and reliable, or are you left with questions about his or her background, prestige, political or religious orientation, or overall reputation?
- Is the author impartial or biased?
- Does the author supply sufficient background information, or does he or she make erroneous assumptions about the reader's previous knowledge?

Review Your Answers to the Analysis and Evaluation Questions

After you record your answers to the analysis and evaluation questions, gather your notes to decide which elements to focus on in your essay. As you sort and organize your material, bear in mind that your rhetorical purpose is to judge the strengths and weaknesses of the reading source according to a set of carefully selected criteria. These criteria will emerge if you follow the same procedures that we outlined for the analysis essay.

1. Look to see if a particular question produced a lengthy, substantive response.
2. See if you can group answers that pertain to similar categories.
3. Select two or more elements for your focus.
4. Return to the relevant parts of the text to check for supporting material.

For a detailed explanation of each procedure, reread page 178.

Decide on an Organizational Plan

To organize your evaluation essay, you can use any of the plans we suggested for the analysis essay:

- Cause and effect
- Argument
- Structure of the reading source

See pages 179–180 for an explanation and brief outline of each pattern. A typical structure for an evaluation is some variation of the format used for an argument essay. We cover argument essays in Chapter 8, but we will give you a brief preview here. We make a distinction between a one-dimensional argument and a two-dimensional argument. To write a unidimensional argument, use the following format:

- State your thesis—your judgment based on three or four criteria that you will use to evaluate the source.
- Allocate one or more body paragraphs to each criterion, developing each with specific evidence from the source.

A two-dimensional argument will assess the source's weaknesses as well as its strengths:

- State your thesis—your evaluation and the criteria for strengths and weaknesses. For example, "Even though Carmichael uses convincing evidence to support his position, he weakens his argument by failing to acknowledge the opposition and making overly broad generalizations."
- Allocate a paragraph or two to acknowledging the source's strengths, substantiating your claims with evidence.
- Allocate paragraphs to discussing the weaknesses.

Drafting

Before you begin writing your preliminary draft, consult the sections on openers, introductions, and conclusions on pages 22–27. Introductory paragraphs of evaluation essays typically include an interest-catching opening sentence, mention of the title and author of the reading source, a thesis disclosing the writer's judgment, mention of the criteria for evaluation, and as much summary of the source as the audience will expect.

Follow your organizational plan as you move into the body of your essay. Be sure to keep your criteria in the forefront as you flesh out your body paragraphs with evidence (quotations, paraphrases, and summaries) from the reading source. Finally, check that you are observing the academic writing conventions (described on page 180).

Revising

Arrange for a classmate or friend to review your preliminary draft and give you feedback. If this is not possible, set the essay aside for a few days and then review it yourself. Respond to the following questions.

✓ *Checklist for Revising an Evaluation Essay*

_____ 1. Can you identify the writer's rhetorical purpose? Is the writer evaluating the reading source in terms of established criteria?

_____ 2. Does everything in the draft lead to or follow from one central meaning? If not, which ideas seem out of place?

_____ 3. Has the writer provided all the information you need to understand the essay?

_____ 4. Do you have enough background about the source, including the title, author, and relevant summary? If not, where do you need more information?

_____ 5. When referring to the source, does the writer supply the necessary documentation?

_____ 6. Are you always able to differentiate the writer's words from those of the author of the reading source? If not, where is there a need for connecting ideas and transitions?

_____ 7. Is the organizational plan appropriate for an evaluation essay? If not, what other organizational pattern do you suggest?

_____ 8. Has the writer made the standards or criteria of evaluation clear to you? If the criteria are unclear, explain your confusion.

_____ 9. When discussing each criterion, does the writer give evidence for the judgment by quoting, paraphrasing, or summarizing relevant parts of the text? Are there any places where additional evidence is needed?

_____ 10. When moving from one evaluative criterion to another, does the writer provide smooth transitions and connecting ideas? If not, where are they needed?

_____ 11. Is the writer's voice appropriate for this type of essay? Why or why not?

_____ 12. Is the opening satisfactory? Why or why not?

_____ 13. Does the essay have an appropriate conclusion?

_____ 14. Is the title suitable for the piece?

_____ 15. Has the writer observed academic writing conventions of using the present tense when explaining how the author uses various techniques and procedures, identifying the author initially by full name and thereafter only by last name, and indenting long quotations in block format?

EDITING

When you are satisfied with your revision, read your paper aloud. Then reread it line by line and sentence by sentence. Check for correct usage, punctuation, spelling, mechanics, manuscript form, and typographical errors. If you are using a word processing program with a spell checker, run the checker on your essay. If your editing skills are not strong, get a friend to read over your work.

ANALYSIS AND EVALUATION OF IMAGES

Academic writing assignments may ask you to analyze and evaluate visual images, such as photographs and paintings, or sources that combine images and language, including advertisements, films, and television programs. These assignments are particularly common in subjects such as art history and communications but you might also receive them in subject areas across the disciplines. In everyday life, we are deluged with visual images that call for interpretation.

The basic approaches to analyzing images are similar to those used for language-based texts. In fact, it has become common in various academic disciplines to view images as "texts" in that they are constructed in the same way that written texts are. Published images often have overt rhetorical goals and are intended for particular target audiences. As with language-based texts, visual texts have content and identifiable genre, organization, and features that are connected to their rhetorical goals.

The following questions will assist you in analyzing and evaluating a variety of images. The questions refer to "the image" under examination, but most of the questions could be applied to collections of images, advertisements, films, and television shows as well as to stand alone images.

QUESTIONS FOR ANALYSIS AND EVALUATION OF IMAGES

Questions about Seeing Content

- What does the image (or images) depict?
- What part of the image captures your eye when you first look at it? What are the other elements of the image, and how do they work with, or against, the prominent element in the image?
- Does the image contain text or have a caption? If so, what is the content of the text, and how does the text affect what we see in the image?
- What is the context of the image?
- What background information is essential to understanding the image?
- At what point in time was the image created?
- Does the image seem to be an authentic representation of what it depicts? What elements add to or detract from its authenticity?
- Is the image's content ambiguous? Are there alternative readings of the image's content?
- In addition to the overt content, does the message contain any signs, symbols, or metaphors that link to content outside of the image itself?

Questions about Seeing Genre, Organization, and Stylistic Features

- How does lighting affect the impression the image makes?
- Is the image in color or black and white? What is the impact of the image's colors or tones?
- Is the image high or low contrast? What is the overall effect of the image's contrast?
- How is the image framed or cropped, and what effect does this have?
- Does the image appear relatively flat, or does it show depth? What impact does depth of field have on the impression the image makes?
- Describe the arrangement of people and objects in the image. What purpose does this arrangement serve?
- Does the white space in the image contribute in any way to its overall effect?
- Does the image appear static, or does it suggest motion? What is the overall effect of the image dynamics?
- Is the image intended to look just like real life, or is it stylized or altered in obvious ways? What accounts for this decision?
- How are people depicted in the image? Do they seem to be posing? Do their eyes or expressions engage the audience? If there is more than one person depicted in the image, how do they interact?
- Can you discern any judgments that were made by the creator of the image that are not highlighted in the previous questions?

- What aspects of the image are most effective in getting your attention?
- If there is a collection of separate images, how are they interrelated?

Questions about Seeing Rhetorical Context

- What do you know about the creator of the image?
- Who is the intended audience for the image, and how is the image shaped for that audience?
- What impact does the image creator want to have on this audience?
- How might various segments of the audience experience the image differently?
- What does the image tell you about its creator's values and opinions?
- Is the image intended to be persuasive?
- How obvious is the rhetorical goal of the image?
- Is the image intended to be a work of art? Is the emphasis more on content or artistry?
- Does the image creator leave elements of the image open to interpretation?
- Does the image imply a story? What is that story?
- How does the image appeal to *logos, pathos,* or *ethos?* (see pages 295–296 for an explanation of these terms).
- Is anything intentionally left out of the image that might alter its meaning?
- What aspects of the image influence its credibility?
- Is the image produced by an individual or an organization that has a political, economic, social, intellectual, or artistic agenda?

While our list of analysis and evaluation questions might prove useful in a fine arts class, it would serve only as a starting point. Classes in art history, painting, photography, and film would, over the course of the semester, provide students with a rich set of analytical and evaluative techniques.

Sociologists and anthropologists often use visual images in their research. In her introductory sociology class, student Hayden Lawson received the following assignment:

> I have placed on reserve in the library a large collection of photographs of everyday American life taken over the last 150 years. Choose several photographs that work together to illustrate a sociological concept covered in our textbook and write a 1,000-word essay that explains how the photographs relate to the concept. Attach photocopies of the images to your paper.

After looking through the images in the library, Hayden selected four photographs. The first of these images, taken during World War II, shows a defense industry worker. The remaining three images, taken in 1948, were part of a collection documenting the cranberry industry.

Hayden used Questions for Analysis and Evaluation of Images (pages 197–198) as she drafted the following essay.

Hayden Lawson

Introduction to Sociology

Prof. Rabinowitz

10 Sept. 2008

Gender Stratification: Visual Evidence

Macionis defines gender stratification as "the unequal
distribution of power, wealth, and privilege between men and
women" (325). As Macionis points out, the basis of gender
stratification is not biological differences between men and women
but rather "cultural conventions" (326). The effects of gender
stratification are particularly obvious in the workplace (350).
Society perceives certain jobs appropriate for men and others for
women based on erroneous assumptions about men's and women's
abilities and cultural assumptions that certain occupations are
more appropriate for one gender than the other. A good illustration
that gender stratification in the workplace is based on cultural
values rather than biological gender differences is the movement of
women into and then out of American heavy industry during the
World War II era. This movement is documented in the photos I have
chosen to analyze of factory workers in the 1940s.

Of the images that characterize American society during the
Second World War, one of the most memorable is that of Rosie the
Riveter, a young female defense industry worker.

As American males entered the armed forces and the
armament factories tooled up for the war, women were needed
to perform heavy industrial work that was traditionally done
by men. There are numerous versions of the Rosie image, but
most depict a robust young woman in overalls, hair tied up in

a kerchief, who is either holding a rivet gun or flexing her arm muscles. "Rosie," a photograph taken in 1944, shows a worker in a Kansas defense plant striking the classic Rosie pose. She faces the camera, smiling and holding a rivet gun, and the muscles in her bared arm are evident. She appears confident and in control, capable of doing what was thought of as a man's job.

Rosie's stint in the factory was short lived. When the war ended in 1945 and men returned to the workforce, many Rosies returned to their roles as housewives and mothers. By 1950, almost 84% of the workers in the U.S. labor force were men (Macionis 333). Some women remained on the factory floor, but the rivet guns and other heavy machinery were handed back to male workers.

A series of photographs taken by C. Hadley Smith in 1948 in a cranberry processing factory illustrate how gender stratification returned to the factory in the post-war period.

4

5

Lawson 3

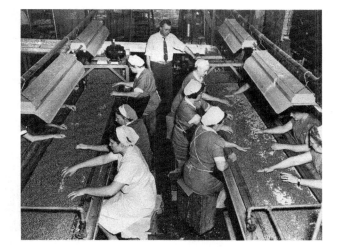

Sorting Tables

The photograph "Sorting Tables" depicts eleven women sorting
cranberries by hand, seated at large tables. In sharp contrast
to the Rosie the Riveter image, the women face down at the
cranberries rather than up at the camera, and in most cases, their
facial features are not evident. The lone male, apparently a
supervisor, is the only person facing the camera directly, and he
stands in the center of the photograph, the position most likely
to catch attention. The women's work involves using only their
hands' fine motor skills rather than muscular strength, and the
fact that some women are invisible except for their hands
highlights that only their hands are important to their work. In
"Rosie," the hands are not evident but the bared arm is a dominant
feature. We cannot see any of the women in "Sorting Tables" head
on, but those we see in profile are apparently expressionless, in
contrast to the strength of character that comes through in the
Rosie the Riveter image. While Rosie wears a sporty kerchief and

Lawson 4

striped shirt, the women in "Sorting Tables" appear to be wearing a work uniform, including aprons and little white hats that remind one of Pilgrim headgear. It is hard to imagine the young woman in "Rosie" tolerating the "Sorting Tables" work environment.

The photographs "Cranberry Cookers" and "Loading Crates" demonstrate the male roles in the cranberry factory.

6

Cranberry Cookers

In "Cranberry Cookers," we see two men operating machinery and one recording data, a job that presumably involves thinking, while in "Loading Crates," two men are lifting cartons onto a dolly. In both photographs, the men are at the center of the image and draw our eyes immediately. We see the face profiles of all five men, enough to give us some sense of their facial features and expressions. The arm muscles of all five men are evident, and they are engaged in "men's work": operating machinery, recording data, and lifting heavy boxes. No women appear in these photographs.

The photographs of the cranberry industry provide a clear example of gender stratification in the workplace. Women are

7

Loading Crates

portrayed in aprons doing jobs that involve only their fingers while men use their muscles and brains and are in control of machinery. It seems likely that the types of jobs that men are doing in the photographs pay more than the women's sorting task. The Rosie the Riveter image provides a visual argument that women are biologically capable of doing "a man's job," but as the cranberry industry photographs show, once society no longer needed women in war industries, women were relegated to "women's work" and were valued less in the factory. This shift indicates that, as Macionis points out, gender stratification is grounded in cultural convention rather than biological differences between men and women.

It's often said that "every picture tells a story." My collection of photos tells a story of the intentions of those originally involved in creating the photos. It seems likely that the composition of the photographs and the selection of which images were printed involved collaboration between the photographer and cranberry industry representatives, and the photos illustrate their values. For example, the fact the women are shown seated on crates rather than chairs indicates that the factory managers not only weren't concerned with the women's comfort but also weren't embarrassed for others to see how they treated female workers. The photographer could have used a camera angle that focused in on a few female sorters and showed much more of their faces as with the photographs of male workers. The decisions that were made in creating the images, both by the photographer and the factory management, illustrate that men's work was more valued than women's work.

It is amazing that in only three years, the image of female factory workers depicted in "Rosie" gave way to that in "Sorting Tables." The fact that American women and men accepted this shift indicates how powerful social norms are in shaping our world views.

9

Work Cited

Macionis, John J. *Sociology*, 9th ed. Upper Saddle River: Prentice
       Hall, 2003. Print.

Exercise 6.5

Compare Hayden Lawson's essay to the questions for analysis and evaluation of images (pages 197–198). Which of those questions did Hayden use as she developed her essay? Pick two questions that Hayden did not draw on and explain how they could be used to either support or contradict Hayden's conclusions.

IN-DEPTH ANALYSIS AND EVALUATION

In-depth analyses and evaluations of a topic, written text, or visual text identify and discuss dimensions that are problematic but not evident to the reader. Often these features are associated with larger problems. Sometimes this process is called "problematizing" a topic or text. In an essay of this type, you dig beneath the surface

- To present a number of facets of the topic, problem, or issue and uncover its various dimensions
- To ask questions about it and examine it from a particular angle or critical lens
- To shed light on a controversy and get to the base of a problem

Your overall rhetorical purpose is to reveal a problem and discuss its complexities. Usually an intense examination of this type will require you to consult reading sources for concepts, constructs, principles, theories, and expert views that you can use to substantiate your analysis and evaluation.

Before we take you through the process of writing an in-depth analysis and evaluation, we would like you to read two sample student essays. In the first essay, "Deinstutionalization: The Past Idea with the Present Misfortunes," Kimberley De Santis analyzes and evaluates a *topic:* deinstitutionalization of people who are mentally ill. In the second essay, "Gender Roles and Advertising," Erica Sanderson analyzes and evaluates a *visual text:* an advertisement for SKYY Vodka. Kim received the following assignment:

> Select a topic you have covered in one of the courses you are taking this semester. Write an essay in which you thoroughly analyze and evaluate the topic for your readers. Explore the topic from different angles. You goal is to present the topic in all its complexities.

De Santis 1

Kimberley De Santis

Professor Kennedy

Composition 101

24 April 2005

Deinstitutionalization: The Past Idea

with the Present Misfortunes

They embellish the streets night and day, harmless to

society, their pain self-evident. Confused by their environment,

they walk without any destination. They are the mentally ill

homeless, and they reside on the streets of our cities. Why are

1

De Santis 2

these sick people on the streets instead of in hospitals? Are there too many occupants in psychiatric wards and not enough vacancies? Are there any vacancies at all? There is much debate about why the homeless mentally ill are in such large numbers on the streets. Many citizens blame the government for the ingenious proposal of deinstitutionalization: the release of mentally ill patients into the community. Beginning in the 1960s, mentally ill people were dismissed from the institutional life and initiated into a lifestyle that they had previously been denied. "Between 1955 and 1996, state mental hospital populations fell from over 550,000 to 59,000" (Zaheer 392). If deinstitutionalization had been a complete success, the mentally ill would be living in community apartments or houses and not sleeping on park benches.

In the past, hospitals housed both borderline and severely mentally ill persons. The inhabitants had conditions such as schizophrenia, manic depressive disorder, autism, panic disorder, and obsessive-compulsive disorder (Torrey 10). Out of those formally committed, 50% to 60% were schizophrenic, 10% to 15% were manic depressive, another 10% to 15% had organic brain diseases such as epilepsy or Alzheimer's, and the remaining few had mental retardation (10). The mentally ill led a life surrounded by other sick persons. Their diseases were not uncommon, but they were placed in the psychiatric hospitals to avoid disruptions that they might cause to mainstream society.

Although there was some concern about disengaging mentally ill patients from institutions, the idea became intriguing. Throughout the 1960s, many people felt that the

2

3

institutionalization of mentally ill patients was morally wrong
(Torrey 143). The government's idea of deinstitutionalization was
welcomed. It allowed the mentally ill patients to be free of state
hospitals and receive care in community-based living centers
(143). President Jimmy Carter and his Commission of Mental Health
defined deinstitutionalization as "the objective of maintaining
the greatest degree of freedom, self-determination, autonomy,
dignity and integrity of mind, and spirit for the individual while
he or she participates in treatment or receives services" (11).
Prior to 1964, mentally ill patients were placed in state
hospitals on the assumption that they were in need of psychiatric
treatment. Their mental well-being was determined by psychiatrists
or psychologists, and sometimes the treatment was completely
involuntary to individuals (143). Deinstitutionalization allowed
those patients who were capable of an independent lifestyle to
pursue residence within the community.

Nineteen sixty-four was a fruitful year for the mentally ill
population. That year the federal Civil Rights Law was passed,
stating that only patients who were a danger to themselves or
others could be committed to institutions (Torrey 143). The
placement of the individuals into the community ensured freedom
that had been previously limited. Communal living allowed the
mentally ill to have a sense of belonging and a feeling of
acceptance in the public realm. For the first time, they could
function as if they were part of the traditional society.

At the time, deinstitutionalization was considerably less
expensive than institutional living. Community-based clinics
averaged about $50 a day, as opposed to psychiatric hospital

De Santis 4

costs of at least $200 a day (Jaroszewski). As former residents
were socialized into the community, they needed to learn to
adjust to diverse lifestyles. Lifestyle stability was provided
by several outpatient programs. Daily activities were monitored,
and staff assisted the patients as much as needed (Jaroszewski).
Everyday activities such as shopping, cooking, hygiene, the
search for employment, paying rent, and cashing checks had to be
taught so that the mentally ill would be successful living in
the community (Long). These reforms benefited the mentally ill by
giving them a sense of security within the society. Society at
large had always ignored the state hospitals and the "crazy"
patients who occupied them. Deinstitutionalization allowed the
patients to become part of the prevalent population. Mental
illness was no longer taboo, nor were its victims.

Thorazine, the first antipsychotic medicine, allowed many   6
mentally ill people to function as if they had no disease at all.
Thorazine and other antipsychotic drugs introduced later did not
cure the ailments, but they helped control the symptoms (Torrey
8). As a result, government and health officials felt it was safe
to discharge patients into the community. It had been said that
medicines and other treatments would be accessible to the needy
persons who had been deinstitutionalized. However, what was not
taken into consideration was how the released patients would
actually receive the medication, rehabilitation, and counseling
(8). Few services were available to the mentally ill, and hence
many persons went untreated. According to psychiatrist E. Fuller
Torrey, "Deinstitutionalization helped create the mental illness
crisis: discharging people from psychiatric hospitals without
ensuring they receive medication and rehabilitation for survival

in the community" (8). Thousands of mentally ill people were without treatment and unable to function appropriately in society.

Many of the patients who were discharged received inadequate care. A 1985 study of 132 patients with schizophrenia, mood disorders, and personality disorders proved that to be true. Thirty-three people were placed with irresponsible families or discharged to public shelters and addresses that turned out to be abandoned buildings or vacant lots. Thirty-four were homeless after one month, forty-four were homeless after three months, and thirty-two remained homeless after six months. Most were able to cash Social Security checks or veterans' benefits, but many had no income and lived on handouts. Many homeless individuals used illegal drugs and alcohol, and some were arrested for bizarre, threatening, or offensive behavior, as well as shoplifting, prostitution, and trespassing (Long). Inadequate government care can be blamed for the misfortunes that the mentally ill individuals experienced.

It is often thought that deinstitutionalization was brought about so that the state no longer had to care directly for the mentally ill. As documented by the U.S. Department of Health and Human Services, programs such as Medicaid, the federal Supplemental Security Income program (SSI), and the Supplemental Security Disability Insurance program (SSDI) provide direct entitlements to mentally ill disabled individuals who live in the community (15). Although these programs provide assistance, many mentally ill homeless live on the streets, and their numbers continue to rise. Therefore, one question to ask the government is, what can be done about this problem?

De Santis 6

Changes have been made to make the governmental system more
rational, systematic, and integrated, but "despite the efforts, the
system remains a 'patchwork of settings,' providers, policies,
administrative sponsors and founders" (U.S. 17). Services as such
are dispersed through a variety of public and private agencies.
These include mental hospitals, general hospitals, veterans'
hospitals, community mental health centers, residential treatment
centers, nursing homes, halfway houses, day treatment centers,
board-and-care homes, outpatient clinics, office-based private
practitioners (including psychologists, psychiatrists, and social
workers), psychosocial rehabilitation programs, clubhouses, and
self-help groups (17). Despite the number of care providers, there
are still the problems of availability, accessibility, and
appropriateness (17). Abolishing the needs of the mentally ill will
be a difficult process. Aid, programs, and communal services provide
some assistance, but a solution to remove the mentally ill from the
streets is a long-term goal that has so far not been accomplished.

Deinstitutionalization marked a new beginning for the
mentally ill. They were no longer involuntarily committed and
hidden away in hospitals. People believed deinstitutionalization
would benefit mentally ill patients by allowing them to function
as part of the mainstream. Unfortunately, deinstitutionalization
has had negative consequences. By 2001, "there [were] over 830,000
mentally ill people in the criminal justice system either in jail,
on probation, or on parole" (Zaheer 392). Another negative result
is the homelessness. Thousands of mentally ill persons struggle to
live on their own on the streets of America. With the proposed
care overlooked, the homeless mentally ill now encounter problems
that they are incapable of solving. Lloyd M. Siegel stated in

De Santis 7

1981, "Patients wander our streets, lost in time, as if in a medieval city. We are protecting their civil liberties much more adequately than we are protecting their minds and their lives" (Torrey 142). The situation is even worse today. Shelters can accommodate only a fortunate few, forcing many others to find shelter anywhere and by any means. As Zaheer points out, "If the number of mentally ill people on the streets and in jail is a measure of the success of deinstitutionalization, then no one will disagree that it has been a complete failure" (393).

We must learn from the experience of the last fifty years. We can no longer push aside homeless mentally ill people just like the garbage and debris they lie next to. More important, we have to rethink the problem and acknowledge that it is bigger than homelessness. As Dr. John A. Talbott explains:

> There must be a reconceptualization of the problem of the treatment and care of the severely and chronically mentally ill. Instead of considering the issue as one of where people should be housed, we must assess the needs of chronic patients and design or revise our services to meet those needs. And this means first and foremost that we must realize that we're not talking merely about psychotherapeutic needs but about medication, resistance to ongoing treatment, medical needs, housing, income, rehabilitation, social services, and what, for want of a better term, has become known as a community support system—that is, a system of supports that enables the chronically mentally ill person to receive the treatments and services he would receive if he were housed in a total institution.

If we do not take the measures Dr. Talbott recommends, the problems of the mentally ill population will continue to worsen.

11

De Santis 8

Works Cited

Jaroszewski, Lea. "Causes of Homelessness: Mental Health
     Issues." *Spare Change* 1996. Web. 8 Mar. 2005. <http://www
     .way.net/wasnew96.html>.

Long, Phillip W. "Mental Illness and Homelessness." *Harvard
     Mental Health Letter* July/Aug. 1990. *Internet Mental
     Health.* Web. 8 Mar. 2005.

Talbott, John A., M.D. "Deinstitutionalization: Avoiding
     the Disasters of the Past." *Psychiatric Services* 55
     (Oct. 2004): 1112-5. *Psychiatryonline.* Web. 1
     April 2005.

Torrey, E. Fuller. *Out of the Shadows: Confronting America's
     Mental Illness Crisis.* New York: Wiley, 1997. Print.

United States Dept. of Health and Human Services. National
     Institute of Mental Health. *Outcasts on Main Street: Report
     of the Federal Task Force on Homelessness and Severe Mental
     Illness.* Washington: GPO, 1992. Print.

Zaheer, David A. "Expanding California's Coerced Treatment for
     the Mentally Ill: Is the Promise of Caring Treatment
     in the Community a Lost Hope?" *Southern California
     Interdisciplinary Law Journal* 10.2 (2001): 385-405.
     LexisNexis Academic. Web. 1 April 2005.

Now read Erica's essay. Erica received the following assignment in her Communications Studies class:

Select an advertisement from a popular magazine with a general readership. Evaluate the ad from the standpoint of the audience's age, gender, occupation, class or income, race or ethnicity. You will identify the target audience for the ad, but you will analyze and evaluate it through the lens of the particular perspective.

Erica Sanderson

Professor C. Kaltefleiter

Introduction to Communication Studies

16 December 2007

Gender Roles and Advertising

A young girl slumping over to touch her Sketcher sneakers, [1] a woman nestling into the arms of a strong man to smell his Calvin Klein perfume, a female modeling the new Gucci purse, its strap in her mouth, a handsome CEO looking at his thousand-dollar wristwatch, a muscular young man wearing a popular brand of underwear—these are images projected at people on a daily basis, whether they are flipping through a gossip magazine, channel surfing on television, or strolling through a city embedded with billboards. Advertisements today are preoccupied with sex, youth, beauty, and weight for both males and females. Ads contain powerful subliminal messages, and some not so subliminal, that enter viewers' subconscious to reaffirm unrealistic desires for perfection and ultimately diminish self-esteem as well as self-acceptance. A critical examination of gender roles, codes, and signs in a contemporary magazine advertisement will uncover the true implications behind an otherwise "innocent" advertisement.

A sexy, thin, scantily clad woman stands seductively in [2] front of a seated businessman, ready to pour him a second round of martinis. The scene has the characteristics of an R-rated movie. However, it's merely the setting for a SKYY Vodka ad in a popular magazine. The intended audience for this ad is adults over twenty-one, since it is a pitch for alcohol. However,

gracing the pages of *People Magazine* the ad can be viewed by
all ages.

The classic little black dress worn by the model in the ad   3
becomes even littler with slits up to the hips, exposed back,
off the shoulder sleeves, and low neckline revealing just the
right amount of cleavage. Standing with her legs apart on either
side of the man's, it seems as if she's about to straddle him.
The ad leaves little to the imagination. The model is the
perfect representation of the sexual objectification of women
and Laura Mulvey's "male gaze":

> In a world ordered by sexual imbalance, pleasure in looking
> has been split between active/male and passive/female. The
> determining male gaze projects its phantasy onto the female
> form which is styled accordingly. In their traditional
> exhibitionist role women are simultaneously looked at and
> displayed, with their appearance coded for strong visual
> and erotic impact so that they can be said to connote to-
> be-looked-at-ness.

In the SKYY Vodka advertisement, the woman has become   4
an object rather than a subject in the eyes of the man,
specifically an object of lust or desire. The ad directs readers
to look at enticing characteristics which appeal to them. This
explains the focused image of the model's long leg being flashed
in the middle of the page. Before even looking at her face, the
viewer is consuming and careening through the curves of her body
and the exposed flawless flesh. The woman stands in front of the
man, martini shaker in hand, about to pour him another drink.
This objectifies her as a servant; she is going to service him,
as he sits comfortably. This portrayal implies that the woman is

lower than the man and should tend to him like a faithful
stereotypical housewife and obey his command for another drink.

From one point of view, the advertisement shows a male
dominated society. The seated man is barely visible. The
eroticized woman is the central focus. The setting appears to
be the man's apartment. He apparently does quite well in his
business as indicated by the sleek sophisticated furniture and
the view of the city skyline in the background. The male is the
successful tycoon while the female just needs to stand there
looking pretty, clear signs of a male run structure. However,
one could view the ad from the opposite perspective. As theorist
Erving Goffman states, "We learn a great deal about the
disparate power of males and females simply through the body
language and poses of advertising" (Kilbourne 265). The body
language communicated by the woman standing over a man is
symbolic of a domineering effect. She is in control of the
situation both socially and sexually as she glares at her
partner like a piece of meat, turning him into the object. In
addition, the apartment could be owned by her and she is merely
satisfying her guest's need for refreshments, playing the ever
lovely hostess.

Goffman, a sociologist who studied how advertising shapes our
notions of male and female behavior, identified certain cultural
codes and signs that are imbedded within advertisements and he
discussed the symbolism behind them, especially in regard to gender
roles (Kilbourne 258-267). The stiletto high heels the woman is
wearing are the ultimate symbol of sexual appeal and femininity,
two things greatly desired by all women. High heels are worn to
make a woman falsely appear to be taller, as power comes with

Sanderson 4

height. They also accent the legs and butt, drawing men's attention to those body parts even more than they usually do. The clacking of stilettos against the floor automatically garners attention, causing heads to turn; these shoes transform a woman into an object. Vodka can be used in all kinds of drinks, but the advertisers chose to use martinis, a sign of class. Martinis signify sleekness and sophistication, the choice drink of a businessman; it's also the usual suspect at high society soirees. Movies often show females seductively sucking the olive, in a gesture suggesting sex. Martinis set the perfect mood for this racy advertisement. Another sign of class is the slicked back hairstyle of the woman, as slicked back hair is seen as sophisticated in the fashion world because it exposes the face, revealing one's facial bone structure. The code of alcohol takes on new meaning: usually alcohol is a means to escape, but here it is a form of communication. It is shown as a way to get a man or woman, to loosen them up, a sort of social instigator. The ad could generate the message to men that they are inadequate in capturing a woman on their own with just their character, that a catalyst is needed to force a woman to succumb to their wishes. They have to intoxicate her. On the other hand, women might interpret this sign to mean that drinking is attractive to a man. Alcohol is sexy and will make you desirable. To loosen up with alcohol is to have fun. The ad could potentially lead both sexes to think that alcohol is necessary for comfortable social interaction.

Other codes are in strong display in the advertisement. The 7 code of the business suit for the man indicates a stereotypical shirt-and-tie male occupation in a corner office with a view. The hotshot, tough, cut-throat businessman, making millions of dollars

Sanderson 5

and getting all the girls, is the ultimate successful masculine
role. This woman in front of him may be just one date in a line
full of potential prospects. Such a message emphasizes the
pressures and expectations society places on men by requiring them
to be wealthy and lucrative. Another cultural sign is the exotic
chair the man is seated in which somewhat resembles an eggshell.
This could be symbolic of the emotional shell men keep themselves
encased in. Most men keep a hard exterior layer so no one can get
too close because men are not supposed to get attached, involved,
or hurt. They have to keep that casing nice and strong so no
emotions escape, because men are not supposed to be sensitive, and
certainly are never to cry. The female model in this advertisement
exhibits the classic stereotypical signs associated with women.
The little black dress makes her vulnerable like a target for male
forays. When going out for a night on the town or a date in this
case, it's almost always expected, nearly required, for a woman to
wear a dress. Her deep crimson nail polish and face full of makeup
are signs of the imperfections she feels she needs to cover up in
order to impress her man, even at her young age. There can be
nothing natural looking when a woman goes out; it's all an act to
appear better, someone unlike her normal self. There is also a
multiplicity of gazes. The viewer looks at the woman who is
looking at the guy who is in turn looking back at her. All of her
concentration is completely devoted to him at this moment. The
stereotypical idea that comes across is that a woman must look
good to please her significant other, not herself.

    Another concept of Goffman's that sheds light on the
advertisement is "licensed withdrawal." "Licensed withdrawal"
revolves around women in ads being removed from situations, hiding

8

Sanderson 6

themselves by turning away, looking down or covering their face. Women are portrayed as "psychologically removed, disoriented, defenseless, spaced out" (Kilbourne 265). In the case of this magazine advertisement, "licensed withdrawal" is directed at both the female and the male figure. The female model is faced toward the man, not the reader. Her head is in a downward gaze and her mouth is shut. She is meant to stand there silently and be a piece of eye candy. There is no real facial expression, not even a smirk. Therefore, no thought or personality is bubbling at the surface. The stance and rigidity of her body is almost robotic. As for the male model, his face is completely hidden as he's sunken into the chair becoming part of the shadows. Almost all the focus is off him. His identity is lost, or maybe seen as unimportant. A man's a man. As long as he's a rich corporate businessman, who cares about the rest? He, too, is simply a chess piece in a game. His personal characteristics, intellect, and charm are hidden to the outsider looking in.

A critical examination of the SKYY Vodka ad reveals the impact advertisements can have on men and women and the potential negative consequences that resonate from them. The degradation of women into sexual objects for male arousal and the portrayal of men as rich, muscular, emotion-ridden balls of masculinity only perpetuate the cycle of stereotypes. They also put continuous pressure on both males and females to transform themselves into the perfect beings they see depicted. The question is, Will these advertising methods ever change? The answer is that this format for advertising may never change because the public allows it to continue, making everyone fall victim to its sadistic tactics.

Sanderson 7

Works Cited

Kilbourne, Jean. "The More You Subtract, the More You Add."

    Gender, Race, and Class in Media. Ed. Gail Dines and Jean

    M. Humez. Thousand Oaks: Sage, 2003. 258-67. Print.

Mulvey, Laura. "Visual Pleasure and Narrative Cinema," *Screen*

    16.3 (Autumn 1975): 6-18. Web. 20 November 2008.

    <https://wiki.brown.edu/confluence/display/MarkTribe/

    Visual+Pleasure+and+Narrative+Cinema>.

"SKYY Vodka." *People Magazine* 3 December 2007: 25. Print.

Erica selected an advertisement for SKYY Vodka that appeared in the December 3, 2007, issue of *People Magazine.* The ad is also featured on the SKYY Vodka Web site. You can access it at http://www.skyy.com/site_map.php. When you are on the site, go to "The Lounge" and click on "SKYY Gallery." You will see a display of eight advertisements. The one Erica selected is the fourth from the right: #54 "The Antagonist," photographed by David LaChapelle.

Notice how each of the student writers employs reading sources. Kimberley draws on six sources to get to the base of the problem of deinstitutionalization. Erica uses two sources for her critique of the vodka advertisement. Toward the beginning of the process, both students asked the journalists' questions: Who? What? When? Where? Why? and How? Notice how each writer provides answers to these questions throughout her essay. Kimberley answers the questions in the following paragraphs:

Who?	Paragraphs 1 and 2
What?	Paragraph 1 and throughout the essay
When?	Chronology in paragraphs 3–6 (the past) and paragraphs 7–10 (the present)
Where?	Paragraphs 1, 2, 5, 7
Why?	Paragraphs 3, 4, 8
How?	Paragraphs 5, 6, 7, 9

Kimberley immediately whets her audience's interest by raising challenging questions that curious readers will want answered; then she introduces and defines the topic, provides a little background, and states the issue. Next, she describes how mentally ill people were treated in the past, identifies them, and explains why they were placed in psychiatric hospitals. In paragraphs 3 through 6, she investigates the causes of the problem, and in the remainder of the essay, she discusses its deleterious effects. Finally, she concludes with recommendations for improving the condition of mentally ill people in the future. Kimberley's goal is to uncover various dimensions of the topic, ferret out problems related to it, and get to the base of these problems. She enlightens her readers by bringing them to a better understanding of why deinstitutionalization of mentally ill people has not been a complete success. Compare Kimberley's essay to Erica Sanderson's.

Erica opens her essay with a series of arresting images from advertisements. She then piques her readers' interest by raising the issue of subliminal messages. At the end of the introduction she states her purpose: to uncover these hidden messages by examining gender roles, codes, and signs in an advertisement in a contemporary magazine. Starting in paragraphs 2 and 3 and continuing throughout the essay, Erica uses the six journalist's questions to dissect the advertisement for her readers. Her description is so detailed that her readers would be able to follow her train of thought even if she had not attached a copy of the SKYY Vodka ad to her paper. With each descriptive passage, Erica probes further to identify a problematic feature of the picture she has been analyzing. In paragraph 2, for example, she introduces the concepts of "Male Gaze" and objectification of women, and she explains their effect.

In paragraph 3 Erica analyzes the image from contrasting points of view in order to show that the ad contains hidden messages about men as well as women. In paragraphs 4 and 5 she anayzes and evaluates the ad in terms of cutural codes and signs that are associated with gender roles: the female model's high heels, the particular type of alcohol, the woman's hairstyle, the role that drinking plays in the situation being depicted, the setting, and the models' attire. In paragraph 6 Erica applies Erving Goffman's concept of "licensed withdrawal" to both the female and the male figures in the ad. In the final paragraph, she reiterates her position about the deleterious effects of ads on both genders. She ends the essay by pointing out that advertisers will continue to send the questionable messages she has described unless the public is more vocal in registering its disapproval.

Exercise 6.6

Read Erica Sanderson's essay, "Gender Roles and Advertising." Then reread Hayden Lawson's essay, "Gender Stratification: Visual Evidence," on pages 199–204. Write a short essay in which you compare the two essays.

WRITING AN IN-DEPTH ANALYSIS AND EVALUATION

Now we take you through the process of writing an in-depth analysis and evaluation. Before you sit down to draft your essay, you will engage in serious intellectual inquiry, closely examining the target topic or text with a view toward identifying and explicating some type of problem.

PREWRITING

Begin by examining your assignment, setting your rhetorical goal, and considering your audience. When you receive the assignment, double-check that it calls for an in-depth analysis and evaluation. If your professor gives you a lot of latitude, be sure to ask what the assignment calls for before you proceed. Your professor may recommend frameworks that you can use to evaluate the topic or text. Erica's assignment offers a number of frames of reference. In-depth analysis and evaluation requires you to draw upon other sources. Ask your professor for advice.

Set your rhetorical goal by asking yourself, Why am I writing this analysis and evaluation? What effect do I hope to have on my audience? Your primary purpose is to explore a topic or text so that your readers will be better able to understand its complexities and comprehend its problematic nature.

For an in-depth analysis and evaluation essay, it is very important to size up your audience. Be sure you know who your readers are and how much they already know about the topic or text. Then adjust your plans accordingly. If your readers have little knowledge, be prepared to give definitions, explain basic concepts, and provide a rich context. If they already know a lot about the topic, you will not have to tell them as much. You can concentrate on finer points and skip over the obvious. In either case, keep in mind that their reason for reading is to obtain better understanding.

Inquire into the Topic or Text

Do a first reading to acquire baseline information. Answer the six journalists' questions: Who? What? When? Where? Why? and How? Summarize your findings in notes or on a chart. Then move on to more probing questions. We recommend that you answer the three sets of questions we present below.

SET 1: QUESTIONS FOR IN-DEPTH ANALYSIS AND EVALUATION

- Who?
- What?
- When?
- Where?
- Why?
- How?

Record Answers in Your Notebook

Delve deeper into the material to uncover a problem or issue. Probe further by asking a second set of questions:

SET 2: QUESTIONS FOR IN-DEPTH ANALYSIS AND EVALUATION

- Why is there a problem?
- How has it been identified?
- Where did it come from?
- When and how has it developed?
- What are its effects, results, consequences?
- What else sheds light on it?

Record Answers in Your Notebook

Delve deeper into the material. Find answers to the third set of questions.

SET 3: QUESTIONS FOR AN IN-DEPTH ANALYSIS AND EVALUATION ESSAY

- Which things and events are most important to consider?
- Who are the experts and what are their views, positions, and concerns? What are the implications?
- What facets, strands, or dimensions of the problem are mentioned in most or all of the reading sources? Are these facets equally important?
- What facets are related? How might they be in conflict?
- Who agrees or disagrees with whom? Which experts see eye to eye and which are in conflict?
- What complexities of the topic or text are revealed by the authoritative sources?
- How might you use interpretations found in the sources?
- How might you use concepts, constructs, or principles found in the sources?
- How might you apply a theory or critical approach found in the sources?

Exercise 6.7

Select either Cyberhood, the topic of Chapter 11, or Adolescent Pregnancy, the topic of Chapter 12. Read the selections in the chapter. In your notebook, record answers to the three sets of analysis and evaluation questions.

Review and Categorize Your Answers to the Three Sets of Questions

Reread the questions and answers while the reading sources are still fresh in your mind. Reexamine your rhetorical purpose, keeping in mind that your goal is to explore the complexities of the topic or text in order to shed light on it and uncover problems for your readers. Group answers into categories. Use the journalists' questions as a base.

WHO?

- Who are the experts and what are their views, positions, and concerns? What are the implications?
- Who agrees or disagrees with whom? Which experts see eye to eye and which are in conflict?

WHAT?

- What things and events are most important to consider?
- What facets, strands, or dimensions of the problem are mentioned in most or all of the reading sources? Are these facets equally important?
- What facets are related? How might they be in conflict?
- What are the effects, results, consequences?

- What complexities of the topic or text are revealed by the authoritative sources?
- What else sheds light on the matter?

WHEN?

- When and how has it developed?
- What are its effects, results, consequences?

WHERE?

- Where did it come from?

WHY?

- Why is this a problem?

HOW?

- How has the problem been identified?
- How might you use interpretations found in the sources?
- How might you use concepts, constructs, or principles found in the sources?
- How might you apply a theory or critical approach found in the sources?

Then group the remaining questions and answers.

- What are the implications of the problem?
- What will it lead to?

After you categorize the questions and answers, return to the relevant parts of the soures you are using for supporting material. Mark passages that you will summarize, paraphrase, and quote.

DRAFTING

Our suggestions for drafting a rhetorical analysis essay apply to in-depth analysis and evaluation essays as well. Consult pages 178–180.

Decide on an Organizational Plan, and Draft Your Essay

Review the organizational plans on pages 15–17. Arrangements that lend themselves to analysis essays are time order (chronology), cause and effect, statement and response, and classification.

REVISING

If your instructor agrees, arrange for a classmate or friend to review your preliminary draft and give you feedback. If this is not possible, set the paper aside for a few days and then review it yourself. Answer the following questions.

✓ *Checklist for Revising an In-Depth Analysis and Evaluation Essay*

_____ 1. Can you identify the writer's rhetorical purpose? Is the writer unpacking the topic or text so that readers can understand its complexities?

_____ 2. Has the writer identified a problem and noted its causes and effects?

_____ 3. Does everything in the draft lead to or follow from one central meaning? If not, which ideas seem to be out of place?

_____ 4. Do you understand the analysis and the terms of the evaluation, and is the writer sensitive to your concerns?

_____ 5. Does the writer provide necessary background information, summary, or description? If not, what is missing?

_____ 6. Does the writer use authoritative sources to substantiate his or her analysis and evaluation?

_____ 7. When referring to sources, does the writer supply the necessary documentation?

_____ 8. Does the writer provide clear transitions and connecting ideas that differentiate his or her own ideas from those of the author?

_____ 9. Does the writer refer to authors by name?

_____ 10. Is the organizational format appropriate for an in-depth analysis essay?

_____ 11. Has the writer made you aware of the complexities of the topic?

_____ 12. Is the basis for the analysis and evaluation clear? If not, explain your confusion.

_____ 13. Does the writer support each point with direct evidence (quotations, paraphrases, summaries) from sources? If not, where are they needed?

_____ 14. When moving from one point of analysis to another, does the writer provide smooth transitions and connecting ideas? If not, where are they needed?

_____ 15. Do you hear the writer's voice throughout the essay? Describe it.

_____ 16. What type of lead does the writer use to open the paper? Is it effective? If not, why not?

_____ 17. Does the paper have an appropriate conclusion? Can you suggest an alternative way to end the essay?

_____ 18. Is the title suitable for the piece? Can you suggest an alternative?

_____ 19. Has the writer followed academic writing conventions, such as writing in present tense when explaining how the author uses particular procedures and techniques, identifying the author initially by full name and thereafter only by last name, and indenting long quotations in block format?

EDITING

When you are satisfied with your revision, read your paper aloud. Then reread it line by line and sentence by sentence. Check for correct usage, punctuation, spelling, mechanics, manuscript form, and typographical errors. If your editing skills are not strong, get a friend to read over your work.

Exercise 6.8

Drawing on one or more articles in Chapter 11 or Chapter 12, write an in-depth analysis and evaluation essay on the topic of Cyberhood or Adolescent Pregnancy. You may focus on whatever aspect of the topic interests you, but whatever your particular focus, your overall goal should be to shed light on the controversy, identify a problem, and discuss implications. Your essay must be substantiated with sound reasoning and convincing examples, and you must make substantial use of source material. Use an organizational plan of your choice, but the paper must have an introduction with a clear thesis statement, well-developed body paragraphs that fit together logically, and a conclusion.

PART IV

Synthesizing Sources

CHAPTER 7

Writing Multiple-Source Essays

As a college writer, you will often compose papers that draw on multiple reading sources. You might write an essay comparing and contrasting two texts or a paper based on several journal articles, a chapter from a book, and a piece from a newspaper. Working with multiple sources is complex because you have to identify consistencies among the texts and then integrate these bits of relevant information with your own ideas. The amount of information you draw from the sources will depend on the topic and the assignment.

In this chapter, we show you how to write five types of papers that draw on multiple sources:

- An essay that compares and contrasts sources
- A summary of multiple sources
- An objective synthesis
- An essay written in response to multiple sources
- A synthesis written for a specific purpose

COMPARING AND CONTRASTING SOURCES

How many times have you received a writing assignment that began "Compare and contrast . . ."? Your social studies teacher may have asked you to contrast the abolitionists' view of slavery with the pro-slavery view, or your English teacher may have told you to compare two characters in a short story. In primary school, you probably wrote reports comparing two types of animals or showing the difference between two countries or states. We use comparison and contrast every day. Asked to describe a new song on the radio, we say, "It has a rap beat, but the lyrics sound more like pop music." We frequently view things in terms of what they are like and unlike.

USES OF COMPARISON AND CONTRAST

Writers use comparison and contrast to describe, explain, and argue. Let us look first at a descriptive paragraph from Leslie Heywood's memoir, *Pretty Good for a Girl*. The setting is the weight room where Heywood works out with the boys on the distance running team. She is describing a confrontation with the coach of the sprinters' team. Identify the comparisons.

> I sit up and there he is: the sprinters' coach. He looks just like—*just like*—Luke Spencer on *General Hospital,* and this is Luke Spencer's year. A few months from now he will rape Laura [and] then marry her, and the whole country will tune in, whether they usually watch the soaps or not, the hype in the papers approaching that reserved for Prince Charles and Princess Di, whose wedding will also happen that month. Like Luke on TV, Coach Luke is gaunt and thin, skin really white, with unruly threads of albino-red hair fanning the air behind him, thinning a bit right on top. He moves quickly, and is sarcastic a lot like he's sarcastic right now, twisting that smile that says he knows it all and knows it right, your place in the universe nothing like his. I look up at him, ready for a fight. He looks at me like you'd look at a rooster who's strutting his stuff just before he's going to get cooked. Not this rooster, mister, not me. I look at him with his own look that says you don't even exist and you'd better get out of my way. His mouth turns up at one corner and he laughs, "Hey, my guys need this bench and you all should go do something else." I don't move.

Did you find the following comparisons between

- Coach Luke and Luke Spencer on *General Hospital?*
- media hype over *General Hospital* and media coverage of the royal wedding?
- Heywood herself and a rooster who's strutting his stuff before he's about to be cooked?

Comparisons add depth to descriptive writing and leave the reader with rich, memorable images.

Next, consider how comparison is used for the purpose of explanation. In the following paragraph, philosophy professor David Rothenberg explains the difference between university students in Finland and in the United States. The passage is from "Learning in Finland: No Grades, No Criticism," an article published in *The Chronicle of Higher Education.*

> The Finnish view is that simply doing the work on one's own time is the point of education. My students always claimed to be too busy, but they rarely seemed stressed or burned out. Students must think, they must write. In Europe, they often save all their thinking for the final project and the final exam at the end of the single course they typically take each semester. In the United States, students and professors communicate all the time—discussing, chatting, bouncing ideas back and forth, at least in small classes. The Finns put more of a boundary between the learned and the learner. Professors are encouraged to pontificate, to put forth information, and the student to sit silently and take it all down.

Last, let us examine how Professor Pat Griffin makes an argument on the basis of similarity. The paragraph is from Griffin's book, *Strong Women, Deep Closets: Lesbians and Homophobia in Sport.* Griffin argues that women athletes possess qualities, talents, and characteristics that are attributed only to male athletes.

Women's serious participation in sport brings into question the "natural" and mutually exclusive nature of gender and gender roles. If women in sport can be tough minded, competitive, and muscular too, then sport loses its special place in the development of masculinity for men. If women can so easily develop these so-called masculine qualities, then what are the meanings of femininity and masculinity? What does it mean to be a man or a woman? These challenges threaten an acceptance of the traditional order in which men are privileged and women are subordinate.

In "A Young Person's Guide to the Grading System" (pages 385–388), Jerry Farber argues that students don't need grades even though they may think otherwise. Farber compares students to addicts:

We're like those sleeping pill addicts who have reached the point where they need strong artificial inducement to do what comes naturally. We're grade junkies— convinced that we'd never learn without the A's and F's to keep us going. (385)

Notice that the quoted passages show writers using comparison and contrast for a precise purpose. Heywood is describing Coach Luke, Rothenberg is explaining the differences between Finnish and American views of higher education, Griffin is making a case for gender equality, and Farber is arguing against grades. Writers may use comparison and contrast simply to explore interesting points of similarity between two subjects or to demonstrate that grounds for comparison actually exist, but more often they describe, explain, or argue.

RHETORICAL PURPOSE FOR COMPARISON-AND-CONTRAST ESSAYS

As a college writer, you will occasionally be asked to compare your own experience with information from reading sources, but more typically you will be required to compare and contrast the views expressed in various texts. Here is a typical assignment.

Compare and contrast two authors' views on assisted suicide: those of Ernest van den Haag in his *National Review* article, "Make Mine Hemlock," and those of Rand Richards Cooper in his *Commonweal* article, "The Dignity of Helplessness: What Sort of Society Would Euthanasia Create?"

Since this is a loosely defined assignment, there are a number of ways you can approach it. The most rudimentary approach is simply to list the similarities and differences in the two authors' views and use the list to compose your essay.

SIMILARITIES

- Neither author is questioning assisted suicide per se.
- Both authors offer some of the same examples.

DIFFERENCES

- Van den Haag is in favor of institutionalizing assisted suicide; Cooper is against it.
- Van den Haag bases his argument on the notion of rights; Cooper claims that this notion is too narrow a framework.

- Van den Haag finds fault with the argument that life is a social duty that no one should shirk; Cooper bases his argument on the "texture of civic life."
- Van den Haag discusses abled individuals' right to commit suicide and also goes into detail about assisted suicide for disabled individuals; Cooper focuses on the elderly.
- Van den Haag goes into detail about the competence of individuals who wish to shorten their life; Cooper does not treat this issue.
- Van den Haag goes into detail about safeguarding the disinterestedness of people who assist with suicides; Cooper predicts that people may act out of self-interest.
- Van den Haag dismisses "slippery slope" arguments; Cooper dwells on the long-range negative consequences of euthanasia.
- Van den Haag says that today people hold the view that "individuals collectively own society, rather than vice versa"; Cooper claims that contemporary society is moving toward communitarianism and interest in togetherness rather than separateness.
- Van den Haag thinks Dr. Kevorkian is courageous; Cooper questions everything Kevorkian has done.
- Van den Haag claims that there are safeguards to ensure that no one is pressured to end his or her life; Cooper claims that the elderly do not have "absolute autonomy" in this matter.

You could easily construct an essay from this list by using a block presentational pattern, allocating a small block to similarities and a large one to differences. The resulting essay would be rather flat because it would simply catalog the similarities and differences. There is nothing intrinsically wrong with this goal, but when it is the only end in mind, it is easy to fall into the trap of doing too much summarizing and too little discussion of similarities and differences. We recommend that you take the process a step further. After you identify similarities and differences, step back and ask yourself what they represent, reveal, or demonstrate. Reflect on the list, select from it, shape it, or expand it. Ask yourself the following questions.

QUESTIONS ABOUT SIMILARITIES AND DIFFERENCES

- Can you select from among the similarities and differences and categorize them in a way that will make your essay more interesting, relevant, eventful, or meaningful?
- Is there a new angle or point of view you can take?
- Can you make the essay functional? Can you create a "rhetorical imperative," that is, write to move or influence a certain group of readers for a specific reason?
- Can you address a more definite audience?
- How can you engage the reader best?
- Can you fashion a richer rhetorical situation?

To illustrate, let us examine a student essay written in response to the assignment on page 230.

Anna Robles

Professor Kennedy

Composition 101

5 May 2005

The Controversy over Assisted Suicide

Paper
opener:
rhetorical
questions

Should competent people, particularly those who are

terminally ill or handicapped, have the right to end their

lives? Or should they be forced to go on living even if they do

not wish to do so? What it comes down to is the question of who

owns life: God, the individual, or the larger society? Many

people believe that suicide is a sin and a transgression against

God and nature. End of discussion. But Ernest van den Haag and

Background,
titles, and
authors

Rand Richards Cooper wish to pursue the matter further. Van den

Haag presents his argument in "Make Mine Hemlock," and Cooper

makes his case in "The Dignity of Helplessness: What Sort of

Society Would Euthanasia Create?" Van den Haag claims that no

one "owns" us. We own ourselves and control our own destinies.

Therefore, any able-bodied person should be permitted to end his

or her life. And disabled people who wish to end their lives

should be given assistance. Cooper disagrees. He thinks it is

wrong to eliminate the stage of life when people become sick and

helpless, and he questions whether we will "be a better, richer,

more humane society for having done so" (14). He also warns that

widespread practice of assisted suicide will present a dire

Thesis

threat to society. Ernest van den Haag and Rand Richards Cooper

have very little in common. They base their arguments on

different assumptions, and they have very different views

of the consequences of assisted suicide.

1

Robles 2

2

Points of
similarity

Both van den Haag and Cooper agree on one point. Dying patients have the right to refuse treatment, and physicians may choose to respect the decision and even help them die. Van den Haag thinks physicians are obligated to assist terminally ill patients. Cooper does not go that far, but he does accept the idea of physicians relieving unnecessary pain. He remarks:

Support
from the
article:
quotation

> In fact, it's not assisted suicide per se I'm questioning, which in other forms has long been practiced unofficially by physicians informing the gravely ill about lethal doses, turning off ventilators to "let nature take its course," and so on. It's the institutionalizing of the practice I'm wondering about, and its effect on our relation to the idea of suffering. (14)

Even though they don't really see eye to eye, this seems to be the only point on which van den Haag and Cooper share any common ground.

3

First
point of
difference

Very different assumptions underlie Van den Haag's and Cooper's arguments. Van den Haag bases his argument on individual rights, whereas Cooper maintains that the notion of individual rights is too narrow a framework. Van den Haag says that neither God nor society "owns" people. They "are thought to own themselves" (60). He explains: "Owners can dispose of what

Van den
Haag

Support
from the
article:
quotation

they own as they see fit. We thus become entitled to control life, including its duration, to the extent nature permits, provided that this control does not harm others in ways proscribed by law" (60). Van den Haag believes that our obligations to ourselves are more important than our obligations to society. He finds fault with the argument that life is a social duty that no one should shirk.

Robles 3

Cooper

Cooper moves his argument outside the framework of the "right" to die. He feels that Americans are obsessed with individual rights: "The appeal of rights is so compelling that it leaves scant room for realities and interests not easily expressed as rights" (12). For Cooper, "our deaths are both solo journeys toward an ultimate mystery and strands in the tapestries of each other's lives" (14). We are interconnected, and this connectedness to one another, the effect that each individual has on "the texture of civic life" (13), is more important than individual rights. In other words, our duty to society outweighs our duty to ourselves.

Support from the article: quotation and paraphrase

Second point of difference

Van den Haag and Cooper also have different opinions about the ramifications of institutionalizing assisted suicide. Cooper points out that if the practice is sanctioned, it will lead unavoidably to undesirable attitudes. He predicts a "creep toward an increased sense of burdensomeness" (12) on the part of the elderly. Viewing themselves as burdens to their loved ones, they will end their lives. Cooper also claims that the ready availability of assisted suicide will transform the way we regard aging. "How often in the assisted-suicide future," he asks, "will someone look at an elderly person and think, consciously or semiconsciously, 'Gee, guess it's about time, huh?'" (13). Cooper sees other negative consequences. He predicts that if we legalize assisted suicide and thus follow what he calls "the quality-of-life, take-me-out-and-shoot-me principle," we will "preempt the infirmities of old age and terminal illness" (13).

Cooper

Support from the article: quotation and paraphrase

4

5

Robles 4

Eventually, we will look askance at disabled and handicapped people of all ages. We will end up thinking, "as Germany did under the Nazis,...of the handicapped as a drain or drag on the healthy body of the rest of us: a pointless deformity; an un-luck; an un-person" (13).

Van den Haag

Van den Haag would accuse Cooper of committing the slippery slope fallacy. Slippery slope arguers predict that one thing will inevitably lead to another more undesirable thing. They also warn of dangerous precedents. Van den Haag says the suggestion that doctors, or anyone else, "would wantonly kill burdensome patients who do not want to die" is unjustified (62). He also thinks the analogy to Nazi Germany is unsound. He argues, "But Nazi practices were imposed on physicians and hospitals by political directives which did not evolve from any prior authority given physicians to assist in suicide. There was no 'slippery slope'" (62). To van den Haag, the slippery slope argument is an "unrealistic nightmare" (62).

Cooper speaks of the importance of accompanying people through terminal illnesses and asks if this is not "one of the core experiences we need to have" (14). Toward the end of his article, he asks, "Whose death is it anyway?" (14), implying that the duty to die, as well as the duty to live, is owed to society. Van den Haag could not disagree more. "Society cannot be shown to have a compelling interest in forcing persons to live against their will," he says. "Moreover, such an interest would hardly justify the cruelty involved" (62).

Margin labels: Van den Haag · Support from the article: quotation · Conclusion

```
                                                      Robles 5

                          Works Cited

    Cooper, Rand Richards. "The Dignity of Helplessness: What Sort

        of Society Would Euthanasia Create?" Commonweal 25 Oct.

        1996: 12-14. Print.

    van den Haag, Ernest. "Make Mine Hemlock." National Review

        12 June 1995: 60-62. Print.
```

Anna does more than list the multitude of differences between van den Haag and Cooper. She describes one area of agreement, and then she selects two points of difference and makes them the focus of her essay: the different assumptions that underlie each author's argument and the views each holds about the consequences of permitting assisted suicide. In paragraph 2, she explains that both van den Haag and Cooper acknowledge that dying patients have the right to refuse treatment and that physicians may choose to respect the decision and even help them die. Next, in paragraphs 3 and 4, she investigates the bases of each author's argument: van den Haag's claims about individual rights and Cooper's claims about civic duty and the needs of society. Then, in paragraphs 5 and 6, Anna discusses Cooper's predictions about the dangers inherent in the legalization of assisted suicide and van den Haag's dismissal of this chain of events.

Exercise 7.1

Return to Anna Robles's essay and consider her rhetorical purpose. Break into groups, and answer the following questions:

1. What do you think prompted Anna to respond to the assignment the way she did?
2. How does Anna view her audience?
3. What impact does she want to have on these readers?
4. What role does Anna assume in relation to the subject matter, the audience, and her own voice?

WRITING AN ESSAY THAT COMPARES AND CONTRASTS SOURCES

To write a comparison-and-contrast essay, follow the same process we outlined in Chapter 1, working through the assignment in *prewriting, drafting, revising,* and *editing.*

PREWRITING

Before you sit down to compose a preliminary draft, read and reread the sources, annotate them, take notes, and plan your essay. The effort you put into these prewriting activities will save time and ensure you of more success than if you move directly from reading the sources to writing your essay. To begin, tailor your reading goal and strategies to the task at hand.

For illustration, we take you through the process Anna Robles followed to address the assignment you just read:

> Compare and contrast two authors' views on assisted suicide: those of Ernest van den Haag in his *National Review* article, "Make Mine Hemlock," and those of Rand Richards Cooper in his *Commonweal* article, "The Dignity of Helplessness: What Sort of Society Would Euthanasia Create?"

Do a First Reading to Get a General Impression of the Source

Since the assignment asks her to compare and contrast van den Haag's and Cooper's views on assisted suicide, Anna's first step is to read the articles to determine how the two authors' views are similar and how they are different. She reads with two questions in mind:

- How are Cooper's and van den Haag's views on assisted suicide similar?
- How are Cooper's and van den Haag's views on assisted suicide different?

After the first reading of the texts, Anna freewrites her reactions, writing nonstop for ten minutes, jotting down whatever comes to her mind.

Reread, Elaborate, and Map Correspondences

Next, she rereads the two articles. The second reading allows her to do two things:

- Tap memory and make associations between previous knowledge and experiences and the reading sources.
- Identify and map correspondences between the two sources.

As Anna performs these activities, she annotates the texts or takes separate notes. As she rereads the selection by van den Haag, she elaborates and identifies places where he agrees or disagrees with Cooper.

van den Haag

Paragraph 11

It is not clear to whom the duty to live could be owed. Once the government no longer legally recognizes God as the authority to which duties are owed, nature cannot have prescriptive authority to force unwilling persons to live, since such authority would have to come from God. Only society is left as the source of this alleged duty. But society cannot be shown to have a compelling interest in

Elaboration

Cooper disagrees. He claims that society should have a compelling interest in keeping people alive because we are all interconnected. He doesn't think society is forcing elderly people to stay alive. He claims

forcing persons to live against their will. Moreover, such an interest would hardly justify the cruelty involved.... *that they really don't want to die; they consent to assisted suicide because they feel helpless and they are convinced they are a burden to society. I don't know what he'd say about cruelty. He seems to think that it is important for people to suffer.*

As she rereads the two sources, she elaborates fully and identifies as many similarities and differences as she can. A rich store of prewriting notes and annotations will be a great help when she writes her essay. When you write a comparison-and-contrast essay, if you have difficulty elaborating on the reading sources, refer to the strategies for elaborating on reading sources on pages 56–58. Here are some additional strategies that will help you compare the two reading sources.

ELABORATING TO UNCOVER COMPARISONS AND CONTRASTS

- Identify points where one source author (1) agrees or disagrees with the other author, (2) says something relevant about the topic that the other author has neglected to say, (3) qualifies ideas stated by the other author, and (4) extends a proposition made by the other author.
- Validate one author's assertion with information provided by the other author.
- Subsume similarities and differences between the sources under subordinate categories.
- Create hierarchies of importance among ideas that are similar or different.
- Make judgments about the relevance of one author's view in relation to the other's view.

As you identify correspondences between the two reading sources, create a *web* (see Figure 7-1). Webbing enables you to link points of similarity and difference. Identify a point of similarity or difference, summarize it in a short phrase, and write it in a box on a sheet of paper. Next, spin out the web by placing each author's ideas around this key idea node. Circle each idea, and draw lines connecting it to the key idea. Where appropriate, connect the circles to each other. When you are finished webbing, you will have a visual display of the points of similarity and difference.

Plan Your Essay

Once you have generated a series of elaborations, you are ready to select and organize your ideas and sketch out a blueprint for your essay. Keep in mind that your purpose is to compare and contrast the views expressed by the two authors. As you review your elaborations, separate the ones dealing with similarities from the ones dealing with differences (see page 230). Mark the text wherever you discover similarities or differences (use symbols: = or √ for similarities, ≠ or × for differences), and create two lists, as we illustrated on page 230.

FIGURE 7-1   Beginning of a Web for Comparison and Contrast

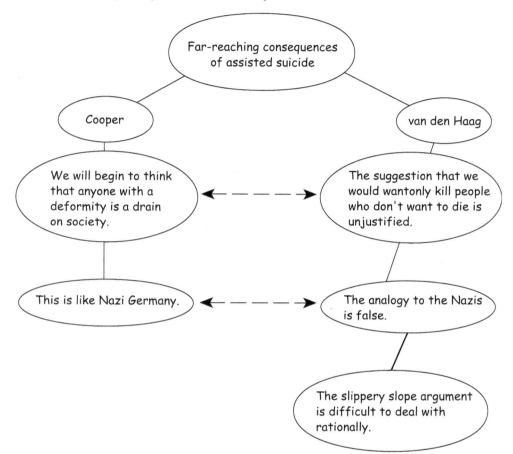

Next, analyze the similarities and differences to discover the points you will discuss. They can be aspects of the subject, major topics, or prominent themes. Categorize the similarities and differences accordingly. See if you can form one or two generalizations. Even if your generalizations have exceptions, they will still be useful.

Usually, writers compare reading sources in order to draw certain conclusions and make particular points clearer to the reader. As we said earlier, you could simply catalog the similarities and differences, but this limited rhetorical purpose leaves little room for you to exercise judgment or analytical skill. The more powerful purpose requires you to select, categorize, and focus.

LIMITED GOAL	MORE POWERFUL GOAL
Catalog all the similarities and differences.	Select from among the similarities and differences, categorize them, and focus the essay on generalizations.

Observe how Anna selected from among the long list of differences between van den Haag and Cooper listed on page 230. She pinpoints two major areas of difference: the assumptions underlying their arguments and their views on the consequences of assisted suicide.

ASSUMPTIONS FOR ARGUMENTS

- Van den Haag says that today we believe that "individuals collectively own society, rather than vice versa." He bases his argument on the notion of rights. He finds fault with the argument that life is a social duty that no one should shirk.
- Cooper argues that the notion of individual rights is too narrow a framework. He claims that we're moving toward communitarianism and togetherness rather than separateness. He bases his argument on the "texture of civic life."

VIEWS ON CONSEQUENCES OF ASSISTED SUICIDE

- Cooper emphasizes long-range negative consequences of euthanasia. Van den Haag dismisses Cooper's "slippery slope" arguments.
- Van den Haag claims there are safeguards to ensure that no one is pressured to end his or her life; Cooper contends that the elderly do not have "absolute autonomy" in this matter.

Once you have decided on your areas of focus, return to the reading sources and search for any relevant material you may have overlooked.

Comparison-and-contrast essays are usually organized in one of two formats: point-by-point or block. Point-by-point arrangement identifies key aspects or facets of the subject that is being compared and contrasted. For the assignment we are working on, that means we would move back and forth between van den Haag and Cooper, comparing and contrasting them on the basis of key points or features of their arguments. Block arrangement presents one side at a time. We would discuss everything van den Haag has to say about the topic before moving on to Cooper. To see how professional writers use these arrangements, read the following passages from an article in which Nancy Henley, Mykol Hamilton, and Barrie Thorne discuss sex differences and sexism in communication.

Point-by-Point Arrangement

There are other sex differences in speech sounds. For boys in our culture, masculinity and toughness are projected by a slightly nasal speech; girls and "gentlemanly" boys have oral, or non-nasal, speech. Males also speak with greater intensity than females. There are differences in the intonation patterns used by each sex: Women have more variable intonations (contrasting levels) than men do; women are said to have more extremes of high and low intonation than men, and to speak with long rapid glides that are absent in men's speech. (174)

Table 7-1 depicts the point-by-point arrangement. Henley, Hamilton, and Thorne explain sex differences in speech sounds by comparing the speech of males and females on the basis of three features: nasality, intensity, and intonation.

TABLE 7-1   Point-by-Point Presentation

Subject	Males	Females	Points of Comparison
Sex differences in speech sounds	Projects masculinity and toughness for boys; oral non-nasal speech for gentlemen	Have oral, non-nasal speech	Nasal quality
	More intensity than females	Less intensity than males	Intensity
	Glides absent	More variable; more extremes of high and low; speak with long, rapid glides	Intonation

Block Arrangement

Self-disclosure is another variable that involves language but goes beyond it. Research studies have found that women disclose more personal information to others than men do. Subordinates (in work situations) are also more likely to self-disclose than superiors. People in positions of power are required to reveal little about themselves, yet typically know much about the lives of others—perhaps the ultimate exemplar of this principle is the fictional Big Brother.

According to the research of Jack Sattel, men exercise and maintain power over women by withholding self-disclosure. An institutional example of this use of power is the psychiatrist (usually male), to whom much is disclosed (by a predominantly female clientele), but who classically maintains a reserved and detached attitude, revealing little or nothing of himself. Non-emotionality is the "cool" of the professional, the executive, the poker player, the street-wise operator. Smart men—those who manipulate others—maintain unruffled exteriors.

Women who obtain authoritative positions may do likewise, but most women have been socialized to display their emotions, thoughts, and ideas. Giving out this information about themselves, especially in a context of inequality, is giving others power over them. Women may not be more emotionally variable than men, but their emotional variability is more visible. This display of emotional variability, like that of variability of intonation, contributes to the stereotype of instability in women. Self-disclosure is not in itself a weakness or negative behavior trait; like other gestures of intimacy, it has positive aspects—such as sharing of oneself and allowing others to open up—when it is voluntary and reciprocal. (176–77)

Table 7-2 depicts the block arrangement. Discussing sex differences in self-disclosure and emotionality, Henley, Hamilton, and Thorne first describe the behavior of males and then describe the behavior of females.

TABLE 7-2   Block Presentation

Sex	Behavior	Points of Comparison
Males	1. Exercise and maintain power over women by withholding personal information.	Self-disclosure,
	2. Are "cool," nonemotional, unruffled.	emotionality
Females	1. Display personal information to people in power.	Self-disclosure,
	2. Appear to be more emotional because they display emotion.	emotionality

Notice that Anna Robles organizes the body paragraphs of her essay on pages 232–236 in a point-by-point arrangement. She covers three points: one point on which van den Haag and Cooper agree and two points on which they disagree. You can visualize this arrangement in a chart or tree diagram (see Figure 7-2). It is beneficial to use some type of graphic organizer as a preliminary outline.

If Anna had used the block comparison pattern, then instead of taking up each of the three points of comparison and alternating between van den Haag and Cooper, she would have presented one side at a time and contrasted the two authors in blocks, one block devoted to van den Haag and the other to Cooper. The pattern is shown in the tree diagram in Figure 7-3.

Exercise 7.2

Rewrite each of the passages on pages 240–241 in the alternative form; that is, recast the point-by-point passage into block format and put the block passage into point-by-point format.

DRAFTING

Anna's next step is to write a preliminary draft of her essay. This will not be a final, polished draft. She will have an opportunity to change her direction, sharpen focus, and make other revisions at a later date. As she is drafting, she follows her outline and keeps the reading sources open. She will consult them often for the quotations, paraphrases, summaries, and other references she will use to support each of her points. When you write your own comparison-and-contrast essay, there are certain conventions you should follow.

CONVENTIONS FOR COMPARISON ESSAYS

- Give your readers some background about the topic.
- Identify the sources by title and author.
- Indicate clearly the focus and thesis of your paper.
- Make clear to your readers the points of comparison you will discuss.

FIGURE 7-2   Diagram for a Point-by-Point Comparison

Subject: Assisted suicide
Sources Being Compared: Van den Haag
                                Cooper
Points of Comparison: 1. Assisted suicide per se
                                2. Assumptions underlying argument
                                3. View of consequences

ASSISTED SUICIDE

OUTLINE FOR A COMPARISON ESSAY WRITTEN IN A POINT-BY-POINT ARRANGEMENT

Paragraph 1   Introduction
Paragraph 2   Similarities between the two authors

Underlying Assumptions of Argument (first major difference)

Very different assumptions underlie van den Haag's and Cooper's arguments. Van den Haag bases his argument on individual rights, whereas Cooper maintains that the notion of individual rights is too narrow a framework.

Paragraph 3   Van den Haag's assumptions
Paragraph 4   Cooper's assumptions

Views on Consequences of Assisted Suicide (second major difference)

Van den Haag and Cooper also have different opinions about the ramifications of institutionalizing assisted suicide.

Paragraph 5   Cooper's views
Paragraph 6   Van den Haag's views
Paragraph 7   Conclusion

- Develop each point of comparison by paraphrasing, summarizing, or quoting relevant points in the readings, or bringing your prior topic knowledge and experience to bear on the text.
- Be sure you discuss the same points for each author. For example, if you discuss assumptions and consequences for van den Haag, discuss the same points for Cooper.

FIGURE 7-3 Tree Diagram for a Block Comparison

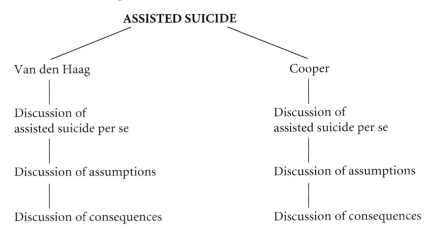

OUTLINE FOR A COMPARISON ESSAY WRITTEN IN A BLOCK ARRANGEMENT

Paragraphs 1 and 2   Same as for the point-by-point essay.

First Block: Van den Haag

Paragraph 3   Assumptions underlying his argument
Paragraph 4   Views on the consequences of assisted suicide

Second Block: Cooper

Paragraph 5   Assumptions underlying his argument
Paragraph 6   Views on the consequences of assisted suicide
Paragraph 7   Conclusion

- Use transitions and verbs that signal similarities and differences to help your readers follow your train of thought:

  also, likewise, in the same way, similarly

  on the contrary, in contrast, even so, however, but, although, despite, in spite of, nevertheless, nonetheless

  on the one hand, on the other hand, not only … but also

  agree, accede, acknowledge, concur, go along, assent

  disagree, counter, deny, retort, contradict, object
- Differentiate your own ideas from those of the authors of the sources.
- Document source material that is paraphrased, summarized, or quoted.

REVISING

If your teacher agrees, arrange to have a classmate or friend review your preliminary draft and give you feedback. If this is not possible, set the paper aside for a few days and then review it yourself. Respond to the following questions.

✓ *Checklist for Revising the First Draft of a Comparison-and-Contrast Essay*

_____ 1. Is the writer's rhetorical purpose clear? (How is the writer attempting to influence or affect readers?)

_____ 2. Does the writer simply catalog similarities and contrasts or focus on key points?

_____ 3. Are the key points clearly expressed in the thesis statement?

_____ 4. Does everything in the essay lead to or follow from one central meaning? (If not, which ideas appear to be out of place?)

_____ 5. Will the reader understand the essay, and is the writer sensitive to the reader's concerns?

        _____ a. Does the writer provide necessary background information about the subject matter, the sources, and their titles and authors? (If not, what is missing?)

        _____ b. Are there clear transitions or connectives that differentiate the writer's own ideas from the ideas in the sources?

        _____ c. Does the writer display an awareness of the authors by referring to them by name?

_____ 6. Is the organizational format appropriate for a comparison-and-contrast essay?

_____ 7. Does the writer use a point-by-point or a block arrangement?

_____ 8. Has the writer clearly stated the points of comparison? (Explain how these criteria or bases for comparison are clear or confusing.)

_____ 9. Does the writer provide transitions and connecting ideas when moving from one source to another or from one point of comparison to the next? (If not, where are they needed?)

_____ 10. Do you hear the writer's voice throughout the entire essay? (Can you describe it?)

_____ 11. Does the writer open the paper in a way that catches the reader's attention?

_____ 12. Does the conclusion simply restate the main idea, or does it offer new insights?

_____ 13. Does the essay have an appropriate title?

_____ 14. Do you have other suggestions you can give the writer for improving this draft?

EDITING

When you are satisfied with your revision, read your paper aloud. This enables you to catch any glaring errors. Then reread the essay line by line and sentence by sentence. Run the spell checker on your essay, and check for grammatical correctness, punctuation, mechanics, manuscript form, and typographical errors. If your editing skills are not strong, get a friend to read over your work.

Exercise 7.3

Make arrangements to have someone review your preliminary draft or, if this is not possible, review it yourself. Answer the questions on page 245. Then use the feedback you receive to revise and edit your paper.

Table 7-3 summarizes the guidelines for comparing and contrasting sources.

TABLE 7-3   Summary of the Guidelines for Comparing and Contrasting Sources

Prewriting: Planning and Preparatory Activities

1. Read the assignment, and decide on your rhetorical purpose.
   • Why are you writing the comparison essay, and what desired effect do you hope to have on your audience?
2. Consider your audience.
   • Are you writing for your professor or for a broader audience?
   • Is your audience in the academic community?
   • Are you writing for a general audience or for specialists?
   • What will your audience already know about the topic?
   • Will you need to explain basic concepts or provide background for the source material to make sense?
   • Will your audience be biased either for or against what the sources say?
   • Can you predict how your audience will react to the sources?
   • What is the overall impact that you wish to have on your audience?
   • How will your writing inform, influence, or change your audience?
3. Read the sources to get a general impression of the content; form, organization, and features; and rhetorical concerns.
   • Reading for information: What is the author's thesis or main point? What are other important points?
   • Reading for form, organization, and features: How does the author get his or her points across? What is the method of presentation? What is the pattern of organization?
   • Reading for rhetorical concerns: What is the author's purpose? How does the author intend to influence the audience? Who is the author, and what is his or her background? To whom is the piece addressed? In what type of publication is it published? What is the author's relationship to the audience?
4. Read the selection you are comparing for the purpose of determining how they are alike or different.
   • In what ways are the selections similar?
   • In what ways do the views in one selection differ from those expressed in the other selection?
5. Reread and elaborate.
   • Tap your memory, and make associations between your background knowledge and the ideas in the reading sources (see the strategies for elaboration of reading sources on page 238).

- Identify points where one source author agrees or disagrees with the other author, says something relevant about the topic that the other author has neglected to say, qualifies ideas stated by the other author, extends a statement made by the other author.
- Validate one author's point with information provided by the other author.
- Subsume similarities and differences between the sources under subordinate categories.
- Create hierarchies of importance among ideas that are similar and those that are different.
- Make judgments about the relevance of one author's view in relation to the other author's.

6. Use webbing to link points of similarity and difference (see page 239).
7. Plan.
   - Review your elaborations.
   - Identify all those that deal with similarities and differences, and place them in categories.
   - Analyze the similarities and differences, asking yourself, "What do these similarities and differences demonstrate? What do they tell us about each of the sources?"
   - Form some kind of generalization based on the significance of the similarities and differences.
   - Formulate your thesis statement.
   - Return to the sources to verify your conclusions.
   - Select an organizational format: point-by-point or block arrangement.

Drafting

1. Write an opening paragraph in which you accomplish these goals:
   - Use an opening that will interest the reader.
   - Announce the topic and disclose a thesis or attitude toward it (the thesis may come later).
   - Indicate the source titles and authors, and provide some summary information about the sources.
   - Establish your voice.
2. Arrange your elaboration notes in paragraphs, and develop each paragraph to its fullest.
3. Compose a concluding paragraph in which you use one of these techniques:
   - Stress the significance of your thesis rather than simply repeating it. Encourage your readers to look beyond the thesis to an important future goal.
   - Predict consequences.
   - Call your readers to action.
   - Use any of the devices for paper openers (see page 23).

Revising

1. If possible, have a classmate or friend read over your first draft and answer the questions on page 245. If no one is available, answer the questions yourself.
2. When you revise, keep the following concerns in mind:
   - Moving from writer-based to reader-based prose
   - Varying sentence length
   - Stressing verbs rather than nouns
   - Using words effectively
   - Detecting sexist language
   - Adding your own voice

1. When you are satisfied with your revision, read your paper aloud. Then reread it line by line and sentence by sentence. Check for correct usage, punctuation, spelling, mechanics, manuscript form, and typos.
2. Run a spell checker on your essay.
3. If your editing skills are not strong, have a friend read over your work.

Exercise 7.4

Read Erika Perotte's essay, "Finding Meaning in Memoir," on pages 187–190. Write an essay comparing Erika's essay to the essay by Anna Robles on pages 232–236.

SUMMARY OF MULTIPLE SOURCES

Summarizing involves focusing in on the key elements of a text and compressing other information, such as examples and details. In Chapter 4, we gave you seven strategies for summarizing sources (see pages 116–120). You won't use all of these strategies at one time. For most assignments, a subset of strategies suffices.

To illustrate the process of summarizing multiple sources, we examine student writer Jamar Williams's summary of three articles on the topic of teen pregnancy. Jamar was asked to write a short, straightforward summary of the views expressed by three authors: Cathy Gulli in her *Maclean's* article, "Suddenly Teen Pregnancy Is Cool?"; Kay Hymowitz in her *City Journal* article, "Gloucester Girls Gone Wild"; and Nancy Gibbs in her *Time* article, "Give the Girls a Break."

Jamar's first challenge was to reduce about nine pages of source material to a short summary. With this goal in mind, he read each article, underlining or highlighting only the most essential information. Then, using the summarizing strategies, he compressed the important information in each article into a single paragraph. Next, he stepped back to look at the larger picture and examine his rhetorical purpose. He asked himself two questions: What is each author's overall purpose? Do these purposes relate to each other in any significant way? Reviewing the articles, he concluded that all three authors focused on explanations for adolescent pregnancy. Gulli argues that girls are getting pregnant because popular culture presents teen pregnancy in a positive light. Taking social factors a step further, Hymowitz contends that today relaxed moral codes and reduced expectations for fathers make it more attractive for young girls to become single parents. Gibbs reasons that teens who decide to give birth may, in fact, be making a responsible, adult decision.

The information about the authors' purposes furnished Jamar with a logical order for his summary and provided him with transitions for moving from one source to the next. As he wrote his draft, he made a special effort to attribute source ideas to the authors by occasionally mentioning their names. He also used transitional words and phrases and provided page references for direct quotations. Here is an annotated version of Jamar's summary.

Jamar Williams

Professor Brown

Academic Writing I

12 October 2008

Summary of Three Articles on Adolescent Pregnancy

Three articles that examine the reasons why teenagers become
mothers are "Suddenly Teen Pregnancy Is Cool?" by Cathy Gulli,
"Gloucester Girls Gone Wild" by Kay Hymowitz, and "Give the Girls
a Break" by Nancy Gibbs. The catalysts for the articles are
twofold: an increase in the birthrate for U.S. teens and an
incident that took place in Gloucester, Massachusetts, where it
was reported that a group of high school girls signed a pact in
which they promised to become pregnant and keep their babies.
Gulli argues that popular culture presents teen pregnancy in a
positive light. Hymowitz contends that social factors, including
relaxed moral codes and reduced expectations for fathers, make it
more attractive for young girls to become single parents. Gibbs
suggests that teens who decide to give birth may, in fact, be
making a responsible, adult decision.

Writing in January 2008 in the Canadian magazine, *Maclean*'s,
Gulli explains that in the U.S. births to teenage mothers have
risen for the first time in fifteen years and recently they have
also risen in England. She expects Canada to have a comparable
increase in the near future. Gulli observes that teen pregnancy
is popularized by the culture. A number of teenage celebrities
have proudly announced that they are having babies, and a teen
pregnancy has been glorified in the film *Juno*, a box-office
success in which the unwed heroine decides to keep her baby.

Margin notes:

Uses a straightforward title

Mentions titles and authors of texts

Provides general framework

Provides attribution

1

2

Williams 2

Gulli offers various experts' explanations for the rise in teen
pregnancies but she believes the fundamental reason for the
increase is that today there is very little shame or stigma
associated with out-of-wedlock births. Being a single teenage
mom is doable and socially accepted.

Provides
transition

Continuing in the same vein as Gulli, Hymowitz attributes
the rise and social acceptance of out-of-wedlock teen births to
changes in contemporary culture. Writing in *City Journal*, she
contends that many working class teenagers have "adolescent
baby lust" which, she says, is understandable since historically
fifteen- and sixteen-year-old girls were considered suitable
for motherhood. Until recently these teens were dissuaded
from having children because of the "no-baby-without-
marriage rule." Today many single women, including teenagers,
are mothers. Hymowitz feels that the epidemic we should
be concerned about is not teen mothers. It is
"fatherlessness."

3

In a July 2008 *Time* magazine article, Gibbs takes issue
with people who have criticized the teen moms at Gloucester
High School. She asks, "What if the 'problem' in evidence at
Gloucester High has more to do with the rejection of abortion
than the acceptance of teen pregnancy?" (2). Gibbs points out
that abortion rates have plummeted, especially for girls aged
fifteen to seventeen. She suggests that the trend is not that
more teens are becoming pregnant. It is that fewer pregnant
teens are having abortions. She says the Gloucester teens
deserve sympathy and respect for accepting the consequences
of their actions.

4

Cites page
number for
quotation

```
                                                      Williams 3

                        Works Cited

Gibbs, Nancy. "Give the Girls a Break." Time 7 July 2008: 36.

        Proquest Research Library. Web. 1 October 2008.

Gulli, Cathy. "Suddenly Teen Pregnancy Is Cool?" Maclean's

        28 January 2008: 40+. Proquest Research Library. Web.

        1 October 2008.

Hymowitz, Kay S. "Gloucester Girls Gone Wild." City Journal

        23 June 2008. Web. 1 October 2008.
```

When you are asked to write a summary of two or more reading sources, you will find the following strategies useful.

STRATEGIES FOR WRITING A SUMMARY OF MULTIPLE SOURCES

- Read each source, annotating it to highlight the important ideas. (If you are writing a short summary, concern yourself with only the most essential information.)
- Reduce each source to its gist by combining important ideas in one or more summary paragraphs (use the summarizing strategies on pages 116–120).
- After you have reduced each source, step back and determine how the authors' purposes relate to one another.
- Decide on your order of presentation.
- Begin with a statement that frames the summary and, if appropriate, gives the titles and authors of the sources.
- As you draft the summary, attribute source ideas to the author.
- Provide transitions in the appropriate places.
- Write a straightforward title.
- Check that you have documented direct quotations and provided a works cited page.

When you are satisfied with your draft, if it is all right with your teacher, give your summary to a classmate or friend and ask that person to use the following checklist to give you some feedback.

✓ Checklist for Revising a Multiple-Source Summary

_____ 1. Has the writer given the piece a straightforward title?
_____ 2. Toward the beginning of the summary, has the writer provided a general statement that provides a framework for the piece?
_____ 3. Has the writer mentioned titles and authors of the sources?
_____ 4. Has the writer explained the author's purpose while summarizing each source?

_____   5. Has the writer attributed the material to the source author (for example, "Celis goes on to say...")?

_____   6. Has the writer provided appropriate transitions or connecting ideas when moving from one source to the next?

_____   7. Has the writer cited page numbers for direct quotations?

_____   8. Has the writer supplied a works cited page?

Exercise 7.5

Select three articles from Chapter 11, Chapter 12, or Chapter 13 of this book. Use the "Strategies for Writing a Summary of Multiple Sources" to write a short, straightforward summary of the three sources.

OBJECTIVE SYNTHESIS

An *objective synthesis* combines separate units or bits of information from two or more reading sources into a coherent whole. When writing an objective synthesis, the first step is to analyze the sources, breaking each one down into separate elements. The next step is to identify common elements and determine the relationships among them. The final step is to recombine the elements into a new composition.

Like a summary, an objective synthesis leaves little room for your own ideas. Your goal is simply to select material from various reading sources and integrate it into a new composition. Writers usually compose objective syntheses when they are engaged in report writing—for example, writing a nonjudgmental survey of sources that address a particular issue. The goal is to repackage information from sources for a new audience.

A psychology professor we know assigns students in his introductory course a series of "microthemes," which are brief overviews of topics of interest to them. Throughout the semester, each student is required to read up on topics and submit twenty-five of these one-page reports, some of which are read to the entire class. Let's examine Christopher Bruno's microtheme on the topic of phobias. Christopher synthesized information from four sources: a dictionary, two encyclopedias, and a psychology textbook.

pho·bi·a *n.* 1. A persistent, abnormal, or illogical fear of a specific thing or situation. 2. A strong fear, dislike, or aversion. —**phobic** *adj.*

—**phobia** *suff.* An intense, abnormal, or illogical fear of a specified thing: *xenophobia.*

—**phobic** *suff.* 1. Having a fear or an aversion for: *xenophobic.* 2. Lacking an affinity for: *lyophobic.*

(American Heritage Dictionary)

Phobia, irrational fear that tends to persist despite reassurance or contravening evidence. Psychoanalytic theory suggests that phobias such as fear of high places, closed spaces, infection, etc., are actually symbolic displacements of more basic but repressed fears and impulses.

(Random House Encyclopedia)

Phobic Neurotic Disorders. These neuroses are characterized by an abnormal fear of a specific object or type of situation. The patient may have one phobia or several, and the degree of disturbance varies considerably among the objects of the phobias. It is believed that in a phobic reaction anxiety originally attached to a specific idea, object, or situation is displaced to something symbolic of the idea, such as dirt, or particular animals, places, or diseases. Phobias are frequent in children as well as adults. The main treatment is psychotherapy.

(Funk & Wagnalls New Encyclopedia)

Phobias

When a person's anxiety is focused irrationally on a particular object or situation, it is called a *phobia.* (The term comes from the Greek word for "fear.") Unlike those with generalized anxiety, people with phobias believe they know what triggers their feeling of dread. The case below is in many ways typical:

> The client was a 30-year-old male who reported intense fear of crossing bridges and of heights. The fear had begun 3 years earlier when he was driving over a large suspension bridge while feeling anxious due to marital and career conflicts. Looking over the side he had experienced intense waves of fear. From that time onward his fear of bridges had become progressively more severe. At first, only bridges similar to the original were involved, but slowly the fear generalized to all bridges. Concurrently, he developed a fear of heights. Just before he came for treatment, he had been forced to dine atop a 52-story building. He had developed nausea and diarrhea and had been unable to eat. This had decided him to seek treatment. [Hurley, 1976, p. 295]

A phobia, then, can be extremely disruptive to a person's life. Ironically, the person may recognize that the fear is irrational, yet still be unable to dismiss it. Only avoidance of the feared object relieves the anxiety. Table 15-1 lists some of the phobias clinicians have encountered.

TABLE 15-1   *Common Phobias*

Phobia	Feared Object or Situation
Acrophobia	High places
Agoraphobia	Open places
Claustrophobia	Enclosed places
Ergasiophobia	Work
Gamophobia	Marriage
Haphephobia	Being touched
Hematophobia	Blood
Monophobia	Being alone
Ocholophobia	Crowds
Taphophobia	Being buried alive
Xenophobia	Strangers

Psychologists have proposed several theories to account for phobias. Freudians have argued that phobias develop as defense mechanisms against dangerous or unacceptable impulses. A man with a bridge phobia, for instance, may be defending against a suicidal urge to jump from a bridge. Learning theorists, in contrast, believe that phobias may result from classical conditioning. A child stung by a bee, for example, may thereafter fear bees because of their past association with pain. Firsthand contact with the feared object is not even needed for this type of classical conditioning to occur. A person may fear swimming in the ocean, for instance, after watching the movie *Jaws*. Here a previously neutral stimulus (ocean water) is repeatedly paired with a terrifying experience (watching people devoured by a shark) until eventually the water alone is enough to generate fear. Other phobias may be instilled through observational learning (Bootzin and Max, 1980). A girl who hears her mother express a terror of heights, for instance, may express the same fear later, even though heights have never been associated with any real danger to her. (Wortman, Loftus, and Marshall 438–39)

After reading the four sources, Christopher took each one apart in order to characterize the different bits of information that it contained. As he moved from one source to the next, he noted information that was repeated. Then he examined information that was not mentioned in the preceding source. For example, both the *American Heritage Dictionary* and the *Random House Encyclopedia* give definitions of phobia, but the encyclopedia also suggests a cause for the condition. The *Funk & Wagnalls New Encyclopedia* includes definition and cause, and also describes the characteristics of patients suffering from phobias and comments on their treatment. The psychology text contributes information to the areas already mentioned and provides new information on various types of phobias.

To help in planning his synthesis, Christopher made a chart to display the relationships among the sources (see Table 7-4).

TABLE 7-4   Comparison of Information in Sources

	American Heritage Dictionary	*Random House Encyclopedia*	*Funk & Wagnalls New Encyclopedia*	**Psychology Textbook**
Definitions	(1) Fear of a specific thing or situation. Fear is persistent, abnormal, and illogical. (2) Strong fear, dislike, aversion.	Irrational fear that persists despite reassurance or contravening evidence.	Type of neuroses; abnormal fear of a specific object or type of situation.	Anxiety focused irrationally on a particular object or situation. Origin is the Greek word for "fear."

	American Heritage Dictionary	*Random House Encyclopedia*	*Funk & Wagnalls New Encyclopedia*	Psychology Textbook
Causes		Psychoanalytical theory suggests that phobias are actually symbolic displacements of more basic but repressed fears and impulses.	Belief that in a phobic reaction anxiety was originally attached to a specific idea, object, or situation, such as dirt or particular animals, places, or diseases.	*Freudians:* Phobias develop as defense mechanisms vs. unacceptable impulses. *Learning theorists:* Phobias result from classical conditioning. Child stung by bee may develop phobia toward bees. Firsthand contact with feared object not necessary. You could fear swimming in ocean after seeing *Jaws*. Phobias can also result from observational learning, e.g., girl fears heights because her mother has fear.
Patients' characteristics			Patient may have one phobia or several. The degree of disturbance varies among the objects of the phobias. Phobias are frequent in children as well as adults.	People know what triggers their feelings of dread. They may recognize the fear as irrational but still be unable to dismiss it. Only avoidance of the feared object relieves anxiety.
Types				Table lists common types of phobias—claustrophobia, xenophobia, acrophobia, etc.
Treatment			Main one is psychotherapy.	
Examples				Story of the man who developed a phobia toward bridges.

After Christopher broke down the sources into parts, identified their common characteristics, and noted other elements, he rearranged these units and integrated them into a single, coherent synthesis. To illustrate, we annotated the draft of his synthesis.

Bruno 1

Christopher Bruno

Professor Mazza

Psychology 101

15 Sept 2005

Phobias Microtheme

Do you feel queasy in high places, uneasy in crowds, or   1

ill at ease in the presence of strangers? If so, you may be

Psychology textbook

acrophobic, claustrophobic, or xenophobic. A *phobia* (the term is

Funk & Wagnalls

derived from the Greek word for "fear") is a type of neurosis or

anxiety. It is an abnormal fear of an object, or situation. The

fear is illogical and irrational because it persists even when

Random House

the patient is reassured or given contravening evidence. People

Psychology textbook

with phobias may know what triggers their feeling of dread and

may recognize the fear as irrational, but they are unable to

dismiss it. The only way they can relieve their anxiety is to

Funk & Wagnalls

avoid the feared object or situation. Phobias are frequent in

children as well as adults, and people can have one or several,

Random House and Funk & Wagnalls

with varying degrees of disturbance. There are various theories

about the causes of phobias. Psychoanalysts suggest that people

with phobias have some basic but repressed fears and impulses,

but they shift the fears to something symbolic of the idea, such

as dirt or particular animals, places, or diseases. In other

Psychology textbook

words, according to these Freudians, phobias develop as defense

Psychology textbook

mechanisms against dangerous or unacceptable impulses. Learning

theorists claim that phobias result from classical conditioning.

A child stung by a bee, for instance, may develop a phobia

Funk &
Wagnalls

toward bees. It isn't even necessary to have firsthand contact

with the feared object. It would be possible to develop a fear

of swimming in the ocean after seeing *Jaws.* Observational

learning can also lead to phobias. A child might be terrified of

heights because she observed her mother's fear of high places. A

common treatment for phobias is psychotherapy.

Christopher's synthesis is much shorter than the combined lengths of the original sources. He was able to compress the originals into fewer words because he did not repeat ideas that recurred in two or more sources. To keep the synthesis to the required one- to two-page length, he also deleted details (the table of common phobias) and examples (the case of the man who was afraid of bridges). If his goal had been to create an even tighter synthesis, Christopher would have eliminated more information and included only the key ideas in each text.

The techniques Christopher used to write his microtheme are appropriate for objective synthesis papers of any length. To write an objective synthesis, use the following strategies.

STRATEGIES FOR WRITING AN OBJECTIVE SYNTHESIS OF MULTIPLE SOURCES

- Read all of the sources.
- Reread the first source, taking it apart and identifying the functions of the various units of information (saying, for example, "This is a definition," "These are reasons," "Here are some of the effects").
- As you move from one source to the next, identify common characteristics ("This source also gives a definition").
- After you have analyzed all the sources, study recurring themes and common characteristics, and organize them in new combinations.
- Decide on the order in which you will present your information.
- Begin with a lead and a straightforward statement of the topic.

Exercise 7.6

Use the following excerpts to compose an objective synthesis. Assume that your rhetorical goal is to inform your readers that language conveys a negative image of both men and women.

1. Discussion of words like *sissy* as insults have been often one-sided: most commentators are content to argue that the female, not the male, is being insulted by such usage. "The implicit sexism" in such terms, writes one commentator, "disparages the woman, not the man" (Sorrels 87). Although the female is being slurred indirectly by these terms, a moment's reflection will show that the primary force of the insult is being directed against the male, specifically the male who cannot differentiate himself from the feminine. Ong argues in *Fighting for Life* that most societies place heavy pressure on males to differentiate themselves from females because the prevailing environment of human society is feminine (70–71). In English-speaking societies, terms like *sissy* and *weak sister,* which have been used by both females and males, are usually perceived not as insults to females but as ridicule of males who have allegedly failed to differentiate themselves from the feminine. (August 118)

2. Whether one looks at elite titles, occupational roles, kinship relationships, endearments, or age-sex categorical designations, the pattern is clear. Terms referring to females are pejorated—"become negative in the middle instances and abusive in the extremes" (Schulz, 1975:69). Such semantic derogation, however, is not evidenced for male referents. *Lord, baronet, father, brother, nephew, footman, bowman, boy, lad, fellow, gentleman, man, male,* and so on "have failed to undergo the derogation found in the history of their corresponding feminine designations" (67). Interestingly, the male word, rather than undergoing derogation, frequently is replaced by a female referent when the speaker wants to debase a male. A weak man, for example, is referred to as a *sissy* (diminutive of *sister*), and an army recruit during basic training is called a *pussy.* And when one is swearing at a male, he is referred to as a *bastard* or a *son-of-a-bitch*—both appellations that impugn the dignity of a man's mother. (Richardson 25–26)

ESSAY WRITTEN IN RESPONSE TO MULTIPLE SOURCES

In Chapter 5, we discussed essays written in response to a single reading source. In this chapter, we explain how to write an essay in which you respond to two or more sources. In this type of essay, you react to the themes or commonalities in the text. To prepare for an essay of this type, you need to read the sources with a particular objective in mind: to establish bases for relating one source to another. Once you identify relationships among the sources, you proceed as you would for any response essay, summarizing the sources and elaborating on them by bringing your previous knowledge to bear on the texts. To a large extent, the summaries and elaborations are governed by the controlling idea of your essay.

A response to multiple sources differs from a summary of sources or an objective synthesis because the writer has a more encompassing purpose. In addition to selecting and combining pieces of information from the various texts, the writer also generates his or her own ideas and incorporates them into the essay. To illustrate how this is done, we annotated an essay by student Matthew J. Williams. Matthew draws on two articles: "Music" by Allan Bloom and "Engaging Students in the Great Conversation" by Neil Postman. He is responding to the following assignment:

> After reading Bloom and Postman, write an essay in which you agree or disagree with the position put forth by these professors. Consider your own experience with music and how it corresponds to or contradicts Bloom's and Postman's main points about the effects of popular music. Engage these men, and with your own powerful voice, converse with them.

Matthew J. Williams

Professor Kennedy

Composition 100

3 October 2000

Who Are They to Judge?

A Reaction to Two Pompous Academics

1

Title reflects writer's stand

Paper opener: quotation

Shakespeare writes in *The Merchant of Venice*, "The man that hath no music in himself, / Nor is not mov'd with concoured of sweet sounds, / Is fit for treasons, stratagems and spoils." Upon

Introduction of sources and authors

concluding Allan Bloom's essay "Music" and Neil Postman's essay "Engaging Students in the Great Conversation," I sat in total disheartenment. Both Bloom and Postman seem to have forgotten what music is all about—the expression of one's soul. So I opened up my desk drawer, picked out a Bob Marley tape, and stuck it in my Walkman. I then had a mild epiphany. I realized that these gentlemen's opinions were not only narrow-minded but also downright erroneous. Both men take an annoyingly pompous position and a highly irritating I-am-better-than-thou attitude. I, for one, have a liking for a wide range of music, from Gregorian chant to common

Thesis

hip-hop. I get the feeling that Bloom and Postman think that I should be canonized for liking the former and sent to hell for liking the latter. I find a lot about Bloom and Postman is wrong: their tone; their disapproval of the media (particularly television) and the educational system; their belief that the current generation no longer listens to classical music and thereby lacks culture, and their association of popular music with sex.

2

First point to which writer is reacting

Tone shows what a person thinks of himself or herself. Both Bloom and Postman take on an overly pompous elitist tone, which tells me that neither man cares about being open-minded. All

Williams 2

they care about is their own opinions on music. I tend to respect people more when they take a more reasonable, double-sided approach. Bloom and Postman deride modern music without offering positive remarks. Admittedly, Bloom makes one good point, saying, "The music of the new votaries...knows neither class nor nation" (132), a sentiment that is completely true. But he fails to realize that his (and many others') stuffy attitudes about classical music explain why modern rock took such a strong hold.

Both Bloom and Postman want to blame the media and the education system for the rise of popular music. They both believe that the television industry promotes only contemporary music and our education system fails to provide culture for us. For instance, Postman, speaking of classical composers, states, "Television tries to mute their voices and render their standards invisible" (2). But what would Christmas be without the National Broadcasting System's airing of "The Nutcracker Suite"? I have also seen such highly revered movies as *Amadeus*, depicting Mozart's life, on national television. Yet Bloom and Postman insinuate that all television is bad, and channels such as MTV are Lucifer himself. They are so opinionated that they fail to mention PBS, A&E, or the Discovery Channel. I think that both men were so busy writing their essays that they didn't carefully examine television programming.

Bloom and Postman claim that the education system fails to teach students "the products of classical art form" (Postman 3). Postman says that schools have only one type of concert: rock concerts. Apparently neither man has been to a high school chorus or band concert lately. Perhaps my upstate New York high

3

4

Second point to which writer is reacting

school was different from its counterparts across the nation in
teaching students the fine arts, though I doubt it. In chorus,
with approximately 150 members out of 400 high school students,
we sang pieces ranging from fugues of the Baroque period to a
medley of Simon and Garfunkel's greatest hits. In band we played
Handel's "Water Music" and a medley of Andrew Lloyd Webber's
compositions from *Phantom of the Opera.* A minimum of two years
of the fine arts, with a passing grade, was required for
graduation. We were exposed to a rich music history but also
taught that popular contemporary music is important too.

Third point
to which
writer is
reacting

Postman's tone makes me believe that he would agree with   5
Bloom's statement that "classical music is dead among the young"
(132). Both authors think that only a small number, if any,
young people in this generation listen to classical music.
Wrong. I was walking down the hall to a friend's room the other
day when I heard a Mozart symphony blaring behind his door. I
was a bit surprised, but I didn't have a heart attack. I enjoy
listening to and performing classical music, as well as popular
music, and the majority of my friends share this attitude.
Obviously, Bloom and Postman have never listened to musical
groups such as Enigma, whose use of Gregorian chant in their
upbeat music got me hooked on this medieval art form.

Bloom and Postman also complain that our society no longer   6
provides us with the culture we need. Their assumptions make
young readers like me feel like commoners, who are not classy
enough to fit the classical mold. Bloom and Postman seem to be
saying that we are reverting to barbarism, like the children in
Lord of the Flies, and that the world is going to hell because

we no longer diligently listen to Mozart or Bach. They are
overlooking the fact that society did not always embrace the
classical music they hold so dear.

Fourth point
to which
writer is
reacting

    Finally there is Postman's belief that rock music is just
setting the stage for sex and Bloom's statement that "young
people know that rock has the beat of sexual intercourse" (136).
When I listen to rock music, I do not have wet dreams. I listen
to music for the musicality and meaning of the particular
artist's soul, not because it is a turn-on. Was Fred Small
talking about sex when he wrote "The Peace Dragon"?

7

    Postman and Bloom don't like popular music, so they find
fault in it. Their numerous personal opinions fail to convince
me of their one-sided view that pop and rock music is bad. I
also get the feeling that neither man actually took the time to

Conclusion

examine rock music. It contains the same elements of meaning as
classical music, despite the different way it is performed.
Perhaps in two or three centuries, the music of today will be
played on public radio stations across the world, as fine pieces
of work. Won't that make Postman and Bloom blush.

8

Works Cited

Bloom, Allan. "Music." *Speculations: Readings in Culture,
    Identity, and Values.* Ed. Charles Schuster and William Van
    Pelt. Englewood Cliffs: Prentice, 1993. 131-43. Print.

Postman, Neil. "Engaging Students in the Great Conversation."
    Reading, Writing, and Thinking. Ed. Isabelle Bradley. New
    York: Houghton, 1978. 1-5. Print.

A response essay allows the writer to draw on personal knowledge and express personal views. In this sense, Matthew's essay is different from the summary of multiple sources on pages 256–257. The summary is entirely dependent on the sources, whereas the response essay includes the writer's own ideas about the topic. Matthew views popular music quite differently from Bloom and Postman and takes offense at their tone and a number of the claims they make in their articles: their disapproval of television and the educational system, their assertion that young people do not listen to classical music and thereby lack culture, and their association of popular music with sex.

Matthew opens his essay with a quotation from *The Merchant of Venice,* a lead that is sure to engage his readers. He then introduces the authors and sources and expresses his reaction. Toward the end of the introductory paragraph, he states his thesis. Next, he devotes a body paragraph to each of the points to which he is reacting: paragraph 2 to Bloom and Postman's tone, paragraph 3 to their condemnation of television and schools, paragraph 4 to their claim that young people do not listen to classical music, and paragraph 5 to their association of popular music with sex. Matthew concludes his essay with an interesting speculation.

To write a straightforward essay in response to multiple sources, use the following strategies.

STRATEGIES FOR WRITING A RESPONSE TO MULTIPLE SOURCES

- Read through all the sources to get a general impression of the content.
- Reread each source, looking for themes or characteristics it shares with the other sources.
- Once you have discovered some commonalities among the sources, express the relationships in a general statement.
- Generate your own reactions (use the strategies for elaborating on texts on pages 56–58).
- Zero in on a single controlling idea or thesis that will govern your essay.
- Study the controlling idea, the sources, and your elaborations, and decide how you will organize your essay: summary followed by response or a pattern of alternating summary and response (for a review of these patterns, see page 156).
- Draft the essay, drawing from your knowledge of the basic features of writing: titles, introductions, sentences, paragraphs, transitions, and so on (see pages 17–27).

When you have completed your essay, if your teacher agrees, ask a classmate or friend to read it over and give you some suggestions for revision. Your reviewer will find the following checklist helpful.

✓ *Checklist for Revising a Multiple-Source Response Essay*

_____   1. Does the writer begin with a title that reflects an overall reaction or stand?

_____   2. Does the essay open with a lead that will interest the reader?

_____   3. Does the writer provide the reader with some background information on the topic?

_____   4. Is there a controlling idea statement, thesis, or mention of the themes or ideas the sources have in common?

_____   5. Does the writer identify the authors and titles of the sources?

_____   6. Does the writer provide sufficient summary information about each source treated in the paper?

_____   7. When moving from one source to the next, does the writer provide transitions or connecting ideas that indicate the relationships between the sources?

_____   8. Does the writer provide an appropriate amount of response?

_____   9. Does the conclusion do more than simply summarize the main points of the paper?

_____   10. Does the writer include parenthetical documentation where it is necessary?

_____   11. Is there a works cited page?

Exercise 7.7

Write a short essay in which you compare Matthew Williams's response to Allan Bloom and Neil Postman to Diane Abramowitz's response to Joshua Quittner in Chapter 5, pages 141–145.

WRITING A SYNTHESIS FOR A SPECIFIC PURPOSE

A synthesis for a specific rhetorical purpose achieves a genuine blend of two sets of ideas: information from various reading sources and your own stored knowledge about the topic. Your aim is to draw from different sources the material you need to support your own thesis. Your objective is not simply to communicate information in the sources, as you would in a summary or an objective synthesis. Nor is it simply to present your general impression of or reaction to the sources. Your goal is to select from the sources information that you can use to develop and support your own thesis.

We use an essay by our student Charlie Fisher as an illustration. Charlie received an assignment that required him to write about the topic of the Internet's effect on human relationships by drawing on three or more sources. As you read Charlie's essay, observe how he uses the readings. Instead of devoting separate paragraphs to each source, he organizes the paragraphs around his own ideas and draws from the sources only the pieces of information that support the point he is trying to make. In each paragraph, he has a specific purpose, and he draws on the sources only insofar as they enable him to fulfill it.

Fisher 1

Charlie Fisher

Academic Writing I

Professor Smith

31 March 2008

The Internet and Relationships in the 21st Century

Title
indicates
writer's
focus

The use of the Internet for communication has become

ubiquitous in our society. It greatly simplifies long distance

communication, and it allows people to be more honest and

confident than they might be in a face-to-face conversation.

Writer's
position

The anonymity of the Internet can also help improve individuals'

sense of identity by allowing them to experiment with different

personality traits online and then apply the ones they feel

most comfortable with to off-line interactions. Of course,

Writer
acknowledges
other
opinions

it is possible to use the Internet to such an extent that it

interferes with one's life and relationships, but this is a

problem associated with all activities available to humans.

As is true in many other cases, one shouldn't indict the

large majority based on the actions of the small minority.

Probably the clearest advantage of the Internet is its

ability to connect people on opposite sides of the globe.

Before the advent of the Internet, the chances of starting a

relationship with someone in another country, state, or even

city were practically nonexistent. Common sense dictates, and

psychological studies have confirmed, that one of the leading

determiners of one's friends is their proximity (Kowalski and

Westen 655). Proximity breeds familiarity, familiarity breeds

affection, and affection often leads to the formation of

relationships, romantic or otherwise. However, with the

1

2

Fisher 2

Internet, people are now able to bypass this superficial

phenomenon. The world has been, as columnist Thomas Friedman

aptly puts it, "flattened." A man living in rural America need

no longer limit his field of social interaction to those within

walking distance. On a dating website, he can find a woman based

on something more meaningful than the fact that she lives across

the street. Without the restrictions of geography, more

important traits can now become the basis of relationships.

Not only does the Internet make it easier to meet people,

it also enhances the quality of relationships by allowing people

to be more honest and open. This is true for several reasons.

First, as Cornell University professor Joe Walther points out,

the anonymity of the Internet "frees...[users]...from worrying

about how they look and sound, so they can focus exclusively

on what they're saying" (qtd. in Biever). Though this may seem

somewhat impersonal, it is helpful for people who are too shy in

public to express themselves effectively when first meeting a

prospective friend or partner. The fact that they are not

actually face-to-face with the person they are talking to makes

them feel safer. If or when it comes time for the two to meet

outside of the virtual world, both parties will be much more

comfortable. Second, while they are communicating online,

neither party needs to know what the other looks like. Once

again, though this may at first sound like a negative aspect,

it is quite positive. With so much emphasis placed on physical

appearance, those who may not fit society's image of what is

handsome or beautiful are often overlooked. The Internet allows

people to ignore such superficial qualities and judge each other

Writer uses two sources to support his position

Writer provides support from source

3

Fisher 3

on personality alone. However trite it may sound, the Internet could very well lead to a world in which it is truly what's inside that counts.

Some people question the Internet's potential to improve communication and enhance human ties. They predict that it will lead to the eventual deterioration of human relationships. Anna Quindlen argues that it is creating a "faceless society" (Quindlen). By this, she means people are increasingly interacting with each other through their computers rather than in real life. Thus, faces are being replaced by computer screens. In her view, this is a problem because facial expressions play a vital role in understanding the true meaning of what is being said. By relying on email, instant messaging, and text messaging, people are unable to communicate effectively.

Yes, if people were cutting themselves off from the real world to such a degree that they had no other human interaction, there would be a serious problem. Using the Internet, or anything else, so much that it overwhelms all other activities is cause to worry. But is this really what is happening? A large number of people use the Internet to stay in contact with distant friends and relatives. Without it, they would have to resort to a telephone call or a letter, both of which are "faceless" tools for communication. In addition, the Internet has made face-to-face contact available where it was previously impossible. With cameras standard items on many new computers, online video messaging is now easier than ever and will surely increase in popularity in the future.

4

5

Writer incorporates opposing position from Quindlen

Writer concedes

Writer provides his own commentary

Fisher 4

Even if a personal relationship is exclusively online and "faceless," it has the potential to enhance one's face-to-face interactions. MIT professor Sherry Turkle recounts the story of a man named Case who, in addition to having an online persona similar to his own real personality, also had one in which he identified himself as a woman and acted more assertive than normal. Because his real personality was very passive, he would sometimes channel his online female persona when he needed to be more forceful (Turkle). Turkle writes, "He tells me that presenting himself as a woman online has brought him to a point where he is more comfortable with confrontation in his RL as a man." The fact that Case was able, through the Internet, to role-play the different parts of his personality has had a therapeutic effect on him. Though not all instances, of course, will involve changing genders online, the ability people have to reinvent themselves on the Internet and try out new personalities can have profound effects on their everyday lives.

Regardless of one's personal opinion, the trend toward online communication is inevitable. Whenever a drastic change such as the Internet is introduced, there will always be those who cry foul. However, in this case much of the criticism is unfounded, and even if it isn't, the great potential of the Internet to improve relationships far outweighs the negatives. As we progress through the 21st century, many of the perceived negatives of the Internet will be forgotten and will be replaced by enthusiasm about how much it has improved our lives.

Support from source

Conclusion makes a projection

6

7

Fisher 5

Works Cited

Biever, Celeste. "Modern Romance." *New Scientist* Apr.-May 2006:
    44-46. *ProQuest Research Library.* Web. 1 Mar. 2008.

Friedman, Thomas. *The World Is Flat: A Brief History of the
    Twenty-First Century.* New York: Farrar, 2005. Print.

Kowalski, Robin, and Drew Westen. *Psychology.* 4th ed. Hoboken:
    Wiley, 2005. Print.

Quindlen, Anna. "The Face in The Crowd" *Newsweek* 20 Mar 2006:
    80. *Proquest Research Library.* Web. 15 March 2008.

Turkle, Sherry. "Cyberspace and Identity." *Contemporary Sociology*
    28 (Nov. 1999): 643-48. Rpt. in *Reading and Writing in the
    Academic Community.* 3rd ed. Ed. Mary Lynch Kennedy and
    Hadley M. Smith. Upper Saddle River: Prentice Hall, 2006.
    461-68. Print.

We annotated portions of Charlie's paper to show you how he integrated his own ideas with paraphrases, quotations, and summaries of the various sources. Notice that he employs the sources to develop his own ideas. The essay is driven by Charlie's ideas, not the ideas presented in the sources.

Exercise 7.8

Compare Charlie's essay to Matthew Williams's essay, a typical response essay in which the writer's primary purpose is to react to ideas presented in the sources.

If you receive a loosely defined assignment like "Write about the Internet and human communication in an essay drawing on three or more outside sources," you will have to read the sources to obtain background information on the topic and identify its dimensions. You will have two goals for the initial reading: to bring your own ideas to bear on the topic by elaborating on and reacting to the material and to identify common elements in the sources.

To achieve the latter goal, read each source searching for the commonalities it shares with the other sources. As you take up each source, ask yourself the following questions.

QUESTIONS FOR IDENTIFYING RELATIONSHIPS AMONG SOURCES

- Does the source text give background information or additional information about points that are presented in other sources?
- Does it provide additional details about points made in other sources?
- Does it provide evidence for points made by another author?
- Are there places where this author contradicts or disagrees with the other authors you have read?
- Are there places where the author supports or agrees with other authors?
- Are there cause-and-effect relationships between this text and the other sources?
- Are there time relationships among the sources?
- Does this text contain elements that can be compared or contrasted with those in other sources?
- Are there other common threads running through this text and the other sources?
- Do the authors of the sources use similar key words or phrases?
- Are there any other ways you can categorize the ideas in the sources?

After you have elaborated on the sources and discovered their common elements, determine the points you wish to get across to your readers. Looking back at Charlie's introductory paragraph, we see that his goal is to explain how the Internet facilitates human communication. Charlie found ample material in the readings to support his position. Drawing on the sources, he accomplishes his goal by explaining how the Internet allows people to communicate across long distances, makes them feel more comfortable relating to others, enables them to focus on substance rather that appearance, and, possibly, gives them tools for improving face-to-face interactions. As Charlie was identifying relationships among the sources, he discovered that one of the authors, Anna Quindlen, disagreed with the others. He acknowledges and responds to Quindlen's criticism of Internet communication in paragraphs 4 and 5 of his essay.

After you have decided on a goal and sketched out your main points, the next step is to locate source information that you can use to develop each point you will make in your essay. This requires you to go back to the sources. Reread them, looking for bits of information that relate to your points. Mark this content in the text, or copy it into your notebook. When you have obtained a sufficient amount of relevant information, you can begin to draft your essay, but first decide whether you will paraphrase, quote, or summarize the supporting information. Here is a recap of the entire process.

STRATEGIES FOR WRITING A SYNTHESIS FOR A SPECIFIC PURPOSE

- Read all the sources to get a general impression of the content.
- Reread each source, elaborating on it by bringing your previous knowledge to bear on the text.
- Determine the elements each text has in common with the other sources by asking the questions for identifying relationships among sources (page 270).
- Decide what points of your own you want to get across to your readers.

- Locate in the sources information that you can use to develop each of your points.
- Draft your essay by quoting, paraphrasing, or summarizing relevant supporting information from the sources and by drawing on your knowledge of the basic features of writing: titles, introductions, sentences, paragraphs, transitions, and so on (see pages 17–27).

When you are satisfied with the draft of your essay, if it is all right with your teacher, ask a classmate or friend to give you suggestions for revision by using the following checklist.

✓ *Checklist for Revising a Synthesis Essay Written for a Specific Purpose*

_____   1. Does the title give you some indication of the writer's attitude toward the topic?

_____   2. Is there an interesting lead that attracts the reader's attention?

_____   3. Does the writer give you sufficient background information on the topic?

_____   4. Does the writer make his or her overall purpose clear to the reader?

_____   5. Can you identify the writer's thesis or expression of point of view?

_____   6. As you read each paragraph, are you aware of the purpose that the writer is trying to accomplish?

_____   7. In each paragraph, does the writer provide sufficient support from the sources?

_____   8. Does the writer include enough of his or her own commentary in each of the paragraphs?

_____   9. Does the conclusion do more than simply summarize the main points of the paper?

_____   10. Does the writer include parenthetical documentation where it is necessary?

_____   11. Is there a works cited page?

Exercise 7.9

This assignment asks you to read another synthesis essay on the topic of technology and human relationships. The essay was written by our student Andrea Siwek. Compare Andrea's synthesis, "Communication Technology's Effect on Interpersonal Relationships," to Charlie Fisher's essay. Comment on each writer's lead; rhetorical purpose; thesis; use of source information to develop each of the points; inclusion of paraphrases, summaries, and quotations; and conclusion.

Andrea Siwek

Professor Smith

Composition 101

1 April 2008

Communication Technology's Effect on Interpersonal Relationships

It is projected that the number of Internet users worldwide
will reach an impressive two billion in 2011 ("Worldwide
Internet Users"). The Internet has capabilities that were once
inconceivable. Information of any kind is now only one click
away, people can communicate instantly despite being separated
by hundreds of miles, and products and services can be ordered
without having to leave the comfort of one's home. Technological
advancements have, in these ways, positively affected quality of
life. In addition, as Jeffrey McQuillen notes, "[T]he increased
ease and time saved afford people the opportunity to become less
interdependent and more autonomous and self-reliant" (McQuillen).
But is this autonomy and independence a good thing? Anna Quindlen
expresses concern about the loss of interdependence:

> The greatest challenge of this century is going to be to
> avoid becoming a faceless society, with all that suggests and
> portends. The change in the way modern human beings know one
> another, and the world, has happened so incrementally and yet
> so quickly that it's almost impossible to assess its ultimate
> psychological cost. Only four decades ago, half a lifetime,
> daily life was different in so many conventions of
> communication. A phone was anchored to the wall, an instant
> message was a hand-delivered greeting card and a blind date
> took place in a restaurant. (Quindlen)

1

I, too, am concerned because even though our society is continually aided by technological advancements, such as the Internet, there are negative social implications in the form of impersonal, dangerous, and socially flawed interpersonal relationships.

The term "computer-mediated communication," also known as CMC, is often used to describe such activities as e-mailing and instant messaging, as well as using chat rooms, message boards, and multi-user domains. These forums enable people to initiate and build relationships without having to meet in the real world (McQuillen). Celeste Biever sees the Internet as a venue for people to experiment with dating in a cheap and safe way. Through online dating services, social networking sites, games, and chat rooms, they can meet far more people than ever before. Pataraporn Jaruhirunsakul cites a study by Lea and Spears (1995) that "has proved that CMC 'increases the field of available' people to meet others, allowing people to overcome the limits of physical proximity" (Jaruhirunsakul). Online, relationships can grow effectively without the constraints of time and space. Writing in 2007, Kaitlyn Starks points out, "Last year, Americans spent upwards of $500 million on online personal ads, and it is predicted that this figure will jump to over $600 million by 2009" (Starks). It is easy for Internet users to find others with shared interests and eventually they may build relationships that may lead to successful matches.

Though online communication has made it possible to find people of shared interest without space and time constraints, it calls for a very different connection than face-to-face interaction. According to McQuillen, there are three key differences between computer-mediated communication and face-to-face communication. The first one is called idealized perception. This speaks to the limited information one can obtain through CMC. Because information is selective, participants may not observe negative attributes, but rather, view whom they are talking to as "the perfect person." The second negative feature of CMC is called elective self-perception or preferred self-presentation. As McQuillen puts it, "One's ability to conceal some aspect (e.g., negative) of self and accentuate others (e.g., positive) is actually enhanced by CMC because of the lack of nonverbal information. The receiver has no (or very limited) information available to test, validate, discredit, or refine the information presented by the sender" (McQuillen). This "preferred self-presentation" can be taken to the extreme when people tell outright lies online and pose as someone else. I think this makes online relationships more dangerous than conventional ones. Even if participants are not being outright deceitful, they are still much less inhibited than if they were in person, so in either case one's identity can be altered through CMC. The final and most evident negative aspect of CMC is the lack of non-verbal cues. Non-verbal cues can be anything from facial expressions to hand gestures to paralanguage. These cues give people a clearer meaning of a given message. Lack of verbal cues can lead to miscommunication. Quindlen brings up an interesting point relating to non-verbal cues, which are unique to face-to-face communication. She cites a story everyone can relate to of a school-aged child being bullied on a playground. It is harder

Siwek 4

for a bully to continue abuse after he witnesses his victim's "wounded eyes" (Quindlen). However, those same expressions cannot be seen behind a computer screen, again making online relationships dangerous.

It's true that computer-mediated communication is important for those who have difficulty with face-to-face communication. As Jaruhirunsakul notes, "McKenna and colleagues (2002) have discovered that people who can better disclose their 'true' or inner self to others on the Internet than in face-to-face settings will be more likely to form close relationships online and will tend to bring those virtual relationships into their 'real' lives" (Jaruhirunsakul). Still, as a society we must be careful not to lose sight of the importance of face-to-face communication skills. Face-to-face communication and relationship building are not easy to develop but they are important and rewarding in the end. It has also been found that "the spontaneous and simultaneous requirements of [face-to-face]...communication place greater demands on cognitive resources" (McQuillen). With correspondence that occurs over the Internet, it is possible to take time to contemplate and refine one's responses. People are no longer required to think on their feet and maintain the ability to respond quickly and efficiently in a conversational setting. Conversational skills are important and they should not be lost by the younger generations.

The Internet, despite its many positive attributes, may have negative consequences for interpersonal relationships. Quindlen puts it eloquently: "The paradox is that all this

4

5

nominal communication has led to enormous isolation, with people hunched over their handhelds or staring into the screen of the computer. There is the illusion of keeping in touch, but always at arm's length." The social consequences of using computer-mediated communication are just beginning to take shape and they may be potentially very detrimental.

Works Cited

Biever, Celeste. "Modern Romance." *New Scientist* Apr.-May 2006: 44-46. *ProQuest Research Library*. Web. 1 Mar. 2008.

Jaruhirunsakul, Pataraporn. "The Study of Love Happens in Computer-Mediated Communication Research." Proc. of Public Policy Development Office, Conf. on Happiness and Public Policy, July, 2007, Bangkok. Web. 17 Mar. 2008.

McQuillen, Jeffrey. "The Influences of Technology on the Initiation of Interpersonal Relationships." *Education* 123.3 (Spring 2003): 616-24. *Communication & Mass Media Complete*. Web. 16 Mar. 2008.

Quindlen, Anna. "The Face in The Crowd" *Newsweek* 20 Mar 2006: 80. *Proquest Research Library*. Web. 15 March 2008.

Starks, Kaitlyn M. "Bye Bye Love: Computer-Mediated Communication and Relational Dissolution." *Texas Speech Communication Journal* 32.1 (Summer 2007): 11-20. *Communication & Mass Media Complete*. Web. 15 Mar. 2008.

"Worldwide Internet Users Top 1.2 B in 2006." *Computer Industry Almanac*. Web. 31 Mar. 2008.

CHAPTER 8

Arguing from Sources

Think about the last time you had an argument.

> With whom were you arguing?
> What was the quarrel about?
> What was your position?
> What was the other person's point of view?
> Did you come to any type of resolution?

Take a few minutes to answer these questions in your journal. After you have finished, compare your experiences with those of your classmates. You will discover one essential similarity: all the arguments involved a disagreement, a division of opinion, or a dispute.

When academic writers "argue," they never pick a fight or hurl accusations at each other. To argue in academic writing means to sort out, investigate, and express an attitude or opinion on a certain topic. In this broad sense, every college paper that expresses a thesis is an argument because the writer's goal is to get the reader to accept his or her perspective, position, or point of view. Even if you are summarizing material or presenting an objective synthesis or comparison and contrast, you are hoping that your reader will accept *your* version of the given information. In most college papers, your intent is to influence your reader in a more direct way. Take the types of academic writing we have discussed in this book: the response essay, in which you explain how you agree or disagree with an author; the analysis and evaluation essay in which you interpret and evaluate a text; the comparison essay, in which you show the similarities or differences between two sets of views; and the synthesis essay, in which you draw on different source materials to support your thesis. Each essay entails an argument of some sort because you are attempting to demonstrate or prove the validity of your view. Writers also use the word *argument* in a more specialized sense, which is in keeping with historical rhetorical tradition.

The term *rhetoric* has a number of different connotations. In everyday conversation, it often means pretentious, empty, or inflated language. In this book, we use *rhetoric* broadly to mean a writer's use of language to achieve an intended effect on an audience. In this chapter, we focus on a particular intended effect: to *persuade* or *convince* your readers of your position. Many of the principles and strategies we discuss are the same ones that ancient rhetoricians used to argue cases, resolve conflicts, and move people to action.

If you were a student living in ancient Greece more than two thousand years ago, instead of taking general education courses, electives, and courses in your major, you would have devoted all your time to rhetoric, a subject that would have prepared you to present eloquent, persuasive arguments. Unlike the academic subjects with which you are familiar, rhetoric is not a content area that deals with a defined body of knowledge. It is a discipline that studies how people consciously and intentionally use written and oral verbal expression to affect an audience. Today, rhetoric examines a wide range of objectives—to inform, motivate, entertain, persuade—but in ancient times, its focus was the strategies and resources needed to convince an audience.

In ancient Greece, knowledge of rhetoric was especially valuable for a young man entering the Greek political assembly, where, because there were no lawyers, each man had to present his own case (women did not participate in the political process, nor did they attend school). A knowledge of rhetoric also enabled young men to become advocates for others, judicial orators, or professional speech writers. Skill in this type of persuasive argument is not as crucial today as it was two millennia ago; nonetheless, the ability to present a clear, logical, compelling defense of your position is important for most college courses.

We differentiate between argument in a broad sense and argument in a narrow, more specialized sense. Sometimes these arguments are called one-sided and two-sided arguments. For both types of argument, your goal is to convince your readers of your perspective, position, or point of view. The specialized, two-sided argument also acknowledges and refutes alternative positions. To illustrate, read the following pair of thesis statements. They are from essays in which the writer discusses the difficulty Asian American students encounter when they try to get parental support for participation in sports.

Thesis A: Argument in the Broad Sense

Asian American parents' value orientation and cultural conditioning predispose them to support their children's academic pursuits but not their participation in sports.

Thesis B: Argument in the Specialized Sense

It is not insensitivity, lack of interest, or ignorance of American sports that predispose Asian American parents to support their children's academic pursuits rather than their participation in sports; it is the parents' value orientation and cultural conditioning.

Both writers claim that two factors account for the parents' reluctance to support sports: the parents' value orientation and their cultural conditioning. Right in the thesis statement, Writer B acknowledges that other explanations exist. It could be that the parents are insensitive to children's needs, or uninterested and uninformed about sports programs. Later, in the body of the essay, Writer B will persuade her readers that her explanations—that value orientation and cultural conditioning account for the parents' lack of support—are more convincing than the other interpretations.

Writer A's objective is to inform her readers about a particular phenomenon and offer explanations for it. Her purpose is not argumentative. She does not set out to persuade readers that one set of explanations is superior to another. Writer A's thesis is not necessarily debatable. She will develop it by offering reasons why the parents encourage their children to pursue academics rather than sports, but she will not argue that the reasons she offers are more valid than explanations offered by others. For Writer B, the topic has become an arguable issue. Writer B has taken it to another level. Now it involves a debate: Which reasons have more explanatory power, the parents' value orientation and cultural conditioning or their insensitivity, lack of interest, and ignorance of American sports? Writer B's purpose is to argue for one set of reasons over another.

ARGUMENT IN THE BROAD SENSE

- Your thesis is not necessarily issue-centered, arguable, or debatable.
- You do not acknowledge explicitly your audience's (conflicting) view.
- Your purpose is usually to explain or present your position. You are not intent on persuading your readers.

ARGUMENT IN THE SPECIALIZED SENSE

- Your thesis is issue-centered, arguable, and debatable.
- You anticipate and acknowledge conflicting views.
- Your purpose is to convince your readers to accept and agree with your position.

The word *argue* derives from a Greek word related to *argent,* "silver or white," denoting brilliance or clarity (which explains why Ag is the chemical abbreviation for silver). From this same word came the name of Argos, the mythological demigod with a hundred eyes. The word implies that a speaker or writer has seized upon an idea, clarified its point, and made its meaning strikingly visible. The goal of the writer of persuasive arguments is to move audiences to thought or action through the clarity of his or her reasoning process.

In this chapter, we will focus on the specialized, two-sided argument. To develop such an argument, you must impart breadth and depth to its focus and make it two-dimensional. Such an argument does not hammer away at one central idea until it exhausts all available evidence and concludes by restating the original proposition:

> The nuclear family consisting of a mother, father, and children is the most appropriate structure for contemporary society.... Thus we see that the nuclear family is the most appropriate structure for modern society.

Instead, it pursues a rounder, perhaps more oblique path if it recognizes its own limitations. It explicitly acknowledges competing hypotheses, alternative explanations, and even outright contradictions:

> The nuclear family consisting of a mother, father, and children is the most appropriate structure for contemporary society, even though it does not serve the needs of every family.

The value of this approach is that it avoids the "tunnel vision" of repeating one and only one proposition. It implies that you have explored competing hypotheses and have weighed the evidence for and against each. Your readers may or may not agree with your conclusion, but they will certainly respect your effort to set it in a broader context.

Exercise 8.1

To develop full, rich, round arguments requires some practice. You can often get this practice by playing with controversial ideas in a creative and free-spirited way. Take an idea, any idea, no matter how preposterous or absurd—for example, "homelessness is a desirable way of life," "the government should allow all immigrants to enter this country," "drugs should be freely available to anyone who wants them," "communities should have the right to prohibit stores from selling pornographic magazines," "public schools should enforce strict dress codes." First, state the idea in your own words. Next, articulate the opposition. Then brainstorm for possible reasons to explain the first idea. After that, brainstorm for possible reasons to explain the second idea. Decide which reasons are most convincing for each position. Rank them in order of strength or importance. Decide which position is most convincing. State that position as the main clause of a sentence. Recast the other position as a subordinate clause linked to the main clause by *because, although, despite,* or some other connective. Finally, try to express the relationship between both clauses: What is the link that brings them together?

THE ARGUMENT ESSAY

Before proceeding further, we would like you to look at an argument essay written by a college student, examine its features, and familiarize yourself with this particular type of writing. Later in the chapter, we discuss the characteristics of an argument essay in more detail. Fiana Muhlberger was asked to write an argumentative essay on one of the topics covered in the anthology section of this textbook. Her audience was to be students in her composition class as well as her instructor. She selected Grades and Learning, the topic of Chapter 10. As you read the essay, take note of the impact Fiana has on you as a reader, and jot down your responses. Does she convince you of her position on the issue? Why or why not? Which features of the essay account for its impact?

Muhlberger 1

Fiana Muhlberger

Professor Smith

Academic Writing II

25 September 2008

Disassemble the Hoops

The lead compares grades to a jail cell

Grades are nothing more than a jail cell for students'

ambition and a cage for students' drive to learn. Students are

1

---

taught at an early age that grades give them value, worth, and status. A's will get you rewards, honors programs, scholarships, and the title of "straight A student." C's mean you're average, nothing special. F's mean you're out of luck: low achieving students are likely to be overlooked in the classroom, skipped over to answer questions, praised for wrong answers, and given

Uses source to support position

little to no help even though they need it the most (Woolfolk 500). Grades move students to do the bare minimum to receive an A. Once they receive the grade, course content ceases to be important and is more often than not completely forgotten. So what have they actually learned? If anything, it is that education is about grades, not a love of learning nor a desire to

Writer's central claim acknowledges opposing view

acquire knowledge. Despite the fact that teachers will argue that they need grades to motivate, discipline, and evaluate students, the current grading system must be weeded out from our classrooms and replaced with a new method of evaluation that will encourage active and long term student learning.

Why do professors give A, B, C, D, and F grades? According to Barbara Gross Davis in her book, *Tools for Teaching,* grades reveal how much students are learning. They are also valuable because they stimulate and motivate students, show them the

Gives background

worth of the work they have done, help them to identify high quality work as compared to unsatisfactory work, make them eligible to receive awards and honors, and communicate their teachers' estimation of their progress (282). Because teachers place such a high value on evaluation, grades are an integral part of the educational system. Colleges did not always use A, B, C, D, and F grading. Mark Durm explains that throughout the

2

nineteenth century, many colleges used descriptive adjectives to evaluate students. It wasn't until 1897 that Mount Holyoke created the letter grade system that is still used today (1-3).

Conciliatory expression

Granted, grades are meant to evaluate students' work and understanding of subject material, but what is the real distinction between an A and an A-, and an A- and a B+? It's indefinable. Does assigning such trivial insignia to the quality of a student's work really measure how much the student has learned? These letters have meaning only because we have attached so much significance to them. A's are worth thousands of dollars in scholarships, acceptance to college and graduate programs, coveted internships, and prestigious jobs. Professor of philosophy Stephen Vogel puts it well: "Grades are money, a currency around which everything revolves." The pressures grades put on students are abundant. It is no wonder that when Cornell University decided to post course listings with median grade averages for the class, the students began to pick gut courses "to pump their GPA's" (Douthat, Ross, Henry, and Poe). This isn't a surprise, because our current educational system demands high GPA's of its students in order for them to achieve a bright future. A statement that psychologist Isidor Finkelstein made in 1913 is still true today: "The evidence is clear that marks constitute a very real and a very strong inducement to work, that they are accepted as real and fairly exact measurements of ability or of performance. Moreover, they not infrequently are determiners of a student's career" (qtd. in Durm 1).

Acknowledges opposing view and refutes it

Conciliatory expression

The claim that the grading system motivates students to better themselves by striving for higher grades has some merit.

3

4

Muhlberger 4

It may be true that students are motivated, but most students find themselves obsessing over the letter on their report card or transcript, rather than focusing on what they actually learn and can take away from the class. In an article in *The Chronicle of Higher Education*, James Lang describes the first time grades "motivated him": "I was so incensed about the grades that I disengaged from that course completely. I was a trained seal jumping through hoops.... But I learned nothing. I remember nothing from the course. In fact, I don't even remember what the course was about." Being obsessed with letter grades often causes students to work just hard enough to boost their GPAs. It doesn't matter if they will not remember any of the material after the course is completed and the final is over. Lang, who is now a professor of English, cites another case of using grades as a motivation, this time in his own classroom. He gave a student a D in hopes that she would start trying harder in his class but the experiment failed and the grade "discouraged the student and caused her to further disengage from the class" by being absent the next class and never attempting to get help for the next assignment as Professor Lang suggested. Grades may increase motivation, but, unfortunately, this is motivation for the wrong reasons.

Professors should motivate students to learn, not motivate them to become "trained seals," as Lang suggests, doing just what's required of them to get an A and never fully engaging with their own learning. Research has shown that the type of motivation students want is motivation to learn. In 2000, Howard Pollio and Hall Beck conducted a study that assessed college

Acknowledgment and rebuttal

Additional support for writer's position

5

students' and instructors' views on grades. They distinguished between those who were learning-oriented and those who were grade-oriented. In the conclusion to the study, they write: "Most students wanted to be more learning and less grade oriented in their personal orientation and for their instructors to afford greater emphasis to learning orientation in teaching their classes." Pollio and Beck go on to say, "Most instructors believed that a strict orientation toward grades yields an undesirable learning environment; despite this, they rely on grades to promote the learning of course material." This is a contradiction. Instructors need to create a favorable learning environment in which students can enrich their minds. Grades will not do this. As English professor Jerry Farber points out, "Grades don't make us want to enrich our minds, they make us want to please our teachers" (441). Instructors should act on their convictions and stop requiring their students to jump through Lang's proverbial hoops.

6

Acknow-
ledges
opposition

Proponents of grades will argue that they are necessary for self-discipline. My English professor gives daily quiz grades in order to ensure that we have done the assigned reading. But is this instilling self-discipline? Farber notes that true self-discipline "is nothing more than a certain way of pleasing yourself" (442), a true desire to make yourself better like revising the same paragraph a thousand times until you're happy with it, by learning the science of cooking because you enjoy it, or by learning how to drive because you want to do it. When

Gives
rebuttal

I was younger, I spent countless hours practicing gymnastics routines until I had perfected them. I did this because I wanted

to excel at gymnastics. I think I would have been less motivated
if I was receiving A, B, and C grades for my routines. As Farber
says, "Learning, actual learning, happens when you want to know"
(441) and the self-discipline needed to do so "is the last thing
anyone is likely to learn for a grade" (442).

When looked at closely, grades actually fail to motivate
or teach self-discipline. If grades teach students anything, it
is a dislike of learning. Students are forced to write, speak,
calculate, evaluate, scientifically prove, and/or mathematically
prove some kind of objective by a certain due date to be marked
with a grade that will seemingly affect their future. No wonder
students hate learning. There's so much pressure on that one
little letter.

Grades fail to motivate and discipline students properly,
but what's worse is they completely fall short of their most
important objective: indicating the degree to which students
have learned what they need for success in later life. Vogel
points out that many colleges have an average grade of an A-.
Yet most "employers and professors deem many students' academic
preparation as lacking ... saying they're unprepared for the real
challenges they are now facing in college and the work world"
("Students Want"). Similarly, McMurtrie, writing in *The
Chronicle of Higher Education*, reports, "The traditional measure
of grades doesn't seem to satisfy employers, lawmakers, or the
public anymore." The reason college and high school graduates
are "deemed unprepared and unsatisfactory" is because grades
have condemned our students to the fate of hoop-jumping seals,
studying only what will be on the test and trying to beat the

7

8

Recap of
argument

Additional
support for
position

Muhlberger 7

system, when they should and need to be active learners engaging their minds in order to better themselves, their community, and our society.

The current grading system needs a complete overhaul. However, it is irrational to suggest that we immediately abolish grades in all colleges, high schools, middle schools, and elementary schools. Students are already conditioned to and invested in our current grading system. Change needs to begin in elementary schools. The primary grades are crucial years when students will either fall in love with learning or just work for the A so mom can put a "Proud Parent of an Honor Student" sticker on her bumper. If grades are abolished at this level, we can weed them out at every subsequent grade level as these first classes advance through the system. Once the first class makes it through the educational system, grades wouldn't be a necessary constraint on students and actual learning will take place.

How should students be evaluated under the new system? There are many different ways this could be accomplished. Students could create portfolios of work: essays, papers, science labs, math projects and problems saved throughout the year that demonstrate they have learned the objectives their teachers required of them. Students could give presentations portraying what they have learned to a panel of educators that would allow for advancement into the next grade. Students could have interviews with a teacher during which the student has to demonstrate an understanding of the course work in order to carry on the conversation.

9

10

Offers plan for action

Gives alternative

Muhlberger 8

None of the alternative methods of assessment need to be linked to letter grades. Teachers could use narrative evaluations to report on students' progress. They could also use descriptions such as Satisfactory, Unsatisfactory, and Incomplete. Some colleges and universities already do this. Faculty at prestigious law schools, for example, Yale and Berkeley, have replaced letter grades with broad categories. Yale uses Honors, Pass, Low Pass, and Fail. Recently Stanford Law abolished grades. Those who advocated the change at Stanford argued that "shifting from the precision of letter grades to broader categories will reduce some pressure and refocus students' and professors' energies on classroom learning" (Guess).

Professors of the Ithaca College Sports Psychology courses do not believe in giving letter grades. Their methods of evaluation include some of the elements listed above but also journals that the students keep to log what they have learned. More importantly, students grade the journals themselves. Skeptics might ask, "Don't all the students just give themselves A's?" Not necessarily. The students enrolled in these classes have to justify the grade they're giving themselves by citing their own work in the class and proving that they know the material. Students have a tendency to be honest when they're forced to confront how much they have actually engaged in a course.

Grade reform needs to become a priority. Much can be done to change the current grading system. There are even more possibilities than I have described. The major goal of all teachers should be to allow students the opportunity to focus on genuine learning instead of on "making the grade." To do so, teachers everywhere need to disassemble the hoops.

Alternative

Alternative

Exhortation to readers

11

12

13

Muhlberger 9

Works Cited

"Students Want to be Challenged." *American Teacher* April 2005:

5. *Proquest Reseach Library.* Web. 14 Sept. 2008.

Douthat, Ross, Terrence Henry, and Marshall Poe. "Gut Check."

The Atlantic Monthly June 2005: 44. *General One File.* Web.

15 Sept. 2008.

Davis, Barbara Gross. *Tools for Teaching.* San Francisco: Jossey,

1993. Print.

Durm, Mark W. "An A Is Not an A Is Not an A: A History of

Grading." *The Educational Forum* 57 (1993): 1-4. Web. 16

Sept. 2008. <http://www.indiana.edu/~educy520/

sec6342/week_07/durm93.pdf>.

Farber, Jerry. "A Young Person's Guide to the Grading System."

The Student as Nigger. New York: Pocket, 1970. 67-72. Rpt.

in *Reading and Writing in the Academic Community.* 3rd ed.

Ed. Mary Lynch Kennedy and Hadley M. Smith. Upper Saddle

River: Prentice Hall, 2006. 441-44. Print.

Guess, Andy. "Stanford Law Drops Letter Grades." *Inside Higher

Ed* 2 June 2008. Web. 14 Sept. 2008.

Lang, James M. "Failing to Motivate." *The Chronicle of Higher

Education,* 3 Dec. 2004: C2. *Proquest Research Library.* Web.

14 Sept. 2008.

McCurtie, Beth. "Colleges Urged to Find Ways to Gauge Learning."

The Chronicle of Higher Education 2 Feb. 2001: A29.

Proquest Research Library. Web. 14 Sept. 2008.

Pollio, Howard R., and Hall P. Beck. "When the Tail Wags the

Dog." *The Journal of Higher Education* 71.1 (Jan/Feb 2000):

84-103. *Proquest Research Library.* Web. 14 Sept. 2007.

Muhlberger 10

Vogel, Stephen. "Grades and Money." *Dissent* 44.4 (Fall 1997).

    Rpt. in *Reading and Writing in the Academic Community*.

    3rd ed. Ed. Mary Lynch Kennedy and Hadley M. Smith. Upper

    Saddle River: Prentice Hall, 2006. 445-48. Print.

Woolfolk, Anita. *Education Psychology*. New York: Pearson, 2007.

    Print.

Exercise 8.2

After reading Fiana Muhlberger's essay, break into small groups, and select a recorder and a reporter. Each member reads to the group his or her answers to the following questions: Does the writer convince you of her position on the issue? Why or why not? Which features of the essay account for its impact? Come up with a group response, and report it to the rest of the class.

Fiana opens the paper with a lead—a metaphor comparing grades to a jail and a cage—to capture the reader's attention. She then uses information from a psychology text to describe how letter grades pigeonhole students. She argues that the grading system may motivate students to get high marks, but this comes at a cost. There is no genuine love of learning because students are preoccupied with grades. Fiana contends that learning will take precedence over grades if the current grading system is abolished and an improved method of evaluation is put in its place. This is Fiana's *central assertion* or *claim*. She knows that her claim will occasion a challenge from others. Many educators will oppose her recommendation on the grounds that grades are needed to motivate, discipline, and evaluate students. Notice that Fiana's thesis is issue-centered, arguable, and debatable, and it acknowledges the opposing view.

> Despite the fact that teachers will argue that they need grades to motivate, discipline, and evaluate students, the current grading system must be weeded out from our classrooms and replaced with a new method of evaluation that will encourage active and long term student learning.

In paragraph 2, Fiana gives her readers background information. She discusses why teachers give grades and she gives a few historical facts about letter grading. In paragraphs 3 and 4, Fiana acknowledges the views of those who defend grading and reveals the holes in their arguments. She opens both of these paragraphs with conciliatory expressions in which she admits that there is some merit to her opponents' views, and then she goes on to expose the weakness of their positions. This is called is called a *refutation* or *rebuttal*.

Paragraph 3 Opposing View

Grades are meant to evaluate students' work and understanding of subject material.

Response to Opposition

These letters have meaning only because we have attached so much significance to them. A's are worth thousands of dollars in scholarships, acceptance to college and graduate programs, coveted internships, and prestigious jobs.

Paragraph 4 Opposing View

The grading system motivates students to better themselves by striving for higher grades.

Response to Opposition

Most students find themselves obsessing over the letter on their report card or transcript rather than focusing on what they actually learn and can take away from the class.

In paragraph 5, Fiana offers additional reasons why the current grading system fails to motivate students to learn. In paragraph 6, she continues to address readers who would find her position unacceptable, acknowledging their positions and explaining why their arguments are ineffective.

Reasons for the Opposing Position

Proponents of grades will argue that they are necessary for self-discipline.

In paragraph 7, Fiana pauses to recap her argument. Then in paragraph 8 she offers additional support for her position.

Grades fail to motivate and discipline students properly, but what's worse is they completely fall short of their most important objective: indicating the degree to which students have learned what they need for success in later life.

In paragraphs 9–12, Fiana lays out a plan of action for overhauling the grading system. In paragraph 9, she cautions that change has to be gradual and incremental, and in paragraphs 10, 11, and 12 she describes alternate methods of evaluating students and reporting on their progress.

Fiana's concluding strategy is to exhort teachers to reform the grading system. Notice that her tone is urgent. Keep in mind that in the conclusion of an argument essay, in addition to recapping your argument, you can use any of the techniques described in Chapter 1—stressing the significance of your thesis, predicting consequences, or calling your readers to action. You can also use the devices for paper openers (see page 23).

All written arguments have basically the same components as Fiana's essay.

COMPONENTS OF ARGUMENT ESSAYS

- Introductory section containing a lead, definition of the issue or problem, and thesis statement
- Section of background information
- Section containing reasons and evidence to support the thesis statement
- Section mentioning opposing views and providing a rebuttal
- Conclusion

FIND AN ISSUE AND STAKE OUT YOUR POSITION

An argument must treat an issue, problem, or question that evokes debate. It begins with a controversial topic and then focuses on aspects of the topic that are open to question. If it begins with the topic of abortion, it might zero in on the issue of whether or not women should have free choice in the matter of abortion. The topic and issue must be genuinely debatable. They cannot be based on subjective opinions, personal preferences, or beliefs on which everyone agrees. Nor should they involve disagreements that are of no practical importance or are not open to legitimate debate. Whether baseball is a better sport than football would not be a suitable topic for an argument essay because sports is a matter of personal preference. Whether or not air pollution is hazardous to health is unacceptable because no one would argue otherwise. Your topic and issue should be arguable and worth arguing about.

In some courses, your professors will stipulate the issues they want you to discuss. For example, in a course on public health and welfare, you might be asked to give your views on whether the government should legalize the use of marijuana for medical purposes. In other courses, your professors will allow you to select your own topics. If this is the case, you must convert the topic into an arguable statement or issue. One way to do this is to ask, What is currently controversial? What do people argue about? Take genetic engineering. If you know something about the topic, you may be aware that although some forms of genetic engineering are beneficial, the prospect of genetically engineering humans is quite scary. If you know very little about the topic, you will have to read up on it to find where the major controversies lie. Once you have discovered the controversial aspects of your topic, convert this information into an issue: whether scientists should use genetic engineering procedures on humans. If you prefer, state your issue as a question: Should scientists use genetic engineering procedures on humans?

Topic: Genetic engineering

Issue: Whether scientists should use genetic engineering procedures on humans

CONVERT A TOPIC INTO A DEBATABLE QUESTION OR ISSUE

1. Identify a suitable topic.
2. Ask, "What is controversial about the topic? What do people argue about?"
3. Convert the controversial aspects of the topic into an arguable question or issue.
4. Double-check that the topic and issue are genuinely debatable and worth arguing about.

Once you have identified an issue, you need to read extensively to learn as much as you can about its complexities. Investigate its history, the context in which it is couched, and the arguments on both sides of the controversy.

As you read, keep in mind that you may have scratched only the surface of the conflict. You may find so much information on your issue that you will have to do a considerable amount of redefining and narrowing.

Be sure to probe both sides of the issue and read with an open mind (even if you have already taken a stand). A useful exercise at this point is what Peter Elbow calls the "believing game." As you encounter various views on the issue, try to see them through the holder's eyes. Even if someone's views are absurd or directly opposite yours, put yourself in that person's place. As Elbow points out, "To do this requires great energy, attention, and even a kind of inner commitment. It helps to think of it as trying to get inside the head of someone who saw things this way—perhaps even constructing such a person for yourself. Try to have the experience of someone who made the assertion" (149).

FORMULATE A MAJOR CLAIM

After you have examined the issue and the reasons why people on both sides of the debate hold particular views on it, you are ready to take a position. In argument essays, your major position is called your *major claim*. A *claim* is an assertion that can be disputed by others.

Major Claim

The government should impose strict guidelines on the genetic engineering of humans because it meddles with evolution.

The above claim argues that the government should take a particular course of action: it should impose strict guidelines on the genetic engineering of humans. Let us look at other claims that one could make regarding the issue of human genetic engineering. Five common types of claims are (1) claims of cause, (2) claims of value, (3) claims of fact, (4) claims of definition, and (5) claims of policy or action.

Claim of cause

The genetic engineering of humans will result in a great divide between the biologically endowed rich who can afford the process and the unenhanced poor who do not have the means to do so.

Claim of value

Any attempt of scientists to improve humans genetically and take evolution into their own hands is a fundamental threat to the human species.

Claim of fact

> Within the next ten years, scientists will have the capability of manipulating human genes.

Claim of definition

> Before we continue the debate over human genetic engineering, we need to make a distinction between reproductive cloning and therapeutic cloning.

Claim of policy or action

> Governments must enact laws that will protect people against genetic discrimination.

Exercise 8.3

Select one of the following topics, convert it into an arguable issue, and express your position in terms of each of the five types of claims.

Global warming
Affirmative action
Censorship of the Internet
Public smoking
Nuclear energy
Gun control
Performance-enhancing steroids
Teenage pregnancy
Preservation of wildlife

DEVELOP YOUR THESIS

A thesis statement may express more than one type of claim. Consider the following thesis which combines a claim of policy or action—the government should impose strict guidelines on the genetic engineering of humans—with a claim of value—genetic engineering meddles with evolution:

```
The government should impose strict guidelines on the genetic
engineering of humans because it meddles with evolution.
```

Thesis statements in argumentative essays may also include the major claims of people on the other side of the controversy. Let's say the opposition's major claim is a claim of cause: that genetic engineering will improve the human species and prevent its extinction. A full blown thesis that states the writer's claim(s) as well as the claim(s) of those on the other side of the debate might be phrased as follows:

```
Although scientists claim that genetic engineering will improve
the human race and prevent its extinction, the government should
impose strict guidelines because it will meddle with evolution.
```

You have three options. You may express the thesis of an argumentative essay:

As a statement of a major claim

> The government should impose strict guidelines on the genetic engineering of humans.

As a statement that expresses more than one type of claim

> The government should impose strict guidelines on the genetic engineering of humans because it meddles with evolution.

As a statement that expresses the major claims of those on the other side of the debate as well the major claims of the writer

> Although scientists claim that genetic engineering will improve the human race and prevent its extinction, the government should impose strict guidelines because it will meddle with evolution.

Regardless of the option you choose, you will discuss opposing viewpoints in the body of your paper.

Exercise 8.4

Look back at Fiana Muhlberger's essay on page 280. Reread the introductory paragraph and answer the following questions about Fiana's thesis:

1. Which of the three options for expressing a thesis did Fiana use?
2. What types of claims are expressed in her thesis?

SUPPORT YOUR THESIS

To defend your claim and disprove your opponents' claims, you need to make a compelling case by presenting convincing reasons. You may have had strong opinions on the issue from the outset ("No, it is immoral to interfere with nature"; "Yes, genetic engineering will prevent people from inheriting deadly diseases"), but opinions are not enough.

An *opinion* is a belief that is not substantiated with evidence or proof. Writing "In my personal opinion" is redundant because by their definition, opinions are personal. Consider the following opinions:

> The school year should not be shortened because young kids usually waste their summers anyway.

> From the time I was thirteen, I worked hard at a job all summer long. Kids should work during the summer and not go to school.

Both statements express personal views, but neither gives firm grounds of support for the view.

A *reason* carries with it the weight of evidence. Read this example:

```
Because our school year is 180 days long but Japan's and Germany's
have from 226 to 243 school days, Japanese and German children
devote more time to learning science and math. A lengthened school
year would allow our students to spend as much classroom time on
science and math as students in other industrialized countries,
and that will help them catch up with the competition.
```

The student who wrote this has provided grounds of support for her view. To make a strong argument, you must support your views with substantial reasons and ground each reason in solid evidence. We explain how to do this later in the chapter.

Exercise 8.5

In your journal, make a claim for one of the following issues or another issue of your choice:

- Whether we should buy American-made goods rather than imports
- Whether rap or heavy metal music promotes violence
- Whether television damages family life
- Whether the United States should extend the school year
- Whether cosmetics firms should be allowed to experiment on animals

Next, state the major reason that you hold your position. Ask yourself two questions: (1) What underlying fact or cause is the basis for my view? (2) Based on this reason, would someone agree or disagree with my position? Now break into small groups and share your positions and reasons with your classmates. As each student explains the issue and gives his or her position and reason for holding it, the other group members should assume a noncommittal position. In other words, if a student in your group explains why she is in favor of lengthening the school year, pretend that you have no opinion on the issue. From your neutral stance, evaluate your classmate's argument. Have you been persuaded to accept his or her view?

MARSHAL SOLID EVIDENCE AND MAKE A STRONG CASE

As we mentioned earlier, rhetoric, the "art of persuasion," was the most important subject in the Greek curriculum over two thousand years ago. At that time, there were no attorneys, and people usually argued their own cases in courts of law. As you can imagine, private citizens were very interested in learning how to present an effective argument that would enable them to win a case. One of the most influential handbooks explaining how to formulate and present arguments was written by the Greek philosopher Aristotle in the fourth century BCE. Much of what Aristotle proposed in *The Rhetoric* is still applicable today. He taught that there are three appeals a person who is arguing a position can make to his or her audience:

The first kind depends on the personal character of the speaker [*ethos*]; the second on putting the audience into a certain frame of mind [*pathos*]; the third on the proof [*logos*]. (1.2.1356)

When we speak of *ethos* today, we mean the way the writer conveys a favorable or creditable impression of himself or herself to the reader. By *pathos* we mean the way the writer takes into account the interests and needs of the reader, and by *logos* we mean the way the writer provides the audience with solid reasons arranged in a logical sequence.

Go back to Fiana's essay on pages 280–289 to look at how she establishes her credibility, interests her audience, and presents a well-reasoned, compelling case.

Make Ethical Appeals

To be ethical is to conduct oneself in accordance with the principles of right and wrong, to make appropriate moral choices, and to have sound fundamental values. These traits make writers credible to their audiences. Readers also expect a writer who is trying to persuade them of something to possess authority, honesty, respect, and competence. There are a number of ways to project a favorable image of oneself and thus make ethical appeals.

WAYS TO MAKE ETHICAL APPEALS

- Establish your authority by exhibiting in-depth knowledge of the subject and drawing on the expert judgments of others.
- Be fair, honest, and accurate.
- Show respect for your audience by using an appropriate tone.
- Divulge your character by drawing on personal experiences that directly support your points.
- Demonstrate competence with correct usage, punctuation, and mechanics.

Establish your authority.   Since you are not likely to be an expert on the issue on which you write, you must learn about it by reading as much as you can. Explore various aspects of the issue, the context in which it is embedded, its history, and the positions held by people on both sides of the debate. One way to write with authority is to draw on respected researchers and reputable experts in the field.

Fiana does an exemplary job of establishing her credibility right at the start of her essay. In the opening paragraph, she projects the image of a writer who can capture the interest of her readers and inform them of the seriousness of the issue and her particular position. In paragraph 2, she demonstrates that she is knowledgeable about the subject and can speak with a sense of authority. Notice how she bolsters her authority with quotations and paraphrases from experts on the subject of grading: Anita Woolfolk, author of a psychology textbook; Barbara Gross Davis, author of a textbook on college teaching; and Mark Durm, author of an article on the history of grading. Fiana maintains this positive image in the remainder of the essay by following a well-developed line of reasoning that takes into account other people's views as well as her own.

Be fair, honest, and accurate.   It is much easier to write a one-sided argument than to examine the issue from the point of view of someone who does not agree with you. But how persuasive is an argument that presents only half of the debate? How convincing would Fiana's argument be if it omitted the views of those who are in favor of grading? Fiana makes her own position more reasonable by taking into account the beliefs and values of those who think differently.

When you make an argument, winning isn't everything. Don't tamper with the evidence, withhold it, take it out of context, or ignore it (especially if it strengthens the case of your opposition). Nor should you bring in irrelevant data or examples or quote a person who has no expertise on the subject under discussion.

Show respect for your audience.   The tone a writer uses in an argument essay reveals his or her attitude toward the subject, people who might not agree with the thesis, and the audience reading the piece. Tone is created with a number of stylistic features, among them choice of vocabulary and level of formality, the inclusion of questions, and the use of first-person (*I, my, mine, we, our*) and second-person (*you, your*) pronouns.

Consider the opening paragraph of Michael Messner's essay, "When Bodies Are Weapons," on the social role that violence plays in constructing masculinity.

> In many of our most popular spectator sports, winning depends on the use of violence. To score and win, the human body is routinely turned into a weapon to be used against other bodies, causing pain, serious injury and death. How do we interpret the social meaning of this violence? Is it socially learned behavior that serves to legitimize masculine power over women? Commentators—both apologists and critics—have made sweeping statements about sports and violence, but their analyses rarely take into account the meanings of violence in sports to athletes themselves. We can begin to understand the broader social meanings of violence in sports by listening to the words of former athletes. (89)

Messner has a reasonable, familiar tone. It is neither overly formal nor uniformly colloquial. Notice how he establishes a relationship with his audience by referring to "*our* most popular sports" in the opening sentence. As he continues, he pulls the readers further into the discussion by asking them questions—"How do we interpret the social meaning of this violence? Is it socially learned behavior that serves to legitimize masculine power over women?"—and by continuing to use the first-person pronoun.

In the following paragraphs from the beginning of William Raspberry's essay, "Racism in the Criminal Justice System Is Exaggerated," the tone is more aggressive.

> There are not more college-age black men in jail than in college. I suspect that old canard was launched when someone said (presumably accurately) that more college-age black men are in jail than in college *dormitories*—a statistic that would leave out off-campus students and almost all technical school and community college enrollees.
>
> So what's the truth? The Justice Department's Bureau of Justice Statistics says that in 1993 approximately 157,000 black males aged 18 to 24 were in local jails and state and federal prisons.
>
> During that same period, according to the education branch of the Census Bureau, 379,000 males in the same age group were in post-secondary education—better than 2 to 1 in favor of college.
>
> The number of incarcerated black men has increased since that period, and I wouldn't be shocked to learn that the number of black college students has gone down. Still, we're not close to having more in jail than in college.
>
> But it isn't just the accuracy of that much-cited statistic that bothers me; it's the *uselessness* of it.

Raspberry's tone is more informal than Messner's. Like Messner, he uses first-person pronouns and directs questions to the reader, but he also uses contractions (*we're, it's, isn't*).

Raspberry reveals more of his attitude. Consider how emphatic he is in the first sentence—"There are not more college-age black men in jail than in college"—and notice how he expresses his feelings by using italics to accentuate words.

We should alert you that some professors may object to first-person pronouns and contractions in academic writing, so before you make these stylistic choices, check with your teacher. To be on the safe side, write in a calm, cool, reasonable tone. Avoid sounding alarmed, aggressive, or abusive. Never use inflammatory language or demeaning words, such as *idiotic, stupid,* or *ridiculous,* when presenting opposing views, and when you respond to the opposition, be conciliatory rather than combative or condescending.

Read paragraph 3 of Fiana's essay, and notice how she responds to those with alternative views by first conceding that they have made a valid point.

> <u>Granted,</u> grades are meant to evaluate students' work and under-
> standing of subject material, <u>but</u> what is the real distinction
> between an A and an A-, and an A- and a B+? It's indefinable.

Notice that she does this again in paragraph 4.

> The claim that the grading system motivates students to better
> themselves by striving for higher grades <u>has some merit.</u> <u>It may be</u>
> <u>true</u> that students are motivated, but most students find themselves
> obsessing over the letter on their report card or transcript,
> rather than focusing on what they actually learn and can take away
> from the class.

We have underlined the words and phrases that contribute to Fiana's conciliatory tone. Think of how her readers would have reacted if she had responded to the opposition as follows:

> <u>Nonsense.</u> <u>It's ridiculous</u> to argue that grades motivate students
> to better themselves. When students receive low grades, they often
> become bitter and disenchanted with the course.

This insulting and condescending tone would have alienated Fiana's readers and done little to persuade them of the validity of her argument.

Divulge your character.   Another way to project a favorable image of yourself is to use as evidence a personal experience that strengthens your argument and substantiates your claims.

Consider a paragraph from an essay in which student Patti Sergent argues that cultural factors limit women's potential and restrict their professional opportunities.

> I got through most of high school with my academic potential
> intact. For me, the adverse cultural impact occurred in my senior
> year during a college advisement session with my guidance coun-
> selor. In my hand, I had transcripts with A's and SAT scores of
> 1350, and in my heart I had a serious interest in chemistry. Mr. Duel
> informed me that "girls should start at a community college
> because many drop out of school to get married within the first
> two years." Though I lost a little of my confidence, I ignored my
> adviser and attended a four-year college, but even there I was
> constantly reminded that "girls," a term I find offensive, make
> better teachers than researchers.

This story tells the readers that the writer is strong, ambitious, and intent on accomplishing her goals. Her experience is credible evidence because it relates directly to the topic at hand.

Demonstrate competence. Readers are more likely to be persuaded by an error-free text than by one that is marred by problems with spelling, punctuation, paragraphing, documentation format, capitalization, and pagination. Before you go public with your paper, read it aloud to another person and then proofread it line by line and word by word.

Limit Emotional Appeals

Writers use emotional appeals to provoke, entice, or arouse the reader and to establish empathy. Though it is important to establish rapport with your readers, be careful not to exploit their emotions. A good piece of advice is to use emotional appeals only as supplements to ethical and logical appeals, not as substitutes for them.

WAYS TO MAKE EMOTIONAL APPEALS

- Draw on firsthand experiences.
- Use concrete examples, anecdotes, stories, comparisons, and contrasts the reader can identify with.
- Use metaphors, similes, and words that evoke particular images and connotations.
- Tie the issue in with the reader's sense of responsibility, civic duty, patriotism, values system, or beliefs.

Draw on firsthand experiences. A personal experience can function both as an ethical appeal that creates a favorable image of the writer and as an emotional appeal that stirs the reader. The example of writer Patti Sergent's encounter with her high-school guidance counselor reveals traits about Patti's character and at the same time creates a sense of indignation in the readers. We are appalled that such a bright young woman was discouraged from pursuing serious study in science. Fiana draws on two experiences in paragraph 6.

```
My English professor gives daily quiz grades in order to ensure
that we have done the assigned readings.

When I was younger, I spent countless hours practicing gymnastics
routines until I had perfected them. I did this because I wanted
to excel at gymnastics. I think I would have been less motivated
if I was receiving A, B, or C grades for my routines.
```

Use concrete examples. In paragraph 11, when Fiana describes alternatives to letter grades, she gives the examples of Yale, Berkeley, and Stanford law schools. Then in paragraph 12 she offers an extended example of authentic assessments at Ithaca College.

Exercise 8.6

Look for other examples, anecdotes, stories, or comparisons and contrasts in Fiana's essay. In your journal, describe the effect that these devices have on you as a reader. Share your findings with the class.

Use metaphors, similes, and evocative language.   Metaphors and similes are comparisons. In a metaphor, the comparison is implicit, and in a simile, it is spelled out. Fiana's lead contains two metaphors: "Grades are nothing more than a jail for students' ambition and a cage for students' drive to learn." Similarly, Jeffrey Goldberg opens "The Color of Suspicion," his article based on interviews with patrol officers about racial profiling, with a metaphor and other words that evoke vivid images:

> Sgt. Mike Lewis of the Maryland State Police is a bull-necked, megaphone-voiced, highly caffeinated drug warrior who, on this shiny May morning outside Annapolis, is conceding defeat.

In his article, Goldberg employs a simile and a sharp comparison:

> The suspects are wearing backward baseball caps and low-slung pants; the woman with them is dressed like a stripper.
> "Is this racial profiling?" Jones asks. A cynical half-smile shows on his face.
> The four buyers are white. Jones and Robinson are black, veterans of the streets who know that white people in a black neighborhood will be stopped. Automatically. Faster than a Rastafarian in Scarsdale.

Writers use metaphorical language to help readers establish connections that create clear-cut pictures in their minds.

Exercise 8.7

Explain the impact each of the following descriptions has on you as a reader.

1. Sgt. Mike Lewis of the Maryland State Police is a thick-necked, loud-spoken police officer who drinks a lot of coffee.
2. "Sgt. Mike Lewis of the Maryland State Police is a bull-necked, megaphone-voiced, highly caffeinated drug warrior."
3. Her clothes were very provocative.
4. She was dressed like a stripper.
5. White people in a black neighborhood will be stopped just as quickly as black people in a wealthy white neighborhood.
6. "White people in a black neighborhood will be stopped. Automatically. Faster than a Rastafarian in Scarsdale."

Appeal to the reader's sense of responsibility, civic duty, patriotism, values system, or beliefs.   This is an effective technique for closing an argument paper. Fiana uses it in her concluding paragraph.

> Grade reform needs to become a priority. Much can be done to change the current grading system. There are even more possibilities than I have described. The major goal of all teachers should be to allow students the opportunity to focus on genuine learning instead of on "making the grade." To do so, teachers everywhere need to disassemble the hoops.

Present Logical Appeals

With logical appeals, you call on your readers' reason and logic. Logical appeals are the linchpins of effective argument essays. Without solid reasons and evidence, the argument falls apart. Four components are central to a logical argument:

- The writer's primary claim, assertion, or thesis
- Reasons that support the central claim
- Assumptions that link the reasons with the central claim
- Evidence that supports the reasons

Fiana's major claim is that the current grading system should be replaced with a method of evaluation that encourages rather than discourages active, long term learning. She offers three reasons for abolishing the current system of grading: grades fail to motivate students to learn; they are not necessary for self-discipline; and they do not indicate the degree to which students have learned what is important for later life. These reasons are based on assumptions that Fiana believes her readers share: first, that the goal of education is learning for its own sake, not for attaining a high grade; second, that students will engage in disciplined learning even when they are not being graded; and, third, that grades do not necessarily predict how prepared one is for life after school. If Fiana's readers do not share her assumptions, the argument will collapse.

Two other components important to an argument are these:

- Consideration of objections raised by people who disagree with the writer's claim and evidence offered in support of these objections
- The writer's refutation of the objections, including reasons the objections do not undermine the writer's argument

Let us examine the evidence Fiana offers to support her position and also the evidence she offers as she presents and refutes the opposition. The main types of evidence writers use are *facts; statistics; examples;* and *expert testimony, statements,* or *other relevant information from acknowledged authorities.* Reread paragraph 5 of Fiana's essay. Examine the various types of evidence she offers in support of her claim that professors should motivate students to learn rather than give them the message that they need to focus on the information on the test.

- She presents the findings of a research study by Howard Pollio and Hall Beck.
- She offers a supporting quotation by English professor Jerry Farber.

Examine the evidence Fiana offers in paragraph 8 to bolster her claim: "Grades fail to motivate and discipline students properly, but what's worse is they completely fall short of their most important objective: indicating the degree to which students have learned what they need for success in later life." She uses two supporting quotations from publications in the field of education, one from *American Teacher* and the other from *The Chronicle of Higher Education.* Now study the evidence she offers as she presents and refutes the opposition in paragraphs 3, 4, 5, 6, and 8.

PARAGRAPH 3

Opposing View

- Grades evaluate students' work and understanding of subject matter.

Refutation

- Statement by Professor Stephen Vogel
- Fact about Cornell University provided by Talia Bar and Asaf Zussman

PARAGRAPH 4

Opposing View

- The grading system motivates students to better themselves by striving for higher grades.

Refutation

- Testimony and specific case of Professor James Lang

Refutation Presented in Paragraph 5

- Results of research study by Pollio and Beck
- Supporting quotation from Farber

PARAGRAPH 6

Opposing View

- Grades are necessary for self-discipline.

Refutation

- Two examples of Fiana's own experiences
- Two supporting quotations by Farber

PARAGRAPH 8

Opposing View

- Grades indicate the degree to which students have learned what they need for success in later life.

Refutation

- Supporting quotation from *American Teacher*
- Supporting quotation from *The Chronicle of Higher Education*

In addition to using the types of support Fiana has employed, you could also supply a personal narrative that relates to the issue at hand. Consider an example from a student who gives his views on the issue of whether children should receive monolingual or bilingual education. Jim Li supplies a personal example to support his point that monolingual education retards immigrant children's educational progress.

An immigrant child should not have his educational progress retarded because of his lack of proficiency in English. Due to mono-lingual education, I wasted two years not acquiring any new knowl-edge except for math, which required very little English. While the other kids in Mr. Baranello's fifth-grade class were busily working on social studies and science assignments, I sat in the far corner of the room engrossed in a thick novel. It was not in English, how-ever. It was in my native language. Except for participating in a one-hour ESL lesson every other day and a daily math lesson, I spent my first year and a half in an American school hardly communicating with anyone. Bilingual education would have served as a transi-tional device for me because for several years I would have received the larger part of instruction in my home language. As Porter points out, this would have led to "better learning of English, better learning of subject matter, and better self-concept" (152).

When you include personal experiences in your argument essays, be sure they relate directly to the reason you are developing.

EVIDENCE TO SUPPORT YOUR REASONS

- Examples based on a similarity to something that happened in the past, a similar case, a hypothetical situation, or relevant experience
- Relevant information: facts, statistics, points of interest
- Statements, testimony, or other relevant information from acknowledged authorities
- Your own personal narrative

Exercise 8.8

Read the selection by Yolanda Moses on pages 458–469. Identify the types of evidence Moses uses, and evaluate the effectiveness of each type.

In addition to offering evidence when presenting their major assertions and the views of their opposition, writers of argument essays may use examples, facts, expert testimony, and other types of evidence in other parts of their essays, especially when giving background information. It is always important to provide context for the issue you are debating. You will have to explain the context in detail in some cases more than in others. The amount of background you provide depends on your audience's familiarity with the subject.

Exercise 8.9

Reread the first two paragraphs on Fiana's essay on pages 280–281 and identify the types of evidence she provides.

Consider Your Audience and Identify Your Readers' Needs

It is important to consider the audience for any essay, but this step is especially critical for an argument. Before sitting down to write, ask yourself the following questions.

QUESTIONS ABOUT AUDIENCE FOR AN ARGUMENT ESSAY

- Are you writing for your professor, your classmates, a broader audience, or a specific group of readers?
- What do your readers already know about the issue? Will you have to explain basic concepts and provide background information for your point of view to make sense?
- How do you want to come across to your audience—as an objective, scholarly authority, or as someone who identifies with your readers and shares their concerns?
- Is your audience noncommittal, or have your readers already taken a stand on the issue you are discussing?

Answers to these questions tell writers a number of things:

- How much effort to expend to attract their readers' attention with the lead sentence and introduction
- How much background information to provide so that readers will thoroughly understand the issue
- How to address readers (objectively or using pronouns like *I, you,* or *we*)
- How to organize their presentation and how much space to devote to opposing views

Fiana made a conscious decision to address her peers as well as her teacher. She decided to open the essay with a few salient examples that would grab readers' attention and then give them background information on teachers' reasons for using grades and on the origins of letter grades. Because of the nature of her audience, she made the tone of the paper friendly and accessible.

The point at which you decide to take up the views of your opponents depends on your audience and the nature of the opposing argument. If you know your readers have good reason to disagree with you, you may want to acknowledge their views early in the paper and devote a good portion of your essay to answering each of their objections. This is the approach taken by Fiana. If you think it will be easy to influence your readers to accept your point of view or if you think their arguments are especially weak, you can dismiss your opposition summarily and get on with discussing your position. Notice that Fiana's thesis statement reflects her order of presentation: "Despite the fact that teachers will argue that they need grades to motivate, discipline, and evaluate students, the current grading system must be weeded out from our classrooms and replaced with a new method of evaluation that will encourage active and long term student learning." Let the pattern of your thesis statement reflect the overall arrangement of your essay.

ORGANIZE AND ARRANGE THE ARGUMENT ESSAY

As we mentioned earlier, some of the principles of argument that were taught in ancient times have been adapted for writers today. *Ad Herennium,* a Latin treatise on Greek rhetorical theory, divides arguments into six parts (Corbett 25):

- Introduction *(exordium)*
- Statement or exposition of the case under discussion *(narratio)*
- Outline of the points or steps in the argument *(divisio)*
- Proof of the case *(confirmatio)*
- Refutation of the opposing arguments *(confutatio)*
- Conclusion *(peroratio)*

Today's principles of organization are not so different. Most modern writers of arguments use some variation of the following divisions:

- Opening
- Explanation of the issue and background
- Writer's thesis
- Presentation of and response to opposing views
- Reasons supporting thesis
- Conclusion

Whether you choose to acknowledge and respond to opposing views early in the essay, as Fiana has done, depends on the situation and the nature of your audience. There is no rule that says that you must arrange your essay in one particular way or another.

TYPICAL ARRANGEMENT OF AN ARGUMENT ESSAY

Title
Introduction

Opener:	Introduce the topic, and interest your reader.
Issue:	Familiarize your reader with the controversy, and give background information the reader needs to know to understand the issue at hand.
Thesis:	Give your stand on the issue and perhaps the view of the opposition.

Body Paragraphs

VARIATION A	VARIATION B
Give opposing views and your refutation.	Present reasons and evidence for your thesis.
Present reasons and evidence for your thesis.	Give opposing views and your refutation.

Conclusion
Recap argument.

Make final appeal to readers.

As we pointed out earlier, there may be times when you have to make a strong case in order to persuade readers who hold views contrary to yours. Using Variation A, you would construct your body paragraphs as follows:

Body Paragraphs

State a conflicting view.

Refute that view.

State another conflicting view.

Refute that view.

State another conflicting view.

Refute that view.

(Continue in this manner as necessary.)

Conclusion

Recap argument.

Make final appeal to readers.

For Exercise 8.10, we reproduce a student essay by Lisa McEttrick. This essay illustrates Variation B.

> Present reasons and evidence for your thesis.
>
> Give opposing views and your refutation.

Lisa's topic is the age of consent for sexual behavior. The issue is whether it is wise to enact legislation that would raise the age of consent and obligate adolescents to secure parental permission to obtain contraceptives or abortions. Lisa's thesis is "Toughening the laws is not a way to protect children; instead, we should provide them with educational programs in the schools."

Exercise 8.10

Read Lisa McEttrick's essay on pages 307–312, and then answer the questions.

1. For whom do you think Lisa is writing this essay: her professor, her classmates, a broader audience, or a specialized group of readers? How did you come to this conclusion?

2. Does Lisa tell her audience enough about the topic that her essay will make sense? What makes you say so?

3. Do you think Lisa views her audience as noncommittal or as strongly opinionated about the issue? Why do you say this?

4. What impression do you have of Lisa? Does she come across as a scholarly, objective authority or as someone who identifies with the readers and shares their concerns?

5. How does Lisa handle opposing views?

6. What reasons does Lisa give to support her position? Cite instances of her use of examples, relevant information from sources, statements or testimony from acknowledged authorities, and personal experience.

7. How does Lisa order her reasons, from weak to strong or strong to weak? What effect does she achieve by this order?

McEttrick 1

Lisa McEttrick

Professor Smith

English 131

8 April 2008

Age of Consent

Should laws regarding age of consent and parental knowledge be made stricter? Toughening up the laws on teen sexual behavior would unintentionally create more problems than we expected. If we raise the age of consent, innocent teens will be prosecuted for experimenting with their peers. Requiring parental permission for contraceptive drugs or abortions will force young girls to forego them altogether and end up pregnant, with an STD, or both. Toughening the laws is not the way to protect children; instead, we should provide them with educational programs in the schools.

The average age of consent worldwide is sixteen, but it ranges from twelve in Zimbabwe, to twenty-one in Madagascar, to the age at which the couple is married in Iran ("Worldwide"). Each culture has its own idea about the age at which young people are ready to engage in sex. Even in our own country we cannot agree. In some states it's fourteen but in most it's sixteen. In California it's eighteen and in other states it depends on the age gap between the two parties. The original age

1

2

of consent, codified in English Common Law and later adopted by
the American colonies, ranged from ten to twelve (Saleton).
Around 1885 it started to rise in order to protect girls'
natural innocence and then it rose further to accommodate the
age of puberty. More recently, the age of puberty has changed
in the other direction: falling instead of rising. Girls are
getting their period shortly after their twelfth birthday. Most
would agree that twelve is not the age that girls are having
sex, but on average earlier puberty means earlier sex (Saleton).

With these numbers in mind, examine the case of twenty-one-
year-old Genarlow Wilson who spent two years of his ten-year
sentence behind bars for receiving oral sex from a fifteen-year-
old girl at a New Year's party when he was seventeen (Koch). Both
parties claimed that the acts were consensual but since they were
engaging in oral sex, not vaginal, consent was not relevant.
Wilson was offered a plea deal that he declined. If he had taken
it, he would have had to register as a sex offender and would no
longer be able to live at home because he had a nine-year-old
sister in the house. As much as he wanted a lesser sentence, he
would not risk not having a home. Genarlow admits to making a
mistake: "I was young then. I did some idiotic things in my teen
years, but you know, every average teen does." He said, "I don't
think any of us made very wise decisions, but I don't think that
any of us can go back then and change what happened" ("Genarlow").

Genarlow is the type of teen we don't want behind bars. It
would be wiser to spend our time and resources on sexual predators,
not teens who are experimenting with peers their own age. Allison
Taylor, executive director of the Texas Council on Sex Offender
Treatment, agrees: "Let's capture the truly 10% who are predators"

(qtd. in Koch). Some states are catching on and lessening the punishment for teen sex offenders. Some do not require teens to register as sex offenders if the age difference is no more than four years and the younger party is at least thirteen. Other states do not even prosecute if the age gap is three years or less. These laws are a step in the right direction in order to differentiate between experimenting adolescents and legitimate sex offenders.

    Critics of lowering the age of consent argue that it opens the door and welcomes sexual predators. According to Roz Prober, president of Beyond Borders, a Winnipeg child advocacy organization, "People are coming to Canada to have sex with children" because in Canada a fourteen-year-old can legally engage in sexual activity with an adult, unless that person is in a position of authority (qtd. in Driedger). A big concern is that adolescents are being lured into prostitution and taken advantage of via the Internet. If the age of consent were raised, parents and other authorities would be able to interfere and rescue their children. Renata Aebi, executive director of the Alliance for the Rights of Children in Vancouver, makes an excellent point: "There's a massive growth industry in the trafficking of children, luring over the Internet. . . . Yes, it will help if we raise the age of consent from 14 to 16 but that protection shouldn't come at the expense of teens' rights to make decisions about their sexuality. Nor should it limit their access to birth control and abortion" (qtd. in Driedger). In order to combat predators taking advantage of young adolescents, we need to educate teens about the danger of online relationships rather than subject them to stricter laws that will restrict them unnecessarily.

Another proposal for stopping sexual predators is to require adolescents to obtain parental consent for contraceptives and/or abortions. According to Texas Representative Kevin Brady, if parents do not have to be notified, a rapist could force contraceptives on the child so she will not get pregnant and no one would ever find out. Brady claims that if parental consent is required, such acts will not go unnoticed. He finds it disgraceful that children as young as nine can get contraceptives without any sort of parental consent. "Unbelievably, from the federal government's standpoint you, the parent, must be kept in the dark. At a time in their young life when children need your help and guidance the most, Washington regulations block you from having a say in their health-care decisions," Brady argues.

6

The truth of the matter is if adolescents want to become sexually active, they are going to find a way to do it, regardless of parental knowledge. If parental knowledge is required to obtain contraceptives, some teens will have sex without protection. Is this the preferable option? Wouldn't it be better if the child were at least safe from pregnancy and STD's? Jan Schakowsky, Congress member since 1988, thinks that to legally require teenage girls to tell their parents about their reproductive choices is to put the lives and health of young women in danger and to deny the reality many of them face today (Schakowsky). According to the American Medical Association, "The desire to maintain secrecy has been one of the leading reasons for illegal-abortion deaths" (qtd. in Schakowsky). Parents need to face the facts that teens aren't going to inform them of all their decisions. Even the best parenting can't stop some adolescents from experimenting with sex at a young age.

7

It is becoming more and more common for teenagers to begin sexual experimenting at a young age. Adolescents within five years of each other's age should be able to experiment with one another without fear of the law. Teen girls should have access to contraceptives freely without fear of their parents condemning their behaviors. As far as sexual predators go, education is the key. If more educational programs are offered in middle and high schools and students are required to attend them for more than one year, teens will gain valuable information about their sexual health.

School programs will teach teens how to access contraceptives and where to go for help if they feel they are being sexually abused. They will learn how to distinguish consensual sex from forced sex. The consequences of STDs and pregnancy will be taught through personal stories and in-depth lessons. Students will know that there is always someone to talk to if they feel like they are being taken advantage of or just need some advice. With these programs in place, students will feel comfortable experimenting with their sexuality without getting involved with the wrong individuals. Unfortunately, sexual predators will always loom on the Internet or elsewhere but we can cut down on the number of teens that fall into their traps by talking more openly about sex and by making strides toward lessening its "taboo" factor. Once we come to terms with the fact that teens are becoming sexually active earlier, we can administer proper education and adequate health care, which will result in better decision making among our nation's young people. These steps will help cut down on sexual abuse and misuse and will make teens feel more comfortable about their sexual health instead of feeling constrained by rules, laws, and regulations.

McEttrick 6

Works Cited

Brady, Kevin. "Symposium: Q: Do Parents always Have a Right to Know When Their Teen Is Seeking Birth Control? Yes: Tear Down the Federally Mandated Wall of Secrecy Between Parents and Young Children." *Insight on the News* 29 Oct.-11 Nov. 2002: 46+. *Proquest Research Library.* Web. 22 March 2008.

Driedger, Sharon Doyle. "Drawing the Line." *Maclean's* 18 Nov. 2002: 106-7. *Proquest Research Library.* Web. 17 March 2008.

"Genarlow Wilson: Plea Deal Would Have Left Me Without a Home." CNN.com 29 Oct. 2007. Web. 19 March 2008.

Koch, Wendy. "States Ease Laws That Punish Teens for Sex with Underage Partners." *USA Today* 25 July 2007: A1. *Proquest National Newspapers.* Web. 25 March 2008.

Saleton, William. "The Mind-Booty Problem: Rethinking the Age of Sexual Consent." *Slate* 27 Sept. 2007. Web. 23 March 2008.

Schakowsky, Jan. "Symposium: Q: Do Parents always Have a Right to Know When Their Teen Is Seeking Birth Control? No: Forcing Parental Notification Will Lead to Deadly Illegal Abortions and Higher Rates of Teen Pregnancy." *Insight on the News* 29 Oct.-11 Nov. 2002: 47+. *Proquest Research Library.* Web. 22 March 2008.

"Worldwide Ages of Consent." *AVERTing HIV and AIDS.* n.d. Web. 20 March 2008.

Exercise 8.11

Write an essay in which you compare Lisa McEttrick's essay to Fiana Muhlberger's essay on pages 280–289.

WRITING AN ARGUMENT ESSAY

Now that you have studied and analyzed two argument essays, you are ready to write one of your own. Select a controversial topic that interests you. Here is a recap of the process we described in this chapter.

PREWRITING

Clarify and Refine the Issue You Will Write About

If you plan to write on a controversial subject that you already know a lot about, you will have no trouble delving beneath the surface and discovering a number of underlying conflicts. Let's say you've read up on the controversy involving the labeling and censoring of certain types of music. Ostensibly, the issue is whether music should be censored. But you perceive a deeper issue. You believe that groups advocating censorship have goals other than protecting youths from "dangerous" lyrics. You think these groups want to suppress all mention of social conditions—drug use, racism, homosexuality, sexual violence—that diverge from the purported norm. Your background knowledge enables you to refine the issue and thus come up with a more innovative slant on the topic.

    If you have not read widely or had experience with the subject, however, you will have to learn more about it by carefully reading the sources your professor recommends. If your professor has not provided a reading list, you must locate relevant sources in the library. Chapter 9 offers useful advice about how to conduct library searches. When you first approach the reading sources, read for answers to the questions, What is controversial about this subject? and What do people argue about?

    Let's say your topic is the annual holiday commemorating Christopher Columbus's discovery of America. You are aware that various groups—Native Americans, Italians, Hispanics—have different views on the appropriateness of parades and other festivities, but you're unsure of the details surrounding the controversy. As you read through the sources, ask yourself, What is so controversial about celebrating Columbus Day? What are these groups arguing about? Your initial reading reveals a major controversy on whether Columbus's conquests should be celebrated or condemned.

    After you have clarified the issue, continue reading the sources, but keep in mind that now your goal is to investigate various aspects of the broad issue so that you can delve beneath the surface and obtain a fresh perspective. For example, if your assignment is to write an essay on gun control, after your initial reading of the sources, you might move from a broad issue like whether handguns should be banned to a more pointed controversy, such as whether law-abiding members of violent communities should be allowed to purchase handguns for self-defense.

Probe Both Sides of the Controversy

As you read through the sources, do your best to understand different positions on the issue. We suggested earlier that you play the "believing game." Take Peter Elbow's advice and get inside the heads of the people who hold views different from your own. Take, for example, the experience of our student Eileen Laureano. Eileen had taken a firm stand on the issue of whether Columbus Day should be celebrated. She felt strongly that since so many Native Americans had perished in the aftermath of Columbus's explorations, Columbus Day should be a time of grief rather than celebration. As Eileen read through her sources, however, she tried to keep an open mind. She pretended that she was a patriotic American who believes that Columbus's contributions should be revered and recognized, and she also tried to see things through the eyes of Italian Americans who believe that by denouncing the celebration, we are depreciating the heritage of their people.

Write Out Clear-Cut Statements of Your Own Position and the Position of Anyone Objecting to Your View

Here is an example.

> *Issue:* Whether rap music has redeeming qualities
>
> *Writer's position/claim based on fact:* Rap music lyrics are a reflection of urban realities.
>
> *Opposing view:* Rap music lyrics are radical, extremist, and dangerous to our youth.

Compose a Thesis That Expresses Your Position As Well As the Position of Those Who Disagree With You

You can express your thesis in either of two ways:

- As a statement of your central claim:

  Rap music lyrics are a reflection of the urban realities of drug use, crime, and violence toward women.

- As a statement that incorporates both your claim and the opposition's:

  Rather than being radical, extremist, and dangerous to youth, rap music lyrics are a reflection of the urban realities of drug use, crime, and violence toward women.

The reason for including the opposing view in your thesis is to let your reader know from the start that your argument will be two-dimensional, not one-sided.

If you have difficulty expressing a lot of information in one sentence, use two or three sentences for your thesis:

> People who claim that rap music lyrics are radical, extremist, and dangerous to youth are seriously mistaken. The lyrics are a reflection of the urban realities of drug use, crime, and violence toward women.

To sum up, make sure that your thesis is issue-centered, arguable, and debatable.

- Be sure to anticipate and acknowledge conflicting views.
- Your purpose is to convince your readers to accept and agree with your position.

Reread the Sources, Formulate Reasons That Back Up Your Thesis and Explain Your Opponents' Views, and Then Locate Various Types of Evidence in Support of the Reasons. Record All This Information in Your Journal

A reason carries the weight of evidence. Be sure that each of your reasons is grounded in facts, statistics, examples, expert testimony, statements, or other relevant information from acknowledged authorities. To see how material from reading sources is eventually incorporated in argument essays, take a look at two excerpts from student papers.

The first is a paragraph in which Eileen Laureano uses facts, statistics, and other relevant information to argue against celebrating Columbus Day.

> Native Americans, in contrast, view the Columbus Day holiday as an insult to their struggles and persecution. The people brought to the "New World" by Columbus's expedition succeeded in exterminating the original inhabitants of the Americas. Many aboriginal nations perished at the hands of the Dutch, English, French, and Spanish. The Tawantinsuyu of the Inca empire were destroyed soon after Columbus's arrival. Theirs was once a civilized nation that ruled over 20 million people and had reached a high level of social, military, agricultural, and handicraft development (Llosa 48). The West Indian population also decreased from 50 million in the fifteenth century to 4 million in the seventeenth century (New Encyclopaedia Britannica 883). If conquest and exploration brought only bloodshed and extermination, then we should have no pride in celebrating this holiday.

In the second excerpt, Jim Li relies on an authority on bilingual education to support his argument that children should receive instruction in their native language as well as in English.

> Rosalie P. Porter, the director of English as a second language and bilingual programs for the Newton, Massachusetts, public schools, points out in her article "The Newton Alternative to Bilingual Education" that second-language learning occurs at varying rates in different individuals. "The ultimate goal is that all students who arrive knowing a language other than English will become bilingual and fully capable of using the second language—English—for social and academic purposes" (150). By combining the mother tongue with English and flexibly catering to the individual's progress, language learning can become most effective.

Use Ethical, Emotional, and Logical Appeals to Establish Credibility, Interest Your Audience, and Present a Well-Reasoned, Compelling Case

Make ethical appeals by exhibiting in-depth knowledge of the subject and drawing on the expert judgments of others; being fair, honest, and accurate; and showing respect for your audience by using an appropriate tone. Divulge your character by drawing on personal experiences that directly support your points, and demonstrate competence with correct usage, punctuation, and mechanics. Make emotional appeals by drawing on firsthand experiences and concrete examples, anecdotes, stories, comparisons, and contrasts the reader can identify with. Also use metaphors, similes, and evocative words that bring to mind particular images and connotations or relate the issue to the reader's sense of responsibility, civic duty, patriotism, values, or beliefs. Make logical appeals with solid reasons and evidence.

DRAFTING

Arrange Solid Reasons in a Logical Sequence

After you have selected information from the reading sources that supports your own reasons and those of your opposition, you need to arrange this material to form the body paragraphs of your essay. There are three common arrangements for argument essays:

1. Writer presents the opposition first, dismisses it, and then gives reasons for his or her own view.
2. Writer first gives reasons for own view and then presents the opposition and refutation.
3. Writer alternates between the views of the opposition and rebuttal and his or her own views.

All three of these arrangements are effective, but there are reasons you might choose one pattern over another. Arrangement 1 works well if the objections you are counteracting are weak and insubstantial. You can respond to them right off and dismiss them summarily. You might also use this arrangement if you intend to work your essay up to a climax, moving from the opposition's views to your refutation, then to your weaker reasons, and finally to your strongest points. If you are addressing a friendly, easily persuadable audience, try arrangement 2. Readers who are predisposed to your position or already on your side will have a vested interest in your views and only a passing interest in the views of the opposition. Arrangement 3 works well when your opponents have a substantial, extended argument that is not easily dismissed. As you take up and challenge the opposition's claims point by point, you can also weave in support for your own views.

Take Your Readers' Level of Interest and Background Knowledge into Account

If your readers already have a stake in the issue, they will be eager to hear what you have to say. Suppose that you are a campus leader writing to persuade students to go along with a proposed increase in the student activity fee. Before voting for or against the increase, students who wish to be informed will be interested in your views. If you don't think your readers are intrinsically interested in the issue, however, open your essay with a lead and an introductory paragraph that will motivate them to read on.

The amount of background you provide also depends on your audience. If you know your readers are knowledgeable about the subject and familiar with the controversy surrounding it, you will not have to do a lot of explaining, defining, or narrating of past events. The topic of record labeling is a good example. If you are writing an argument essay to your classmates about the censorship of song lyrics, you can assume that most of them know a fair amount about the controversy. Conversely, if your purpose is to convince your class-mates that history justifies Irish Americans' financial support of the Irish Republican Army, you will have to supply historical information and explanations that place the controversy in a contemporary context.

Decide How You Want to Come Across to Your Audience

Undoubtedly, you want your audience to view you as someone who is knowledgeable and believable. The best way to establish your credibility is to provide your readers with a two-dimensional argument that rests on solid reasons and is documented with reliable sources. If you simply offer opinions or unsubstantiated reasons, your readers will feel no compulsion to accept your view.

Whether you write in a professional or a personal voice depends on the context of the situation. Some teachers require impersonal third-person writing; others allow the use of *I, we,* and *you.* Some arguments lend themselves to scholarly, objective prose; others work better when the writer uses *I, we,* and *you* to identify personally with the issue and pull the readers into the controversy.

REVISING

If it is all right with your instructor, have a classmate or friend read over your first draft and answer the questions listed below. If no one is available, answer the questions yourself.

After you have produced a first draft of your essay, use the following checklist to revise your work.

✓ *Checklist for Revising an Argument Essay*

_____ 1. Does the writer organize the discussion around the discernible purpose of persuading or convincing an audience?

_____ 2. Does the writer move beyond the purpose of simply synthesizing or comparing and contrasting opposing views?

_____ 3. Is the argument two-dimensional, taking into account both sides of the issue, or is it one-sided?

_____ 4. Does the writer use the conventions (not necessarily in this order) that the reader expects to find in an argument essay?

   _____ a. Explanation of the issue

   _____ b. Arguable thesis

   _____ c. Background information

   _____ d. Support for the position being argued

   _____ e. Mention of the conflicting position

   _____ f. Writer's response to the opposition

   _____ g. Conclusion

_____ 5. Does the writer present reasons rather than opinions?

_____ 6. Are the reasons supported with evidence?

_____   7. Does the writer draw on reliable sources?

_____   8. Does the writer make a favorable, creditable impression?

_____   9. Does the writer display an awareness of the audience's needs by setting a context for the reader in the following ways?

      _____ a. Giving appropriate background information

      _____ b. Mentioning authors and titles of sources when necessary

      _____ c. Supplying necessary documentation for sources

      _____ d. Providing clear connectives that differentiate his or her ideas from those of the writers of the sources

EDITING

When you are satisfied with your revision, read your paper aloud. Then reread it line by line and sentence by sentence. Check for correct usage, punctuation, spelling, mechanics, manuscript form, and typographical errors. If your editing skills are not strong, get a friend to read over your work.

CHAPTER 9

Researching Sources and Writing Research Papers

ASSIGNMENTS THAT REQUIRE RESEARCH

To this point in the textbook, you may have been writing essays by drawing on the reprinted sources in Part V. Many of your professors will ask you to write about specified materials, such as textbooks, reserve readings, handouts, or class readings, but they will also ask you to conduct independent research. These research-based assignments may be as short as a one-page critique of an article of your choice, involving under an hour of library research, or as long as a thirty-page term paper requiring a minimum of twenty sources, involving many trips to the library over a period of weeks. Whatever the paper length or time commitment, the success of the entire project depends on the skills of information retrieval you will learn in this chapter.

EXAMPLES OF WRITING TASKS THAT MAY REQUIRE RESEARCH

- Reviews of books that you choose yourself
- Summaries or critiques of journal articles that you have to find yourself
- Short reports on issues currently in the news
- Essays analyzing literature that draw on published literary criticism
- Reviews of the literature in particular topic areas
- Term papers

Although you will find the techniques covered in this chapter useful for *any* assignment that involves research, our examples focus on a research assignment that has three specific characteristics:

- It allows the student to choose a topic.
- It involves using a range of information sources.
- It requires sustained effort over a period of weeks.

These features call for special skills as well as the skills you have already learned in this book. Depending on the specific research assignment, you may need any or all of the writing processes discussed in Chapters 2 through 8. The approach to reading academic sources presented in Chapter 2 is crucial to library research, as are paraphrasing, quoting, and summarizing covered in Chapters 3 and 4. In addition, the ability to respond to sources (Chapter 5), analyze and evaluate sources (Chapter 6), synthesize ideas from a variety of sources (Chapter 7), and develop arguments (Chapter 8) will help you with research-based writing projects. Indeed, if you have mastered the skills in Chapters 2 through 8, you are well on the way to writing good research papers.

Exercise 9.1

The exercises in this chapter assume that you are working on a research assignment specified by your instructor. If you do not have an assignment, you must come up with a topic to complete the exercises. You might consider a topic of special interest or one that is an extension of the readings in Part V. Do one page of freewriting about your research interests.

RESEARCH AND THE WRITING PROCESS

Research is an intellectually complex activity that goes beyond knowing how to "look things up" using indexes and search engines. Good research involves careful thought and creativity as well as the ability to locate information. Let us demonstrate how research functions as part of the overall writing process.

RESEARCH AND THE WRITING PROCESS

Prewriting

- Set a research schedule.
- Select a topic.
- Develop a research strategy.
- Conduct research in your college library.
- Use electronic catalogs and periodical databases.
- Locate information on the World Wide Web.
- Collect information through surveys and interviews.
- Evaluate information sources.
- Excerpt relevant information from sources.

Drafting

- Synthesize sources.
- Argue, analyze, and evaluate.

- Draft a thesis.
- Derive a plan.
- Create an outline.
- Write from your outline.

Revising

- Revise based on readers' comments.

Editing

- Check for correct usage, punctuation, spelling, mechanics, manuscript form, and typographical errors.

Exercise 9.2

Speculate on how you can make sense of your research topic. What are the areas of confusion, ambiguity, disagreement, or uncertainty? What information might you collect that would help clarify your understanding of the topic? Freewrite one page in response to these questions.

PREWRITING

SET A RESEARCH SCHEDULE

Short assignments based on research may not require a special allocation of time, but assignments that ask students to locate a number of sources call for special planning. A major pitfall of research is failing to allow enough time. You must always allow for the unexpected in research assignments. Even the most knowledgeable researchers can encounter hitches that require more time than they had anticipated. Topics that initially seem promising may prove impossible to research; the sources that you need may be unavailable; preliminary research may show you that your initial research question is naive and must be modified; or you may have the required number of sources on the topic but find they don't fit together in a coherent argument. When students use the World Wide Web for research, they tend to allot less time for the research process because the Web seems to provide immediate, almost effortless access to source material. As we explain later in this chapter, using the Web as a means of circumventing library-based research is usually a mistake because it is difficult, and sometimes impossible, to conduct effective Web searches in a range of academic subject areas. Careful research takes time, and there are no reliable shortcuts.

The following chart provides general advice on the time required for research.

ASSIGNMENT	TIME TO COMPLETE RESEARCH AND WRITING	LIBRARY VISITS
Single source, topic specified by assignment	1 week	1
Single source, student's choice of topic	1 week	2
Up to five sources, topic specified by assignment	2 weeks	3
Up to five sources, student's choice of topic	2 weeks	4
Up to ten sources, topic specified by assignment	3 weeks	6
Up to ten sources, student's choice of topic	3 weeks	7
More than ten sources	4 weeks	8

You may be surprised by the number of library visits that we recommend. Remember that we allow for the unexpected challenges that often arise in the research process. If you set aside the recommended time, you will avoid getting caught short even if things do not go smoothly.

Once you estimate how much time your research project will take, make yourself a schedule. We illustrate with our student Kristen. Kristen received the following assignment in her composition course:

Write an eight- to ten-page research paper that addresses an issue related to a specific academic discipline that would be of interest to other first-year college students. Use at least ten sources of information.

Using our calculations as a guide, Kristen estimated that she would need at least four weeks for this assignment. She then created a schedule by specifying the work to be done and the corresponding deadlines:

Research Paper Deadlines

October 3	Settle on preliminary topic
October 6	Attend library orientation tour (10:30 a.m.)
October 7	Write a list of questions I want my research to answer, and brainstorm a list of key terms that pertain to my topic
October 10–14	Locate information (allow time for library visits each evening)
October 16	Outline the paper
October 17–21	Write the first draft, and if necessary, return to the library to fill in any missing information
October 24–26	Revise draft
October 27–29	Edit draft
October 30	Turn in final draft

Exercise 9.3

Establish a schedule for your research paper assignment. First, decide which tasks you have to do. Then create a timeline that specifies the date by which you will complete each task. Make sure you allot enough time for library research following the guidelines on page 322.

SELECT A TOPIC

Your instructor may specify a topic for the focus of your research. In a history course, you might receive the following assignment: "Working from press releases published within a month of the atomic bomb blasts at Hiroshima and Nagasaki, discuss how the American government justified its use of nuclear weapons to end World War II." This assignment tells you that you need to consult newspapers published in the late summer of 1945 and look for articles that contain government statements on A-bomb explosions over Japan. If you receive an open-ended assignment like Kristen's, however, you won't know where to begin the search for information. You will first have to narrow and focus the topic. Kristen turns to the following strategies.

STRATEGIES FOR GENERATING TOPICS

- *Freewrite in response to the assignment.* Write nonstop for ten minutes, using any cues in the assignment to generate ideas. Then search your freewriting for useful ideas.
- *Brainstorm.* Create a list of words and phrases in response to the assignment. Then read over the list and look for similarities, patterns, and connections.
- *Use research tools.* Consult general subject headings in indexes, either electronic or paper, to narrow the topic.
- *Consult with your professor.* Ask your professor to suggest topics in his or her discipline.

Kristen begins her topic search by freewriting:

> This assignment asks me to write about an academic topic that other first-year students would find interesting. What would that be? The course I am taking this semester that interests me most is sociology. Many of the issues that come up in that course would interest a wide range of people, not just social science scholars, since they pertain to how our society functions. It might be interesting to research how our society will change in the twenty-first century. I guess I could write about the impact of technology, like how the Internet and e-mail will affect interpersonal relationships and workplace interactions. Another issue we discussed in sociology class was how the traditional nuclear family is being replaced by new family structures, including single-parent and gay-parent families. Class members disagreed on whether this change in family structure is positive or negative for children, parents, and society as a whole. Perhaps I could collect more information on how the American family is changing and what the impact of the changes will be.

As you narrow your topic and begin your search for information, also think about your purpose. One purpose could be to provide the reader with a survey of perspectives on a topic; another could be to argue a particular point of view. If you are researching a topic on which you already have definite opinions, you may have a thesis in mind before you consult the information sources. But if you are investigating a new area, you should start thinking about your purpose as soon as you start working with the sources.

When Kristen begins her research, she is not sure what point she wants to prove, but she knows her audience. She narrows her topic and collects information that will appeal to first-year students and make sense to them. Her readers will not have the benefit of her hours of research, so they may need careful explanations of ideas that are self-evident to Kristen.

Kristen's general topic, changes in American family structure, is still too broad to research efficiently. The following strategies will help her refine her research goals.

STRATEGIES FOR FOCUSING YOUR RESEARCH GOALS

- *What do you already know about the topic?* In what ways could you expand on this knowledge by turning to sources? What uncertainties do you have about the topic that might be answered in sources?

- *What are your personal feelings on the topic?* What are your values and beliefs on this topic? How might you find sources that support or contradict your views, values, or beliefs?

- *From what perspectives can you view the topic?* What are common beliefs on the subject? What do experts on the topic believe? What do those most directly affected by the topic believe?

- *What might your own audience need to know about the topic?*

As you work to focus your topic, it may be helpful to visit the library. Reference librarians can evaluate your topic and give you specific suggestions for narrowing it. When Kristen asks a reference librarian for help in narrowing her topic, he demonstrates how to use a computerized index to current magazines and journals to browse through subject headings related to the American family. (Later in this chapter, we discuss computerized indexes and subject headings in detail.) The librarian explains that by looking up a major subject heading related to her topic and then examining its subheadings or related subjects, Kristen may discover ways to narrow her focus. He also suggests that she scan the titles of articles that are listed under a promising subheading to get a sense of how other writers have narrowed the topic. Finally, he suggests that she locate and look through several articles whose titles indicate that they will provide a survey of information or opinions related to her topic.

Following the librarian's suggestion, Kristen first uses General OneFile, a database that includes articles from a wide range of academic and popular periodicals. Kristen first tries the subject heading "Family" and finds that it has a long list of subdivisions and related subjects. She scans through the list and notes that several of the related subjects, such as "Family leave" and "Family values," are terms used by politicians campaigning for office. With this in mind, she returns to the reference desk and asks the librarian how she can find articles on what the candidates currently campaigning for the nation's presidency have said about family values. He shows Kristen how to use a computerized newspaper index to search for articles that focus on two topics: presidential candidates and family values. (Later in the chapter, we explain how to search simultaneously for two subjects.) She leaves the library with copies of several relevant articles. Though her topic is not yet precisely defined, she thinks that she will link the political rhetoric on family values with the more research-oriented material she studied in her sociology class. Kristen now has a sense of direction and is ready to investigate her topic in more depth.

Even though you may begin with a clear sense of direction, you may shift emphasis or narrow or expand your topic as your research continues. Don't be so committed to your initial topic that you ignore information indicating that a different focus might be more appropriate or more interesting. If you have a thesis in mind, regard it as a first attempt to make sense of the issue without the benefit of all the relevant information. As you collect information, you may find that your preliminary thesis does not fit with all the facts and may need to be altered or even abandoned entirely. Thesis statements may be subject to revision as you research and write. If you cling to your initial thesis in spite of the information you collect, you may produce a paper that is inconsistent, illogical, or confusing.

Since you may have to shift direction, it is important to gather and evaluate information well in advance of your project's due date. Leave yourself enough time to shift emphasis and look for other information sources. With complex topics, you may need to make several shifts before you arrive at an approach that you can sustain throughout a lengthy paper.

Exercise 9.4

In one page of freewriting, analyze your research goals and objectives. Do you know where to begin? To what extent have you narrowed your topic? Do you have a preliminary thesis? Have you located some information on your topic? Do you have to alter your focus in response to this information? What must you do before you move on to the next stage?

DEVELOP A RESEARCH STRATEGY

Once you have defined your topic, you need a plan of attack that will guide your search for information. We call this plan your *research strategy*. Think about the various types of sources that will meet your needs.

Whatever research strategy you devise, it should be flexible enough to accommodate the unexpected. As we mentioned earlier, you may need to change your goals during the research process. We wish we could give you an orderly sequence of research activities that would work for any assignment, but in practice, research often does not proceed as planned, and even the elaborate strategies described in textbooks may not lead you to the information you need. Flexibility is the most basic principle of library research.

The following questions will help you derive your research strategy.

QUESTIONS TO CONSIDER WHEN DETERMINING YOUR RESEARCH STRATEGY

- What are the assignment specifications?
- Who is your audience?
- What level of complexity or scope of coverage do you intend to achieve?
- What indexing terms (search vocabulary) will provide access to the information you want?

Assignment Specifications

Your research strategy may be determined largely by the demands of the assignment. Research assignments sometimes specify the types of sources that should be used. An assignment on the contemporary American family might call for "current articles from at least three periodicals," "both books and periodicals," "sources that focus on parenting," "sources written by conservatives as well as liberals," or "evidence from sociological research studies." In addition, the assignment might encourage students to search on the

World Wide Web or might specify that students use a library rather than the Web. Each of these directives calls for a particular research strategy. Kristen's assignment specifies a required number of sources but allows her to choose which types.

Audience

Remember that your readers must be able to grasp your ideas, so you need to draw on sources that are appropriate for them. Since Kristen's audience is first-year students, she decides to look for sources meant for a general audience of educated readers.

Level of Complexity or Scope of Coverage

Another part of your research strategy is to consider the variety of perspectives on your topic and decide which ones you will investigate. A major function of research is to explore the full complexity of an issue by examining a range of different opinions. For instance, if you were writing a research paper on trade protectionism for an economics class, you would try to locate sources that are critical of protectionism as well as supportive of it. For her research on changes in family structure, Kristen looks for the perspectives of those who defend the traditional nuclear family as well as those who champion alternative family structures. Your research strategy should include making a list of the differing perspectives you hope to find. Add to this list any new perspectives you encounter as you read the various sources.

Indexing Terms (Search Vocabulary)

To complete your research strategy, produce a list of words or phrases associated with your topic. Anticipate the words that might be used to describe or categorize the subject. These are the terms you will use to look up your topic in catalogs and indexes or on the World Wide Web. For her paper on the American family, Kristen compiles the following search vocabulary list.

Search Vocabulary

> families (or family)
> American families (or family)
> divorce
> family values
> family values and politics
> nuclear families (or family)
> single mothers (or mother)
> single fathers (or father)
> single-parent families (or family)
> families and politics
> families and elections
> family policy
> family structure

gay families (or family)
lesbian families (or family)
children
child rearing

Variations in spelling and punctuation as well as the differences between singular and plural forms may affect your search results, particularly if you use an electronic index or search engine. Note that Kristen's list reminds her to check both the singular and the plural of her search terms. She might also try both "single-parent families" and "single parent families." Slight differences such as these can determine whether or not a search is successful.

Be expansive, and list as many terms as you can. Then add to your list when you locate sources that suggest additional terms. You need a rich list of search terms because it is often hard to guess which ones will result in useful information.

Exercise 9.5

Outline a strategy for obtaining information for your research topic that takes into consideration the assignment specifications, your intended audience, and the level of complexity or scope of coverage. Then compile a list of search terms that you think will provide access to relevant information on your topic.

CONDUCT RESEARCH IN YOUR COLLEGE LIBRARY

In the twenty-first century, students typically come to college with some idea of how to locate information online. We find, however, that our current first-year students have less experience using libraries than did students of previous generations. Two decades ago, students and scholars working on research papers spent many hours in academic libraries tracking down and reading source material. Libraries housed all of the books, periodicals, and other sources of information that they needed as well as the indexes and catalogs that helped them locate these sources. As they worked on research projects, students learned how their libraries were organized and what resources they contained.

Our current students are less familiar with libraries because they conduct much or all of their research from their home computers. Indeed, it is now possible to do extensive research on certain topics without traveling to the library at all. It is, however, vitally important that students learn to use college libraries. If they rely solely upon what they can access from their home computers, students will miss out on the following advantages of college libraries:

ADVANTAGES OF ACADEMIC LIBRARIES FOR RESEARCHERS

- Expert collection development and quality control
- Extensive collections of books and other resources that are not available in electronic form
- Systematic organization and careful indexing
- Expert staff of reference librarians

A college library collection is developed specifically to serve the needs of academic researchers. Books, periodicals, and other materials are chosen either by librarians who specialize in collection development or faculty experts in particular fields of study. Because the collection is built systematically, an academic library collection is much more likely to include the important works in a particular discipline. Your library may also include special collections for programs of study that are highlighted at your college.

Currently, relatively few books are available in full-text online versions; thus with the exception of periodicals, most of the scholarly sources in your college library's collection are probably not available online. Classic scholarship in many field is contained principally in books. In addition to books, libraries may include maps, photographs, microforms, artifacts, and other objects that can only be viewed and analyzed by actually traveling to the library.

Libraries arrange and index sources with the needs of researchers in mind. The overarching goal of every library is to help users find the resources they are looking for. In contrast, the World Wide Web is constructed by millions of individuals with myriad goals such as financial gain and political advocacy. Information sources on the Web may be arranged to promote those agendas, and Web search engines may also reflect the biases of various commercial and political interests. Libraries make conscious effort to avoid those biases and to place the needs of library users ahead of those of information providers, and that perspective guides the way information is arranged and indexed.

A final advantage of conducting research in your college library is that you can get help from reference librarians, whose major responsibility is to help students and faculty members with research. Reference librarians can show you how to use the library's collection and also how to access sources available online from remote sites, including material on the World Wide Web. A few minutes spent discussing your research needs with a reference librarian can be more productive than hours of surfing the Web.

Take advantage of opportunities to learn about your library early in your academic career. Your library reference department may offer library orientation sessions, reference skills workshops, and credit-bearing courses on information resources. When you receive an assignment that requires research, begin, as did Kristen, with a trip to your library rather than a search on the Web. While your Web search may yield quick results, a library trip may guide you more efficiently to the sources you need.

Exercise 9.6

Take a self-guided tour of your college library. Start by getting a guide or a map that shows how your campus library is organized. Next locate the reference desk. Do not confuse it with the circulation desk, the place where items are checked out. The librarians at the reference desk provide one-on-one research assistance. Find out what days and hours reference librarians are available and what services they provide. Find out how the collection is organized. Does your library use the Library of Congress or the Dewey Decimal classification system? Are periodicals shelved with books or separately? Are other formats (recordings, microfilms, and so on) shelved separately? Are there any subject-specific (music, science, and so forth) libraries on your campus? You should be able to answer these questions on the basis of materials that you can get at the reference desk. Now tour the library and make sure you can find the principal elements of the collection.

Library Catalogs

The library catalog contains a description of each item in the collection and indexes items by subject, title, and author. Catalogs typically list not only books but also periodicals (magazines, journals, and newspapers), pamphlets, audio recordings (reel-to-reel and cassette tapes, LPs, and CDs), sheet music, microforms (microfilm, microfiche, and microcards), motion pictures, video recordings (films, video cassettes, and DVDs), computer data files, images (graphics and photos), three-dimensional artifacts, and maps. Note that the central library catalog provides the titles of periodicals (*New York Times, College English, Newsweek,* and so forth) and date range of holdings for periodicals but does not describe individual articles. On pages 331–344, we explain how to find particular periodical articles on a given subject.

In most academic libraries, the catalog is computerized and can be searched by subject, title, or author. Your library houses computer workstations linked to the online catalog, but the catalog may also be accessible from other computer workrooms across campus or even from your dorm room or home.

Figure 9-1 depicts a computer catalog entry that Kristen located in her research on contemporary family structure. Notice that the sample entry includes a *call number* for the item: HQ756.P65 1996. This number indicates the item's subject area and its shelving location. You are probably familiar with the Dewey Decimal call numbers used in most primary and secondary schools. College libraries typically use the Library of Congress system rather than the Dewey Decimal system, and the call number in Figure 9-1 is based on the Library of Congress system.

FIGURE 9-1 Sample Computer Catalog Entry

Location:	General Stacks
Call Number:	HQ756 .P65 1996
Number of Items:	1
Status:	Not Charged
Author:	Popenoe, David, 1932–
Title:	Life without father : compelling new evidence that fatherhood and marriage are indispensable for the good of children and society/David Popenoe.
Publisher:	New York : Martin Kessler Books, c1996.
Description:	viii, 275 p. ; 25 cm.
ISBN:	0684822970
Notes:	Includes bibliographical references (p. 229–264) and index.
Subjects:	Fatherless families United States.
	Fatherhood United States.
	Fathers United States.
	Paternal deprivation United States.
	Children of single parents United States.
	United States social conditions.
OCLC Number:	33359622

The initial parts of either Library of Congress or Dewey call numbers indicate the general subject area. The following chart lists the basic Library of Congress subject areas and the corresponding Dewey subject headings.

LIBRARY OF CONGRESS	DEWEY
A—General Works	000—Generalities
B—Philosophy; Psychology; Religion	100—Philosophy and Related Disciplines
C—Auxiliary Sciences of History	200—Religion
D—General and Old World History	900—History; Geography
E, F—American History	
G—Geography; Maps; Recreation; Anthropology	
H—Social Sciences (Economics; Sociology)	300—Social Sciences
J—Political Science	
K—Law	
L—Education	
M—Music	700—The Arts
N—Fine Arts	
P—Linguistics; Languages; Literature	400—Language
	800—Literature
Q—Science	500—Pure Science
R—Medicine	600—Applied Science; Technology
S—Agriculture	
T—Technology	
U—Military Science	
V—Naval Science	
Z—Bibliography; Library Science	

Books and other materials are shelved systematically by call numbers. As an example, let's consider the parts of the call number based on the Library of Congress system for David Popenoe's *Life without Father:* HQ756.P65 1996. On the library shelves, books are alphabetized according to the letters indicating the general topic area—HQ in our example. Within each general topic area, items are arranged in ascending numerical order according to the topic subdivision, in this case 756. For books, items within the subdivision are arranged alphabetically by the first letter of the author's last name and then numerically by an additional file number to ensure that each book in the collection has a unique call number. In our example, P is the first letter of Popenoe's name and 65 is the additional file number. Finally, 1996 is the book's date of publication. Call numbers can get more complex than our example indicates, but the same filing and shelving principles apply. Call numbers not only provide a shelving address for an information source but ensure that items on the same topic are stored together. Thus if you locate one item on your subject, you may find others in the immediate vicinity.

Electronic catalogs may index the library collection according to a number of different source characteristics, such as media type or publication date, but the subject, author, and title indexes are the ones most frequently used by researchers. Kristen located Popenoe's book and others by conducting subject searches using the search vocabulary from her brainstorming list. A subject search on the term "fathers" led her to Popenoe's book.

Library-Based Periodical Indexes

As we noted, the central library catalog lists titles of periodical holdings but does not provide information on the articles that these periodicals contain. The tools used to access periodical articles are developed by commercial companies that sell their indexes to academic libraries. On page 324, we mentioned that Kristen used *General OneFile,* an electronic periodical index, to help narrow her research topic. *General OneFile* surveys thousands of periodicals—popular magazines as well as a selection of specialized academic and professional journals—and assigns each article to one or more subject areas. Articles are also indexed by article titles, authors' names, publication titles, year of publication, and a number of other document characteristics.

Queries.   You begin searching an electronic database by typing in a *query,* which is typically one or more words that are related to your topic of interest. In response, the retrieval system attempts to match the query with relevant information sources in the system's database. Though systems vary in their precise search strategies, most compare the specific words in queries to indexes or word lists compiled from all the information sources. Some indexes are created by subject-area professionals who read sources and then assign indexing terms that describe their contents; others are merely lists of all the words that occur in the text of the source, often ranked by frequency or prominence in the document.

In addition to subject indexes, systems may include indexes based on a variety of bibliographic elements. Author, title, and subject are the standard indexes available for searching library catalogs, but many systems index other items, such as publication date, language, personal name, geographic name, and source type (book, video, audio, and so forth). Often you can examine several indexes with a single query; for example, you could search for sources on single-parent families that were published after 1995. In databases that provide the full text of magazine, journal, or newspaper articles, the words used in each article may be indexed so that you can actually search the articles' contents.

Each item in a retrieval system index points to one or more electronic *records* for individual sources that are related to the index item. A record contains a description of a source and an indication of where it can be found. In some cases—for instance, when searching the World Wide Web—the record may provide a direct electronic link to the complete version of the source (see Figure 9-2).

The limitations of database retrieval systems.   Information retrieval systems are designed to be "user friendly." For instance, if you mistakenly type "family valus" as your query, the system may respond, "Did you mean: 'family values'?" Or if you type in the query "1st family," the system may automatically guide you to the equivalent indexing term "first family." Responses such as this may give the impression that the system is able to understand the user's intentions and thus possesses a rudimentary form of artificial intelligence. User-friendly interfaces are helpful, but don't expect an information retrieval system to do any of your thinking for you. It is primarily a word-matching tool and can only make even

FIGURE 9-2   How an Information Retrieval System Works

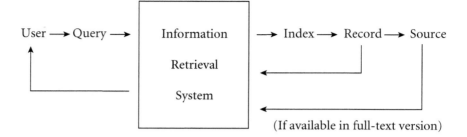

the simplest inferences about your research interests and your intentions. If you have the impression that the system will somehow figure out what you are interested in and guide you to the relevant sources, you may actually fail to locate the most useful information.

Conducting a subject search.   Using the *General OneFile* database, Kristen enters the term "family" as a subject search, and as Figure 9-3 shows, she discovers that a number of subject headings contain the word *family*. Kristen notes that the subject heading containing the single

FIGURE 9-3

From Gale. *General OneFile.* ©, a part of Cengage Learning, Inc. Reproduced by permission. www.cengage.com/permissions.

word *family* has subdivisions, so she decides to browse through them. Figure 9-4 shows one screen of "family" subdivisions. From this and subsequent screens, Kristen chooses the subdivisions "analysis," "political aspects," and "social aspects," which seem closest to her topic. Figure 9-5 shows a screenshot of references listed under the "political aspects" subheading. Kristen peruses the lists of sources under each relevant subject heading and subheading. For titles that look promising, she views the complete records for the articles, which include publication information and in some cases the full text. Kristen returns to the initial results from searching for "family" as a subject heading (see Figure 9-3), browses through the "related subjects" listed under "family," and notes that "family studies" and "family values" are subject headings of possible interest. She examines the lists of sources under these subject headings and compiles a list of those that seem most relevant to her paper topic.

There are scores of different periodical indexes that vary widely in topic area and organizational structure. Some, such as *General OneFile, Academic Search Premier,* and *ProQuest Research Library,* cover a vast range of subject areas; other indexes deal with limited topic areas or academic disciplines. Kristen consults a specialized index in her research on contemporary family structure: SocINDEX, which focuses on literature in sociology and related disciplines. SocINDEX operates in a similar fashion to General OneFile and other nonspecialized electronic indexes; however, some specialized indexes can be baffling

FIGURE 9-4

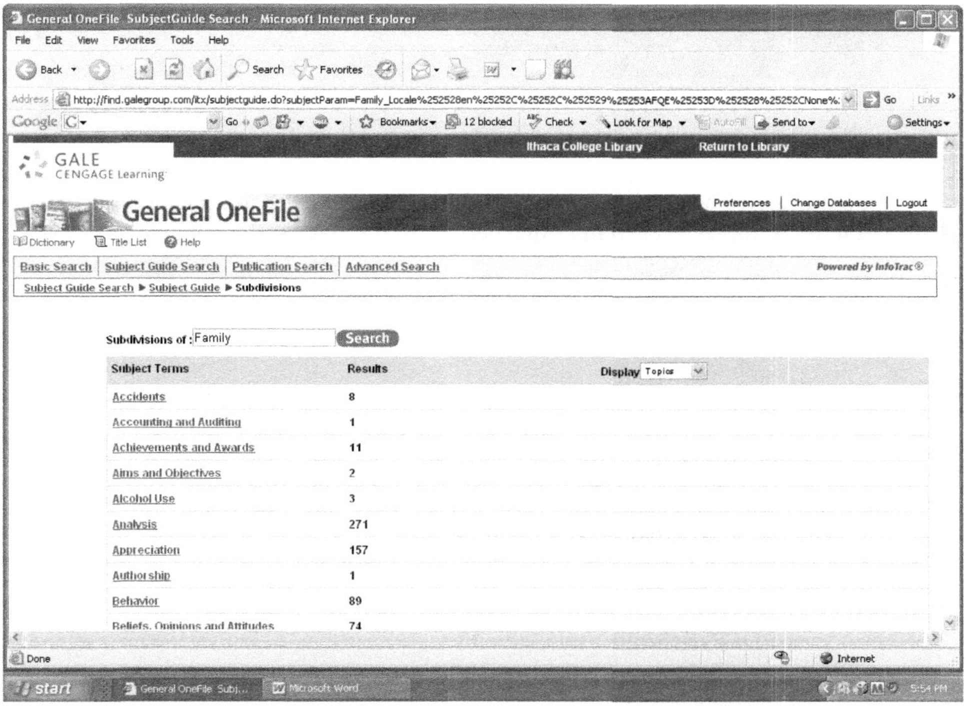

From Gale. *General OneFile.* ©, a part of Cengage Learning, Inc. Reproduced by permission. www.cengage.com/permissions.

FIGURE 9-5

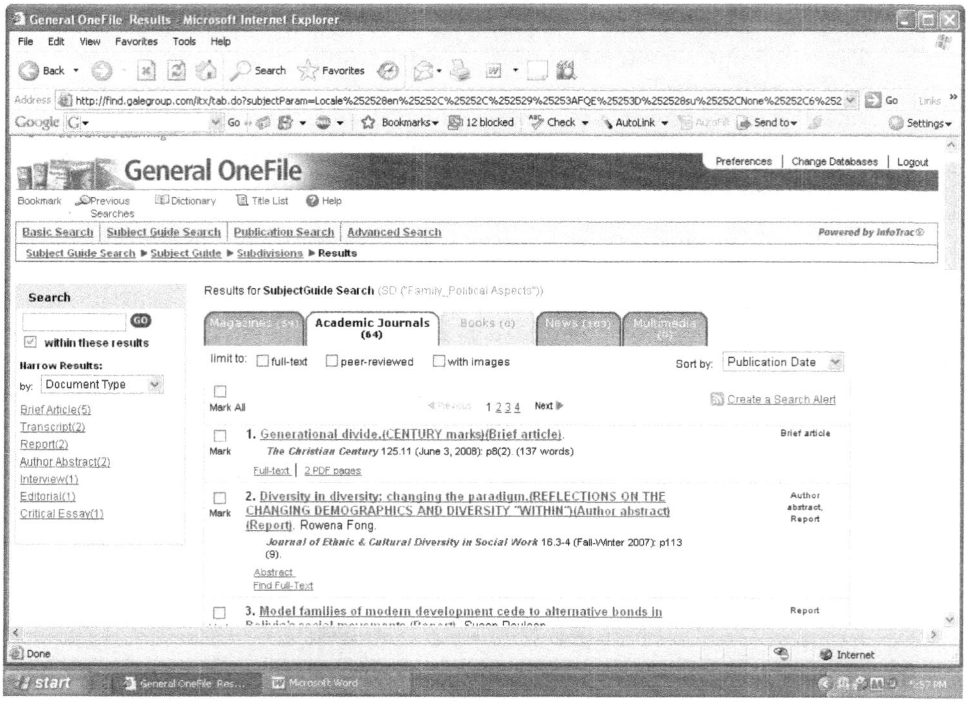

From Gale. *General OneFile*. ©, a part of Cengage Learning, Inc. Reproduced by permission. www.cengage.com/
permissions.

to the novice, so you may need the help of a reference librarian the first time you use them.
Other examples of current online periodical indexes are the following:

Alternative Press Index

AP Images

Biological Abstracts

Business Source Premiere

Contemporary Women's Issues

ERIC (education)

Ethnic Newswatch

GPO Access (federal publications)

GreenFile (environmental issues)

Historical Abstracts

MEDLINE (health and medicine)

MLA International Bibliography

Music Index Online

National Newspaper Index

PsycINFO (psychology)

ScienceDirect

SPORTDiscus (athletics)

Note that the names of online periodical indexes sometimes change as they evolve and combine. Consult your reference librarian for a current list of titles.

Often periodical indexes provide abstracts of articles, which are short summaries of the articles' contents. Keep in mind that abstracts are intended only to help researchers decide which articles are most relevant to their interests; they are not meant to circumvent careful reading of the entire article. Do not rely on abstracts as information sources; they are only access tools. It is considered dishonest to cite an article in a research paper if you read only the abstract and not the full text.

Academic libraries typically provide electronic versions of periodical indexes. Your library may devote specific computer workstations to one or several selected electronic periodical indexes or may link its electronic indexes so that they can all be accessed, along with the library's online catalog, from each library workstation. These services may be accessible from computer workrooms outside the library or even from your dorm room, depending on your college's computer network.

As more periodicals become available in electronic form, many academic libraries are cutting back on the number of paper or microform versions in their collections and instead providing online access to periodicals. Your library may have computer workstations where you can locate, read, and print out full-text versions of the articles you need.

Exercise 9.7

Select a topic, or use one assigned by your professor. Go to the library and find two books and two periodical articles on your topic. Use a computerized access tool, either an online library catalog or a periodical database, to find at least one of these sources, and if possible, have the computer print out the record for the source. Photocopy the table of contents of the book or periodical, and on the photocopy, circle the chapter or article that is relevant to your topic. Submit the computer printout and the photocopies to your instructor.

USE ELECTRONIC CATALOGS AND PERIODICAL DATABASES

Subject Headings and Their Subdivisions

Using an electronic library catalog of a periodical database such as *General OneFile,* you can, with most topics, search by subject and quickly obtain a list of possible sources. As we explained on pages 326–327, you first brainstorm a list of words or phrases that seem to describe your topic area. Then, you conduct subject searches using those terms. With a good list of search terms and access to your library catalog and various periodical databases, you should be able to locate sources related to virtually any subject area. But this is not the end of the research process by any means. It's relatively easy to get search results, but getting database "hits" does not mean you have adequately researched your topic.

When you work with large databases such as *General OneFile,* which provides access to millions of articles, any subject search is likely to retrieve hundreds or even thousands of articles, more than you can even skim. When confronted with these long lists of sources, you may be inclined to work with those at the top of the lists, which are typically the most recently published. The problem with this strategy is that search terms can only approximate your interests, and you must actually examine the sources retrieved by the search to determine which will be most useful. While recently published sources are often desirable, the best sources for your purposes may have been published several years ago and might be buried deep in a source list.

A broad search may retrieve thousands of sources, far more than you can carefully review, but a narrow search may miss the material that would best serve your purposes. For example, imagine that you are writing a research paper for a sociology class on the impact that human cloning would have on American society. If you use the expressions "cloning" or "human cloning" to search the World Wide Web, you will retrieve hundreds of information sources, only some of which will be relevant to your topic. If you use a more exclusive query such as "human cloning regulation," you will probably retrieve useful sources concerning legal restrictions on cloning, but you may not obtain more speculative pieces on the potential impact of human cloning.

With large databases, perhaps the best strategy is to conduct four or five relatively narrow searches, trying out a range of search terms. This technique enables you to zero in on relevant sources and expand recall beyond what would be achieved with a single query. The following table illustrates how Kristen applies this approach using the search vocabulary she generated (see page 326) and the *General OneFile* database. Recall that Kristen has partially narrowed her topic (pages 323–324) and is now looking for sociological studies of the family. The subject subdivisions listed are generated automatically by the *General OneFile* database.

SUBJECT SEARCH TERM	SUBDIVISION	NUMBER OF ARTICLES RETRIEVED
Family		11,765
Families		(see Family)
Family values		147
Family values	Social aspects	9
Family values	Research	4
Nuclear family		22
Single mothers		1,237
Single mothers	Social aspects	235
Single fathers		162
Single fathers	Social aspects	24
Gay family		Not a subject heading
Lesbian family		Not a subject heading
Family structure		Not a subject heading
Family policy		1,970
Family policy	Social aspects	94

As she applies her search vocabulary to the database, Kristen discovers additional search terms that did not occur to her initially. For example, when she retrieves the results for the subject Nuclear family, Kristen selects the "Related subjects" link that *General OneFile* provides and is guided to two subject headings: Family, Extended family. Kristen adds the term "extended family" to her search vocabulary list, since she realizes this is an important aspect of both traditional and modern families that she did not consider initially. When she tries "Gay family" as a subject search, she finds that *General OneFile* does not use that term as a subject heading, but the database provides a list of its closest matches to "Gay family," which includes the term "Gay parents." Once again, Kristen adds this term to her search vocabulary list. When she tries the search term "Family structure," it does not match a *General OneFile* subject heading; but in the closest match list, Kristen sees the term "Family studies," which she adds to her own search vocabulary list. In the early stages of your research, be aware of and explore the subject headings that surface as you work with databases. Follow avenues that open up as you work with databases.

At this stage, Kristen reduces as well as adds to her search vocabulary list. For example, when she examines the first few documents that she retrieved with the search term "Family policy" and the subheading "Social aspects," she sees that the articles are about family planning and population control, topics that are not directly relevant to her research topic. She decides to cut "Family policy" from her list. Her preliminary research is largely a process of figuring out how the database indexes the material related to her topic. This process takes time, but ultimately it may help Kristen avoid spending hours poring through sources that don't turn out to be relevant.

Boolean Searching

As she scans through her search results, Kristen notices that many of the subject terms she used are still relatively broad, and she has retrieved more sources than she has the time to read. She decides to narrow her search further using the Boolean operators AND, OR, and NOT. Boolean operators are used to link search elements in logical relationships, as indicated in the following chart:

FIRST SUBJECT HEADING	BOOLEAN OPERATOR	SECOND SUBJECT HEADING	RESULT
single fathers	AND	single mothers	Each source retrieved is about both single fathers and single mothers.
single fathers	OR	single mothers	Retrieves all sources that are about either single fathers or single mothers.
single fathers	NOT	single mothers	Retrieves all sources about single fathers but excludes any that are also about single mothers.

Most electronic library catalogs and periodical databases allow users to create complex searches using Boolean operators. Boolean searches can be very specific to your research topic, and they can take full advantage of the potential of electronic databases. For example, let's assume that you want information on the national debate over welfare reform that occurred in 1996. If you enter the subject heading "welfare reform," the Boolean opera-tor AND, and the publication year "1996," the computer will respond as follows:

1. Create a list of all items that have the subject heading "welfare reform."
2. Create a list of all items that have a publication year of 1996.
3. Compare list 1 and list 2 and create a new list of all items that have "welfare reform" as a subject heading *and* were published in 1996.
4. Return to the researcher the total number of items in list 3 and, if requested, the refer-ence for each item in list 3.

Note that AND and NOT narrow the search by placing limits on the first search term, while OR expands the search by adding a second term to the query. The Boolean AND sometimes confuses researchers who associate the word *and* with addition and hence think that the operation will increase the number of sources retrieved. The Boolean AND actu-ally places more restrictions on searches and usually cuts down on the number of hits. The Boolean operator that increases the number of sources retrieved is OR. The query "welfare reform" AND "occupational training" retrieves only articles that covered both welfare reform and job training efforts. By contrast, the query "welfare reform OR occupational training" locates three types of articles: those that focus exclusively on welfare reform, those that focus exclusively on job training, and those that cover both topics.

The Boolean operator NOT excludes specific items from the retrieval process. For example, the expression "welfare reform NOT occupational training" identifies articles on welfare reform but excludes articles that concern job training.

Some information retrieval systems allow you to use Boolean operators in algebraic expressions to piece together complex search statements such as the following:

((subject = welfare reform) OR (subject = occupational training)) AND (pub-lication year = 1996)

In order to use Boolean operators on the *General OneFile* database, Kristen needs to select the "Advanced Search" option. While some databases launch to Boolean searching mode at startup, many start with single subject searching as the default mode and provide Boolean operators as a user option which will have a label such as "Advanced Search," "Expert Search," or "Power Search." Kristen uses Boolean logic to construct several queries that are narrower than her previous searches:

Results from *General OneFile* Database Search

FIRST SUBJECT TERM	BOOLEAN OPERATOR	SECOND SUBJECT TERM	NUMBER OF ARTICLES RETRIEVED
family	AND	politics	623
family	AND	elections	185
family values	AND	nuclear family	5
family values	AND	politics	8
family values	AND	elections	5
single fathers	AND	single mothers	9
single mothers	AND	family values	0
single fathers	AND	family values	0

Notice that by using the AND operator, Kristen is able to draw in both aspects of her topic: American family values and American political discourse. Databases typically allow you to link at least three subjects using Boolean operators; *General OneFile* allows you to use as many as nine AND operators in a single query. The ability to use Boolean operators is critical to researchers because their topics are typically more complex than the concepts captured by the individual database subject headings.

Kristen decides to use the search narrowing functions built into the *General OneFile* software in order to reduce the scope of several of her subject searches. The following table describes the results of using several of those search-narrowing functions:

Results from *General OneFile* Database Search

SUBJECT QUERY	FUNCTION USED TO NARROW THE SEARCH	NUMBER OF DOCUMENTS RETRIEVED
family AND elections		185
family AND elections	peer-reviewed academic journals	10
family AND elections	publication year 2008	12

Database software typically allows you to limit your search by publication type and date, which are the factors that are usually of most interest to researchers. Many databases allow you to limit your searches according to other document features, for example, whether or not the document contains images.

Full Text Searching

In our earlier examples, Kristen was using Boolean operators and other database software features to narrow the scope of her search, since various items in her search vocabulary, such as "family," "family values," and "politics," generated numerous document hits, more than she could easily scan. Because so much is written about American families, both in scholarly and popular sources, subject searches on topics connected to the concept "family" usually generate a lot of document hits. For other topics, however, it may be difficult to locate relevant subject headings on electronic databases. For example, if you were researching the topic of photograph copyright, you might find a document that references the Supreme Court's landmark decision in the 1884 case of Burrow-Giles Lithographic Co. v. Sarony. You want to find out more about this particular case, so you conduct subject searches on *General OneFile, Proquest Research Library,* and *Academic Search Premier,* but get no results. To broaden your search, you might try "all text" or "full document" options rather than subject searches. While these options vary somewhat depending upon the database you are using, in general they search through the abstracts, citations, and the actual texts of documents for the terms in the search query. The following table shows the results of conducting full text searches for "Burrow-Giles Lithographic Co. v. Sarony" on several different databases:

DATABASE	SEARCH OPTION	NUMBER OF DOCUMENTS RETRIEVED
General OneFile	"entire document"	23
Proquest Research Library	"citation and document text"	7
Academic Search Premier	"all text"	33

Database software varies in how it matches the words in the query to those in the text of the document. The most straightforward approach is to search documents for the precise phrase in the query. For example, a search for "youthful offenders" would retrieve only documents that include the word "youthful" followed immediately by the word "offenders." In certain databases, the user activates this exact match function by placing quotation marks around the words in the search query. Some systems are sensitive to the proximity of words within documents and allow users to specify in their queries a maximum separation distance for words in the query. For instance, a query for "youthful offenders" could specify that no more than two words should separate "youthful" and "offenders," which would retrieve documents that include the phrase "youthful nonviolent offenders" but not "the youthful appearance of many violent offenders." Database software may also rank sources by the number of times they include the words in the query, since documents in which those words occur frequently are more likely to be useful to the researcher than documents that include only occasional uses of the words.

Comparing Results from Different Databases

Once you become familiar with a particular database and have used it successfully to research a topic, it is tempting to stick with it; however, it is best to use multiple databases, particularly in the early stages of your research. It is true that the same articles and books may be accessed from different databases, and thus searches conducted on multiple databases may be redundant to a degree; however, the indexing terms vary enough among databases that a particular query may yield different results as you move among databases.

Kristen decides to try her search vocabulary on two other general purpose databases: *Academic Search Premier* and *Proquest Research Library*. Notice how her results differ from those she obtained on *General OneFile*:

Results from *Academic Search Premier*

FIRST SUBJECT TERM	BOOLEAN OPERATOR	SECOND SUBJECT TERM	NUMBER OF ARTICLES RETRIEVED
family	AND	politics	351
family	AND	elections	93
family values	AND	nuclear family	3
family values	AND	politics	5
family values	AND	elections	11
single fathers	AND	single mothers	11
single mothers	AND	family values	4
single fathers	AND	family values	0

Results from *Proquest Research Library*

FIRST SUBJECT TERM	BOOLEAN OPERATOR	SECOND SUBJECT TERM	NUMBER OF ARTICLES RETRIEVED
family	AND	politics	1,305
family	AND	elections	324

family values	AND	nuclear family	0
family values	AND	politics	0
family values	AND	elections	0

Kristen's last three queries on *Proquest Research Library* yield no document hits, which suggests to her that "family values" is not a subject heading on that particular database. She enters "family values" as a single subject query and confirms that *Proquest* does not use that particular subject heading; however, that database does respond to the query with a list of "suggested topics about" family values. Kristen picks several of those suggested topics and uses them to construct subject searches with the following results:

Results from *Proquest Research Library*

SUBJECT QUERY	NUMBER OF ARTICLES RETRIEVED
family life AND values AND politics	39
family life AND values AND elections	17

Another approach Kristen tries is to use the phrase "family values" as a *citation and abstract* query on *Proquest Research Library.* This search feature examines the various elements in the citation for the source (author, article title, journal or magazine title, and so forth) as well as the source *abstract,* which is a brief summary of the source. *Proquest* does not use "family values" as a subject heading, but if the phrase "family values" occurs in a source title or abstract, then there is a good chance that the content of the source will pertain to the topic of family values. This strategy results in 1899 document hits, far too many to scan through, so Kristen uses Boolean operators to limit the search as follows:

Results from *Proquest Research Library*

ABSTRACT/ CITATION SEARCH TERM		FIRST SUBJECT TERM		SECOND SUBJECT TERM	NUMBER OF ARTICLES RETRIEVED
family values					1,899
family values	AND	nuclear family			1
family values	AND	gays and lesbians			11
family values	AND	politics	AND	elections	4

Recall that Kristen wants to compare the political rhetoric on family values with the more research-oriented material she studied in her sociology class. All-purpose databases like *General OneFile, Proquest Research Library,* and *Academic Search Premier* do cover a range of academic journals including some that publish sociological research. Kristen decides that she will also try a database that focuses specifically on sociology: SocINDEX.

Results from *SocINDEX With Subject* Database Search

FIRST SUBJECT TERM	BOOLEAN OPERATOR	SECOND SUBJECT TERM	NUMBER OF ARTICLES RETRIEVED
family values			221
family values	AND	nuclear family	4
family structure			1,858
family structure	AND	family values	0
family structure	AND	nuclear family	6
family structure	AND	single parents	88
family values	AND	single parents	1
family structure	AND	gay parents	14
family structure	AND	lesbian parents	0
family values	AND	gay parents	0
family values	AND	politics	0

Notice that "family structure," one of the items on Kristen's initial search vocabulary list that did not produce results on the generic databases, is a subject heading on SocINDEX. As you move from one database to the next, revisit your search vocabulary list and try various terms, not just the ones that worked on other databases.

Using One Source as a Bridge to Others

Once you have located a source that is relevant to your research, you can often use the subject headings and other characteristics of that source to locate additional information on your topic. When she is searching on *Academic Search Premier,* Kristen locates a source on family values and politics that she thinks will be useful for her paper. She notes the following information:

Author:	Arlene Skolnick
Author's bio:	Member of the Board of Directors of the Council on Contemporary Families and Visiting Scholar at New York University Department of Sociology.
Article title:	"Rethinking the Politics of the Family."
Publication:	*Dissent*
Date:	Fall 2004
Subject heading assigned to the source by *Academic Search Premier:*	Family, Women, Political parties, Conservatives, Political participation, Party affiliation

Kristen reasons that since Skolnick is a sociologist, she may have written additional article on American families, so Kristen enters an author and subject query on *Academic Search Premier:*

AUTHOR		SUBJECT TERM	NUMBER OF ARTICLES RETRIEVED
Skolnick, Arlene	AND	family	7

Kristen also tries additional subject searches using some of the subject headings that she noticed among those associated with Skolnick's article:

FIRST SUBJECT TERM		SECOND SUBJECT TERM	NUMBER OF ARTICLES RETRIEVED
conservatives	AND	family	18
conservatives	AND	family values	4
party affiliation	AND	family	6
party affiliation	AND	family values	0
party affiliation	AND	women	11
party affiliation	AND	single parents	1
party affiliation	AND	gay parents	0

Since she acquired new search vocabulary items from her work with Skolnick on *Academic Search Premier,* Kristen returns to *General OneFile* to try out these new search terms and see if they yield additional results:

DATABASE	FIRST SUBJECT TERM		SECOND SUBJECT TERM	NUMBER OF ARTICLES RETRIEVED
General OneFile	conservatives	AND	family	0
General OneFile	conservative	AND	family	41
General OneFile	conservative	AND	family values	0
General OneFile	party affiliation	AND	family	4
General OneFile	party affiliation	AND	women	13
General OneFile	party affiliation	AND	single parents	0
General OneFile	party affiliation	AND	gay parents	0

Kristen is also able to use articles she finds on periodical indexes as a bridge to books on her topic. She enters "Skolnick, Arlene" as a subject search on her college library's online book catalog and finds that the library has four books coauthored by Skolnick on the American family. As she peruses the sources she located through online databases, Kristen notices several are book reviews. One of the books being reviewed seems directly relevant to her topic: *Queer Family Values: Debunking the Myth of the Nuclear Family,* written by Valerie Lehr. Kristen switches from the online database to her college library's catalog and finds that a copy is available.

Kristen locates another article that provides a bridge to others sources: "The New Family Values Crusaders" written by Judith Stacey. Within the first few paragraphs, Stacey mentions the "central players" in a group of social scientists who were, in the mid 1990s, asserting the notion that the American family was in danger: Barbara Dafoe Whitehead, David Blankenhorn, David Popenoe, and Jean Bethke Elshtain. Kristen assumes that these scholars have published on the topic of the family, and tries a series of database queries, specifying each in turn as author and also using the subject term of "family." Indeed, she finds these authors have published articles and, in some cases, books on the topic. Taken together, these resources provide Kristen with a clear understanding of the position these scholars took on the status of the American family and the influence it had on both conservative and liberal politicians. She plans on using this information in her essay to explain how social science scholarship has influenced the political debate over family values.

The particular path that Kristen takes in her research is unique; it is determined by the demands of her topic but also by her own ingenuity as a researcher. Notice that her research process is dynamic. She is not merely "looking things up" but rather probing, exploring, and investigating. Good researchers are creative thinkers who strategize and see connections among ideas. Don't pursue a "hit and run" research strategy by merely entering queries until you get some hits and then printing out a few sources from on the top of your document list. Take the time to explore available databases and experiment with various queries. Follow up on leads that come to the surface as you conduct research. Exercise your mind and have some fun!

Using Additional Search Features: Truncation and Wild Cards

Computerized retrieval systems usually allow you to truncate or shorten search terms. Instead of typing in the search statement "politically correct movement," you might enter "political* AND correct*" on a system where * is used as a truncation symbol. This query would retrieve "politically correct movement," "political correctness," and other variations on this terminology. It is often wise to truncate words in search statements, particularly when you are unsure of the precise indexing terms used in the database.

A query wild card is a symbol, typically a question mark, which indicates a missing letter in a query that could take on any character value. For example, the query "wom?n" would retrieve "woman" and "women."

LOCATE INFORMATION ON THE WORLD WIDE WEB

The World Wide Web is aptly named; it encases the globe in a web of data pathways consisting of electrical wires, fiber optic cables, and wireless signals. These pathways link together millions of Web sites, which are locations on the Web created and maintained by organizations or individuals. While Web sites range widely in purpose, content, size, and organization, they are often collections of texts and/or images. The content of a Web site is displayed on one or more Web pages, which vary in length from a single computer screen to the equivalent of hundreds of screens that users may scroll through. A Web site usually has a home page that indicates the basic purpose of the site; for large sites, the home pages may provide links to various Web pages contained within the site or to Web pages on other sites.

For the next few pages, we will discuss Web research that is conducted through search engines such as Google and AltaVista, but in point of fact, most library catalogs and periodical databases, the resources we discussed on pages 331–344, are also accessed through the World Wide Web and are considered Web products. Some students may have difficulty understanding the distinction we are about to make between library-based and Web-based resources, and indeed, these two realms become more intertwined as time goes on. Since a single computer interface may provide access to the library catalog, periodical databases, and Web search engines such as Google, the user may see them as equally reliable means of accessing information. But as we will explain, it is important for researchers to understand the distinctions among these access tools.

The growth of the World Wide Web has made it easy to locate certain types of information. Using a Web search engine such as Google, a guitar player can, within minutes, find Web sites with product information on new and used guitars, chords for the latest songs, and discographies for famous guitarists. This information would take hours to collect without the Web. The Web works well in this case for several reasons. Since thousands of amateur musicians and music fans use the Web to share information, its popular music resources are vast and probably cover any guitar, song, or guitarist. Also, search queries about guitars, guitar music, and guitarists are relatively easy to formulate because they are based on straightforward names (Fender, Purple Haze, Jimi Hendrix). Finally, amateur guitarists are looking for information that is interesting or useful, but they may not be concerned with precision. For example, amateurs are satisfied with playable chord progressions that sound close to the original recording; they don't need authentic musical transcriptions.

The World Wide Web does not work as well for academic researchers as it does for hobbyists. One difficulty is that books and academic journals remain the standard vehicles for scholarly communication, and these publications are not necessarily available on the Web. Thus there is no guarantee that the Web will provide access to important scholarly resources on your topic. Another problem is that the Web is not arranged and indexed with the needs of the academic researcher in mind, so you may have difficulty locating material on your subject even when it is available on the Web. A final difficulty is that academic researchers care very much about reliability and accuracy, but the Web has no effective quality control. Anyone can establish a Web page and disseminate any information; thus, the Web has expanded tremendously the opportunity for publishing material that has no basis in fact. Some Web pages use graphics that appear very professional, but the content on those pages is merely uninformed opinion or is slanted to sell a product or service. For instance, if Kristen used the query "family," she might be directed to Web pages of divorce lawyers and family therapists advertising their services. Commercial Web pages, usually indicated by Web addresses that end in ".com," are often specifically designed to attract search engines so that the services or products promoted by such sites receive maximum exposure. Some commercial sites provide information useful to researchers, but others are biased and manipulative.

Despite its limitations, researchers often find the World Wide Web useful, and in some cases it is essential. When Kristen wants to find the positions of current candidates for office on family values, she turns to their campaign Web sites. The Web sites are, in many cases, the official media outlets for the campaigns and thus are more author-itative than newspaper articles that report secondhand on the candidates' statements. Many branches of the federal and state governments use the Web as their primary means of disseminating information. Some academic and popular periodicals publish online, either as a fee-based service or for free. The Web's importance to researchers will undoubtedly increase in the years to come as more and more resources come online.

In order to connect to Web sites, you need a computer that has Web browser soft-ware, such as Internet Explorer or Mozilla Foxfire, and is linked to a Web service com-pany, such as AOL or Roadrunner. While you are a student, your college may provide you with Web access. Computers in your campus library, classrooms, and technology workrooms may link to the Web, and your dormitory room may have wall jacks that allow you to connect your own computer to the Web. If you live off campus, your college may provide a dial-up service for Web access. Figure 9-6 illustrates the pathways involved when a user connects to the Internet, accesses a search engine, and is directed to the search results.

FIGURE 9-6   Searching the World Wide Web

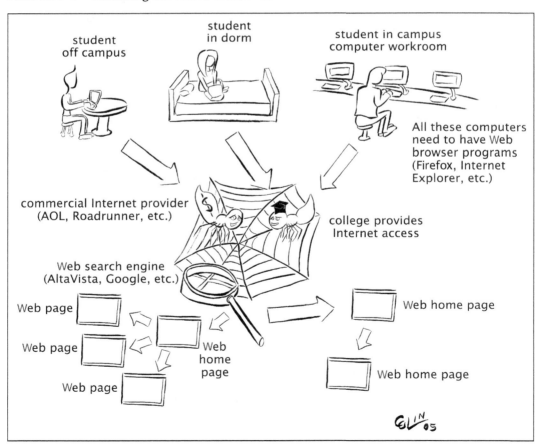

URLs

Each Web site is identified by its *universal resource locator,* more commonly called its URL. If you want to visit a particular Web site, you can travel there through cyberspace by typing its URL into the appropriate window of your Web browser.

URLs have a particular structure:

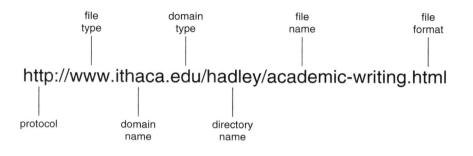

The domain type provides important information about the nature of the Web site. In our example, the domain type is .edu, which is reserved for Web sites associated with educational institutions. The URL domain types .com and .net indicate a Web site established by a commercial business; .org is used by nonprofit organizations and advocacy groups, and .gov by governmental organizations. The affiliation of the Web site producer gives you some indication about the rhetorical goals of the site. If, for instance, you are seeking information about the effectiveness of a new drug for lowering cholesterol, it would be important to know if the Web site you are visiting is associated with a commercial drug producer, a non-profit health advocacy group, a university where researchers study cholesterol, or a government agency involved in drug regulation. Of course, you cannot judge the quality and objectivity of a Web site's information based on its URL alone. For example, while the cholesterol-reduction drug producers want you to buy their products, they are obligated by law to provide accurate information to the public; thus, their .com corporate Web sites might give you just the information you need to compare the functions of various drugs. But as we explained in our earlier discussion of critical reading (see pages 70–72), it is important to factor in the authors' rhetorical goals when you analyze and evaluate sources.

U.S. government Web sites house a wealth of information about American society. In the course of her research, Kristen investigates the Web site of the federal government (http://usgov .gov). She finds Web links related to the American family and follows them to *ChildStats.gov* (http://www.childstats.gov), the official Web site of the Federal Interagency Forum on Child and Family Statistics, which provides up-to-date information on American family structure.

Common Domain Types

DOMAIN SUFFIX	NATURE
.com	Commercial and business entities
.net	Network organization or network administration
.org	Public and nonprofit organizations, business, and groups

DOMAIN SUFFIX	NATURE
.info	Nonprofit; intended for informative sites
.edu	Education; reserved for educational institutions (most are postsecondary)
.gov	Federal and local U.S. government sites
.mil	Department of Defense and military sites

Web Search Engines

Your instructors may give you the URLs of specific Web sites that they want you to visit in connection with their courses. Their syllabi or online assignment sheets may even provide links that allow you to travel directly to these sites. In other cases, however, you may need to "surf" the Web on your own to locate information, and for this purpose, you need to use a Web search engine, which is a tool that combs the Web looking for sites related to your search term. When you type your query into a search engine, it responds with a list of Web sites that correspond as closely as possible to the words or phrases you provided. Search engines use a variety of methods for locating information, so entering the same words or phrases on two search engines can generate strikingly different results; thus, it is wise to search for your topic on several engines. Another approach is to use a *metasearch engine* which examines the databases of multiple search engines. For example, the metasearch engine WebCrawler accesses Ask, Google, Live Search, and Yahoo.

If you have Web access through a service provider such as AOL or Roadrunner, a search engine may appear on your home page when you first link to the Web. Once you are on the Web, you may travel, free of charge, to various search engines, including the following:

EXAMPLES OF SEARCH ENGINES

AltaVista (http://altavista.com)

Ask (http://www.ask.com)

Google (http://www.google.com)

Google Scholar (http://scholar.google.com)

Live Search (http://www.live.com)

Yahoo (http://search.yahoo.com)

EXAMPLES OF METASEARCH ENGINES

DogPile (http://www.dogpile.com)

Mamma (http://www.mamma.com)

Webcrawler (http://webcrawler.com)

Since search engines are elements of the dynamic Web industry, be aware that their names and URLs may change.

Once you are connected to the Web, you may travel to these search engines by typing in their URLs. You will also see links to these search engines on various Web pages, such as on your library home page.

Large or complex Web sites often have internal search engines that provide access just to Web pages included within the site. Your college's home page may include a window labeled "search" where you can type in keywords and receive a list of Web pages maintained on your campus that are related to your query. If you type in "psychology," the search engine might return links to the Web pages of your psychology department, the various faculty members in the psychology department, student organizations for psychology majors, and so on.

The list of Web sites that a search engine returns in response to your query is, in most cases, arranged in order of relevance to your query, with the most relevant sources at the top of the list. Figure 9-7 shows the AltaVista home-page search window where Kristen typed in her query "family structure values." Figure 9-8 is a partial list of sources that AltaVista returned in response to Kristen's query.

We mentioned earlier that library-based subscription services typically allow you to search with more precision than is possible on the Web. There are, however, several ways to make Web searching more precise. First, make sure that you generate an extensive list of search terms and use several of them simultaneously to restrict the search to the most relevant items. Notice that in the previous example based on an AltaVista search, Kristen combined the terms *family structure* and *family values* to narrow her search to sources that address both issues.

Another way to increase the precision of your Web search is to select the advanced or expert search option. When you start up most search engines, they are configured for simple keyword searches of all available indexes. All too often, these keyword searches yield thousands of hits, most of which are not useful. To refine your search and take advantage of features such as Boolean operators, you may need to shift to advanced searching mode. Figure 9-9 shows the Advanced Web Search screen from AltaVista.

Notice how the advanced search option allows users to narrow their searches. The "all of these words" option is equivalent to the Boolean AND function, while "any of these words" is the same as the Boolean OR, and "none of these words" replicates the Boolean NOT. The "this exact phrase" option is the same as placing quotation marks around a query so that it searches for precise phrase matches. In the "Search with . . . this boolean expression" window, users can create their own Boolean expressions and combine the AND, OR, and NOT functions in algebraic expressions that capture complex search logic. Under "Date:" users can specify a timeframe (any time, within the past week, within the past two weeks,

FIGURE 9-7 AltaVista Home Page

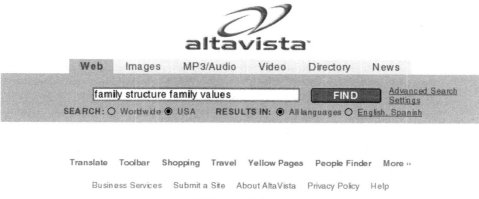

FIGURE 9-8 Search Results from AltaVista

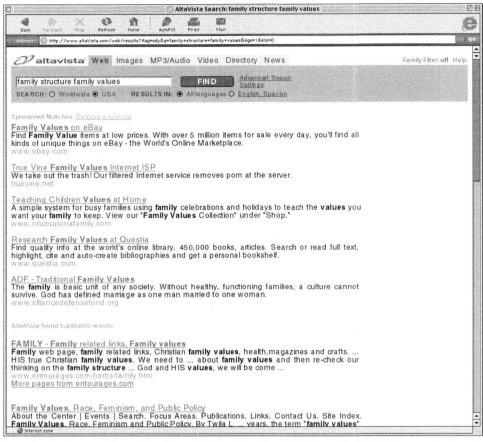

Reproduced with permission of Yahoo! Inc. © 2005 by Yahoo! Inc. YAHOO! and the YAHOO! logo are trademarks of Yahoo! Inc.

within the past month, and so on) or a date range (beginning with 1980). The "File type:" option allows users to limit the file formats (text, PDF, html, and so forth) of the documents that their searches will retrieve. This option might be important if your computer is only able to read certain types of files. Using the "Location" windows, users can limit their searches to certain types of sites (.com, .edu, .gov, .org, and so forth) or to sites that share a certain root URL (for instance, http://whitehouse.gov to limit the search to White House Web sites). These various options on the advanced search page allow for much more precise searches than does the keyword search available on the search engine home page.

Here are several additional searching techniques to improve your efficiency and success when you conduct research on the World Wide Web:

1. Read all the help screens or searching tips that accompany the particular search engine you are using. Each search engine has unique characteristics that you must understand if you are to take full advantage of its potential.

FIGURE 9-9 AltaVista Advanced Web Search Page

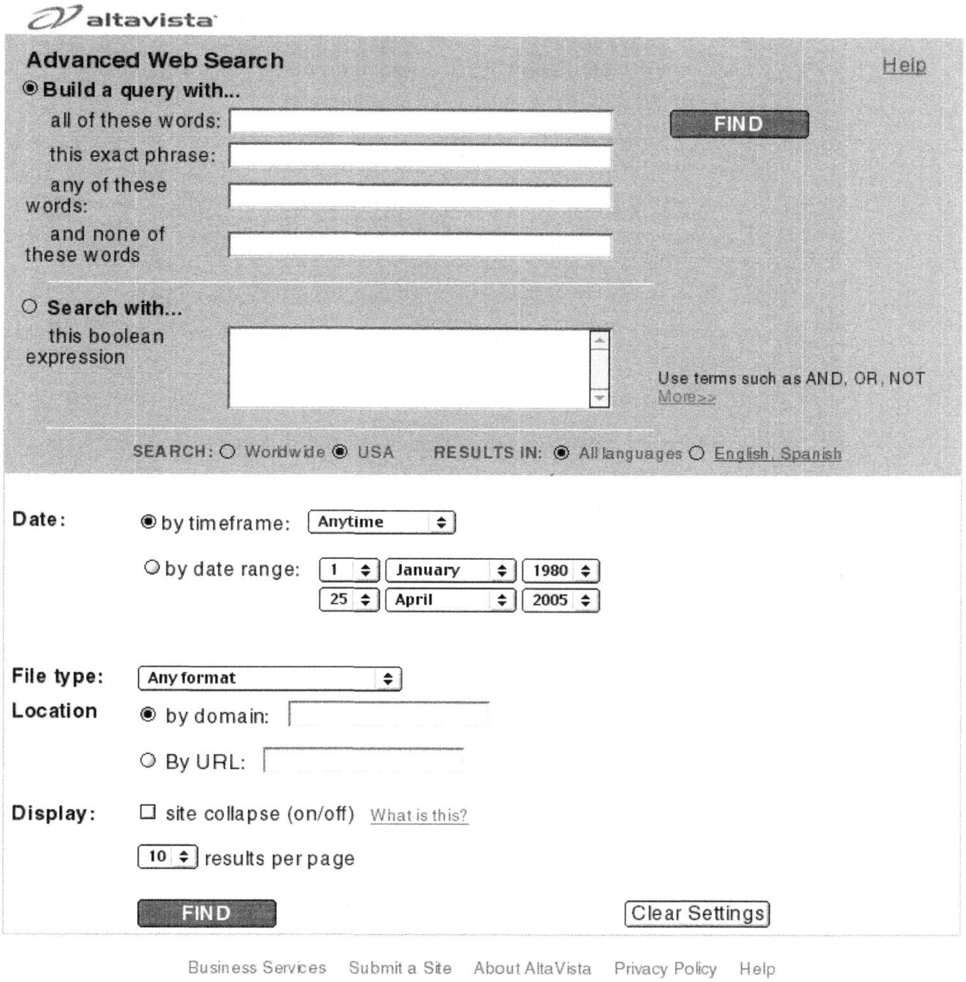

2. Try your query on several different search engines. Given that the Web search engines are not precise research tools, it often helps to experiment with several and find which responds best to your particular query.

3. Look for electronic sources that have comparable print versions, and steer away from sources that have no print equivalents. Unsubstantiated opinion does sometimes appear in print, but as a general principle, information that finds its way into print is more reliable than information that is available only on the Web.

4. Evaluate the reliability of Web sources. Researchers should always question the reliability of sources, even if they come from an academic library. It is very important to evaluate Web-based sources. With the computer tools currently available, anyone can create a professional-looking Web page and stock it with content that is completely absurd. Ask yourself the following questions about Web sites:

- What is the overall goal of the Web site? Do the authors of the Web site have motives other than presenting the objective truth? For instance, does the site advocate a particular political agenda or sell a product?
- Is the site produced by a reputable organization? Does it provide a mailing address and phone number? Does it invite inquiries?
- Do the authors of the Web site identify themselves? Do they provide any evidence of their expertise or credibility? For example, do they possess training or experience in the topic area covered by their site? Do they demonstrate that they are aware of the standard scholarly or professional literature in the topic area?
- Do the authors distinguish between opinion and fact? Do they provide nonanecdotal evidence to substantiate their conclusions? Do they cite published sources?
- When was the site created? How often is it updated? When was it last updated?

Your college reference librarians may have additional suggestions on how to improve search precision. They are experienced Web users and know how best to use the Web to answer your particular research questions.

COLLECT INFORMATION THROUGH SURVEYS AND INTERVIEWS

In most cases, the bulk of the material you use in research papers will come from published sources; however, depending on your topic and assignment, it might be appropriate to use information collected through informal interviews and surveys. For example, imagine you are writing a research paper for a psychology class on how birth order (only child, first born, middle child, last born, and so on) affects personality. The psychological literature contains numerous studies on this topic, but you might also interview students in your dorm who represent each of the birth order positions and use these "cases in point" as concrete illustrations of the conclusions reached in the psychological studies. You might also survey twenty or thirty students representing a range of birth orders to see if their perceptions of the relationship between birth order and personality match the research findings.

Informal interviews and surveys provide only anecdotal information and are not a reliable basis for firm conclusions. Still, anecdotes are often useful for explaining a concept or framing an interesting introduction or closing for a research paper. Informal surveys may help you sharpen your research question or identify trends that warrant more careful investigation. Although an informal survey is not sufficient to challenge the conclusions of published studies, it may be useful to note a significant difference between informal and published research results. For instance, imagine that a student researcher conducts an informal survey in a college dorm on the interaction between birth order and personality. If the results of this informal survey differ from published conclusions, the student might suggest in his or her paper that additional formal research should be conducted to see if the published conclusions still hold for the current college-age population.

A final advantage of conducting informal surveys and interviews is that they get you directly involved with the topic. This hands-on approach helps increase your interest, particularly for topics that are rather dry if research is restricted to published sources alone.

Even if you do not end up using the anecdotal information you collect, the experience of getting actively involved with the topic will lead to a better final product.

Whenever you conduct informal interviews or surveys, keep in mind the following principles:

1. Make sure you comply with college regulations concerning the use of human subjects. These regulations are typically applied in more formal research studies, but your college may have guidelines even for informal interviews and surveys. Check with your instructor if you are unsure of your college's human subject policies.

2. Whatever your college's policies are, make sure you respect the privacy of your interview or survey subjects. Do not repeat their responses in casual conversation, and do not use subjects' actual names in your research paper unless there is a clear reason to do so and you have obtained their permission.

3. Establish clear goals for your questions. Interview or survey questions should be intended strictly to establish facts, record beliefs about what is fact, or record personal feelings or values.

4. Try asking the same question worded in several different ways. Sometimes a slight change in wording prompts a different response from a subject. It is often difficult to predict the precise wording that will convey your question most effectively.

5. Don't ask questions that betray a bias. Say you are surveying or interviewing last-born children to research a possible link between birth order and personality. You would indicate a bias if you asked, "In what ways did your parents and older siblings spoil you?" A more neutral question would be, "How did your parents and older siblings treat you? Did they treat other family members in the same way or differently?"

6. Do not press anyone who seems reluctant to consent to an interview or complete a survey. Many people prefer not to discuss their personal lives, particularly when someone is taking notes on what they say.

EVALUATE INFORMATION SOURCES

As you search for source material, you are constantly judging whether it has direct relevance to your topic. Don't excerpt information that is only remotely related. If you collect a lot of information without exercising judgment, you may get a false sense of how well your research is proceeding. You could have a large number of sources and still not have the information needed to develop the paper in the direction you intend. As you locate and work with sources, ask yourself how they fit in with your overall goals for the research paper. To what parts of the topic do the sources pertain? Do they support your preliminary thesis? What perspectives on the topic do they represent? Make sense of each source as you examine it. Don't wait until you have completed your research.

By urging you to exercise judgment in choosing sources, we are not suggesting that you ignore ideas that conflict with your own. Remember that your thesis is preliminary and subject to change. You may shift your point of view after you read some of the arguments presented in the sources.

In addition to evaluating the sources' relevance to your topic, you should also judge their comparative quality and credibility. Don't think you can have complete confidence in a source simply because you found it in a library. Libraries include wildly opinionated, even bizarre sources along with those that are logical and objective. There is nothing wrong with an author expressing a strong opinion, but it is a mistake for researchers to view all opinions as equally valid. Since research is a quest for understanding, researchers must work with the sources that are most helpful in making sense of the issue.

As you analyze sources, it is always helpful to speculate on the author's rhetorical purpose, as we described in Chapter 2 (pages 70–72). What are the author's reasons for writing? Who is the author's intended audience? How does the author want to influence this audience? The answers to these questions will help you understand the source better and figure out whether it is appropriate for your paper. For instance, if you are writing for a public health course on the impact that smoking in public places has on nonsmokers, you may be skeptical of information from the Tobacco Institute, an organization that represents the interests of the tobacco industry. If you are writing on spending priorities for public education, you may find useful information in a teachers' union publication, but you should keep in mind the union's desire to increase teachers' salaries and benefits. If you think about writers' motives, you can put their ideas in proper perspective.

Exercise 9.8

Locate two sources that pertain to your research topic but clearly differ in perspective, authoritativeness, or credibility. Write a one-page paper that compares the usefulness of these sources for your research purposes.

EXCERPT RELEVANT INFORMATION FROM SOURCES

The basic skills for excerpting information from library sources—paraphrasing, quoting and summarizing—are covered in Chapters 3 and 4 of this book. Here we discuss the special problems associated with the sheer number of sources you are working with for a research paper. A common problem is that a researcher loses track of the exact source for an important piece of information. Each time you excerpt a passage from a source, whether you hand-copy, reword, or photocopy, be sure you carefully record a complete citation to the source. Record the exact page numbers where specific pieces of text are located. When you draft your paper, you will cite the source as well as the page for each paraphrase, summary, and quotation. We give citation formats in Appendix A. The following chart summarizes the bibliographic information that you need to record.

INFORMATION YOU NEED FOR YOUR CITATION

Book

Author(s), title, publisher, city of publication, date of publication, pages where the information you excerpted is located

Magazine

Author(s), title of article, name of magazine, date (day, month, year), inclusive pages for entire article, pages where the information you excerpted is located

Scholarly Journal

Author(s), title of article, name of journal, volume number, year of publication, inclusive pages for entire article, pages where the information you excerpted is located

Newspaper

Author(s), title of article, name of newspaper, date (day, month, year), inclusive pages for entire article, pages where the information you excerpted is located

Web Site

Author(s), title of document, Web site name, date of electronic publication, organization associated with the site, date that you (the researcher) accessed the site, electronic address (URL) of the site

Web-Based Version of Source That Is Also Available in Print

Complete information for the Web site as well as complete publication information for the print version.

Another common difficulty is failing to distinguish adequately between paraphrases and quotations in research notes and thus including in the research paper an author's exact words without indicating that fact. This is an unintentional but serious form of plagiarism. Be very meticulous about your use of quotation marks as you take notes. Reread our discussion of plagiarism on pages 89–90.

There is also a danger of excerpting too much information. Some students compulsively collect every scrap of information that is remotely related to their topic, thinking that they will make sense of it all at their leisure. Don't bury yourself with paper, whether it is note cards, pages of notes, or photocopies of sources. Excerpt only what you think you might use. As we stressed earlier, research is a sense-making process. It is hard to make sense of something when you are overwhelmed with information. In the next section, we discuss how to judge the usefulness of sources as you locate them.

Much has been written on how you should record information that you excerpt from sources. Some textbooks strongly recommend index cards for research notes because cards can be grouped and rearranged easily. You can cut up pages from your research notebook or photocopies of sources and group these pieces just as you can note cards. Another alternative is to record your research notes on a computer and use word processing or outlining programs to organize the information. We recommend that you try various methods of recording excerpts and decide what works best for you.

In addition to notes that record specific pieces of information from the sources, you should keep a separate set of notes for preliminary thesis statements, organizational plans, or other important ideas that occur to you during the process of research.

Exercise 9.9

Read Kristen's paper on pages 364–376, noting the ways in which she excerpted information from sources. What method of excerpting predominates? Approximately what percentage of the paper is made up of source excerpts compared to the student's own ideas? Do you think this relative proportion is appropriate?

DRAFTING

Synthesize Sources

The research paper is, by its very nature, a synthesis. The power of research is its ability to bring together information from various sources to illuminate an issue, possibly in ways that the source authors did not anticipate. The researcher can be creative at all stages of the research process, but it is the act of synthesis that offers special opportunities for originality. You may be able to make connections among sources that have previously gone unnoticed or to structure information in new ways. Through synthesis, you give shape to the information. This is the ultimate goal of the research process.

In Chapter 7, we discussed five types of syntheses: a compare-and-contrast essay, a summary of multiple sources, an objective synthesis, an essay written in response or reaction to multiple sources, and a synthesis with a specific purpose. For a quick review, see the strategies for synthesizing on pages 257 and 270. You may use any of these approaches in research papers, depending on the assignment specifications and your goals.

Argue, Analyze, and Evaluate

It is common for long research papers to include more than one type of synthesis. Argument (Chapter 8), analysis (Chapter 6), and evaluation (Chapter 6) may also be important elements in a research paper. Reread Kristen's research paper on pages 364–376, paying special attention to where she uses argument, analysis, and evaluation.

Draft a Thesis

We mentioned earlier in this chapter that you may have a working thesis in mind when you begin researching. If not, one may emerge as you collect information. The following procedure will help you generate a working thesis from your research notes.

GENERATING A THESIS

1. Scan your research notes quickly, noting any general trends, main concepts, or overall patterns.
2. Freewrite for ten minutes on what you think your research might tell your reader.
3. Reduce your freewriting to several sentences that explain what you want to say to your reader.

After scanning her research notes, Kristen freewrites the following paragraph:

> From the sources I read, it seems as if a lot of the current attention to the American family comes from political debates about "family values." One thing that the politicians seem to agree on is that the traditional nuclear family is declining. Some politicians think that this change means that family values are also declining, but others think that a new set of family values is developing that is positive in its own way. Whatever their viewpoint, politicians often use the expression "family values" in a vague way. It's hard to pin down what they have in mind. However, the articles I read that were written by sociologists were much

clearer on exactly how family values are changing and what the advantages and disadvantages of those changes might be. I can use the observations of the sociologists to make better sense of what the politicians are talking about in the political debate over family values.

Kristen rereads her freewriting and condenses it into a preliminary thesis:

The political debate over family values has to do with the fact that the traditional nuclear family is declining. But the politicians use expressions like "family values" in a vague way and do not always explain exactly what they are thinking. The writings of sociologists on the family are more objective; the issues are clearer. I will try to use sociology to explain the issues that are at the base of politicians' positions on family values.

This is still a preliminary thesis. Compare it with the thesis excerpted from the final version of Kristen's research paper:

```
To a large extent, the debate over family values revolves around
whether this transformation represents the decline of the American
family or an opportunity to strengthen and improve families. The
sociological literature on the evolution and current status of the
American family helps clarify the issues that are at the core of
this political debate. I will use the findings of sociologists who
study the American family to analyze issues that lie at the core
of the political controversy over family values.
```

Notice that Kristen's final thesis is refined, more fully developed, and more coherent. The main purpose of a preliminary thesis is to focus your research activities, but sometimes you may need to depart from the initial thesis as you understand more about the topic.

Exercise 9.10

Draft a preliminary thesis statement for your own research paper. Ask a classmate to read your thesis statement and orally paraphrase it. Did your intentions come through?

DERIVE A PLAN

A research paper can follow one organizational plan or a combination of the plans we have discussed in this book. Review the major organizational plans presented on page 16.

A plan may occur to you as you conduct research. You may see that the information you collect from various sources fits into an obvious pattern, or you may borrow a plan from one of your sources. You might also consider how you might use the source information to support your thesis.

If no obvious pattern emerges from the information you collected, systematically examine your research notes. Derive one or more possible plans by categorizing the notes. If you use note cards, sort them into piles, grouping related information, to see what patterns appear. Try several grouping schemes to find what works best.

As Kristen sorts her note cards into piles, she fits them into five main categories:

1. Facts about how the traditional American nuclear family is fading and the new structures that are taking its place
2. Evidence that shifting cultural values caused changes in family structure
3. Evidence economic factors caused changes in family structure
4. Evidence that nontraditional family structures are harmful to children
5. Evidence that nontraditional family structures do not harm children

Kristen thinks about these five categories, reconsiders her preliminary thesis, and comes up with the following plan.

- Thesis: The political debate over family values has to do with the fact that the traditional nuclear family is declining. But the politicians use expressions like "family values" in a vague way and do not always explain exactly what they are thinking. The writings of sociologists on the family are more objective; the issues are clearer. I will try to use sociology to explain the issues that are at the base of politicians' positions on family values.

- First, I need to explain how the American family has changed over time. In particular, I need to trace the decline of the traditional nuclear family and the rise of alternative family structures.

- Next, I will explain the sociological evidence that decline of the traditional nuclear family results from a shift in cultural values.

- Then I will explain the evidence that economic conditions, not cultural values, have led to the increase in nontraditional families.

- Next, I will give the evidence that nontraditional families are harmful to children.

- Finally, I will examine the evidence that nontraditional families are viable structures for raising children.

CREATE AN OUTLINE

Throughout this book, we have discussed working from organizational plans as you draft essays. We have described these plans as outlines that do not include much detail. Detailed outlines are required for research projects. Because research writers must juggle many sources and deal with issues in depth, they need an outline that will keep them on task and provide a unifying framework for information from various sources. A pitfall of research paper writing is becoming bogged down in the details from sources and failing to clarify the relationships among ideas. If you draft your research paper working from a detailed outline, it will be easier to write, and in the end, your train of thought will be more evident to your audience.

Some instructors call for a traditional outline based on the following structure. Note that such an outline requires at least two entries at each successive level.

I.
  A.
    1.
      a.
        i.
        ii.
      b.
    2.
  B.
II.

The formal outline provides a clear hierarchical structure that is useful for imposing order on a complicated topic with a number of discrete subtopics. Here is a portion of a formal outline for a paper on contemporary family structure.

IV. Advantages of families in which both parents work
  A. Financial security
    1. The majority of families need two incomes to survive.
    2. Welfare reform is based on the premise that both parents are capable of earning money.
    3. Children derive significant benefits from the family's financial security.
  B. Gender role equality
    1. Home responsibilities are shared.
      a. Housecleaning and maintenance
      b. Food preparation
      c. Child rearing
    2. Men and women retain economic autonomy.
    3. Men and women hold equal authority over and responsibility for the fate of the family.
V. Disadvantages of having two working parents

With some topics or certain collections of sources, however, you may feel constrained if you have to force the material into this hierarchy. In these cases, free-form outlining, which allows the writer to determine his or her own structure, may come closer to reflecting your actual thinking. Here is a draft of Kristen's free-form outline based on the organization plan shown earlier. Notice that she expands on the organizational plan as she begins to plug in ideas from some of her sources.

> Thesis: The political debate over family values has to do with the fact that the traditional nuclear family is declining. But the politicians use expressions like "family values" in a vague way and do not always explain exactly what they are thinking. The writings of sociologists on the family are more objective; the issues are clearer.

I will try to use sociology to explain the issues that are at the base of politicians' positions on family values.

Changes in the American family in the 20th century

Katz and Stern (2007)

- nuclear families: 55% in 1900, 25% in 2000 (p. 91)
- rates of out-of-wedlock birth increased since 1970 (p. 91)
- 30% of households, single woman is head (p. 91)

Trimberger (2007)

- current out-of-wedlock birth rate at 2.5% (p. 83)
- more Americans currently living alone than in families with children (p. 82)

Bouchey (2007)

- 1/3 American children raised by single parent

Popenoe (1997)

- half of American marriages now end in divorce

Evidence that changes in "family values" led to structural changes in the family

Popenoe (1999)

- "highly expressive or self-focused individualism" (p. 30)
- "Playboy-style sexual opportunism and rejection of responsibilities" (p. 30)
- women see the nuclear family as an "oppressive institution" (p.30)
- sexual revolution led to sex outside marriage and divorce
- must restore "cultural importance of voluntary, lifelong monogamy" (p. 30)

Whitehead (1997)

- divorce comes to be viewed as an issue of what is best for adults, not for children

Elshtain (2000)

- children who grow up without "experience of seeing married life" do not develop family values

Evidence that American family has changed in response to economic conditions

Skolnick (1997)

- Since 1965, economy has not favored the "family-sustaining career opportunities"

Boushey (2007)

- Women entered workforce out of economic necessity even though the women's movement did open up career opportunities and reproductive options

Skolnick (2006)

- Homemaking no longer a viable career for women, so traditional family had to give way to other forms

Stacey (1994) and Skolnick (2004, p. 46)

- provide list of economic factors that changed family structure
- "Talk about family change is almost totally disconnected from the discussion of technology and economy" (Skolnick, 2006, p. 47).

Evidence that children are harmed by being raised in nontraditional familes

   Whitehead (2007)

      – Single mothers lack access to "two of the most effective sources of
        self-sufficiency-professional jobs and marriage" (p. 6)

   Gallagher and Blankenhorn (1997)

      – List drugs, psychological problems, violence, and abuse as risks of nontradi-
        tional families (p. 13)

   Elshtain (2000) and Popenoe (1997)

      – Children who don't live with both parents are two to three times more likely
        to develop psychological and behavioral problems

   Whitehead (1997)

      – Intact families allow parents to invest more time in their children

Evidence that children are not harmed by being raised in nontraditional families

   Skolnick (1997), Stacey (1994), and Ehrenreich (1996)

      – Impact of divorce on children is exaggerated
      – Stacey (p. 120) and Ehrenreich show weaknesses in research by Wallerstein
        that is most often cited to show that divorce is harmful to children

   Ehrenreich (1996)

      – Media distorts the impact of divorce and typically depicts divorce as bad

   Stacey (1994)

      – Social scientists think that the quality of relationships within families is
        more important than family structure (p. 120)

Evidence that homosexual parenting is not harmful

   Many politicians are opposed to gay marriage and gay parenting on moral/religious grounds
   Perrin (2002)

      – Review of the literature shows that children of gay and lesbian parents are not
        substantially different from their peers raised by straight parents. "Apparently
        parents' sexual orientation has no measurable effect on the quality of parent-
        child relations or on children's health or social adjustment" (p. 129)

Advantages of postmodern families

   Sherer (1996)

      – Postmodern families more flexible and can adapt to the times.

   Mack-Canty and Wright (2004)

      – Research shows feminist parents led to happier families and personal growth

   Bouchey (2007)

      – Research shows that working mothers actually spend more time with their
        children than stay-at-home moms

Conclusion: Comment on current election year and the continuing family values debate

Exercise 9.11

Create an outline for your research paper. Ask a classmate to read the outline and answer the following questions: (1) What is the overall plan for the paper? (2) Does each point in the outline relate clearly to the overall goal? Revise your outline in response to your classmate's comments.

WRITE FROM YOUR OUTLINE

Use your outline as a guide for drafting. Group your notes or note cards according to the points in your outline, and draft the essay paragraph by paragraph. Keep in mind our advice on developing paragraphs (pages 25–27), introductions (pages 22–24), and conclusions (page 27). Be sure to include complete references for all source information. It is easy to lose track of where information came from if you do not record this information in the first draft.

As you draft your essay, you may find that you need to depart from your outline. The outline is intended to serve as a guide, not a straitjacket. If you discover new patterns or ideas in the process of writing, don't hesitate to include them in your essay.

Exercise 9.12

As you reread Kristen's essay on pages 364–376, compare her outline to her final draft. Where did she expand on the outline as she wrote her draft? Note in the margin the types of synthesis that she uses to develop her paper. Then explain how you will use synthesis strategies in your own research process.

Exercise 9.13

Based on your outline, write a first draft of your research paper. Don't hesitate to include new ideas or patterns you discover as you write.

REVISING

REVISE BASED ON READERS' COMMENTS

One result of going through the research process is that you become engrossed in the material; that makes it difficult for you to view your writing objectively. It is important to get feedback on your draft to see if your message gets through to the audience. You may ask your reader to use the following checklist as a feedback guide, or you may work alone and apply the checklist to the draft yourself.

✓ *Checklist for Revising a Research Paper*

_____	1. Is the paper written on a sufficiently narrow topic?
_____	2. Can you understand the writer's research goals?
_____	3. Does the writer present a clear thesis?
_____	4. Does the writer make sense of the information from sources?
_____	5. Can you discern the research paper's form (multisource comparison and contrast, summary of multiple sources, objective synthesis, essay of response to multiple sources, synthesis with a specific purpose, argument, analysis, or evaluation)?
_____	6. Is the information from sources organized according to a clear plan?
_____	7. Does the writer use information from sources convincingly?
_____	8. Are the writer's assertions substantiated with material from sources?
_____	9. Does the writer provide transitions among sources and among pieces of information?
_____	10. Is the writer's voice appropriate for this type of essay? Why or why not?
_____	11. Is the opening satisfactory? Why or why not?
_____	12. Does the essay have an appropriate conclusion?
_____	13. Is the title suitable for the piece?
_____	14. Can you identify the source for each piece of information?
_____	15. Does the paper end with a list of works cited that includes all sources referred to in the text of the paper?

Exercise 9.14

If your teacher agrees, have a classmate or friend review your preliminary draft and give you feedback. If this is not possible, set the essay aside for a few days and then review it yourself. Use the checklist for revising a research paper.

EDITING

When you are satisfied with your revision, read your paper aloud. Then reread it line by line and sentence by sentence. Check for correct usage, punctuation, spelling, mechanics, manuscript form, and typographical errors. If your editing skills are not strong, get a friend to read over your work. Keep in mind the following concerns:

✓ *Checklist for Editing a Research Paper*

_____	1. Are all your sentences complete?
_____	2. Have you avoided run-on sentences, both fused sentences and comma splices?

_____ 3. Do pronouns have clear antecedents, and do they agree in number, gender, and case with the words for which they stand?

_____ 4. Do all subjects and verbs agree in person and number?

_____ 5. Is the verb tense consistent and correct?

_____ 6. Have you used modifiers (words, phrases, subordinate clauses) correctly and placed them where they belong?

_____ 7. Have you used matching elements in parallel constructions?

_____ 8. Are punctuation marks used correctly?

_____ 9. Are spelling, capitalization, and other mechanics (abbreviations, numbers, italics) correct?

Exercise 9.15

Use the editing checklist as you work to complete your research paper.

As Kristen drafts her essay, she uses the American Psychological Society (APA) manuscript and documentation style. The APA style is commonly used in the social sciences, and Kristen's instructor suggested that APA format might be appropriate for her topic. Appendix A provides a comparison of MLA and APA styles.

```
                                                   Family Values 1

    Kristen Lester

    Academic Writing I

    Professor Smith

    October 30, 2008

                   Family Values in an Election Year

        It seems that each election year, conservative, moderate,       1

    and liberal candidates go to considerable lengths to express

    their strong support for "family values." Since 1976, the phrase

    "family values" has been used in every Republican Party national

    platform (Quindlen, 2007). "Strong families, blessed with

    opportunity, guided by faith, and filled with dreams are the

    heart of a strong America" read the 2004 Democratic Party
```

platform ("Strong at home," 2004). In a speech given on Father's

Day 2008, Barack Obama identified absent fathers as a major cause

of problems in black communities, an argument that sociologist

Michael Eric Dyson claimed was calculated to sway "those whites

still on the fence about whom to send to the White House." In an

election year, everyone seems anxious to play the family values

card, and with good reason. In a 2007 USA Today/Gallup poll, 75%

of Americans said that the candidates' positions on "family

values" would have an important influence on their votes in the

next presidential election (Carroll, 2007).

The assumption underneath this dialogue is that the

American family is endangered and needs reinforcement.

Unfortunately, the political rhetoric around family values often

degenerates to posturing that lacks precision and clarity. What

exactly are "family values," and how are they in peril? Without

a doubt, American families have changed significantly in recent

years. The traditional nuclear family, with a breadwinner

father, homemaker mother, and children, has been on the decline,

and it is being replaced by what sociologist David Elkind calls

the "postmodern family," a term that encompasses various types

of domestic units such as single-parent families, dual-income

families, and remarried families (as cited in Scherer, 1996,

p. 4). To a large extent, the debate over family values revolves

around whether this transformation represents the decline of the

American family or an opportunity to strengthen and improve

families. The sociological literature on the evolution and

current status of the American family helps clarify the issues

that are at the core of this political debate. I will use the

findings of sociologists who study the American family to

analyze issues that lie at the core of the political controversy over family values.

Social scientists agree that Americans are now living less frequently in traditional nuclear families than they did in the past. In 1900, 55% of households were traditional nuclear families (two married parents and children) as opposed to 25% in 2000 (Katz & Stern, 2007, p. 91). Twenty-five percent of children are currently born out of wedlock (Trimberger, 2007, p. 83) and the rates of out-of-wedlock birth increased 404% for white women and 82% for black women between 1970 and 2000 (Katz & Stern, 2007, p. 91). Around a third of all American children are being raised by a single parent, who in most cases is employed (Boushey, 2007). In 1900, almost all single mothers were widows, whereas in 2000, "most were either divorced, separated, or never married" (Katz & Stern, 2007, p. 91). There are currently more Americans living alone than there are households with a married couple and one or more children (Trimberger, 2007, p. 82) and in 30 percent of families, the head of household is a single woman (Katz & Stern, 2007, p. 91). Fifty percent of American marriages end in divorce (Popenoe, 1997). Politicians who refer to dramatic structural changes in the American family could certainly find support in social science research. Without a doubt, the American family has changed during the latter part of the twentieth century.

When politicians call for a return to "family values," they often seem to imply that Americans merely have to recommit themselves to the traditional nuclear family, which will then change the larger society. This suggests that family structure is largely a function of Americans' belief systems, and that it will shift along with those beliefs. Some social scientists do support

the notion that values determine social structure. David Popenoe

(1999) believes that the shift in family structure resulted from

social movements of the 1960s and 1970s, particularly "highly

expressive or self-focused individualism" (p. 30), feminism,

"female economic pursuit" (p. 30), and the sexual revolution.

According to Popenoe, the modern nuclear family was a key to

American and European social stability, but this social structure

was threatened by cultural changes that placed more emphasis on

personal liberation than on family unity. The impact on males was

to encourage "Playboy-style sexual opportunism and rejection of

responsibilities" and on females to view "the modem nuclear family

as an oppressive institution" (Popenoe, 1999, p. 30). The sexual

revolution undermined the idea that sex should take place only

within a marriage and made divorce more acceptable. Whitehead

(1997) points out that attitudes toward divorce changed so that

"society no longer defined divorce as a social or family event,

with multiple stakeholders, notably the children whose interests

must be represented and served. Instead, it saw divorce as an

individual and psychological event with a single stakeholder, the

initiating adult." According to Elshtain (2000), the situation

worsens as antifamily cultural values are passed on to children:

> We see that more and more children are growing up with
>
> little or no experience of seeing married life, hence no
>
> living examples of what it means for two people to commit
>
> themselves to one another over time.... Over the past three
>
> or four decades, the message American children receive from
>
> the wider culture is one that is high on romance and sex
>
> but hostile or, at best, indifferent to marriage ...
>
> [;consequently,] we have not been imparting to the next

Family Values 5

generation a set of fundamental norms and beliefs about the
meaning and purposes, responsibilities and freedom, of
marriage and family life.

Popenoe maintains that we Americans need to reexamine our
cultural values with regard to the family: "If the nuclear
family is to be revived, *we must restore the cultural importance
of voluntary, lifelong monogamy*" (Popenoe, 1999, p. 30). Many
politicians echo Popenoe's explanation for the collapse of the
American family and call for a return to traditional family
values in order to resurrect the nuclear family.

Other social scientists, however, believe that American
family structure has changed largely in response to economic
conditions rather than shifting cultural values.

> Since 1965, two major developments have had a profound
> impact on families. One was the shift at the end of the
> postwar boom to a lean-and-mean postindustrial economy that
> stripped family-sustaining career opportunities from many
> blacks and noncollege-educated adults of all demographic
> groups. Young adults in the family-forming stage of life
> have been hit especially hard by an insecure and uncertain
> job market. (Skolnick, 1997)

While some conservative politicians and certain social
scientists point to feminism as a reason that fewer women stay
home with young children, sociologists more often cite economic
pressures. Boushey (2007) points out that while the women's
movement made it possible for more females to obtain better
jobs, most women enter the workforce out of economic necessity:

> Mothers work because they can and also because they have
> to. The feminist revolution opened up job opportunities and

the Pill allowed women to choose when to have a family. But

for most families, if Mom's at work it's because she has to

be. Who can raise a family on just one income? How can a

single mother even contemplate not working now that we've

closed the welfare offices?...And the higher the family

income, the more likely it is that Mom has a job and works

full time. In recent decades, the families that were

upwardly mobile were those who had a working wife.

From this perspective, women's participation in the workforce   8

is a response to economic conditions rather than a voluntary

assertion of feminist values. In this day and age, demographic

and economic changes make it unnecessary and impractical for

homemaking to be a lifetime career (Skolnick, 2006). When both

parents work, the economic pressures on the family lessen. Just

as the rise of the traditional nuclear family was a response to

industrialization, the current shift away from the traditional

family has the same driving force: a changing economic reality

(Skolnick, 2006). As this example indicates, Americans are not

entirely free to choose their "family values," but often must

organize their family life to accommodate social conditions in

the larger society.

The [revisionist social scientists]...have it backwards

when they argue that the collapse of traditional family

values is at the heart of our social decay. The losses in

real earnings and in breadwinner jobs, the persistence of

low-wage work for women and the corporate greed that has

accompanied global economic restructuring have wreaked far

more havoc on Ozzie and Harriet Land than the combined

effects of feminism, sexual revolution, gay liberation, the

counterculture, narcissism, and every other value flip of

the past half-century. (Stacey, 1994, pp. 120-121)

Skolnick (2004) adds to Stacey's list of factors responsible for

social problems "growing inequality; a new economic insecurity

that reaches far up into the middle class; a mismatch between the

needs of families and the demands of employers for longer hours

and lower labor costs; declining public services; rising costs

for housing, healthcare and education; and on and on" (p. 46).

According to Skolnick, Americans understand that family life has

changed and that the world in general has changed, but they don't

perceive the relationship between the two. "Talk about family

change is almost totally disconnected from the discussion of

technology and economy" (Skolnick, 2004, p. 47). According to

this perspective, politicians tend to blame declining moral

values for social problems because it absolves them, to some

extent, from addressing the complex causes of those problems.

A common assumption in political rhetoric is that children

are better off in traditional nuclear families than in other

household types. One might think that candidates for office

cannot afford to alienate the huge and growing population of

single parents, but much political rhetoric implies that single-

parent families are unacceptable structures in which to raise

children. This notion receives some support from social

scientists such as Barbara Defoe Whitehead, who argues that

single motherhood is detrimental to the mothers themselves and

their children. Single mothers typical lack access to "two of the

most effective sources of self-sufficiency—professional jobs and

marriage" and as as result their children often begin life "at

the bottom of the [economic] ladder" (Whitehead, 2007). Based on their review of "large-scale studies," Gallagher and Blankenhorn (1997) paint a dire picture of the consequences for children growing up in single parent families: "Children raised outside of intact marriages are more likely to be poor, to have trouble in school, to report psychological problems, to commit violence against themselves and others, to use drugs, and to experience sexual and physical abuse" (p. 13). Research studies indicate that the rate of mental and behavioral problems is two to three times higher for children who are not living with both parents (Elshtain, 2000; Popenoe, 1997). According to Whitehead (1997), "Nondisrupted two-parent households simply have a greater capacity to make higher and often longer-term investments of time and money in their children than the fast-growing alternatives: one-parent, stepparent, and foster-parent families."

However, many social scientists maintain that the breakup of a marriage does not stop effective parenting and that effects of divorce on children are often exaggerated (Skolnick, 1997). A study by California therapist Judith Wallerstein is most commonly cited when measuring these effects (Ehrenreich, 1996). According to Ehrenreich, Wallerstein found that 41% of children whose parents are divorced are "doing poorly, worried, underachieving, deprecating, and often angry" years after the split. Ehrenreich, however, points out that this report lacks credibility because it focused on just sixty couples. More important, two-thirds of them were without "adequate psychological functioning" previous to the divorce. Stacey (1994) points out that Wallenstein's research compares the children of divorce with all other children, but not specifically with children living in families with problematic marriages but no divorce. Without that comparison, Stacey says

11

Family Values 9

that the research tells us nothing about the real impact of
divorce (p. 120).

Divorce is typically portrayed on television and in films   12
as devastating for all involved, but "just as there are bad
divorces, there are good divorces too," Constance Ahron points
out (as cited in Ehrenreich, 1996). Both parents do, in many
cases, remain financially and emotionally responsible for their
children. The situation after divorce sometimes even improves
when families are relieved of constant fighting and abuse. As
divorce has become more acceptable, its effects have become less
harsh. Stacey (1994) maintains that "most social scientists do
not agree that a family's structure is more important than the
quality of the relationships" (p. 120). She agrees that children
of divorced parents do have more social difficulties, in
general, than children of parents who stay together, but she
points out that it may be the hostility within the home, not the
divorce itself, that is responsible for the children's problems.

Homosexual parenting is more often opposed by conservative   13
politicians than by moderates or liberals. Currently, states and
municipalities recognize the rights of same-sex couples to varying
degrees, with liberals generally supporting those rights and
conservatives challenging them. Of all the political debates over
the American family, this one is perhaps the least informed by
sociological research. However, such research does exist. Perrin
reviewed the sociological literature on gay and lesbian parenting
and concluded that children of gays or lesbians are not
significantly different from their peers raised by straight
parents. "It appears that the psychosocial adjustment of children
is influenced more strongly by family processes and interactions

than by the number and sexual orientation of their parents"
(Perrin, 2002, p. 125). Overall, the strength of attachment to
their parents is comparable in families with gay, lesbian and
straight parents (p. 126). Some of these children do have
difficulty coming to grips with their parents' sexual orientation,
but others not only accept their gay and lesbian parents but also
develop closer relationships with them than is typical in straight
families (p. 127). The sociological research provides no support
for the view expressed by some politicians that gay and lesbian
parenting is incompatible with good family values. As Perrin
states, "Apparently parents' sexual orientation has no measurable
effect on the quality of parent-child relationships or on
children's mental health or social adjustment" (p. 129).

A number of social scientists embrace the postmodern family
and argue that politicians should do more to support it rather than
pine for the traditional nuclear family. David Elkind says that the
postmodern family "is more fluid and more flexible....It mirrors the
openness, complexity, and diversity of our contemporary lifestyle"
(as cited in Scherer, 1996, p. 4). In their literature review,
Mack-Canty and Wright (2004) cite research showing that personal
growth and family happiness are enhanced in families where "parents
identify with feminist principles and parent from feminist
perspectives." Boushey (2007) points out that working mothers
actually spend more time with their children but less on housework.
It seems possible that postmodern families will be more responsive
than traditional nuclear families to the new economic,
technological, and cultural changes facing American families today.
We are presented with new challenges and opportunities to which
postmodern families are highly responsive.

14

15

As the current election year unfolds, we will undoubtedly witness more political battles over what is best for the American family: a return to traditional family values and structures, or an effort to improve the success of the various postmodern family forms. What is the reality beneath the political rhetoric? Are we weakening the most basic social element of our society, or are we gaining a flexibility that the family will need to survive in the twenty-first century? The sociological literature does not provide definite answers to these questions even though it may clarify the underlying issues. When seeking answers to these questions, it is essential to consider which structure is most suitable for raising children so that they grow up to be both autonomous and socially responsible. Children must feel like an important part of their parents' lives and need to be embraced with love, care, and guidance. When these qualities are provided, both individual happiness and social harmony will follow.

References

Boushey, H. (2007, March). Values begin at home, but who's home? *The American Prospect, 18*, A2-4. Retrieved October 5, 2008, from Proquest Research Library database.

Carroll, J. (2007, December). Public: "Family values" important to presidential vote. *The Gallup Poll Briefing, 97.* Abstract retrieved October 8, 2008, from Proquest Research Library database.

Family Values 13

Dyson, M. E. (2008, June 30). The blame game. *Time, 171,* 38.

Ehrenreich, B. (1996, April 8). In defense of splitting up: The
     growing anti-divorce movement is blind to the costs of bad
     marriage. *Time, 147,* 80. Retrieved October 5, 2008, from
     Proquest Research Library database.

Elshtain, J. B. (2000, March). Philosophic reflections on the
     family at millennium's beginning. *World and I, 15,* 312.
     Retrieved October 5, 2008, from General OneFile database.

Gallagher, M., & Blankenhorn, D. (1997, July/August). Family
     feud. *The American Prospect,* 12-16. Retrieved October 9,
     2008, from Proquest Research Library database.

Katz, M.B., & Stern, M. J. (2007, Fall). American families: Changes
     in the twentieth century. *Dissent, 54,* 90-92. Retrieved
     October 8, 2008, from Proquest Research Library database.

Mack-Canty, C., & Wright, S. (2004, October) Family values as
     practiced by feminist parents. *Journal of Family Issues,
     25,* 851-880. Retrieved October 10, 2008, from Sociology:
     A Sage Full Text Collection database.

Perrin, E. (2002). *Sexual orientation in child adolescent health
     care.* New York: Kluwer. Retrieved October 12, 2008, from
     SocINDEX database.

Popenoe, D. (1997, September-October). Family trouble (divorce).
     American Prospect, 16. Retrieved October 12, 2008, from
     General OneFile database.

Popenoe, D. (1999, July-August). Can the nuclear family be
     revived?" *Society, 36,* 28-30. Retrieved October 9, 2008,
     from SocINDEX database.

Quindlen, A. (2007, September 3). Disinvited to the party. *Newsweek,*
     68. Retrieved October 5, 2008, from General OneFile database.

Family Values 14

Scherer, M. (1996). On our changing family values: A conversation with David Elkind. *Educational Leadership, 53,* 4-9.

Skolnick, A. (1997, September-October). Family trouble (divorce). *American Prospect,* 16. Retrieved October 12, 2008, from General OneFile database.

Skolnick, A. (2004, Fall). Special series: Rethinking the politics of the family. *Dissent, 51,* 45-47. Retrieved October 8, 2008, from Proquest Research Library database.

Skolnick, A. (2006, Fall). Beyond the "M" word. *Dissent, 53,* 81-87. Retrieved October 5, 2008, from Academic Search Premier database.

Stacey, J. (1994, July 25-August 1). The new family values crusaders. *The Nation, 259,* 119-122. Retrieved October 10, 2008, from General OneFile database.

Strong at home, respected in the world: The 2004 Democratic national platform for America. (n.d.). Retrieved October 15, 2008, from http://www.democrats.org/pdfs/2004platform.pdf

Trimberger, E. K. (2007, Spring). Further beyond the "M" word. *Dissent, 54,* 82-84. Retrieved October 8, 2008, from Proquest Research Library database.

Whitehead, B. D. (1997, September/October). Family trouble (divorce). *American Prospect,* 16. Retrieved October 5, 2008, from Proquest Research Library database.

Whitehead, B. D. (2007, January 26). Single mothers: The costs of going it alone. *Commonweal 134,* 6. Retrieved October 5, 2008, from Proquest Research Library database.

PART V

Reading Selections

CHAPTER 10

Grades and Learning

In our hometown of Ithaca, New York, the Lehman Alternative Community School offers all courses on credit/no-credit basis rather than assigning A–F grades. In lieu of grades, teachers provide end-of-semester assessments, typically several paragraphs for each student, that describe what students learned and indicate the quality of their work. During the four years of high school, each student compiles a portfolio that includes examples of his or her strongest work on essays, exams, lab reports, and other projects. The completed portfolio is the primary requirement for high-school graduation.

One of the goals of the credit system used at the Lehman Alternative Community School is to help students focus on learning rather than on grades. A common critique of A–F grading is that it encourages students to think of the grade itself as the primary purpose of education and makes instructors "teach to the test" rather than attend to the individual needs of each student. At the same time, however, there is a growing movement in America for raising educational standards, a component of which is a call for tougher grading, to motivate higher levels of achievement. Grade inflation is often cited for undermining the integrity of our educational system and devaluing high-school and college diplomas.

The readings in this chapter analyze the relationship between grades and learning. "Zen and the Art of Grade Motivation," Liz Mandrell's personal essay based on her experience as a high-school English teacher, concludes that grades are a necessary incentive for most high-school students. Jerry Farber, in his public essay "A Young Person's Guide to the Grading System," argues that the A–F grading system has all but destroyed students' motivation to learn and that learning is meaningful only when students have a genuine desire for intellectual growth. In "Grades and Money," another public essay, Steven Vogel suggests that the current generation of college students sees grades, rather than knowledge and understanding, as the reward for the effort they invest in academic work and that our society encourages this perception. Finally, Stephen Ray Flora and Stacy Suzanne Poponak's research study entitled "Childhood Pay for Grades Is Related to College Grade Point Averages" concludes that rewarding children early on for performing well in school encourages them to value academic work as they move through the education system.

Zen and the Art of Grade Motivation

Liz Mandrell

A former high-school English teacher, Liz Mandrell is a teacher-consultant with the Morehead Writing Project, Kentucky. She is currently teaching in the English Department at Morehead State University.

This article was originally published in English Journal, *a publication of the professional group, National Council of Teachers of English. The audience for* English Journal *is secondary-school English teachers.*

Prereading

In the initial paragraphs of her article, Mandrell describes a situation in which students felt "burdened by the academic system." Think of a specific college or high-school class in which you felt particularly burdened. Would removing the competition for grades have reduced that burden? Would you have learned as much without the grades? Freewrite for ten minutes in response to these questions.

Educators have long questioned the validity of grades with regards to determining the intellectual ability of students, and have sought more valid means of evaluation with performance events, portfolios, and exit interviews. The bottom line is that grades, by any other name, have and always will play a major role in education and in life. I recently decided to push the grade envelope with a group of students who were obviously burdened by the academic system, and here is what I found.   1

I knew something was up when I heard them wishing they were still in Junior English. Kyle said something about how she missed Mrs. Thornton. Lewis mentioned how nice Mrs. Thornton was and how well she treated them. I felt like saying, "O.K. What is wrong? Where have I strayed from the prescribed teacher behavior?" I didn't have to wait long to know my error.   2

Chris stood up, waiting to see if I would extend the scepter toward him. Chris is the indisputable King of the Cliffs Notes. He cleared his throat like any good defense attorney awaiting permission to make the opening statement; I waited patiently.   3

"Yes, Chris. Did you have something to say?" I said, noticing tension edging around the room like a toothless man at a dentist's convention.   4

"Yes, ma'am. Uh ... I think I speak for the rest of the class, ... I ... uh, we think that there is entirely too much put on us, ma'am," he said.   5

(For the record, I'm only 29, hardly worthy of the matronly title of "ma'am," a title I've repeatedly asked him to assign only to his Sunday School teacher, his mother, his grandmother and really, really old women.)   6

"You think there is entirely too much put upon you?" I said. "What does that mean exactly?"   7

"That means, ma'am, that we are having trouble, I mean, we are ... well, this isn't the only class we have, you know," he said, finally, with a pained, constipated look on his face.   8

"Yeah, you are giving us too much work," chimed in Lewis. Lewis is an extremely 9
bright student, well-read, and self-motivated. I could count on Lewis to get all my obscure
pop culture jokes. I could also count on Lewis to apologize for every statement he made.
"I'm sorry, but ... really, I'm sorry, but it's way too much work," he said, picking gum off his
black Chuck Chriss, avoiding eye contact.

(Just for the record and to avoid being arrested by the Homework Police, I checked 10
with Mrs. Thornton, their Junior English teacher. The homework burden in her class
sentenced my homework load to the old folks home. No contest. I was not an ogre.)

"Yeah, and some of us have GPAs to watch," said Robin as she jumped into the fray. 11
Robin is a young Katie Couric, all smiles and perky nose, but racked with journalistic
ambition and biting cynicism. She continued, "Right now there are four other people who
are valedictorians, but I'm the only one taking an AP class. Do you think it is right to let
someone take three hours of Small Engine Repair and be valedictorian?"

"Robin, you could have taken Small Engine Repair instead of this class," I posed as 12
a possible alternative. A look of aversion crossed their collective class face, thinking of the
horrors and mysteries of vocational education that bubbled beyond the doors of the Vo-
Tech building. After several other members of the class jumped onto the Let's Trash the
AP Curriculum hay wagon and took me on several trips around the field, I began to
despair. A not-so-peaceful, not-so-easy feeling crept over me like a snagged pair of nylon
underwear. I was not going to change my beautiful curriculum, resplendent with Dostoevsky,
Woolf, Camus, and Conrad. I would not substitute my diligently planned, carefully imple-
mented syllabus for some shallow bimbo syllabus just because they couldn't hack the work.
Besides they were all doing very well in the class. Why were they complaining?

Meeting Everyone's Needs

I went home a lonely woman, a teacher betrayed by her craft. I had many decisions to make, 13
and not many answers were available. As I often do when I need time to meditate, I went to
my office (the tub), lit a couple of candles, and began to devise a way to meet everyone's
needs. Teachers are masters at meeting everyone's needs; I can do this, I assured myself, I've
been doing this all my life. After lying like a slug in boiling water for several hours, I had
come to no sound conclusions, save that my skin was peeling like a shrimp boat captain's
bare back after a day on the delta. (I'm not sure where that hyperbole came from ... I may be
watching my *Forrest Gump* video just a little too much. Hi, I'm The Teacher ... People call me
The Teacher.)

Getting out of the tub, I noticed my husband had been reading my worn copy of 14
Robert Pirsig's *Zen and The Art of Motorcycle Maintenance* (1974, New York: Morrow) and
had left it lying on the dresser. I'll resist the urge to say the clouds parted and angels sang,
but at that moment I realized that I had been given the opportunity to teach as if grades
didn't matter, as if they didn't exist, as if the quality of learning was my only objective. I
could teach with no direction save that of curiosity, no lesson plans, only with an eye on
Quality Learning. I could be a student also, a fellow sponge, thirsting for the definitions of
life and its lessons.

Here was an occasion to grant all my students As and teach as if learning was our only 15
goal. I'd like to say that all education is just learning for learning's sake, but my students
were scholarship obsessed and that translated into slavery to the *A*. Why not be a liberator,

unlocking the rusty grade manacles that had fettered their natural, childlike creative selves for the last twelve years? These students were hard working and mature; they could handle such freedom. I resolved to try the idea on my department chairperson the next morning.

The chair thought it was a great idea, but advised me not to air this notion about too much. A little too liberal, she said. Remember this is the South. I told my students the next day that I was granting them a 98% for this six weeks only on an experimental basis. They were stunned for a moment, a look on their faces as if a pardon from the President had come two minutes before a firing squad had lowered their paltry carcasses in the dirt.

Eventually they caught the spirit of the moment, and started spouting off about how school had destroyed their education, how AP had ruined them, how they even looked critically and analytically at the *TV Guide*. They shouted with celebration of freedom and liberty hereforeto not experienced within the classroom walls. They stood on the desks and recited "O Captain, My Captain." They hoisted me on their shoulders, carrying me through the halls shouting "Carpe Diem!"

(O.K. O.K. Maybe those last couple of things didn't really happen, but they were plenty excited about this new system.)

They signed contracts that stated that they would learn for the sake of curiosity and learning, and that, at intervals, they would turn in proof, products of some sort, that they were actually learning. Everyone signed the contracts with gleeful flourish, smug in the self-assurance that they would benefit from this experiment, sail above the banal mediocrity that grades had held them to, and actualize themselves in ways they never thought possible with traditional education. I decided to start them out with a book that would reveal whether or not there was truth to their pious pleas to give them knowledge or give them death. I assigned *Crime and Punishment* over winter break.

The New System

Did they succeed? No. They started out heartily enough, joining into the discussion with zest, researching items of interest that had popped up during discussion. During those first two weeks, I thought I had hit upon the secret of teaching. They were more alive than I'd ever seen them.

My first journal entry upon returning from winter break was as follows:

Today was the first day back after break and I was wondering whether *Crime and Punishment* would have been read. They surprised me. They had read it, although I think Chris may have only read the Cliffs Notes which is O.K. since he'll pay for being a slacker later on in life. (Author's Note: Who am I kidding? Chris will never have to pay for not reading *Crime and Punishment*. Just another lie teachers tell themselves to make it through the day.) Cooper was as animated as I have seen her during the discussion. She was very vocal, answering several questions as well as elaborating on points to which I alluded. Overall, we had an excellent session. There was no hesitation or time wasted. We worked right to the bell.

Four weeks later my entry was as follows:

On Friday, I asked that they turn in a product, any product of our learning to share with the rest of the group. Only three students did so. Chris, Lewis and Cooper submitted something, something less than they are able to do. Robin, Kyle and Anita did not turn in anything.

16

17

18

19

20

21

22

One day I typed a simple message on the computer and left the room. I asked each of   *23*
them to answer the question truthfully with a simple sentence that would not betray their
identities. The question I asked was: "Did you or did you not read *Crime and Punishment*
and *Sons and Lovers* in their entirety for this class? If you read half of each and finished your
reading with a set of Cliffs Notes, I do not consider that as having read the entire book." The
students responded:

> I did not finish reading the books but plan to.

> I read half of the books and the Cliffs Notes just as I have all year.

> I read most of both books and plan to finish them later.

> I read both them (sic) Cliffs Notes.

> I did read the books.

> I sat home and read all of the books, twice.

It had begun. The all-consuming lethargy accompanying their senior year was   *24*
only advanced by this new and improved style of learning. Our search for quality, our
enterprise for truth had fallen into despair. By the end of the six weeks, I was carrying
the discussions completely, having questioned the class and received no response.
Many of them offered explanations, "I admit. I have nothing." With the absence of
grades, the class had relaxed and become so slack that quality was no longer our objective; getting to class on time and having something intelligent to say was now our goal.
I was perplexed. Had I not met their needs? Had I not devised a brilliant plan whereby
we learned without the grade?

Are Grades Necessary?

Back to the tub. I was currently taking a class at a nearby university to fulfill a master's degree   *25*
requirement. I tried to think how large my motivation would be if my professor announced
one evening she would no longer be giving us grades. Would I read my 60-page assignments,
write two 10- to 12-page critical papers on some obscure eighteenth-century British author
and join in the discussion with such gusto? No, I would not perform to the degree that I
was currently engaging myself in the class. I probably wouldn't even be taking the class if it
wasn't a university requirement. However, I had enjoyed the class a great deal and learned
some very valuable lessons about my culture and myself from studying eighteenth-century
England.

Maybe grades are necessary. Maybe I am a product of a carrot-at-the-end-of-the-stick   *26*
world and can only be motivated by a grade, a paycheck, a bonus, a public pat on the back
instead of knowing, quietly and contentedly, that what I do is fulfilling, distinctive, and
important. Am I saying that without the grade, the paycheck, the bonus, the public recognition I would just be an amoeba in a petri dish, content to remain in the same spot until my
remote ran out of batteries or my Pepsi went hot? How frightening!

At the end of the six weeks, I was wearied, and my students had spun themselves   *27*
into such a state of lethargy, I was afraid I would never be able to deprogram them. I asked

my students to look back over our experiment and reflect on paper. Their responses were varied, but honest.

Six strange weeks. That is what it was. Indeed it was a noble experiment. It could have been a relief not to worry about grades, but then I had to deal with my conscience. What I learned about myself at times frightened me. I am lazy. I read the books at my own pace and finished them all save *Jude the Obscure,* but I felt guilty for not having read them in time for discussion. Signed, Lewis   *28*

I did not learn more or put more emphasis on learning due to the project. I learned about myself—and pushing myself to do work that really wasn't required of me. As a learner. I'm sorry I didn't benefit. I work harder and learn more when I know the grade is on the line. Signed, Chris   *29*

Our experiment helped me in a few ways. I was free from stress over the assignments due. I was allowed to work at my own pace, and I didn't have to worry about being up to par. My work was basically done for my own enjoyment, not to earn an *A* in the class and remain as valedictorian with a 4.0. However, the experiment did affect me in a negative way. I became lazy as the infamous Senioritis began to flow through my body. I realized that without some outside force staying on my back—whether it be a teacher, a grade, a boss or a definite deadline—I may waste away into a bum and spend the rest of my life roaming the streets of New York visiting soup kitchens. Signed, Robin.   *30*

This six weeks has been the most bizarre in my learning history. For once, I felt that I actually did things for myself, not for a grade. Each day I have looked forward to coming to English because I found it to be a relaxing environment with no pressure. This six weeks I have at last been able to declare myself a PROCRASTINATOR! I have a severe case of Senioritis gnawing at me. I need more self discipline. Signed, Anita   *31*

I really liked this experiment. I really learned the freedom of not having to worry about grades. But in all actuality, I don't care about grades anyway. I really liked this set grade thing. However, I also realize how unrealistic it really is. I'm a procrastinator and that is in everything, not just this class. I am ready to be placed back on the regular grading schedule. Signed, Cooper   *32*

I really enjoyed it. As far as being self motivated as I thought I would be in the beginning, I wasn't. I did get off to a good start. It was easy to concentrate and absorb while I knew I had an automatic *A.* However, since I am a senior, I have Senioritis and I find it hard to be motivated about anything. Thanks a lot! Signed, Kyle   *33*

My conclusions from this experiment are simple.   *34*

Conclusion

Learning must somehow be linked to a product. That product must be measured or graded to gauge the worth of the product according to the merit it deserves. Somewhere in a parallel universe where students do their homework and read *Crime and Punishment* for fun, I'm sure grades are abolished, but here on Planet Earth, I will continue to award grades, whether it be an *A,* a Distinguished, or a Very, Very Good.   *35*

READING FOR CONTENT

1. Why did Mandrell's students feel they were overburdened by schoolwork? List the students' complaints.
2. When Mandrell notices Pirsig's *Zen and the Art of Motorcycle Maintenance* lying on the dresser, she has an epiphany. What was her realization, and how did her students react to it?
3. Describe Mandrell's "home office."
4. Compare the students' performance during the first two weeks of Mandrell's experiment with their performance during the next four weeks.
5. Compare Mandrell's experience as a student in a university course with her students' experience.
6. Summarize the students' reflections in paragraphs 28 to 33.
7. What does Mandrell conclude from her experiment?

READING FOR GENRE, ORGANIZATION, AND STYLISTIC FEATURES

1. Explain how Mandrell uses the problem-solution format to organize her article.
2. In paragraph 2, Mandrell uses a simile to compare her student, Chris, to a "good defense attorney." Cite other instances of similes, for example, those in paragraphs 4, 12, 13, and 16, and comment on their effectiveness.
3. Mandrell uses other forms of figurative language. Explain the function of the metaphors in paragraphs 3, 11, 14, 15, and elsewhere.
4. Would you describe Mandrell's tone as serious or humorous? Support your position with examples from the text.

READING FOR RHETORICAL CONTEXT

1. Mandrell's article was originally published in *English Journal* for an audience of high school English teachers. Which features of the article are especially appealing to these readers?
2. Which features of the article do you find most convincing? Do you identify more with Mandrell or with her students? Explain your answer.
3. Mandrell's article was originally published in 1997. Do you think her argument will still be convincing to readers today? Explain why or why not.

WRITING ASSIGNMENTS

1. Describing the students in her AP English class, Mandrell explains, "[M]y students were scholarship obsessed and that translated into slavery to the *A*" (paragraph 15). Does this description apply to all high school students or only to those in advanced classes? Drawing on your own experience, write an essay in response to this question.
2. Write a proposal for how students might learn effectively without grades. Make sure you take into account the failure of Mandrell's experiment. Address the proposal to the president of your university.
3. Mandrell's title, "Zen and the Art of Grade Motivation" is an allusion to Robert Pirsig's *Zen and the Art of Motorcycle Maintenance,* which Mandrell mentions in paragraph 14. Do some research to find out more about Pirsig's book. Draw on the sources you find to write a short essay in which you explain how Pirsig's work relates to Mandrell's article.

A Young Person's Guide to the Grading System

Jerry Farber

Jerry Farber, a professor of English and comparative literature at San Diego State University, is the author of many books and articles of social and literary criticism. His work had an impact on the student movement of the late 1960s and early 1970s.

Farber's essay was first published in 1969 in a collection of essays and stories entitled The Student as Nigger. *Farber uses the analogy in the title to describe students as slaves of teachers and administrators.*

Prereading

In the first paragraph of his essay, Farber asks the reader to consider what grades do for learning. Freewrite for ten minutes in response to this prompt.

There's no question that the grading system is effective in training people to do what they're told. The question is: What does it do for learning? 1

Grades focus our attention. But on what? On the test. Academic success, as everyone knows, is something that we measure not in knowledge but in grade points. What we get on the final is all-important; what we retain after the final is irrelevant. Grades don't make us want to enrich our minds; they make us want to please our teachers (or at least put them on). Grades are a game. When the term is over, you shuffle the deck and begin a new round. Who reads his textbooks after the grades are in? What's the point? It doesn't go on your score. 2

Oddly enough, many of us understand all of this and yet remain convinced that we need to be graded in order to learn. When we get to college, twelve years of slave work have very likely convinced us that learning is dull, plodding and unpalatable. We may think we need to be graded: we assume that without the grades we'd never go through all that misery voluntarily. But, in fact, we've been had. We've been prodded with phony motivations so long that we've become insensitive to the true ones. We're like those sleeping pill addicts who have reached the point where they need strong artificial inducement to do what comes naturally. We're grade junkies—convinced that we'd never learn without the A's and F's to keep us going. Grades have prevented us from growing up. No matter how old a person is—when he attends school, he's still a child, tempted with lollipops and threatened with spankings. 3

Learning happens when you *want* to know. Ask yourself: did you need grades to learn how to drive? To learn how to talk? To learn how to play chess—or play the guitar—or dance—or find your way around a new city? Yet these are things we do very well—much better than we handle that French or Spanish that we were graded on for years in high school. Some of us, though, are certain that, while we might learn to drive or play chess without grades, we still need them to force us to learn the things we don't really want to learn—math, for instance. But is that really true? If for any reason you really want or need some math—say, algebra—you can learn it without being graded. And if you don't want it and don't need it, you'll probably never get it straight, grades or not. Just because you pass a subject doesn't mean you've learned it. How much time did you spend on algebra and 4 geometry in high school? Two years? How much do you remember? Or what about grammar? How much did all those years of force-fed grammar do for you? You learn to talk (without being graded) from the people around you, not from gerunds and modifiers. And as for writing—if you ever do learn to write well, you can bet your sweet ass it won't be predicate nominatives that teach you. Perhaps those subjects that we would never study without being graded are the very subjects that we lose hold of as soon as the last test is over.

Still, some of us maintain that we need grades to give us self-discipline. But do you   5
want to see real self-discipline? Look at some kid working on his car all weekend long. His parents even have to drag him in for dinner. And yet, if that kid had been compelled to work on cars all his life and had been continually graded on it, then he'd swear up and down that he needed those grades to give him self-discipline.

It is only recently—and out of school—that I have begun to understand self-discipline   6
in writing. It grows out of freedom, not out of coercion. Self-discipline isn't staying up all night to finish a term paper; that's slave work. Self-discipline is revising one paragraph fanatically for weeks—for no other reason than that you yourself aren't happy with it. Self-discipline is following a problem through tedious, repetitive laboratory experiments, because there's no other way of finding out what you want to know. Or it can be surfing all day long every single day for an entire summer until you are good at it. Self-discipline is nothing more than a certain way of pleasing yourself, and it is the last thing anyone is likely to learn for a grade.

Coercion inside school probably leads many of us to develop our self-discipline in areas   7
untouched by the classroom. Who knows? If movie-going, dancing and surfing were the only required subjects, there might well be a poetic renaissance. I suspect that most kids fool around with writing on their own at some point—diaries, poetry, whatever—but this interest rarely survives school. When you learn that writing is intellectual slave work, it's all over.

Do you think you're a lazy student? No wonder! Slaves are almost always lazy.   8

Suppose I go to college; I want to be a chemist or a high school teacher or an   9
accountant. Are grades really my only reason for learning the field? Is getting graded going to turn me on to my subject? Or is it more likely to turn me off? How sad this is. History is so engrossing. Literature is so beautiful. And school is likely to turn them dull or even ugly. Can you imagine what would happen if they graded you on sex? The race would die out.

Wouldn't it be great to be free to learn? Without penalties and threats, without having   10
to play childish competitive games for gold and silver stars? Can you even imagine what the freedom to learn might be like?

Perhaps this kind of freedom sounds attractive to you but you're convinced that it isn't   11
suited to our society. Even if the grading system can be shown to work against learning, you may assume that grades are still necessary to *evaluate* people—to screen people for various kinds of work.

But think about it. Do you really believe that the best way to determine someone's   12
qualifications is to grade him—A, B, C, D, F—week by week, day by day, in everything he studies for sixteen years of school? Is this monstrous rigmarole honestly necessary in order to determine who gets which jobs?

There are far better ways to determine a person's qualifications. Many fields already   13
do their own screening by examination; the bar exam is one instance. In some areas—journalism, for example—supervised on-the-job experience would probably be the most effective screening and qualifying technique. Other fields might call for a combination

of methods. Engineers, for example, could be qualified through apprenticeship plus a demonstration of reasonable competency on exams at various levels—exams on which they would, of course, get an unlimited number of tries.

In a great many fields, no screening technique is necessary at all. Countless employers, public and private, require a college degree for no really good reason, simply because it enables their personnel departments to avoid making any meaningful individual evaluation and because it indicates some degree of standardization. There is no reason why a person should be forced to spend four years of his life in college just to get a decent job and then discover that he would have been much better off working in the field itself for four years and pursuing his own learning interests on a less rigid and formal basis.   *14*

Still it might be argued that eliminating grades entirely would require too sudden a shift in our society. I would maintain that the sudden shift is desirable. In any case, though, society is not likely to face the simultaneous abandonment of grading by every school in the country. Furthermore, on a campus where there is enormous resistance to abolishing grades, one could put forth a fairly good half-way compromise—the Credit system—which is, from my point of view, worth trying even though it falls short of what should be the real goal: no grades at all.   *15*

Under this system, some courses could be made totally free of grading: basic algebra, say, or drawing or poetry writing. The rest would be run on a Credit basis. If you meet the minimum requirements of a course, you get credit for it. No A's or C's or silver stars. Just credit. And if you don't meet the requirements, nothing happens. You don't lose anything or get penalized; you just don't get credit for that course. This is NOT the Pass-Fail System. Pass-Fail is a drag; if you don't pass a course, you get hurt. Under the Credit system you simply either get credit or you don't. All that your record shows is the courses you've earned credit for (not the ones you've attempted). And when you get credit for enough courses, you can get some kind of certification or credential, if you want one, according to the number and type of courses you've taken. And there should be not just a few assembly-line four-year degrees: AB, BS, and so on; there should be scores of more meaningful and varied certifications and degrees. Or maybe there should be none at all, just a list of the courses for which you have credit.   *16*

What's wrong with that? College becomes something more like a place for learning and growth, not fear and anxiety. It becomes a learning community, not a gladiatorial arena where you're pitted in daily battle against your fellow students. In elementary and secondary schools, of course, there is an even weaker pretext for grading and even more to be gained by its abolishment.   *17*

And we mustn't be too quick to assume that abolishing A's and F's would make our colleges still more overcrowded. If we eliminate the pointless Mickey-Mouse requirements that are foisted on everyone, if we eliminate the gold-star games and all the administrative paperwork and class busywork that go along with them, if we reduce the overwhelming pressure for a meaningless, standardized degree, then perhaps we'll end up with learning facilities that can accommodate even more students than the number that get processed in the factories that we currently operate.   *18*

And if an employer wants not just degrees but grade-point averages too, the colleges will explain that that's not what they are there for. Graduate schools, for their part, will probably not present a serious problem. They already put heavy emphasis on criteria other than GPA's. They stress interviews, personal recommendations: most of them already give their own entrance exams anyway. Besides, the best graduate schools will probably be delighted to get some *live* students for a change.   *19*

But what about the students themselves? Can they live without grades? Can they learn   *20*
without them? Perhaps we should be asking ourselves: can they really learn *with* them?

READING FOR CONTENT

1. Farber compares students to "sleeping pill addicts" and calls them "grade junkies." Explain the similarities between students and individuals who are addicted to drugs.

2. Farber give four examples of self-discipline. Cite each example and explain how it differs from self-discipline imposed by grades.

3. Explain what Farber means when he says that if humans were graded on sex, "the race would die out" (paragraph 9).

4. Do employers need grades to evaluate people's ability to do a job? What other measures of evaluation could they use?

5. Summarize "the credit system" and explain how it differs from traditional systems of grading.

6. Why does Farber propose "the credit system" instead of recommending the abolishment of grading?

7. If colleges and universities abandoned A's and F's, how would this change in the grading system affect these institutions?

READING FOR GENRE, ORGANIZATION, AND STYLISTIC FEATURES

1. If you were to add subtitles to Farber's essay, where would you place them and what would they be?

2. Would you describe Farber's tone as formal and reverent or informal and irreverent? Cite examples from the text to support your view.

3. Farber uses a large number of examples. Cite the ones that relate especially to you and explain why you find them appealing.

4. In paragraph 18, Farber uses the device of repetition. What other stylistic devices does he use in his essay? Give examples.

READING FOR RHETORICAL CONTEXT

1. Instead of giving his readers a ready-made "guide" to grading, Farber engages them in a conversation about grades. Explain how he engages his readers and draws them into the conversation.

2. As Farber explains his position against grades, he acknowledges arguments that his readers might make in favor of grades: that grades are needed for learning, self-discipline, and evaluation. Explain how Farber refutes each of these three claims.

3. Farber's essay was published over forty years ago. Do you think it has appeal for readers today? Which aspects of the essay are timely and which are dated?

WRITING ASSIGNMENTS

1. In paragraphs 4 to 6, Farber gives a number of examples of learning for its own sake as compared to learning for a grade. Write an essay describing experiences in which you learned something without being graded.

2. Reread Farber's remarks about writing in paragraphs 4, 6, and 7. Then write an essay in response. Describe your experiences with writing. Are they comparable to or different from Farber's? Did formal lessons on grammar teach you to write? Have you ever worked on a piece of writing in order to please yourself rather than a teacher? Did you ever "fool around with writing" on your own, for example, writing stories, journal entries, or poems? Did school assignments dampen your enthusiasm for writing?

3. Write an essay in which you analyze Farber's argument and evaluate its effectiveness.

4. Write an essay in which you respond to the questions at the end of Farber's article. Can students "live without grades"? "Can they learn without them?" "Can they really learn with them?" (paragraph 20).

Grades and Money

Steven Vogel

Steven Vogel is a professor of philosophy at Denison University. He is the author of Against Nature: The Concept of Nature in Critical Theory *(SUNY Press 1996), as well as articles published in* Environmental Ethics, Social Theory and Practice, Philosophy Today, Research in Philosophy and Technology, Praxis International, Dissent, *and other journals.*

This article was originally published in Dissent, *a magazine of independent social thought. It provides in-depth analysis of a range of American and global social and political issues.*

Prereading

The title of Vogel's article suggests that there is a relationship between grades and money. What do you anticipate that relationship might be? Freewrite for ten minutes in response to this question.

When I was a college student, back in the early seventies, people I knew made it a point not to talk about their grades. To this day, I have no idea how my friends did in college— they all graduated, which I guess means they did well enough. Today some are lawyers, doctors, businesspeople, software designers, bed-and-breakfast hosts, and so forth, but I'd be hard-pressed to guess who were the straight-A students among them and who barely squeaked through.   *1*

Me, I'm a college professor, teaching philosophy at a small private liberal-arts college in the Midwest. And what strikes me today is how different my students are: they talk about their grades *all the time*. They argue and gossip about them, complain to me and my colleagues about them, orient their whole college lives, as far as I can tell, around them. I say this not to sound self-righteous or holier than they—openness about grades is probably healthier than the kind of highfalutin' squeamishness we exhibited—but rather to explain the difficulty I feel in really *understanding* grades, in grasping what exactly they are and what   *2* they're for. My students are much better at it than I am. When they come into my office to ask (usually in despair or anger) why they got the grade they did in my class, I'm always a little confused, and a little embarrassed, for them and for me: *why* exactly are we talking about this? I always think. Of course it's particularly embarrassing because I've been teaching, and assigning grades, for twelve years, and I guess from my students' point of view it's the most important thing I do. (As far as I'm concerned, it's just a twice-yearly annoyance, and furthermore an impossibility: what exactly *is* the difference between a B− and a C+? Damned if I know.)

No, I don't understand grades that well. But when I read last winter that President Clinton was proposing to grant tax deductions for tuition to all college students who maintain B averages, something about it felt wrong to me, and I started to wonder why.

Everybody in the world of higher education, and most people outside, too, pays lip service to the idea that the point of education is, well, to *get educated*. It's the learning that's the goal, we say, not the grade; we want our students to learn about history and philosophy and literature and science and art and mathematics because doing so will make them better people, better citizens of a democracy. The point is to develop talents, attitudes, habits of mind that are good in themselves, that will improve their lives (and the lives of their fellow citizens); we say that education itself is such a good. If this is true, then grades must play a secondary role; they can serve a motivating function, but ought never to be mistaken for the goal of the process as such.

This is what we *say,* but it is not the way we act, and it is certainly not the way most of our students see the situation. For them the goal of going to class, writing papers, taking exams, and so on, is simply the grade itself. When I ask a student why a higher grade in a course is so important, I'm often told it's because it will increase the grade point average (GPA); when I ask why the GPA is important, I'm told that it's necessary for getting into a good postgraduate school, which is in turn important for getting a good job, which is important for making lots of money. Everything is important *for* something else, in this litany; nothing is important for itself. Except, of course, money.

It's money that's the crux of it. An important part of what we're teaching in college— not what we intend to teach, but what we do teach nonetheless—is how to think about money, what its relation is to value and effort and self-worth. Anyone entering this society surely needs to know all this; it's arguably the most important skill our culture demands. But of course we don't use real money to teach this skill—that would be too expensive and risky. Instead, we use grades. In my college, like most others, grades *are* money. They're the currency around which everything revolves.

What grades *ought* to be is a report, nothing more: how did the student do, how much did he or she learn, how much were his or her skills and critical self-consciousness and knowledge of the world expanded? A serious student might indeed want to know that at the end of the course—might want it to check his or her work, might even want to use it as a carrot or a stick. But we don't use grades as a report; we use them, in myriad ways, as money. We talk about "docking" students' grades for turning in papers late or missing classes, like finance companies assessing a late fee; we offer "contracts," whereby students are promised certain grades for doing a certain amount of work. My dean tells me that the syllabus I give to students at the beginning of the semester *is,* legally speaking, a contract, and has been interpreted by the courts as such—it must specify how I will calculate grades at the end of the term, and woe to me if I say that the final exam will count 30 percent and later change my mind and make it 35 percent. Students expect that their grade will indicate the amount of time they have put into the course, as if they were hourly workers, and many faculty agree that it's important to consider "effort" when they "award" grades.

The relationship between me and the students is really an exchange relationship: they provide me with work of a certain quality and I reward it—pay for it—by giving them a certain grade. This all seems so obvious to everyone that it's never even remarked upon, even though it is entirely different from, and even incompatible with, what we normally say about the relationship in the classroom—which is that it's one where I'm a teacher helping my students learn. Their learning isn't something they "give" me, not something I'm supposed to pay them for. Nothing real is exchanged in the classroom, and so the model of money is out of place there. But we're all so used to it everywhere else that we don't even notice. Yet applying it in the classroom produces perverse results. *8*

If grades are money, and if the product for which they pay is learning, then it's perfectly rational for students to try to minimize that learning while maximizing their "return," and looking for loopholes or strategies that will produce the best possible grade for the least possible effort. And they do: I'm constantly amazed by the mathematically sophisticated understanding students instantly develop of whatever new grading scheme I announce, and by their ability to find ambiguities and possible avenues for creative interpretation in it. Their incentive is thus *not* to learn, or to learn as little as possible while maintaining a good GPA—while I am placed in the position of having to figure out new ways to trick them into learning by designing ingenious new ways to grade. *9*

On the faculty side, the situation is more pleasant, if no less perverse. If grades are money, for us they are funny money, Monopoly money, because it costs us nothing to give them out—and no more, except in terms of our self-image, to give out an A than a C. Thus we get to play out our own fantasies about money—we can be skinflints, stingily giving out one or two A's a year, or spendthrifts, spreading high grades everywhere, or, like that guy on the show about the millionaire, looking for needy cases (troubled students, applicants to tough graduate programs) upon whom to generously bestow our wealth. Since we all want to be loved, and since the students seem to care so damned much, the misers are few. The result, as any economist will tell you, is inflation; in many of the best colleges the average grade is around A−. *10*

If grades are money, then learning is a cost—a painful effort one undergoes only for the reward it produces. That the learning or the effort might itself be the reward—which is what we *say* about education—makes no sense or is sentimental rubbish. The effect of turning grades into money is to commodify learning, making it appear as something that is painful in itself and useful only for what it can buy. This is exactly the opposite of what education ought to be about. *11*

I point all this out to my students when I can, often giving a heartfelt speech on the first day of the course about what I think grades are and how they ought not to be taken so seriously. The students look at me as though I'm crazy. *12*

In the last few years, my college has begun to offer merit scholarships, which is to say financial aid to very good students without requiring them to prove financial need; this is one of the ways we have helped to build up an excellent honors program that has been a real boon to the institution. But one characteristic of these scholarships is that to keep them students must maintain a certain GPA—generally a B average and sometimes even higher. Here the analogy between money and grades is not merely an analogy: a B can now literally be worth thousands of dollars. One day a student came to me for advice on her course *13* schedule and informed me that, although she'd like to try a philosophy course sometime, she couldn't risk it because she wasn't sure what her grade would be. When I tried out one of my lines about how "the important thing is learning, not grades," she looked back at me fiercely and explained that if her GPA dropped even a little bit she would lose her scholarship, worth ten thousand dollars; how dare I tell her grades aren't important? I had no response. She was right. She kept the scholarship, and never learned philosophy.

By tying grades to money, we give students incentives not to take risks. Very good and well-prepared first-year students often come to me to explain that they would rather take Calculus One than Calculus Two, even though they have already taken calculus in high school—or rather, *because* they have; that way they are guaranteed a good grade. These honors students are in some ways the worst in terms of their fixation on grades and their constant and creative search to find ways to manipulate the system; their skill at doing so, after all, has gotten them where they are today.   *14*

When I heard that President Clinton was offering tax deductions for B's, I imagined my own college's program turned into national policy, and I blanched. Did we really want to write the current grading system into tax law?   *15*

As it turned out, that aspect of the proposal disappeared in the final tax bill. Everybody seemed a little dubious about the idea of turning college professors into agents of national tax policy. But the deeper questions were never asked: about why we so easily accept the equation between grades and money that the proposal implied, about what grades really are for and why we take them for granted. What was wrong with Clinton's well-meaning proposal was that it sent the wrong message. Few noticed because we are all so in thrall to instrumentalism and commodfication—and because we no longer feel sure what education is for or why we value it. We let grades count as money—we let education count as money—because money, nowadays, is the only value we know.   *16*

READING FOR CONTENT

1. How do the attitudes of Vogel's current students toward grades differ from those of Vogel and his classmates when they were undergraduates in the early 1970s?
2. Explain what Vogel means when he says that people pay lip service to the true goals of education.
3. Compare and contrast the practice of using grades as a "report" and using grades as "money."
4. Why does Vogel believe that he has "to figure out ways to trick [students] into learning by designing ingenious ways to grade them" (paragraph 9)?
5. Explain what Vogel means when he says that grades are "funny money" for professors.
6. Why do Vogel's students think his views on grading are crazy?
7. According to Vogel, what has been the effect of merit-based scholarship?
8. Why does tying grades to money prevent students from taking risks?

READING FOR GENRE, ORGANIZATION, AND STYLISTIC FEATURES

1. Describe Vogel's opening strategy.
2. Describe and give examples of the evidence Vogel offers to support his claim that grades are money.

3. Explain how Vogel's essay is an extended analogy.

4. Why does Vogel, at the beginning of the third paragraph, state that he doesn't understand grades even though he is writing an analytical essay about grades?

READING FOR RHETORICAL CONTEXT

1. Who is Vogel's intended audience? Is Vogel attempting to change the behavior of this audience? Explain your answer.

2. How might a professor who takes grades seriously respond to Vogel's piece?

WRITING ASSIGNMENTS

1. Write an essay in which you summarize the parallels Vogel draws between grades and money.

2. Should grades determine financial aid and scholarships? Draw on Vogel's article to write an essay that weighs the pros and cons of tying financial aid to grades.

3. Using Vogel's article as a base, compare and contrast students' views on grades with the views of professors.

4. Write an essay in which you agree or disagree with Vogel's claim that students are constantly looking for loopholes and strategies for outwitting the grading system.

5. Write an essay in response to Vogel's final statement: "We let grades count as money—we let education count as money—because money, nowadays, is the only value we know."

Childhood Pay for Grades Is Related to College Grade Point Averages

Stephen Ray Flora and Stacy Suzanne Poponak

Stephen Ray Flora is Associate Professor of Psychology at Youngstown State University. He is author of The Power of Reinforcement *(SUNY Press 2004). When this article was published, Stacy Suzanne Poponak was a graduate student at Youngstown State University. She is now a doctoral student at the University of Notre Dame.*

This article was originally published in Psychological Reports, *a bimonthly journal featuring scholarly research studies in the field of psychology.*

Prereading ▬

Do you think parents should pay elementary school children for high grades? Freewrite for ten minutes in response to this question.

Summary.—*In a sample of 87 college students from four junior level courses, being paid for earning good grades in childhood was related to higher college GPAs relative to students who were not paid for good grades in childhood.*

Reproduced with permission of authors and publishers from: Flora, S.R. & Poponak, S.S. Childhood pay for grades is related to college grade point averages. *Psychological Reports*, 2004, 94, 66.
© Psychological Reports 2004.

Despite their demonstrated effectiveness, the use of reinforcement programs, especially   *1*
the use of tokens and money, have been argued against based on the pervasive idea that
"extrinsic rewards undermine intrinsic interest" (see Cameron, Banko, & Pierce, 2001 for
review). Conversely, learning research suggests that reinforcing students' performance on
academic tasks should "condition reward value" to academic behaviors, resulting in increased
enjoyment, academic engagement (e.g., Eisenberger, 1992), and *higher* GPAs relative to
students who were not reinforced for earning good grades. The present study surveyed
Youngstown State University college students from four junior level classes on whether
their parents ever paid them for earning good grades, if they enjoyed college, and in three
classes students were asked if they were rewarded for good grades in other ways. Finally, the
participating students' college GPAs were obtained.

Eighty-seven percent (45 of 52) of students who were not paid, and 91% (32 of 35) of   *2*
students who were paid, reported enjoying college. Only 51% of students (18 of 35) who
were not paid reported being rewarded by their parents in other ways for earning good
grades. Conversely, 89% of students (24 of 27) paid for earning good grades were also
rewarded in other ways, e.g., praise, dinners, treats, trips. Students who were paid for earning
good grades in childhood had significantly *higher* mean college GPAs than students who
were not paid: 3.29 vs. 2.88, respectively ($t_{85} = 3.35, p < .01$). These results suggest that reinforcement for academic work conditions reward value of academic work and helps to *create*
intrinsic interest in academic behaviors.

References

CAMERON, J., BANKO, K. M., & PIERCE, W. D. (2001) Pervasive negative effects of rewards on intrinsic
motivation: the myth continues. *The Behavior Analyst,* 24, 1–44.

EISENBERGER, R. (1992) Learned industriousness. *Psychological Review,* 99, 248–267.

READING FOR CONTENT

1. In the context of the first sentence in Flora and Poponak's study, what are "extrinsic rewards" and what is "intrinsic interest"?
2. Paraphrase the first sentence in Flora and Poponak's study, which explains a reason that paying for grades might hurt children.
3. Paraphrase the second sentence in Flora and Poponak's study, which explains a reason that paying for grades might help children.
4. How did Flora and Poponak conduct their study and what were their results?
5. Paraphrase the last sentence of the study in which Flora and Poponak state their conclusions from the data they collected.

READING FOR GENRE, ORGANIZATION, AND STYLISTIC FEATURES

1. Label in the margin of the article these standard components of a research study: (a) statement of the problem, (b) description of the procedure, (c) research results, (d) conclusions from the study.
2. Create a simple table that presents the research results that Flora and Poponak obtained.

READING FOR RHETORICAL CONTEXT

1. Researchers value objectivity. Do you think Flora and Poponak approached their study objectively? What is the basis for your answer?

2. What aspects of Flora and Poponak's article indicate that it is intended for an academic audience? How could it be modified for a more general audience?

WRITING ASSIGNMENTS

1. Imagine you are a parent of an eight-year-old child who states that his classmates are being paid by their parents for their grades and wants you to pay for high grades as well. Write a response to your child that draws on Flora and Poponak's study in a simplified form that an eight-year-old child could understand.

2. Imagine that you are a third-grade teacher. Write a letter to the parents of the children in your class explaining your views on giving children monetary rewards for grades.

WRITING ASSIGNMENTS FOR CHAPTER 10

1. Write a straightforward summary of the views expressed in three of the selections in this chapter. For advice, refer to "Summary of Multiple Sources," pages 248–258.

2. Imagine you are establishing a college devoted to maximizing student learning and you have free rein to establish any grading system you choose. Describe the system you envision and draw on the articles in this chapter to provide a rationale for your choice.

3. Write an in-depth analysis and evaluation of the relationship between the grading system and learning. What complexities of the topic are revealed by the four selections in this chapter? Do the authors see eye to eye? Who agrees or disagrees with whom? Before you begin, read the section, "In-Depth Analysis and Evaluation," pages 205–225.

4. Write an essay in which you compare and contrast the views of Liz Mandrell in "Zen and the Art of Grade Motivation" and Jerry Farber in "A Young Person's Guide to the Grading System." Read "Comparing and Contrasting Sources," pages 228–247.

5. Write an essay in which you agree or disagree with the positions put forth by Jerry Farber and Stephen Vogel. Consider your own experience with the grading system and how it affirms or contradicts the two authors' points about the effects of grading. Engage these authors and with your own powerful voice, converse with them. For pointers, read "Essay Written in Response to Multiple Sources," pages 258–264.

6. Drawing on the four selections in this chapter, write an essay in which you argue for or against Stephen Vogel's claim, "[W]e no longer feel sure what education is for or why we value it." Before you begin, return to Chapter 8 and read the advice on how to write an argument essay.

CHAPTER 11

Cyberhood

According to *Internet World Stats,* as of October 8, 2008, 1,463,632,361 people were accessing the Internet. Every year the number of new users grows exponentially as people flock to the Web to communicate with one another and search for knowledge, news, and entertainment. The focus of Chapter 11 is online communication and its effect on our social relationships, our sense of self, and our understanding of community. In recent years, we have seen an explosion in online socializing. In 2006 Harvard student Mark Zuckerberg founded *Facebook,* and within two years nine million college students had subscribed to it. Now, open to the public, *Facebook* has over a hundred million users. As more and more of us become members of "cyberhoods," we see that our social norms are rapidly changing. Tools such as *Facebook* updates, mobile-phone text messages, and two-line messages or "tweets" on Twitter provide us with continuous online contact with friends and acquaintances. Some of us are always connected. Is this a good thing? The authors of the selections in this chapter ask us to contemplate this question.

Joseph Weizenbaum who was a pioneer of artificial intelligence and one of the foremost computer scientists in the United States, warned of the danger or our reliance on digital technology:

> We must ... admit that we are intoxicated with science and technology, that we are deeply committed to a Faustian bargain that is rapidly killing us spiritually and will soon kill us physically.... We must live one day at a time in the real world peopled by genuine human beings, not images, a world in which word and deed are inherently valued, not the engineered applause of some abstract audience. (Weizenbaum 11)

Weizenbaum and a host of pundits who examine the social impact of technology fear that we are losing our sense of what it means to be human. They argue that technology cuts us off from society and nature and fragments our personal identities. Others contend that the Internet can be used to affirm identity and build community because it has the potential to strengthen relationships. The readings in Chapter 11 focus on this controversy. In "Modern Romance," Celeste Biever discusses online dating and questions whether cyber romance will work when it moves offline. In a scholarly article entitled "Cyberspace and Identity," Sherry Turkle explains how online systems make it possible for people to experiment with virtual identities in ways that may contribute to their development as human beings. In the final selection, "Is There a There in Cyberspace?" John Perry Barlow compares physical and virtual communities by presenting the advantages and disadvantages of each arrangement.

Modern Romance

Celeste Biever

Celeste Biever is the biomedical news editor for New Scientist *magazine.*
New Scientist is a weekly international magazine that reports on current events and developments in the fields of science, technology, and the environment.

Prereading

Respond to the following questions in your journal:

- Do you or would you feel comfortable dating online? Why or why not?
- Do you think online dating is safe? Why or why not?

He was a strapping 28-year-old with a mane of brown hair, she a dazzling redhead in a white strapless vest and tight trousers. Garth Fairlight of London, UK, and Pituca Chang of Irvine, California, first met watching fireworks and eating burgers at a Fourth of July party in 2003. It wasn't quite love at first sight, but after protesting against high taxes together, the chemistry became obvious. Two months later she moved in, and by November they were married.   *1*

It sounds like a fairy-tale romance, but it actually happened—in the online fantasy world of Second Life, that is. Garth and Pituca are actually screen names, and the pair are at least 20 years older than they look inside the game, where players appear as cartoon versions of themselves—called avatars—and communicate by typing messages.   *2*

If the idea of a cyber-romance doesn't turn you on, perhaps you should take a closer look. The couple insist the feelings they have for each other are real and that they were madly in love long before they met face to face. "The love part happened in the game," says Pituca, but she and Garth are now engaged to be married in real life. Catherine Smith, marketing director at Linden Lab in San Francisco, California, which produces Second Life, says the pair are just one of many couples who have got married inside the game. Others say that getting hitched in real life is rarer, but it happens.   *3*

While love in virtual worlds may still be unusual, less intense online relationships have become commonplace. A study completed last month by the non-profit Pew Internet & American Life Project based in Washington DC found that 74 per cent of single internet users in the US have taken part in at least one online dating-related activity, including sites   *4* specifically devoted to finding a match, while 15 per cent of American adults (that's 30 million people) say they know someone who has been in a long-term relationship with a partner they met online. So what's the big attraction?

The internet has some clear advantages over the real world as a place to meet people,   5
says Dan Ariely, who studies online dating at the Massachusetts Institute of Technology's Media Lab. "The problem of meeting people in modern life is very real. Online relationships are a way to experiment cheaply and in a nondangerous way with romantic life." Moreover, you can meet far more people online than you could ever hope to in a bar or in the office. And because online games and chat rooms often have a theme, they allow users to home in on people with whom they share interests. Some online dating sites, including Match.com and eHarmony, apply algorithms that their creators claim can pick out couples most likely to be a successful match.

However, it is the nature of online interactions themselves that intrigues psychologists   6
and sociologists. There is growing evidence that communicating online is more conducive to openness than a face-to-face rendezvous. "We tend to interact differently online," says Ren Reynolds, a virtual-world consultant based in the UK. "We tend to be more honest, more intimate with people."

This is known as the "hyperpersonal" effect, a term coined in 1996 by Joe Walther of   7
Cornell University in New York (Communication Research, vol 23, p 3). Walther says that communicating by typed message gives people time to construct their responses. It also frees them from worrying about how they look and sound, so they can focus exclusively on what they're saying. Without the cues that we rely on to form impressions during face-to-face encounters, such as facial expressions and mannerisms, people can build more positive impressions of each other without being confronted with a jarring reality that might put them off.

Nick Yee of Stanford University, California, studies how the hyperpersonal effect oper-   8
ates in virtual worlds, where people get to know each other "from the inside out". "In real life we judge a person by their physical appearance and then we get to know their character and values. In a massively multiplayer online role-playing game, the reverse is true," he writes on the virtual worlds blog Terra Nova. This is an experience that Erika, who is in her early 20s and moved to the UK from the US after meeting her husband Damien inside Second Life, has also enjoyed. "In real life you are usually first attracted to someone by their looks," she says. "However, online you can't touch or look. All you can see is their personality."

Online communication can also encourage people to take risks, because there is   9
always the opportunity to simply disappear if things become awkward or embarrassing. And while it is certainly easy to lie online, it turns out it's even easier to tell the truth. In a 2002 study, Walther showed that people communicating online were much more likely to disclose personal details about themselves (*Human Communication Research,* vol 28, p 317). Experts believe that this is because people are shielded from disapproving facial expressions and awkward consequences.

So what happens when online couples finally meet in the flesh? Katelyn McKenna of   10
Israel's Ben Gurion University suggested in 2002 that an attraction sparked online that might not have taken off in real life can be strong enough to survive even when the relationship moves offline. Her research shows that meeting someone "inside out" might, in some cases, be preferable to meeting them the right way round. When Pituca decided to meet Garth in London, exactly one year after they had first met in the game, things went swimmingly. "I'm there at Heathrow, and when I saw her come out, I immediately knew it was

her," says Garth. "It felt like she had been on a business trip but that we had been together our whole life."

However, it seems the hyperpersonal effect also has a flip side. Although it brings *11* greater intimacy and self-disclosure, it also encourages a hyperactive imagination that can result in dashed hopes. "You have less information and therefore individuals fill in the gaps with what they would like to believe," says Nicole Ellison, who is based at Michigan State University in East Lansing and studies self-disclosure in online dating sites.

The internet has pitched us into a new era of romance that offers greater opportu- *12* nities to meet the right partner and a better environment for intimate and honest communication. But it also plays by different rules. Plenty of people who have tried to make online relationships work in real life have been disappointed. For some, it's best to enjoy cyber-romance for what it is. Whether or not it's love, it can certainly be life-changing.

READING FOR CONTENT

1. In which ways does the Internet offer more advantages for meeting people than the real world?
2. Explain what Joe Walther means by the "hyperpersonal" effect.
3. Why are people more likely to divulge more about themselves online than offline?
4. What is the flip side of the "hyperpersonal effect"?

READING FOR GENRE, ORGANIZATION, AND STYLISTIC FEATURES

1. Biever opens the article with a scenario and picks up the example again in paragraph 10. What does the story of Garth Fairlight and Pituca Chang add to the article?
2. What is the effect of the questions Biever asks the reader in paragraphs 4 and 10?
3. Biever relies heavily on sources. Make note of the places where she refers to sources and explain how these sources support her points.

READING FOR RHETORICAL CONTEXT

1. What effect did this article have on you? What effect do you think it had on readers of the *New Scientist* magazine?
2. Do you think Biever gives a balanced view of cyber-romance? Why or why not?

WRITING ASSIGNMENTS

1. Using "Modern Romance" as a base, write a brief essay on the pros and cons of online dating.
2. Biever cites a study from the Pew Internet and American Life Project that discovered that 74 percent of unmarried Internet users have engaged in online dating. Write an essay in which you (a) discuss the implications of this statistic and (b) speculate about what it reveals about contemporary society and culture.
3. Explore the online dating services Biever mentions in her article—Match.com, eHarmony.com—or other popular dating sites. Write an essay addressed to your classmates in which you argue for or against expending the energy needed to participate in online dating.

Cyberspace and Identity

Sherry Turkle

Sherry Turkle is the Abby Rockefeller Mauzé Professor of the Social Studies of Science and Technology at the Massachusetts Institute of Technology (MIT). She is the author of Psychoanalytic Politics: Jacques Lacan and Freud's French Revolution *(Guilford 1992);* The Second Self: Computers and the Human Spirit *(Simon and Schuster 1984); and* Life on the Screen: Identity in the Age of the Internet *(Simon and Schuster 1995). For additional biographical information, see http://www.mit.edu/~sturkle/.*

This article originally appeared in Contemporary Sociology, *a scholarly journal published by the American Sociological Association.* Contemporary Sociology *contains reviews and critical discussions of recent work in sociology and important trends and issues in the field.*

Prereading ▄

Think of a time when you assumed temporarily a personality or identity that differs from whom you really are. You might think of a situation where you assumed an online identity or a real-world situation in which you intentionally gave the impression that you were a different type of person than you really are. Describe the experience. Was it positive or negative?

We come to see ourselves differently as we catch sight of our images in the mirror of the machine. Over a decade ago, when I first called the computer a "second self" (1984), these identity-transforming relationships were most usually one-on-one, a person alone with a machine.[1] This is no longer the case. A rapidly expanding system of networks, collectively known as the Internet, links millions of people together in new spaces that are changing the way we think, the nature of our sexuality, the form of our communities, our very identities. In cyberspace, we are learning to live in virtual worlds. We may find ourselves alone as we navigate virtual oceans, unravel virtual mysteries, and engineer virtual skyscrapers. But increasingly, when we step through the looking glass, other people are there as well.

Over the past decade, I have been engaged in the ethnographic and clinical study of how people negotiate the virtual and the "real" as they represent themselves on computer screens linked through the Internet. For many people, such experiences challenge what they have traditionally called "identity," which they are moved to recast in terms of multiple windows and parallel lives. Online life is not the only factor that is pushing them in this direction; there is no simple sense in which computers are causing a shift in notions of identity. It is, rather, that today's life on the screen dramatizes and concretizes a range of cultural trends that encourage us to think of identity in terms of multiplicity and flexibility.

1

2

---

[1]*For a fuller discussion of the themes in this essay, see Turkle (1995).*

Virtual Personae

In this essay, I focus on one key element of online life and its impact on identity: the creation and projection of constructed personae into virtual space. In cyberspace, it is well known, one's body can be represented by one's own textual description: The obese can be slender, the beautiful plain. The fact that self-presentation is written in text means that there is time to reflect upon and edit one's "composition," which makes it easier for the shy to be outgoing, the "nerdy" sophisticated. The relative anonymity of life on the screen—one has the choice of being known only by one's chosen "handle" or online name—gives people the chance to express often unexplored aspects of the self. Additionally, multiple aspects of self can be explored in parallel. Online services offer their users the opportunity to be known by several different names. For example, it is not unusual for someone to be BroncoBill in one online community, ArmaniBoy in another, and MrSensitive in a third.

The online exercise of playing with identity and trying out new identities is perhaps most explicit in "role playing" virtual communities (such as Multi-User Domains, or MUDs) where participation literally begins with the creation of a persona (or several); but it is by no means confined to these somewhat exotic locations. In bulletin boards, newsgroups, and chat rooms, the creation of personae may be less explicit than on MUDs, but it is no less psychologically real. One IRC (Internet Relay Chat) participant describes her experience of online talk: "I go from channel to channel depending on my mood. . . . I actually feel a part of several of the channels, several conversations. . . . I'm different in the different chats. They bring out different things in me." Identity play can happen by changing names and by changing places.

For many people, joining online communities means crossing a boundary into highly charged territory. Some feel an uncomfortable sense of fragmentation, some a sense of relief. Some sense the possibilities for self-discovery. A 26-year-old graduate student in history says, "When I log on to a new community and I create a character and know I have to start typing my description, I always feel a sense of panic. Like I could find out something I don't want to know." A woman in her late thirties who just got an account with America Online used the fact that she could create five "names" for herself on her account as a chance to "lay out all the moods I'm in—all the ways I want to be in different places on the system."

The creation of site-specific online personae depends not only on adopting a new name. Shifting of personae happens with a change of virtual place. Cycling through virtual environments is made possible by the existence of what have come to be called "windows" in modern computing environments. Windows are a way to work with a computer that makes it possible for the machine to place you in several contexts at the same time. As a user, you are attentive to just one of the windows on your screen at any given moment, but in a certain sense, you are a presence in all of them at all times. You might be writing a paper in bacteriology and using your computer in several ways to help you: You are "present" to a word processing program on which you are taking notes and collecting thoughts, you are "present" to communications software that is in touch with a distant computer for collecting reference materials, you are "present" to a simulation program that is charting the growth of bacterial colonies when a new organism enters their ecology, and you are "present" to an online chat session whose participants are discussing recent research in the field. Each of these activities takes place in a "window," and your identity on the computer is the sum of your distributed presence.

The development of the windows metaphor for computer interfaces was a technical innovation motivated by the desire to get people working more efficiently by "cycling through" different applications, much as time-sharing computers cycled through the computing needs of different people. But in practice, windows have become a potent metaphor for thinking about the self as a multiple, distributed, "time-sharing" system.

The self no longer simply plays different roles in different settings—something that people experience when, for example, one wakes up as a lover, makes breakfast as a mother, and drives to work as a lawyer. The windows metaphor suggests a distributed self that exists in many worlds and plays many roles at the same time. The "windows" enabled by a computer operating system support the metaphor, and cyberspace raises the experience to a higher power by translating the metaphor into a life experience of "cycling through."   *8*

Identity, Moratoria, and Play

Cyberspace, like all complex phenomena, has a range of psychological effects. For some people, it is a place to "act out" unresolved conflicts, to play and replay characterological difficulties on a new and exotic stage. For others, it provides an opportunity to "work through" significant personal issues, to use the new materials of cybersociality to reach for new resolutions. These more positive identity effects follow from the fact that for some, cyberspace provides what Erik Erikson ([1950]1963) would have called a "psychosocial moratorium," a central element in how he thought about identity development in adolescence. Although the term *moratorium* implies a "time out," what Erikson had in mind was not withdrawal. On the contrary, the adolescent moratorium is a time of intense interaction with people and ideas. It is a time of passionate friendships and experimentation. The adolescent falls in and out of love with people and ideas. Erikson's notion of the moratorium was not a "hold" on significant experiences but on their consequences. It is a time during which one's actions are, in a certain sense, not counted as they will be later in life. They are not given as much weight, not given the force of full judgment. In this context, experimentation can become the norm rather than a brave departure. Relatively consequence-free experimentation facilitates the development of a "core self," a personal sense of what gives life meaning that Erikson called "identity."   *9*

Erikson developed these ideas about the importance of a moratorium during the late 1950s and early 1960s. At that time, the notion corresponded to a common understanding of what "the college years" were about. Today, 30 years later, the idea of the college years as a consequence-free "time out" seems of another era. College is pre-professional, and AIDS has made consequence-free sexual experimentation an impossibility. The years associated with adolescence no longer seem a "time out." But if our culture no longer offers an adolescent moratorium, virtual communities often do. It is part of what makes them seem so attractive.   *10*

Erikson's ideas about stages did not suggest rigid sequences. His stages describe what people need to achieve before they can move ahead easily to another developmental task. For example, Erikson pointed out that successful intimacy in young adulthood is difficult if one does not come to it with a sense of who one is, the challenge of adolescent identity building. In real life, however, people frequently move on with serious deficits. With incompletely resolved "stages," they simply do the best they can. They use whatever materials they have at hand to get as much as they can of what they have missed. Now virtual social life can play a role in these dramas of self-reparation. Time in cyberspace reworks the notion of the moratorium because it may now exist on an always-available "window."   *11*

Expanding One's Range in the Real

Case, a 34-year-old industrial designer happily married to a female co-worker, describes his   *12*
real-life (RL) persona as a "nice guy," a "Jimmy Stewart type like my father." He describes his
outgoing, assertive mother as a "Katharine Hepburn type." For Case, who views assertiveness
through the prism of this Jimmy Stewart/Katharine Hepburn dichotomy, an assertive man is
quickly perceived as "being a bastard." An assertive woman, in contrast, is perceived as being
"modern and together." Case says that although he is comfortable with his temperament
and loves and respects his father, he feels he pays a high price for his own low-key ways. In
particular, he feels at a loss when it comes to confrontation, both at home and at work. Online,
in a wide range of virtual communities, Case presents himself as females whom he calls his
"Katharine Hepburn types." These are strong, dynamic, "out there" women who remind Case
of his mother, who "says exactly what's on her mind." He tells me that presenting himself as a
woman online has brought him to a point where he is more comfortable with confrontation in
his RL as a man.

Case describes his Katharine Hepburn personae as "externalizations of a part of myself."   *13*
In one interview with him, I used the expression "aspects of the self," and he picked it up
eagerly, for his online life reminds him of how Hindu gods could have different aspects or
subpersonalities, all the while being a whole self. In response to my question "Do you feel
that you call upon your personae in real life?" Case responded:

> Yes, an aspect sort of clears its throat and says, "I can do this. You are being so amazingly
> conflicted over this and I know exactly what to do. Why don't you just let me do it?"...
> In real life, I tend to be extremely diplomatic, nonconfrontational. I don't like to ram my
> ideas down anyone's throat. [Online] I can be, "Take it or leave it." All of my Hepburn
> characters are that way. That's probably why I play them. Because they are smart-
> mouthed, they will not sugar-coat their words.

In some ways, Case's description of his inner world of actors who address him and are able
to take over negotiations is reminiscent of the language of people with multiple-personality
disorder. But the contrast is significant: Case's inner actors are not split off from each other
or from his sense of "himself." He experiences himself very much as a collective self, not
feeling that he must goad or repress this or that aspect of himself into conformity. He is at
ease, cycling through from Katharine Hepburn to Jimmy Stewart. To use analyst Philip
Bromberg's language (1994), online life has helped Case learn how to "stand in the spaces
between selves and still feel one, to see the multiplicity and still feel a unity." To use computer
scientist Marvin Minsky's (1987) phrase, Case feels at ease cycling through his "society of
mind," a notion of identity as distributed and heterogeneous. Identity, from the Latin *idem,*
has been used habitually to refer to the sameness between two qualities. On the Internet,
however, one can be many, and one usually is.

An Object to Think with for Thinking About Identity

In the late 1960s and early 1970s, I was first exposed to notions of identity and multiplicity.   *14*
These ideas—most notably that there is no such thing as "the ego," that each of us is a mul-
tiplicity of parts, fragments, and desiring connections—surfaced in the intellectual hot-
house of Paris; they presented the world according to such authors as Jacques Lacan, Gilles
Deleuze, and Félix Guattari. But despite such ideal conditions for absorbing theory, my
"French lessons" remained abstract exercises. These theorists of poststructuralism spoke

words that addressed the relationship between mind and body, but from my point of view had little to do with my own.

In my lack of personal connection with these ideas, I was not alone. To take one example, for many people it is hard to accept any challenge to the idea of an autonomous ego. While in recent years, many psychologists, social theorists, psychoanalysts, and philosophers have argued that the self should be thought of as essentially decentered, the normal requirements of everyday life exert strong pressure on people to take responsibility for their actions and to see themselves as unitary actors. This disjuncture between theory (the unitary self is an illusion) and lived experience (the unitary self is the most basic reality) is one of the main reasons why multiple and decentered theories have been slow to catch on—or when they do, why we tend to settle back quickly into older, centralized ways of looking at things.   *15*

When, 20 years later, I used my personal computer and modem to join online communities, I had an experience of this theoretical perspective which brought it shockingly down to earth. I used language to create several characters. My textual actions are my actions—my words make things happen. I created selves that were made and transformed by language. And different personae were exploring different aspects of the self. The notion of a decentered identity was concretized by experiences on a computer screen. In this way, cyberspace becomes an object to think with for thinking about identity—an element of cultural bricolage.   *16*

Appropriable theories—ideas that capture the imagination of the culture at large—tend to be those with which people can become actively involved. They tend to be theories that can be "played" with. So one way to think about the social appropriability of a given theory is to ask whether it is accompanied by its own objects-to-think-with that can help it move out beyond intellectual circles.   *17*

For example, the popular appropriation of Freudian ideas had little to do with scientific demonstrations of their validity. Freudian ideas passed into the popular culture because they offered robust and down-to-earth objects-to-think-with. The objects were not physical but almost-tangible ideas, such as dreams and slips of the tongue. People were able to play with such Freudian "objects." They became used to looking for them and manipulating them, both seriously and not so seriously. And as they did so, the idea that slips and dreams betray an unconscious began to feel natural.   *18*

In Freud's work, dreams and slips of the tongue carried the theory. Today, life on the computer screen carries theory. People decide that they want to interact with others on a computer network. They get an account on a commercial service. They think that this will provide them with new access to people and information, and of course it does. But it does more. When they log on, they may find themselves playing multiple roles; they may find themselves playing characters of the opposite sex. In this way, they are swept up by experiences that enable them to explore previously unexamined aspects of their sexuality or that challenge their ideas about a unitary self. The instrumental computer, the computer that does things for us, has revealed another side: a subjective computer that does things to us as people, to our view of ourselves and our relationships, to our ways of looking at our minds. In simulation, identity can be fluid and multiple, a signifier no longer clearly points to a thing that is signified, and understanding is less likely to proceed through analysis than by navigation through virtual space.   *19*

Within the psychoanalytic tradition, many "schools" have departed from a unitary view of identity, among these the Jungian, object-relations, and Lacanian. In different ways,   *20* each of these groups of analysts was banished from the ranks of orthodox Freudians for such suggestions, or somehow relegated to the margins. As the United States became the center of psychoanalytic politics in the mid-twentieth century, ideas about a robust executive ego began to constitute the psychoanalytic mainstream.

But today, the pendulum has swung away from that complacent view of a unitary self. Through the fragmented selves presented by patients and through theories that stress the decentered subject, contemporary social and psychological thinkers are confronting what has been left out of theories of the unitary self. It is asking such questions as, What is the self when it functions as a society? What is the self when it divides its labors among its constituent "alters?" Those burdened by post-traumatic dissociative disorders suffer these questions; I am suggesting that inhabitants of virtual communities play with them. In our lives on the screen, people are developing ideas about identity as multiplicity through new social *practices* of identity as multiplicity.

With these remarks, I am not implying that chat rooms or MUDs or the option to declare multiple user names on America Online are causally implicated in the dramatic increase of people who exhibit symptoms of multiple-personality disorder (MPD), or that people on MUDs have MPD, or that MUDding (or online chatting) is like having MPD. I am saying that the many manifestations of multiplicity in our culture, including the adoption of online personae, are contributing to a general reconsideration of traditional, unitary notions of identity. Online experiences with "parallel lives" are part of the significant cultural context that supports new theorizing about nonpathological, indeed healthy, multiple selves.

In thinking about the self, *multiplicity* is a term that carries with it several centuries of negative associations, but such authors as Kenneth Gergen (1991), Emily Martin (1994), and Robert Jay Lifton (1993) speak in positive terms of an adaptive, "flexible" self. The flexible self is not unitary, nor are its parts stable entities. A person cycles through its aspects, and these are themselves ever-changing and in constant communication with each other. Daniel Dennett (1991) speaks of the flexible self by using the metaphor of consciousness as multiple drafts, analogous to the experience of several versions of a document open on a computer screen, where the user is able to move between them at will. For Dennett, knowledge of these drafts encourages a respect for the many different versions, while it imposes a certain distance from them. Donna Haraway (1991), picking up on this theme of how a distance between self states may be salutory, equates a "split and contradictory self" with a "knowing self." She is optimistic about its possibilities: "The knowing self is partial in all its guises, never finished, whole, simply there and original; it is always constructed and stitched together imperfectly; and therefore able to join with another, to see together without claiming to be another." What most characterizes Haraway's and Dennett's models of a knowing self is that the lines of communication between its various aspects are open. The open communication encourages an attitude of respect for the many within us and the many within others.

Increasingly, social theorists and philosophers are being joined by psychoanalytic theorists in efforts to think about healthy selves whose resilience and capacity for joy comes from having access to their many aspects. For example, Philip Bromberg (1994), insists that our ways of describing "good parenting" must now shift away from an emphasis on confirming a child in a "core self" and onto helping a child develop the capacity to negotiate fluid transitions between self states. The healthy individual knows how to be many but to smooth out the moments of transition between states of self. Bromberg says: "Health is when you are multiple but feel a unity. Health is when different aspects of self can get to know each other and reflect upon each other." Here, within the psychoanalytic tradition, is a model of multiplicity as a state of easy traffic across selves, a conscious, highly articulated "cycling through."

From a Psychoanalytic to a Computer Culture?

Having literally written our online personae into existence, they can be a kind of Rorschach test. We can use them to become more aware of what we project into everyday life. We can use the virtual to reflect constructively on the real. Cyberspace opens the possibility for identity play, but it is very serious play. People who cultivate an awareness of what stands behind their screen personae are the ones most likely to succeed in using virtual experience for personal and social transformation. And the people who make the most of their lives on the screen are those who are able to approach it in a spirit of self-reflection. What does my behavior in cyberspace tell me about what I want, who I am, what I may not be getting in the rest of my life?

25

As a culture, we are at the end of the Freudian century. Freud after all, was a child of the nineteenth century; of course, he was carrying the baggage of a very different scientific sensibility than our own. But faced with the challenges of cyberspace, our need for a practical philosophy of self-knowledge, one that does not shy away from issues of multiplicity, complexity, and ambivalence, that does not shy away from the power of symbolism, from the power of the word, from the power of identity play, has never been greater as we struggle to make meaning from our lives on the screen. It is fashionable to think that we have passed from a psychoanalytic culture to a computer culture—that we no longer need to think in terms of Freudian slips but rather of information processing errors. But the reality is more complex. It is time to rethink our relationship to the computer culture and psychoanalytic culture as a proudly held joint citizenship.

26

References

Bromberg, Philip. 1994. "Speak that I May See You: Some Reflections on Dissociation, Reality, and Psychoanalytic Listening." *Psychoanalytic Dialogues* 4 (4): 517–47.

Dennett, Daniel. 1991. *Consciousness Explained.* Boston: Little, Brown.

Erikson, Erik. [1950] 1963. *Childhood and Society,* 2nd Ed. New York: Norton.

Haraway, Donna. 1991. "The Actors are Cyborg, Nature is Coyote, and the Geography is Elsewhere: Postscript to 'Cyborgs at Large.'" In *Technoculture,* edited by Constance Penley and Andrew Ross. Minneapolis: University of Minnesota Press.

Gergen, Kenneth. 1991. *The Saturated Self: Dilemmas of Identity in Contemporary Life.* New York: Basic Books.

Lifton, Robert Jay. 1993. *The Protean Self: Human Resilience in an Age of Fragmentation.* New York: Basic Books.

Martin, Emily. 1994. *Flexible Bodies: Tracking Immunity in America Culture from the Days of Polio to the Days of AIDS.* Boston: Beacon Press.

Minsky, Martin. 1987. *The Society of Mind.* New York: Simon & Schuster.

Turkle, Sherry. [1978] 1990. *Psychoanalytic Politics: Jacques Lacan and Freud's French Revolution.* 2nd Ed. New York: Guilford Press.

———. 1984. *The Second Self: Computers and the Human Spirit.* New York: Simon & Schuster.

———. 1995. *Life on the Screen: Identity in the Age of the Internet.* New York: Simon & Schuster.

READING FOR CONTENT

1. What does Turkle mean by "identity play" (paragraph 4) and what are some of the ways people play with their identities on the Internet?
2. Define Erik Erikson's concept of "psychological moratorium" and explain how virtual communities offer adolescents that moratorium today (paragraphs 9–11).
3. Explain what an "appropriable" theory is and give an example of such a theory (paragraphs 17–19).
4. Summarize the shift in how scholars view the self that is described in paragraphs 20 and 21. Since this is a particularly difficult passage, you may need to rely on strategies for handling complex readings that are provided on pages 74–78.
5. According to Turkle, what cultural forces are leading us to reconstruct our notion of identity as unitary and autonomous and instead think of "self" as manifesting multiplicity and flexibility (paragraphs 14–24)?
6. Compare the negative aspects of "mutiplicity" that Turkle mentions in paragraph 22 with the positive aspects she presents in paragraph 23.
7. According to Turkle, what can we gain by analyzing our online lives (paragraph 25)?

READING FOR GENRE, ORGANIZATION, AND STYLISTIC FEATURES

1. Explain the function of the subheadings in Turkle's article.
2. Notice how Turkle writes from the first person point of view in this scholarly article. How does her use of "I" affect her argument?
3. How does the example of Case, the young man who experiments with various online personalities, support Turkle's argument?
4. How does Turkle use the windows metaphor (paragraphs 6–8) and the metaphor of multiple drafts (paragraph 23–24) to advance her argument?
5. Comment on the way Turkle cites sources and employs them to her advantage.

READING FOR RHETORICAL CONTEXT

1. Read Professor Turkle's homepage—http://www.mit.edu/~sturkle/—and its links to Turkle's publications, presentations, activities, interviews and profiles. Use this information to write a paragraph on Turkle's background and credibility.
2. What are the social practices that prompted Turkle to write "Cyberspace and Identity"?
3. "Cyberspace and Identity" was originally published in a 1999 issue of *Contemporary Sociology*. Do you think it would still merit the attention of sociologists today? Why or why not?
4. Reread the last two paragraphs and paraphrase the points that Turkle is trying to get across to her readers.

WRITING ASSIGNMENTS

1. According to Turkle, trying out new identities in cyberspace gives some people "an uncomfortable sense of fragmentation" and offers others "possibilities for self-discovery" (paragraph 5). Write an essay in which you describe how you feel about creating multiple online identities.

2. The *New York Times Magazine,* September 7, 2008, featured an article by Clive Thompson, "I'm So Totally, Digitally Close to You: How News Feed, Twitter and Other Forms of Incessant Online Contact Have Created a Brave New World of Ambient Intimacy," about the loss of anonymity on the Internet. Thompson writes, "When cyberspace came along in the early '90s, it was celebrated as a place where you could reinvent your identity—become someone new" (47), but it doesn't work that way today. Thompson quotes University of Maryland sociologist Zeynep Tufekci's remarks about the Internet:

   > If anything, it's identity-constraining now.... You can't play with your identity if your audience is always checking up on you. I had a student who posted that she was down-loading some Pearl Jam, and someone wrote on her wall, "Oh, *right,* ha-ha—I know you, and you're not into *that.*"

   Thompson continues to quote Tufekci: "You know the old cartoon? 'On the Internet, nobody knows you're a dog?' On the Internet today, *everybody* knows you're a dog! If you don't want people to know you're a dog, you'd better stay away from a keyboard" (47).Write an essay in which you argue that today we can no longer enjoy the type of anonymous, consequence-free "identity play" that Turkle describes in her 1999 article.

3. Toward the end of her article, Turkle says we need to reflect upon our online lives by asking "What does my behavior in cyberspace tell me about what I want, who I am, what I may not be getting in the rest of my life" (paragraph 25). Write a self-reflective essay in response to this question.

Is There a There in Cyberspace?

John Perry Barlow

John Perry Barlow, a lyricist for the Grateful Dead, operated his family's cattle ranch in Wyoming from 1971 to 1988. He is one of the founders of the Electronic Frontier Foundation, an advocacy group for preserving free speech in digital media. Barlow has been called the Thomas Jefferson of the online community for his famous essay, "A Declaration of the Independence of Cyberspace." An essayist and lecturer, Barlow is a Fellow at Harvard Law School's Berkman Center for Internet and Society.

   "Is There a There in Cyberspace?" was originally published in a special issue of Utne Reader *entitled "Cyberhood vs. Neighborhood" in spring 1995.*

Preading

Write nonstop for fifteen minutes about what you already know about the differences between online communities and real life communities.

"There is no there there."
> Gertrude Stein (speaking of Oakland)

"It ain't no Amish barn-raising in there . . ."
> Bruce Sterling (speaking of cyberspace)

I am often asked how I went from pushing cows around a remote Wyoming ranch to my present occupation (which *Wall Street Journal* recently described as "cyberspace cadet"). I haven't got a short answer, but I suppose I came to the virtual world looking for community.   *1*

Unlike most modern Americans, I grew up in an actual place, an entire nonintentional community called Pinedale, Wyoming. As I struggled for nearly a generation to keep my ranch in the family, I was motivated by the belief that such places were the spiritual home of humanity. But I knew their future was not promising.   *2*

At the dawn of the 20th century, over 40 percent of the American workforce lived off the land. The majority of us lived in towns like Pinedale. Now fewer than 1 percent of us extract a living from the soil. We just became too productive for our own good.   *3*

Of course, the population followed the jobs. Farming and ranching communities are now home to a demographically insignificant percentage of Americans, the vast majority of whom live not in ranch houses but in more or less identical split level "ranch homes" in more or less identical suburban "communities." Generica.   *4*

In my view, these are neither communities nor homes. I believe the combination of television and suburban population patterns is simply toxic to the soul. I see much evidence in contemporary America to support this view.   *5*

Meanwhile, back at the ranch, doom impended. And, as I watched the community in Pinedale growing ill from the same economic forces that were killing my family's ranch, the Bar Cross, satellite dishes brought the cultural infection of television. I started looking around for evidence that community in America would not perish altogether.   *6*

I took some heart in the mysterious nomadic City of the Deadheads, the virtually physical town that follows the Grateful Dead around the country. The Deadheads lacked place, touching down briefly wherever the band happened to be playing, and they lacked continuity in time, since they had to suffer a new diaspora every time the band moved on or went home. But they had many of the other necessary elements of community, including a culture, a religion of sorts (which, though it lacked dogma, had most of the other, more nurturing aspects of spiritual practice), a sense of necessity, and most importantly, shared adversity.   *7*

I wanted to know more about the flavor of their interaction, what they thought and felt, but since I wrote Dead songs (including "Estimated Prophet" and "Cassidy"), I was a minor icon to the Deadheads, and was thus inhibited, in some socially Heisenbergian way, from getting a clear view of what really went on among them.   *8*

Then, in 1987, I heard about a "place" where Deadheads gathered where I could move   *9*
among them without distorting too much the field of observation. Better, this was a place I
could visit without leaving Wyoming. It was a shared computer in Sausalito, California,
called the Whole Earth 'Lectronic Link, or WELL. After a lot of struggling with modems, ser-
ial cables, init strings, and other Computer arcana that seemed utterly out of phase with
such notions as Deadheads and small towns, I found myself looking at the glowing yellow
word "Login:" beyond which lay my future.

"Inside" the WELL were Deadheads in community. There were thousands of them   *10*
there, gossiping, complaining (mostly about the Grateful Dead), comforting and harassing
each other, bartering, engaging in religion (or at least exchanging their totemic set lists),
beginning and ending love affairs, praying for one another's sick kids. There was, it seemed,
everything one might find going on in a small town, save dragging Main Street and making
out on the back roads.

I was delighted. I felt I had found the new locale of human community—never mind   *11*
that the whole thing was being conducted in mere words by minds from whom the bodies
had been amputated. Never mind that all these people were deaf, dumb, and blind as para-
mecia or that their town had neither seasons nor sunsets nor smells.

Surely all these deficiencies would be remedied by richer, faster communications   *12*
media. The featureless log-in handles would gradually acquire video faces (and thus
expressions), shaded 3-D body puppets (and thus body language). This "space" which I
recognized at once to be a primitive form of the cyberspace William Gibson predicted in
his sci-fi novel *Neuromancer,* was still without apparent dimensions of vistas. But virtual
reality would change all that in time.

Meanwhile, the commons, or something like it, had been rediscovered. Once again,   *13*
people from the 'burbs had a place where they could encounter their friends as my fellow
Pinedalians did at the post office and the Wrangler Café. They had a place where their hearts
could remain as the companies they worked for shuffled their bodies around America. They
could put down roots that could not be ripped out by forces of economic history. They had
a collective stake. They had a community.

It is seven years now since I discovered the WELL. In that time, I co-founded an orga-   *14*
nization, the Electronic Frontier Foundation, dedicated to protecting its interests and those
of other virtual communities like it from raids by physical governments. I've spent countless
hours typing away at its residents, and I've watched the larger context that contains it, the
Internet, grow at such an explosive rate that, by 2004, every human on the planet will have
an e-mail address unless the growth curve flattens (which it will).

My enthusiasm for virtuality has cooled. In fact, unless one counts interaction with   *15*
the rather too large society of those with whom I exchange electronic mail, I don't spend
much time engaging in virtual community, at all. Many of the near-term benefits I anticipated from it seem to remain as far in the future as they did when I first logged in. Perhaps
they always will.

Pinedale works, more or less, as it is, but a lot is still missing from the communities   *16*
of cyberspace, whether they be places like the WELL, the fractious newsgroups of USENET,
the silent "auditoriums" of America Online, or even enclaves on the promising World
Wide Web.

What is missing? Well, to quote Ranjit Makkuni of Xerox Corporation's Palo Alto   *17*
Research Center, "the *prana* is missing," *prana* being the Hindu term for both breath and

spirit. I think he is right about this and that perhaps the central question of the virtual age is whether or not *prana* can somehow be made to fit through any disembodied medium.

Prana is, to my mind, the literally vital element in the holy and unseen ecology of rela- 18
tionship, the dense mesh of invisible life, on whose surface carbon-based life floats like a thin film. It is at the heart of the fundamental and profound difference between information and experience. Jaron Lanier has said that "information is alienated experience," and, that being true, *prana* is part of what is removed when you create such easily transmissible replicas of experience as, say, the evening news.

Obviously a great many other, less spiritual, things are also missing entirely, like body 19
language, sex, death, tone of voice, clothing, beauty (or homeliness), weather, violence, veg-
etation, wildlife, pets, architecture, music, smells, sunlight, and that ol' harvest moon. In short, most of the things that make my life real to me.

Present, but in far less abundance than in the physical world, which I call "meat 20
space," are women, children, old people, poor people, and the genuinely blind. Also mostly missing are the illiterate and the continent of Africa. There is not much human diversity in cyberspace, which is populated, as near as I can tell, by white males under 50 with plenty of computer terminal time, great typing skills, high math SATs, strongly held opinions on just about everything, and an excruciating face-to-face shyness, especially with the opposite sex.

But diversity is as essential to healthy community as it is to healthy ecosystems (which 21
are, in my view, different from communities only in unimportant aspects). I believe that the principal reason for the almost universal failure of the intentional communities of the '60s and '70s was a lack of diversity in their members. It was a rare commune with any old people in it, or people who were fundamentally out of philosophical agreement with the majority.

Indeed, it is the usual problem when we try to build something that can only be 22
grown. Natural systems, such as human communities, are simply too complex to design by the engineering principles we insist on applying to them. Like Dr. Frankenstein, western civ-
ilization is now finding its rational skills inadequate to the task of creating and caring for life. We would do better to return to a kind of agricultural mind-set in which we humbly try to re-create the conditions from which life has sprung before. And leave the rest to God.

Given that it has been built so far almost entirely by people with engineering degrees, 23
it is not so surprising that cyberspace has the kind of overdesigned quality that leaves out all kinds of elements nature would have provided invisibly.

Also missing from both the communes of the '60s and from cyberspace are a couple of 24
elements that I believe are very important, if not essential, to the formation and preservation of a real community: an absence of alternatives and a sense of genuine adversity, generally shared. What about these?

It is hard to argue that anyone would find losing a modem literally hard to survive, 25
while many have remained in small towns, have tolerated their intolerances and created entertainment to enliven their culturally arid lives simply because it seemed there was no choice but to stay. There are many investments—spiritual, material, and temporal—one is willing to put into a home one cannot leave. Communities are often the beneficiaries of these involuntary investments.

But when the going gets rough in cyberspace, it is even easier to move than it is in the 26
'burbs, where, given the fact that the average American moves some 12 times in his or her life, moving appears to be pretty easy. You cannot only find another bulletin board service (BBS) or newsgroup to hang out in; you can, with very little effort, start your own.

And then there is the bond of joint suffering. Most community is a cultural stockade erected against a common enemy that can take many forms. In Pinedale, we bore together, with an understanding needing little expression, the fact that Upper Green River Valley is the coldest spot, as measured by annual mean temperature, in the lower 48 states. We knew that if somebody was stopped on the road most winter nights, he would probably die there, so the fact that we might loathe him was not sufficient reason to drive on past his broken pickup. *27*

By the same token, the Deadheads have the Drug Enforcement Administration, which strives to give them 20-year prison terms without parole for distributing the fairly harmless sacrament of their faith. They have an additional bond in the fact that when their Microbuses die, as they often do, no one but another Deadhead is likely to stop to help them. *28*

But what are the shared adversities of cyberspace? Lousy user interfaces? The flames of harsh invective? Dumb jokes? Surely these can all be survived without the sanctuary provided by fellow sufferers. *29*

One is always free to yank the jack, as I have mostly done. For me, the physical world offers far more opportunity for *prana* rich connections with my fellow creatures. Even for someone whose body is in a state of perpetual motion, I feel I can generally find more community among the still-embodied. *30*

Finally, there is that shyness factor. Not only are we trying to build community here among people who have never experienced any in my sense of the term, we are trying to build community among people who, in their lives, have rarely used the word *we* in a heartfelt way. It is a vast club, and many of the members—following Groucho Marx—wouldn't want to join a club that would have them. *31*

And yet... *32*

How quickly physical community continues to deteriorate. Even Pinedale, which seems to have survived the plague of ranch failures, feels increasingly cut off from itself. Many of the ranches are now owned by corporate types who fly their Gulfstreams in to fish and are rarely around during the many months when the creeks are frozen over and neighbors are needed. They have kept the ranches alive financially, but they actively discourage their managers from the interdependence my former colleagues and I require. They keep agriculture on life support, still alive but lacking a functional heart. *33*

And the town has been inundated with suburbanites who flee here, bringing all their terrors and suspicions with them. They spend their evenings as they did in Orange County, watching television or socializing in hermetic little enclaves of fundamentalist Christianity that seem to separate them from us and even, given their sectarian animosities, from one another. The town remains. The community is largely a wraith of nostalgia. *34*

So where else can we look for the connection we need to prevent our plunging further into the condition of separateness Nietzsche called sin? What is there to do but to dive further into the bramble bush of information that, in its broadest forms, has done so much to tear us apart? *35*

Cyberspace, for all its current deficiencies and failed promises, is not without some very real solace already. *36*

Some months ago, the great love of my life, a vivid young woman with whom I intended to spend the rest of it, dropped dead of undiagnosed viral cardiomyopathy two days short of her 30th birthday. I felt as if my own heart had been as shredded as hers. *37*

We had lived together in New York City. Except for my daughters, no one from Pinedale had met her. I needed a community to wrap around myself against colder winds than fortune had ever blown at me before. And without looking, I found I had one in the virtual world.

On the WELL, there was a topic announcing her death in one of the conferences to which I posted the eulogy I had read over her before burying her in her own small town of Nanaimo, British Columbia. It seemed to strike a chord among the disembodied living on the Net. People copied it and sent it to one another. Over the next several months I received almost a megabyte of electronic mail from all over the planet, mostly from folks whose faces I have never seen and probably never will.

They told me of their own tragedies and what they had done to survive them. As humans have since words were first uttered, we shared the second most common human experience, death, with an openheartedness that would have caused grave uneasiness in physical America, where the whole topic is so cloaked in denial as to be considered obscene. Those strangers, who had no arms to put around my shoulders, no eyes to weep with mine, nevertheless saw me through. As neighbors do.

I have no idea how far we will plunge into this strange place. Unlike previous frontiers, this one has no end. It is so dissatisfying in so many ways that I suspect we will be more restless in our search for home here than in all our previous explorations. And that is one reason why I think we may find it after all. If home is where the heart is, then there is already some part of home to be found in cyberspace.

So ... does virtual community work or not? Should we all go off to cyberspace or should we resist it as a demonic form of symbolic abstraction? Does it supplant the real or is there, in it, reality itself?

Like so many true things, this one doesn't resolve itself to a black or a white. Nor is it gray. It is, along with the rest of life, black/white. Both/neither. I'm not being equivocal or whishy-washy here. We have to get over our Manichean sense that everything is either good or bad, and the border of cyberspace seems to me a good place to leave that old set of filters.

But really it doesn't matter. We are going there whether we want to or not. In five years, everyone who is reading these words will have an e-mail address, other than the determined Luddites who also eschew the telephone and electricity.

When we are all together in cyberspace we will see what the human spirit, and the basic desire to connect, can create there. I am convinced that the result will be more benign if we go there open-minded, open-hearted, and excited with the adventure than if we are dragged into exile.

And we must remember that going to cyberspace, unlike previous great emigrations to the frontier, hardly requires us to leave where we have been. Many will find, as I have, a much richer appreciation of physical reality for having spent so much time in virtuality.

Despite its current (and perhaps in some areas permanent) insufficiencies, we should go to cyberspace with hope. Groundless hope, like unconditional love, may be the only kind that counts.

In Memoriam, Dr. Cynthia Homer (1964–1994).

READING FOR CONTENT

1. What features of the Whole Earth 'Lectronic Link (WELL) appealed to Barlow?
2. Explain what Barlow means when he says "the *prana* is missing" from virtual communities.
3. List the nonspiritual things that are missing from online communities.
4. Describe how Barlow's physical community of Pinedale has deteriorated.
5. Explain what Barlow means when he says, "Cyberspace, for all its current deficiencies and failed promises, is not without some very real solace already" (paragraph 36).

READING FOR GENRE, ORGANIZATION, AND STYLISTIC FEATURES

1. If you were to write subheadings for the major divisions of Barlow's essay, what would they be? Write subheadings for the following groups of paragraphs: 1–13, 14–32, 33–41, 42–47.
2. Explain the significance of the two quotations that preface Barlow's essay.
3. Notice the places where Barlow asks questions: paragraphs 17, 24, 29, 35, and 42. What effect do these questions have on his readers?
4. Underline the various transitional words and expressions Barlow uses to begin paragraphs in the essay, for example, "Indeed" (22), "Also missing" (24), "But" (26), "And then there is" (27), "By the same token" (28), "Finally" (31), and explain how these transitions function.
5. The genre of "Is There a There in Cyberspace?" is personal essay. What features of the writing differentiate it from formal academic writing?

READING FOR RHETORICAL CONTEXT

1. Review Barlow's homepage, http://homes.eff.org/~barlow/, and then explain how Barlow's background gives credibility to the argument he makes in "Is There a There in Cyberspace?"
2. What does Barlow's use of terms such as "Heisenbergian" (paragraph 8) and "Manichean" (paragraph 43) and his reference to Nietzche (paragraph 35), tell you about his conception of his readers? Google these references and then paraphrase the sentences in which each occurs in the essay.
3. Describe Barlow's purpose in writing the essay. What does he want his readers to take away from it?

WRITING ASSIGNMENTS

1. Write a personal essay in which you describe the physical neighborhood and community of your youth. Express your views on whether this neighborhood could be replicated in "cyberhood."
2. Drawing on "Is There a There in Cyberspace?," write an essay in response to Barlow's statement: "I believe the combination of television and suburban population patterns is simply toxic to the soul" (paragraph 5).
3. Writing over a decade ago, Barlow claims, "There is not much human diversity in cyberspace." Reread paragraph 20 and write an essay in which you agree or disagree that there is still a lack of diversity in cyberspace today.

4. Write a formal evaluation of "Is There a There in Cyberspace?" Revise your essay with the "Checklist for Revising an Evaluation Essay" on pages 195–196.

5. Read "A Declaration of Independence of Cyberspace" on Barlow's homepage (http://homes.eff.org/~barlow/) or play it on YouTube (http://www.youtube .com/watch?v=vFA4YegJIWM). Barlow wrote this manifesto in 1996, almost ten years after he joined WELL, the Deadhead online community he describes in "Is There a There in Cyberspace?" Write an essay in which you compare the views Barlow expresses in "Is There a There in Cyberspace?" with those he conveys in "A Declaration of Independence of Cyberspace."

WRITING ASSIGNMENTS FOR CHAPTER 11

1. Use the "Strategies for Writing a Response to Multiple Sources," pages 263–264, to write a response essay that engages the ideas presented in the three reading selections in this chapter.

2. Synthesize ideas from at least two of the readings in this chapter to explain how one can take advantage of modern technology and still avoid its drawbacks. Use the "Checklist for Revising a Synthesis Essay Written for a Specific Purpose," Chapter 7, page 271, to revise your essay.

3. Drawing on the readings in this chapter, write an essay in which you argue point A or point B:

   A. Technology cuts us off from society and nature and fragments our personal identities.

   B. Technology can be used to affirm identity, build community, and strengthen relationships.

   Review Chapter 8, "Arguing from Sources," before writing your essay.

4. Using a reading in this chapter as your base, write a short research essay on one of the following topics: (a) the Internet as a place for developing serious relationships, (b) the Internet as a place to gain knowledge of self and a stronger sense of identity, (c) the Internet as a place for building genuine community. Review Chapter 9, "Researching Sources and Writing Research Papers," before writing your paper.

CHAPTER 12

Adolescent Pregnancy

During the second half of the 20th century, adolescent pregnancy was thought to be an undesirable condition. A common perception was that young girls lacked the maturity and financial resources to make good parents, and the responsibilities of early motherhood would severely limit their educational and career opportunities. While Americans remained divided on the issues of abortion and birth control, they agreed that social policies should discourage adolescent pregnancies. In regions where public schools offered sex education, a primary goal was to reduce pregnancy rates among young girls. Social policies, including sex education and public health programs, substantially reduced teen pregnancies in the final decades of the twentieth century.

As we moved into the twenty-first century, more young girls began to have babies. According to the National Center for Health Statistics, the teen birth rate for girls fifteen to nineteen increased 3 percent during the year 2005. This statistical trend was accompanied by a wave of media attention. The plot of *Juno,* one of the most popular films of 2007, is driven by decisions a sixteen-year-old girl (Juno) makes involving her pregnancy. Included are decisions (1) to have unprotected sex with her boyfriend, (2) to accept the pregnancy as her own problem to solve, (3) to have and then not to have an abortion, (4) to give up her baby for adoption, (5) to offer the baby to a specific wife and husband she located through an advertisement, (6) to decline the offer of money for the baby, (7) to reject the romantic overtures of the husband, (8) to give the baby to the wife alone, after the couple splits up, and (9) to get back together with the boyfriend who fathered the baby. Juno makes all of these decisions on her own, with little guidance from others. The film affirms the notion that young girls can handle the responsibilities of pregnancies.

In spring of 2008, newspapers and magazines across the nation reported on a dramatic rise in teen pregnancies in the town of Gloucester, Massachusetts. Supposedly, the increase resulted from a pact made by fifteen- and sixteen-year-old girls to become pregnant and raise their children together. Media commentary on the events in Gloucester often referenced *Juno* and speculated on the motivations of girls who are, under the law, too young to consent to sex but still decide to become mothers.

The readings in this chapter examine the reasons that teens become mothers. In "Gloucester Girls Gone Wild," Kay Hymowitz suggests various social factors, including relaxed moral codes and reduced expectations for the father, that make it attractive for young girls to become single parents. Cathy Gulli's article "Suddenly Teen Pregnancy Is Cool?" examines a wide range of explanations for teenage pregnancy and ultimately argues that today young, unmarried women and girls have "cultural permission" to give birth to babies out of wedlock. In "Give the Girls a Break," Nancy Gibbs suggests that the incident in Gloucester may indicate that an increasing number of teens are rejecting abortion and deciding to become moms instead. In this chapter, we include a research study conducted by Carol Cowley and Tillman Farley: "Adolescent Girls' Attitudes Toward Pregnancy: The Importance of Asking What the Boyfriend Wants." Cowley and Farley's major finding is that boyfriends' opinions have a significant influence on whether adolescent girls choose to become mothers.

Gloucester Girls Gone Wild

Kay S. Hymowitz

Kay Hymowitz is the William E. Simon Fellow at the Manhattan Institute and a contributing editor to City Journal. *She is the author of* Marriage and Caste in America: Separate and Unequal Families in a Post-Marital Age *(2006),* Liberation's Children: Parents and Kids in a Postmodern Age *(2003), and* Ready or Not: What Happens When We Treat Children as Small Adults *(1999).*

The article was originally published in City Journal *on June 23, 2008.* City Journal *is a quarterly magazine devoted to urban affairs and urban policy.*

Prereading ▬

Why do you think teenage girls become pregnant? Do they do it willingly or is teen pregnancy usually an accident? Respond in your journal.

The nation's latest what's-the-matter-with-kids-today story comes from Gloucester, Massachusetts, and it's a jaw-dropper. According to *Time,* a group of 15- and 16-year-old girls at Gloucester High School made a "pregnancy pact"—an agreement that they would all get pregnant and then raise their kids together. And at least on the first part of the pledge, they've evidently been successful, with one of the baby mamas choosing a 24-year-old homeless guy as her co-parent.

Depressing, no? But the story could have one upside: it might expose the folly of much of what has passed for wisdom about teen pregnancy. I say might because so far the media seem to be having trouble grasping what happened in this old, largely Catholic fishing town. Just about every report has pondered the question of whether Gloucester kids were getting

1

2

the necessary sex education and birth control. "Currently Gloucester teens must travel about 20 miles (30 km) to reach the nearest women's health clinic; younger girls have to get a ride or take the train and walk," observed *Time*. "But the notion of a school handing out birth control pills has met with hostility." Yet what's most striking in the Gloucester story was that these girls had every intention of getting pregnant, and knew exactly how to get the job done. Unless someone has figured out how to force young people to take birth-control pills, sex education is completely beside the point.

To be fair, reporters are simply repeating the primary narrative about teen pregnancy that public-health experts and family planning organizations like Planned Parenthood have long advanced. That narrative asserts that kids wind up pregnant because they can't get birth control, or feel too ashamed to ask for it, or, worse, don't even know that you can find yourself with a baby if you don't use it. The problem of teen pregnancy is especially acute in the United States, say the experts, because Americans have so many hang-ups about sex and won't talk candidly with their children about it. Hence the experts' answer to our national conundrum: European- and preferably Swedish-style sex education, teaching kids how to use condoms and to "make good decisions." 3

The dominant narrative may have had some truth to it in the pre–Madonna/Paris Hilton era. But it ignores several key changes in contemporary teenaged life—changes that the Gloucester posse has graciously illustrated for us. First, many young women who become pregnant these days either want to have a baby (as in Gloucester) or are, at the very least, open to the idea. In order for birth control to work, you have to use it religiously, and the only way you use it religiously is if you really, really don't want to get pregnant. Yet researchers like Kathryn Edin and Maria Kefalas in *Promises I Can Keep* find that's not the case for many low-income mothers. They describe young women who speak longingly about the "joys of motherhood" and who find the middle-class penchant for putting off motherhood until the later twenties incomprehensible. As rates of out-of-wedlock pregnancy have increased recently among women with a high school diploma and even those with a year or two of college, the same thinking seems to have spread to working-class communities like Gloucester. 4

Put another way, übersocialized middle-class experts, journalists, and policy makers aren't addressing the fact that girls tend to like babies. In most cultures in human history, 15- or 16-year-olds were seen as viable mothers (only after being married off, of course), so biological urge coincided with social need. But in more complex societies like ours, in which a long period of education and wealth accumulation is necessary to prepare for an advanced labor market and marriage, adolescent baby lust poses a big problem. 5

In the past, the problem was held at bay by a combination of sexual reticence, social disapproval, and a no-baby-without-marriage rule, since it wasn't easy to find a presentable boy ready to sign on to a life sentence at 16. No more. Sexual reticence is now deemed something on the order of a Victorian perversion. Social disapproval? Nowhere evident. The Gloucester school's superintendent found that most townspeople greeted with a yawn the news that local teen pregnancy rates were soaring, the Boston Globe reported. Doubtless, too, the girls noticed that Disney star Jamie Lynn Spears was about to make her dad a grandfather. (It's a girl, by the way: congratulations, Jamie Lynn!) And what about the Gloucester girls' own classmates, carrying their adorable babies to the school's day care center every day? 6

Then there's the point compellingly made by Kathleen Parker in her new book *Save the Males*: Americans aren't all that keen on fathers these days. A girl eyeing her cousin's cute little baby girl used to believe that she had to find a husband before she could have one of her 7 own. Now, she can bypass the husband problem and just spend a little leisure time with the homeless guy on Main Street. Who cares if Dad is an addict or a tramp? They're all bums—or jerks—anyway. It's worth recalling that experts defined teen pregnancy as a social problem only in the 1980s, when they claimed to discover an "epidemic" of young mothers. In fact, teen mothers had always been commonplace, but before 1970 they generally got married before reaching the delivery room. In their wisdom, experts decided that the problem was only that the mothers were too young—a genuine concern, true—but went mum on the disappearance of husbands.

As a result, we got an epidemic all right—of fatherlessness. The antics in Massachusetts aside, teen pregnancy has actually declined over the past 15 years. Yet out-of-wedlock birthrates keep rising, largely because of single young women in their twenties. If some bored and aimless teens decide to give single motherhood a whirl, who can be surprised?   *8*

READING FOR CONTENT

1. According to Hymowitz, why is it irrelevant to ask whether the Gloucester girls received sex education and birth control?

2. What is the "dominant narrative" about teen pregnancy, and, according to Hymowitz, why is it wrong?

3. What does research say about low-income women's desire for motherhood?

4. Why are "sexual reticence, social disapproval, and a no-baby-without-marriage rule" no longer deterrents for adolescent pregnancy?

5. According to Hymowitz, we shouldn't be surprised that teens want "to give single motherhood a whirl." Explain why this is so.

READING FOR GENRE, ORGANIZATION, AND STYLISTIC FEATURES

1. Review the "Typical Arrangement of an Argument Essay" in Chapter 8, pages 305–306. Explain which of the two variations Hymowitz uses to organize her article.

2. How does Hymowitz refute people who hold views different from her own? Is she conciliatory or combative? Cite examples.

3. Comment on Hymowitz's tone. Is it formal or informal, reverent or irreverent?

4. Does Hymowitz make ethical, emotional, and logical appeals to her audience? Review the three types of appeals on pages 295–303 and explain which types Hymowitz uses in her article. Cite examples.

5. Review the types of claims presented on pages 292–293. What is Hymowitz's major claim? Would you describe it as a claim of cause, value, fact, definition, or action?

READING FOR RHETORICAL CONTEXT

1. Describe the event that prompted Hymowitz to write the article. For additional information, do a Google search using the term "Gloucester Girls."

2. In paragraphs 4 and 7, Hymowitz draws on expert sources. What effect does the information have on her readers?

3. Comment on Hymowitz's credibility as a writer.

WRITING ASSIGNMENTS

1. Summarize Hymowitz's argument in 200 words or less.

2. Write an essay in response to the following quotation:

   > In fact, teen mothers had always been commonplace, but before 1970 they generally got married before reaching the delivery room. In their wisdom, experts decided that the problem was only that the mothers were too young—a genuine concern, true—but went mum on the disappearance of husbands. (paragraph 7)

3. Write a rhetorical analysis of "Gloucester Girls Gone Wild." Before you begin your essay, review the section on Rhetorical Analysis on pages 171–181.

4. Using Hymowitz's remarks about historical precedent in paragraph 5 as your base, write a brief research essay on the history of women's age for marriage. For pointers on database searching, see Chapter 9.

Suddenly Teen Pregnancy Is Cool?

Cathy Gulli

Cathy Gulli is an associate editor and regular contributor to Maclean's *magazine.*

The article was originally published in Maclean's *magazine.* Maclean's *is a leading Canadian magazine. Published weekly, it focuses on Canadian current affairs. "Suddenly Teen Pregnancy Is Cool?" was the cover story for a January 2008 issue of the magazine.*

Prereading

Read the introductory paragraph of the article and respond to Cathy Gulli's question: "How could a wealthy preteen idol ... be just several months away from adolescent, out-of-wedlock motherhood?"

When Jamie Lynn Spears, the 16-year-old sister of Britney, announced that she was pregnant last month in *OK!*, the magazine sold a record two million copies and had to run a second printing of the issue to keep up with demand. How could a wealthy preteen idol with her own hit Nickelodeon show, and the good sister to her chaotic older kin, be just several months away from adolescent, out-of-wedlock motherhood? "I didn't believe it because Jamie Lynn's always been so conscientious. She's never late for her curfew," lamented mother Lynne Spears. She got over the shock in a week, and then Jamie Lynn, ever conscientious, notified the press that she would be having, keeping and raising the baby with her mama in Louisiana. "I'm just trying to do the right thing," said the star of Zoey 101.

Only a few days earlier, the film *Juno* had been released to instant and unanimous applause from such diverse sources as *The New Yorker, Christianity Today* and *Film Freak*

1

2

Central. Suddenly the heroine of a hit movie-a comedy no less-could be a smart, motivated, white, middle-class girl, just 16, who matter-of-factly chooses to have a baby and an open adoption rather than an abortion. No big deal.

Unplanned pregnancy is now a pop-culture staple. Movies like *Knocked Up* and *Waitress,* and celebrity moms including Nicole Richie and Jessica Alba, are part of a trend that's sweeping teen culture along with it: *American Idol* star Fantasia Barrino became a mom at 17, and the last season of *Degrassi: The Next Generation* ended with Emma realizing she might be pregnant. "The media is awash in it," says David Landry, senior research associate at the Guttmacher Institute in New York, a non-profit organization focused on sexual and reproductive health. Even *Grey's Anatomy* had a teen pregnancy storyline last year, and just last week so did *Gossip Girl.*

"As an idea, teen pregnancy is more socially accepted," says Andrea O'Reilly, a women's studies professor at York University in Toronto, and director of the Association for Research on Mothering. Evidence of a less outraged reaction was best summarized by Hollywood's most sought-after paparazzi muse, Lindsay Lohan: "Why does everyone think it's such a big deal?" she replied when asked what she thought of Jamie Lynn's situation.

Then came the statistical data confirming that something—something real—was happening: in 2006, for the first time in 15 years, the teen birth rate in America actually increased, said a report by the National Center for Health Statistics (NCHS), a branch of the U.S. Centers for Disease Control. Meanwhile, in England, the number of pregnancies among females under age 18 also rose in 2005—to the highest point since 1998, according to the U.K.'s Department for Children, Schools and Families.

So far, the numbers aren't rising in Canada, but our statistics are a couple of years old—from 2005. Some experts say that when data does become available, we'll see the same rise as our neighbours. "Overall trends for these three countries tend to mirror each other," says Alex McKay, research coordinator of the Sex Information and Education Council of Canada. "If we're seeing an increase in the teen birth rate in the U.S. and the U.K.," he continues, "it is quite likely we may see the same thing occur in Canada."

In an era when not getting pregnant should be easy, explanations for the jump in births among teens are speculative, if not elusive. Data on abortion rates or contraception use are outdated, so there's little way of knowing for sure how much of the increase is due to a rise in unprotected sex or a possible decline in abortion rates. Some experts say it's just a blip, a statistical aberration we'll see corrected next year. Others believe the problem is institutional, that ineffective abstinence-only programs are to blame in the U.S. Or that we may have simply maxed out how much teen pregnancy can be prevented. "Whenever you try to improve things it's easiest in the beginning," says Bill Albert, deputy director of the National Campaign to Prevent Teen and Unplanned Pregnancy, based in Washington.

Those who see the signs of something more profound offer a range of explanations: a celebrity culture that downplays the hard work of motherhood; ever-changing family structures that normalize non-traditional arrangements; children who live at home longer than ever with parental support and aren't expected, if they have kids of their own, to marry the father.

Invariably though, it seems teen pregnancy has become more accepted. A Denver high school is considering implementing a four-week maternity leave for students so they can recover and get used to the baby without penalties for missing class. In Canada, there is a recognition that teen moms should receive more help too: "Schools try to offer flexibility to young mothers," says Marcia Powers-Dunlop, chief of social work with the Toronto District School Board's northwest region. Consequently, many girls don't drop out, she's observed, "because there isn't the stigma that there once was." Jamie Lynn, for her part, was photographed recently toting a GED study book to get her high-school equivalency degree.

"There's a redefining of motherhood," says O'Reilly. "Teen moms are saying, why can't I be a mother now?" She believes that as older women are gaining acceptance as new mothers, adolescent girls are claiming their maternal rights too. "Before, the time of motherhood was so restricted. Now it's okay at 48. So why not at 18?" The feminist motherhood movement, as O'Reilly refers to the growing show of support for moms of all ages, has people questioning societal expectations about when is the right time to have children. "It's part of a larger revisioning of motherhood: queer mothers, old mothers, young mothers. That wasn't possible 20 years ago."

Suffice to say, the rising American teen birth rate in 2006 is something of an eye-opener. Between 1991 and 2005, the United States saw a 34 per cent decrease in the birth rate among those aged 15 to 19. But in 2006, that relatively steady decline was reversed. Suddenly, among 15- to 17-year-olds, the rate was up three per cent to 22 babies per 1,000 females, and 18- and 19-year-olds jumped four per cent to 73 births for every 1,000. "That took us by surprise," admits Stephanie J. Ventura, head of the reproductive statistics branch at NCHS. And the rise was spread over almost every ethnic group except for Asians; births among black, native, Hispanic and white teenagers rose. While no specific data was collected on the income of teen mothers, Albert says that with three in 10 girls getting pregnant by age 20, "you realize this is not [just] 'poor folk.' The problem is spread wide."

In England and Wales, the birth rate per 1,000 females under age 20 rose to 45.5 in 2006 compared to 44.8 the year before. Not a huge leap, but it's already one of the highest rates in the developed world. The United Nations' last comprehensive tally of G8 countries, from 2004, showed the U.K. has the third-highest teen birth rate, with 26.8 births per 1,000, slightly lower than Russia (28.2) and well above Japan (5.6), France (7.8), Italy (6.7) and Germany (11). The U.S. soars above them all, at 41.8 per 1,000 females.

Canada ranks exactly in the middle, with a teen birth rate of 13.4 per 1,000 as of 2005 (or 14.5 in 2003, as stated in the UN report), but that's still down 45 per cent over the last decade. Domestically, we've come a long way. In 1995, teens aged 15 to 19 had 24.3 births per 1,000. And among the under-15 age group, the number of births per 1,000 plummeted nearly 60 per cent between 1995 and 2004. (Teen births, of course, are not the same thing as teen pregnancies, which include births and abortions and therefore capture the broader picture of how many adolescents are actually dealing with pregnancy, one way or another. Like birth rates, pregnancy rates also showed declines through the late 1990s and early to mid-2000s in the U.S., the U.K. and Canada, but the latest numbers are between two and five years old.)

What no one knows in Canada, for now, is what's been happening in the last couple of years. McKay suggests Canada should consider rises in other countries as foreshadowing of what could be happening here. "Although there are profound differences between Canada and the United States," he says, "both countries have seen a persistent long-term decline in teen pregnancy rates over the last quarter-century." That both our southern neighbour and England have seen reversals means "there's a fairly big probability we will see the same," he continues. Adds David Quist, executive director of the Ottawa-based Institute of Marriage and Family Canada, an arm of Focus on the Family: "Often Canada follows the U.S. in trends like this."

10

11

12

13

14

And the U.S., before seeing the jump in its teen birth rate in 2006, first witnessed a flattening out. "The rate of decline had slowed in the last few years," explains Ventura, "so maybe that was an early indication that it was about to reverse." Similarly, England's birth rate has barely budged since 2000. [15]

In Canada, the declining teen birth rate has also levelled off—from 14.9 births per 1,000 in 2002 to 13.6 in 2004 to 13.4 births one year later. [16]

So what if this isn't a blip? It could be that teens are just following what is really a nationwide trend in the U.S. Across all ages (from 15 to 44) the birth rate is up, according to the NCHS. Between 2005 and 2006, more women had babies than had since 1961—in excess of 4.2 million. And the 2006 fertility rate was the highest it had been since 1971. Explanations for the overall increase are as elusive as for the rising teen birth rate. [17]

"The short answer is none of us really know why the rates went up," says Albert. For teens, many blame the rise on abstinence-only programs, which have bloomed in the U.S. since 1996, with more than $1 billion in federal funding. Critics say they deny teens information that could help them make safer decisions when they do have sex. "There is precious little evidence to suggest that abstinence-only interventions work," says Albert. But he's reluctant to put much stock in arguments for or against abstinence-only, since these programs existed during the major declines between 1996 and 2005. [18]

In Canada, the federal government has assembled guidelines for sex education, but programs differ by school board, school and classroom, says McKay. He believes programs are not uniform enough across the country to make a consistent contribution to the health of Canadian youth. "The extent and quality of sex education varies from excellent to nonexistent. And unfortunately, the non-existent is more common," he says. [19]

Poor access to emergency contraception and abortion also may explain the increase in teen births. "There are more limits now on abortions—[longer] waiting periods, fewer abortion providers," says Landry. As well, they often require travel, parental permission, and large fees. Plus, he adds, teens may be more reluctant to terminate because it has become "such a politicized, divisive issue." Meanwhile, pharmacies can sell the morning after pill only to females 18 or older; younger girls need a doctor's note, a problem since the medication must be administered within 72 hours of having sex. [20]

The situation isn't much better in Canada. The morning-after pill, while readily available, requires a consultation with a pharmacist, which costs up to $45 plus the drug fee. And according to a 2007 report by the Canadian Federation for Sexual Health, less than one in six hospitals provided abortions in 2006, and many provinces do not have full health insurance coverage for terminations done in clinics. Without the option to terminate a pregnancy, we'll see a rise in births, says O'Reilly. [21]

Or it could be that teen birth rates have simply gone as low as they can. After all, says Landry, the vast majority of adolescents have sex: "In some ways, it's amazing that we have had this long a run in the decline in birth rates." After several years of getting the message about teen pregnancy out to the most receptive adolescents, "it may be that we're down to very difficult cases," says Albert. [22]

It doesn't seem to be the case that teens generally are less sexually prudent than earlier generations. The age of first sexual experience hasn't gotten any younger—17 in the U.S., and 16.5 in Canada. The use of condoms and hormonal birth controls had increased as of 2002 in the States, and in Canada, contraception use has risen—nearly 87 per cent of teens have safe sex. (This further suggests that abstinence-only programs may not work.) And [23] adolescents here aren't having any more sex than earlier generations either. "In some ways, [teens] tend to be more conservative now than they were in the past," says McKay.

During the 1960s and '70s, sex was a rite of passage equated with youthful rebellion and liberation, he surmises. Today, many "teens have sex for reasons associated with pleasure, relationships and exploration. It's done in a different context." 24

The fact that "babies!" tops the list of news categories at www.people.com suggests that pregnancy—celebrity, teen, unplanned, out-of-wedlock, whatever—has moved into a new realm of acceptance. "It's no longer a scary word," says Ottawa-based sex therapist Sue McGarvie. "It's been normalized." Entertainment tabloids, which have long featured style-watch lists, have turned their attention to the latest accessory in Hollywood—protruding bellies. And teens, heavy consumers of such media, are getting the message that "having a baby is the new handbag," says Nicole Fischer, 17, who lives in Calgary and just gave birth to her son Cristian five months ago. 25

"Popular culture is showing a more positive representation of young mothers," says O'Reilly. Today, having an unexpected baby can be more of an image-enhancer than a shameful faux pas. It's part of a larger trend to make motherhood chic and happening, she says: "If you're 18, you want a baby on your hip, a miniskirt, and a guitar on your back." In many ways, celebrities have helped prove that motherhood isn't "the end of coolness or sexiness for women, or the end of the line," says Ariel Gore, a Portland, Ore.–based blogger and author of *Breeder: Real-Life Stories from the New Generation of Mothers,* among other books. 26

Trite as it may sound, Albert says social norms are shaped by star culture. "The Britneys of this world and the Angelina Jolies may have an effect. To ignore it would be Pollyannaish." Of course, to say it's all positive would also be wrong, says O'Reilly. "The glamour and romance quickly goes—when you're having morning sickness [or] in childbirth for two days. That whole [Hollywood mom] culture worries me," she continues, "because that's not how motherhood is." 27

However misguided, Powers-Dunlop says that some teens "no longer think there's a big deal" about having sex—and so, presumably, getting pregnant. As someone in daily contact with adolescents, she says that premarital sex now is a way of life. It is not unusual for her to get calls about 12- and 13-year-olds who are expecting babies. "That would have been unheard of a while ago," she says. "And yet it's no longer cause for panic." 28

Celebs aside, rising teen birth rates may also have to do with home life, Powers-Dunlop adds, where casual sex may be observed among single parents. "There's a lot of families separating and divorcing, and parents having new partners but not getting married. There's a message that this is a natural," she explains. "It's no longer love then sex." In fact, the ever-more diverse family structures happening today—gay parents, multi-faith and race marriages, open relationships, step and half-siblings, and single-parent adoption or in vitro fertilization—may relieve some of the old shock of teen parenthood. 29

And now that more adult children live at home with their folks for longer—60 per cent of Canadians aged 20 to 24 did last year—teens may feel they'll have more support in raising their child, just like Jamie Lynn Spears is counting on her mother's help. (Fischer, meanwhile, is living with the family of her boyfriend, who fathered the baby.) 30

One trend observed by Pauline Paterson, director of the YWCA's girls and family programs in Scarborough, Ont., is a phenomenon called "multi-daddying." Teen moms are actually having more than one baby with various fathers as a way of forming bonds with 31 new men in their lives—and it's yet another way that adolescents are putting their stamp on parenthood and establishing new family models.

Of course, few people would say they encourage adolescent motherhood. Actress Eva Mendes, during the launch of her antifur PETA ads, said of unplanned births, "It's an epidemic and I don't want to catch it!" Lily Allen, the 22-year-old singer, admonished teen pregnancy in *Marie Claire*. Soon after, she announced that she was surprised but "thrilled" to be expecting a child too.

The main difference these days is that the severe shame and stigmatization teens used to face when they got pregnant has lessened—if only slightly, says Kayla Clark, 18, who got pregnant despite using two forms of birth control. She gave birth to son William almost two years ago. That change is partly because parents, teachers and health care workers are realizing that much worse things can befall an adolescent. "Now parents worry about serious drugs, HIV or AIDS," says O'Reilly, not to mention gang violence. In *Juno*, for example, the parents heaved a huge sigh of relief when the big news their daughter had come to confess turned out to be pregnancy—they were terrified she had been expelled or was addicted to drugs.

There's also recognition that offering support to pregnant teens doesn't necessarily have to mean it's being encouraged. "Taking away the stigma isn't going to cause a bunch of young women to get pregnant," says Gore. She suggests the rising birth rate may be a backlash to the intense campaigns against teen pregnancy throughout the last decade. Adolescents may be rebelling against the idea that they can't be parents. Gore also believes that teens may be more open to motherhood after witnessing their own moms suffer health problems or constant fatigue because they put off having kids until later in life. "I don't think there's anything intrinsically wrong with teen parenting," Gore says. Her beef is with the need for more social services to help adolescent mothers cope.

There are some indications support is taking priority. Louise Dean Centre in Calgary is one of only a few schools in Canada that cater exclusively to pregnant teens and young mothers aged 14 to 20. "They feel more comfortable that [motherhood] hasn't ended their life," says teacher Alison Orpe. "It's just taken it in a different direction." And groups for adolescent moms, like the one run by Scarborough's YWCA, provide a dinner and community support twice a week for teens and their babies. The group is constantly at maximum capacity, with 150 attending.

Fischer, who says she was "the perfect child" of her family, and got pregnant after having sex for the first time, is among the students at Louise Dean. She has big plans to become a legal assistant. "My grades are up and I know I'm going to college," she says. "I know there is a way out. But you have to be responsible enough to make the choices."

Increasingly, teens are proving that they can pull off adolescence and motherhood at once. "There are some huge pregnancy success stories," McGarvie says. "It's not necessarily all bad." Many young mothers are finding "motivation, tenacity and purpose" in their new role, continues O'Reilly, and this propels them to stay in school so they can later find work and establish a good life for their growing family. As much as we may not like to admit it, adds McKay, "there are many young women who are perfectly capable of bearing a child in their late teens and leading healthy and productive lives for themselves and providing a good upbringing for their children."

Part of this empowerment is tied up in the fact that unplanned pregnancy no longer automatically means that girls must have a secret abortion or put their baby up for closed

32

33

34

35

36

37

38

adoption—as *Juno* shows. Nor do they automatically have to marry the father of their baby. McKay says we are undergoing a profound transformation in the control women are exhibiting over their reproductive fate. Clark lives on her own with the baby in subsidized housing and will begin studying exercise science at the University of Lethbridge in September. She says that while she debated both termination and open adoption, she couldn't bear giving up her claim to motherhood. "I couldn't be part of life knowing that I [wouldn't be] a mom anymore," she says.

"It's a rescripting of what we know as a teen mom," says O'Reilly. Historically, they   39
were demonized, or worse: they were known as "the disappeared," she says. "You were shipped off to Aunt Martha's" for an abortion or to put the baby up for adoption. Now, "there's more cultural permission to be a young mother than 10 or 20 years ago," believes O'Reilly. "It's not a death sentence."

READING FOR CONTENT

1. Reread paragraph 4 and summarize the four explanations for the rise in teenage births.
2. What explanations are offered by people who see the increase in the teen birth rate as indicative of a larger social problem?
3. What indicators show that teen pregnancy is more accepted today than in the past?
4. For someone who hasn't read Gulli's article, explain the "feminist motherhood movement."
5. Summarize the seven reasons that are given for the rising teen birth rates in paragraphs 18–25.
6. According to Gulli, what aspects of teens' home life may contribute to their acceptance of premarital sex and pregnancy?
7. What types of support are offered to teen mothers?
8. What social factors contribute to teenage mothers' sense of empowerment?
9. Paraphrase Gulli's thesis or major claim.

READING FOR GENRE, ORGANIZATION, AND STYLISTIC FEATURES

1. Comment on the effectiveness of Gulli's lead and introductory paragraph. What is the effect on the reader?
2. If you were to insert subtitles into this article, where would you place them and what would they be?
3. How would you describe Gulli's point of view, voice, and tone? Does Gulli use the first person (I, we), the second person (you), or the third person (he, she, it, they)?

READING FOR RHETORICAL CONTEXT

1. "Suddenly Teen Pregnancy Is Cool?" was written for a Canadian magazine. Which aspects of the article will appeal to the Canadian readership, and which will interest an international audience?
2. In this article, Gulli draws on eight acknowledged authorities. Make note of each of these references and explain how each contributes to Gulli's agenda.

3. Gulli also quotes actresses, a teacher, and teen moms. Make note of each of these references and explain how each contributes to Gulli's agenda.

4. Comment on the number of facts and statistics in the article. What effect do paragraphs 11, 12, and 13 have on the reader?

WRITING ASSIGNMENTS

1. Review Chapter 4, "Summarizing Sources," and then write a summary essay of Gulli's article.

2. In paragraph 26, Gulli writes, "Today, having an unexpected baby can be more of an image-enhancer than a shameful faux pas." Do you agree or disagree? Write an essay in response.

3. According to Gulli, "Unplanned pregnancy is now a pop-culture staple" (paragraph 3). Do you think celebrities shape our rules of conduct and societal expectations? Write an essay in response.

4. Write an essay in which you argue for or against the new family model of "multi-daddying" that Gulli describes in paragraph 31.

Give the Girls a Break

Nancy Gibbs

Nancy Gibbs is Editor-at-Large and the award-winning author of over one hundred cover stories for Time *magazine.*

The article was originally published in Time *magazine. Published weekly,* Time *is a widely circulated magazine of news and current events.*

Prereading

In this selection, Nancy Gibbs offers her interpretation of the incident involving the Gloucester girls' pregnancy pact. Does the title give you a clue about her attitude toward the pregnant teens? In your journal, write a paragraph predicting what that attitude will be.

You know you've found a perfect cultural touchstone when everyone brushes past it on the way to opposite conclusions. The tale of the Gloucester High School "pregnancy pact" has exposed many culprits, many causes and much confusion over what it actually tells us about anything larger than the luck and judgment of 18 now infamous teenage girls.   *1*

When my TIME colleague Kathleen Kingsbury first quoted Gloucester High principal Joseph Sullivan as saying that the reason pregnancies at his school quadrupled this year   *2* was that a group of sophomore girls "made a pact to get pregnant and raise their babies together," the story made headlines from here to Australia—but no one could agree about what it meant. If only Massachusetts hadn't rejected federal funds for abstinence-only education, lamented Tony Perkins of the Family Research Council. If only the school health clinic had been allowed to dispense birth control pills, countered its medical director, Dr. Brian Orr, who resigned over the contraception ban. If only No Child Left Behind hadn't diverted funds from better health education, charged Gloucester mayor Carolyn Kirk. If only Mars had not been in Leo in the eighth house, suggested Monica at Astrology Mundo, who had predicted a flare-up of teen sex around the summer solstice. The culture was an irresistible target, after movies like *Juno* "glamorized" unwed motherhood; if only the school's "marauding narcissistic sluts" hadn't followed the toxic example of movie stars and the Spears sisters, wrote some bloggers, who longed for the return of the scarlet letter.

I wonder if the critics would be so quick to condemn if they viewed the story another way. There is certainly troubling anecdotal evidence that some of the girls set out to get pregnant together. But other girls talk about a different kind of resolution. What if the "problem" in evidence at Gloucester High has more to do with the rejection of abortion than the acceptance of teen pregnancy? 3

It is easy for a school to know how many students give birth each year, but—especially in a heavily Catholic town like Gloucester—it is impossible to know how many pregnancies are terminated. Birthrates are not the same as pregnancy rates, and the national trends in both tell an interesting story. While 750,000 teens become pregnant every year, that is the lowest level in 30 years, according to the Guttmacher Institute, down 36% from a peak in 1990. Abortion rates have fallen even faster; since the late 1980s, the abortion rate for girls ages 15 to 17 has fallen 55%, and this year the overall U.S. abortion rate is at its lowest level since 1974. 4

At the same time, we are in the middle of a baby boomlet; the 4.3 million babies born in 2006 were the most since 1961. And among teenage girls, though the birthrate has generally been falling for the past two decades, it did rise 3% in 2006 for girls 15 to 17. No one can quite explain why this is. 5

Which brings us back to Gloucester. What if the visible leap in pregnancies is part of a different trend, which the national studies confirm: not necessarily more kids having sex or more girls getting pregnant but instead more of those who do deciding to have the baby rather than abort it? Consider Lindsey Oliver, a Gloucester student who says she found herself pregnant despite being on the Pill. She told Good Morning America that she made her own pact with friends to help them get through their unplanned pregnancies together. She and her boyfriend, a 20-year-old community-college student, talked about trying to do the right thing in a difficult situation. 6

Whether a girl—or a woman—decides to end a pregnancy or see it through is as complex an emotional and moral and medical calculation as she ever faces. But I wonder if some soft message has taken hold when the data suggest that more women facing hard choices are deciding to carry the child to term. This has been the mission of the crisis-pregnancy-center movement, the more than 4,000 centers and hotlines and support groups around the country that aim to talk women out of having abortions and offer whatever support they can. If not in Hollywood, then certainly in Gloucester, teen parents and their babies face long odds against success in life. Surely they deserve more sympathy and support than shame and derision, if the trend that they reflect is not a typical 7 teenager's inclination to have sex but rather a willingness to take responsibility for the consequences.

What if the visible leap in pregnancies reflects not necessarily more girls getting pregnant but more kids deciding to have the baby rather than abort it?   8

READING FOR CONTENT

1. A touchstone is a reference point, criterion, or standard by which something is judged. Why does Gibbs refer to the Gloucester incident as "a perfect cultural touchstone"?
2. According to Gibbs, what reasons do people give for the Gloucester teens' actions?
3. According to Gibbs, how does the national abortion rate compare to the birth rate?
4. Gibbs believes that the rise in pregnancies is due to a new trend. Explain this trend.
5. What has caused the trend?

READING FOR GENRE, ORGANIZATION, AND STYLISTIC FEATURES

1. Study the organization of the Gibbs article. Explain how paragraphs 1–3 function in comparison to paragraphs 4–7.
2. Describe Gibbs's tone. What is the effect of the rhetorical questions she asks in paragraphs 3 and 6?
3. How does the device of repetition function in this article? Look at the repetition of "If only…" in paragraph 2 and "I wonder" in paragraphs 3 and 7.
4. Describe the types of evidence Gibbs uses to support her argument and explain why they are effective.

READING FOR RHETORICAL CONTEXT

1. "Give the Girls a Break" is a short article published in a national news magazine. Is Nancy Gibbs writing as a reporter or a commentator? How would you describe her purpose?
2. How convincing is Gibbs's argument? Explain why she has or has not persuaded you to accept her point of view.
3. In paragraph 2, Gibbs cites a reference to the Gloucester teens as "marauding narcissistic sluts." In contrast, how does Gibbs want her readers to view the Gloucester girls?

WRITING ASSIGNMENTS

1. Summarize this brief article by reducing it to a single paragraph.
2. Do you have relatives, friends, or acquaintances who became parents in their teenage years? If so, write an essay describing their situation. Have they been able to support themselves and their children without economic hardship? Have they been subject to social disapproval or have they received the sympathy and support that Gibbs describes in paragraph 7 of her article?
3. Write an essay in which you argue for or against Gibbs's explanation for the rise in the U.S. birth rate.

Adolescent Girls' Attitudes Toward Pregnancy: The Importance of Asking What the Boyfriend Wants

Carol Cowley, MSN, NP and Tillman Farley, MD

Carol Cowley holds a Master of Science in Nursing Degree and is a registered Nurse Practitioner. Tillman Farley is a physician who specializes in Obstetrics and Gynecology.

The article was originally published in 2001 in The Journal of Family Practice, *a peer-reviewed scientific journal specializing in family medicine. The readership for this monthly journal consists of primary care physicians and researchers in the field of family health.*

Prereading

Most of the media coverage and scholarly analysis of adolescent pregnancy focuses on young mothers. The role of young fathers is rarely analyzed. In your journal, write a paragraph explaining why you think the responsibilities of fathers are seldom discussed.

Adolescent Girls' Attitudes Toward Pregnancy

The Importance of Asking What the Boyfriend Wants

Carol Cowley, MSN, NP, and Tillman Farley, MD

Brighton and Fort Lupton, Colorado

- **Objective**   We evaluated the factors associated with attitudes toward pregnancy among girls presenting to an adolescent health clinic to better predict which girls are at the highest risk of pregnancy.

- **Study Design**   We used a cross-sectional provider-administered survey design.

- **Population**   A total 202 girls aged 13 to 18 years presenting consecutively for reproductive health services to an adolescent care clinic were interviewed about their desire for pregnancy. Girls found to be already pregnant at the initial visit (n = 54) were removed from analysis.

- **Outcomes Measured**   The main outcome measured was desire for pregnancy. Subjects were grouped by those desiring pregnancy (n = 16), those desiring to avoid pregnancy (n = 107), and those ambivalent about pregnancy (n = 25).

- **Results**   The girls who were ambivalent about pregnancy were not significantly different from the girls desiring pregnancy. In unadjusted analysis, girls desiring pregnancy or who were ambivalent about it were more likely to be Hispanic, unemployed, to not attend school, to live with neither natural parent, and to have lived away from home for more than 2 weeks. In adjusted analysis, the reported attitude of the boyfriend toward having a child was the only significant predictor of adolescent girls' attitude toward pregnancy.

- **Conclusions**   The best predictor of an adolescent girl's attitude toward pregnancy is her perception of her boyfriend's desire for a baby. Primary care providers should include boyfriends in any efforts to delay pregnancy in at-risk adolescent girls. Teenagers who are ambivalent about whether they want to be pregnant do not differ significantly from those desiring pregnancy, and should be considered just as high risk.

- **Key Words**   Adolescent pregnancy, risk factors, attitudes, boyfriend. *(J Fam Pract 2001;50:603–607)*

Key Points

- When assessing risk for pregnancy in a teenaged girl, the most important question to ask may be whether she thinks her boyfriend wants her to be pregnant.

- Girls who are ambivalent about whether they want to be pregnant are very similar to those desiring pregnancy, and should be considered at high risk for pregnancy.

- Primary care providers should encourage communication between teenaged girls and their partners, and actively involve partners in the pregnancy and parenting discussion.

Early adolescent childbearing is associated with a wide range of adverse consequences and restricted life opportunities for young girls and the children they bear.[1–5] Helping adolescents delay early childbearing has long been a goal of healthcare providers, researchers, and policymakers.[6,7] Although the adolescent pregnancy rate in the United States is decreasing in most groups,[8] it is still disturbingly high, particularly among Hispanic girls.

Most efforts to prevent or delay adolescent pregnancy have been directed at providing birth control, but this intervention is likely to fail if teens are not interested in preventing pregnancy. Although several studies have examined the factors and motivations underlying adolescent contraceptive behavior,[9–13] teen attitudes toward pregnancy are still poorly understood.[14] Adolescents may not share the same negative view of their childbearing as do adults concerned with preventing it. Retrospective studies suggest that as many as 60% to 80% of teenaged pregnancies are "unintended."[15,16] Other studies examining pregnant and parenting adolescents' attitudes toward childbearing suggest that the percentage of pregnancies that are truly unintended may be lower than commonly believed.[10,17–19] A significant percentage of never-pregnant adolescents harbor either highly ambivalent or positive attitudes toward early childbearing.[19–21] A better understanding of the factors associated with a desire for pregnancy among adolescents may help health care providers better predict the most at-risk adolescents.

•Submitted, revised, March 5, 2001.

From the Salud Family Health Centers, Brighton, Colorado (C.C. T.F.) and the University of Colorado Department of Family Medicine, Fort Lupton (T.F.).

Results of this study were presented at the North American Primary Care Research Group meeting in Florida in November 2000.

Our study investigated factors associated with adolescent desire for pregnancy among girls seeking reproductive health services at an adolescent clinic. Earlier studies have examined the attitudes of girls presenting for pregnancy testing, or who were already enrolled in prenatal care.[9] No other studies have specifically looked at the factors associated with non-pregnant adolescents' attitudes toward pregnancy, or the role of the boyfriend in influencing those attitudes.

Methods

Setting

This study was conducted in an adolescent health clinic within a migrant/community health center in a town with a population of 10,000, 25 miles from a major midwestern city. The clinic was staffed by a nurse practitioner and an adolescent health educator. The full spectrum of adolescent problems are dealt with in this clinic, but most visits are for pregnancy testing, birth control counseling, and checks for sexually transmitted diseases (STDs). Ninety-eight percent of visits are by females. The clinic serves patients aged 12 through 20 years, and has been operating in its current location for 20 years. The clinic offers completely confidential services to those who request it, with no parental notification or consent required.

Subjects

Girls aged 13 to 18 years presenting consecutively for reproductive health services were eligible for this study. Girls were excluded if they had delivered a baby in the previous 12 months, had a miscarriage or a therapeutic abortion in the previous 6 months, or were currently using a hormonal method of contraception. A total of 202 girls were initially eligible and all agreed to participate. Because studies have shown that a woman's attitude toward pregnancy changes once she is aware of being pregnant, we subsequently decided to also exclude those girls already pregnant at the initial visit (n = 54), leaving 148 subjects in the final data analysis. All subjects spoke either Spanish or English.

Data Collection

After obtaining informed consent, each girl underwent an extensive, semistructured interview exploring her attitude toward pregnancy, childbearing, and contraceptive use. All interviews were done by 1 of the 2 clinicians working in the adolescent clinic (a 35-year-old adolescent health educator and a 40-year-old obstetric nurse practitioner). Both clinicians were white women who had been working in this clinic for more than 15 years. The health educator was fluent in Spanish. A girl's attitude toward pregnancy was determined by a series of questions. Other information elicited included ethnicity, age, school attendance, employment status, social habits (alcohol and tobacco use, current dating, current sexual activity), family structure, whether the subject had ever lived away from home for more than 2 weeks, age of her boyfriend, boyfriend's attitude about pregnancy, and confidentiality of the initial visit. Obstetric and gynecologic histories of each girl were also obtained. After the interview, pregnancy testing was done, if indicated.

Data Analysis

Based on the interview, each girl was categorized as desiring pregnancy, wishing to avoid pregnancy, or being ambivalent about pregnancy. Girls desiring pregnancy were so similar to girls who felt ambivalent about pregnancy that these girls were grouped together in the final analysis and compared against those girls wishing to avoid pregnancy.

Data were analyzed using the SAS statistical program (version 8.0). We used chi-squared testing for unadjusted analysis of factors associated with adolescent attitudes toward pregnancy. Unadjusted associations with a P value greater than .2 were included in multiple logistic regression analysis to adjust for multiple variables, and to calculate odds ratios and 95% confidence intervals. The final multiple logistic regression model included only those variables found to retain significance at P less than .05.

Results

Demographic characteristics of the participants are shown in Table 1. Of the 148 girls, almost all (92%) were currently dating, and most (88%) were sexually active with their partner. Ninety-six percent had never been pregnant previously, 86% had never used hormonal contraception, and 84% had never had a Papanicolaou test or an STD screening.

The mean age of subjects' boyfriends was 18.4 years, with an age range of 13 to 30 years. One third of the girls lived with both of their biological parents, and 78% lived with at

**TABLE 1   Demographic Characteristics
of Study Population (N = 148)**

Ethnicity	n (%)
Hispanic	66 (44.6)
Non-Hispanic White	82 (55.4)
Age, years*	
13 to 14	22 (14.9)
15 to 16	69 (46.6)
17 to 18	57 (38.5)
Family structure	
Lives with both natural parents	54 (36.5)
Lives with natural mother	49 (33.1)
Lives with boyfriend	14 (9.5)
Lives with other relative	13 (8.8)
Lives with natural father	12 (8.1)
Lives with husband	3 (2.0)
Lives with other non-relative	2 (1.4)
Lives by herself	1 (<1)

*Mean age = 16.0 years.

least one biological parent. Three were already married at the time of initial visit. Almost half (46%) described their enrollment visit as confidential.

One hundred seven (56.4%) of the girls were categorized as wishing to avoid pregnancy, 16 girls (19.8%) as desiring pregnancy, and 25 girls (23.7%) as ambivalent about whether they wanted to be pregnant. Unadjusted analysis comparing girls desiring pregnancy with those feeling ambivalent revealed only 1 significant difference: girls desiring pregnancy were more likely to report that their boyfriends wanted a baby. So, in the final analysis, these girls were grouped together, and compared with the girls wishing to avoid pregnancy (Table W1*).

Unadjusted analysis of the 148 subjects is shown in Table 2. Girls wishing to avoid pregnancy differed from girls desiring or ambivalent about pregnancy in 6 different parameters: ethnicity, school attendance, employment status, family structure, time spent away from home, and desire of boyfriend to have a baby. There was no significant association between a girl's age and her attitude toward pregnancy ($P = .48$). Notably, the mean age difference between girls and their boyfriends was not significantly associated with desire for pregnancy.

In multivariate analysis of characteristics of the girls themselves, factors significantly associated with a positive attitude toward pregnancy were Hispanic ethnicity, having lived away from home for more than 2 weeks, and having left school (Table 3).

When boyfriend characteristics and attitudes were added to the analysis, all subject characteristics ceased to be significant, leaving the perception of the boyfriends' desire for pregnancy as the only significant variable.

Discussion

We found the strongest predictor of an adolescent girl's attitude toward pregnancy was her stated belief about whether her boyfriend wanted a baby. In light of the powerful influence of the girl's perception of her boyfriend's attitude toward pregnancy, no other factors are significantly associated with her own attitude toward pregnancy. This finding suggests that family physicians and other health care providers working with teenaged girls should include the boyfriend in any discussions aimed at delaying pregnancy.

Girls ambivalent about pregnancy are markedly similar to those desiring it, differing only in the degree to which they believe their boyfriends want a baby. It may be that some of the ambivalence about pregnancy arises from a difference of opinion between the girl and her boyfriend. Girls ambivalent about pregnancy were least likely to know their boyfriend's opinion on the subject. It may be that young girls who are ambivalent about pregnancy are also those with more limited interpersonal communication skills, making it difficult for them to discuss critical reproductive health issues with their partners. Health care providers may have a role in facilitating improved communication between girls and their partners by specifically addressing partner communication when seeing girls individually, as well as by inviting their partners to be present and more actively involved in clinic visits. Interventions focused solely on providing information about and access to contraception are unlikely to be sufficient in strengthening a girl's motivation to delay pregnancy. More appropriate and effective interventions may be those that explore the extent to which her partner's attitudes shape her own critical reproductive health decisions, and encourage greater dialogue between a girl and her partner with respect to contraceptive and childbearing decisions.

---

*Table W1 can be found on the *JFP* Web site at www.jfponline.com

TABLE 2   Comparison of Girls Desiring Pregnancy or Ambivalent About Pregnancy with Those Wishing to Avoid Pregnancy

Variable	Girls Desiring Pregnancy or Ambivalent About It (N = 41)	Girls Wishing to Avoid Pregnancy (N = 107)	Unadjusted Odds Ratio (95% CI) for Desiring Pregnancy
CHARACTERISTICS OF STUDY PARTICIPANT			
Mean age, years	16	16	
Hispanic, no. (%)	28 (68)	38 (35)	3.9 (1.8–8.4)
No longer in school, no. (%)	20 (49)	15 (14)	5.8 (2.6–13.3)
Unemployed, no. (%)	33 (83)	65* (61)	3.0 (1.2–7.3)
Does not live with any natural parent, no. (%)	16 (39)	17 (16)	3.4 (1.5–7.6)
Currently uses alcohol, no. (%)	24[†](60)	63 (59)	1.0 (0.5–2.2)
Has lived away from home for at least 2 weeks, no. (%)	30 (73)	39 (36)	4.8 (2.1–10.6)
CHARACTERISTICS OF BOYFRIEND			
Mean age	18.3 years (14–24)	18.0 years (13–25)	
Age > 18	17[‡] (46)	35 (36)	1.5 (0.7–3.2)
Mean age difference in years between subject and her boyfriend	2.35	2.0	
Information missing	4	11	
BOYFRIEND'S ATTITUDE TOWARD PREGNANCY			
Wants a child, no. (%)	23[‡] (62)	2[§] (2)	78.9 (16.7–371.5)
Doesn't want a child, no. (%)	4[‡] (11)	93[§] (95)	.007 (.002–.026)
Ambivalent about having a child, no. (%)	3[‡] (8)	2[§] (2)	4.1 (0.7–25.8)
Subject does not know what boyfriend wants, no. (%)	7[‡] (19)	1[§] (1)	22.6 (2.7–191.4)
Information missing	4	9	

* N–65
[†] N–24
[‡] N–37
[§] N–98
CI denotes confidence interval.

TABLE 3   Adjusted Odds Ratio for Desiring Pregnancy (N = 148)

	Adjusted Odds Ratios (95% CI) for Desiring Pregnancy
MODEL EXCLUDING BOYFRIEND VARIABLES	
Girl has lived away from home for >2 weeks	3.0 (1.3–7.2)*
Hispanic	3.5 (1.5–8.0)*
Not in school	3.8 (1.6–9.4)*
MODEL INCLUDING BOYFRIEND VARIABLES	
Boyfriend does not want a baby*	1.0 (reference)
Boyfriend wants a baby*	146.6 (29.2–736.6)
Boyfriend ambivalent about baby*	19.1 (2.8–131.6)
Subject does not know what boyfriend wants*	89.2 (9.7–818.0)

*As reported by the study subjects.
CI denotes confidence interval.

Although several studies have been done on the contraceptive behavior of adolescent girls, to our knowledge no other studies have focused on evaluating the influence of the boyfriend's perceived attitude toward childbearing on nonpregnant adolescent girls' desire for a child. Our study did not support other studies' findings showing that girls desiring pregnancy are more likely to have older boyfriends.[22] In our study population, neither boyfriend age nor the age difference between the girl and her boyfriend were significantly associated with the girl's desire to become pregnant.

Limitations

Our study has several limitations. We did not talk with the boyfriends themselves, but instead were limited to what the girls reported about their boyfriends. The girls' perceptions of their boyfriends' attitudes toward pregnancy may be more a reflection of the girls' own desires. Also, we do not know what the girls really thought about pregnancy, only what they reported to us. It may be that more girls desired pregnancy, but were not willing to admit it. Our study did not use a previously validated questionnaire to determine "intendedness" of pregnancy. Because of the difficulty in ascribing motivations to adolescent behavior and reported attitudes, the entire concept of intendedness of pregnancy may not be relevant when discussing adolescent pregnancies.[18, 23] However, the semistructured interview used in our study elicited a rich and detailed explanation of attitudes toward such topics as birth control, pregnancy, and influences of family and boyfriend.

Our study results may not be generalizable to other adolescent populations. Our study sample was from a mostly rural area, and the only minority group represented was Hispanic. The vast majority of girls visiting our community health center are from low socioeconomic groups. It is not clear that our results would be true for other ethnicities or for girls from higher socioeconomic levels.

Conclusions

A boyfriend's desire for a baby is best predictor of an adolescent girl's attitude toward pregnancy. The most effective interventions may be those that explore the extent to which a boyfriend's attitude shapes a girl's critical reproductive health decisions. Primary care providers should include boyfriends in any efforts to delay pregnancy in at-risk adolescent girls and should encourage greater dialogue between the girl and her partner with respect to contraceptive and childbearing decisions.

Acknowledgments

The authors would like to acknowledge the following people for their assistance with this study: Kathy Beamis, for help with data collection; Sherry Holcomb, MS. and Debbi Main, PhD. for help with data analysis; the University of Colorado Primary Care Faculty Development Fellowship group, for review and suggestions.

References

1. Maynard RA, ed. Kids having kids: the economic cost and social consequences of teen pregnancy. Washington DC. Urban Institute Press, 1997.

2. Grogger J, Bronars S. The socioeconomic consequences of teenage childbearing: findings from a natural experiment. Fam Plan Perspect 1993: 25:156–161.

3. Hardy JB, Shapiro S, Astone NM, Miller TL, Brooks-Gunn J, Hilton SC. Adolescent childbearing revisited: the age of innercity mothers at delivery is a determinant of their children's self-sufficiency at age 27–33. Pediatrics 1997; 100:802–09.

4. Resnick MD, et al., Protecting adolescents from harm: findings from the National Longitudinal Study on Adolescent Health. JAMA 1997; 287: 823–32.

5. Alan Gutumacher Institute. Sex and American teenagers. New York: AGI. 1994.

6. Kirby D. No easy answers: research findings on programs to reduce teen pregnancy. Washington DC: The Campaign to Prevent Teen Pregnancy, 1997.

7. National Campaign to Prevent Teen Pregnancy. Whatever happened to childhood? the problem of teen pregnancy in the United States. Washington, DC, 1997.

8. State specific pregnancy rates among adolescents—United States, 1992–95. MMWR June 26, 1998; 47:497–504.

9. Bloom KC, Hali DS. Pregnancy wantedness in adolescents presenting for pregnancy testing. Am J Matern Child Nurs 1999; 24:296–300.

10. Stevens-Simon C, Kelly L, Cox A. Why pregnant adolescents say they did not use contraception prior to conception. J. Adolesc Health 1996; 19:48–53.

11. Stevens-Simon C, Lowy R. Teenage childbearing: an adaptive strategy for the socioeconomically disadvantaged or a strategy for adapting to socioeconomic disadvantage? Arch Pediatr Adolesc Med 1995; 149:912–15.

12. Emans J, Grace E, Woods E, et al. Adolescent's compliance with the use of oral contraceptives. JAMA 1987; 257: 3377–81.

13. Levinson RA. Reproductive and contraceptive knowledge, contraceptive self-efficacy, and contraceptive behavior among teenage women. Adolescence 1995; 30:65–85.

14. Coley RL, Chase-Lansdale PL. Adolescent pregnancy and parenthood: recent evidence and future directions. Am Psychol 1998; 53:152–66.

15. Henshaw SK. Unintended pregnancy in the United States Family Plan Perspect 1998; 30: 24–29, 46.

16. Institute of Medicine. The best intentions. Unintended pregnancy and the well-being of children and families. Washington DC. National Academy Press, 1995.

17. Trussel J, Vaughan B, Stanford J. Are all contraceptive failures unintended pregnancies? Evidence from the 1995 National Survey of Family Growth. Family Plan Perspect 1999; 5:246–47, 260.

18. Rubin V, East P. Adolescents' pregnancy intentions. J Adolesc Health 1999; 24:313–20.

19. Zabin L, Astone N, Emerson M. Do adolescents want babies? The relationship between attitudes and behavior. J Res Adolesc 1993; 3:67–86.

20. Zabin LS, Sedivy V, Emerson MR. Subsequent risk of childbearing among adolescents with a negative pregnancy test. Fam Plan Perspect 1994; 26:212.

21. Rainey DY, Stevens-Simon C, Kaplan DW. Self-perception of infertility among female adolescents. Am J Dis Child 1993; 147:1053–56.

22. Spingarn RW, DuRant RH. Male adolescents involved in pregnancy: associated health risk and problem behaviors. Pediatrics 1996; 98:262–68.

23. Sable M. Pregnancy intentions may not be a useful measure for research on maternal and child health outcomes. Family Plan Perspect 1999; 5:247–50.

READING FOR CONTENT

1. According to Cowley and Farley, why do we have a poor understanding of teenagers' attitudes toward pregnancy?

2. Cowley and Farley examine factors that other studies investigating teen attitudes toward pregnancy have not considered. What are these factors?

3. What method did Cowley and Farley use to select their subjects and why did they reduce the original number of 202 to 148?

4. Describe the data Cowley and Farley collected.

5. In their final analysis, why do Cowley and Farley combine the group of girls "desiring pregnancy" with the group "ambivalent about pregnancy"?

6. Summarize the demographic characteristics of the 148 subjects.

7. How do "girls wishing to avoid pregnancy" differ from the girls in the rest of the sample?

8. What is the major finding of Cowley and Farley's study, and what does this finding suggest to healthcare providers?

9. List the limitations of Cowley and Farley's study.

READING FOR GENRE, ORGANIZATION, AND STYLISTIC FEATURES

1. Cowley and Farley follow the prescribed format for a research study. The study is organized into five sections: introduction, methods, results, discussion, and conclusion. Reread each section and describe its contents.

2. The Results section of a research study usually contains some type of graphic display, for example, figures or tables, of the data. Do the three tables in the Cowley and Farley study help you to understand the data? Why or why not?

3. Why do you think it is important for researchers to include a section on the limitations of the study? Do you agree with Cowley and Farley's comments about the limitations? Did you notice any other limitations?

4. Comment on the voice and sentence structure. Do you think passive voice (e.g., "This study *was conducted....*") and lengthy complex sentences are appropriate for an article of this type? Why or why not?

READING FOR RHETORICAL CONTEXT

1. Research studies begin with an abstract like the one in paragraph 1. What do you think is the function of the abstract? Why would it appeal to readers of *The Journal of Family Practice?*

2. In the introductory section of the study, how do Cowley and Farley convince their readers of the need for the type of research they are conducting?

3. In the Discussion section, Cowley and Farley talk about the potential significance of their findings. What are the implications for health care professionals?

WRITING ASSIGNMENTS

1. Cowley and Farley's review of the research on teen pregnancy found that some studies suggest that "as many as 60% to 80% of teenaged pregnancies are 'unintended,'" while others suggest that "the percentage of pregnancies that are truly unintended may be lower than commonly believed." What do you think? Write an essay in which you present your position.

2. Are you surprised by the finding that 92 percent of the 148 girls were dating and 88 percent were sexually active? Write an essay in response to these statistics.

3. Write an essay in which you evaluate Cowley and Farley's study and principal finding: "A boyfriend's desire for a baby is the best predictor of an adolescent girl's attitude toward pregnancy." Given the limitations of the study, especially the fact that the researchers did not interview the girls' boyfriends, how much weight does this finding have? What types of additional research would strengthen this finding?

4. If you were to conduct a study on adolescent pregnancy, what major question would you hope to answer? Design a small study that might answer your research question. Include the setting and subjects, the method you will use for collecting data (e.g., interviews, surveys), and the procedures you will use to analyze the data.

WRITING ASSIGNMENTS FOR CHAPTER 12

1. Write an essay in which you thoroughly analyze and evaluate the topic of adolescent pregnancy. Use the selections in this chapter to present the topic in all its complexity. Reread the section of in-depth analysis and evaluation, pages 205–224, before you begin.

2. In their discussion of the rising birth rate among young single women and teens, Kay Hymowitz, Cathy Gulli, and Nancy Gibbs agree on some points and disagree on others. Write an essay in which you compare and contrast the three authors' views and explain which of the three positions is the most compelling. Review the material on comparing sources, pages 228–248, before you begin.

3. Write an essay in which you synthesize the main points of the four selections in this chapter. Consult "Strategies for Writing an Objective Synthesis of Multiple Sources," page 257, before you write the paper.

4. Using evidence from the articles in this chapter as a base, write an essay in which you argue that the conditions and services available today make it relatively easy for single young women to have babies. Reread Chapter 8, "Arguing from Sources," before you begin this project.

5. Cowley and Farley discovered that the "attitude of the boyfriend toward having a child was the only significant prediction of the adolescent girls' attitude toward pregnancy." To what extent do Hymowitz, Gulli, and Gibbs discuss the role of boyfriends or adolescent fathers? Drawing on the selections in this chapter as well as on sources you locate on your own, write an essay on the topic of adolescent fathers. For assistance locating sources, reread Chapter 9, "Researching Sources and Writing Research Papers."

CHAPTER 13

Creativity and Ownership

Should creations of the mind—music, literature, art, film, plays, photography, software, and other intellectual works—be protected and regulated by law, or should we be able to borrow, transform, and share these works freely? According to United States copyright law, creators have the exclusive rights to their work, and we are prohibited from using it without their authorization.

Copyright is not granted in perpetuity. The protection usually extends seventy years after the death of the author. In the U.S., works published prior to 1923 are in the public domain. This means they are available to anyone for any purpose. The limited duration of copyright allowed Walt Disney to draw inspiration from older sources with impunity. The fairy tales collected by Jacob and Wilhelm Grimm in the early 1800s are the bases for films such as *Snow White, Sleeping Beauty,* and *Cinderella.* Disney was allowed to make as many changes to the tales as he wished. But if you were to download a copyrighted song from the Web, you could not alter it in any way unless you first obtained the copyright owner's approval. If we had included Abraham Lincoln's 1863 Gettysburg Address in this book, we could have done so without paying a copyright permissions fee. If we had used Dr. Martin Luther King Jr.'s speech, "I Have a Dream," without permission, we would have been guilty of the crime of copyright infringement.

Some experts feel that copyright laws are overly restrictive. Lawrence Lessig, one of the authors in this chapter, founded the Free Culture Movement to promote the sharing of creative works because he feels that strict copyright and intellectual property laws hamper creativity. Other experts think copyright laws are too permissive. They argue that authors should be guaranteed exclusive rights to their creations. The dichotomy is epitomized by two quotations from Chapter 13:

> Ideas arise, evolve through collaboration, gain currency through exposure, mutate in new directions, and diffuse through imitation. The constant borrowing, repurposing, and transformation of prior work are as integral to creativity in music and film as they are to fashion. (Bollier and Racine 446)

> [A] work of art is more than an idea. . . . We have different words for art and idea because they are two different things. The flow and proportion of the elements

441

of a work of art, its subtle engineering, even its surface glosses, combine substance and style indistinguishably in a creation for which the right of property is natural and becoming. (Helprin 449)

Do you agree with the first quotation or the second one? Is it in the public interest to give exclusive rights to the creators of intellectual works, or are we harmed by such legislation? Keep these questions in mind as you read the four selections in this chapter.

In the first reading, "Why Crush Them?," Lawrence Lessig questions why there is no provision of "fair use" (limited sampling without the author's permission) for sound recordings. Lessig bemoans the fact that every teenager who remixes a song on the Internet is guilty of criminal behavior. In the second selection "Control of Creativity?" David Bollier and Laurie Racine compare the music and film industries to the fashion industry. They point out that fashion designers know that "creativity cannot be bridled and controlled." Bollier and Racine argue that the music and film industries should recognize this truism. In the third selection, "A Great Idea Lives Forever. Shouldn't Its Copyright?," fiction writer Mark Helprin makes a case for extending the duration of copyright protection as a means of compensation for authors and their families. Finally, musicologist David Hajdu examines how the "remix culture" is transforming the way recording artists and their fans view music. His piece is entitled "I, Me, Mine."

Why Crush Them?

Lawrence Lessig

Lawrence Lessig is Professor of Law at Stanford Law School and the founder and director of Stanford's Center for Internet and Society. A foremost authority on copyright issues, he is the author of five books: Codev2 *(downloadable as a Wiki at http://www.socialtext.com/, 2007);* Code v2, and Other Laws of Cyberspace *(2006);* Free Culture: How Big Media Uses Technology and the Law to Lock Down Creativity *(2004);* The Future of Ideas: The Fate of the Commons in a Connected World *(2001); and* Code, and Other Laws of Cyberspace *(1999).*

The article was originally published in Newsweek. Newsweek *is a weekly news magazine that is distributed worldwide and has a circulation of over four million readers.*

Prereading

Do you think that amateur musicians should be allowed to sample music and lyrics without the composers' and songwriters' permission? Write two to three paragraphs in response to this question.

In the next five years, there will be more than a billion additional machines for making music in the world. Not pianos or guitars, but computers. These computers are increasingly changing the way music gets made. A whole host of "composers" use these machines to create powerful new compositions. And as these creators can become experts without

1

20 years of piano lessons, these machines are inviting a much wider range of creative souls to express their creativity.

Much of this music follows in the footsteps of hip-hop. Using powerful (but cheap) digital technologies, any kid can now remix sounds found on an ordinary CD and, after adding his or her own style, produce a new creative work. And while the genre has developed far beyond what hip-hop originally was, the inspiration is the same: how do you take found creativity, and make it something new?

Nor is music the only place where this remix culture is flourishing. University of Southern California researcher Mimi Ito describes an emerging anime music video (AMV) culture, in which tens of thousands of kids take Japanese anime recorded from TV and then, using personal computers, recut these anime to fit them to popular songs or, in some cases, popular movie trailers. "You don't understand how important this is," one American father told me after I had described to an audience this emerging form of art. "My son couldn't get into college until he showed them his AMVs."

Remix in art is, of course, nothing new. What is new is the law's take on this remix. For while the law of copyright protected Louis Armstrong as he made "fair use" of the compositions of his jazz contemporaries, courts in the United States have held that there's no fair-use right to a sound recording at all. Any sample taken without permission, however small, is "piracy." And such is the view of almost all in the movie industry. In his recent book, *Darknet,* J. D. Lasica describes asking seven major studios for permission to include short clips from popular movies in his own home movie. Lasica promised he would not show the film to anyone except his family. All but one denied the request. Asked if he could use two 10-second clips of Daffy Duck, for example, Warner Brothers wrote, "we do not . . . allow our material to be edited or altered in any way."

It is said by many that the Internet has changed things. And indeed, for an enlightened few, it has. The rock band Wilco discovered that it sells more albums, and more concert tickets, when it makes its music relatively freely available on the Net. Warner Music now seems to be singing the same song.

But the change we rarely notice is the effective change the law has made to the right of creators to use this technology to create. The tradition of remix was alive and well before digital technologies came along—for the rich, at least. Digital technologies then democratized that tradition, extending the power to create broadly. But according to copyright law, remix in the world of digital technologies is presumptively illegal unless expensive permissions are secured. As one producer described to me, "It cost us $40,000 to make the CD, and then $200,000 to clear the rights to the music we remixed." Or as another documentary filmmaker described: digital technologies made it possible to produce a powerful new political documentary for less than $50,000, but it cost more than $50,000 to clear the rights to the news clips used in that documentary. And these are the lucky ones, the ones who can afford the permission. For the average kid, there is no such luck. Thus, rather than welcoming a new generation of creators, the law calls them "pirates," and rallies technology companies to build the tools to stop this "piracy."

We can build those tools. We can drive these new creators underground. We can reinforce a system in which remixing is legal only for those who can afford high-priced lawyers. But the question governments should be asking is: why? Just at the moment when digital technologies give to our kids the most extraordinary power of creativity, why shut it down? If Shakespeare and Disney and Miles Davis were not pirates, what principled reason is there to condemn their digital equivalents?

READING FOR CONTENT

1. According to Lessig, what is technology's effect on creative expression?
2. What is the "anime music video culture"?
3. Explain why remixing is "nothing new." What precedents are there?
4. Explain why sampling without permission is considered to be piracy in both the music industry and the film industry.
5. What is Lessig's opinion of "digital criminals"?

READING FOR GENRE, ORGANIZATION, AND STYLISTIC FEATURES

1. In paragraphs 1, 2, and 3, how does Lessig persuade his readers that remixing is a widespread phenomenon?
2. In paragraph 6, Lessig quotes a music producer and a documentary filmmaker. How do these quotations further Lessig's argument?
3. Comment on the organization of the article. How do paragraphs 1–3 function in comparison to paragraphs 4–7?

READING FOR RHETORICAL CONTEXT

1. How does Lessig's background prepare you for the position he takes in his article?
2. In paragraph 4, how does J. D. Lasica's experience affect the reader? How does it bolster Lessig's argument?
3. Explain whether you think the length and style of Lessig's article are appropriate for readers of *Newsweek*.

WRITING ASSIGNMENTS

1. Write an essay in response to the question Lessig asks in paragraph 2: "How do you take found creativity and make it something new?"
2. Write an essay in which you argue for or against the position Lessig takes in this article.
3. Write a brief research essay on the Disney Corporation and copyright law. For an ironic view, see Professor Eric Faden's video in which Disney characters explain copyright law. You can access the video at Free Government Information: http://freegovinfo.info/node/1204.

Control of Creativity?

David Bollier and Laurie Racine

David Bollier is a political strategist, journalist and author who focuses on issues related to the effect digital technologies are having on culture. He is Senior Fellow at the Norman Lear Center of the Annenberg School of Communications, University of Southern California, and the author and coauthor of eleven books. His most recent books are Viral Spiral: How the Commoners Built a Digital Republic of Their Own *(2009);* Ready to Share: Fashion and the Ownership of Creativity *(2006), coauthored with Laurie Racine; and* Brand Name Bullies: The Quest to Own and Control Culture *(2005).*

Laurie Racine is Senior Fellow at the Norman Lear Center of the Annenberg School of Communications, University of Southern California. With David Bollier, she has coauthored Ready to Share: Fashion and the Ownership of Creativity *(2006) and codirected the Lear Center project Creativity, Commerce, and Culture, which explores intellectual property rights in digital environments.*

The article was originally published in The Christian Science Monitor, *an international newspaper focusing on current events.*

Prereading

Do you think the fashion industry controls creativity in the same way that the music and film industries do? Respond in your journal.

Why do fashion, film, and music—the sultans of cool in our culture, the shapers of our consciousness—take such radically different approaches to the control of creativity?   *1*

The music and film industries continue to battle over the need to expand copyright protection, and to limit sharing and reuse of prior work. The fashion industry, driven by similar market interests, employs a modus operandi that accepts rather than rejects derivation and appropriation as creative tools.   *2*

The contrast is particularly fascinating, given the dependence of each of these industries on our shared cultural heritage, which we call the "commons." The music and film industries' resources are being sapped in ongoing battles about the scope of legal protection that their CDs and DVDs should enjoy and whether prior works may be freely reused. These industries are unusually possessive: Their attorneys have gone after consumers who played DVDs on non-Windows software ("piracy"), Girl Scouts who sang copyrighted songs around the campfire ("no performance license"), and kids who set up their own Harry Potter fan websites ("trademark violation").   *3*

By contrast, the fashion industry long has accepted that creativity is too large and fugitive an essence to be owned outright as property. Fashion is a massive industry that thrives in a competitive global environment despite minimal legal protections for its creative design. While many people dismiss fashion as trivial and ephemeral, its economic importance and cultural influence are enormous. US apparel sales alone were $180 billion a few years ago, supporting an estimated 80,000 garment factories, and fashion is a major force in music, entertainment, and other creative sectors.   *4*

It is precisely because fashion pervades so many aspects of our lives that we fail to appreciate the "social ecology" that supports it—the open sharing, unauthorized innovations, and creative appropriations. To be sure, the fashion industry aggressively protects its brand names and logos, utilizing trademarks and licensing agreements. In most cases, however, the actual creative design of garments is not owned by anyone. The couturier dress   *5* worn by a Hollywood starlet on the red carpet can be knocked off immediately and legally appear days later on department store racks.

The Hollywood studios and major record labels consider it self-evident and axiomatic that creativity must be strictly controlled through copyright law, lest it be "stolen" and creators forced out of business. It is a significant point that creators, especially individual artists, need effective, reliable ways to be paid for their work—and copyright offers one important vehicle. But the fashion industry has a deeper faith in the power of creativity. Despite scant legal protection, fashion businesses invest enormous sums in each new season's creative cycle—and reap substantial profits year after year.   6

For virtually all players in fashion, some form of derivation, recombination, imitation, revival of old styles, and outright knockoff is the norm. Few denounce, let alone sue, the appropriator for "creative theft." They're too busy trying to stay ahead of the competition through the sheer power of their design and marketing prowess.   7

The fashion world understands that creativity is a collaborative and community affair. It's far too big, robust, and evolving for any one player to "own" as a legal entitlement. Long lineages of couturiers from Balenciaga to Ungaro, Chanel to Lagerfeld, and Gucci to Tom Ford have shown that designers necessarily must learn, adopt, and adapt from those who have blazed previous trails. If one were to deconstruct their work, an evolutionary chain of distinct themes, references, design nuances, and outright appropriations could be discerned.   8

Occasionally someone may protest a "rip-off" and get murmurs of sympathy. And the counterfeiting of brand-name products is rightly condemned as theft. However, in general, creative derivation is an accepted premise of fashion. Indeed, the industry's growth and prosperity have been built upon the famous maxim of Isaac Newton, "If I have seen further, it is by standing on the shoulders of giants."   9

Is it possible that the fashion industry, long patronized as a realm of the ephemeral and insubstantial, is the real bellwether for future ideas of "ownership" of creative content?   10

Through fashion we have a ringside seat on the ecology of creativity in a world of networked communication. Ideas arise, evolve through collaboration, gain currency through exposure, mutate in new directions, and diffuse through imitation. The constant borrowing, repurposing, and transformation of prior work are as integral to creativity in music and film as they are to fashion.   11

Although the music and film industries acknowledge the cultural commons as a source of inspiration, they then turn around and try to claim exclusive ownership of the results. The Disney Company, for example, has "taken private" dozens of folk stories and literary classics while contributing nothing to the public domain. Such one-way privatization of our culture makes it difficult for new creators to build from works that were themselves derivative at an earlier point.   12

Creativity can endure only so much private control before it careens into a downward spiral of sterile involution. If it is to be fresh, passionate, and transformative, creativity must have the room to breathe and grow, "unfettered and alive."   13

The legendary designer Coco Chanel understood this reality. She once said, "Fashion is not something that exists in dresses only; fashion is something in the air. It's the wind that blows in the new fashion; you feel it coming, you smell it . . . in the sky, in the street; fashion has to do with ideas, the way we live, what is happening."   14

The fashion world recognizes that creativity cannot be bridled and controlled and that *15* obsessive quests to do so will only diminish its vitality. Other content industries would do well to heed this wisdom.

READING FOR CONTENT

1. Explain why Bollier and Racine view the music and film industries as "unusually possessive."
2. Notice how Bollier and Racine define their terms. What definitions do they give for "cultural commons" and "social ecology"?
3. Under what conditions would the fashion industry accuse someone of theft?
4. Why do Bollier and Racine object to "one-way privatization of culture" (paragraph 12)?
5. Explain how Bollier and Racine defend the fashion industry from claims that it is trivial and insubstantial.
6. What do Bollier and Racine think will happen to creativity if it is over-controlled?

READING FOR GENRE, ORGANIZATION, AND STYLISTIC FEATURES

1. What is the function of the rhetorical questions in paragraphs 1 and 10?
2. How would you describe Bollier and Racine's tone? Do you think the tone is serious in paragraph 3?
3. In paragraph 6, how do Bollier and Racine acknowledge the validity of views contrary to their own and then how do they refute those views?

READING FOR RHETORICAL CONTEXT

1. What is the main point that Bollier and Racine wish to get across to the readers of their article?
2. Bollier and Racine quote Isaac Newton in paragraph 9 and Coco Chanel in paragraph 14. How do these quotations strengthen their argument?
3. Which parts of Bollier and Racine's argument will their readers find most persuasive? Cite the passages.

WRITING ASSIGNMENTS

1. Summarize the differences between the industry of fashion and the industries of music and film with respect to their approach to creativity and "creative theft."
2. Write an argumentative essay in which you either defend or oppose Bollier and Racine's claim: "Ideas arise, evolve through collaboration, gain currency through exposure, mutate in new directions, and diffuse through imitation. The constant borrowing, repurposing, and transformation of prior work are as integral to creativity in music and film as they are to fashion."
3. Write an essay in which you agree or disagree with Bollier and Racine's position: "that creativity cannot be bridled and controlled and that obsessive quests to do so will only diminish its vitality" (paragraph 15).

A Great Idea Lives Forever. Shouldn't Its Copyright?

Mark Helprin

Mark Helprin is a fiction writer and essayist. He is the author of three collections of short stories: A Dove of the East and Other Stories, Ellis Island and Other Stories, *and* The Pacific and Other Stories; *five novels:* Refiner's Fire, Winter's Tale, A Soldier of the Great War, Memoir from Antproof Case, *and* Freddy and Fredericka; *and three children's books:* Swan Lake, A City in Winter, *and* The Veil of Snows.

The article was originally published in the New York Times, *a daily newspaper published in New York City. The* New York Times *has the third largest circulation in the United States. The paper has won ninety-eight Pulitzer Prizes and many other awards for journalism.*

Prereading ▰

Do you think the creative property of authors, artists, musicians, and filmmakers should be afforded the same protections as their physical property (houses, cars, and boats)? Respond in your journal.

What if, after you had paid the taxes on earnings with which you built a house, sales taxes on the materials, real estate taxes during your life, and inheritance taxes at your death, the government would eventually commandeer it entirely? This does not happen in our society to houses. Or to businesses. Were you to have ushered through the many gates of taxation a flour mill, travel agency or newspaper, they would not suffer total confiscation.

Once the state has dipped its enormous beak into the stream of your wealth and possessions they are allowed to flow from one generation to the next. Though they may be divided and diminished by inflation, imperfect investment, a proliferation of descendants and the government taking its share, they are not simply expropriated.

That is, unless you own a copyright. Were I tomorrow to write the great American novel (again?), 70 years after my death the rights to it, though taxed at inheritance, would be stripped from my children and grandchildren. To the claim that this provision strikes malefactors of great wealth, one might ask, first, where the heirs of Sylvia Plath berth their 200-foot yachts. And, second, why, when such a stiff penalty is not applied to the owners of Rockefeller Center or Wal-Mart, it is brought to bear against legions of harmless drudges who, other than a handful of literary plutocrats (manufacturers, really), are destined by the nature of things to be no more financially secure than a seal in the Central Park Zoo.

The answer is that the Constitution states unambiguously that Congress shall have the power "*to promote the Progress of Science and useful Arts,* by securing for limited Times to Authors and Inventors the exclusive Right to their respective Writings and Discoveries." (The italics are mine, the capitalization was likely James Madison's.)

It is, then, for the public good. But it might also be for the public good were Congress to allow the enslavement of foreign captives and their descendants (this was tried); the seizure of Bill Gates's bankbook; or the ruthless suppression of Alec Baldwin. You can always

1

2

3

4

5

make a case for the public interest if you are willing to exclude from common equity those whose rights you seek to abridge. But we don't operate that way, mostly.

Furthermore, one should not envy the perpetrators of sensationalist trash, but rather admire them, in the hope that someday, somehow, without prostituting, debasing and degrading oneself while recklessly destroying what is left of the literary culture, one might enjoy a fraction of their wealth. They represent, however, only a small fraction of writers, and their good fortune is a poor excuse for seizing either their property or that of their leaner colleagues.   6

And Barnes & Noble is able to publish price-reduced non-copyrighted works not so much because it saves the 10 percent to 15 percent of revenue that would go to the gruel-eating authors, but because it saves the 50 percent that would go to the publishers. Booksellers that publish their own titles benefit not from escaping the author's copyright, but the previous publisher's exercise of a grant of rights (limited, authors take note, to 35 years). "Freeing" a literary work into the public domain is less a public benefit than a transfer of wealth from the families of American writers to the executives and stockholders of various businesses who will continue to profit from, for example, "The Garden Party," while the descendants of Katherine Mansfield will not.   7

Absent the government's decree, copyright holders would have no exclusivity of right at all. Does not then the government's *giveth* support its *taketh*? By that logic, should other classes of property not subject to total confiscation therefore be denied the protection of regulatory agencies, courts, police and the law itself lest they be subject to expropriation as payment for the considerable and necessary protections they too enjoy? Should automobile manufacturers be nationalized after 70 years because they depend on publicly financed roads? Should Goldman Sachs be impounded because of the existence of the Securities and Exchange Commission?   8

Why would the framers, whose political genius has not been exceeded, have countenanced such an unfair exception? Jefferson objected that ideas are, "like fire, expansible over all space, without lessening their density at any point, and, like the air in which we breathe, move and have our physical being, incapable of confinement or exclusive appropriation."   9

But ideas are immaterial to the question of copyright. Mozart and Neil Diamond may have begun with the same idea, but that a work of art is more than an idea is confirmed by the difference between the "Soave sia il vento" and "Kentucky Woman." We have different words for art and idea because they are two different things. The flow and proportion of the elements of a work of art, its subtle engineering, even its surface glosses, combine substance and style indistinguishably in a creation for which the right of property is natural and becoming.   10

And in Jefferson's era 95 percent of the population drew its living from the land. Writers and inventors were largely those who obtained their sustenance from their patrimony or their mills; their writings or improvements to craft were secondary. No one except perhaps Hamilton or Franklin might have imagined that services and intellectual property would become primary fields of endeavor and the chief engines of the economy. Now they are, and it is no more rational to deny them equal status than it would have been to confiscate farms, ropewalks and other forms of property in the 18th century.   11

Still, it is the express order of the Constitution, long imprinted without catastrophe upon the fabric of our history. But given the grace of the Constitution it is not surprising to find the remedy within it, in the very words that prohibit the holding of patents or copyrights in perpetuity: "for limited Times."   12

The genius of the framers in making this provision is that it allows for infinite adjustment. Congress is free to extend at will the term of copyright. It last did so in 1998, and   13 should do so again, as far as it can throw. Would it not be just and fair for those who try to extract a living from the uncertain arts of writing and composing to be freed from a form of confiscation not visited upon anyone else? The answer is obvious, and transcends even justice. No good case exists for the inequality of real and intellectual property, because no good case can exist for treating with special disfavor the work of the spirit and the mind.

READING FOR CONTENT

1. According to Helprin, why is it unfair to limit copyright protection to seventy years after an author's death?

2. Explain why Helprin believes that the U.S. Constitution abridges authors' rights.

3. To whom is Helprin referring when he speaks of writers who are "perpetrators of sensationalism"?

4. Paraphrase the point Helprin is making in paragraph 7.

5. Explain some of the differences between the era of Jefferson and the framers of the Constitution, and the era we live in now.

6. According to Helprin, when one is discussing the duration of copyright, why is it important to consider the Constitution's phrase "securing for limited Time"?

7. Paraphrase Helprin's thesis.

READING FOR GENRE, ORGANIZATION, AND STYLISTIC FEATURES

1. How does Helprin's opening paragraph set up the distinction between physical property and intellectual property?

2. Explain what Helprin accomplishes by using figurative language, for example: "once the state has dipped its enormous beak into the stream of your wealth" (paragraph 2) and "to be no more financially secure than a seal in the Central Park Zoo" (paragraph 3).

3. In paragraphs 8 and 9, Helprin asks a string of rhetorical questions. How do these questions further his argument?

4. Comment on Helprin's writing style.

READING FOR RHETORICAL CONTEXT

1. Given Mark Helprin's background, why would you expect him to hold the views he has espoused?

2. Helprin refers to writers like himself as "harmless drudges," "gruel-eating authors," and "leaner colleagues." What effect do these descriptions have on the reader?

3. List and explain the effectiveness of the various types of evidence Helprin uses to further his argument. Which evidence will his readers find most convincing?

WRITING ASSIGNMENTS

1. Write an essay in which you evaluate the effectiveness of Helprin's argument.

2. Write an essay in response to Helprin's statement: "No good case exists for the inequality of real and intellectual property, because no good case can exist for treating with special disfavor the work of the spirit" (paragraph 13).

I, Me, Mine

David Hajdu

David Hajdu, a professor of journalism at Columbia University, writes a monthly column on music and popular culture for The New Republic. *Professor Hadju is the author of* The Ten-Cent Plague: The Great Comic-Book Scare and How It Changed America; Lush Life: A Biography of Billy Strayhorn; *and* Positively 4th Street: The Lives and Times of Joan Baez, Bob Dylan, Mimi Baez Farina and Richard Farina.

The article was originally published in The New Republic, *a biweekly magazine focusing on politics and the arts.*

Prereading

Respond to the first two sentences of Hajdu's article. In a sense, do you think you "own" the music you strongly identify with, even if that music is written and performed by others? Answer this question in your journal.

The urge to make the work our own is elemental to the act of encountering art, and we try to satisfy it in many ways. We look at a painting or listen to a piece of music and take it in, hoping that it will prove to be not only an expression of human feeling but also a stimulus to it; we expect art to move us in a personal way. Or we buy the artwork or a copy of it, making our ownership literal (if not always legal, in case of downloading bootleg digital files). Or we wear our esteem for the work like a fashion label, for the social or professional status it confers. Or we draw inspiration from the work and apply it to things we make ourselves, using whatever of it serves our needs. In one way or another, to experience art of any kind is to appropriate it, and to be a devotee of any art or artist is to be a claimant.

In the music world, recording technology has greatly complicated the issues of ownership, authorship, and proprietary rights by simplifying the acquisition of creative property. Since the rise of sampling and downloading, digital technology has transferred many of the privileges of authorship from what was once an elite of professional musicians to the iPod-ed masses. Anyone with a laptop and home mixing software such as GarageBand (a substitute for both the garage and the band) or Pro Tools (an electronic kit to help amateurs sound as if they are not) can put together technically impressive multi-track recordings. To generate the music for those tracks, home producers have for some time now been able to extract snippets from any recordings in the digital domain, doctor them electronically, edit them, and perhaps even use traditional instruments and vocal tracks. The exponential growth in the popularity of such home recording over the past several years has helped fill the pages of MySpace with fragmentary sound-alike songs, while providing countless musical neophytes with gratifying quasi-creative experiences and inflated conceptions of their musical talent. As the record industry burns to ash, record-making is thriving in the same sense that moviemaking, of a sort, is booming on YouTube—that is, in the diminished form of derivative, perfunctory goofing around, the products of which may have momentary entertainment value, especially to their creators.

Some rock acts that made their reputations as sonic experimenters a long decade ago, *3*
such as Radiohead and Nine Inch Nails, seem humbled in the presence of the shape-shifting
creature that popular music has become in the digital age. Both those bands recently made
high-profile attempts at Web innovation that are essentially acts of capitulation, if not desperation. Radiohead made lots of news when the band released its first album since 2003, *In
Rainbows*, through its website in a plan that allowed downloaders to pay whatever price they
chose—a great publicity stunt in the form of a vast, universal tip jar. After too many listeners
decided to drop in too few coins, the band released another version of the album, priced
conventionally. More recently, Trent Reznor made the new Nine Inch Nails album *The Slip*
available through the band's website, for free. In an announcement of the release on his site,
Reznor wrote, "thank you for your continued and loyal support over the years—this one's on
me." A CD release of *The Slip*, at a price to be determined, will follow in July, at which time
Reznor and the latest incarnation of his band will have begun a national tour, for which seats
will likely cost at least four or five times the price of a CD.

There is nothing wrong with—or new about—giving away samples to entice customers *4*
to pay for other, profitable goods. The technique has long been common in the narcotics
trade and in the marketing of supermarket cheeses. More interesting than the fact that Radiohead and Nine Inch Nails have provided albums to listeners for free or for cheap are the
efforts that both bands have recently made to come to terms with the phenomenon of home
record-making. Radiohead and Nine Inch Nails have each now ventured into "open-source
remixing," a growing sphere of digital play in which enthusiasts are granted access to the
stems of a song—the individual parts of a multi-track recording, each of which might have,
say, the drums or the bass line or a guitar part—in order to manipulate them or add to them
at home. In differing ways and to differing degrees, both bands are opening up their
processes, making public the component parts of their music to give fans the feeling of col-
laborating with their idols—shadow-dancing with the rock stars. Through open-source
remixing, music fans who might have been just listeners are assuming a kind of ownership
which is, on its face, revolutionary, but which is, ultimately, illusory.

Radiohead, in April, made available for purchase through iTunes the five stems, one *5*
for each of the five band members' instruments, that make up "Nude," a single from *In Rainbows*. (Side note: in the group's native Britain, more than half of all singles are still released
as seven-inch vinyl records, as well as on CD and as downloads; it seems to me that the survival of 45s there has to do with both an English reverence for the tradition that vinyl represents and a frugal English reluctance to throw away perfectly good record players.) With
each of the stems going for iTunes's usual per-song price of 99 cents, "Nude" costs five times
as much to buy in parts as it costs as a song. This is to be expected. To break anything sellable
into bits is to grant each of those bits a value that justifies a price.

"Nude," like several of the songs on *In Rainbows*, is one that fans of the band have long *6*
known in multiple earlier incarnations. At concerts in 1998, the tune was a soul ballad
framed around the sound of a Hammond organ. By 2005, Thom Yorke was doing the song
in solo performances, strumming it gently on the acoustic guitar and murmuring it like an
emo navel-gazer. On *In Rainbows*, it opens with a swirling cloud of synth effects and settles
into a shuffling bass-driven groove. (The terse lyrics center on the phrase "Don't get any big
ideas/They're not gonna to happen," a blunt plea to resist the sexual imagination.) A wisp of
a piece unaligned to a fixed arrangement, it is suited to remixing; indeed, Radiohead has
itself been toying with the song for ten years.

To encourage remixes of "Nude" (and purchases of its stems), Radiohead sponsored a competition and started posting submissions on the band's site. By mid-May, more than 2,200 remixes of the song had been posted and voted on by fans (and, presumably, also automatic-voted on by the digital ringers that hackers can conjure and viral-marketing services can provide for pay). I started listening to the posted remixes (and casting votes, nay and yea, for some of them) shortly after the first went up in April, and over a month's time I got to hear about two hundred versions of "Nude." I did the listening in spurts, taking in a post or two when I felt in the mood, to prevent the repetition of the tune from having the effect of torture.

A great many of the "Nude" remixes I have heard are attempts to change the overall mood of the song by doctoring the tonal colors and redistributing the weights of the musical elements. In a high number of cases, the bass line that dominates the In Rainbows version recedes, and new beats of all sorts take over: intricate and realistic-sounding drum patterns are among the easiest things to generate with software such as GarageBand. The gently pulsing waltz pattern of the official release gives way to heavy beats, often in the propulsive 4/4 basic to rock and hip-hop. Since GarageBand can change the time signature, the tempo, or the key of a song with a few mouse clicks, all those features of the composition get transformed in various "Nude" remixes, with results that can only with a snicker be called mixed. Much of the alteration and ornamentation in the "Nude" remixes seem arbitrary, stunty, or inappropriate. In nearly a dozen of the hundred remixes ranked highest on the Radiohead site, fans added keyboard tracks that oversimplified the already simple chords of the tune or simply got the chords wrong. Re-harmonization is not at all uncommon in the realm of interpretive music; but its point is generally to reconsider, rather than to reduce or to misrepresent, the original music.

The way GarageBand works, the process of personalizing music is highly regimented—that is, depersonalized. For each creative decision involved in customizing a track, the software provides a handy drop-down menu of options. What kind of guitar sound would you like, "Arena Rock" or "Glam" or "Clean Jazz"? What sort of vocals, "Female Basic" or "Epic Diva"? The system transforms music-making into shopping, and it provides the same illusion of individual expression that we find in the mall. Now we can make our sound in the same way we create our own look—by mixing and matching a handful of items from the racks of the same stores that everyone else in America is choosing from. After all, what does "Clean Jazz" mean, other than "Banana Republic"?

Trent Reznor, in a grand gesture of magnanimity, has made the stems of the last several Nine Inch Nails albums (including White Teeth from 2005 and Year Zero from last year) available for remixing, at no cost, through the NIN site. A longtime hero among rock techheads for the loving noisy artifice of his one-man-band recordings, Reznor is so eager to be aligned with the home-remixing phenomenon that he has sponsored a compilation album of fan remixes of songs from White Teeth and Year Zero. Called The Limitless Potential, the album of twenty-one selections is free for downloading, although the individual stems of the tracks that the fans contributed are not accessible for further remixing through the Nine Inch Nails site. (Evidently the "open" in opensourcing has its limits.) Most of the Nine Inch Nails remixes posted, like the "Nude" remixes, are efforts to move the songs from one mode—industrial rock, the style Reznor practically invented in the 1980s—to some other style: house music, or psychedelia, or an approximation of funk. The remixes tend to take lateral steps, hopping

7

8

9

10

across category lines from stylistic box to box. They do not, as a rule, try to differ from the originals in point of view or depth or aesthetic value; they seek to differ primarily in kind.

Despite its obvious debts to the Web era, home remixing in one sense suggests a return to the musical culture of the days before sound recording on wax cylinders, around the turn of the last century. In their capacity as remixers, members of the musical public are again assuming participatory roles, interpreting compositions at home, much as late Victorians played sheet music in parlor musicales. There is also a social component to both spheres of participation, as remixers post their efforts, listen to one another's, and vote on them. I spent a good part of a weekend making my own remix of "Nude." (For the record, I added some wan obligato lines on guitar and concocted a vocal counter-melody, which I sang with the essential assistance of a pitch-correction plug-in.) Dissatisfied with the results, I decided not to post them, and I feel as if my remix, as one unposted, is not real in the same way that the worst remixes on the Radiohead website are. In the ballooning community of remixers, as in the rest of the Web universe, to post is to be.

11

I was further deterred from submitting my remix to the "Nude" competition by the "terms and conditions" of submission. Despite the fact that remixers can not only amend the elements of the Radiohead recording but also add tracks of their own devising—new beats, different chords, additional melodies (such as the admittedly weak guitar and vocal lines I made up), even whole new sets of lyrics (or spoken language)—Radiohead claims full ownership of every part of the remixes sent its way. Every part: not just the original stems, but every bit of music anyone might add to a submitted track. The fine print specifies, "All rights in and to any remixed versions ('Remixes') of the song 'Nude' ('the Song') created by the Entrant shall be owned by Warner/ Chappell Music Ltd ('WCM') and to the extent necessary the Entrant hereby assigns all rights in the Remixes of the Song to WCM throughout the World for the full life of copyright and any and all extensions and renewals thereof. . . . Thom Yorke, Jonny Greenwood, Colin Greenwood, Ed O'Brien and Phil Selway will be registered and credited as the sole writers and WCM the publishers of the Remixes of the Song created by the Entrant."

12

If this is legal, it is also extortionate and an act of terrible hypocrisy—a revocation of the promise of creative ownership that is drawing people to remixing, the promise that Radiohead has been eager to exploit, in large print, to sell its stems. The very idea of remixing implies remaking, and that carries with it a legitimate claim of ownership—aesthetic, ethical, and legal. If most of the remixes on both the "Nude" site and Nine Inch Nails's Unlimited Potential album speak unpersuasively for remixing's potential, they are not definitive proof of remixing's limits. For the moment, Yorke and his band have a message for fans loaded with GarageBand and an urge to own a part of Radiohead: Don't get any big ideas. They're not going to happen.

13

But more troubling even than the hypocrisy of a few rock stars is the narcissism at the heart of the phenomenon of home remixing—the notion that to take a work of creative expression and make it "ours" is to improve it. It is a colossal mistake to coerce an expression of others into an expression of ourselves. The premise of open-source remixing is that finally we can admire nobody so much as ourselves. But in music, as in all art and love and politics, there is usually more to gain in trying to understand what belongs, uniquely and idiosyncratically and serendipitously, to somebody else.

14

READING FOR CONTENT

1. Explain how amateur musicians can use technology to create their own recordings.
2. Why does Hajdu view Radiohead and Nine Inch Nails's online offers as "acts of capitulation, if not desperation"?
3. What is "open-source remixing," and how have Radiohead and Nine Inch Nails capitalized on it?
4. What is Hajdu's opinion of the amateur remixes he has listened to?
5. Explain how GarageBand works by paraphrasing paragraph 9.
6. What reasons does Hajdu give for not posting his remix of "Nude"?
7. Explain why Hajdu accuses Radiohead and Nine Inch Nails of acts that are extortionate and hypocritical.
8. What is Hajdu's attitude toward amateur musicians who engage in home remixing?

READING FOR GENRE, ORGANIZATION, AND STYLISTIC FEATURES

1. Comment on the appropriateness or inappropriateness of Hajdu's title.
2. How does the first paragraph set the stage for the argument that follows?
3. What is the function of paragraphs 6, 7, and 8? How do they contribute to Hajdu's argument?
4. Describe the analogy Hajdu uses in paragraph 9 and comment on its effectiveness.
5. Describe the analogy Hajdu uses in paragraph 11 and comment on its effectiveness.
6. Describe Hajdu's tone. Look especially at paragraph 4, Hajdu's use of parenthetical expressions, his analogies, and his word choice.

READING FOR RHETORICAL CONTEXT

1. What recent incidents in the music world prompted Hajdu to write his article?
2. Do you think Hajdu speaks with sufficient authority? Give examples of passages that impress you.
3. How does Hajdu's personal experience—his attempt to remix "Nude"—affect you as a reader?
4. Comment on the appropriateness of Hajdu's article for readers of *The New Republic*.

WRITING ASSIGNMENTS

1. Do you think open-source remixing is illusory or revolutionary? Using "I, Me, Mine" as your base, write a brief essay in response to this question.
2. Write an essay in which you analyze and evaluate the effectiveness of Hajdu's argument.
3. Write a letter to Warner/Chappell Music Ltd. in which you object to the company's claim to "full ownership of every part of the remixes sent its way" (paragraph 12).
4. Write an essay in which you agree or disagree with Hajdu's claim that "narcissism [is] at the heart of the phenomenon of home mixing—the notion that to take a work of creative expression and make it 'ours' is to improve it" (paragraph 14).

WRITING ASSIGNMENTS FOR CHAPTER 13

1. Both Lawrence Lessig and David Hajdu write about the remix culture. Write an essay in which you compare and contrast both authors' views. Refer to "Comparing and Contrasting Sources," pages 228–248.

2. Are creative works derivative or totally original? Do artists and writers create their works of art from nothing, or are they produced by recombining and remixing bits of works that already exist? Drawing on the articles in this chapter, write an essay in response to these questions. Consult "Strategies for Writing a Response to Multiple Sources," pages 263–264.

3. How important is it that artists, authors, and designers reap all of the financial benefits from their creations? Drawing on David Bollier and Laurie Racine's "Control of Creativity?," Mark Helprin's "A Great Idea Lives Forever. Shouldn't Its Copyright?," and one other selection in this chapter, write an essay in response to this question. Consult "Strategies for Writing a Response to Multiple Sources," pages 263–264.

4. Drawing on library sources as well as the selections in this chapter, write an essay in which you trace the history of copyright legislation in the United States. When did it start and what did it regulate? When did the law expand? What were the amendments to it? What does copyright legislation cover today? What are the implications of the law for works produced with digital technologies? Read over Chapter 9, "Researching Sources and Writing Research Papers," before you tackle this assignment. The United States Copyright Office is a good place to begin your research: http://www.copyright.gov.

5. The capacity to digitize virtually any form of information has made it relatively easy for anyone with access to the Internet and a CD burner to locate, exchange, and copy texts, songs, and images. Many applaud this easy access to information. Musicians, artists, writers, film makers who control the rights to information sources assert that free copying amounts to theft of their intellectual property. Legal battles over music sampling are well-publicized examples of this conflict. What is the cultural impact of the struggle between those who champion free access to information and those who argue for copyright protection? Research this topic thoroughly and write an essay in which you argue your position. Consult Chapters 8 and 9 for this assignment.

CHAPTER 14

Race and American Society

Race affects American society in profound ways. To some Americans, racism remains the most challenging issue facing the nation. The color of people's skin determines how they are treated in all areas of daily life; racial discrimination is prevalent; and racism is tightly woven into the fabric of American society. Other commentators say that race no longer matters; minorities have achieved equality; and we are moving toward a colorblind society.

Race is a slippery concept. Earlier thinking maintained that race is biologically determined. Modern biology and anthropology have challenged this notion and found it to be false. Humans belong to one species, the human race. As Ian Haney Lopez, a legal scholar at the University of California, Berkeley, points out:

> There are no genetic characteristics possessed by all Blacks but not by non-Blacks; similarly, there is no gene or cluster of genes common to all Whites but not to non-Whites. One's race is not determined by a single gene or gene cluster, as is, for example, sickle cell anemia. Nor are races marked by important differences in gene frequencies, the rates of appearance of certain gene types. The data compiled by various scientists demonstrates, contrary to popular opinion, that intra-group differences exceed inter-group differences. That is, greater genetic variation exists within the populations typically labeled Black and White than between these populations. This finding refutes the supposition that racial divisions reflect fundamental genetic differences.

Despite findings to the contrary, many people still conceive of race as biologically determined, and some think that certain "races" are intellectually superior to others. They fail to understand that racial designations are social constructs. Society determines our notions about race, and these social perceptions are constantly evolving. Earlier in our history, the term "white" was reserved for people of English heritage. In the nineteenth century, immigrant groups from Mediterranean countries were not considered white. Today the boundaries of "white" are expanding.

The race question has figured dominantly in United States history. The U.S. was conceived of as a white nation. Southern states would never have ratified the Constitution if Blacks

457

had been given the right to citizenship. In fact, the nation has upheld a racial conception of citizenship. The Naturalization Act of 1790 limited the right of people from other countries to become citizens unless they were "free white persons," that is, people of white English heritage. In 1870 the law was broadened to include people of African descent, but it continued to exclude Asians. Immigrants of all races were not eligible for citizenship until 1952.

Former male slaves and their progeny were not granted citizenship until the Fourteenth Amendment was passed in 1868, and although the Fifteenth Amendment gave them the right to vote in 1870, many Blacks remained disenfranchised because of poll taxes and literacy requirements. These barriers, along with segregated schools, racial profiling, discrimination in employment, and a host of other roadblocks built into the system are examples of institutional racism. Sometimes an institution's treatment of people of different races is unwitting, and other times it is intentional.

The authors of the two selections in this chapter ask penetrating questions about America's racialized history and American contemporary society. The topic of "Race, Higher Education, and American Society" is affirmative action in higher education. Yolanda T. Moses explains why people of color have traditionally been underrepresented in higher education, and she argues that elite colleges and universities should institute policies that will rectify past and present discrimination. In the second selection, "A More Perfect Union," President Barack Obama discusses the destructive nature of racism and calls upon all Americans to come together in order to counteract the negative social, political, and economic effects of racism; heal the wounds of this divided nation; and perfect our union.

Race, Higher Education, and American Society

Yolanda T. Moses

Yolanda T. Moses is Professor of Anthropology at the University of California–Riverside. Her research interests include cultural change and the relationship between cultural diversity and public policy. She has served as president of the City University of New York, the American Association for Higher Education, and the American Anthropological Association. In addition, she has been a member of the board of trustees of the Ford Foundation and Dean and Professor of Anthropology at California State Polytechnic University–Pomona. She is the coauthor of How Real Is Race?: A Sourcebook on Race, Culture, and Biology *(2007) and* Strategies in Teaching Anthropology *(1999).*

The article was originally published in The Journal of Anthropological Research, *a scholarly journal that publishes original research from across the globe in all areas of anthropology. It is based on a JAR Distinguished Lecture that was originally delivered by Professor Moses and later edited into publishable form by Lawrence Straus.*

Prereading

How much does race matter on your college campus? Is diversity promoted or merely tolerated? Are there any racial tensions or animosities? Are any of the deeper racial problems in our society reflected in your school? Freewrite for ten minutes in response to these questions.

This article explores three connected premises: first, that folk beliefs about the immutable nature of race are prevalent in society today; second, that there is a social and cultural reluctance to discuss the American racialized worldview; and, third, that there is the potential for American policy makers and society at large to reembrace biological determinism and social Darwinism at the millennium. The author suggests that anthropologists have a major role to play in educating a wider public about race, cultural pluralism, and diversity in education. Anthropologists should do this by (1) articulating for a general audience what race is and what it is not; (2) providing an anthropological analysis of higher education as a public right or a public good; (3) providing an anthropological analysis of the contemporary American culture of education and educational success; and (4) explaining American paradoxical behavior concerning affirmative action.

"Race, higher education, and American society" are three topics that I care deeply about and have written and talked about separately on many other occasions. In this article I want to bring them together in a way that helps me to lay out three major observations that I have been thinking about as I go about my work as an anthropologist, as a spokesperson for higher education—especially public higher education—and as someone who still believes in the potential of American society to deliver on its promise of an equitable, culturally pluralistic society.

The first observation is that the folk beliefs about the fixed, immutable nature of biological "race" are alive and well in American culture today. Anthropologists have made pronouncements that there is no such thing as biological race, that "it's not race, it's clines," and that race is socially and culturally constructed (Brace 1982; Goodman 1996; Mukhopadhyay and Moses 1997). But I contend that recent academic policies and/or state initiatives (for example, in California and Washington State) that in effect restrict access by people of color, women, and poor Whites to higher education are not *logical* from an educational, quality-of-life, or economic perspective. They neither correlate with national polls on diversity nor do they correlate necessarily with the values of the presidents, faculties, and staffs on campuses across the country that must enforce these policies. Something else is going on. I am concerned that well-meaning educators may unwittingly buy into social Darwinist theories which will then be used by those who want to keep "the other" (minorities and women) in their place.

The second and even more disturbing observation is how this racial worldview is not even talked about directly—but it is hidden in buzzwords within a vocabulary of respectability. This vocabulary is made up of words like "excellence," "quality," or "qualified"—as in "we want to hire the most qualified person." The word "merit" is used as if it is itself a unilinear measure, and the Scholastic Aptitude Test (SAT) has taken on almost holy dimensions in its applications, *contrary* to what research shows about its lack of predictability for measuring the success of women or people of color. Why is this happening now, at this point of time in American cultural history?

Third, and perhaps the most disturbing of all, is the potential for reasonable people at the end of the twentieth century and of the millennium to get back into a nineteenth-century biologically determinist mode of accepting the notions of fixed racial, gender, and class hierarchies all over again. We have seen that in the nineteenth century, these stereotypes and "scientific truths" helped to justify the social, economic, and political status quo in European colonies in Africa and Asia, as well as in the Americas (Smedley 1993). What is the motivation today, precisely at a time when American demographics are more complex than ever?

Finally, I will discuss ways in which anthropologists *can* and do make a difference   5
in educating ourselves, our students, and a wider public about how to get clarity and understanding concerning the issues of race, racism, human diversity, and American cultural values. We must give voice to that which remains unspoken and is *deafening* in its silence.

Race: Is It Biological or Cultural?

Race—A New Paradigm

Modern anthropology's roots lie in nineteenth-century European natural history traditions,   6
with their focus on the classification and comparison of human populations and their search for indicators of "mental capacity." Cultural anthropologists such as L.H. Morgan and E.B. Tylor worked with physical anthropologists of the time to "scientifically" reconstruct human prehistory and to rank human groups along a unilinear evolutionary path from "savagery" to "civilization." Morgan considered mental development crucial to a group's evolutionary progress. Physical indicators of evolutionary rank were developed, including such attributes as the degree of facial projection and the position of the foramen magnum. Measurements of cranial dimensions and proportions ("the cephalic index") were initially proposed as indicators of advancement. Cranial size and the weight and morphological complexity of the brain were other measures used to infer the "mental capacity" of various groups (e.g., "races," sexes, immigrant groups) according to their "natural" "intellectual endowments," which presumably identified their overall evolutionary rank (Mukhopadhyay and Moses 1997:518).

Efforts to refine devices for measuring linked physical and mental traits existed well   7
into the twentieth century. Such endeavors stimulated the development of psychometrics and the intelligence tests first used in World War I on nearly two million American military recruits. Consistent with Euro-American racial ideology, these tests were eventually put to civilian use. Psychologists interpreted results of these tests as indicators of heredity-based, innate intelligence and compared group scores to support ideologies of natural racial superiority and inferiority (Mukhopadhyay and Moses 1997:518). Anthropology helped establish an elaborate set of ideological principles, based on racial and biological determinism, which to this day deeply influence how the world understands human variation and its relations to human behavior. This racial worldview has provided a rationale for slavery, colonial and neocolonial domination, racial segregation, and discrimination and miscegenation laws, and it has fueled the eugenics and anti-immigration movements in the United States.

On the other hand, anthropology—both cultural and biological—played a major   8
role in twentieth-century attempts to transform and dismantle the American racial worldview. From Franz Boas, who as early as 1897 questioned the key assumption in American racial ideology, to the rise of population genetics in the 1930s to 1950s, American anthropologists have sought to dismantle the Euro-American racial worldview. A paradigm shift was in the making, from old typological and morphological definitions of static races to the consideration of dynamic populations with overlapping physical distributions of traits. Yet even the rise of population genetics was not sufficient to eradicate the old racial worldview.

To those who wanted to maintain "racial" purity, population genetics actually offered a way to potentially identify and eradicate "bad" genes, such as the genes for homosexuality, criminal behavior, etc.

During the 1940s, anthropologists reexamined the racial worldview themes in view of Nazism and genocide. In the 1950s and the 1960s, anthropologists focused on the problems with the old racial classifications and argued for the socially and culturally constructed meaning of "race." Ashley Montagu was instrumental in disseminating new anthropological insights to the wider, nonanthropological community. Research by anthropologists in the 1960s and 1970s helped to refine the "deficit" models, which argued that African American schoolchildren lacked the verbal capacities of their Euro-American counterparts. By the 1980s, anthropology appeared to have successfully challenged—at least within the profession—central elements in the racial worldview, particularly the existence of "biological races" within the species *Homo sapiens,* as well as the common belief that American racial categories are universal, longstanding, and rooted in nature.

Unfortunately this shift within the anthropological community appears to have had little external impact. The American racial worldview seems to be alive and well in the popular imagination, among some of our most prominent political leaders, in the halls of academia, and even among some of our anthropological colleagues. This is strikingly apparent in the widespread attention paid to the book *The Bell Curve* (Herrnstein and Murray 1994), a 1990s version of racial determinism. It is also telling in the more popular pronouncements of radio talk-show hosts and newspaper articles that treat race as if it were still an operative biological phenomenon. "Racism"—the attitudinal, behavioral, and institutional manifestation of the American racial ideology—continues to be pervasive in American society. We anthropologists clearly must do a better job at disseminating our findings about race to a wider audience.

As we shift to make "race" once again the center of anthropological inquiry and praxis, we will engage both cultural and biological anthropologists in the common enterprise of reintroducing a more unified anthropological voice into contemporary conversations on race and human diversity. Here I would like to discuss the concept of "race" as it relates to the controversies in higher education that swirl around notions of intelligence and the question of who is still lacking access to higher education in this country.

Over the past five to seven years, practitioners have been revisiting and reexamining the nature of race in both biological and cultural anthropology (e.g., Harrison 1995; Goodman 1996; Lieberman and Jackson 1995; Blakey 1987; Marks 1995; Sacks 1994; Shanklin 1994). The conclusion of most of us is that "race" does not exist as a biological phenomenon, but rather that it is socially and culturally constructed. Having said that, we also have said how important it is to understand that this statement does not explain why people *look* different. Most lay people, and some cultural anthropologists, do not know how to explain human variability in ways that are easily understood. So, in the absence of reasonable anthropological explanation, many people tend to fall back on what they know, or what they think they know. The media and peers tend to reinforce uninformed stereotypes, and eventually these stereotypes become belief. For example, why were the sociobiological themes of Shockley's and Jensen's writings so popular with conservatives in the 1970s, and why was *The Bell Curve* such a best-seller only recently? Just a few years ago I proposed that it was because both books reinforce easy stereotypes that have long been held in this society, namely, that people of color and women are inferior to White males, and that our cultural

9

10

11

12

institutions subliminally reinforce these notions in many ways, from advertising to loan policies, to work laws, to wages.

No one, of course, would admit to doing this, and some of it may even be subliminal, but the result is that stereotypes about particular people having certain innate characteristics get reinforced. You fill in the blanks: "Asians are smart," "Blacks are good athletes," "Latins are good lovers," etc. We live in a society preconditioned to the suggestion of fixed racial and biological categories. In times of scarcity, these stereotypes often serve as justifications to restrict access to the benefits of society.   *13*

How does this play out in higher education? There is the tendency for elected officials in conservative governments not to put funds where they think they are not going to do any good. This part is fiscal conservatism, but it also reflects a nineteenth-century racialized view of minorities that underlies recent challenges to affirmative action and access to universities—a belief that certain people cannot learn. This viewpoint manifests itself in popular initiatives such as Proposition 209 in California, which incidentally was coordinated by an anthropologist, Glen Custred. It has also been evident in recent cases in Texas and Michigan. I argue that these activities really mask the truth and perpetuate myths about the realities of racism in this country in general and in higher education in particular. Four of these myths are: (1) we don't need help for people of color and women because racism and sexism have ended, (2) university curricula already have been sufficiently broadened, (3) the potential for underrepresented minorities to succeed is limited since they are inherently inferior, and (4) grades and test scores constitute "merit."   *14*

The Role of Higher Education in American Society

The United States was originally founded as a nation that provided educational opportunities for wealthy, elite, White males. Women, people of color, and poor White males were not originally written into the Constitution as full citizens. It took the Thirteenth, Fourteenth, and Fifteenth Amendments for slaves and the Nineteenth Amendment for women to become voters in this country. "Race," class, and gender issues have always been parts of the landscape of American cultures; it is still so today. "Race," class, and gender have also always played roles in higher education in this country. Over the years the development of the U.S. populist notions of higher education took hold in the following ways: *15*

1. The creation of municipal colleges began to address the fact that there were vast numbers of poor, immigrant people who could not afford a college education. (The City College of New York was founded in 1847, although women were not included until 1870, when Hunter College was founded.)   *16*

2. The Morrill Act of 1868 created land-grant colleges and universities. It established state universities that began as resources for farmers, stressing agricultural field stations. Early entrants were farmers, who were not selected against for putative reasons of academic "merit."   *17*

3. With World War II and the G.I. Bill, the federal government once again provided an opportunity for an even wider group of Americans to take advantage of higher education than ever before. These were generally working-class White males and people of color who had served their country in the military and who were rewarded with the opportunity to obtain postsecondary education. My father, for example, was a beneficiary of the G.I. Bill, both to attend refrigeration school and to buy a new house. He   *18*

got his certificate, but he was unable to get a job in his newly acquired trade. This move of millions of Americans into colleges and universities was unprecedented and led to the further democratization of higher education in the U.S.

4. The 1954 *Brown v. Topeka* Supreme Court decision and the Civil Rights Movement of the 1960s for the first time brought Blacks, women, and other underrepresented minorities into universities that had discriminatory admissions policies, especially in the South and in the Southwest.

19

There are over 3,700 institutions of higher education in the United States. From the inception of our populist notions of democracy and education, there has been differential access to them. Sociologists Gunnar Myrdal and W.E.B. Dubois both said that "race" would be the major problem for us to solve in the twentieth century. How does the most successful country in the world step up to the plate to talk about race and to tackle racism at the individual, institutional, and societal levels? If we do not do so, I would suggest, as others do, that our status as a great nation will be diminished. As a nation, we must embrace the diversity that is our destiny. Our universities and colleges are the place to engage the central issues of our cultural variety.

20

The demographics of colleges and universities have changed during the last three decades. For example, the percentage of women attending college in the United States has increased from 44 percent in 1961 to 53 percent in 1991. In 1961 Whites comprised 97 percent of the total college population; in 1994 they comprised only 78 percent. Blacks comprised 2 percent in 1961; in 1994, 12 percent. The number of Latinos attending college has also increased over the past ten years. While women and men had previously been graduating at the same rates, over the past two years, data show that women have now surpassed men in college graduation rates—29 percent versus 26 percent (Day and Curry 1998). Greater access to higher education for minorities has translated into better performance on standard school tests for their children. Grissmer, Kirby, Berends, and Williamson (1994) showed tremendous increases in the verbal and math proficiency scores of Black thirteen-to-seventeen-year-olds between 1970 and 1990 as measured by the National Assessment of Educational Progress (NAEP) Test. While the scores of Whites increased approximately 0.1 standard deviation over that time period, those of Blacks increased by more than 0.6 standard deviations, and those of Hispanic seventeen-year-old students increased 0.2 standard deviations in math and more than 0.5 standard units in verbal skills (Grissmer et al. 1994).

21

Despite these gains, the majority of students of color, when they do go to college, go to community colleges and less-selective four-year colleges and universities. So, if the majority of students of color go on to less-selective colleges and universities, then why is there a need for affirmative action in higher education? Affirmative action came into existence as an Executive Order of the President of the United States to make equal opportunity a reality for those who were not able to immediately step up to the "starting line." President Lyndon Johnson justified the need for affirmative action at a speech at Howard University:

22

> You do not wipe away the scourge of centuries by saying: You are now free to go where you want, and do as you desire.... You do not take a person who for years has been hobbled by chains and liberate him, bring him to the starting line of a race and then say you are free to compete with all of the others, and still justly believe that you have been completely fair. (Citizens' Commission on Civil Rights 1984; quoted in Wightman n.d.:27)

23

Opponents of affirmative action argue that the Civil Rights Movement encouraged us to advocate a color-blind society in exchange for equality. Jones (1997:524)

24

points out that, to the contrary, the Civil Rights Movement actually encouraged the removal of race as a barrier to opportunity and sought to minimize its negative impact. Affirmative action has been highly criticized because of the aggressive racial- and gender-based admissions policies that elite universities have put in place to recruit more students of color and women. If you will recall, back in 1978, in the highly celebrated Bakke decision, the issue revolved around whether a White male, Alan Bakke, had been deprived of a slot in medical school in favor of a less-qualified minority person. In ruling on this case, the Supreme Court said that a college or university could use race as one of many factors in admissions. I remember being at the Stanford University Center for Advanced Studies in the Behavioral Sciences in the summer of 1978, where I participated in a summer program called "Biological Difference and Social Inequality." The Bakke case was very much the topic of conversation. There was a split among the interdisciplinary team of researchers in the program as to whether they supported the idea. Some said that individual merit should count and that, despite past discrimination, "race" (or gender) should not be given preferential consideration in the university admissions process.

Today, twenty-one years later, the concept of affirmative action is just as highly contested with the lawsuits that have been filed in Texas (Hopwood) and in Michigan (Center for Individual Rights). Americans tend to favor the idea of equal opportunity but shy away from and dislike the idea of quotas and preferential treatment. Race and gender should not be given special consideration in admissions according to the Regents of the University of California, as well as other trustees of universities across the country.   25

I propose that both race and class beliefs are operating to help to maintain the status quo of exclusivity as to who goes to elite universities and colleges. In addition to a potential for increased income, graduation from an elite institution bestows upon the graduate the "right" friends, the best networks, the "right" contacts, the "right" job opportunities, and the general ability to develop relationships with people and a lifestyle that spell out "he is upper or upper-middle class" and "he/she fits in." The old cliché, "it's not what you know, it's who you know," takes on added meaning. How you walk and talk, whom you date, what parties you go to, what fraternities you pledge, etc., are often a part of the package you get when you are lucky enough to get into an elite university. I argue that affirmative action measures put White males and to a certain extent White females at a disadvantage when race is taken into account, and White males are likewise somewhat disadvantaged when gender is taken into account. Affirmative action programs create criteria which their networks, alumni, connections, legacy, social milieu, contacts, and parents' donations can't help them under affirmative action, while privilege is disadvantaged. So arguments of "fairness," "color blindness," and "race neutrality" become the buzzwords. Thus White males and females become disadvantaged, discriminated against by the system that has been set up to correct historical systemic discrimination. The sacrosanct ideal of individual rights is being pitted against what is best for the society.   26

Race, Class, and Test Scores

As I stated earlier, in this section I am going to discuss how salient words such as "merit" and "quality" are used in the admissions process and how a single standardized test such as the SAT figures more prominently, not less, in the arguments used by conservatives to describe why minorities are not qualified (read "worthy") to attend elite institutions. The   27

SAT exam and the vocabulary of "worthiness" that tends to be used in connection with it create an artificial environment that reinforces the myth that individual merit and intelligence can only be measured by scores on such tests. The fact that minorities and women consistently do worse on these tests is assumed to mean that there must be some underlying immutable, natural reason for this.

The conservative arguments conveniently tend to ignore that "race" and "racism" are class issues and cut across class barriers as well. Education and money often cannot overcome the discrimination that even wealthy people of color (Blacks, Latinos, and Native Americans) experience in this country (Jones 1997). All group characteristics play a defining role in determining the experience and access to opportunities for an individual. Though this disparity exists across all class levels, the literature shows that the disadvantages of the poor are really exacerbated by race. While it is true that many Euro-American people are poor, it is almost exclusively Latinos and African Americans who live in concentrated poverty (Taylor 1998).

28

The isolated urban ghettos in which poor Blacks and Latinos live present fewer opportunities for educational or economic opportunity than the more economically integrated neighborhoods where low-income Whites tend to live. These neighborhoods where Blacks and Latinos tend to live were created over a long period of time through discriminatory policies and practices (Taylor 1998). The research literature also shows how positive the impact is on low-income minority students who attend school in economically and racially integrated settings. But since Blacks and Latinos tend to live in areas with a high concentration of poverty, the schools they attend tend to afford little or no opportunity for them to receive a superior education. This type of evidence counters the assumption that all low-income children, regardless of "race" or ethnicity, are disadvantaged equally. This is one of the premises underlying replacing the use of "race" with "class" as a plus factor in admissions criteria at the University of California and elsewhere.

29

Merit and Test Scores

Wightman (n.d.) looks at the history of standardized test use and the evolution of tests as the principal screening device in determining admission to higher education. She argues that those who are against affirmative action and other race-conscious policies base their arguments on the common notion that there are concrete ways of measuring merit that are fairly precise and scientific. And they argue that any departures from these supposedly valid tests result in unfair discrimination against individuals who are more deserving. Wightman shows that although a test may be statistically sound, policies based on such narrow definitions of merit tend to exclude students whose qualifications do not give them the experiences they need. These policies reinforce the status quo and continue to create a homogenous student body. Wightman's (n.d.) findings can be summarized as follows:

30

1. Factors that determine *merit* and *capacity for success*—a mixture of ability, talent, and motivation—are *not* measured by standardized tests.

31

2. Misuse of test scores for purposes beyond which they were validated have had a systematic, adverse impact on minority applicants to higher education institutions. There is a consistent difference of one standard deviation between Blacks and Whites, but

32

this difference has not been presented as attributable to environmental factors and says nothing about capacity to achieve if given the opportunity. We are left with the perception that there is something "natural" about the differences.

3. A predictable differential validity exists among the different "racial" and ethnic groups that take these tests. Its origins are unknown. If the source of this differential predictive validity is unknown, then its well-documented existence calls into question the utility of considering the test scores of *all* applicants in a uniform way (especially if the goal is to be inclusive and not exclusive).   *33*

4. Evidence shows that minorities are excluded when only test scores and grade-point averages are given in *substantial numbers*. However, when admitted, despite lower numerical indicators, most students succeeded.   *34*

I argue the point that "merit" is a cultural construct that has historically benefited certain elite people. Merit has always been multidimensional, but it has become more and more unidimensional as it is used to keep the club elite. Bowen and Bok (1998) show that letting minorities in through aggressive affirmative action has worked and worked well in the elite colleges and universities. Though we are only talking about a small group of people who get into these programs, Bowen and Bok's book, *The Shape of the River* (1998), shows that affirmative action policies have worked for the past twenty-five years to bring a small elite group of minorities into the most prestigious colleges and universities in the country. In the final part of the article, I would like to revisit this issue of access to elite universities and colleges.   *35*

Is It Race or Racism?

I have painted a picture in this article that Americans and American popular culture are reinforcing some of the premises that we used in the nineteenth century to justify the social hierarchy and the power base of Europeans in a colonialized world of White landowners, to justify slavery, and later to establish Jim Crow laws in the United States, in order to maintain the status quo of Whites in a social hierarchy that had put them in a privileged position. Those systems of social inequality were maintained through a pervasive and widely held belief that some groups were more wanting than others and that Whites should benefit from their superior *racial* status by having superior social status.   *36*

Today, while it is not quite so blatant, still there is the denial of the continuing impact of institutional racism: policies and practices in every segment of American society that work to keep poor people poor and poor people of color doubly disenfranchised.   *37*

One prime example that I use from my own institution is that since 1847, when the taxpayers of New York City had to support "The Free Academy," which later became City College, there has been a distrust of "those people" and their ability to learn. In the nineteenth century, the immigrants were from Southern and Eastern Europe. Today they are from the world diaspora (especially Latin America, Africa, and Southeast Asia), as well as from the poor neighborhoods of New York City.   *38*

The current anti-affirmative action arguments place the blame on the shoulders of the minority groups, rather than society, to make the claim as to why disparities exist in grades and test scores between people of color (except Asians) and Whites. By ignoring centuries of institutional racism, as well as evidence that discrimination in housing,   *39* employment, health, and education continue to exist, the only supposed causes that are left are biological or natural.

Anthropologists must guard against this tendency in American culture to *not* talk about race and racism. The silence is deafening. How can we as anthropologists participate in the discussions about the importance of diversity and access in higher education? How can we provide opportunities for our students and the public at large to understand difference and differential performance in a nonbiological racialized way? I will discuss these issues in the last section.   *40*

Conclusion

What is it that anthropology brings to the discussion of access, "race," cultural pluralism, and diversity in higher education?   *41*

The first thing we bring to the discussion is a clear articulation for public use of what "race" is and what it is not. Based on the path I have taken with this article, it is clear that we must point out to the general public that the concept of biological "race" no longer exists, that "race" is culturally constructed, and that "racism" is alive and well both in American society in general and in higher education in particular.   *42*

Second, anthropology can provide the lenses through which the country can examine its often paradoxical behavior toward higher education in a democratic society. Is it a public right or a public good? Who should have access to it and under what conditions? From elite universities to open-access institutions, where are the contradictions and paradoxes, what are the policy issues that need to be addressed?   *43*

Third, anthropologists should be able to describe the contemporary culture of education and educational success. In our postcapitalist, consumer-oriented society, what students need to do to be successful is often at odds with what popular culture reinforces. Young people in contemporary American culture are reinforced to be consumers of goods and services, to have a short attention span, and not to want to work hard on homework. Hence, science and mathematics are not pursued in high schools because they are harder and take more time to do the required work. American students, by and large, are not less intelligent than high school students in the countries where more math and science work is required; they are just more lazy and less challenged.   *44*

So, how does this scenario play out along class, race, and ethnic lines?   *45*

Upper- and upper-middle-class students tend to get tutored, mentored, and advised by family members who have gone to college on how to prepare for the SAT and for the college admission process, as well as on how to negotiate the environment once the student gets there.   *46*

First-generation immigrant students present a different picture. They are often successful in secondary and postsecondary school because their families have not been in the United States long enough to have absorbed negative educational value habits. In addition, the families of first-generation immigrant students, while seeking better economic and political conditions, are often slow to give up their own cultural values. So the students often get reinforcement for success from their families' values, rather than negative reinforcement from their peer groups or from society at large. This may also help to explain why certain immigrant groups (such as Asian, Eastern European, South American, and Caribbean students) often do better than students who have spent their lives going through domestic inner-city school systems.   *47*

Working-class students of all ethnicities are at a disadvantage under this system. They are not always challenged or motivated to study because the payoffs (a good college education   *48* and employment) seem far away and there is no clear path for them to see how to achieve them. Working-class students who do make it to university are at risk, because they do not understand the educational culture nor do they have the familial support systems to help them. As a matter of fact, some African American and Latino students have been shown to actually shy away from being seen as successful in high school (Fordham 1996). Colleges and universities that have been successful with this cohort of students have used a variety of measures, including the involvement of peers, faculty, and parents as mentors and role models.

Fourth, we can explain why people are so upset with affirmative action policies that support the ideology of equal opportunity. After all, affirmative action is really only operative in elite institutions, where access to this kind of education is a limited good and where the people who have historically had access are now at a disadvantage under a system of racial/gender preferences. The executive branch of the government has mandated that societal needs override individual "merit" to achieve a level playing field for all citizens. This kind of anthropological analysis challenges biologically deterministic arguments about merit and shows how systems of inequality can construct biological categories to maintain favored position status. Anthropology has a critical role to play in the study of and advocacy for the establishment of a more just American society and culture, one in which diversity is not only accepted but genuinely regarded as a common good.[1]

Note

1. The text of the *JAR* Distinguished Lecture was edited into publishable form by Lawrence Straus.

References Cited

Blakey, M.L., 1987, Skull Doctors: Intrinsic Social and Political Bias in the History of American Physical Anthropology, with Special Reference to the Work of Aleš Hrdlička. Critique of Anthropology 7(2):7–35.

Bowen, W., and D. Bok, 1998, The Shape of the River: Long-Term Consequences of Considering Race in College and University Admissions. Princeton, N.J.: Princeton University Press.

Brace. C.L., 1982, Comment on Redefining Race: The Potential Demise of a Concept in Physical Anthropology. Current Anthropology 23:648–49.

Day, J., and A. Curry, 1998, Educational Attainment in the United States: March 1997. Pp. 20–505 in Current Population Reports: Population Characteristics, Census Bureau. Washington, D.C.: U.S. Department of Commerce, Economic and Statistics Administration.

Fordham, S., 1996, Blacked Out: Dilemmas of Race, Identity and Success at Capital High. Chicago: University of Chicago Press.

Goodman, A., 1996, The Resurrection of Race: The Concept of Race in Physical Anthropology in the 1990s. Pp. 174–86 in Race and Other Misadventures: Essays in Honor of Ashley Montague in His Ninetieth Year (ed. by L.T. Reynolds and L. Lieberman). Dix Hills, N.Y.: General Hall Publishers.

Grissmer, D., S.N. Kirby, M. Berends, and S. Williamson, 1994, Student Achievement and the Changing Family. Santa Monica, Calif.: Rand.

Harrison, F., 1995, The Persistent Power of "Race" in the Cultural and Political Economics of "Racism." Annual Review of Anthropology 24:47–74.

Herrnstein, R.J., and C. Murray, 1994, The Bell Curve: Intelligence and Class Structure in American Life. New York: Free Press.

Jensen, A.R., 1974, How Biased Are Culture Loaded Tests? Genetic Psychology Monographs 90:185–244.

Jones, J.A., 1997, Prejudice and Racism. 2nd ed. New York: McGraw Hill.

Lieberman, L., and F. Jackson, 1995, Race and Three Models of Human Origin. American Anthropologist 97:237–42.

Marks, J., 1995, Human Biodiversity: Genes, Race and History. New York: Aldine de Gruyter.

Mukhopadhyay, C., and Y.T. Moses, 1997, Reestablishing Race in Anthropological Discourse. American Anthropologist 99(3):527–33.

Sacks, K., 1994, How Did Jews Become White Folks? Pp. 78–102 in Race (ed. by S. Gregory and R. Sanjek). New Brunswick, N.J.: Rutgers University Press.

Shanklin, E., 1994, Anthropology and Race. Belmont, Calif.: Wadsworth Publishing.

Shockley, W., 1987, Jensen's Data on Spearman's Hypotheses: No Artifact. Behavioral and Brain Sciences 10:512.

Smedley, A., 1993, Race in North America: Origin and Evolution of a Worldview. Boulder, Colo.: Westview Press.

Taylor, W.L., 1998, Racism and the Poor: Integration and Affirmative Action as Mobility Strategies. In Locked in the Poorhouse: Cities, Race, and Poverty in the United States (ed. by F.R. Harris and L.A. Curtis). Lanham, Md.: Rowman and Littlefield Publishers.

Wightman, L., n.d., Standardized Testing and Equal Access: A Tutorial. In A Compelling Interest: Weighing the Evidence on Racial Dynamics in Higher Education (ed. by M. Chang, D. Witt, J. Jones, and K. Hakuta). Unpublished work in author's possession.

READING FOR CONTENT

1. In the nineteenth century, how did anthropologists attempt to link humans' physical traits with their mental traits along an evolutionary continuum?

2. What are the positive and negative contributions of anthropologists described in paragraph 7 and paragraph 8?

3. According to Moses, how does the anthropological view of race as socially and culturally constructed contrast with the American worldview of race?

4. How does Moses define "racism"?

5. Explain what Moses means when she says, "We live in a society preconditioned to the suggestion of fixed racial and biological categories" (paragraph 13).

6. According to Moses, what four myths hide the reality of racism in higher education (paragraph 14)?

7. Summarize the position Moses takes in paragraph 20.

8. What is the ongoing affirmative action debate in higher education?

9. According to Moses, what are the benefits of attending an elite university?

10. How does Moses explain the phenomenon that, on average, people of color and women do worse on the SAT than European-American males (paragraphs 28–35)?

11. How does Moses define "institutional racism" and what examples of institutional racism does she give?

12. Summarize Moses' explanation of how anthropology can help advance our understanding of the role of diversity in higher education (paragraphs 41–49).

13. Explain what Moses means when she says, "Affirmative action is only operative in elite institutions" (paragraph 49).

READING FOR GENRE, ORGANIZATION, AND STYLISTIC FEATURES

1. The genre of the Moses selection is scholarly research article. What aspects of the article identify it as a piece of academic writing?

2. Since the article is complex, Moses lays out a plan for her readers and uses sequencers and certain words and phrases to focus the readers' attention. Point out the places where Moses provides this assistance to her audience.

3. Moses's article is divided into six major sections. Summarize each section in three sentences or less.

4. Notice the questions Moses poses in paragraphs 3, 4, 12, 14, 22, 40, 41, 43, and 45. Examine each question and comment on the function it serves.

5. Review the five types of claims presented on pages 292–293. Which of these claims is Moses making?

READING FOR RHETORICAL CONTEXT

1. In her first paragraph, how does Moses position herself with respect to her topic and audience?

2. What assumptions does Moses make about the educational level and age of her audience?

3. Turn back to pages 295–303 to review the ethical, emotional, and logical appeals that a writer who is arguing a position can make to his or her readers. Then explain how Moses makes each of these appeals.

WRITING ASSIGNMENTS

1. In paragraph 14, Moses alludes to California's Proposition 209 and movements to ban affirmative action in Texas and Michigan. Research state-level legislation that prohibits the use of sex, race, and ethnicity in making admissions decisions in higher education. Then write an essay explaining how these laws have affected women, black, Latino, and Asian students.

2. Write an essay in which you debunk the four myths (paragraph 14) that perpetuate racism in higher education.

3. Write an essay in response to the following excerpt from paragraph 35 of Moses's article: "I argue the point that 'merit' is a cultural construct that has historically benefited certain elite people."

4. In paragraph 21, Moses notes that the percentage of women enrolled in colleges in the United States increased from 44 percent in 1961 to 53 percent in 1991. Conduct research to see if the gender gap has widened since 1991 or remained the same. Then write an essay describing the trends in enrollment.

5. Do you think American students are "more lazy and less challenged" than students in other countries, and do you agree that "this scenario play(s) out along class, race, and ethnic lines"? Write an essay in which you argue for or against the position Moses takes in paragraphs 44–49.

6. Do you think colleges and universities should change the focus of affirmative action policies away from race to economic class? Write an essay in which you argue your position.

A More Perfect Union

Barack Obama

Barack Obama, a former United States Senator from Illinois, was elected President of the United States in 2008. He was the first African-American to be nominated for the office of president. Mr. Obama was president of the Harvard Law Review *and a member of the Illinois Senate. He is the author of* Dreams from My Father: A Story of Race and Inheritance *(1995) and* The Audacity of Hope: Thoughts on Reclaiming the American Dream *(2006).*

"A More Perfect Union" is a speech Mr. Obama delivered while he was campaigning for president. He delivered it on March 18, 2008, to an audience at the National Constitution Center in Philadelphia, Pennsylvania. The following is the text of that speech provided by his presidential campaign.

Prereading

Read and respond to the opening quotation from the Preamble to the United States Constitution. Do you think the United States is a "perfect union," or are there factions and disunion in our country? Respond in your journal.

"We the people, in order to form a more perfect union."

Two hundred and twenty-one years ago, in a hall that still stands across the street, a group of men gathered and, with these simple words, launched America's improbable experiment in democracy. Farmers and scholars, statesmen and patriots who had traveled across an ocean to escape tyranny and persecution finally made real their declaration of independence at a Philadelphia convention that lasted through the spring of 1787.

The document they produced was eventually signed but ultimately unfinished. It was stained by this nation's original sin of slavery, a question that divided the colonies and brought the convention to a stalemate until the founders chose to allow the slave trade to continue for at least twenty more years, and to leave any final resolution to future generations.

Of course, the answer to the slavery question was already embedded within our Constitution—a Constitution that had at its very core the ideal of equal citizenship under the law; a Constitution that promised its people liberty, and justice, and a union that could be and should be perfected over time.

3

And yet words on a parchment would not be enough to deliver slaves from bondage, or provide men and women of every color and creed their full rights and obligations as citizens of the United States. What would be needed were Americans in successive generations who were willing to do their part—through protests and struggle, on the streets and in the courts, through a civil war and civil disobedience and always at great risk—to narrow that gap between the promise of our ideals and the reality of their time.

4

This was one of the tasks we set forth at the beginning of this campaign—to continue the long march of those who came before us, a march for a more just, more equal, more free, more caring and more prosperous America. I chose to run for the presidency at this moment in history because I believe deeply that we cannot solve the challenges of our time unless we solve them together—unless we perfect our union by understanding that we may have different stories, but we hold common hopes; that we may not look the same and we may not have come from the same place, but we all want to move in the same direction—towards a better future for our children and our grandchildren.

5

This belief comes from my unyielding faith in the decency and generosity of the American people. But it also comes from my own American story.

6

I am the son of a black man from Kenya and a white woman from Kansas. I was raised with the help of a white grandfather who survived a Depression to serve in Patton's Army during World War II and a white grandmother who worked on a bomber assembly line at Fort Leavenworth while he was overseas. I've gone to some of the best schools in America and lived in one of the world's poorest nations. I am married to a black American who carries within her the blood of slaves and slaveowners—an inheritance we pass on to our two precious daughters. I have brothers, sisters, nieces, nephews, uncles and cousins, of every race and every hue, scattered across three continents, and for as long as I live, I will never forget that in no other country on Earth is my story even possible.

7

It's a story that hasn't made me the most conventional candidate. But it is a story that has seared into my genetic makeup the idea that this nation is more than the sum of its parts—that out of many, we are truly one.

8

• • •

[At this point in the speech Obama addressed controversial remarks about race made by his former pastor, Jeremiah Wright.]

The fact is that the comments that have been made and the issues that have surfaced over the last few weeks reflect the complexities of race in this country that we've never really worked through—a part of our union that we have yet to perfect. And if we walk away now, if we simply retreat into our respective corners, we will never be able to come together and solve challenges like health care, or education, or the need to find good jobs for every American.

9

Understanding this reality requires a reminder of how we arrived at this point. As William Faulkner once wrote, "The past isn't dead and buried. In fact, it isn't even past." We do not need to recite here the history of racial injustice in this country. But we do need to remind ourselves that so many of the disparities that exist in the African-American community today

10

can be directly traced to inequalities passed on from an earlier generation that suffered under the brutal legacy of slavery and Jim Crow.

Segregated schools were, and are, inferior schools; we still haven't fixed them, fifty years after *Brown v. Board of Education,* and the inferior education they provided, then and now, helps explain the pervasive achievement gap between today's black and white students.   *11*

Legalized discrimination—where blacks were prevented, often through violence, from owning property, or loans were not granted to African-American business owners, or black homeowners could not access FHA mortgages, or blacks were excluded from unions, or the police force, or fire departments—meant that black families could not amass any meaningful wealth to bequeath to future generations. That history helps explain the wealth and income gap between black and white, and the concentrated pockets of poverty that persists in so many of today's urban and rural communities.   *12*

A lack of economic opportunity among black men, and the shame and frustration that came from not being able to provide for one's family, contributed to the erosion of black families—a problem that welfare policies for many years may have worsened. And the lack of basic services in so many urban black neighborhoods—parks for kids to play in, police walking the beat, regular garbage pick-up and building code enforcement—all helped create a cycle of violence, blight and neglect that continue to haunt us.   *13*

This is the reality in which Reverend Wright and other African-Americans of his generation grew up. They came of age in the late fifties and early sixties, a time when segregation was still the law of the land and opportunity was systematically constricted. What's remarkable is not how many failed in the face of discrimination, but rather how many men and women overcame the odds; how many were able to make a way out of no way for those like me who would come after them.   *14*

But for all those who scratched and clawed their way to get a piece of the American Dream, there were many who didn't make it—those who were ultimately defeated, in one way or another, by discrimination. That legacy of defeat was passed on to future generations—those young men and increasingly young women who we see standing on street corners or languishing in our prisons, without hope or prospects for the future. Even for those blacks who did make it, questions of race, and racism, continue to define their worldview in fundamental ways. For the men and women of Reverend Wright's generation, the memories of humiliation and doubt and fear have not gone away; nor has the anger and the bitterness of those years. That anger may not get expressed in public, in front of white co-workers or white friends. But it does find voice in the barbershop or around the kitchen table. At times, that anger is exploited by politicians, to gin up votes along racial lines, or to make up for a politician's own failings.   *15*

And occasionally it finds voice in the church on Sunday morning, in the pulpit and in the pews. The fact that so many people are surprised to hear that anger in some of Reverend Wright's sermons simply reminds us of the old truism that the most segregated hour in American life occurs on Sunday morning. That anger is not always productive; indeed, all too often it distracts attention from solving real problems; it keeps us from squarely facing our own complicity in our condition, and prevents the African-American community from forging the alliances it needs to bring about real change. But the anger is real; it is powerful; and to simply wish it away, to condemn it without understanding its roots, only serves to widen the chasm of misunderstanding that exists between the races.   *16*

In fact, a similar anger exists within segments of the white community. Most working- and middle-class white Americans don't feel that they have been particularly   *17* privileged by their race. Their experience is the immigrant experience—as far as they're concerned, no one's handed them anything, they've built it from scratch. They've worked hard all their lives, many times only to see their jobs shipped overseas or their pension dumped after a lifetime of labor. They are anxious about their futures, and feel their dreams slipping away; in an era of stagnant wages and global competition, opportunity comes to be seen as a zero sum game, in which your dreams come at my expense. So when they are told to bus their children to a school across town; when they hear that an African American is getting an advantage in landing a good job or a spot in a good college because of an injustice that they themselves never committed; when they're told that their fears about crime in urban neighborhoods are somehow prejudiced, resentment builds over time.

Like the anger within the black community, these resentments aren't always expressed in polite company. But they have helped shape the political landscape for at least a generation. Anger over welfare and affirmative action helped forge the Reagan Coalition. Politicians routinely exploited fears of crime for their own electoral ends. Talk show hosts and conservative commentators built entire careers unmasking bogus claims of racism while dismissing legitimate discussions of racial injustice and inequality as mere political correctness or reverse racism.   18

Just as black anger often proved counterproductive, so have these white resentments distracted attention from the real culprits of the middle class squeeze—a corporate culture rife with inside dealing, questionable accounting practices, and short-term greed; a Washington dominated by lobbyists and special interests; economic policies that favor the few over the many. And yet, to wish away the resentments of white Americans, to label them as misguided or even racist, without recognizing they are grounded in legitimate concerns— this too widens the racial divide, and blocks the path to understanding.   19

This is where we are right now. It's a racial stalemate we've been stuck in for years. Contrary to the claims of some of my critics, black and white, I have never been so naïve as to believe that we can get beyond our racial divisions in a single election cycle, or with a single candidacy—particularly a candidacy as imperfect as my own.   20

But I have asserted a firm conviction—a conviction rooted in my faith in God and my faith in the American people—that working together we can move beyond some of our old racial wounds, and that in fact we have no choice if we are to continue on the path of a more perfect union.   21

For the African-American community, that path means embracing the burdens of our past without becoming victims of our past. It means continuing to insist on a full measure of justice in every aspect of American life. But it also means binding our particular grievances—for better health care, and better schools, and better jobs—to the larger aspirations of all Americans—the white woman struggling to break the glass ceiling, the white man who's been laid off, the immigrant trying to feed his family. And it means taking full responsibility for our own lives—by demanding more from our fathers, and spending more time with our children, and reading to them, and teaching them that while they may face challenges and discrimination in their own lives, they must never succumb to despair or cynicism; they must always believe that they can write their own destiny.   22

Ironically, this quintessentially American—and yes, conservative—notion of self-help found frequent expression in Reverend Wright's sermons. But what my former pastor too   23 often failed to understand is that embarking on a program of self-help also requires a belief that society can change.

The profound mistake of Reverend Wright's sermons is not that he spoke about *24* racism in our society. It's that he spoke as if our society was static; as if no progress has been made; as if this country—a country that has made it possible for one of his own members to run for the highest office in the land and build a coalition of white and black, Latino and Asian, rich and poor, young and old—is still irrevocably bound to a tragic past. But what we know—what we have seen—is that America can change. That is true genius of this nation. What we have already achieved gives us hope—the audacity to hope—for what we can and must achieve tomorrow.

In the white community, the path to a more perfect union means acknowledging that *25* what ails the African-American community does not just exist in the minds of black people; that the legacy of discrimination—and current incidents of discrimination, while less overt than in the past—are real and must be addressed. Not just with words, but with deeds—by investing in our schools and our communities; by enforcing our civil rights laws and ensuring fairness in our criminal justice system; by providing this generation with ladders of opportunity that were unavailable for previous generations. It requires all Americans to realize that your dreams do not have to come at the expense of my dreams; that investing in the health, welfare, and education of black and brown and white children will ultimately help all of America prosper.

In the end, then, what is called for is nothing more, and nothing less, than what all *26* the world's great religions demand—that we do unto others as we would have them do unto us. Let us be our brother's keeper, Scripture tells us. Let us be our sister's keeper. Let us find that common stake we all have in one another, and let our politics reflect that spirit as well.

For we have a choice in this country. We can accept a politics that breeds division, and *27* conflict, and cynicism. We can tackle race only as spectacle—as we did in the OJ trial—or in the wake of tragedy, as we did in the aftermath of Katrina—or as fodder for the nightly news. We can play Reverend Wright's sermons on every channel, every day and talk about them from now until the election, and make the only question in this campaign whether or not the American people think that I somehow believe or sympathize with his most offensive words. We can pounce on some gaffe by a Hillary supporter as evidence that she's playing the race card, or we can speculate on whether white men will all flock to John McCain in the general election regardless of his policies.

We can do that. *28*

But if we do, I can tell you that in the next election, we'll be talking about some other *29* distraction. And then another one. And then another one. And nothing will change.

That is one option. Or, at this moment, in this election, we can come together and say, *30* "Not this time." This time we want to talk about the crumbling schools that are stealing the future of black children and white children and Asian children and Hispanic children and Native American children. This time we want to reject the cynicism that tells us that these kids can't learn; that those kids who don't look like us are somebody else's problem. The children of America are not those kids, they are our kids, and we will not let them fall behind in a 21st century economy. Not this time.

This time we want to talk about how the lines in the Emergency Room are filled with *31* whites and blacks and Hispanics who do not have health care; who don't have the power on their own to overcome the special interests in Washington, but who can take them on if we do it together.

This time we want to talk about the shuttered mills that once provided a decent life for men and women of every race, and the homes for sale that once belonged to Americans from every religion, every region, every walk of life. This time we want to talk about the fact that the real problem is not that someone who doesn't look like you might take your job; it's that the corporation you work for will ship it overseas for nothing more than a profit. *32*

This time we want to talk about the men and women of every color and creed who serve together, and fight together, and bleed together under the same proud flag. We want to talk about how to bring them home from a war that never should've been authorized and never should've been waged, and we want to talk about how we'll show our patriotism by caring for them, and their families, and giving them the benefits they have earned. *33*

I would not be running for President if I didn't believe with all my heart that this is what the vast majority of Americans want for this country. This union may never be perfect, but generation after generation has shown that it can always be perfected. And today, whenever I find myself feeling doubtful or cynical about this possibility, what gives me the most hope is the next generation—the young people whose attitudes and beliefs and openness to change have already made history in this election. *34*

There is one story in particularly that I'd like to leave you with today—a story I told when I had the great honor of speaking on Dr. King's birthday at his home church, Ebenezer Baptist, in Atlanta. *35*

There is a young, twenty-three-year-old white woman named Ashley Baia who organized for our campaign in Florence, South Carolina. She had been working to organize a mostly African-American community since the beginning of this campaign, and one day she was at a roundtable discussion where everyone went around telling their story and why they were there. *36*

And Ashley said that when she was nine years old, her mother got cancer. And because she had to miss days of work, she was let go and lost her health care. They had to file for bankruptcy, and that's when Ashley decided that she had to do something to help her mom. *37*

She knew that food was one of their most expensive costs, and so Ashley convinced her mother that what she really liked and really wanted to eat more than anything else was mustard and relish sandwiches. Because that was the cheapest way to eat. *38*

She did this for a year until her mom got better, and she told everyone at the roundtable that the reason she joined our campaign was so that she could help the millions of other children in the country who want and need to help their parents too. *39*

Now Ashley might have made a different choice. Perhaps somebody told her along the way that the source of her mother's problems were blacks who were on welfare and too lazy to work, or Hispanics who were coming into the country illegally. But she didn't. She sought out allies in her fight against injustice. *40*

Anyway, Ashley finishes her story and then goes around the room and asks everyone else why they're supporting the campaign. They all have different stories and reasons. Many bring up a specific issue. And finally they come to this elderly black man who's been sitting there quietly the entire time. And Ashley asks him why he's there. And he does not bring up a specific issue. He does not say health care or the economy. He does not say education or the *41* war. He does not say that he was there because of Barack Obama. He simply says to everyone in the room, "I am here because of Ashley."

"I'm here because of Ashley." By itself, that single moment of recognition between that young white girl and that old black man is not enough. It is not enough to give health care to the sick, or jobs to the jobless, or education to our children.   42

But it is where we start. It is where our union grows stronger. And as so many generations have come to realize over the course of the two hundred and twenty-one years since a band of patriots signed that document in Philadelphia, that is where the perfection begins.   43

READING FOR CONTENT

1. How was the Constitution "stained by this nation's original sin of slavery"?
2. Explain what Mr. Obama means when he says, "[T]he most segregated hour in American life occurs on Sunday morning" (paragraph 16).
3. Explain the ways in which both black anger and white anger have been counterproductive.
4. A controversy over Mr. Obama's pastor, Jeremiah Wright, prompted him to make this speech. What is his criticism of Reverend Wright in paragraphs 22, 23, and 24?
5. In paragraphs 30 to 33, Mr. Obama outlines his platform. What are the changes he pledged to make as president of the United States?
6. Summarize the story Mr. Obama tells at the end of the speech and explain how it supports his central position.

READING FOR GENRE, ORGANIZATION, AND STYLISTIC FEATURES

1. How does the opening quotation from the Constitution set the stage for the theme of the speech?
2. Cite the places where Mr. Obama threads this theme throughout the speech.
3. What is the function of paragraphs 11–13? What would be lost if Mr. Obama had omitted them from the speech?
4. Throughout the speech, Mr. Obama uses parallelism in his sentences. For an example, look at paragraph 17:

   > So when they are told to bus their children to a school across town; when they hear that an African American is getting an advantage in landing a good job or a spot in a good college because of an injustice that they themselves never committed; when they're told that their fears about crime in urban neighborhoods are somehow prejudiced, resentment builds over time.

   Point to other passages where effective parallelism is used.
5. Cite the paragraphs in which Mr. Obama compares and contrasts the experiences and attitudes of blacks and whites.
6. In paragraphs 30 to 33, what effect does Mr. Obama achieve by repeating the phrase, "This time"? Cite other places in the speech where he uses repetition.
7. What is the function of paragraphs 35–42? Why do you think Mr. Obama left this story to the end of the speech?

READING FOR RHETORICAL CONTEXT

1. Explain the significance of the setting of the speech: the National Constitution Center in Philadelphia, Pennsylvania.

2. In paragraph 7, Mr. Obama explains that he is half white and half black: "I am the son of a black man from Kenya and a white woman from Kansas." What effect will paragraph 7 have on his audience? Throughout the speech, how does he speak to people of both races?

3. What does the speech reveal about Mr. Obama's religious and spiritual values? Cite passages to support your opinion.

WRITING ASSIGNMENTS

1. Write an essay about your own personal experiences with racism and explain whether or not racism still manifests itself today.

2. How were slaves shortchanged by the Constitution? Do research on how the members of the Constitutional Convention handled the issue of slavery and explain the compromises that were made.

3. Using the speech as your base, write an essay in response to the following quotation from paragraph 25: "['A More Perfect Union'] requires all Americans to realize that your dreams do not have to come at the expense of my dreams."

4. Writing about "A More Perfect Union," George Lakoff, a renowned linguist who is the Goldman Distinguished Professor of Cognitive Science Linguistics at the University of California, states:

   > What makes this great speech great is that it transcends its immediate occasion and addresses in its form as well as its words the most vital of issues: what America is about; who are, and are to be, as Americans; and what politics should be fundamentally about.

   Using Lakoff's comment as your base, write an essay in which you analyze Mr. Obama's speech.

5. Mr. Obama's "A More Perfect Union" has been compared to "I Have a Dream" by Martin Luther King, Jr. (August 28, 1963). Write an essay in which you compare the two speeches. The text of "I Have a Dream" is available at www.stanford.edu/group/King/publications/speeches/address_at_march_on_washington.pdf. You can view both speeches on YouTube. Barack Obama's is available at http://www.youtube.com/watch?v=pWe7wTVbLUU and Martin Luther King's at http://www.youtube.com/watch?v=iEMXaTktUfA.

WRITING ASSIGNMENTS FOR CHAPTER 14

1. In "Race, Higher Education, and American Society," Yolanda Moses writes, "'Racism'—the attitudinal, behavioral, and institutional manifestation of the American racial ideology—continues to be pervasive in American society" (paragraph 10). Write an essay in which

you describe the extent to which Barack Obama would agree or disagree with this statement. Before you begin your essay, review the section on comparing and contrasting sources in Chapter 7, pages 228–248.

2. In "Race, Higher Education, and American Society," Yolanda Moses asks, "How does the most successful country in the world step up to the plate to talk about race and to tackle racism at the individual, institutional, and societal levels?" (paragraph 20). Drawing on Moses's article, Barack Obama's "A More Perfect Union," and your own experiences and ideas, write an essay in which you answer this question. Refer to the "Writing a Synthesis for a Specific Purpose," pages 264–276.

3. Both Moses and Obama criticize the media for "unmasking bogus claims of racism" (Obama, paragraph 18) and treating race "as if it were an operative biological phenomenon" (Moses, paragraph 10). Do you think the media have an accurate understanding of race? Does media coverage play up racial stereotypes? Conduct research and write an essay on the mainstream media's coverage of race. Consult Chapter 9, Researching Sources and Writing Research Papers.

4. Both Moses and Obama discuss systemic or institutional racism. Moses considers the use of standardized testing to be a form of institutional racism. Obama cites factors such as segregated schools and legalized discrimination. Using the two selections in this chapter as your base, write an essay in which you compare institutional racism to the bigotry and bias of racist individuals.

5. Moses observes that there is a "tendency in American culture to *not* talk about race and racism." She says, "The silence is deafening" (paragraph 40). Write an essay in which you explain how Barack Obama has broken the silence and spoken candidly about many of the issues in Moses's article.

APPENDIX A

Documenting Sources

MLA DOCUMENTATION STYLE

Chapters 3–8 contain essays written according to the MLA (Modern Language Association) rules for page format (margins, page numbering, titles, and so forth) and source documentation. In addition to providing many examples that illustrate MLA style, we describe MLA guidelines for using parenthetical documentation to cite sources that you summarize (86–87), paraphrase (97), or quote (104–109) and for constructing a works cited list (87–88). As a college student, you may need to document materials that differ from our earlier examples. The first section of the appendix is an MLA "quick guide" that includes examples of how to document the types of sources that students use most often in academic papers. For an exhaustive discussion of MLA documentation style, see the *MLA Manual and Guide to Scholarly Publishing*, 3rd edition.

MLA QUICK GUIDE

The following examples illustrate how to document in MLA style the types of sources that most often appear in college students' essays.

Printed Books

Book with one author

> Brody, Miriam. *Manly Writing: Gender, Rhetoric, and the Rise of Composition*. Carbondale: Southern Illinois UP, 1993. Print.

Two or more books by the same author (alphabetize by title)

> Kennedy, William J. *Jacopo Sannazaro and the Uses of the Pastoral*. Hanover: UP of New England, 1983. Print.

> ---. *Rhetorical Norms in Renaissance Literature*. New Haven: Yale UP, 1978. Print.

Book with two authors

> Kramnick, Isaac, and R. Laurence Moore. *The Godless Constitution: The Case against Religious Correctness.* New York: Norton, 1996. Print.

Article, essay, poem, or short story that is reprinted in an edited textbook anthology, after appearing initially in a periodical

> Vogel, Steven. "Grades and Money." *Dissent* Fall 1997: 102-4. Rpt. in *Reading and Writing in the Academic Community.* 3rd ed. Ed. Mary Lynch Kennedy and Hadley M. Smith. Upper Saddle River: Pearson, 2006. 445-48. Print.

Article, essay, poem, or short story that appears in print for the first time in an edited anthology

> McPherson, Diane. "Adrienne Rich." *Contemporary Lesbian Writers of the United States: A Bio-Bibliographical Critical Sourcebook.* Ed. Sandra Pollack and Denise D. Knight. Westport: Greenwood, 1993. 433-45. Print.

Section, chapter, article, essay, poem, short story, or play in a book with one author

> Brown, Cory. "Drought." *A Warm Trend.* Wesley Chapel: Swallow's Tale, 1989. 29. Print.

Signed article in a reference work

> Flanagan, David. "Carver, Wayman (Alexander)." *New Grove Dictionary of Jazz.* 2nd ed. 2002. Print.

Printed Periodicals

Article, essay, poem, or short story in an academic or professional journal

> Mirskin, Jerry. "Writing as a Process of Valuing." *College Composition and Communication* 46.3 (1995): 387-410. Print.

Article, essay, poem, or short story in a magazine

> Quindlen, Anna. "Disinvited to the Party." *Newsweek* 3 Sept. 2007: 68. Print.

Article in a newspaper

> Henderson, Dave. "It's All About Respect." *Ithaca Journal* 12 Dec. 2002: 9B. Print.

Online Sources

Magazine or journal article obtained through a library-based online subscription service

> Scott, Sarah. "Do Grades Really Matter?" *Maclean's* 10 Sept. 2007:
>   35-36. *General OneFile.* Web. 3 Aug. 2008.

Periodical available online

> Kerr, Tom. "Buried Alive on San Quentin's Death Row." *Counterpunch*
>   4 Sept. 2007: n.p. Web. 11 Aug. 2008.

Document on organization's Web site

> Jackson, Jerome A. "Ivory-Billed Woodpecker (Campephilis principalis)."
>   *The Birds of North American Online.* Cornell Lab of Ornithology.
>   N.d. Web. 2 Aug. 2008.

Personal Web site

> Smith, Colin. Home page. *Outpoor: The Colin Smith Site.* N.p. 2004-07.
>   Web. 8 Aug. 2008.

Document available on the Web that would be difficult to locate without having the URL

> Mulvey, Laura. "Visual Pleasure and Narrative Cinema," *Screen* 16.3
>   Autumn 1975. 6-18. Web. 20 November 2008. <https://wiki.brown.edu/
>   confluence/display/MarkTribe/Visual+Pleasure+and+Narrative+Cinema>.

Other Common Sources

College Course

> Mahan, Katharyn Howd. Poetry II. Ithaca College, Ithaca. 14 April
>   2008. Lecture.

Film

> *Juno.* Dir. Jason Reitman. Fox Searchlight, 2007. Film.

Television or radio program

> "Court Silences MIT Students Over Subway Hacking" Narr. Melissa Block
>   and Robert Siegel. *All Things Considered.* Natl. Public Radio.
>   WEOS, Geneva, 11 Aug. 2008. Radio.

Interview

> Hall, Donald. Personal interview. 19 Apr. 2001.
>
> Grahn, Judy. Telephone interview. 23 Mar. 2000.

Performance of music, dance, or drama

> Chick Corea Electrik Band. Dir. Chick Corea. Bailey Hall, Cornell U.,
>   Ithaca. 15 Oct. 1985. Performance.

Public Presentation

> Wang, Jack. "Castrated Fathers: The Anxiety of Male Authorship in
>   Asian American Literature." Northeast Modern Language Association
>   Conference. Cambridge. April 2005. Panel.

Recording: CD

> Cohen, Leonard. *Ten New Songs.* Sony, 2001. CD.

APA DOCUMENTATION STYLE

While MLA documentation style is an important standard in the humanities, APA (American Psychological Association) style is used widely in the social sciences. APA style differs from MLA style in many details, but both share the basic principles of including source names and page numbers (APA also adds the publication date) in parentheses within the text of the paper and of listing complete publication information for each source in an alphabetized list. Below is a point-by-point comparison of APA and MLA styles. For a complete explanation of APA style, consult the *Publication Manual of the American Psychological Association,* 5th edition.

COMPARISON OF MLA AND APA DOCUMENTATION STYLES

MLA

> The question has been answered before (O'Connor 140-43).
>
> O'Connor has already answered the question (140-43).

APA

> The question has been answered before (O'Connor, 2002, pp. 140-143).
>
> O'Connor (2002) has already answered the question (pp. 140-143).

APA parenthetical citations include the year of publication; provide the abbreviations p. or pp., which stand for page or pages; and include the redundant hundreds digit in final page numbers. Commas separate authors, years, and page numbers.

MLA

> Jones originally supported the single-factor explanation ("Infant
> Sensory") but later realized that the phenomenon was more complex
> ("New Theory").

APA

> Jones originally supported the single-factor explanation (2001)
> but later realized that the phenomenon was more complex (2007).

In MLA parenthetical citations, abbreviated titles are used to distinguish between different works by the same author, while APA uses year of publication to make that distinction.

MLA

```
                            Works Cited
   Dyson, Michael Eric. "The Blame Game." Time 30 June 2008: 38. Print.
   Katz, Michael B., and Mark J. Stern. "American Families: Changes in the
        Twentieth Century." Dissent Fall 2007: 90-92. Proquest Research
        Library. Web. 6 Oct. 2008.
   Poponoe, David. (1999). "Can the Nuclear Family Be Revived?" Society,
        36.5 (1999): 28-30. SocINDEX. Web. 9 Oct. 2008.
```

APA

```
                            References
   Dyson, M. E. (2008, June 30). The blame game. Time, 171, 38.
   Katz, M. B., & Stern, M. J. (2007, Fall). American families: Changes in
        the twentieth century. Dissent, 54(4), 90-92. Retrieved October 6,
        2008, from Proquest Research Library database.
   Poponoe, D. (1999). Can the nuclear family be revived? Society, 36(5),
        28-30. Retrieved October 9, 2008, from SocINDEX database.
```

- For **MLA** style papers title the source page "Works Cited," whereas in **APA** style papers title the page "References."
- For **Works Cited** lists, include authors' complete names; for **References** lists, use only authors' last names and first and middle initials.
- For **Works Cited** lists, when there are two or more authors, invert the first author's name, insert a comma and the word "and," and give the second author's first name and surname in the common order. For **References** lists, when there are two or more authors, invert all the names. After the first author's name, insert a comma and an ampersand (&).
- For **Works Cited** lists, capitalize major words in the titles of books and periodicals and use italics for all words in those titles. For **References** lists, capitalize only the first word and all proper nouns of the titles (and subtitles) of books. Capitalize all major words in the titles of periodicals. Use italics for book and periodical titles.
- For **Works Cited** lists, provide book data in the following sequence: author, title of book, city of publication, shortened form of the publisher's name, date of publication. For **References** lists, provide book data in the following sequence: author, date of publication, title of the book, place of publication, publisher.
- For **Works Cited** lists provide journal article data in the following sequence: author, title of the article, title of the journal, volume number, date of publication, inclusive pages. For **References** lists, provide journal article data in the following sequence: author, date of publication, title of the article, title of the journal, volume number, inclusive pages.

APPENDIX B

Editing for Correctness

SENTENCE STRUCTURE

CLAUSES AND SENTENCES

All sentences are made up of subjects and verbs. The *subject* is the part of the sentence that names someone or something: the doer. The *verb* is the part that states, asserts, or

485

predicates something about the subject: that tells what the doer does. The word *predicate* means to proclaim, affirm, or state an attribute or quality. That's why the verb is sometimes called the *predicate* or *predicate verb*. Let's say we are writing about Sherry Turkle, one of the authors whose work appears in Chapter 11 of this book. *Sherry Turkle* is our subject. What do we want to proclaim about Turkle? She writes about machine-human interaction. Our sentence becomes

Sherry Turkle writes about machine-human interaction.

Another name for this brief sentence is an *independent clause.*

All clauses have subjects and predicates, but only some clauses are sentences. To qualify as a bona fide sentence, a clause has to express a complete thought; for example, *Sherry Turkle writes about machine-human interaction.* We call this an *independent clause,* and to show that it is self-contained, we begin it with a capital letter and end it with a period.

Sentences may contain more than one independent clause, as the examples by Stephen Vogel and Jerry Farber illustrate.

Vogel

I imagined my own college's program turned into national policy, and I blanched. (392)

Farber

Self-discipline isn't staying up all night to finish a term paper; that's slave work. (386)

Vogel combines or coordinates his independent clauses with a *coordinating conjunction* preceded by a comma, and Farber joins his with a semicolon. Perhaps you once learned FANBOYS as a mnemonic device for remembering the seven coordination conjunctions: *for, and, nor, but, or, yet, so.*

Note that conjunctions do not always signal a clause boundary. Each of the following sentences contains only one clause:

Sherry Turkle and her associates write about machine-human interaction.

Sherry Turkle writes and lectures about machine-human interaction.

Sherry Turkle and her associates write and lecture about machine-human interaction.

Sherry Turkle and her associates is a compound subject, meaning that it includes two or more elements that are the actors in the sentence. Similarly, *writes and lectures about machine-human interaction* is a compound verb, since two or more actions are described by the sentence.

A clause with a compound subject or verb implies two or more simpler clauses:

Compound:	Sherry Turkle and her associates write about machine-human interaction.
Implied clause:	Sherry Turkle writes about machine-human interaction.
Implied clause:	Sherry Turkle's associates write about machine-human interaction.

A clause that has a compound subject or compound verb is still considered a single clause even though it implies two or more simple clauses.

Sentences may also contain an independent clause and one or more additional clauses called *dependent clauses*. These clauses are called *dependent* because they depend on the independent or main clause for their existence. Without the independent clause, they make no sense. Consider Farber's sentence from page 386:

> If movie-going, dancing, and surfing were the only required subjects, there might be a poetic renaissance.

If Farber isolated the independent clause, it would still make sense to us.

> There might be a poetic renaissance.

If he broke off the dependent clause, we would be baffled.

> If movie-going, dancing, and surfing were the only required subjects.

We would ask, "What would happen if movie-going, dancing, and surfing were the only required subjects?" It is easy to identify a dependent clause because it begins with a *subordinating conjunction,* such as the word *if* in the above example. *Sub* means *under* in Latin, so you can think of the subordinating conjunction and dependent clause as being under the control of the independent clause. The most frequently used subordinating conjunctions are *after, although, as, as if, as long as, as much as, as soon as, as though, because, before, even if, even though, how, if, inasmuch, in order that, now that, since, so that, than, that, though, unless, until, when, whenever, where, whereas, wherever, whether, while.* See if you can find the subordinating conjunctions and dependent clauses in other Farber sentences.

> When the term is over, you shuffle the deck and begin a new round.

> Learning happens when you want to learn.

> Countless employers, public and private, require a college degree for no really good reason, simply because it enables their personnel departments to avoid making any meaningful individual evaluations and because it indicates some degree of standardization.

Whenever you use a subordinating conjunction to form a dependent clause, make sure you connect the dependent clause to an independent clause. If you don't, you will produce a sentence fragment. We give you tips for avoiding fragments later in this section.

At this point, we analyze the structure of more complicated sentences. Here is one a student wrote in an essay about public school drug-testing policies:

> Drug testing advocates feel that extracurricular activities are privileges, not rights, so if students want to participate, they must abide by all school district rules and policies, including drug tests.

The first step is to see if there is more than one independent clause. The tip-off is the presence of a coordinating conjunction or a semicolon. The sentence contains the coordinating conjunction *so* preceded by a comma. Since coordinating conjunctions join independent clauses of equal weight, the clauses on each side of *so* could be written as separate sentences.

> Drug testing advocates feel that extracurricular activities are privileges, not rights. If students want to participate, they must abide by all school district rules and policies, including drug tests.

Next, study the two sentences we isolated above to see if they contain any dependent clauses. Here, your signal is a subordinating conjunction (see the list of subordinating conjunctions on page 487). The first sentence contains *that,* and the second begins with *if.*

> Drug testing advocates feel that extracurricular activities are privileges, not rights.

> If students want to participate, they must abide by all school district rules and policies, including drug tests.

So, all told, the student's sentence is composed of two independent and two dependent clauses:

- Drug testing advocates feel (independent)
- that extracurricular activities are privileges, not rights (dependent)
- if students want to participate (dependent)
- they must abide by all school district rules and policies, including drug tests (independent)

Sentence Fragments

(Make sure you understand the earlier section on clauses and sentences before you read this material.)

A *sentence fragment* looks like a sentence in that it starts with a capital letter and ends with a period, but it does not contain an independent clause and thus is not a correct sentence. The most common type of fragment is a dependent clause masquerading as a full-blown sentence. Two cues enable us to see through this disguise: the fragment begins with a subordinating conjunction, and it is not attached to an independent clause. Here is an excerpt from a student paper:

```
Police search teenagers more frequently than adults. Because
teenagers are perceived as more likely to violate the law and less
likely to have the power to resist searches.
```

The first sentence is a short, independent clause that can stand alone. Now read the second, longer sentence aloud. The subordinating conjunction *because* is a red flag, so right off, you know the sentence is a dependent clause. Taken by itself, it states a cause but doesn't give an effect. You're shaking your head asking, "Because teens are perceived this way, what happens?" You can fix the error either by removing the subordinating conjunction or by attaching the dependent clause to the independent clause in the preceding sentence.

> Police search teenagers more frequently than adults. Teenagers are perceived as more likely to violate the law and less likely to have the power to resist searches.

> Police search teenagers more frequently than adults because teenagers are perceived as more likely to violate the law and less likely to have the power to resist searches.

Fragments can be difficult to detect because, as you saw in the above excerpt, they don't sound wrong when you read them in context. You have to read them separately to detect the problem. In the context of a paragraph, a fragment may make perfect sense and not stand out as incomplete. Nonetheless, we can give you advice for identifying fragments: start at the end of your paper and work backwards as you proofread. This practice breaks up the flow of thought and helps you to think about each sentence in isolation rather than in context.

The most common ways to repair a sentence fragment are to combine the fragment with a nearby sentence that contains an independent clause or to convert the fragment into a grammatically complete sentence by eliminating the subordinating conjunction. See how these two solutions apply to the fragment in the following example.

Original

Some say that cloning is acceptable as long as it is only for research. While others say that cloning is useful to create replacement organs.

Solution 1, Sentence Combining

Some say that cloning is acceptable as long as it is only for research, while others say that cloning is useful to create replacement organs.

Solution 2, Eliminate the Subordinating Conjunction

Some say that cloning is acceptable as long as it is only for research. Others say that it is useful to create replacement organs.

Run-On Sentences and Comma Splices

(Make sure you understand the earlier section on clauses and sentences before you read this material.)

Separate your independent clauses with periods, semicolons, coordinating conjunctions, or conjunctive adverbs. If you don't, you will write run-on sentences or comma splices. Run-on sentences, also called fused sentences, occur when two independent clauses are lumped together with nothing separating them.

Economic pressures compel college students to enter the work force after graduation few go directly on to pursue advanced degrees.

Comma splices occur when two independent clauses are tied together with a comma.

Economic pressures compel college students to enter the work force after graduation, few go directly on to pursue advanced degrees.

Notice that the second independent clause begins with a pronoun. To avoid sounding repetitive, the writer uses *few* to stand for *college students*. The writer doesn't realize that *few* has become the legitimate subject of an independent clause: "Few go directly on to pursue advanced degrees."

What is the motivation for the comma splice? The writer may think that because the ideas in the two independent clauses are closely related, she should separate them with a comma, a punctuation mark that is less emphatic than a period. Commas are not strong enough to separate independent clauses, however. The writer should have used a semicolon. A semicolon is strong enough to be used in place of a period; a comma is not.

> Economic pressures compel college students to enter the work force after graduation; few go directly on to pursue advanced degrees.

Three other ways to fix run-on sentences and comma splices are to join the independent clauses with a coordinating conjunction, link them with a conjunctive adverb, or combine them after converting one of the clauses to a dependent clause.

Coordinating conjunction Choosing from among FANBOYS *(for, and, nor, but, or, yet, so)*, the most appropriate conjunction is *so*.

> Economic pressures compel college students to enter the work force after graduation, so few go directly on to pursue advanced degrees.

Conjunctive adverb *Conjunctive adverbs* are words or phrases that join two independent clauses. They are usually preceded by a semicolon and followed by a comma. Common conjunctive adverbs are *accordingly, also, alternatively, as a result, besides, consequently, for example, for instance, furthermore, hence, however, in addition, indeed, in fact, instead, meanwhile, moreover, nevertheless, of course, on the other hand, otherwise, then, therefore, thus*. The most logical connectors for our sample sentence are *hence, consequently, therefore,* and *as a result*.

> Economic pressures compel college students to enter the work force after graduation; therefore, few go directly on to pursue advanced degrees.

Conversion of independent clause to dependent clause To make one independent clause subordinate to another independent clause, select an appropriate subordinating conjunction and use it to head up the dependent clause. See the list of subordinating conjunctions on page 487.

> Since economic pressures compel college students to enter the work force after graduation, few go directly on to pursue advanced degrees.

If you wish, you can move the clauses around.

> Few college students go directly on to pursue advanced degrees because of economic pressures.

To summarize, we have discussed five ways to correct run-ons and comma splices.

1. Write each independent clause as a sentence.
2. Join the independent clauses with a semicolon.
3. Join the independent clauses with a coordinating conjunction.
4. Join the independent clauses with a conjunctive adverb.
5. Convert one of the clauses to a dependent clause.

All five options are legitimate, but one may be preferable to another depending on the context and the relationship you want to express.

A common misconception is that the number of words in a sentence plays a role in determining whether it is a run-on, a comma splice, or a grammatically correct structure. But consider the following examples:

Grammatically Correct Sentence

While it could be argued that sentencing violent youthful offenders as adults is a more effective deterrent than sending them to the juvenile justice system where they may get a mere slap on the wrist, incarcerating young people in adult prisons lessens significantly their chances of receiving rehabilitation services and developing into productive citizens.

Comma Splice

Many youth commit serious crimes, they deserve adult sentences.

You can't use sentence length to judge whether or not a sentence is grammatically correct. You must analyze its clause structure.

ELLIPTICAL CONSTRUCTIONS

As you edit your work, you should also look for elliptical clauses. An *elliptical clause* is a clause that makes sense even though some of the words have been left out.

There are two reasons why you should examine elliptical clauses when you edit your writing. One is to make sure that the omission of words does not confuse your readers. The other is to double-check that the elliptical clause modifies the appropriate words in the sentence. Consider the following sentence from a student essay.

```
The author could very well offend some feminists and women's
rights advocates when he recommends that after birth the mother
should stay home for at least eighteen months.
```

The elliptical clause is *after (she gives) birth.* But the sequence of the sentence misleads readers. At first, we read it to mean *After her birth, the mother should stay home.* To avoid ambiguity, the student should have fleshed out the clause.

The author could very well offend some feminists and women's rights advocates when he recommends that after she gives birth, the mother should stay home for at least eighteen months.

Here is another example of a bothersome elliptical construction.

While practicing civil disobedience, a police officer confronted the demonstrators.

Again, the way to correct the dangling elliptical clause is to flesh it out by inserting a subject and predicate.

While the demonstrators were practicing civil disobedience, a police officer confronted them.

Elliptical constructions make your writing more concise and help you to avoid belaboring the obvious. But be sure they do not cause problems for your readers.

Dangling Constructions

As you edit your writing, make sure that whenever you use modifiers—words or groups of words, phrases, participles, or clauses—to describe other elements in the sentence, you place these modifiers in the appropriate position. Here is a sentence from an essay on eating disorders. The student is describing the tragedy that befell a bulimic girl named Theresa.

```
Weakened from the strain of purging, her mom took her to the emer-
gency room.
```

The sentence says that Theresa's mother was weakened from the purging. We can repair the sentence in one of two ways. We can leave the modifier as is and revise the independent clause to make *Theresa* the subject.

> Weakened from the strain of purging, Theresa was taken to the emergency room by her mom.

Or we can convert the modifier to a dependent clause. Don't forget that a dependent clause starts with a subordinating conjunction and contains a subject and a verb.

> Because Theresa was weakened from the strain of purging, her mom took her to the emergency room.

A rule of thumb is to keep the modifier close to, if not next to, the words it describes. By placing *weakened from the strain of purging* directly next to *Theresa,* we avoid confusion. See what happens when the modifier is separated from the word it describes in the following sentence.

> It is difficult to argue for curfews with intensity.

The writer gives the impression that *curfews* are intense. If she moves the phrase *with intensity* closer to *argue,* the word it describes, she will eliminate the ambiguity. She could leave the modifier as is and place it after the verb.

> It is difficult to argue with intensity for curfews.

Or she could convert the phrase *with intensity* to an adverb and put it after *argue.*

> It is difficult to argue intensely for curfews.

Parallel Structure

Parallel structures are words, phrases, or clauses that have equivalent weight and identical form. We underlined the parallel structures in a sentence from Michael J. Budds's article on rock and roll.

> Although still shocking in some quarters, moreover, <u>the casual use of profanities,</u> <u>the graphic references to sexual behaviors and drug use,</u> and <u>the open attacks on cultural "sacred cows"</u> have not been exclusive to rock and roll.

The three parallel elements are comparable in that each consists of a noun modified by a phrase:

NOUN	PREPOSITIONAL PHRASE
casual use	of profanities
graphic references	to sexual behaviors and drug use
open attacks	on cultural "sacred cows"

Now look at an example of faulty parallelism.

> Americans focus too much on making money, consuming goods, and prestige.

The sentence lists three objectives. The first two have the same form: an *-ing* verb (or gerund) + a noun. The third takes the form of a noun. The -ing verb is missing. For consistency, we have to insert an –ing verb before *prestige.*

> Americans focus too much on making money, consuming goods, and attaining prestige.

When you double-check that your parallel structures are in the same form, don't overlook sentences that contain correlative conjunctions: *either ... or, neither ... nor, both ... and, whether ... or, not only ... but also.* Make sure you use these conjunctions to join structures that have the same form.

> The president urged Congress either to pass the bill or to offer an amendment.

The constructions following *either* and *or* are comparable: to pass the bill or to offer an amendment. Our students are fond of the *not only ... but also* construction, but they frequently use it incorrectly.

> Young women suffering from anorexia are not only physically debilitated but also are mentally depressed.

Following the guideline that the structures following *not only* and *but also* should be equivalent, we can change the sentence in either of the following ways:

> Young women suffering from anorexia are not only physically debilitated but also mentally depressed.

> Young women suffering from anorexia not only are physically debilitated but also are mentally depressed.

VERBS

SUBJECT–VERB AGREEMENT

A serious error that makes readers wince is lack of agreement between subjects and verbs. As you edit your writing, check that all your subjects match up with your verbs. When the subject refers to a single person or thing, the verb usually ends in *s*. In the following sentence, the subject, *candidate,* is singular, so the verb, *stumps,* ends in *s*.

> The senatorial candidate stumps for votes all summer.

And when the subject refers to more than one person or thing, the subject ends in *s*.

> The senatorial candidates stump for votes all summer.

But, as the following example illustrates, this is not always the case.

> Jazz, rock, and rap have African American roots.

Most college students handle subject–verb agreement with relative ease, but the situation can be tricky when the subject and verb are separated by a group of words, a prepositional phrase, or a dependent clause. Let us examine three sentences written by our students. In the first example, a group of words comes between the subject and verb.

```
Farber, as well as Vollmer and other authors, question the value
of grades.
```

The writer should have ignored the intervening words and made the verb agree with Farber.

```
Farber, as well as Vollmer and other authors, questions the value
of grades.
```

In the second sentence, a propositional phrase separates the subject and the verb.

```
One of the tests show a connection between eating disorders and
depression.
```

Because the phrase *of the tests* breaks up the subject and verb, the writer got confused and made the verb agree with *tests,* the word closest to it, instead of with the word *One,* the subject of the sentence. If she had ignored the phrase, she would have written *One . . . shows.* In the third sentence, a clause comes between the subject and the verb.

A law that allows teenagers to be searched more readily than adults are unfair and unconstitutional.

Law is the subject, but since the word *adults* appears immediately before the verb, the writer chose the plural verb. She should have written "A *law . . . is . . . .*"

TENSE SWITCHING

Unexpected shifts in verb tense are often confusing to the reader. Writers may have good reasons to shift verb tense (past, present, future, and so on) within a piece of writing or even within a sentence, as the following example shows:

Youth curfew laws started in inner cities but are now common in the suburbs.

The sentence shifts tense from past to present because it describes where curfew laws originated and goes on to explain where they are currently found. The shift in tense makes sense. In the following sentence, the tense change is illogical.

Another idea that some think is better than establishing youth curfews was to start a special juvenile court.

The sentence starts in the present (*think*) but then shifts to the past *was* for no good reason. It doesn't make sense that an idea people are considering in the present would take a past-tense verb.

Shifts in tense are more common between sentences than within sentences, as in the following example:

Grades provide a motivation for meeting homework deadlines and paying attention in boring classes, but do they actually promote learning? In high school, I became an expert at getting top grades. My strategy was to fill in the study guides based on just skimming the textbook and then to look over the study guide just before the test. I don't actually read the book. I was not concerned with learning the material; only the grade was important to me.

The description of how the student saw grades during high school starts in the second sentence, which is in the past tense: "In high school, I became an expert ...." The third sentence is also in the past tense ("My strategy was ..."), but in the fourth sentence, there is a shift into the present tense: "I don't actually read the book." The tense shift is illogical, since earlier sentences established that the events being described in the paragraph happened in the past.

PRONOUNS

The Latin prefix *pro* means *for*. That's why we say pronouns stand in *for* nouns, other pronouns, and noun phrases. A *noun phrase* is the subject of a sentence along with all the words that modify or describe it. In the following sentence, the noun phrase is *Steven Vogel, a professor of philosophy at Denison University.*

> Steven Vogel, a professor of philosophy at Denison University, wrote "Grades and Money."

If we use pronouns to replace the nouns and noun phrases in this sentence, we arrive at a three-word sentence: *He wrote it.* Take a look at a sentence from Vogel's article. We underlined the pronouns.

> The relationship between <u>me</u> and the students is really an exchange relationship: <u>they</u> provide <u>me</u> with work of a certain quality and <u>I</u> reward <u>it</u>—pay for <u>it</u>—by giving <u>them</u> a certain grade.

Notice the two pronouns *they* and *them* refer to *students,* and the pronoun *it* refers to *work of a certain quality.* The word or words the pronoun refers to is called its antecedent. *Antecedent* comes from the Latin words *ante,* meaning *before,* and *cedere,* meaning *to go.* In a sentence, the antecedent is the word or words that go before the pronoun in that the pronoun refers to it. In the above example, *students* is the antecedent of *they* and *them,* and *work of a certain quality* is the antecedent of *it.* As you edit your writing, make sure your pronouns

- have clear antecedents.
- match up with their antecedents.
- are consistent.

CLEAR ANTECEDENTS

Your readers should not have to stop reading to ask, "What does the pronoun refer to?" as we had to do when we read the following sentence in a student's paper:

```
When parents restrict their children's rights, they typically suffer
in the long run.
```

The antecedent for *their* is clear: it refers back to *parents,* the only noun that precedes it in the sentence. But what is the antecedent of *they?* Does it refer to *parents* or to *children?* Does the writer mean that children suffer from not having rights, or does she mean that parents suffer, perhaps from their children's rebellion against restrictions? Look carefully at the pronouns in your writing. When more than one noun precedes a pronoun, make sure your readers know which of the nouns is the pronoun's antecedent.

Another form of ambiguity that will give your readers grief is a pronoun that has no reference at all. It is common to hear people speak of "they" when they are referring to the government or the officials in charge, as in the following sentence.

They should amend the Constitution to clarify the age at which teenagers get full adult rights.

They refers to legislators who have the power and authority to amend the Constitution. In academic writing, you should avoid vague references. They are generally unacceptable despite that they are common in conversation.

OTHER MISMATCHES BETWEEN PRONOUNS AND THEIR ANTECEDENTS

Watch out for other mismatches between pronouns and their antecedents. Sometimes writers inadvertently use plural pronouns to refer to singular nouns or singular pronouns to refer to plural nouns. In an essay about eating disorders, one of our students wrote

```
Another myth is that when a person is finally treated, they are cured
of the sickness.
```

Since *person* is singular, the pronoun has to be singular. We fix the mismatch either by changing the number of the noun or by changing the number of the pronoun.

Another myth is that when a person is finally treated, he or she is cured of the sickness.

Another myth is that when people are finally treated, they are cured of the sickness.

When checking for agreement in number, it helps to draw an arrow between the pronoun and its antecedent. Arrows make the mismatches between singular nouns and plural pronouns more visible.

Sometimes we use pronouns to refer to other pronouns. A common blunder is to use plural pronouns to refer to indefinite pronouns, such as *anybody, anyone, anything, everybody, everyone, everything, nobody, no one, nothing, somebody, someone, something*. These pronouns are called *indefinite* because they don't refer to anyone or anything in particular. Consider the following sentence:

We know that everyone wants their vote to be counted.

Everyone is singular in form. You can see this because it takes a singular verb, *wants*. Therefore, it requires a singular pronoun.

We know that everyone wants his or her vote to be counted.

You hear sentences with mismatches between pronouns and indefinite pronouns every day, and you may even read them in publications. But to be on the safe side, you should avoid using plural pronouns to refer to singular, indefinite pronouns in your own writing.

PRONOUN CONSISTENCY

The last pronoun problem we discuss is pronoun consistency. Writers use different points of view. When they are emphasizing their own experience, they use the first-person point of view, as William Bennett does in "What Hath the Beatles Wrought? Rock-&-Roll and the Collapse of Authority."

> I'm a lover of early rock-and-roll music. I played guitar in the 1950s, have a juke box in my home today, and still enjoy the good stuff. At the same time, I'm a strong critic of current hyperviolent, hateful, exceedingly sexualized and vulgar music.

Writers use the second-person point of view to directly address the reader, as we have done in this book.

> You hear sentences with mismatches between pronouns and indefinite pronouns every day, and you may even read them in publications. But to be on the safe side, you should avoid using plural pronouns to refer to singular indefinite pronouns.

And, like Michael J. Budds, they use the third-person point of view, the perspective that is commonplace in academic writing:

> No musical repertory in Western civilization has aroused more controversy than rock and roll. No musical repertory has attracted so many powerful and self-righteous opponents.

Maintaining a consistent point of view is important in writing. As you edit your papers, check that you have not shifted among first, second, and third person within a sentence or within a set of related sentences. It makes logical sense for a train of thought to stay in the first, second, or third person. Notice the shift in person in the following sentence.

> Extracurricular activities are privileges and not rights. So if high school students want to participate, then you must abide by all the rules that accompany the school district's policies, including drug testing.

The writer begins in the third person and abruptly shifts to the second person, *you,* for no logical reason. Shifts to the second person often occur in sentences that start with a generalization and then apply that generalization to the reader. In this case, the generalization is *high school students,* a class of people. Here's another example in an excerpt from a student paper.

> Another myth is that eating disorders are only about food, but they really concern how you perceive your body and what is happening to you emotionally. For many people, the disorder is the focus of life. They block out painful memories, feelings, and emotions with food.

The writer switches from the myth about eating disorders to *you* and starts talking to the reader. Shifts in perspective are confusing. As a rule of thumb, make sure your sentences maintain a consistent point of view.

MISUSED WORDS

Certain groups of words and phrases in the English language are tricky. One such group contains words that sound alike or are spelled alike but have different meanings. Writers can easily mix up *to, too,* and *two; lead* (to guide), *lead* (the metal), and *led* (the past tense of to guide: *lead*); and *their, there,* and *they're.* Another group consists of words that are close enough in sound and spelling to cause confusion, such as *affect* and *effect; choose* and *chose.* And a third group is made up of everyday blunders. Following is a list of the misused words and phrases and the blunders that we see most frequently in student papers.

MISUSED WORDS

accept/except: *Accept* means receive; *except* means excluding.

affect/effect: *Affect* means influence; *effect* means result.

all ready/already: *All ready* means fully prepared; *already* means happened by this time.

amount/number: *Amount* is used with things that can't be counted; *number* is used with things that can be counted.

choose/chose: *Choose* is the present tense of the verb; *chose* is the past tense.

its/it's: *Its* is a possessive pronoun; *it's* is a contraction for *it is.*

know/no: *Know* means to possess knowledge; *no* expresses refusal or means not at all.

lead/led: *Lead* is the present tense of the verb *to lead; led* is the past tense.

loose/lose: *Loose* means to turn free or make less tight; *lose* means to fail to win or to cease to have.

passed/past: *Passed* is the past tense of the verb *to pass,* meaning to go across or through; *past* is a preposition meaning at the farther side of.

principal/principle: *Principal* means chief or head of a school; *principle* means a basic truth or law.

that/who: Use *that* to refer to objects and animals without names; use *who* to refer to people.

their/there/they're: *Their* means belonging to them; *there* refers to location; *they're* is the contraction for they are.

then/than: *Then* refers to time; *than* refers to comparison.

to/too/two: *To* is the preposition; *too* is the adverb meaning also; *two* is the number.

who's/whose: *Who's* is a contraction for *who is; whose* is the possessive case of who or which.

your/you're: *Your* is the possessive case of you; *you're* is the contraction for *you are.*

BLUNDERS

alright	for	all right
alot	for	a lot
different than	for	different from
irregardless	for	regardless
thru	for	through
could of, should of, would of	for	could have, should have, would have
afterwards	for	afterward
towards	for	toward
being that, being as, on account of, due to the fact that	for	because
plus (as a conjunction)	for	and
'til (or till)	for	until
thusly	for	thus
firstly, secondly, thirdly	for	first, second, third
use to	for	used to
suppose to	for	supposed to
themself (or themselfs)	for	themselves

Your professor may want to add his or her favorite faux pas to this list. If you would like to review a more comprehensive list of commonly confused words, check out Paul Brians's Common Errors in English from his book *Common Errors in English Usage,* http://www.wsu.edu:8080/~brians/errors/errors.html. Since there are so many confusing words in English, a smart move is to start a list of your own and refer to it when you are editing your papers. When you complete an essay, use the find or search function on your word processing program to locate each occurrence of the words on your list and check to see that you have used the correct forms. This technique counteracts the natural tendency to read over misused words that sound correct to the ear. Using find or search functions, you can check a long paper in just a few minutes.

PUNCTUATION

COMMAS

Many of our students place commas by feel rather than by rule. Many of you probably do the same thing. This is understandable, since there is no definitive set of rules for writers to follow. Professional and academic writers vary in their comma placement habits, so when you read books and articles, you see a range of patterns for comma use. Some writers generously sprinkle their prose with commas, as illustrated by this excerpt from *The Autobiography of Malcolm X* in which Malcolm X assesses his leadership qualities:

> I had, as one asset, I knew, an international image. No amount of money could have bought that. I knew that if I said something newsworthy, people would read or hear of it, maybe even around the world, depending upon what it was. More immediately, in New York City, where I would naturally base any operation, I had a large, direct personal following of non-Muslims.

Other writers use commas sparingly.

> The financial crisis in the last years of Phillip II's reign was enough in itself to check Spanish action in northern Europe. Peace with France in 1598 was a recognition that Spain could not fight a war on three fronts simultaneously. In the Low Countries the transfer of sovereignty to the archdukes was a belated attempt to end the struggle with the northern provinces by peaceful means and to close one of the gaping holes of Spanish expenditure. The Archduke Albert was a realist and he used his sovereignty to reduce commitments still further. On his own initiative he sent an ambassador to London to open negotiations with the new king of England, James I, and he urged Madrid to take the dispute to the conference table; the policy bore fruit in the Treaty of London (1604) which ended the long Anglo-Spanish war. (Lynch 53–54)

It would be handy if you could follow your own instincts for comma placement rather than learn rules. But if those instincts are not grounded in a strong understanding of language structure and knowledge of traditional punctuation conventions, comma placement will be random and inconsistent. For skilled writers who have this background, comma placement may become reflexive, but many first-year students do not have an intuitive sense of where commas are needed. To help you out, we build on our earlier discussion of sentence structure to provide a list of comma rules that will enable you to punctuate effectively.

In assembling our rules, we reflect a modern trend to use commas sparingly. We combine overlapping rules to create a streamlined but functional list. We don't want you to be so overwhelmed by the sheer number of comma rules that you revert to the instinctive approach to punctuation.

SEVEN RULES FOR USING COMMAS

1. Use commas before coordinating conjunctions *(for, and, nor, but, or, yet, so)* to join independent clauses.

   > Computer scientists argue that machine intelligence can only advance, so it is likely that computers will become increasingly humanlike in their thinking.

   Notice the comma comes before the conjunction, *so,* not after it. Don't be tempted to fire off a comma automatically at every conjunction. Commas are optional when the two independent clauses are short.

   > Jake arrived and Abigail left.

   When conjunctions connect the elements in compound subjects and verbs, commas are not needed.

   > Computers and calculators have advanced at an astonishing rate.

   > Computers calculate and compare much faster than humans.

2. Use commas after introductory words, phrases, and clauses. The comma signals the reader to pause.

   > Unquestionably, General Lee's decisions at the Battle of Gettysburg were correct.

   > In the light of overwhelming evidence, it should be clear to all that Lee is not to be blamed for what happened at Gettysburg.

   > If Longstreet had trusted Lee's judgment and ordered the attack at the appropriate time, the outcome would have been vastly different.

   When an independent clause is followed by a dependent clause beginning with *if, after, before, unless, until,* or *when,* you do not need a comma.

   > The outcome would have been vastly different if Longstreet had trusted Lee's judgment and ordered the attack at the appropriate time.

3. Use commas between items in a list. The commas substitute for *and.*

   > On the other hand, many psychologists argue that computers will never exhibit the deep emotions, complex motives, and developmental growth that underlie human thinking.

4. Use commas to separate speaker tags and direct quotations.

   > Michael J. Budds writes, "As the twentieth century reaches its end, the circumstances surrounding rock and roll are more complicated than ever and as controversial as ever."

"If grades are money, then learning is a cost—a painful effort one undergoes only for the reward it produces," says Steven Vogel (391).

According to Frude, "People willingly talk to machines about their personal problems." He believes this trend will strengthen in the future (34).

Don't use a comma when the quotation is an integral part of the sentence.

I have observed that people "willingly talk to machines about their personal problems" (Frude 34).

Sherry Turkle concedes that "there is no simple sense in which computers are causing a shift in notions of identity" (400).

5. Use commas to set off nonessential information from the rest of the sentence.

Frude, who has studied psychology, thinks that many mental patients could be helped by computerized therapy sessions.

We read an article by Sherry Turkle, a professor at M.I.T.

Scientists who design computers have similar hopes.

In the third example, the clause *who design computers* is essential to the meaning. Therefore, the sentence does not take a comma.

6. Use commas to separate transitional and parenthetical expressions from the rest of the sentence.

Many leading psychologists, however, believe that there are basic differences between computer and human intelligence that can never be overcome.

Most scientists believe, on the other hand, that computers can equal or surpass humans in logical thinking and mathematics.

7. Use commas to separate items in dates, addresses, personal titles, and numbers.

On August 30, 2005, he began his undergraduate studies at Wooster College, Wooster, Ohio, with the intention of studying American history.

The article was written by Jacob Yale, Ph.D.

There are computer memory chips that can store the equivalent of 1,500 books.

APOSTROPHES

We use apostrophes to indicate ownership, signal omission, and form the plurals of letters and words. Today, the most common use of apostrophes is to form possessives of nouns and indefinite pronouns (see the list of indefinite pronouns on page 496). But when apostrophes were first introduced into the English language, their primary function was to indicate omitted letters. Shakespeare begins Sonnet 105 with the line

Let not my love be cal'd Idolatrie. (1609 edition)

Let not my love be called idolatry. (modernized version)

We tell you this because when you form possessives, it helps to think of the apostrophe as a replacement for *of*.

The professor's class = the class of the professor

Michael Budds's position = the position of Michael Budds

The people's arguments = the arguments of the people

Here's how to use an apostrophe to show possession:

1. When a noun or indefinite pronoun ends in any letter but *s*, add *'s*

    Farber's main point is that grades destroy self-discipline.

    The people's representative in court is the district attorney.

    This year everyone's vote will be counted.

2. When a singular noun ends in *s*, add *'s*

    The boss's position angered the union.

    We will read several of Henry James's novels this semester.

3. When a plural noun ends in *s*, add only the apostrophe

    Students' SAT scores show less about their potential than their high-school grades do.

    Keep in mind that a plural noun that does not end in *s* takes *'s*.

    The women's movement gained momentum.

4. Never punctuate possessive pronouns (*his, hers, its, ours, yours, theirs, whose*) with apostrophes.

    The government announced its decision last April.

Use apostrophes to signal omission. We still use apostrophes to indicate that letters have been left out. The apostrophe replaces the *n* and the *o* in *cannot* to form the contraction *can't*. In a contraction, the apostrophe replaces the letters that have been dropped. Use this principle when you proofread your papers. It will tell you if your apostrophes are in the right place. The student who writes *did'nt* needs to remind herself that the contraction combines *did not*. The omitted letter is *o*; therefore, the apostrophe goes after the *n*: *didn't*.

Also use apostrophes to signal omission when referring to years and dates.

Erikson developed his theories of identity in the '50s and '60s.

The Class of '01 contributed ten thousand dollars.

Use apostrophes to form the plural of lowercase letters of the alphabet and words.

I'm always astonished when clerks at checkout counters ask me how many *n's* there are in *Kennedy*.

My students put too many *however's* in their essays.

Keep in mind that capital letters, letter combinations, Arabic numbers, and acronyms are pluralized by adding *s,* not *'s:* Fs, Ps and Qs, 3s, HMOs. Never use an apostrophe to indicate the plural of personal names. Put *The Smiths* on your mailbox, not *The Smiths'.*

Sometimes our students add apostrophes to constructions that already indicate possession. The apostrophes are superfluous in the following sentence:

> The rights of minors' can be regulated more stringently than the rights of adults'.

The phrases *of minors* and *of adults* signal possession. There is no need for apostrophes. However, you would have to insert apostrophes if you omitted the two *of's.*

> Minors' rights can be regulated more stringently than adults'.

After *adults,* the noun, *rights,* is understood. In comparisons with a noun understood, don't forget the apostrophe.

SEMICOLONS AND COLONS

Students shy away from semicolons and colons because they're not sure how to use them. They are handy punctuation marks, so it makes sense to add them to your repertoire.

Semicolons

Read the following sentence from Sherry Turkle's "Cyberspace and Identity."

> When they log on, they may find themselves playing multiple roles; they may find themselves playing characters of the opposite sex.

Why doesn't Turkle separate the two independent clauses with a period? It's because a period brings the reader to a complete stop—the writer says, "That's one idea, and here's a different one." The semicolon tells the reader to slow down—the writer says, "Here's one idea, and here's a closely related one." Turkle's first clause tells us that people play multiple roles, and the second clause tells us that those roles may be their gender opposites. This illustrates the main reason for using a semicolon: to indicate the close connection between the two halves of a sentence. Here are two more examples, these taken from student papers.

> The American family is in a time of trial; economic and social changes are exerting more and more pressure as time goes by.

> Families aren't falling apart; they are experiencing a different type of world that is constantly changing.

The first use of semicolons, then, is to separate two independent clauses that are close in meaning.

The second use of semicolons is to separate independent clauses when the second clause begins with a conjunctive adverb and phrase. Recall our discussion of conjunctive adverbs or phrases on page 490.

> According to Barret and Robinson, children of gay parents may experience stress as they come to terms with their parents' sexual orientation; however, the authors conclude that this struggle often helps the children develop into adults who are tolerant and appreciate diversity.

The third use of semicolons is to subdivide long lists when items in the series contain commas.

> This semester we will have three tests that cover usage topics: commas, semicolons, colons, and apostrophes; spelling, word confusions, and word choice; and run-ons, fragments, pronoun selection, and subject-verb agreement.

The semicolons enable the writer to separate the eleven items into three subunits.

Colons

Don't mix up colons and semicolons. A colon balances a period on top of another period, whereas a semicolon balances a period on top of a comma. Colons have two principal uses.

1. Use colons after independent clauses that introduce quotations, questions, or lists.

   > Barret and Robinson argue that children of gay parents are no different than any other children: "Some do well in just about all activities; some have problems, and some are well adjusted."

   > Critics of the contemporary American family pose a tough question: How can our families adjust to the economic upheavals of the last twenty years?

   > Three family structures are becoming more common: single-parent families, childless couples, and two-parent families in which both parents work.

   Do not use a colon when the list is preceded by a form of the verb *to be* or by *such as, for example, including,* or *especially.*

   > Three family structures are single-parent families, childless couples, and two-parent families in which both parents work.

2. Use a colon after an independent clause to announce something more. What comes after the colon develops what came before it. The colon functions this way in Sherry Turkle's sentence.

   > The instrumental computer, the computer that does things for us, has revealed another side: a subjective computer that does things to us as people, to our view of ourselves and our relationships, to our ways of looking at our minds. (404)

   The first clause says the computer has revealed another side. The colon says, "Get ready to hear what this other side is."

APPENDIX C

Revising for Style

STRATEGIES FOR IMPROVING STYLE

- Avoid inflated language.
- Vary the structure and length of your sentences.
- Strengthen your verbs.
- Make your writing concise by cutting ineffective words and expressions and eliminating needless repetition.
- Liven up your writing with detail.
- Avoid sexist language.

AVOID INFLATED LANGUAGE

For many years, a bone of contention in the academic community has been whether first-year college students should be taught to write in a style that has the ring of formal academic discourse or in a more personal style that uses everyday language. The debate is not whether one of these two styles of writing should be taught to the exclusion of the other, but rather which should receive more emphasis and in what order they should be introduced. One perspective is that college students should be immediately initiated into formal academic writing; another view is that they need to develop a strong, clear, personal voice before they move on to more formal academic styles.

Our emphasis in this book is on expanding your awareness of stylistic differences, both in the texts you read and in your own writing. For that purpose, in the anthology section of the book we include reading selections that are written in informal styles as well as formal styles. Our goal is to help you understand that academic writing contexts require you to comprehend and produce a range of writing styles. This may occur within the confines of a single course. For example, your American history professor might assign both a research paper on the political impact of immigration and a reflective essay on how your own family's immigration stories have affected your perspectives. The first essay requires a relatively formal style, whereas the second permits a style that is more personal and conversational. In

505

this book, rather than focus on any particular style, we want you to become more sensitive to style in general and better able to analyze the stylistic decisions you make as you write.

Though we want to make you aware of the diversity of stylistic options available to academic writers, we don't want to give the impression that all stylistic choices students make are equally good. We have already mentioned that for certain writing tasks, some stylistic responses make more sense than others. There are also cases in which style is just plain bad, regardless of context. This occurs when students attempt to imitate the language and complexity of academic writing but don't know enough about academic discourse to be successful. Consider the following examples from student papers. Please understand that we are not poking fun at these students. We are using their writing to illustrate a problem that is widespread, even among advanced students and scholars.

Example 1

```
Before we are alive, we are born into a ready-made culture which
is unquestioned by those already alive in our to be culture.
```

The student is trying to convey the idea that every person is born into a culture whose members already share certain values and assumptions. In the attempt to make the sentence sound complex, the writer obscures this concept, and the result is a sentence that we have to read several times to understand.

Example 2

```
Arguments supporting genetic engineering development to continue
are arguments that create substantial consideration in the minds
of scientists and the public as well.
```

Here the student is unnecessarily wordy in an apparent attempt to achieve a sophisticated tone. The result sounds awkward and stilted. A simpler and better sentence would be "Both scientists and the public are skeptical about arguments that support genetic engineering."

Example 3

```
The subject of violence in American society is something that must be
a concern of the public across the country if we are to do something
about the problem of violence in the streets of our major cities.
```

The assertion is simple: "Americans must become more aware of urban violence as a first step in solving the problem," and it can be stated in sixteen rather than thirty-eight words. The writer takes an approach that many students believe is valued in the academic community: Use as many words as possible to communicate your idea. When professors ask you to elaborate on ideas, they usually mean be specific and add concrete detail. They don't want you to say the same thing using a greater number of words. But is simpler and shorter always better? Not necessarily. Writers must continually balance the desire to explore ideas fully with the need to be clear and succinct.

All of the above examples may result from student writers attempting to mimic styles that are beyond their reach. It is good to stretch your stylistic muscles, but it takes experience and training to become a style heavyweight.

In his textbook *Writing with Style,* John Trimble describes how reaching for words that sound "academic," may actually damage a student's sense of language:

> Most of us write as if we're paid a dime a word. We've been conditioned, I suppose, by school assignments calling for more words than we have ideas. That gets us into the habit of phrase-stretching—a hard habit to break. Then, too, it's easier to think in long, ready-made phrases, which have the added attraction of sounding elegant.... This habit of thinking in prefab phrases slowly dulls our sensitivity to words as words. It's inevitable. (53)

As we noted earlier, students sometimes think that their professors value inflated language in which content takes a back seat to verbiage. They expect to be rewarded for writing what they term *b.s.* Our experience indicates that this perception is based on campus legend more than on fact. Surveys taken on one of our campuses revealed that most faculty members value clarity of expression and organization of ideas over all other writing traits. They are not impressed with big words and long sentences if clarity is compromised. Consider the following sentence from a first-year student's essay on gender roles. From context, we could figure out what the student means: that due to industrialization, male muscle power is less essential to society than it once was.

> In society today, it would be difficult for any individual to deny the fact that with the advance of modern industry, there is a shift in the direction of decreasing marginal utility of males.

Notice that the phrase "it would be difficult for any individual to deny the fact" contributes nothing to the central meaning of the sentence and serves only to increase sentence length. "Marginal utility" has a very specific meaning in the field of economics: it concerns how consuming additional units of a particular commodity or service affects the consumer's level of satisfaction. The student may have encountered the concept of marginal utility in an economics course and thought that his sentence would sound more sophisticated if he used the phrase, but "marginal utility" does not make sense in his sentence and only confuses the reader. The student's effort to use inflated language hides his intended meaning.

A common piece of advice contained in writing style manuals is to avoid overblown language that confuses the reader and suggests that the writer is more concerned with making an impression than with communicating ideas. This advice is a central theme in the most widely distributed book on style of the last hundred years, *The Elements of Style,* written originally by William Strunk, Jr., in 1919 when he taught at Cornell University, and later revised by the essayist and novelist E. B. White. This slim volume advises students, "Write in a way that comes easily and naturally to you, using words and phrases that come readily to hand." Strunk and White also caution students against using overblown language: "Do not overwrite. Rich, ornate prose is hard to digest, generally unwholesome, and sometimes nauseating.... Avoid fancy words."

Strunk and White's advice on style is similar to George Orwell's suggestions in his famous essay "Politics and the English Language" (1946): "Never use a long word where a short one will do.... Never use a foreign phrase, a scientific word, or a jargon word if you can think of an everyday English equivalent." As an illustration, Orwell translates the following passage from the Bible into the ugly, overblown style that he opposes:

Ecclesiastes

I returned and saw under the sun, that the race is not to the swift, nor the battle to the strong, neither yet bread to the wise, nor yet riches to men of understanding, not yet favor to men of skill; but time and chance happeneth to them all.

Orwell's Revision

Objective consideration of contemporary phenomena compels the conclusion that success or failure in competitive activities exhibits no tendency to be commensurate with innate capacity, but that a considerable element of the unpredictable must invariably be taken into account.

Notice that Orwell eliminated all the clear, concrete examples from the biblical passage and substituted wordy generalizations. Simple language such as "time and chance" is converted into vague and verbose phrases such as "a considerable element of the unpredictable." "I returned and saw under the sun" becomes "Objective consideration of contemporary phenomena compels the conclusion." The clarity and elegance of the biblical passage is destroyed by the paraphrase.

Like Orwell, Strunk and White recommend that students avoid words that sound pretentious when simpler words will convey meaning just as directly. We agree with this advice, but we would add that people trained in particular academic disciplines and professions use complex language, including specialized vocabularies, because it makes communication with their target audiences clearer and more efficient. Look, for example, at an excerpt from Roger C. Schank's study of how human memory is organized. Schank is one of the world's experts on artificial intelligence.

Scripts conform to the terminal scenes of MOPs. They are subject to TPS, produce CDs, and contain memories, so they are a special kind of MOP. However, MOPs tend to organize information in general about an area and thus one level of suborganization in MOPs are the methods of filling the various strands of the MOP. That is what scripts are: standardized memory chunks that are particular methods of filling one or more strands in a MOP. (485)

Schank's language is replete with specialized terminology, all of which makes sense to scholars in natural-language processing, a field that investigates how people converse with computers. Whatever your college major, an important part of your course of study is learning the specialized language of your discipline. You must practice this language when you speak and write. The trick is to gain that experience, which sometimes involves taking risks, without creating sentences that sound unnatural or can't be understood. This requires equal measures of courage and caution.

As you work on style, keep in mind that academic writing standards for style change over time. It used to be that scholars shied away from the first-person pronoun *I,* and they sanctioned the use of the passive voice. In many disciplines, scholars now write in less formal language. At one time, scientific articles were written strictly in the third person. Now, certain respected publications accept articles that use first-person references to the author or coauthors. As standards shift, it is difficult for writing teachers, much less their students, to keep up with the conventions in various disciplines. Sometimes students encounter old-school professors who are not receptive to informal style in any context. Sometimes students themselves are inflexible. They arrive at college with the impression that good style is governed by a series of absolute rules, such as "Never use *I*" or "Don't begin a sentence with *and*." As a result, they resist the notion that stylistic choices vary according to particular circumstances.

VARY THE STRUCTURE AND LENGTH OF YOUR SENTENCES

Skilled writers vary sentence length to break up the rhythm, make the prose more lively, and highlight important ideas. Often, writers put their basic assertions in short sentences in order to draw attention to them. They use longer sentences for details, examples, or qualifications. In the following excerpt from renowned science writer Carl Sagan, we separated the sentences so that you can see their relative lengths, and we placed the shorter sentences in bold type. Notice how Sagan makes his most important points in the short sentences and then uses the longer sentences to expand on those points with details and examples.

> **Science is a way of thinking more than it is a body of knowledge.**
>
> Its goal is to find out how the world works, to seek what regularities there may be, to penetrate to the connections of things—from subnuclear particles, which may be the constituents of all matter, to living organisms, the human social community, and hence to the cosmos as a whole.
>
> **Our intuition is by no means an infallible guide.**
>
> Our senses may be distorted by training and prejudice or merely because of the limitations of our sense organs, which, of course, perceive directly but a small fraction of the phenomena of the world.

The writer's strategy is to make the key points in short sentences and put the detailed explanation in longer sentences.

As you make a conscious effort to vary the length of your sentences, you can use a number of strategies. Sentence expansion and sentence combining will help you to create long sentences, and sentence division will help you with shorter ones.

Strategies for Expanding Sentences

1. Use prepositional phrases to add more information to the sentence.
2. Introduce or end the sentence with a phrase that contains a verb.
3. Add an introductory clause or a sentence-ending clause.
4. Place a modifier at the beginning, middle, or end of the sentence.

Strategies for Combining Sentences

1. Combine two sentences (independent clauses) with a coordinating conjunction: *for, and, nor, but, or, yet, so.* You may have learned to remember these seven conjunctions as FANBOYS.

2. Combine two sentences (independent clauses) with a conjunctive adverb: *however, consequently, thus, furthermore, nevertheless, then, certainly, besides, similarly.* See page 490 for a more complete list of conjunctive adverbs.

3. Convert one of the independent clauses to a dependent clause that begins with a subordinating conjunction—*since, if, because, while, unless*—that shows the relationship between the two clauses. See page 487 for a more complete list of subordinating conjunctions.

4. Collapse two sentences together by changing the word order and adding connecting words.

Strategies for Dividing Longer Sentences

1. Search for coordinating conjunctions *(for, and, nor, but, or, yet, so)* and for adverbial conjunctions (*however, nevertheless, consequently, thus,* and so on). Then divide the sentences at these points.

2. Search for subordinating conjunctions (*if, when, unless, because, although,* and so on). Then break up the sentence by turning the dependent clause into an independent clause.

3. Look for other incidents of *and* or *but* in the sentence and insert a period before the conjunction.

STRENGTHEN YOUR VERBS

Verbs can make or break your sentences. That's why every book on writing improvement advises writers to strengthen their verbs. In *Wild Mind: Living the Writer's Life,* prose stylist Natalie Goldberg puts it best:

> I am amazed by the power of verbs. They carry the energy for a sentence. They are the action. Think of sentences without them: Vivian a tire onto the rack; Fido a lamb chop. Verbs are the stars that light up the dark sky: Vivian *hoisted* a tire onto the rack. Fido *devoured* a lamb chop. They are the joint that moves the sentence, like the elbow that connects the upper and lower arm. (213)

As you revise your writing, replace limp, lifeless verbs with "stars that light up the sky." Look for weak verbs, such as forms of the verb *to be (is, are, was, were, be, being, been),* and replace them with robust, full-bodied verbs. Sentences structured around *to be* verbs depend heavily on nouns to convey their meaning. Notice the two occurrences of the verb *is* and the large number of nouns in the following sentence. We underlined the nouns and italicized the verbs.

The <u>creation</u> of an overall <u>design</u> for a <u>computer system</u> *is* the <u>responsibility</u> of a <u>systems analyst</u>, whereas the <u>implementation</u> of the <u>design plan</u> *is* often the <u>duty</u> of a <u>computer programmer</u>.

One way to revise the sentence is to ask, Who does what? The doers are the systems analyst and the computer programmer. The actions are *design the computer system* and *implement the design plan*. We revised the sentence to read

The <u>systems analyst</u> *designs* the <u>computer system</u>, and the <u>computer programmer</u> *makes* the <u>system</u> *work*.

We replaced "implementation of the design plan" with a simpler expression, "makes the system work." Most important, we got rid of the cumbersome nominalizations, *creation* and *implementation*. *Nominalization* is the practice of making nouns from verbs or adjectives by adding suffixes *(-ance, -ence, -tion, -ment, -sion)*. Such nouns are often accompanied by prepositional phrases, for example, *creation of an overall design, implementation of the design plan,* and *duty of a computer programmer.* As you revise, watch out for strings of prepositional phrases, nominalizations, and forms of the verb *to be*.

Let's examine another sentence that cries out for stylistic revision.

The rights of teenagers have been a debate between parents and their children for generations.

This sentence sounds awkward and stilted. Once again, ask yourself, Who does what? Parents and children debate. *Debate* is a more powerful verb than the colorless verb *has been*. As you rewrite the sentence, be quick to identify the subject and the action the subject is taking.

In each generation, parents and their children debate the issue of teenagers' rights.

But academic writers sometimes prefer the passive over the active. Occasionally, passive voice is a more desirable fit in the sentence. Other times, it is a required convention in the academic field. Consider the following example:

Technology is often described as a double-edged sword that can work to our benefit or detriment depending upon how it is applied.

This sentence tells how technology is described by people in general. Trying to add a subject by naming all those people would be awkward and unwieldy. Certain academic fields sanction the use of passive voice. It is prevalent in the sciences and social sciences, though we should mention that the active voice is becoming more accepted in these fields. A rule of thumb is, unless your professor requests it, avoid passive voice whenever possible. Use it only in special cases.

Just as the passive voice is sometimes useful, so are *be* verbs and nominalization. We don't mean to suggest that writers should never use them. Problems in style arise only when these forms are overused. Although there is no absolute rule, you should look closely when you find more than one *be* verb or one nominalization per sentence. You need not analyze the nouns and verbs in every paper you write, but it's a good idea to check periodically to see the direction your style is taking. Over time, you will find that less analysis is necessary because you'll use more active verbs and fewer prepositions and nominalizations.

Summary of Strategies for Strengthening Verbs

- Ask, Who does what? Then place the subject—the performer of the action— toward the beginning of the sentence and put the verb—the action—after it.
- Replace colorless, lifeless verbs, especially forms of *to be,* with vivid, powerful verbs.
- Get rid of cumbersome nominalizations. If necessary, convert nouns to verbs.
- Change passive voice to active voice.

MAKING YOUR WRITING CONCISE BY CUTTING INEFFECTIVE WORDS AND EXPRESSIONS AND ELIMINATING NEEDLESS REPETITION

Make your writing concise by cutting ineffective words and expressions and eliminating needless repetition. One of the most painful tasks you will perform as a writer is getting rid of material you don't need. Some prose stylists call this cutting the fat or pruning deadwood. It's difficult to pare down your writing if you don't know what to eliminate. You need to train yourself to identify the fat.

Six elements add excess weight to your writing: (1) intensifiers, (2) redundant modifiers and words that imply other words, (3) hedges, (4) worn-out words, (5) overused expressions, and (6) needless repetition.

INTENSIFIERS

absolutely, actually, basically, certainly, clearly, definitely, especially, extremely, funda-mentally, generally, just, obviously, particularly, perfectly, practically, quite, rather, really, severely, significant, simply, so many, surely, totally, utterly, very

---

Intensifiers are supposed to provide force and emphasis to a word, but when you overuse them, you clutter up your writing. Avoid these fillers whenever possible. If necessary, replace them with more precise, forceful words.

REDUNDANT MODIFIERS AND WORDS THAT IMPLY OTHER WORDS

completely finish, each and every individual, end result, free gift, final outcome, first and foremost, future plans, given (before a noun), important essentials, past history, period of time, red in color, shiny in appearance, sudden crisis, terrible tragedy, true facts, various differences, very unique

---

We put the superfluous words in bold type. Some of these words and expressions are redundant, and others can be inferred from context or details your reader already knows.

HEDGES

almost, appears, attempt, can, could, I believe, I think, in some ways, it seems that, may, most, often, oftentimes, perhaps, possibly, probably, seem, suggests, to a certain extent, try, usually, virtually

---

You may think you are exercising modesty and restraint when you use these words and expressions, but in reality you will come across to your readers as timid and unsure. Use them sparingly.

WORN-OUT WORDS

a bit, a little, basic, beautiful, better, bunch, certain, choose, definitely, effective, emphasize, excellent, great, important, interesting, kind of, main, nice, perfect, pretty, sometimes, specific, stuff, think, thing, try, use

---

OVERUSED EXPRESSIONS

according to the experts, as everyone knows, cause for concern, despite the fact that, for future reference, gives me great hope, little or no effect, if you want my honest opinion, in conclusion, in due course, in essence, in my opinion, in the event that, in the strongest possible terms, in view of the fact, it appears to be the case, on the contrary, on the other hand, obviously, room for improvement, strongest possible terms, there is no doubt, under the impression, window of opportunity

---

NEEDLESS REPETITION

When you are revising your writing, in addition to shaving off intensifiers, redundant modifiers, words that imply other words, hedges, and worn-out words and expressions, cut out simple word repetition. When you repeat the same word or word root within a sentence, you make your writing sound unsophisticated. Needless repetition establishes a Dick and Jane tone, gives the impression that you didn't take the time to choose words carefully, or creates an echo in your readers' minds that distracts them and forces them to reread. See how removing repetition improves our students' sentences.

Original

Students often attend college for personal growth, both intellectual and personal.

Revision

Students often attend college for both personal and intellectual growth.

Repetition of *personal* made the sentence awkward. The problem was easily remedied.

Original

It gives an individual a competitive edge over the competition.

Revision

It gives an individual a competitive edge.

Competitive and *competition,* which derive from the root word *compete,* are repetitive. We eliminated *over the competition* because, by definition, *a competitive edge* implies that competition exists.

LIVEN UP YOUR WRITING WITH DETAIL

Often, what separates an A-level paper from less successful writing is the writer's attention to detail. In *Writing Down the Bones,* a best-selling book on writing, Natalie Goldberg advises writers to use showing statements, even in academic writing.

> Some general statements are sometimes very appropriate. Just make sure to back each one with a concrete picture. Even if you are writing an essay, it makes the work so much more lively. Oh, if only Kant or Descartes had followed these instructions, "I think therefore I am"—I think about bubble gum, horse racing, barbeque, and the stock market; therefore, I know I exist in America in the twentieth century. Go ahead, take Kant's *Prolegomena to Any Future Metaphysic* and get it to show what he is telling. We would all be a lot happier. (69)

You will make your readers a lot happier if you liven up your writing with the strategies for adding detail that we present in the box below:

Strategies for Adding Detail

- Add descriptive adjectives.
- Substitute precise, powerful words for vague, lackluster words.
- Insert specific facts.
- Crack open general statements with sentences containing pointed, specific information.
- Add concrete examples.
- Break open a general statement by supplying an illustration.

AVOID SEXIST LANGUAGE

When you reread your drafts, double-check that you have not used sexist language. Use the masculine pronouns *he* and *his* and nouns that end in *-man* or *-men* only when they refer to a male or when you want to point out that a group is composed entirely of males. Don't use these forms to refer to women. Instead, use the following strategies.

Strategies for Avoiding Sexist Language

- Use expressions that recognize both sexes (his or her, she or he).
- Use plural pronouns (they, their).
- Use nouns that are not gender-specific (mail carrier, police officer).
- Revise the sentence to avoid the need for a pronoun entirely.

Credits

TEXT

Front Matter

Corbett, Edward. *Classical Rhetoric for the Modern Student*. 3rd ed. New York: Oxford UP, 1990. Print.

Elbow, Peter. *Writing With Power*. New York: Oxford, 1998. Print.

Elbow, Peter. *Writing Without Teachers*. New York: Oxford, 1973. Print.

Flower, Linda. "Writer-Based Prose: A Cognitive Basis for Problems in Writing." *College English* Sept. 1979: 19–37. Print.

Haas, Christina, and Linda Flower. "Rhetorical Reading and the Construction of Meaning." *College Composition and Communication* 39 (1988): 167–83. Print.

Murray, Donald. *The Craft of Revision*. New York: Holt, 1991. Print.

Scardamalia, Marlene, and Carl Bereiter. "Knowledge Telling and Knowledge Transforming in Written Composition." *Advances in Applied Psycholinguistic*s. Ed. Sheldon Rosenberg, Boston: Cambridge UP, 1987. Vol. 2, 143. Print.

Shaughnessy, Mina. *Errors and Expectations*. New York: Oxford UP, 1977. Print.

Stein, Victoria. "Elaboration: Using What You Know." *Reading-to-Write: Exploring a Cognitive and Social Process*. Eds. Linda Flower et al. New York: Oxford UP, 1990. 144–48. Print.

Chapter 1

Beaumont, Jeff. "Nunez and Beyond: An Examination of Nunez v. City of San Diego and the Future of Nocturnal Juvenile Curfew Ordinances." *Journal of Juvenile Law* 19 (1998): 84–122. *LexisNexis Academic*. Web. 3 Sept. 2008.

Berry, Eleanor. "The Free Verse Spectrum" *College English* 59 (1997): 873–97. Print.

Bloom, Benjamin. S., et al., eds. *Taxonomy of Educational Objectives; The Classification of Educational Goals, by a Committee of College and University Examiners*. New York: Longmans, 1956. Print.

Carroll, Lee Ann. "Pomo Blues: Stories from First-Year Composition." *College English* 59 (1997): 916–33. Print.

Elbow, Peter. *Writing With Power*. New York: Oxford, 1998. Print.

Elbow, Peter. *Writing Without Teachers*. New York: Oxford, 1973. Print.

Joy, Bill. "Why the Future Doesn't Need Us." *Wired* April 2000: 238. Print.

Kellogg, Ronald T., and Bascom A. Raulerson III. "Improving the Writing Skills of College Students." *Psychonomic Bulletin & Review* 14.2 (2007): 237–43. *Academic Search Premier*. Web. 27 Aug. 2008.

Knowles, John. *A Separate Peace*. New York: Macmillan, 1969. Print.

Lamott, Anne. *Bird by Bird*. New York: Pantheon, 1994. Print.

Lunsford, Andrea A., and Karen J. Lunsford. "'Mistakes are a Fact of Life': A National Comparative Study." *College Composition and Communication* 59:4 (2008): 781–806. Print.

Turkle, Sherry. "Computational Technologies and Images of the Self." *Social Research* 64.3 (1997): 1093–112. *Academic Search Premier*. Web. 27 Aug. 2008.

Turkle, Sherry. "Cuddling Up to Cyborg Babies." *UNESCO Courier* Sept. 2000: 43–45. *Academic Search Premier*. Web. 27 Aug. 2008.

Chapter 2

Budds, Michael J. "From Fine Romance to Good Rockin'—and Beyond: Look What They've Done to My Song." *Bleep! Censoring Rock and Rap Music*. Eds. Betty Houchin Winfield and Sandra Davidson. Westport: Greenwood, 1999. 1–8. Print.

Friere, Paulo. *Pedagogy of the Oppressed*. Trans. Myra Bergman Ramos. New York: Seabury, 1970. Print.

Kierkegaard, Søren. "Fear and Trembling." *Fear and Trembling and the Sickness unto Death*. Trans. Walter Lowrie. Princeton: Princeton UP, 1941. Print.

Ong, Walter J., S.J. *The Presence of the Word: Some Prolegomena for Cultural and Religious History*. New York: Simon, 1967. 137. Print.

Papalia, Diane, and Sally W. Olds. *Human Development*. New York: McGraw, 1978.

Selzer, Jack. "Rhetorical Analysis: Understanding How Texts Persuade Readers." Eds. Charles Bazerman and Paul Prior. *What Writing Does and How It Does It*. Mahwah: Erlbaum, 2004. Print.

Chapter 3

Bambara, Toni Cade. "The Lesson." *Gorilla, My Love*. New York: Random, 1972. 87–96. Print.

Budds, Michael J. "From Fine Romance to Good Rockin'—and Beyond: Look What They've Done to My Song." *Bleep! Censoring Rock and Rap Music*. Eds. Betty Houchin Winfield and Sandra Davidson. Westport: Greenwood, 1999. 1–8. Print.

Cooper, Rand Richards. "The Dignity of Helplessness: What Sort of Society Would Euthanasia Create?" *Commonweal* 25 Oct. 1996: 12–15. Print.

Dickens, Charles. *A Tale of Two Cities.* 1859. New York: Pocket, 1957. Print.

Drizin, Steven. "Juvenile Justice: A Century of Experience." *Current* Nov. 1999: 3+. Print.

Dyson, Michael Eric. "2 Live Crew's Rap: Sex, Race, and Class." *Christian Century* Jan. 1991: 7–8. Print.

Frude, Neil. *The Intimate Machine.* New York: New American Library, 1983. Print.

Gates, David. "Decoding Rap Music." *Newsweek* 17 Mar. 1990: 60–63. Print.

Goode, Stephen, and Timothy W. Maier. "Inflating the Grades." *Insight on the News* 25 May 1998: 8–11. *Proquest Research Library.* Web. 4 Sept. 2008.

Goodwin, Doris Kearns. *The Fitzgeralds and the Kennedys.* New York: Simon, 1987. Print.

Grant, Linda. "What Sexual Revolution?" *Sexing the Millennium: Women and the Sexual Revolution.* New York: Grove, 1994. Print.

Heker, Liliana. "The Stolen Party." *Other Fires: Short Fiction by Latin American Women.* Ed. Alberta Manual. New York: Random, 1982. 152–58.

Krauthammer, Charles. "First and Last, Do No Harm." *Time* 15 Apr. 1996: 83. Print.

Laing, R. D. *The Politics of Experience.* New York: Ballantine, 1967. Print.

Leo, John. "When Life Imitates Video." *U.S. News and World Report* 3 May 1999: 14. Print.

Luckman, Joan, and Karen C. Sorensen. *Medical-Surgical Nursing.* Philadelphia: Saunders, 1974. Print.

Moffatt, Michael. "College Life: Undergraduate Culture and Higher Education." *Journal of Higher Education* Jan.–Feb. 1991: 44–61. Print.

Monaco, James. *How to Read a Film.* New York: Oxford UP, 1977. Print.

O'Donnell, Philip. "Ours and Theirs: Redefining Japanese Pop Music." *World and I.* July 1998: 186+. Print.

Rothenberg, David. "Learning in Finland: No Grades, No Criticism." *Chronicle of Higher Education* 23 Oct. 1998: B9+. Print.

Scherer, Joanna Cohan. "Historical Photographs as Anthropological Documents: A Retrospective." *Visual Anthropology* 3 (1990): 367–409. Print.

"Should Children Be Tried As Adults?" *Jet* Nov. 1999: 52. Print.

Stansky, Lisa. "Age of Innocence." *ABA Journal* Nov. 1996: 61–66. Print.

Stephens, Gene. "High-Tech Crime Fighting: The Threat to Civil Liberties." *Futurist* July–Aug. 1990: 20–25. Print.

Talbot, Margaret. "The Maximum Security Adolescent." *New York Times Magazine* 10 Sept. 2002: 41–47+. Print.

Young, Lise A. "Suffer the Children: The Basic Principle of Juvenile Justice Is to Treat the Child, Not Punish the Offense." *America* 22 Oct. 2001: 19+. Print.

Zuger, Abigail, and Steven H. Miles. "Physicians, AIDS, and Occupational Risk: Historical Traditions and Ethical Obligations." *Journal of the American Medical Association* 258 (1987): 1924–28. Print.

Chapter 4

Brown, Ann. L., and Jeanne D. Day. "Microrules for Summarizing Texts: The Development of Expertise." *Journal of Verbal Learning and Verbal Behavior.* 22.1 (1983): 1–14. Print.

Sagan, Carl. "In Defense of Robots." *Broca's Brain.* New York: Ballantine, 1980. 280–92. Print.

Chapter 5

Stein, Victoria. "Elaboration: Using What You Know." *Reading-to-Write: Exploring a Cognitive and Social Process.* Eds. Linda Flower et al. New York: Oxford UP, 1990. 144–48. Print.

Chapter 6

Vidal, Gore. "The Four Generations of the Adams Family." *Matters of Fact and Fiction: Essays, 1973–1976.* New York: Random, 1978. 153–74. Print.

Chapter 7

August, Eugene. "Real Men Don't: Anti-Male Bias in English." *University of Dayton Review* Winter 1986–Spring 1987: 115–24. Print.

Cooper, Rand Richards. "The Dignity of Helplessness: What Sort of Society Would Euthanasia Create?" *Commonweal* 25 Oct. 1996: 12–15. Print.

Griffin, Pat. *Strong Women, Deep Closets: Lesbians and Homophobia in Sport.* Champaign: Human Kinetics, 1998. 16–18. Print.

Henley, Nancy, Mykol Hamilton, and Barrie Thorne. "Womanspeak and Manspeak: Sex Differences and Sexism in Communication, Verbal and Nonverbal." *Beyond Sex Roles.* Ed. Alice Sargent. 2nd ed. St. Paul: West, 1985. 168–85. Print.

Heywood, Leslie. *Pretty Good for a Girl: A Memoir.* New York: Free Press, 1998. Print.

Richardson, Laurel. "Gender Stereotyping in the English Language." *The Dynamics of Sex and Gender: A Sociological Perspective.* 3rd ed. New York: Harper, 1988. 19–26. Print.

Rothenberg, David. "Learning in Finland: No Grades, No Criticism." *Chronicle of Higher Education* 23 Oct. 1998: B9+. Print.

van den Haag, Ernest. "Make Mine Hemlock." *National Review* 12 June 1995: 60–62. Print.

Chapter 8

Aristotle. *The Rhetoric.* Trans. W. Rhys Roberts. *The Rhetoric and Poetics of Aristotle.* Ed. Friedrich Solomon. New York: Modern Library, 1954. Print.
Corbett, Edward. *Classical Rhetoric for the Modern Student.* 3rd ed. New York: Oxford UP, 1990. Print.
Elbow, Peter. *Writing Without Teachers.* New York: Oxford, 1973. Print.
Goldberg, Jeffrey. "The Color of Suspicion." *New York Times Magazine* 20 June 1999: 51+. Print.
Messner, Michael A. "When Bodies Are Weapons." *Sex, Violence, and Power in Sports: Rethinking Masculinity.* Eds. Michael A. Messner and Donald F. Sabo. Freedom: Crossing, 1994. 89–98. Print.
Porter, Rosalie P. "The Newton Alternative to Bilingual Education." *Annals of the American Academy of Political and Social Science* Mar. 1990: 147–50. Print.
Raspberry, William. "Racism in the Criminal Justice System Is Exaggerated." *Washington Post* Natl. weekly ed. 15–21 Apr. 1996. Print.

Chapter 10

Farber, Jerry. "A Young Person's Guide to the Grading System." *The Student as Nigger.* New York: Pocket, 1970. 67–72. Print.
Flora, Stephen Ray, and Stacy Suzanne Poponak. "Childhood Pay for Grades Is Related to College Grade Point Averages." *Psychological Reports* 94 (2004): 66. Print.
Mandrell, Liz. "Zen and the Art of Grade Motivation." *English Journal* Jan. 1997: 28–31. Print. Copyright 1997 by the National Council of Teachers of English. Reprinted with permission.
Vogel, Steve. "Grades and Money." *Dissent* Fall 1997: 102–04. Print.

Chapter 11

Barlow, John Perry. "Cyberhood vs. Neighborhood." *Utne Reader* March–April 1995: 50–57. Print.
Biever, Celeste. "Modern Romance." *New Scientist* 29 April–5 May 2006: 44–45. Print. © New Scientist Magazine.
Internet World Stats: Usage and Population Statistics. n.d. Web. 8 Oct. 2008.
Thompson, Clive. "I'm So Totally, Digitally Close to You: How News Feed, Twitter and Other Forms of Incessant Online Contact Have Created a Brave New World of Ambient Intimacy." *New York Times Magazine* 7 Sept. 2008: 42–47. Print.
Turkle, Sherry. "Cyberspace and Identity." *Contemporary Sociology* 28 (Nov. 1999): 643–48. Print.
Weizenbaum, Joseph. "Technological Detoxification." *Technology Review* Feb. 1980: 10–11. Print.

Chapter 12

Cowley, Carol, and Tillman Farley. "Adolescent Girls' Attitudes Toward Pregnancy: The Importance of Asking What the Boyfriend Wants." *Journal of Family Practice* 50 (July 2001): 603–07. Print.
Gibbs, Nancy. "Give the Girls a Break." *Time* 7 July 2008: 36. Print.
Gulli, Cathy. "Suddenly Teen Pregnancy Is Cool?" *Maclean's* 28 Jan. 2008: 40–44. Print.
Hymowitz, Kay S. "Gloucester Girls Gone Wild." *City Journal* 23 June 2008. Web. 4 Aug. 2008.

Chapter 13

Lessig, Lawrence. "Why Crush Them?" *Newsweek* 28 Nov. 2005: 48. Print.
Bollier, David, and Laurie Racine. "Control of Creativity?" *Christian Science Monitor* 9 Sept. 2003: 9. Print.
Helprin, Mark. "A Great Idea Lives Forever. Shouldn't Its Copyright?" *New York Times* (late edition (East coast)) 20 May 2007: 4.12. Print.
Hajdu, David. "I, Me, Mine" *New Republic* 25 June 2008: 34–37. Print. Reprinted by permission of THE NEW REPUBLIC, © 2008, *The New Republic,* LLC.

Chapter 14

Lakoff, George. "Much More than Race: What Makes a Speech Great." *Open Left.* 24 March 2008. Web. 25 September 2008.
Lopez, Ian F. Haney. "The Social Construction of Race: Some Observations on Illusion, Fabrication, and Choice." *Harvard Civil Rights-Civil Liberties Law Review* 29 (Winter, 1994). Print.
Moses, Yolanda T. "Race, Higher Education, and American Society." *Journal of Anthropological Research* 55 (Summer 1999): 255. Print.
Obama, Barack. "A More Perfect Union." Philadelphia: National Constitution Center. 18 March 2008. Address.

Appendix A

MLA Manual and Guide to Scholarly Publishing, 3rd ed. New York: MLA, 2008.
Publication Manual of the American Psychological Association, 5th ed. Washington: APA, 2001.

Appendix B

Barret, Robert L., and Bryan E. Robinson. "Children of Gay Fathers." *Redefining Families*. Ed. Adele Eskeles Gottfried, and Allen W. Gottfried. New York: Plenum, 1994. Print.

Bennett, William. "What Hath the Beatles Wrought? Rock-&-Roll and the Collapse of Authority." *The American Enterprise* May–June 1997: 72. Print.

Budds, Michael J. "From Fine Romance to Good Rockin'—and Beyond: Look What They've Done to My Song." *Bleep! Censoring Rock and Rap Music*. Eds. Betty Houchin Winfield and Sandra Davidson. Westport: Greenwood, 1999. 1–8. Print.

Frude, Neil. *The Intimate Machine*. New York: Penguin, 1983. Print.

Lynch, John. *The Hispanic World in Crisis and Change: 1590–1700*. Oxford: Blackwell, 1992. 53–54. Print.

X, Malcolm, and Alex Haley. *The Autobiography of Malcolm X*. New York: Grove, 1966. 309. Print.

Appendix C

Goldberg, Natalie. *Wild Mind: Living the Writer's Life*. New York: Bantam, 1990. Print.

———. *Writing Down the Bones: Freeing the Writer Within*. Boston: Shambala, 1986. Print.

Orwell, George. "Politics and the English Language." *A Collection of Essays*. New York: Harbrace, 1953. Print.

Sagan, Carl. "Can We Know the Universe? Reflections on a Grain of Sand." *Broca's Brain*. New York: Ballantine, 1980. Print.

Schank, Roger C. "Reminding and Memory Organization: An Introduction to MOPs." In *Strategies for Natural Language Processing*. Eds. Wendy G. Lehnert and Martin H. Ringle. Hillsdale, NY: Lawrence Erlbaum, 1982. Print.

Strunk, William, Jr., and E. B. White. *The Elements of Style*. 2nd ed. New York: MacMillan, 1972. Print.

Trimble, John R. *Writing with Style: Conversations on the Art of Writing*. 2nd ed. Upper Saddle River: Prentice, 2000. Print.

PHOTOS

Index